arihant
SUCCESS AND NOTHING LESS

AF819898

Be a TOP SCORER
in ISC Exams 2025

i Succeed

15 Sample Question Papers

with Quick Study Notes

Physics 12th

AUTHOR
Sayonika Jana
M.Sc *(Physics)*

List of *i Succeed* Sample Papers for ISC 12

- Physics
- Chemistry
- Mathematics
- Biology
- Accounts
- Economics
- Commerce
- English Language
- Literature in English

Arihant Prakashan
(School Division Series)

Administrative & Production Offices

Regd. Office
'Ramchhaya' 4577/15, Agarwal Road, Darya Ganj, New Delhi -110002
Tele: 011- 47630600, 43518550

Head Office
Kalindi, TP Nagar, Meerut (UP) - 250002
Tel: 0121-7156203, 7156204

Sales & Support Offices
Agra, Ahmedabad, Bengaluru, Bareilly, Chennai, Delhi, Guwahati, Hyderabad, Jaipur, Jhansi, Kolkata, Lucknow, Nagpur & Pune.

PRICE ₹275.00

PO No : TXT-XX-XXXXXXX-X-XX

Published by Arihant Publications (India) Ltd.

For further information about the books published by Arihant, log on to www.arihantbooks.com or e-mail at info@arihantbooks.com

Follow us on

i Succeed

SAMPLE QUESTION PAPERS

THE **BEST CHOICE** OF TEACHERS & STUDENTS, Why?

01 Exact Exam Pattern

All Sample Papers have been designed on the actual exam format of ISC

02 Complete Syllabus

Complete coverage of syllabus through different types of questions across all the sample papers

03 Latest Specimen & Examination Question Paper

Latest Specimen & ISC examination Question Paper with detailed solutions.

04 Detailed Solutions

Step-by-step solutions to help you understand concepts and improve problem-solving skills.

05 Quick Study Notes

Focused revision of the whole syllabus through Quick Study Notes.

06 All Type of Questions

Coverage of all type of exam pattern questions, analysis, understanding, recall, application & evaluation.

Free Doubt Solving APP

To help you sort out your doubts at any time any place.

i Succeed

Physics Class 12

i Succeed

Course Structure

2024-25

There will be two papers in the subject.

PAPER I : Theory	70 marks
PAPER II : Practical	15 marks
Project Work	10 marks
Practical File	5 marks

PAPER I THEORY 70 Marks

S. No.	UNIT	TOTAL WEIGHTAGE
1.	Electrostatics	14 Marks
2.	Current Electricity	
3.	Magnetic Effects of Current and Magnetism	16 Marks
4.	Electromagnetic Induction and Alternating Currents	
5.	Electromagnetic Waves	2 Marks
6.	Optics	18 Marks
7.	Dual Nature of Radiation and Matter	7 Marks
8.	Atoms and Nuclei	6 Marks
9.	Electronic Devices	7 Marks
	Total	70 Marks

Note

(i) Unless otherwise specified, only S. I. Units are to be used while teaching and learning, as well as for answering questions.

(ii) All physical quantities to be defined as and when they are introduced along with their units and dimensions.

(iii) Numerical problems are included from all topics except where they are specifically excluded or where only qualitative treatment is required.

1. ELECTROSTATICS

(i) **Electric Charges and Fields** Electric charges; conservation and quantisation of charge, Coulomb's law; superposition principle and continuous charge distribution. Electric field, electric field due to a point charge, electric field lines, electric dipole, electric field due to a dipole, torque on a dipole in uniform electric field.

Electric flux, Gauss's theorem in electrostatics and its applications to find field due to infinitely long straight wire, uniformly charged infinite plane sheet and uniformly charged thin spherical shell.

(a) Coulomb's law, SI unit of charge; permittivity of free space and of dielectric medium. Frictional electricity, electric charges (two types); repulsion and attraction; simple atomic structure-electrons and ions; conductors and insulators; quantization and conservation of electric charge; Coulomb's law in vector form; (position coordinates r_1, r_2 not necessary). Comparison with Newton's law of gravitation; Superposition principle ($\mathbf{F}_1 = \mathbf{F}_{12} + \mathbf{F}_{13} + \mathbf{F}_{14} + \ldots$).

(b) Concept of electric field and its intensity; examples of different fields; gravitational, electric and magnetic; Electric field due to a point charge $\mathbf{E} = \mathbf{F}/q_0$ (q_0 is a test charge); $\mathbf{E}$ for a group of charges (superposition principle); a point charge q in an electric field $\mathbf{E}$ experiences an electric force $\mathbf{F}_E = q\mathbf{E}$. Intensity due to a continuous distribution of charge i.e. linear, surface and volume.

(c) Electric lines of force: A convenient way to visualize the electric field; properties of lines of force; examples of the lines of force due to (i) an isolated point charge (+ve and −ve); (ii) dipole; (iii) two similar charges at a small distance;(iv) uniform field between two oppositely charged parallel plates.

(d) Electric dipole and dipole moment; derivation of the $\mathbf{E}$ at a point, (1) on the axis (end on position) (2) on the perpendicular bisector (equatorial i.e. broad side on position) of a dipole, also for $r >> 2l$ (short dipole); dipole in a uniform electric field; net force zero, torque on an electric dipole: $\tau = \mathbf{p} \times \mathbf{E}$ and its derivation.

(e) Gauss's theorem: the flux of a vector field; $Q = vA$ for velocity vector $\mathbf{v} || \mathbf{A}$, $\mathbf{A}$ is area vector. Similarly, for electric field $\mathbf{E}$, electric flux $\phi_E = EA$ for $\mathbf{E} || \mathbf{A}$ and $\phi_E = \mathbf{E} \cdot \mathbf{A}$ for uniform $\mathbf{E}$. For non-uniform field $\phi_E = \int d\phi = \int \mathbf{E} \cdot d\mathbf{A}$. Special cases for $\theta = 0°, 90°$ and 180°. Gauss's theorem, statement: $\phi_E = q/\epsilon_0$ or $\phi_E = \oint \mathbf{E} \cdot d\mathbf{A} = q/\epsilon_0$ where ϕ_E is for a closed surface; q is the net charge enclosed, ϵ_0 is the permittivity of free space. Essential properties of a Gaussian surface.

Applications: Obtain expression for $\mathbf{E}$ due to 1. an infinite line of charge, 2. a uniformly charged infinite plane thin sheet, 3. a thin hollow spherical shell (inside, on the surface and outside). Graphical variation of E vs r for a thin spherical shell.

(ii) **Electrostatic Potential, Potential Energy and Capacitance** Electric potential, potential difference, electric potential due to a point charge, a dipole and system of charges; equipotential surfaces, electrical potential energy of a system of two point charges and of electric dipole in an electrostatic field.

Conductors and insulators, free charges and bound charges inside a conductor. Dielectrics and electric polarisation, capacitors and capacitance, combination of capacitors in series and in parallel. Capacitance of a parallel plate capacitor, energy stored in a capacitor.

(a) Concept of potential, potential difference and potential energy. Equipotential surface and its properties. Obtain an expression for electric potential at a point due to a point charge; graphical variation of E and V versues r, $V_P = W/q_0$; hence $V_A - V_B = W_{BA/q_0}$ (taking q_0 from B to A) $= (q/4\pi\varepsilon_0)(1/r_A - 1/r_B)$; derive this equation; also $V_A = q/4\pi\varepsilon_0 \cdot 1/r_A$; for $q > 0, V_A > 0$ and for $q < 0, V_A < 0$. For a collection of charges V = algebraic sum of the potentials due to each charge; potential due to a dipole on its axial line and equatorial line; also at any point for $r >> 2l$ (short dipole). Potential energy of a point charge (q) in an electric field $\mathbf{E}$, placed at a point P where potential is

V, is given by $U = qV$ and $\Delta U = q(V_A - V_B)$. The electrostatic potential energy of a system of two charges = work done $W_{21} = W_{12}$ in assembling the system; U_{12} or $U_{21} = (1/4\pi\varepsilon_0)\, q_1 q_2 / r_{12}$. For a system of 3 charges $U_{123} = U_{12} + U_{13} + U_{23} = \frac{1}{4\pi\varepsilon_0}\left(\frac{q_1 q_2}{r_{12}} + \frac{q_1 q_3}{r_{13}} + \frac{q_2 q_3}{r_{23}}\right)$. For a dipole in a uniform electric field, derive an expression of the electric potential energy $U_E = -\,\mathbf{p}\cdot\mathbf{E}$, special cases for $\phi = 0°, 90°$ and 180°.

(b) *Capacitance of a conductor $C = Q/V$; obtain the capacitance of a parallel-plate capacitor ($C = \varepsilon_0 A/d$) and equivalent capacitance for capacitors in series and parallel combinations. Obtain an expression for energy stored $\left(U = \frac{1}{2}CV^2 = \frac{1}{2}QV = \frac{1}{2}\frac{Q^2}{C}\right)$ and energy density.*

(c) *Dielectric constant $K = C'/C$; this is also called relative permittivity $K = \varepsilon_r = \varepsilon/\varepsilon_0$; elementary ideas of polarization of matter in a uniform electric field qualitative discussion; induced surface charges weaken the original field; results in reduction in **E** and hence, in potential difference (V); for charge remaining the same $Q = CV = C'V' = K \cdot CV'$; $V' = V/K$; and $E' = E/K$; if the capacitor is kept connected with the source of emf, V is kept constant $V = Q/C = Q'/C'$; $Q' = C'V = K \cdot CV = K \cdot Q$ increases; For a parallel plate capacitor with a dielectric in between, $C' = KC = K \cdot \varepsilon_0 \cdot A/d = \varepsilon_r \cdot \varepsilon_0 \cdot A/d$. Then $C' = \frac{\varepsilon_0 A}{(d/\varepsilon_r)}$; for a capacitor partially filled dielectric, capacitance, $C' = \varepsilon_0 A/(d - t + t/\varepsilon_r)$.*

2. CURRENT ELECTRICITY

Mechanism of flow of current in conductors. Mobility, drift velocity and its relation with electric current; Ohm's law and its proof, resistance and resistivity and their relation to drift velocity of electrons; V-I characteristics (linear and non-linear), electrical energy and power, electrical resistivity and conductivity.

Temperature dependence of resistance and resistivity.

Internal resistance of a cell, potential difference and emf of a cell, combination of cells in series and in parallel, Kirchhoff's laws and simple applications, Wheatstone bridge, metre bridge. Potentiometer-principle and its applications to measure potential difference, to compare emf of two cells; to measure internal resistance of a cell.

(a) *Free electron theory of conduction; acceleration of free electrons, relaxation time τ; electric current $I = Q/t$; concept of drift velocity and electron mobility. Ohm's law, current density $J = I/A$; experimental verification, graphs and slope, ohmic and non-ohmic conductors; obtain the relation $I = v_d enA$. Derive $\sigma = ne^2\tau/m$ and $\rho = m/ne^2\tau$; effect of temperature on resistivity and resistance of conductors and semiconductors and graphs. Resistance $R = V/I$; resistivity ρ, given by $R = \rho \cdot l/A$; conductivity and conductance; Ohm's law as $\mathbf{J} = \sigma\mathbf{E}$.*

(b) *Electrical energy consumed in time t is $E = Pt = VIt$; using Ohm's law $E = \left(\frac{V^2}{R}\right)t = I^2Rt$. Potential difference $V = P/I$; $P = VI$; Electric power consumed $P = VI = V^2/R = I^2R$; commercial units; electricity consumption and billing.*

(c) *The source of energy of a seat of emf (such as a cell) may be electrical, mechanical, thermal or radiant energy. The emf of a source is defined as the work done per unit charge to force them to go to the higher point of potential (from – ve terminal to + ve terminal inside the cell) so, $\varepsilon = dW/dq$; but $dq = Idt$; $dW = \varepsilon dq = \varepsilon Idt$. Equating total work done to the work done across the external resistor R plus the work done across the internal resistance r; $\varepsilon Idt = I^2R\,dt + I^2 r dt$; $\varepsilon = I(R + r)$; $I = \varepsilon/(R + r)$; also $IR + Ir = \varepsilon$ or $V = \varepsilon - Ir$ where Ir is called the back emf as it acts against the emf ε; V is the terminal potential difference. Derivation of formulae for combination for identical cells in series, parallel and mixed grouping. Parallel combination of two cells of unequal emf. Series combination of n cells of unequal emf.*

(d) *Statement and explanation of Kirchhoff's laws with simple examples. The first is a conservation law for charge and the 2nd is law of conservation of energy. Note change in potential across a resistor $\Delta V = IR < 0$ when we go 'down' with the current (compare with flow of water down a river), and $\Delta V = IR > 0$ if we go up against the current across the resistor. When we go through a cell, the – ve terminal is at a lower level and the + ve terminal at a higher level, so going from – ve to + ve through the cell, we are going up and $\Delta V = +\,\varepsilon$ and going from + ve to – ve terminal through the cell, we are going down, so $\Delta V = -\,\varepsilon$. Application to simple circuits. Wheatstone bridge; right in the beginning take $I_g = 0$ as we consider a balanced bridge, derivation of $R_1/R_2 = R_3/R_4$ [Kirchhoff's law not necessary]. Metre bridge is a modified form of Wheatstone bridge, its use to measure unknown resistance. Here $R_3 = l_1$ and $R_4 = l_2$; $R_3/R_4 = l_1/l_2$. Principle of Potentiometer: fall in potential $\Delta V \propto \Delta l$; auxiliary emf ε_1 is balanced against the fall in potential V_1 across length l_1. $\varepsilon_1 = V_1 = Kl_1$; $\varepsilon_1/\varepsilon_2 = l_1/l_2$; potentiometer as a voltmeter. Potential gradient and sensitivity of potentiometer. Use of potentiometer: to compare emfs of two cells, to determine internal resistance of a cell.*

3. MAGNETIC EFFECTS OF CURRENT AND MAGNETISM

(i) **Moving Charges and Magnetism**

Concept of magnetic field, Oersted's experiment. Biot-Savart law and its application. Ampere's Circuital law and its applications to infinitely long straight wire, straight and toroidal solenoids (only qualitative treatment). Force on a moving charge in uniform magnetic and electric fields, cyclotron. Force on a current carrying conductor in a uniform magnetic field, force between two parallel current-carrying conductors-definition of ampere, torque experienced by a current loop in uniform magnetic field; moving coil galvanometer - its sensitivity. Conversion of galvanometer into an ammeter and a voltmeter.

(ii) **Magnetism and Matter**

A current loop as a magnetic dipole, its magnetic dipole moment, magnetic dipole moment of a revolving electron, magnetic field intensity due to a magnetic dipole (bar magnet) on the axial line and equatorial line, torque on a magnetic dipole (bar magnet) in a uniform magnetic field; bar magnet as an equivalent solenoid, magnetic field lines; Diamagnetic, paramagnetic and ferromagnetic substances, with examples. Electromagnets and factors affecting their strengths, permanent magnets.

(a) *Only historical introduction through Oersted's experiment. [Ampere's swimming rule not included]. Biot-Savart law and its vector form; application; derive the expression for B (i) at the centre of a circular loop carrying current; (ii) at any point on its axis. Current carrying loop as a magnetic dipole. Ampere's circuital law: statement and brief explanation. Apply it to obtain* **B** *near a long wire carrying current and for a solenoid. Only formula of* **B** *due to a finitely long conductor.*

(b) *Force on a moving charged particle in magnetic field* $\mathbf{F}_B = q(\mathbf{v} \times \mathbf{B})$; *special cases, modify this equation substituting* $d\mathbf{l}/dt$ *for v and I for q/dt to yield* $\mathbf{F} = Id\mathbf{l} \times \mathbf{B}$ *for the force acting on a current carrying conductor placed in a magnetic field. Derive the expression for force between two long and parallel wires carrying current, hence, define ampere (the base SI unit of current) and hence, coulomb; from Q = It. Lorentz force.*

(c) *Derive the expression for torque on a current carrying loop placed in a uniform* **B**, *using* $\mathbf{F} = I\mathbf{l} \times \mathbf{B}$ *and* $\tau = \mathbf{r} \times \mathbf{F}$; $\tau = NIAB\sin\phi$ *for N turns* $\tau = \mathbf{m} \times \mathbf{B}$, *where the dipole moment* $\mathbf{m} = NI\mathbf{A}$, *unit:* A-m^2. *A current carrying loop is a magnetic dipole; directions of current and* **B** *and* **m** *using right hand rule only; no other rule necessary. Mention orbital magnetic moment of an electron in Bohr model of H-atom. Concept of radial magnetic field. Moving coil galvanometer; construction, principle, working, theory* $I = k\phi$, *current and voltage sensitivity. Shunt. Conversion of galvanometer into ammeter and voltmeter of given range.*

(d) *Magnetic field represented by the symbol* **B** *is now defined by the equation* $\mathbf{F} = q_0(\mathbf{v} \times \mathbf{B})$; **B** *is not to be defined in terms of force acting on a unit pole, etc.; note the distinction of* **B** *from* **E** *is that* **B** *forms closed loops as there are no magnetic monopoles, whereas* **E** *lines start from + ve charge and end on – ve charge. Magnetic field lines due to a magnetic dipole (bar magnet). Magnetic field in end-on and broadside-on positions (No derivations). Magnetic flux* $\phi = \mathbf{B} \cdot \mathbf{A} = BA$ *for B uniform and* $\mathbf{B} \| \mathbf{A}$; *i.e. area held perpendicular to for* $\phi = BA(\mathbf{B} \| \mathbf{A})$, $B = \phi/A$ *is the flux density [SI unit of flux is weber (Wb)]; but note that this is not correct as a defining equation as* **B** *is vector and* ϕ *and* ϕ/A *are scalars, unit of B is tesla (T) equal to* 10^{-4} *gauss. For non-uniform* **B** *field,* $\phi = \int d\phi = \int \mathbf{B} \cdot d\mathbf{A}$.

(e) *Properties of diamagnetic, paramagnetic and ferromagnetic substances; their susceptibility and relative permeability. It is better to explain the main distinction, the cause of magnetisation (M) is due to magnetic dipole moment (m) of atoms, ions or molecules being 0 for dia, > 0 but very small for para and > 0 and large for ferromagnetic materials; few examples; placed in external* **B**, *very small (induced) magnetisation in a direction opposite to* **B** *in dia, small magnetisation parallel to* **B** *for para, and large magnetisation parallel to* **B** *for ferromagnetic materials; this leads to lines of* **B** *becoming less dense, more dense and much more dense in dia, para and ferro, respectively; hence, a weak repulsion for dia, weak attraction for para and strong attraction for ferro magnetic material. Also, a small bar suspended in the horizontal plane becomes perpendicular to the* **B** *field for dia and parallel to* **B** *for para and ferro. Defining equation* $H = (B/\mu_0) - M$; *the magnetic properties, susceptibility* $\chi_m = (M/H) < 0$ *for dia (as M is opposite H) and > 0 for para, both very small, but very large for ferro; hence relative permeability* $\mu_r = (1 + \chi_m) < 1$ *for dia, > 1 for para and >> 1 (very large) for ferro; further,* $\chi_m \propto 1/T$ *(Curie's law) for para, independent of temperature (T) for dia and depends on T in a complicated manner for ferro; on heating ferro becomes para at Curie temperature. Electromagnet: its definition, properties and factors affecting the strength of electromagnet; selection of magnetic material for temporary and permanent magnets and core of the transformer on the basis of retentivity and coercive force (B-H loop and its significance, retentivity and coercive force not to be evaluated).*

4. ELECTROMAGNETIC INDUCTION AND ALTERNATING CURRENTS

(i) **Electromagnetic Induction** Faraday's laws, induced emf and current; Lenz's Law, eddy currents. Self-induction and mutual induction. Transformer.

(ii) **Alternating Current** Peak value, mean value and RMS value of alternating current/voltage; their relation in sinusoidal case; reactance and impedance; *L-C* oscillations (qualitative treatment only), *L-C-R* series circuit, resonance; power in AC circuits, wattless current. AC generator.

(a) *Electromagnetic induction, magnetic flux, change in flux, rate of change of flux and induced emf; Faraday's laws. Lenz's law, conservation of energy; motional emf* $\varepsilon = Blv$, *and power* $P = (Blv)^2/R$; *eddy currents (qualitative);*

(b) *Self-Induction, coefficient of self-inductance,* $\phi = LI$ *and* $L = \dfrac{\varepsilon}{dI/dt}$; *henry = volt. Second/ampere, expression for coefficient of self-inductance of a solenoid* $L = \dfrac{\mu_0 N^2 A}{l} = \mu_0 n^2 A \times l$.
Mutual induction and mutual inductance (M), flux linked $\phi_2 = MI_1$; *induced emf* $\varepsilon_2 = \dfrac{d\phi_2}{dt} = M\dfrac{dI_1}{dt}$. *Definition of M as* $M = \dfrac{\varepsilon_2}{dI_1/dt}$ *or* $M = \dfrac{\phi_2}{I_1}$. *SI unit henry. Expression for coefficient of mutual inductance of two coaxial solenoids.* $M = \dfrac{\mu_0 N_1 N_2 A}{l} = \mu_0 n_1 N_2 A$
Induced emf opposes changes, back emf is set up, eddy currents. Transformer (ideal coupling): principle, working and uses; step up and step down; efficiency and applications including transmission of power, energy losses and their minimisation.

(c) *Sinusoidal variation of V and I with time, for the output from an AC generator; time period, frequency and phase changes; obtain mean values of current and voltage, obtain relation between RMS value of V and I with peak values in sinusoidal cases only.*

(d) *Variation of voltage and current in AC circuits consisting of only a resistor, only an inductor and only a capacitor (phasor representation), phase lag and phase lead. May apply Kirchhoff's law and obtain simple differential equation (SHM type),* $V = V_0 \sin\omega t$, *solution* $I = I_0 \sin\omega t$, $I_0 \sin(\omega t + \pi/2)$ *and* $I_0 \sin(\omega t - \pi/2)$ *for pure R, C and L circuits respectively. Draw phase (or phasor) diagrams showing voltage and current and phase lag or lead, also showing resistance R, inductive reactance* X_L; $(X_L = \omega L)$ *and capacitive reactance* X_C, $(X_C = 1/\omega C)$. *Graph of* X_L *and* X_C *versus f.*

(e) *The L-C-R series circuit: Use phasor diagram method to obtain expression for I and V, the potential difference across R, L and C; and the net phase lag/lead; use the results of 4(e), V lags I by* $\pi/2$ *in a capacitor, V leads I by* $\pi/2$ *in an inductor, V and I are in phase in a resistor, I is the same in all three; hence draw phase diagram, combine* V_L *and* V_C *(in opposite phase; phasors add like vectors) to give* $V = V_R + V_L + V_C$ *(phasor addition) and the max. values are related by* $V_m^2 = V_{Rm}^2 + (V_{Lm} - V_{Cm})^2$ *when* $V_L > V_C$ *Substituting potential difference = current × resistance or reactance, we get* $Z^2 = R^2 + (X_L - X_C)^2$ *and* $\tan\phi = (V_{Lm} - V_{Cm})/V_{Rm} = (X_L - X_C)/R$ *giving* $I = I_m \sin(\omega t - \phi)$, *where* $I_m = V_m/Z$ *etc. Special cases for R-L and R-C circuits. [May use Kirchhoff's law and obtain the differential equation] Graph of Z versus f and I versus f.*

(f) *Power P associated with L-C-R circuit* $= \frac{1}{2}V_0 I_0 \cos\phi = V_{rms} I_{rms} \cos\phi = I^2_{rms} R$; *power absorbed and power dissipated; electrical resonance; bandwidth of signals and Q factor (no derivation); oscillations in an LC circuit* ($\omega_0 = 1/\sqrt{LC}$).
Average power consumed averaged over a full cycle $\overline{P} = (1/2) V_0 I_0 \cos\phi$, *power factor* $\cos\phi = R/Z$. *Special case for pure R, L and C; choke coil (analytical only),* X_L *controls current but* $\cos\phi = 0$, *hence* $\overline{P} = 0$, *wattless current; LC circuit; at resonance with* $X_L = X_C$, $Z = Z_{min} = R$, *power delivered to circuit by the source is maximum, resonant frequency* $f_0 = \frac{1}{2\pi\sqrt{LC}}$.

(g) *Simple AC generators: Principle, description, theory, working and use. Variation in current and voltage with time for AC and DC Basic differences between AC and DC.*

5. ELECTROMAGNETIC WAVES

Basic idea of displacement current. Electromagnetic waves, their characteristics, their transverse nature (qualitative ideas only). Complete electromagnetic spectrum starting from radiowaves to gamma rays elementary facts of electromagnetic waves and their uses.

Concept of displacement current, qualitative descriptions only of electromagnetic spectrum; common features of all regions of electromagnetic spectrum including transverse nature (**E** and **B** perpendicular to **c**); special features of the common classification (gamma rays, X-rays, UV rays, visible light, IR, microwaves, radio and TV waves) in their production (source), detection and other properties; uses; approximate range of λ or *f* or at least proper order of increasing *f* or λ.

6. OPTICS

(i) **Ray Optics and Optical Instruments** Ray Optics: Reflection of light by spherical mirrors, mirror formula, refraction of light at plane surfaces, total internal reflection and its applications, optical fibres, refraction at spherical surfaces, lenses, thin lens formula, lens maker's formula, magnification, power of a lens, combination of thin lenses in contact, combination of a lens and a mirror, refraction and dispersion of light through a prism.

Optical instruments: Microscopes and astronomical telescopes (reflecting and refracting) and their magnifying powers and their resolving powers.

(a) *Reflection of light by spherical mirrors. Mirror formula: its derivation; R = 2f for spherical mirrors. Magnification.*

(b) *Refraction of light at a plane interface, Snell's law; total internal reflection and critical angle; total reflecting prisms and optical fibres. Total reflecting prisms: application to triangular prisms with angle of the prism 30°, 45°, 60° and 90° respectively; ray diagrams for refraction through a combination of media,* ${}_1n_2 \times {}_2n_3 \times {}_3n_1 = 1$, *real depth and apparent depth. Simple applications.*

(c) *Refraction through a prism, minimum deviation and derivation of relation between n, A and* δ_{min}. *Include explanation of* $i - \delta$ *graph,* $i_1 = i_2 = i$ *(say) for* δ_m; *from symmetry* $r_1 = r_2$; *refracted ray inside the prism is parallel to the base of the equilateral prism. Thin prism. Dispersion; Angular dispersion; dispersive power, rainbow-ray diagram (no derivation). Simple explanation.*

(d) *Refraction at a single spherical surface; detailed discussion of one case only-convex towards rarer medium, for spherical surface and real image. Derive the relation between* n_1, n_2, u, v *and R. Refraction through thin lenses: derive lens maker's formula and lens formula; derivation of combined focal length of two thin lenses in contact. Combination of lenses and mirrors (silvering of lens excluded) and magnification for lens, derivation for biconvex lens only; extend the results to biconcave lens, plano convex lens and lens immersed in a liquid; power of a lens* $P = 1/f$ *with SI unit dioptre. For lenses in contact* $1/F = 1/f_1 + 1/f_2$ *and* $P = P_1 + P_2$. *Lens formula, formation of image with combination of thin lenses and mirrors.*

[Any one sign convention may be used in solving numericals].

(e) *Ray diagram and derivation of magnifying power of a simple microscope with image at D (least distance of distinct vision) and infinity; Ray diagram and derivation of magnifying power of a compound microscope with image at D. Only expression for magnifying power of compound microscope for final image at infinity.*

Ray diagrams of refracting telescope with image at infinity as well as at D; simple explanation; derivation of magnifying power; Ray diagram of reflecting telescope with image at infinity. Advantages, disadvantages and uses.

(ii) **Wave Optics** Wave front and Huygen's principle. Proof of laws of reflection and refraction using Huygen's principle. Interference, Young's double slit experiment and expression for fringe width(β), coherent sources and sustained interference of light, Fraunhofer diffraction due to a single slit, width of central maximum.

(a) *Huygen's principle: wavefronts-different types/shapes of wavefronts; proof of laws of reflection and refraction using Huygen's theory.*

[Refraction through a prism and lens on the basis of Huygen's theory not required].

(b) *Interference of light, interference of monochromatic light by double slit. Phase of wave motion; superposition of identical waves at a point, path difference and phase difference; coherent and incoherent sources; interference: constructive and destructive, conditions for sustained interference of light waves [mathematical deduction of interference from the equations of two progressive waves with a phase difference is not required]. Young's double slit experiment: set up, diagram, geometrical deduction of path difference* $\Delta x = d\sin\theta$, *between waves from the two slits; using* $\Delta x = n\lambda$ *for bright fringe and* $\Delta x = (n + \frac{1}{2})\lambda$ *for dark fringe and* $\sin\theta = \tan\theta = y_n/D$ *as y and* θ *are small, obtain* $y_n = (D/d)n\lambda$ *and fringe width* $\beta = (D/d)\lambda$.

Graph of distribution of intensity with angular distance.

(c) *Single slit Fraunhofer diffraction (elementary explanation only). Diffraction at a single slit: experimental setup, diagram, diffraction pattern, obtain expression for position of minima,* $a\sin\theta_n = n\lambda$, *where n = 1, 2, 3... and conditions for secondary maxima,* $a\sin\theta_n = (n + \frac{1}{2})\lambda$; *distribution of intensity with angular distance; angular width of central bright fringe.*

7. DUAL NATURE OF RADIATION AND MATTER

Wave particle duality; photoelectric effect, Hertz and Lenard's observations; Einstein's photoelectric equation-particle nature of light. Matter waves-wave nature of particles, de-Broglie relation; Conclusion from Davisson-Germer experiment (Qualitative only).

(a) Photoelectric effect, quantisation of radiation; Einstein's equation $E_{max} = h\nu - W_0$; threshold frequency; work function; experimental facts of Hertz and Lenard and their conclusions; Einstein used Planck's ideas and extended it to apply for radiation (light); photoelectric effect can be explained only assuming quantum (particle) nature of radiation. Determination of Planck's constant (from the graph of stopping potential V_s *versus* frequency f of the incident light).

Momentum of photon $p = E/c = h\nu/c - h/\lambda$.

(b) de-Broglie hypothesis, phenomenon of electron diffraction (qualitative only). Wave nature of radiation is exhibited in interference, diffraction and polarisation; particle nature is exhibited in photoelectric effect. Dual nature of matter: particle nature common in that it possesses momentum p and kinetic energy *KE*. The wave nature of matter was proposed by Louis de-Broglie, $\lambda = h/p = h/mv$.

Davisson and Germer experiment; qualitative description of the experiment and conclusion.

8. ATOMS AND NUCLEI

(i) **Atoms** Alpha-particle scattering experiment; Rutherford's atomic model; Bohr's atomic model, energy levels, hydrogen spectrum.

Rutherford's nuclear model of atom (mathematical theory of scattering excluded), based on Geiger-Marsden experiment on α-scattering; nuclear radius r in terms of closest approach of α-particle to the nucleus, obtained by equating $\Delta K = \frac{1}{2}mv^2$ of the α-particle to the change in electrostatic potential energy ΔU of the system $U = \frac{2e \times Ze}{4\pi\varepsilon_0 r_0} = r_0 \sim 10^{-15}$ m = 1 Fermi; atomic structure; only general qualitative ideas, including atomic number *Z*, neutron number *N* and mass number *A*. A brief account of historical background leading to Bohr's theory of hydrogen spectrum; formulae for wavelength in Lyman, Balmer, Paschen, Brackett and Pfund series. Rydberg constant. Bohr's model of H-atom, postulates (*Z* = 1); expressions for orbital velocity, kinetic energy, potential energy, radius of orbit and total energy of electron. Energy level diagram, calculation of ΔE, frequency and wavelength of different lines of emission spectra; agreement with experimentally observed values. [Use nm and not Å for unit of λ].

(ii) **Nuclei** Composition and size of nucleus, Mass-energy relation, mass defect; binding energy per nucleon and its variation with mass number; Nuclear reactions, nuclear fission and nuclear fusion.

(a) *Atomic masses and nuclear density; Isotopes, Isobars and Isotones – definitions with examples of each. Unified atomic mass unit, symbol* u, 1u = 1/12 *of the mass of* ^{12}C *atom* = 1.66×10^{-27} *kg). Composition of nucleus; mass defect and binding energy, BE* = $(\Delta m)\,c^2$. *Graph of BE/nucleon versus mass number A, special features-less BE/nucleon for light as well as heavy elements. Middle order more stable [see fission and fusion] Einstein's equation* $E = mc^2$. *Calculations related to this equation; mass defect/binding energy, mutual annihilation and pair production as examples.*

(b) ***Nuclear Energy*** *Theoretical (qualitative) prediction of exothermic (with release of energy) nuclear reaction, in fusing together two light nuclei to form a heavier nucleus and in splitting heavy nucleus to form middle order (lower mass number) nuclei, is evident from the shape of BE per nucleon versus mass number graph. Also calculate the disintegration energy Q for a heavy nucleus (A = 240) with BE/A ~ 7.6 MeV per nucleon split into two equal halves with A = 120 each and BE/A ~ 8.5 MeV/nucleon; Q ~ 200 MeV. Nuclear fission: Any one equation of fission reaction. Chain reaction- controlled and uncontrolled; nuclear reactor and nuclear bomb. Main parts of a nuclear reactor including their functions - fuel elements, moderator, control rods, coolant, casing; criticality; utilization of energy output - all qualitative only. Fusion, simple example of* $^1\text{H} \rightarrow {}^4\text{He}$ *and its nuclear reaction equation; requires very high temperature ~* 10^6 *degrees; difficult to achieve; hydrogen bomb; thermonuclear energy production in the sun and stars. [Details of chain reaction not required].*

9. ELECTRONIC DEVICES

(i) Semiconductor Electronics: Materials, Devices and Simple Circuits. Energy bands in conductors, semiconductors and insulators (qualitative ideas only). Intrinsic and extrinsic semiconductors *p* and *n*-type, *p-n* junction.

(ii) Semiconductor diode: *I-V* characteristics in forward and reverse bias, diode as a rectifier; special types of junction diodes: LED, photodiode, solar cell and Zener diode and its characteristics, Zener diode as a voltage regulator.

(a) *Energy bands in solids; energy band diagrams for distinction between conductors, insulators and semiconductors-intrinsic and extrinsic; electrons and holes in semiconductors.*
Elementary ideas about electrical conduction in metals [crystal structure not included]. Energy levels (as for hydrogen atom), 1s, 2s, 2p, 3s, etc. of an isolated atom such as that of copper; these split, eventually forming bands of energy levels, as we consider solid copper made up of a large number of isolated atoms, brought together to form a lattice; definition of energy bands-groups of closely spaced energy levels separated by band gaps called forbidden bands. An idealised representation of the energy bands for a conductor, insulator and semiconductor; characteristics, differences; distinction between conductors, insulators and semiconductors on the basis of energy bands, with examples; qualitative discussion only; energy gaps (eV) in typical substances (carbon, Ge, Si); some electrical properties of semiconductors. Majority and minority charge carriers-electrons and holes; intrinsic and extrinsic, doping, p-type, n-type; donor and acceptor impurities.

(b) *Junction diode and its symbol; depletion region and potential barrier; forward and reverse biasing, V-I characteristics and numericals; half wave and a full wave rectifier. Simple circuit diagrams and graphs, function of each component in the electric circuits, qualitative only. [Bridge rectifier of 4 diodes not included]; elementary ideas on solar cell, photodiode and light emitting diode (LED) as semi conducting diodes. Importance of LED's as they save energy without causing atmospheric pollution and global warming. Zener diode, V-I characteristics, circuit diagram and working of Zener diode as a voltage regulator.*

Preparation Assessment Zone

Welcome to the Preparation Assessment Zone !

In this section, you'll find **ISC Specimen Paper** and **Board Examination Paper 2024** to help you assess your readiness. Attempt these papers to familiarize yourself with the exam format and identify areas that need improvement.

Progress Tracker **Tick the papers as you complete them.**

- ☐ ISC Specimen Paper
- ☐ Board Exam Paper 2024

ISC Specimen Paper

Session 2024-25

Physics (Code 861)

Class 12

General Instructions

1. This paper is divided into four Sections- A, B, C and D. Answer all questions.
2. **Section A** consists of one question having sub-parts of one mark each.
3. **Section B** consists of seven questions of two marks each.
4. **Section C** consists of nine questions of three marks each.
5. **Section D** consists of three questions of five marks each.
6. Internal choices have been provided in two questions each in Section B, Section C and Section D.

- No. of Questions : 20
- No. of Sections : 4
- Time Alloted : 3 Hrs.
- Max. Marks : 70

Section A [14 Marks]

1. A. In questions (i) to (vii) below, choose the correct alternative (a), (b), (c) or (d) for each of the questions given below:

(*i*) Figure below shows a circuit containing an ammeter *A*, a galvanometer *G* and a plug key *K*. When the key is closed, • *Analysis* [1]

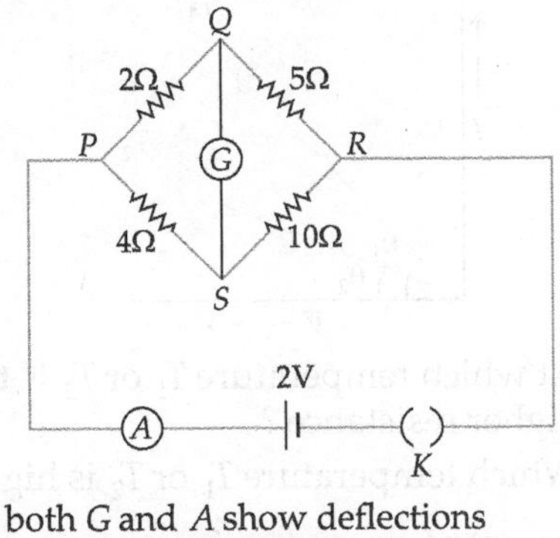

(a) both *G* and *A* show deflections

(b) neither *G* nor *A* shows deflection

(c) *G* shows deflection but *A* does not

(d) *A* shows deflection but *G* does not

(*ii*) A circular coil having *N* turns of radius *R* carrying a current *I* is used to produce a magnetic field *B* at its centre *O*. If this coil is opened and rewound such that the radius of the newly formed coil is 2 *R* carrying the same current *I*, what will be the magnetic field at the centre *O*? • *Analysis* [1]

(a) $2B$ (b) B (c) $\frac{B}{2}$ (d) $\frac{B}{4}$

(*iii*) Magnetic susceptibility of a diamagnetic substance • *Recall* [1]

(a) decreases with the increase in its temperature

(b) is not affected by the change in its temperature

(c) increases with increase in its temperature

(d) first increases, then decreases with increase in its temperature

(*iv*) The de-Broglie wavelength of an electron in the first Bohr's orbit of hydrogen atom is equal to • *Understanding* [1]

(a) diameter of the first orbit

(b) circumference of the first orbit

(c) radius of the second orbit

(d) $\frac{h}{2\pi}$

(*v*) An ideal *p-n* junction diode offers • *Recall* [1]

(a) zero resistance in forward as well as reverse bias

(b) infinite resistance in forward as well as reverse bias

(c) zero resistance in forward but infinite resistance in reverse bias

(d) infinite resistance in forward but zero resistance in reverse bias

(*vi*) Given below are two statements marked Assertion and Reason. Read the two statements and choose the correct option.
Assertion An astronomical telescope has an objective lens having large focal length.
Reason Magnifying power of an astronomical telescope varies directly with focal length of the objective lens. • *Understanding* [1]

(a) Both Assertion and Reason are true and Reason is the correct explanation for Assertion.

(b) Both Assertion and Reason are true but Reason is not the correct explanation for Assertion.

(c) Assertion is false and Reason is true.

(d) Both Assertion and Reason are false.

(*vii*) Given below are two statements marked, Assertion and Reason. Read the two statements and choose the correct option.
Assertion If critical angle of glass-air pair ($\mu_g = 3/2$) is θ_1 and that of water-air pair ($\mu_w = 4/3$) is θ_2, then the critical angle for the water-glass pair will lie between θ_1 and θ_2.
Reason A medium is optically denser, if its refractive index is greater. • *Analysis* [1]

(a) Both Assertion and Reason are true and Reason is the correct explanation for Assertion.

(b) Both Assertion and Reason are true but Reason is not the correct explanation for Assertion.

(c) Assertion is false and Reason is true.

(d) Both Assertion and Reason are false.

B. Answer the following questions briefly.

(*i*) Current I flowing through a metallic wire is gradually increased. Show graphically how heating power (P) developed in it varies with the current (I). • *Application* [1]

(*ii*) Explain why core of a transformer is always laminated? • *Recall* [1]

(*iii*) Why does a car driver use a convex mirror as a rear-view mirror? • *Recall* [1]

(*iv*) Represent diagrammatically how the incident planar wavefronts of wavelength λ pass through an aperture of size d, when d is approximately equal to λ? • *Understanding* [1]

(*v*) What is meant by "Dual nature of matter"? • *Recall* [1]

(*vi*) What happens when an electron collides with a positron? • *Recall* [1]

(*vii*) What energy conversion takes place in a solar cell? • *Recall* [1]

Section B [14 Marks]

2. (*i*) A dielectric slab of dielectric constant K and thickness t is introduced between the two plates of a capacitor of plate- separation d (> t) and common area A. The capacitance of this system is given as

$$C = \frac{\varepsilon_0 A}{(d-t) + \left(\frac{t}{K}\right)}$$

How does the capacitance C modify in each of the following cases? • *Application* [2]

(a) The dielectric slab covers half the distance of separation between the two plates.

(b) The whole space between the plates is filled with the dielectric.

Or

(*ii*) In given figure, the current-voltage graphs for a conductor are given at two different temperatures T_1 and T_2. • *Analysis* [2]

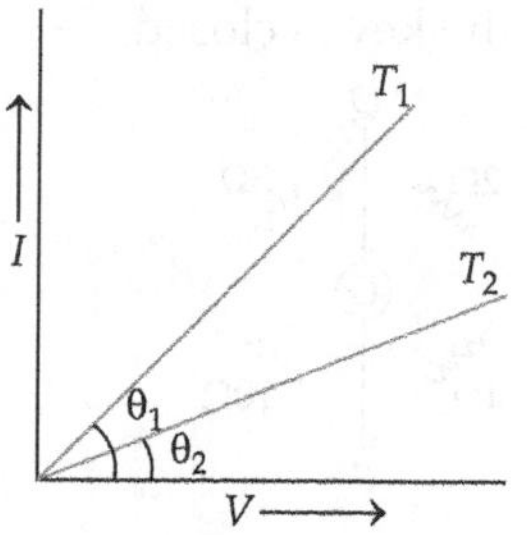

(a) At which temperature T_1 or T_2 is the higher resistance ?

(b) Which temperature T_1 or T_2 is higher?

3. Arrangement of an oxygen ion and two hydrogen ions in a water molecule is shown in figure. Calculate electric dipole moment of water molecule. Express your answer in terms of e (charge on hydrogen ion), l and θ. • *Application* [2]

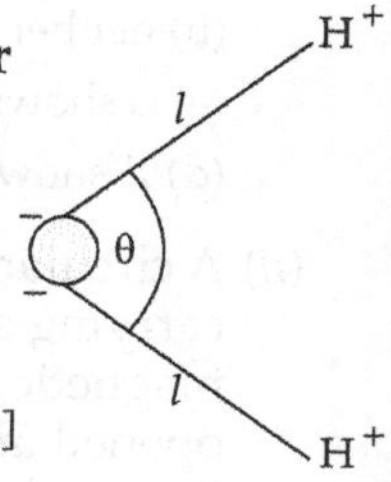

4. (*i*) Figure below shows a part of an electric circuit. • *Application* [2]

(a) Apply Kirchhoff's junction rule to the junction *A* to find current flowing through the 5 Ω resistor.

(b) Apply Kirchhoff's loop rule to the loop *ABDA* to find current flowing through the 7Ω resistor.

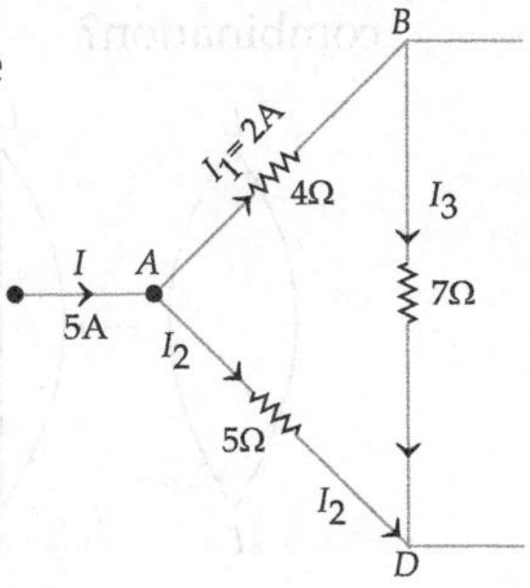

Or (*ii*) In a potentiometer, a cell is balanced against 110 cm when the circuit is open. A cell is balanced at 100 cm when short-circuited through a resistance of 10 Ω. Find the internal resistance of the cell. • *Application* [2]

5. Figure below are two long, parallel wires carrying current in the same direction such that $I_1 < I_2$. • *Recall* [2]

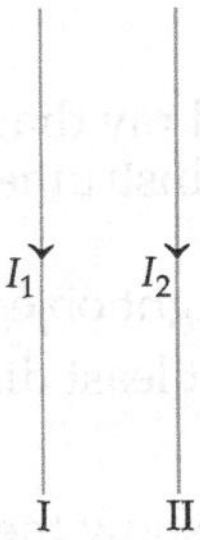

(*i*) In which direction will wire I_1 move?

(*ii*) If the direction of the current I_2 is reversed, then in which direction will the wire I_1 move now?

6. (*i*) The focal length of a double convex lens is equal to the radius of curvature of either surface. What is the refractive index of its material? • *Application* [1]

(*ii*) What is meant by a thin prism? • *Recall* [1]

7. (*i*) Name the electromagnetic radiation that has been used in obtaining the image below • *Recall* [1]

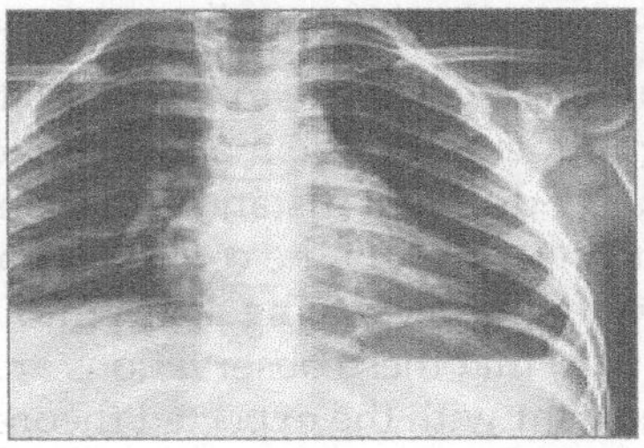

(*ii*) What is the wavelength range of electromagnetic radiation used in radio broadcast? • *Recall* [1]

8. How does stopping potential in photoelectric emission vary, if

(*i*) the intensity of the incident radiation increases? • *Recall* [1]

(*ii*) the frequency of incident radiation decreases? • *Understanding* [1]

Section C [27 Marks]

9. "A uniformly charged conducting spherical shell for the points outside the shell behaves as if the entire charge of the shell is concentrated at its centre". Show this with the help of a proper diagram and verify this statement. • *Recall* [3]

10. (*i*) Study the two circuits shown in figure below. The cells in the two circuits are identical to each other. The resistance of the load resistor *R* is the same in both circuits.

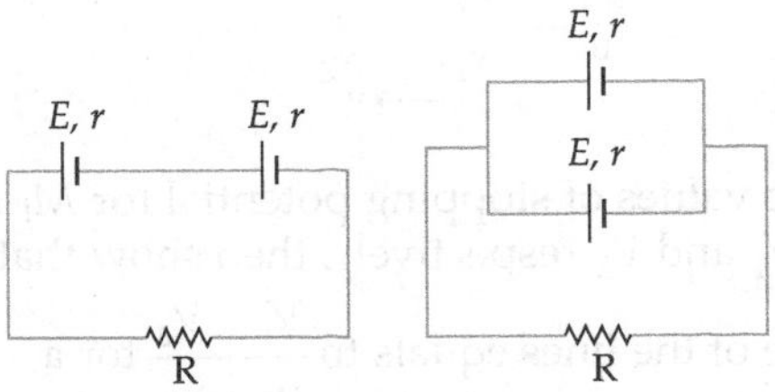

If the same current flows through the resistor *R* in both circuits, calculate the internal resistance of each cell in terms of the resistance of resistor *R*. Show your calculations. • *Application* [3]

Or (*ii*) The drift velocity of electrons in a conductor connected to a battery is given by

$v_d = -e\frac{E\tau}{m}$, where *e* is the charge of the electron, *E* is the electric field, τ is the average time between collisions and *m* is the mass of the electron.

Based on this, answer the following • *Analysis* [3]

(a) How does the drift velocity change with a change in the potential difference across the conductor?

(b) A copper wire of length l is connected to a source. If the copper wire is replaced by another copper wire of the same area of cross-section but of length $4l$, how will the drift velocity change? Explain your answer.

11. A galvanometer of resistance 100 Ω gives a full-scale deflection for a potential difference of 200 mV. • *Application* [3]

(*i*) What must be the resistance connected to convert the galvanometer into an ammeter of the range 0-200 mA?

(*ii*) Determine resistance of the ammeter.

12. (*i*) A student records the following data for the magnitudes (B) of the magnetic field at axial points at different distances x (as shown in figure below) from the centre O of a circular coil of radius a carrying a current I. Verify (for any two) that these observations are in good agreement with the expected theoretical values of B. • *Application* [3]

x	$x=0$	$x=a$	$x=2a$	$x=3a$
B	B_0	$\frac{B_0}{2\sqrt{2}}$	$\frac{B_o}{5\sqrt{5}}$	$\frac{B_0}{10\sqrt{10}}$

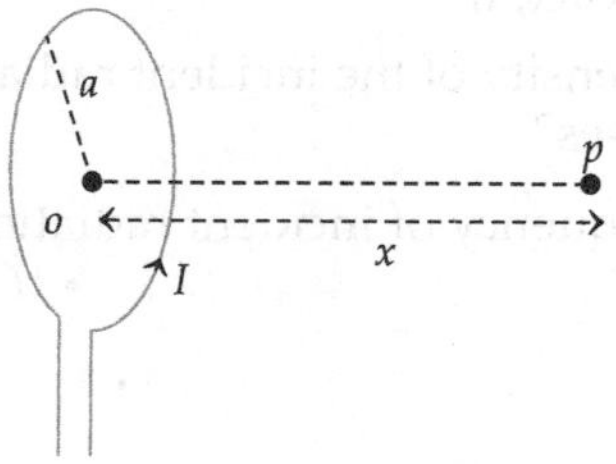

Or

(*ii*) An electron moving along positive X-axis with a velocity of $8\times10^{-7}\ ms^{-1}$ enters a region having uniform magnetic field $B=1.3\times10^{-3}$ T along positive Y-axis. • *Application* [3]

(a) Explain why the electron describes a circular path.

(b) Calculate the radius of the circular path described by the electron.

13. With the help of a neatly drawn labelled diagram, prove the law of reflection on the basis of Huygens' wave theory. • *Recall* [3]

14. A lens of focal length f is divided into two equal parts and then these parts are put in a combination as shown in figure . • *Application* [3]

(*i*) What is the focal length of L_1?

(*ii*) What is the focal length of the final combination?

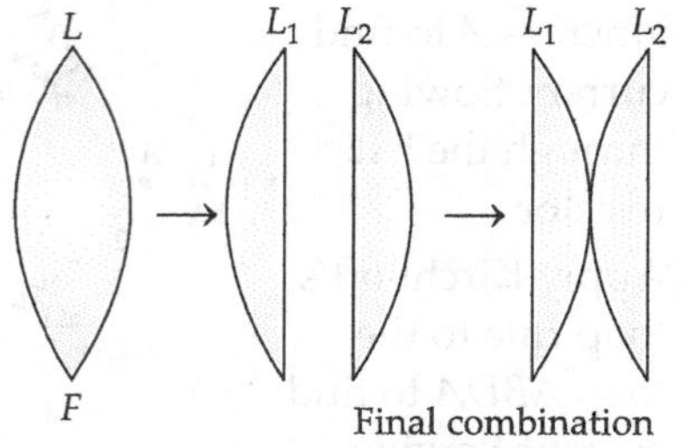

15. In Young's double slit experiment, how is interference pattern affected when the following changes are made • *Understanding* [3]

(*i*) Slits are brought closer to each other.

(*ii*) Screen is moved away from the slits.

(*iii*) Red coloured light is replaced with blue coloured light.

16. (*i*) A virologist studies details of a virus with the help of an instrument. Name the instrument used by him. • *Recall* [1½]

(*ii*) Draw a labelled ray diagram of an image formed by this instrument, assuming • *Recall* [1½]

(a) a small upright object.

(b) image lies at least distance of distinct vision

17. The graphs below show the variation of the stopping potential V_S with the frequency (ν) of the incident radiations for two different photosensitive materials M_1 and M_2.

Express work function for M_1 and M_2 in terms of Planck's constant (h) and threshold frequency and charge of the electron (e).

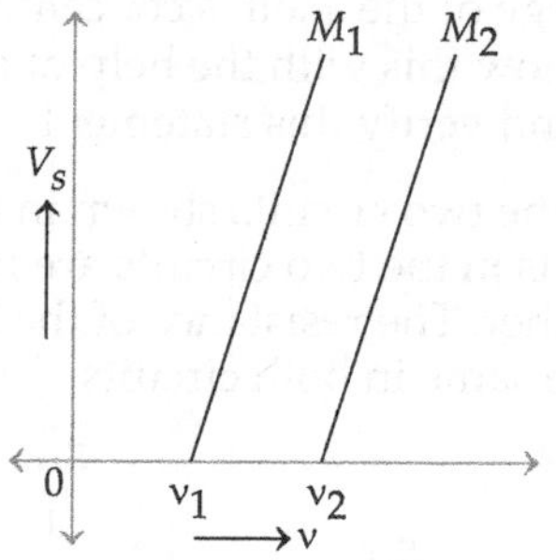

If the values of stopping potential for M_1 and M_2 are V_1 and V_2 respectively, then show that the slope of the lines equals to $\frac{V_1 - V_2}{\nu_1 - \nu_2}$ for a frequency, $\nu > \nu_2$ and also $\nu > \nu_1$. • *Analysis* [3]

Section D [15 Marks]

18. (*i*) The magnetic field through a single loop of wire, 12 cm in radius and 8.5 Ω resistance, changes with time as shown in graph below. The magnetic field is perpendicular to the plane of the loop. [5]

(a) Find the induced emf for the time intervals 0 to 2.0 s, 2.0 to 4.0 s and 4.0 to 6.0 s. • *Application*

(b) Hence, plot induced current as a function of time. • *Application*

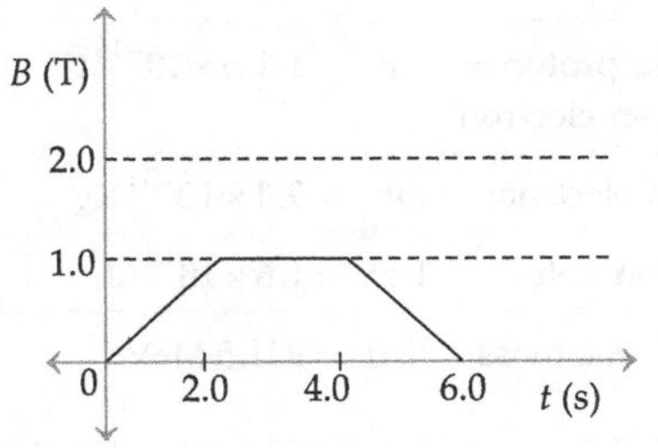

Or (*ii*) Three students, X, Y and Z performed an experiment for studying the variation of AC, with frequency in a series *L-C-R* circuit and obtained the graphs as shown below. They all used

(I) an AC source of the same emf and

(II) inductance of the same value. [5]

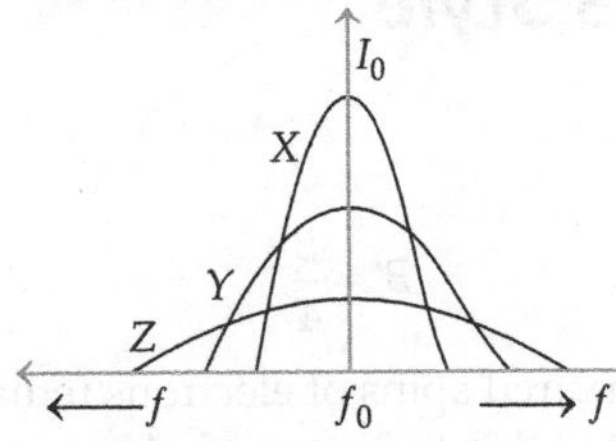

(a) Who used minimum resistance? • *Analysis*

(b) In which case will the quality *Q* factor be maximum? • *Analysis*

(c) What did the students conclude about the nature of impedance at resonant frequency (f_0)? • *Analysis*

(d) An ideal capacitor is connected across 220 V, 50 Hz and 220 V, 100 Hz supplies. Find the ratio of current flowing through it in the two cases. • *Application*

19. (*i*) (a) Find the binding energy per nucleon of ^{235}U based on the information given below.

	Mass (u)
Mass of neutral $^{235}_{92}$U	235.0439
Mass of a proton	1.0073
Mass of a neutron	1.0087

(b) Find the energy released during the following fission reaction.

$$^{235}_{92}\text{U} + {}^{1}_{0}n \rightarrow {}^{236}_{92}\text{U} \rightarrow {}^{90}_{36}\text{Kr} + {}^{143}_{56}\text{Ba} + 3\,{}^{1}_{0}n$$

	Mass (u)
^{235}U	235.0439
^{90}Kr	89.9195
^{143}Ba	142.9206
^{1}n	1.0087

• *Application*

(c) During Rutherford's gold foil experiment, it was observed that most of the α-particles did not deflect. However, some showed a deflection of 180°. What hypothesis was made to justify the deflection of α-particle by 180°? • *Recall* [5]

Or

(*ii*) (a) Define unified atomic mass unit. • *Recall*

(b) Calculate its energy equivalent. • *Application*

(c) In an atom X, electrons absorb the energy from an external source. This energy "excites" the electrons from a lower-energy level to a higher energy level around the nucleus of the atom. When electrons return to the ground state, they emit photons.
Figure below is the energy level diagram of atom X with three energy levels, $E_1 = 0.00$ eV, $E_2 = 1.78$ eV and $E_3 = 2.95$ eV.
The ground state is considered 0 eV for reference. The transition of electrons takes place between levels E_1 and E_2.

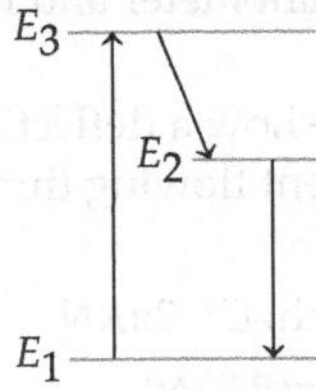

I. What wavelength of radiation is needed to excite the atom to energy level E_2 from E_1? • *Application*

II. Suppose the external source has a power of 100 W. What would be the rate of photon emission? • *Application* [5]

20. Sanya performed an experiment of obtaining characteristic curves of a junction diode. When she forward biased it, she found that beyond forward voltage $V = V_k$, the conductivity is very high. When she reverse biased the diode, she found that a very small current (of about a few microamperes) flows in the diode. It remained constant even though she varied the voltage. [5]

(*i*) In given figure, which one of the diodes is forward biased? • *Recall*

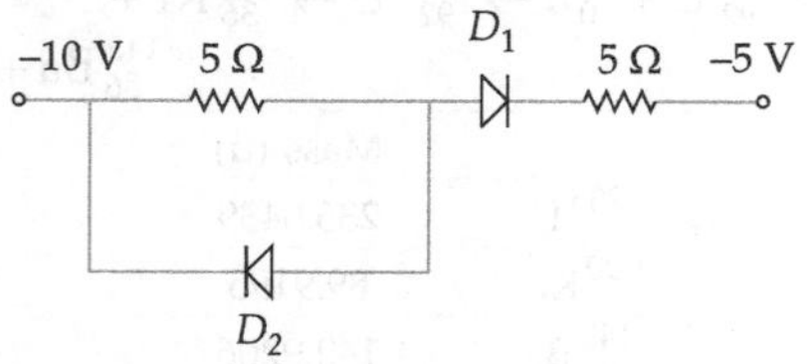

(*ii*) What is meant by a saturation current? • *Application*

(*iii*) When applied voltage during forward bias is small, why does no current flow in the diode? • *Recall*

(*iv*) The circuit shown in the figure below contains two diodes, each with a forward resistance of 50 Ω and with infinite resistance during reverse bias. If the battery voltage is 6V, then calculate the current through the 100 Ω resistance. • *Application*

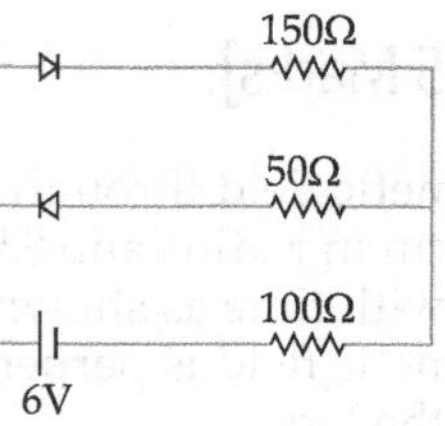

Useful constants and Relations

Planck's constant	h	$= 6.6 \times 10^{-34}$ J-s
Speed of light in vacuum	c	$= 3 \times 10^{8}\ ms^{-1}$
Charge of a proton = Charge of an electron	e	$= \pm 1.6 \times 10^{-19}$ C
Mass of an electron	m	$= 9.1 \times 10^{-31}$ Kg
One electron volt	1 eV	$= 1.6 \times 10^{-19}$ J
Unified atomic mass unit	1 u	= 931.5 MeV

Solutions *in Topper's Style*

1. A. (*i*) (*d*) *A* shows deflection but *G* does not. When key is closed, the galvanometer is connected in parallel with a very low resistance, it will not show any deflection because most of the current by passes the galvanometer and flows through the low resistance.

The ammeter will show a deflection as it measures the current flowing through the circuit.

(*ii*) (*d*) The initial length, $C = 2\pi RN$

New length, $C' = 2\pi(2R)N'$

Since, new length and old length are equal, we have $N' = \dfrac{N}{2}$

Old magnetic field, $B = \dfrac{\mu_0 NI}{2R}$

New magnetic field, $B' = \dfrac{\mu_0 N' I}{2R'}$

On substituting values N' and R', we get

$$\therefore \quad B' = \frac{\mu_0 NI}{4R \cdot 2} \left[\because B = \frac{\mu_0 NI}{2R} \right]$$

$$B' = \frac{B}{4}$$

(*iii*) (*b*) The paired spins of electrons remains unaffected due to increase in temperature, hence diamagnetism is independent of temperature.

(*iv*) (*b*) According to the de-Broglie's hypothesis, the wavelength λ of a particle is given by

$$\lambda = \frac{h}{p}$$

The de-Broglie wavelength of the electron in the first orbit is equals to the circumference of that orbit, i.e. $2\pi r_1$, where r_1 is the radius of the first Bohr orbit. This ensures that the electron's wave fits exactly into the orbit, forming a standing wave with an integer number of wavelengths around the circle.

(*v*) (*c*) When the diode is forward biased, it allows current to flow freely with no voltage drop and when the diode is reverse biased, it does not allow any current to flow, behaving like an open circuit. Thus, in forward bias, the resistance is effectively zero and in reverse bias, it is infinite.

(*vi*) (*a*) Both A and R are true and R is the correct explanation for A.

The magnifying power of an astronomical telescope is given by $M = \frac{f_o}{f_e}$

From the above relation, it can be said that the magnifying power is directly proportional to the focal length of the objective lens, not the focal length of the eyepiece.

(*vii*) (*c*) The critical angle for the water-glass pair (θ_{wg}) is less than both θ_1 and θ_2 and will not lie not between them.

Also, a medium is optically denser, if its refractive index is greater. Hence, Assertion is false and Reason is true.

B. (*i*)

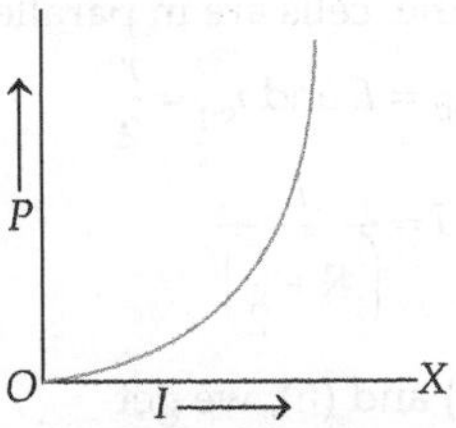

(*ii*) The core of a transformer is always laminated to reduce energy losses due to eddy currents. Laminations increase the electrical resistance of the core, minimising these currents and thus improving efficiency.

(*iii*) A car driver uses a convex mirror as a rear view mirror because it forms diminished image and hence provides a wider field of view, allowing the driver to see more area behind the vehicle.

(*iv*)

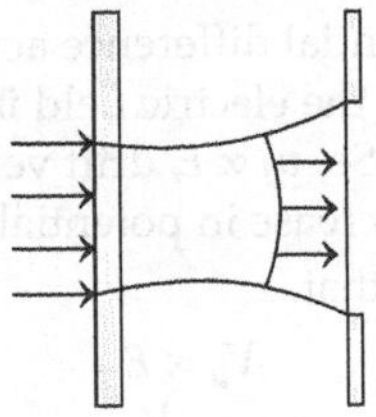

(*v*) The dual nature of matter refers to the concept that particles, such as electrons and photons, exhibit both wave-like and particle like nature.

(*vi*) When an electron collides with a positron, they annihilate each other, producing gamma ray photons.

(*vii*) In a solar cell, light energy is converted into electrical energy.

2. (*i*) (a) Substitute $t = \frac{d}{2}$ in the following equation,

$$\therefore \quad C = \frac{\varepsilon_0 A}{(d-t) + \frac{t}{k}} \quad ...(i)$$

$$C = \frac{\varepsilon_0 A}{\left[\left(d - \frac{d}{2}\right) + \frac{d}{2k}\right]} = \frac{2\varepsilon_0 AK}{[d(k+1)]}$$

(b) Substitute, $t = d$

So, $$C = \frac{k\varepsilon_0 A}{d}$$

Or

(*ii*) (a) The slope of the *I-V* graph gives the conductance,

$$R = \frac{V}{I} = \frac{1}{\tan\theta}$$

$$\therefore \quad \theta_1 > \theta_2$$

$$\tan\theta_1 > \tan\theta_2$$

So, resistance at T_1 < resistance at T_2.

(b) The resistance of a conductor rises with temperature, therefore $T_2 > T_1$.

3. Electric dipole moment is given by

$$p = q \times l \quad ...(i)$$

where, *q* is charge and *l* is distance between two charges.

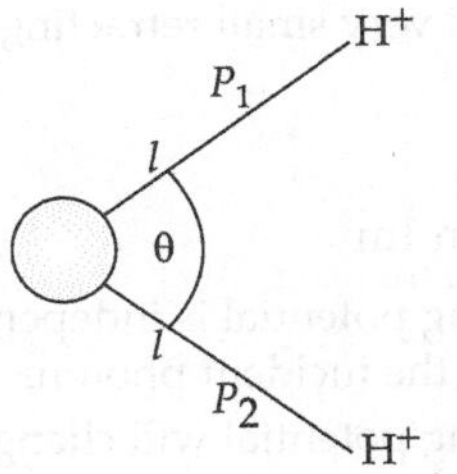

Using Eq. (i), we get

$$p_1 = p_2 = e \times l$$

Net dipole moment, $p' = 2p\cos\alpha = 2e \times l \cos\left(\frac{\theta}{2}\right)$

4. (*i*) (a) According to the Kirchhoff's junction rule to the junction *A*,

$$I = I_1 + I_2$$

$$5 = 2 + I_2$$

$$I_2 = 5 - 2 = 3\text{A}$$

(b) Apply Kirchhoff's loop rule to the loop *ABDA*,

$$I_1 \times 4 + I_3 \times 7 = I_2 \times 5$$

$$2 \times 4 + I_3 \times 7 = 3 \times 5$$

$$8 + 7I_3 = 15$$

$$I_3 = \frac{15-8}{7}$$

Hence, $I_3 = 1\text{A}$

Or

(*ii*) Given, resistance, $R = 10\ \Omega$

$$l_1 = 110 \text{ cm}$$

$$l_2 = 100 \text{ cm}$$

Internal resistance, $r = ?$

$$r = R\left(\frac{l_1}{l_2 - 1}\right) = 10\left(\frac{110}{100-1}\right) = 11.11\Omega$$

5. (*i*) Two long parallel wires carrying current in the same direction attract each other, therefore, it will move towards I_2.

(*ii*) Two long, parallel wires carrying current in the opposite direction repel each other, therefore it will move away from I_2.

6. (*i*) Focal length of a lens is given by

$$\frac{1}{f}=(\mu-1)\left(\frac{1}{R_1}+\frac{1}{R_2}\right)$$

By the given information, we have

$$R_1=R_2=f$$

$$\frac{1}{f}=(\mu-1)\left(\frac{1}{f}+\frac{1}{f}\right)$$

$$(\mu-1)=\frac{1}{2}$$

So, $\mu=1.5$

(*ii*) A thin prism is a transparent, triangular prism which has a very small refracting angle, i.e. less than 4°.

7. (*i*) X-rays

(*ii*) Greater than 1m

8. (*i*) The stopping potential is independent of the intensity of the incident photon.

(*ii*) The stopping potential will change with the frequency of the incident photon.

9. A uniformly charged spherical shell of radius R carrying charge density σ.

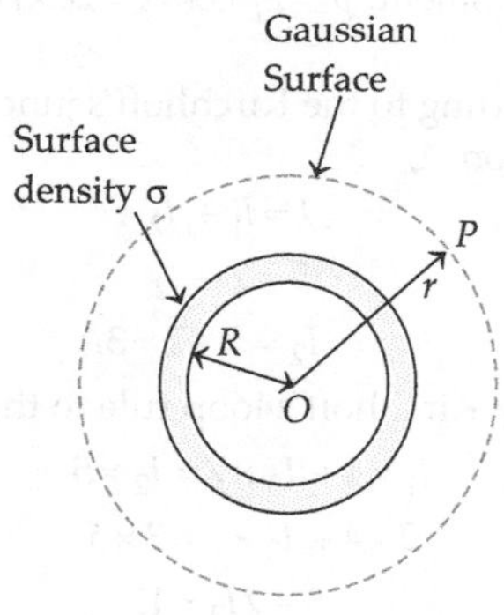

According to the Gaussian surface, a sphere of radius $r>R$ and with centre O, passing through P.

E and ΔS (area vector) at every point are parallel.

Hence, flux through each of the area element,

$$\Delta\phi=E\cdot\Delta S$$

Summing over all ΔS,

$$\Delta\phi=E\cdot 4\pi R^2$$

The charge enclosed is $\sigma\times 4\pi R^2$.

By Gauss's law, $E\times 4\pi r^2=\frac{q}{\varepsilon_0}=\frac{\sigma\times 4\pi R^2}{\varepsilon_0}$

$$E=\frac{\sigma R^2}{\varepsilon_0 r^2}=\frac{q}{4\pi\varepsilon_0 r^2}$$

According to the coulomb's law, this formula is exactly similar to the field produced by a point charge q placed at the centre O.

10. (*i*) $I=\frac{E}{(R+r)}$

where, $E=$ the emf of the cell

and $r=$ internal resistance of the cell.

In circuit 1, the cells are in series.

$\therefore$ $E_{eq}=2E$ and $r_{eq}=2r$

Hence, $I=\frac{2E}{(R+2r)}$ ...(i)

In circuit 2, the cells are in parallel.

$\therefore$ $E_{eq}=E$ and $r_{eq}=\frac{r}{2}$

$\therefore$ $I=\frac{E}{\left(R+\frac{r}{2}\right)}$ ...(ii)

From Eqs. (i) and (ii), we get

$$\frac{2E}{(R+2r)}=\frac{E}{\left(R+\frac{r}{2}\right)}$$

$$2\left(R+\frac{r}{2}\right)=R+2r$$

$$2R+r=R+2r$$

$$\therefore\quad r=R$$

Or

(*ii*) (a) If the potential difference across the conductor is increased, the electric field inside the conductor increases. So, $v_d\propto E$, drift velocity also increases with an increase in potential difference.

(b) We know that,

$$V_d\propto E$$

But $E=\frac{V}{l}$

Hence, when length increases to $4l$, drift velocity becomes $\left(\frac{1}{4}\right)$th of the original value.

11. (*i*) Given, galvanometer of resistance, $G=100\,\Omega$

Potential difference, $V_g=200$ mV

$I=200$ mA

Resistance to be connected to the galvameter to convert to an ammeter.

$$S=I_gG/(I-I_g)$$

Here, $I_g=V_g/G=200/100=2$ mA

$\therefore$ $S=2\times10^{-3}\times100/(0.2-0.002)=1.01\,\Omega$

(*ii*) The resistance of the ammeter,

$$\frac{1}{R}=\frac{1}{100}+\frac{1}{1.01}=0.999\,\Omega$$

12. (*i*) The expression for B at an axial point of a circular coil carrying current is

For N turns

$$B=\frac{\mu_0}{4\pi}\frac{2NI(\pi a^2)}{r^3}$$

For $N=1$ turn

$$B=\frac{\mu_0}{4\pi}\frac{2I(\pi a^2)}{r^3}$$

At the centre, $x=0$;

$$B=\frac{\mu_0}{2}\frac{I}{a}$$

At $x=a$; $B=\dfrac{B_0}{2\sqrt{2}}$

At $x=2a$; $B=\dfrac{B_0}{5\sqrt{5}}$

At $x=3a$; $B=\dfrac{B_0}{10\sqrt{10}}$

Or (*ii*) (a) The electron describes a circular path because force exerted by the magnetic field is always perpendicular to its velocity, hence it provides the necessary centripetal force to the electron.

(b) Given, $v=8\times10^{-7}\ \text{ms}^{-1}$

$$B=1.3\times10^{-3}\ \text{T}$$

We know that, $\dfrac{e}{m}=\dfrac{v}{Br}$

$$\frac{1.6\times10^{-19}}{9.1\times10^{-31}}=\frac{8\times10^{-7}}{1.3\times10^{-3}\times r}$$

$$r=\frac{8\times10^{-7}\times9.1\times10^{-31}}{1.6\times10^{-19}\times1.3\times10^{-3}}$$

So, $r=0.35$ m

13. Let 1, 2, 3 be the incident rays and 1′, 2′, 3′ be the corresponding reflected rays.

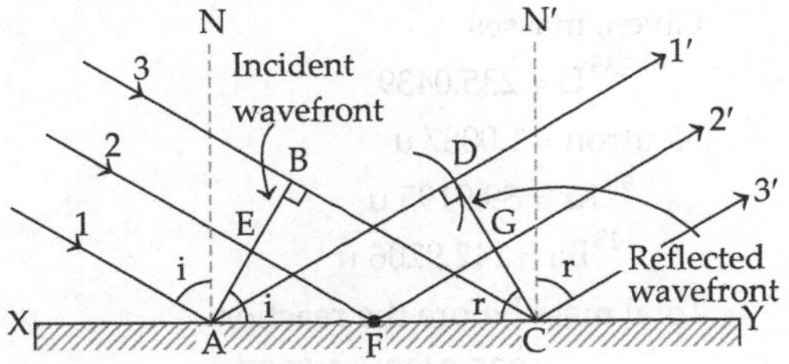

If c is the speed of the light, t is the time taken by light to go from B to C or A to D or E to G through F, then

$$t=\frac{EF}{c}+\frac{FG}{c} \quad \ldots(i)$$

In ΔAEF, $\sin i=\dfrac{EF}{AF}$

In ΔFGC, $\sin r=\dfrac{FG}{FC}$ or $t=\dfrac{AF\sin i}{c}+\dfrac{FC\sin r}{c}$

$$\Rightarrow t=\frac{AC\sin r+AF(\sin i-\sin r)}{c} \quad [\because FC=AC-AF]$$

For rays of light from different parts on the incident wavefront, the values of AF are different. But light from different points of the incident wavefront should take the same time to reach the corresponding points on the reflected wavefront.

So, t should not depend upon AF. This is possible only, if

$$\sin i-\sin r=0$$

i.e. $\sin i=\sin r$

or $\angle i=\angle r$ ...(ii)

which is the **first law of reflection.**

Further, the incident wavefront AB, the reflecting surface XY and the reflected wavefront CD are all perpendicular to the plane of the paper. Therefore, incident ray, normal to the mirror XY and reflected ray all lie in the plane of the paper. This proves the **second law of reflection.**

14. (*i*) The focal length of L_1,

$$\frac{1}{f}=(\eta-1)\left(\frac{2}{R}\right)$$

(*ii*) The focal length of the final combination,

$$\frac{1}{f_1}=(\eta-1)\left(\frac{1}{R}\right)$$

$$f_1=2f$$

$$\frac{1}{f_2}=(\eta-1)\left(\frac{2}{R}\right)$$

$$f_2=f$$

15. (*i*) Fringe width is given by

$$\beta=\frac{\lambda D}{d}$$

where, λ is the wavelength of light, D is the distance between the slits and the screen and d is the distance between the slits.

If d decreases, β increases.

(*ii*) If the screen is moved away from the slits (i.e., D increases) the fringe width β will increase. This means the fringes will be farther apart.

(*iii*) When red light is replaced by blue light, λ decreases and thus β decreases.

16. (*i*) The instrument used by a virologist to study details of a virus is a compound microscope.

(*ii*)

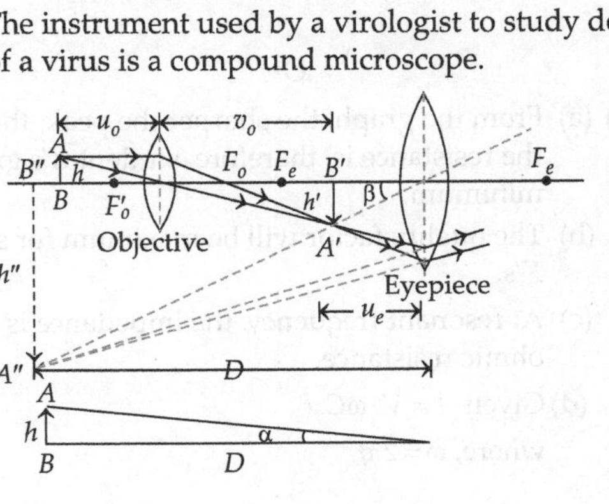

17. Work function for metals M_1 and M_2,

$$W_{01} = \frac{h\nu_{01}}{e} \text{ and } W_{02} = \frac{h\nu_{02}}{e}$$

Stopping potential of metal 1 and 2 are

$$V_1 = \left[\frac{h}{e}\right]\nu - \left[\frac{h}{e}\right]\nu_1$$

$$V_2 = \left[\frac{h}{e}\right]\nu - \left[\frac{h}{e}\right]\nu_2$$

$$\therefore \quad V_1 - V_2 = \left[\frac{h}{e}\right](\nu_1 - \nu_2)$$

$$\left[\frac{h}{e}\right] = \frac{V_1 - V_2}{\nu_1 - \nu_2}$$

18. (*i*) (a) Area of the circular loop $= \pi r^2$

$$= 3.14 \times (0.12)^2 \text{ m}^2 = 4.5 \times 10^{-2} \text{ m}^2$$

$$E = \frac{-d\phi}{dt} = -\frac{d}{dt}(BA)$$

$$= -A\frac{dB}{dt} = -A \cdot \frac{B_2 - B_1}{t_2 - t_1}$$

For $0 < t < 2\text{s}$,

$$E_1 = -4.5 \times 10^{-2}\left\{\frac{1-0}{2-0}\right\}$$

$$= -2.25 \times 10^{-2} \text{ V}$$

$$\therefore \quad I_1 = \frac{E_1}{R} = \frac{-2.25 \times 10^{-2}}{8.5} = -2.6 \times 10^3 \text{A}$$

$$= -2.6 \text{ mA}$$

For $4\text{s} < t < 6\text{s}$,

$$I_3 = \frac{-4.5 \times 10^{-2}}{8.5} \times \left(\frac{0-1}{6-4}\right) \text{A} = 2.6 \text{ mA}$$

(b)

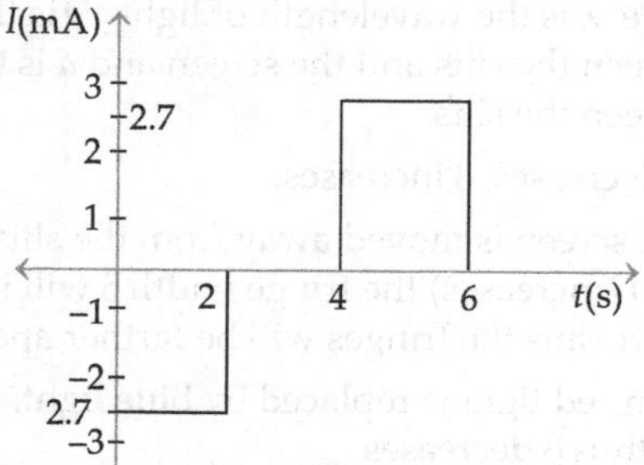

Or

(*ii*) (a) From the graph, the sharper the peak, the lower the resistance is, therefore, student *X*'s graph is minimum.

(b) The quality factor will be maximum for student *X*'s.

(c) At resonant frequency, the impedance is equal to ohmic resistance.

(d) Given, $I = V \cdot \omega C$

where, $\omega = 2\pi f$

For 50 Hz : $I_1 = V \cdot 2\pi \times 50 \times C$

For 100 Hz : $I_2 = V \cdot 2\pi \times 100 \times C$

Ratio of current $\frac{I_1}{I_2} = \frac{V \cdot 2\pi \cdot 50}{V \cdot 2\pi \cdot 100}$

$$= \frac{50}{100} = \frac{1}{2}$$

The ratio of current flowing through it in the two cases is 1:2.

19. (*i*) (a) Given,

Mass of $^{235}U_{nucleus} = 235.0439$

Number of protons $(Z) = 92$

Number of neutrons $(N) = 235 - 92 = 143$

Mass of a proton = 1.0073 u

Mass of a neutron = 1.0087 u

Total mass of proton and neutron

$$= 92 \times 1.0073 + 143 \times 1.0087$$

$$= 92.6716 + 144.2441$$

$$= 236.9157 \text{ u}$$

Mass defect,

$$\Delta m = \text{Total mass} - \text{Mass of } ^{235}\text{U}$$

$$= 236.9157 - 235.0439$$

$$= 1.8718 \text{ u}$$

Convert mass defect to energy

1 atomic mass unit (u) = 931.5 MeV

Binding energy $= \Delta m \times 931.5$

$$= 1.8718 \times 931.5$$

$$= 1743.58$$

Binding energy per nucleon $= \frac{1743.58}{235}$

$$= 7.49 \text{ MeV}$$

(b) $^{235}_{92}\text{U} + ^{1}_{0}n \longrightarrow ^{236}_{92}\text{U} \longrightarrow ^{90}_{36}\text{Kr} + ^{143}_{56}\text{Ba} + 3^{1}_{0}n$

Given, masses

$^{235}\text{U} = 235.0439$

Neutron = 1.0087 u

$^{90}\text{Kr} = 89.9195$ u

$^{143}\text{Ba} = 142.9206$ u

Total mass before the reaction

$$= 235.0439 + 1.0087$$

$$= 236.0526 \text{ u}$$

Total mass after the reaction

$$= 89.9195 + 142.9206 + 3(1.0087)$$

$$= 235.8662 \text{ u}$$

Mass defect (Δm) =

$236.0526 - 235.8662 = 0.1864$ u

$$\theta = \Delta m \times 931.5 \text{ MeV}$$

$$= 0.1864 \times 931.5 \text{ MeV}$$

$$= 173.63 \text{ MeV}$$

(c) Rutherford hypothesised that the atom has a small, dense, positively charged nucleus that cause the deflection of α-particles by 180°.

Or

(*ii*) (a) A standard unit of mass that quantifies mass on a atomic or molecular scale.

(b) The value of E can be calculated (in MeV)

$$1 \text{ amu} = \frac{1}{12} \times \text{mass of one carbon atom}$$

$$= \frac{1}{12} \times \frac{12}{N}$$

$$1 \text{ amu} = \frac{1}{N} \text{ gram}$$

$$1 \text{ u} = \frac{1}{6.0221 \times 10^{23}}$$

$$= 1.6605 \times 10^{-24} \text{ g}$$

$$1 \text{ u} = 1.6605 \times 10^{-27} \text{kg}$$

$$E = mc^2$$

$$= 1.6605 \times 10^{-27} \times (3.0 \times 10^8)^2$$

$$= \frac{1.4924 \times 10^{-10}}{1.6022 \times 10^{-13}} \text{ MeV}$$

$$= 931.5 \text{ MeV}$$

(c) I. The wavelength of radiation is needed to excite the atom to energy level E_1 to E_3 are

$$\lambda = \frac{hc}{\Delta E}$$

$$= 1.24 \times 10^{-6}/2.95 = 420.3 \text{ nm}$$

When the laser transition takes place between E_1 and E_2.

$\therefore$ The wavelength of the beam of laser produced will be

$$\lambda = \frac{hc}{\Delta E} = 1.24 \times 10^{-6}/1.78$$

$$= 696.6 \text{ nm}$$

II. Energy of photon = 1.78 eV

$$= 1.78 \times 1.602 \times 10^{-19} \text{ J}$$

$$= 2.8516 \times 10^{-19} \text{ J}$$

Photons emitted per second = power (energy emitted per second)/energy of each photon

$$= 100 \text{ W} / 2.8516 \times 10^{-19} \text{J}$$

$$= 3.506 \times 10^{20}$$

20. (*i*) D_2 is forward biased because in D_2, p-side is connected to higher voltage, than n-side.

(*ii*) Saturation current is that current which remains constant even on increasing the potential difference.

(*iii*) Due to the potential barrier or barrier potential difference, no current flows in the diode when applied voltage during forward bias is small.

(*iv*)

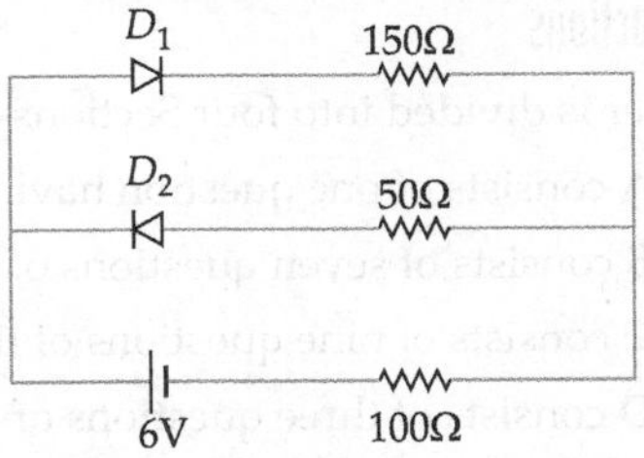

Ignoring 50 Ω because D_2 is reverse biased and offers infinite resistance. By Ohm's law,

$$I = \frac{V}{R} = \frac{6}{(50 + 150 + 100)}$$

$$= \frac{6}{300} = 0.02 \text{ A}$$

Write your Roll No.

Board Exam Paper 2024

Physics 12th (Code 861)

No. of Ques : 20 No. of Sections : 4 Time : 3 Hrs. Max. Marks : 70

General Instructions

1. This paper is divided into four Sections- A, B, C and D. Answer all questions.
2. **Section A** consists of one question having sub-parts of one mark each.
3. **Section B** consists of seven questions of two marks each.
4. **Section C** consists of nine questions of three marks each.
5. **Section D** consists of three questions of five marks each.
6. Internal choices have been provided in two questions each in Section B, Section C and Section D.

Section A [14 Marks]

1. (A) In questions (i) to (vii) given below, choose the correct alternative (a), (b), (c) or (d) for each of the questions.

(i) If potential difference between the two ends of a metallic wire is doubled, then drift speed of free electrons in the wire [1]

(a) remains same (b) becomes double

(c) becomes four times (d) becomes half

(ii) A meter bridge is balanced with a known resistance (R) in the left hand gap and an unknown resistance (S) in the right hand gap. Balance point is found to be at a distance of l cm from the left hand side. When the battery and the galvanometer are interchanged, balance point will [1]

(a) shift towards left

(b) shift towards right

(c) remain same

(d) shift towards left or right depending on the values of R and S

(iii) Lorentz force in vector form is [1]

(a) $F = Bqv\sin\theta$ (b) $\mathbf{F} = q(\mathbf{v} \times \mathbf{B})$

(c) $\mathbf{F} = q(\mathbf{B} \times \mathbf{v})$ (d) $\mathbf{F} = \mathbf{v}(q \times \mathbf{B})$

(iv) **Assertion** (A) When an electric current is passed through a moving coil galvanometer, its coil gets deflected.

Reason (R) A circular coil produces a uniform magnetic field around itself when an electric current is passed through it. [1]

(a) Both Assertion and Reason are true and Reason is the correct explanation for Assertion.

(b) Both Assertion and Reason are true but Reason is not the correct explanation for Assertion.

(c) Assertion is true and Reason is false.

(d) Assertion is false and Reason is true.

(v) When a ray of white light is incident obliquely on the first surface of a prism, then [1]

(a) red colour is deviated most
(b) green colour is deviated most
(c) yellow colour is deviated most
(d) violet colour is deviated most

(vi) The de-Broglie wavelength (λ) associated with a moving electron having kinetic energy (E) is given by [1]

(a) $\frac{2h}{\sqrt{2mE}}$ (b) $\frac{2\sqrt{2mE}}{h}$
(c) $\frac{h}{\sqrt{2mE}}$ (d) $\sqrt{2mhE}$

(vii) The majority charge carriers in a p-type semiconductor are [1]

(a) electrons
(b) holes
(c) protons
(d) ions

B. Answer the following questions briefly.

(i) In an electric dipole, what is the locus of a point having zero potential? [1]

(ii) Three identical cells each of emf e are connected in parallel to form a battery. What is the emf of the battery? [1]

(iii) Three bulbs B_1 (230V, 40W), B_2 (230V, 60W) and B_3 (230V, 100W) are connected in series to a 230V supply. Which bulb glows the brightest? [1]

(iv) Explain the meaning of the following statement Curie temperature for soft iron is 770°C. [1]

(v) What type of wavefronts are associated with a point source of light? [1]

(vi) What is pair production? [1]

(vii) In semiconductor physics, what is the function of a rectifier? [1]

Section B [14 Marks]

2. (i) A hollow sphere of radius R has a point charge q at its centre. Electric flux emanating from the sphere is X. How will the electric flux change, if at all, when [2]

(a) radius of the sphere is doubled?
(b) charge q is replaced by an electric dipole?

Or

(ii) In case of an infinite line charge, how does intensity of electric field at a point change, if at all, when

(a) charge on it is doubled?
(b) distance of the point is halved? [2]

3. (i) What is meant by the statement : "Relative permittivity of water is 81"?

(ii) Can a body be given a charge of 2.2×10^{-19} C? Give a reason for your answer. [2]

4. (i) What type of transformer is used in a mobile phone charger?

(ii) Why is the core of a transformer made of soft iron and not of steel? [2]

5. (i) Name the electromagnetic radiation whose frequency is 10^{11} Hz.

(ii) What is the speed of radio waves in vacuum? [2]

6. Draw a labelled graph showing the variation in intensity of diffracted light with diffracting angle in a single slit Fraunhofer diffraction experiment. [2]

7. (i) Figure given below is the energy level diagram for hydrogen atom. Study the transitions shown and answer the following questions. [2]

(a) State the type of spectrum obtained.
(b) Name the series of spectrum obtained.

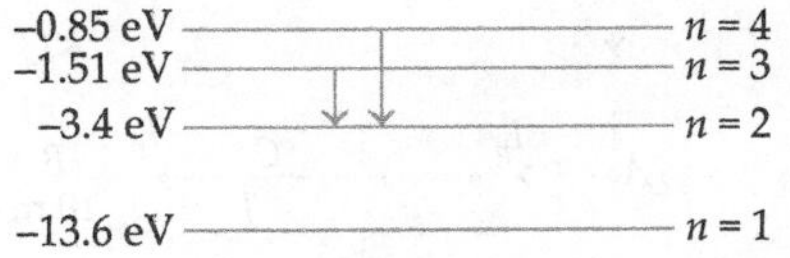

Or

(ii) In a nuclear reactor, state the use of the following.

(a) Graphite rods
(b) Cadmium rods [2]

8. With reference to a semiconductor diode, define the following terms. [2]

(i) Depletion region
(ii) Potential barrier

Section C [27 Marks]

9. Obtain an expression for equivalent capacitance C when three capacitors C_1, C_2 and C_3 are connected in series. [3]

10. (i) The following figure shows two batteries E_1 and E_2 having emfs of 18 V and 10 V and internal resistances of 1 Ω and 2 Ω respectively. W_1, W_2 and W_3 are uniform metallic wires *AC*, *FD* and *BE* having resistance of 8 Ω, 6 Ω and 10 Ω respectively. *B* and *E* are mid-points of the wires W_1 and W_2. Using Kirchhoff's laws of electrical circuits, calculate the current flowing in the wire W_3. [3]

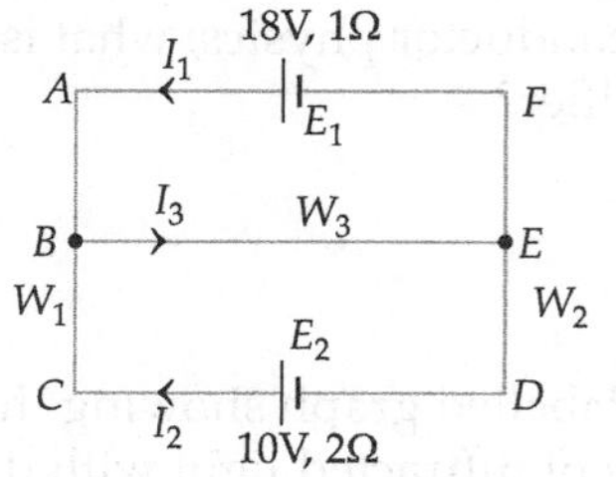

Or

(ii) Figure given below shows a potentiometer circuit in which the driver cell *D* has an emf of 6 V and internal resistance of 2 Ω. The potentiometer wire *AB* is 10 m long and has a resistance of 28 Ω. The series resistance *R* is of 20 Ω. [3]

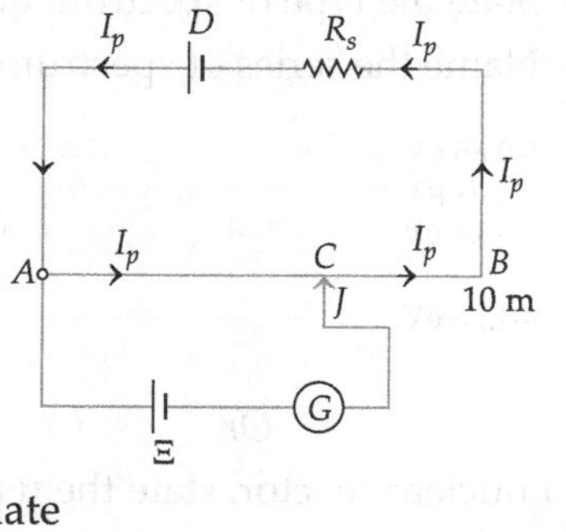

Calculate

(a) the current I_p flowing in the potentiometer wire *AB* when the jockey (*J*) does not touch the wire *AB*.

(b) emf of the cell X, if the balancing length *AC* is 4.5 m.

11. Using Biot-Savart's law, show that magnetic flux density *B* at the centre of a current carrying circular coil of radius *R* is given by [3]

$$B = \frac{\mu_0 I}{2R}$$

where, the terms have their usual meanings.

12. Figure given below shows an infinitely long metallic wire *YY′* which is carrying a current *I′*. *P* is a point at a perpendicular distance *r* from it. [3]

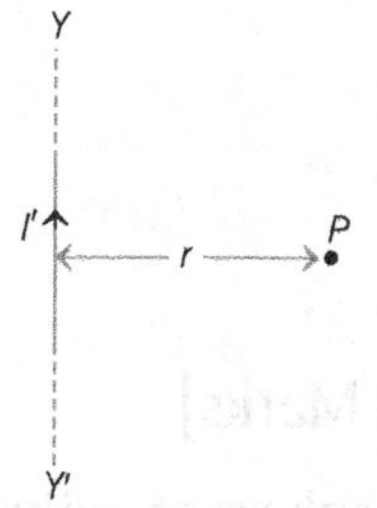

(i) What is the direction of magnetic flux density *B* of the magnetic field at the point *P*?

(ii) What is the magnitude of magnetic flux density *B* of the magnetic field at the point *P*?

(iii) Another metallic wire *MN* having length *l* and carrying a current *I* is now kept at the point *P*. If the two wires are in vacuum and parallel to each other, how much force acts on the wire *MN* due to the current *I′* flowing in the wire *YY′*?

13. (i) Using Huygens' wave theory, show that (for refraction of light) [3]

$$\frac{\sin i}{\sin r} = \text{constant}$$

where, the terms have their usual meanings. You must draw a neat and labelled diagram.

Or

(ii) In Young's double slit experiment, show that

$$\beta = \frac{\lambda D}{d}$$ [3]

where, the terms have their usual meanings.

14. Figure given below shows a ray of monochromatic light LM incident on the first surface AB of a regular (equilateral) glass prism ABC. The emergent ray grazes the adjacent surface AC. Calculate the angle of incidence. (Refractive index of glass = 1.5) [3]

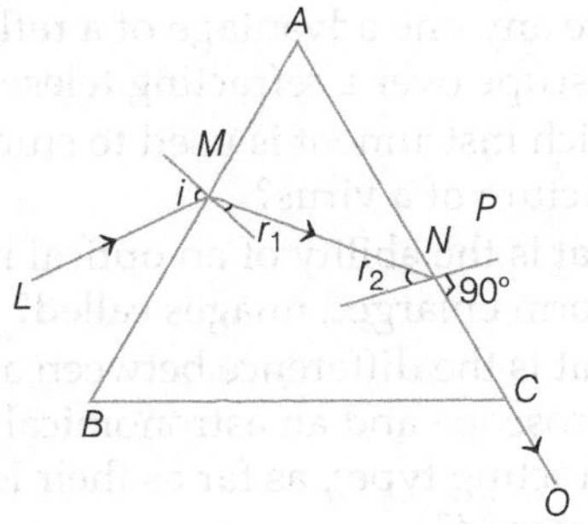

15. A student is performing an experiment to determine focal length of a convex lens by using lens formula, i.e. by no parallax method. The examiner gives some instructions to the student. The student responds to each instruction as per her understanding of the experiment. [3]

State whether the student's response is correct or incorrect. Give a reason for your answer.

(i) **EXAMINER** Image formed by the lens is magnified. Reduce the size of the image.
STUDENT moves the lens towards the object pin.

(ii) **EXAMINER** Plot a graph of $(1/v)$ against $(1/u)$.
STUDENT takes $(1/v)$ on Y-axis and $(1/u)$ on X-axis.

(iii) **EXAMINER** Write the relation between the optical power (P) and the focal length (f) of the convex lens.
STUDENT writes $P = 2f$.

16. (i) In an experiment on photoelectric effect, how does stopping potential change, if at all, when intensity of incident monochromatic UV-radiation is increased? [3]

(ii) Ultraviolet light is incident on metals P, Q and R, having work functions 8e V, 2e V and 4e V respectively.

(a) Which metal has the lowest threshold frequency for photoelectric effect?

(b) For which metal is the value of E_{max} minimum?

(**Note** E_{max} is maximum kinetic energy of the emitted photoelectrons).

17. (i) What is meant by forward biasing of a semiconductor diode? [3]

(ii) Draw a labelled characteristic curve (I-V graph) for a semiconductor diode during forward bias.

Section D [15 Marks]

18. (i) (a) A 220 V, 50 Hz AC source is connected to a coil having coefficient of self-inductance of 1H and a resistance of 400 Ω. Calculate [5]

(I) the reactance of the coil.

(II) the impedance of the coil.

(III) the current flowing through the coil.

(b) Draw a labelled graph showing variation of impedance (Z) of a series L-C-R circuit *versus* frequency (f) of the AC supply. Mark the resonant frequency as f_o.

Or

(ii) (a) When current flowing through a solenoid decreases from 5A to 0 in 20 millisecond, an emf of 500 V is induced in it. [5]

(I) What is this phenomenon called?

(II) Calculate coefficient of self-inductance of the solenoid.

(b) (I) RMS value of an alternating current flowing in a circuit is 5A. Calculate its peak value.

(II) State any one difference between a direct current (DC) and an alternating current (AC).

19. (i) (a) On the basis of Bohr's theory, derive an expression for the radius of the nth orbit of an electron of hydrogen atom. [5]

(b) Calculate the energy released in the following nuclear fusion reaction

$${}^{2}_{1}H + {}^{2}_{1}H \longrightarrow {}^{4}_{2}He + \text{energy}$$

Mass of ${}^{2}_{1}H$ = 2.014102 u

Mass of ${}^{4}_{2}He$ = 4.002604 u

Or

(ii) (a) Calculate mass defect and binding energy of $^{20}_{10}$Ne nucleus, given [5]

Mass of $^{20}_{10}$Ne = 19.992397u,

Mass of $^{1}_{1}$H = 1.007825u,

Mass of $^{1}_{0}n$ = 1.008665u.

(b) State the Bohr's postulate of angular momentum of an electron.

(c) (I) What is the velocity of an electron in the 3rd orbit of hydrogen atom, if its velocity in the 1st orbit is v_0?

(II) Radius of the 1st orbit of hydrogen atom is r_0. What will be the radius of the 4th orbit?

20. Read the passage given below and answer the questions that follow. [5]

There are two types of optical instruments : Microscopes and Telescopes.

Microscopes are used to magnify very tiny objects whereas telescopes are used to study distant objects. Both of them deploy convex lenses. In his telescope, Newton used a large parabolic mirror to collect light from the stars and reduce aberrations.

(i) Rohit observed the launch of Chandrayan 3 with the help of an optical instrument. Name the instrument used by him.

(ii) State any one advantage of a reflecting telescope over a refracting telescope.

(iii) Which instrument is used to study the structure of a virus?

(iv) What is the ability of an optical instrument to form enlarged images called?

(v) What is the difference between a compound microscope and an astronomical telescope (refracting type), as far as their lenses are concerned?

Useful Constants and Relations

1.	Charge of a proton	e	1.6×10^{-19} C
2.	Speed of light in vacuum	c	3×10^{8}ms^{-1}
3.	Unified atomic Mass	1u	931 MeV

Solutions *in Topper's Style*

1. (A) (i) (*b*) Drift speed is given as

$$v_d = \frac{eE}{m}\tau \quad \text{and} \quad E = \frac{V}{l}$$

Put value of E in v_d,

$$v_d = \frac{eV}{ml}\tau \Rightarrow v_d \propto V$$

So, if potential difference is doubled, then v_d also becomes double.

(ii) (*c*) If the galvanometer and battery are interchanged, the position of balance point remains unchanged. Hence, the galvanometer will show no current. Interchanging the resistors R and S can change the balance point.

(iii) (*b*) Expression for Lorentz force is given as

$$\mathbf{F} = q(\mathbf{v}\times\mathbf{B})$$

where, q is charge of the particle, $\mathbf{v}$ is velocity of the particle and $\mathbf{B}$ is the magnetic field in which the particle is moving.

(iv) (*c*) Assertion is true and Reason is false.

When an electric current is passed through a moving coil galvanometer, its coil gets deflected as when a current carrying coil is placed in a uniform magnetic field, it gets deflected because of torque acting on it. A non-uniform magnetic field is produced around the circular coil when an electric current is passed through it.

(v) (*d*) Shorter wavelengths (like violet) deviate more in a prism due to increased refraction, whereas longer wavelengths (like red) deviate least. The deviation of light in a prism is dependent on its wavelength. Hence, violet colour deviates the most.

(vi) (*c*) The de-Broglie wavelength (λ) associated with a moving electron is given as

$$\lambda = \frac{h}{p} \quad \text{...(i)}$$

and kinetic energy, $E = \frac{1}{2}mv^2 = \frac{p^2}{2m}$

$\Rightarrow \qquad p = \sqrt{2mE} \qquad \ldots\text{(ii)}$

From Eqs. (i) and (ii), we get

$$\lambda = \frac{h}{\sqrt{2mE}}$$

(vii) (*b*) The majority charge carriers in a *p*-type semiconductor are holes.

(B) (i) The locus of a point having zero potential is a vertical straight line which is the perpendicular bisector (equatorial line) of an electric dipole.

(ii) In a parallel combination, the total emf of the battery will be the same as that of the individual emf of the cells.

(iii) In series combination, the same current flows through each bulb. Resistance, $R = \frac{V^2}{P}$ or $R \propto \frac{1}{P}$

Therefore, the resistance of 40 W bulb is highest for the given three bulbs.

Heat produced, $H = I^2Rt$ or $H \propto R$, so maximum heat is produced in 40 W bulb.

As a result of it, 40 W bulb will glow more brightly than the other two bulbs.

(iv) Soft iron is a ferromagnetic material. So, above 770°C temperature, it loses its permanent magnetic field and the magnetism completely disappears. Above this temperature, the ferromagnetic material behaves as a paramagnetic substance.

(v) Light point sources are connected to spherical wavefronts.

(vi) When an energetic γ-ray photon falls on a heavy substance, it is absorbed by some nucleus of the substance and an electron and a positron are produced.

This phenomenon is called pair production and may be represented by the equation

$$h\nu \longrightarrow {}_{+1}\beta^0 + {}_{-1}\beta^0$$

(vii) The process of converting alternating voltage/current into direct voltage/current is called rectification. Diode is used as a rectifier for converting alternating current/voltage into direct current/voltage.

2. (i) (a) Using Gauss' theorem, we have

Electric flux, $\phi_E = \frac{q}{\varepsilon_0}$

So, making the radius of the sphere double does not change the electric flux emanating from the sphere.

(b) Since, the total charge of an electric dipole is zero. So, if charge *q* is replaced by an electric dipole, then electric flux will be zero.

Or (ii) The intensity of electric field at a point due to infinite line charge is given as

$$E = \frac{\lambda}{2\pi\varepsilon_0 r}$$

where, λ is the uniform line charge density and *r* is the magnitude of radial distance.

(a) If charge on line charge conductor is doubled, electric field will remain same as it is independent of charge.

(b) If distance of the point is halved, the electric field will become double, i.e.

$$E' = \frac{\lambda}{2\pi\varepsilon_0\left(\frac{r}{2}\right)} = 2\left(\frac{\lambda}{2\pi\varepsilon_0 r}\right) = 2E$$

3. (i) Relative permittivity (ε_r) of water is the ratio of absolute permittivity (ε) and permittivity of free space (ε_0).

i.e., $\varepsilon_r = \frac{\varepsilon}{\varepsilon_0}$

It means that permittivity of water is 81 times that of free space.

(ii) No, because 8.6×10^{-19}C is not an integral multiple of quantum of charge which is 1.6×10^{-19}C.

4. (i) Mobile phone charger contains a step-down transformer to convert the input of 220 V to a working output voltage of around 5 V, since it works on the simple principle of conversion of AC (alternating current) to DC (direct current).

(ii) Soft iron loses all its magnetic properties when the current in the coil is switched OFF, whereas steel does not lose its magnetic properties when the current is stopped. Soft iron has high coercivity and low retentivity.

5. (i) Infrared radiation has frequency range 3×10^{11} Hz to 4×10^{14} Hz.

(ii) Radio wave is an electromagnetic wave. These waves do not require any material medium for propagation and travel in vacuum with the speed of light. i.e., 3×10^8 m/s.

6. Intensity distribution for Fraunhofer diffraction at a single slit.

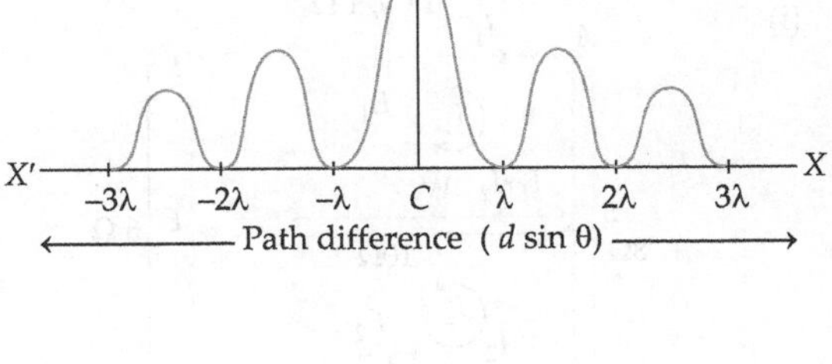

7. (i) (a) Electron goes from higher to lower energy state. So, the spectrum is emission spectrum.

(b) Balmer series

Or

(ii) (a) In a nuclear reactor, graphite rods control the rate of fission reactions by moderating neutron speed.

(b) Cadmium rods absorb excess neutrons to regulate reactor power output.

8. (i) The region on either side of the junction which becomes depleted (free) from the mobile charge carriers is called depletion region or depletion layer. The width of depletion region is of the order of 10^{-6} m.

(ii) The potential difference developed across the depletion region is called the potential barrier. It depends on dopant concentration in the semiconductor and temperature of the junction.

9. When a potential difference (V) is applied across several capacitors connected end-to-end in such a way that, sum of potential differences across all the capacitors is equal to the applied potential difference V, then these capacitors are said to be connected in series.

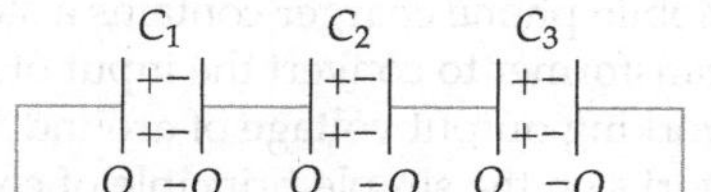

The potential difference across the separate capacitors are given by

$$V_1 = \frac{Q}{C_1},\ V_2 = \frac{Q}{C_2} \text{ and } V_3 = \frac{Q}{C_3}$$

However, the potential difference across the series combination of capacitors is V volt

where, $V = V_1 + V_2 + V_3$ ...(i)

Let C_s represents the equivalent capacitance, then

$$V = \frac{Q}{C_s} \quad \text{...(ii)}$$

Combining Eqs. (i) and (ii), we get

$$\frac{Q}{C_s} = \frac{Q}{C_1} + \frac{Q}{C_2} + \frac{Q}{C_3} \Rightarrow \frac{1}{C_s} = \frac{1}{C_1} + \frac{1}{C_2} + \frac{1}{C_3}$$

10. (i)

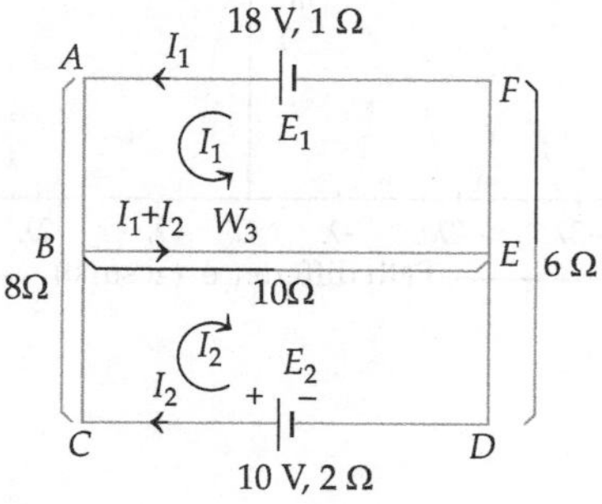

Applying equation in loop $AFEBA$,

$$3I_1 + 1I_1 + 4I_1 + 10(I_1 + I_2) = 18 \quad \text{...(i)}$$

and in loop $BCDEB$,

$$3I_2 + 2I_2 + 4I_2 + 10(I_1 + I_2) = 10 \quad \text{...(ii)}$$

From Eqs. (i) and (ii), we get

$$18I_1 + 10I_2 = 18 \quad \text{...(iii)}$$

$$10I_1 + 19I_2 = 10 \quad \text{...(iv)}$$

From Eq. (iv), $I_1 = \frac{10 - 19I_2}{10}$ ...(v)

Substitute value of Eq. (v) in Eq. (iii), we get

$$\frac{18}{10}(10 - 19I_2) + 10I_2 = 18$$

$$\Rightarrow \frac{180}{10} - \frac{342}{10}I_2 + 10I_2 = 18$$

$$\Rightarrow \frac{(-342 + 100)}{10}I_2 = 18 - \frac{180}{10}$$

$$\Rightarrow I_2 = 0$$

From Eq. (v), $I_1 = \frac{10 - 19I_2}{10} = \frac{10}{10} = 1$ A

$$I_3 = I_1 + I_2 = 1\text{A}$$

Or

(ii)

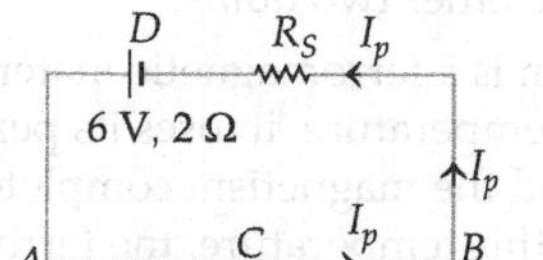

(a) The current flowing in the potentiometer wire AB when the jockey (J) does not touch the wire AB,

$$I_p = \frac{V}{R_{net}} = \frac{6\text{V}}{R_{AB} + R_s + r}$$

$$= \frac{6}{28 + 20 + 2} = \frac{6}{50} = 0.12 \text{ A}$$

(b) When the jockey is moved to point B, potential drop will be

$$V_{AB} = I_p \cdot R_{AB}$$

$$\Rightarrow = 0.12 \times 28 = 3.36 \text{ V}$$

Length of the wire AB is 10 m, so potential gradient,

$$K = \frac{V_{AB}}{L} = \frac{3.36}{10} = 0.336\ \Omega / \text{m}$$

The length of the wire AC is 4.5 m in the null deflection position or balancing position, then potential difference between points A and C,

$$V_{AC} = 0.336 \times 4.5 = 1.512 \text{ V}$$

∴ The emf of cell X is 1.512 V.

11. Consider a circular coil of radius R and carrying a current I in the direction as shown in figure. Suppose the entire circular coil is divided into a large number of current elements, each of length dl.

According to Biot-Savart's law, the magnetic field dB at the centre O of the coil due to the current element Idl is given by

$$B = \frac{\mu_0}{4\pi} \frac{I(d\mathbf{l} \times \mathbf{R})}{R^3} \quad ...(i)$$

The magnitude of dB at the centre O is

$$dB = \frac{\mu_0}{4\pi} \frac{Idl \times R \sin\theta}{R^3}$$

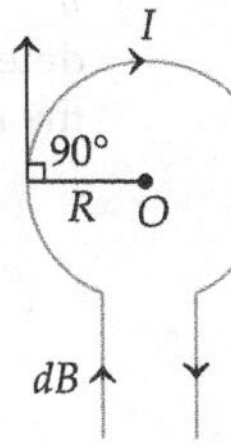

$$\Rightarrow \quad dB = \frac{\mu_0}{4\pi} \frac{Idl \sin\theta}{R^2}$$

$$\therefore \quad B = \int dB = \int \frac{\mu_0}{4\pi} \frac{Idl \sin\theta}{R^2}$$

$$\theta = 90^\circ \quad \Rightarrow \quad \sin 90^\circ = 1$$

$$\therefore \quad B = \frac{\mu_0}{4\pi} \frac{I}{R^2} \int dl$$

$$\int dl = \text{Total length of the coil} = 2\pi R$$

$$\Rightarrow \quad B = \frac{\mu_0}{4\pi} \frac{I}{R^2} (2\pi R) = \frac{\mu_0 I}{2R}$$

12. (i) According to right hand thumb rule, the direction of magnetic flux density B of the magnetic field at the point P is downward and into the paper.

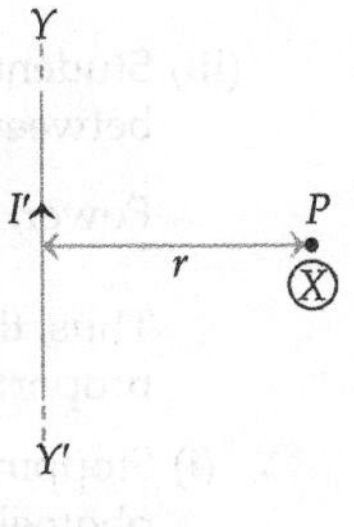

(ii) Magnitude of magnetic flux density B of the magnetic field at the point P is $B = \frac{\mu_0 I}{2\pi r}$

(iii) Force between two current-carrying parallel conductors per unit length is given by

$$F = \frac{\mu_0}{4\pi} \cdot \frac{2I_1 I_2}{r}$$

Force on wire MN having length l and carrying a current I due to long metallic wire YY',

$$F = \frac{\mu_0}{4\pi} \frac{2I' I}{r} \cdot l$$

13. (i) Let 1, 2, 3 be the incident rays and 1′, 2′, 3′ be the corresponding refracted rays.

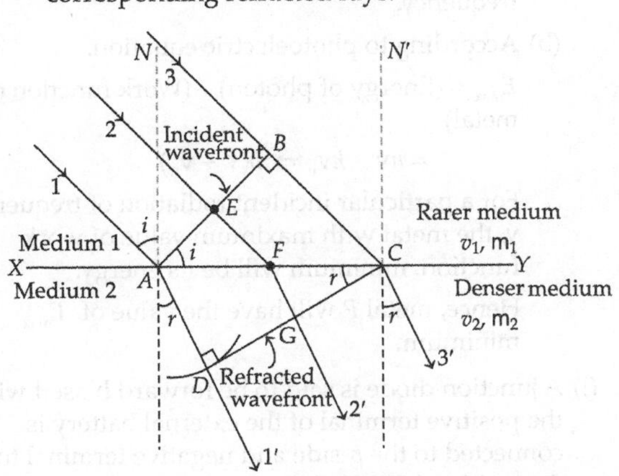

If v_1, v_2 are the speeds of light in the two media and t is the time taken by light to go from B to C or A to D or E to G through F, then $t = \frac{EF}{v_1} + \frac{FG}{v_2}$

In ΔAFE, $\quad \sin i = \frac{EF}{AF}$

In ΔFGC, $\quad \sin r = \frac{FG}{FC}$

$$\Rightarrow \quad t = \frac{AF \sin i}{v_1} + \frac{FC \sin r}{v_2}$$

$$\Rightarrow \quad t = \frac{AC \sin r}{v_2} + AF\left(\frac{\sin i}{v_1} - \frac{\sin r}{v_2}\right)$$

$[\because FC = AC - AF]$

For rays of light from different parts on the incident wavefront, the values of AF are different. But light from different points of the incident wavefront should take the same time to reach the corresponding points on the refracted wavefront. So, t should not depend upon AF. This is possible only, if

$$\frac{\sin i}{V_1} - \frac{\sin r}{V_2} = 0$$

$$\Rightarrow \quad \frac{\sin i}{\sin r} = \frac{v_1}{v_2} \quad ...(i)$$

Now, if c represents the speed of light in vacuum, then $\mu_1 = \frac{c}{v_1}$ and $\mu_2 = \frac{c}{v_2}$ are known as the **refractive indices** of medium 1 and medium 2, respectively. In terms of refractive indices, Eq. (i) can be written as

$$\mu_1 \sin i = \mu_2 \sin r$$

$$\Rightarrow \quad \mu = \frac{\sin i}{\sin r}$$

This is known as **Snell's law of refraction.**

Or

(ii) Suppose S_1 and S_2 are two fine slits, a small distance d apart. They are illuminated by a strong source S of monochromatic light of wavelength λ. MN is a screen at a distance D from the slits.

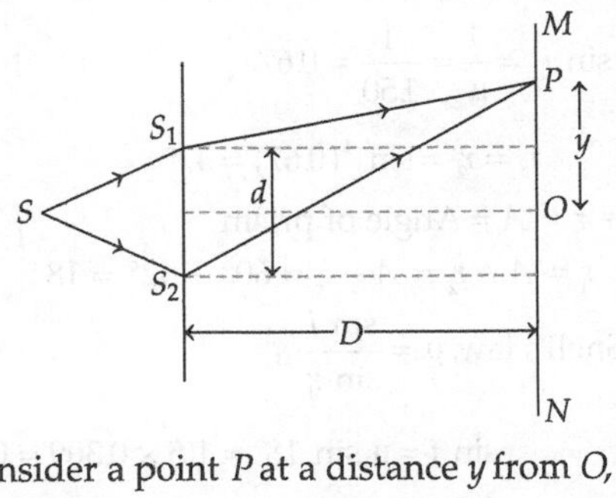

Consider a point P at a distance y from O, the centre of screen.

The path difference between two waves arriving at point P is equal to $S_2P - S_1P$.

Now, $(S_2P)^2 - (S_1P)^2$

$$= \left[D^2 + \left(y + \frac{d}{2}\right)^2\right] - \left[D^2 + \left(y - \frac{d}{2}\right)^2\right] = 2yd$$

Thus, $S_2P - S_1P = \dfrac{2yd}{S_2P + S_1P}$

But $S_2P + S_1P \approx 2D \quad \therefore \quad S_2P - S_1P \approx \dfrac{dy}{D}$

For constructive interference (Bright fringes)

Path difference $= \dfrac{dy}{D} = n\lambda$, where, $n = 0, 1, 2, 3, \ldots$

$\therefore \quad y = \dfrac{nD\lambda}{d} \quad [\because n = 0, 1, 2, 3, \ldots]$

Hence, for $n = 0$, $y_0 = 0$ at O central bright fringe

for $n = 1$, $\quad y_1 = \dfrac{D\lambda}{d}$ for 1st bright fringe

for $n = 2$, $\quad y_2 = \dfrac{2D\lambda}{d}$ for 2nd bright fringe

for $n = n$, $\quad y_n = \dfrac{nD\lambda}{d}$ for nth bright fringe

The separation between two consecutive bright fringes is $\beta = \dfrac{nD\lambda}{d} - \dfrac{(n-1)D\lambda}{d} = \dfrac{D\lambda}{d}$

Fringe width of dark fringes is also same.

14. Consider the given figure

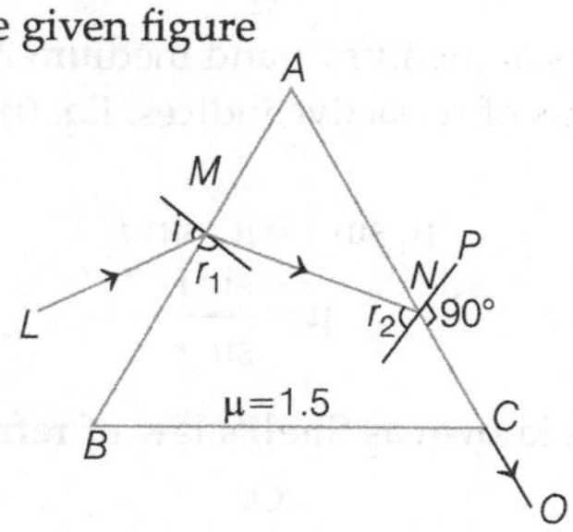

The refracted ray NO will just suffer total internal reflection or grazes the surface AC, if it is incident at the critical angle i_c, i.e. $r_2 = i_c$.

Now, for face AC,

$$\sin i_c = \frac{1}{\mu} = \frac{1}{1.50} = 0.67$$

$\Rightarrow \quad i_c = r_2 = \sin^{-1}(0.67) = 42°$

But $r_2 + r_1 = A =$ Angle of prism

$\Rightarrow \quad r_1 = A - r_2 = A - i_c = 60° - 42° = 18°$

From Snell's law, $\mu = \dfrac{\sin i}{\sin r_1}$

$\Rightarrow \quad \sin i = \mu \sin 18° = 1.5 \times 0.309 = 0.4635$

$\Rightarrow \quad i = \sin^{-1}(0.4635) = 27.61°$

Thus, angle of incidence, $i \approx 28°$

15. (i) Student's response is incorrect. On decreasing the distance between lens and object, image formed by lens is magnified but increasing the distance between lens and object, forms a small size image.

(ii) Student's response is correct. The graph between $\dfrac{1}{u}$ and $\dfrac{1}{v}$ for a thin convex lens in order to determine its focal length is plotted as shown in the figure.

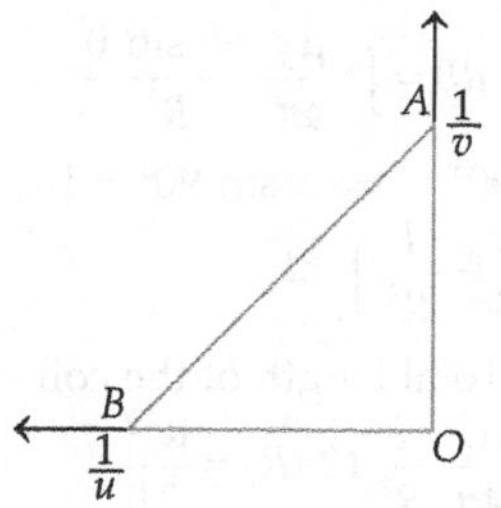

(iii) Student's response is incorrect. The correct relation between the optical power and focal length is

Power, $P = \dfrac{1}{f(\text{in m})}$

Thus, the power of lens or mirror is inversely proportional to the focal length.

16. (i) Stopping potential does not change at all, only photoelectric current increases linearly with increase in intensity of incident monochromatic UV-radiation.

(ii) (a) Threshold frequency is given by

$$\nu_0 = \frac{\phi_0}{h}$$

So, $\quad \phi_0 \propto \nu_0$

Thus, metal having less work function will have the lowest threshold frequency.

Thus, metal Q has the lowest threshold frequency.

(b) According to photoelectric equation,

E_{max} = (Energy of photon) – (Work function of metal)

$$= h\nu - h\nu_0 \Rightarrow h(\nu - \nu_0)$$

For a particular incident radiation of frequency ν, the metal with maximum value of work function, minimum will be its energy.

Hence, metal P will have the value of E_{max} minimum.

17. (i) A junction diode is said to be forward biased when the positive terminal of the external battery is connected to the p-side and negative terminal to the n-side of the diode.

(ii) *I-V* characteristic for a diode during forward bias.

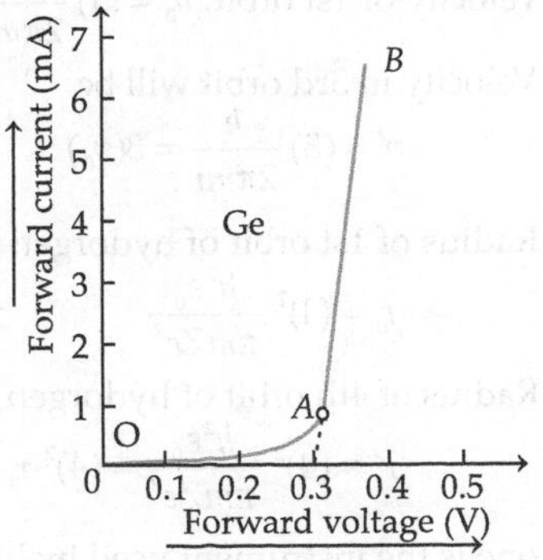

18. (i) (a) I. Reactance of coil,

$X_L = 2\pi fL$

$= 2 \times 3.14 \times 50 \times 1$

$= 314\ \Omega$

II. Impedance of coil,

$Z = \sqrt{R^2 + X_L^2}$

$= \sqrt{(400)^2 + (314)^2}$

$= \sqrt{160000 + 98596}$

$= \sqrt{258596}$

$= 508.5\ \Omega$

III. Current flowing in coil,

$I = \frac{V}{Z}$

$I = \frac{220}{508.5}$ A

$= 0.43$ A

(b) At $f = f_0$, $Z = R$. This is the minimum value of impedance.

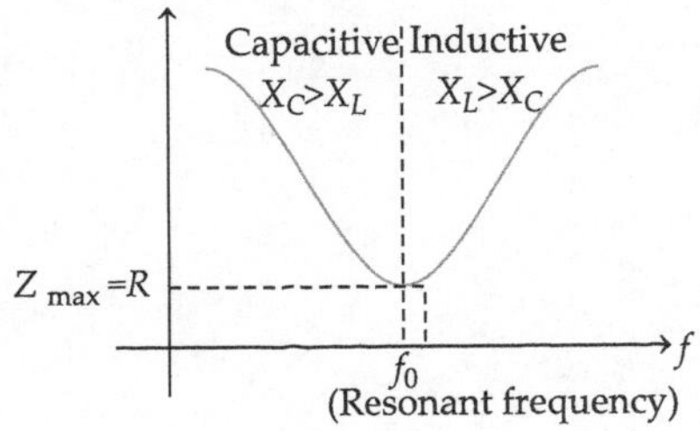

Or

(ii) (a) I. Self-inductance of long solenoid.

II. Given, $\Delta I = -5$ A, $\Delta t = 20 \times 10^{-3}$ s

$e = 500$ V, $L = ?$

$\therefore$ Induced emf, $e = -L\frac{\Delta I}{\Delta t}$

$\Rightarrow \quad 500 = -L\left(\frac{-5}{20 \times 10^{-3}}\right) \Rightarrow L = 2$ H

(b) I. Peak value of current $I_0 = \sqrt{2}\ I_{rms}$

$= \sqrt{2} \times 5 = 7.07$ A

II. Alternating current (AC) is the current of magnitude varying with time and direct current (DC) is the current of constant magnitude.

19. (i) (a) A hydrogen-like atom consists of a tiny positively charged nucleus and an electron revolving in a stable circular orbit around the nucleus.

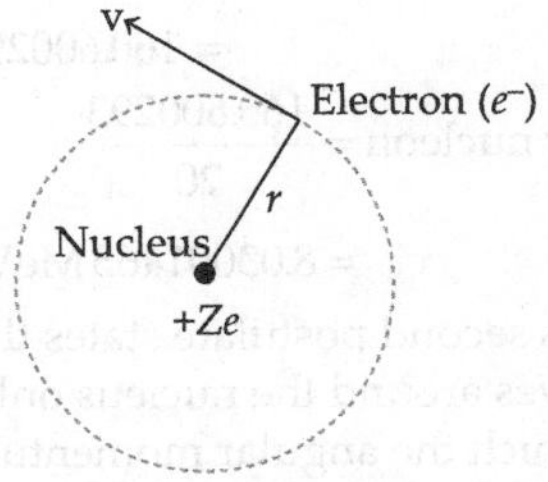

Let *e*, *m* and *v* be respectively the charge, mass and velocity of the electron and *r* be the radius of the orbit. The positive charge on the nucleus is *Ze*, where *Z* is the atomic number. As, the centripetal force is provided by the electrostatic force of attraction, we have

$$\frac{mv^2}{r} = \frac{1}{4\pi\varepsilon_0} = \frac{(Ze) \times e}{r^2} \text{ or } mv^2 = \frac{Ze^2}{4\pi\varepsilon_0 r} \quad \ldots(i)$$

From the second postulate, the angular momentum of the electron is

$$mvr = \frac{nh}{2\pi} \quad \ldots(ii)$$

where, $n = (1, 2, 3, \ldots..)$ is the principal quantum number.

From Eqs. (i) and (ii), we get

$$r = \frac{n^2h^2\varepsilon_0}{\pi mZe^2}$$

This is the equation for the radii of the permitted orbit.

According to this equation, $r_n = n^2$

Since, $n = 1, 2, 3, \ldots.$

For Bohr radius, $n = 1$ and $Z = 1$

So, $\quad r_1 = \frac{h^2\varepsilon_0}{\pi me^2}$

(b) Mass of reactants $= 2.014102 \times 2 = 4.028204$ u

Mass of products $= 4.002604$ u

Mass defect, $\Delta m =$ Mass loss

$= (4.028204 - 4.002604)$ u $= 0.0256$

Energy released, $E = \Delta mc^2$

$= 0.0256 \times 931 = 23.84$ MeV

Or

(ii) (a) In a nucleus of $^{20}_{10}Ne$

Number of protons $= 10$

Number of neutrons $= 20 - 10 = 10$

Total mass of 10 protons and 10 neutrons
$= 10m_p + 10m_n = 10(m_p + m_n)$
$= 10 \times (1.007825 + 1.008665)$
$= 10 \times 2.01649\,u = 20.1649\,u$

Mass defect, $\Delta m = 20.1649 - 19.992397$
$= 0.172503\,u$

Total binding energy $= 0.172503 \times 931$
$= 160.600293$ MeV

E_b per nucleon $= \frac{160.600293}{20}$

$= 8.03001465$ MeV/nucleon

(b) Bohr's second postulate states that the electron revolves around the nucleus only in those orbits for which the angular momentum is some integral multiple of $h/2\pi$.

Thus, angular momentum of the orbiting electron is quantised, i.e. $L = \frac{nh}{2\pi}$

for any permitted (stationary) orbit, $mvr = \frac{nh}{2\pi}$

(c) I. Velocity of 1st orbit, $v_0 = (1)\frac{h}{2\pi mr}$

Velocity in 3rd orbit will be

$v' = (3)\frac{h}{2\pi mr} = 3(v_0)$

II. Radius of 1st orbit of hydorgen atom,

$r_0 = (1)^2 \frac{h^2\varepsilon_0}{\pi m Ze^2}$

Radius of 4th orbit of hydorgen atom will be

$r' = (4)^2 \frac{h^2\varepsilon_0}{\pi m Ze^2} = (4)^2\, r_0 = 16r_0$

20. (i) Telescope is the instrument used by him.

(ii) The mirror can be made parabolic to reduce spherical aberration.

(iii) Microscopes are used to magnify very tiny structure of a virus.

(iv) Resolving power of a microscope.

(v) In compound microscope, objective lens has smaller aperture and smaller focal length than the eye-piece, while in telescope, the objective lens has a larger aperture and larger focal length than the eye-piece.

Proficiency Building Zone

Welcome to the Proficiency Building Zone !

This section contains **15 Sample Question Papers** designed to enhance your problem-solving skills and proficiency. Use these papers to practice regularly and track your progress. Remember, consistent practice is key to mastering Physics.

Progress Tracker Tick the papers as you complete them.

- ☐ Sample Paper 1 _____ (Fill your score)
- ☐ Sample Paper 2 _____ (Fill your score)
- ☐ Sample Paper 3 _____ (Fill your score)
- ☐ Sample Paper 4 _____ (Fill your score)
- ☐ Sample Paper 5 _____ (Fill your score)
- ☐ Sample Paper 6 _____ (Fill your score)
- ☐ Sample Paper 7 _____ (Fill your score)
- ☐ Sample Paper 8 _____ (Fill your score)
- ☐ Sample Paper 9 _____ (Fill your score)
- ☐ Sample Paper 10 _____ (Fill your score)
- ☐ Sample Paper 11 _____ (Fill your score)
- ☐ Sample Paper 12 _____ (Fill your score)
- ☐ Sample Paper 13 _____ (Fill your score)
- ☐ Sample Paper 14 _____ (Fill your score)
- ☐ Sample Paper 15 _____ (Fill your score)

SQP Code : **PB-1/15** Series *i*-**Succeed 1-25/15** Roll No.

Sample Question Paper 01

Physics 12th (Code 861)

General Instructions

1. This paper is divided into four Sections- A, B, C and D. Answer all questions.
2. **Section A** consists of one question having sub-parts of one mark each.
3. **Section B** consists of seven questions of two marks each.
4. **Section C** consists of nine questions of three marks each.
5. **Section D** consists of three questions of five marks each.
6. Internal choices have been provided in two questions each in Section B, Section C and Section D.

Time : 3 Hrs.

Max. Marks : 70

Section A (14 Marks)

1. **A.** In questions (i) to (vii) below, choose the correct alternative (a), (b), (c) or (d) for each of the questions given below.

(*i*) If 10 A of current is flowing through a circular coil of 200 turns and radius 7 cm, then the magnitude of the magnetic moment of the current loop becomes • *Understanding* [1]

(a) 25.5 JT^{-1} (b) 30 JT^{-1} (c) 30.8 JT^{-1} (d) 32 JT^{-1}

(*ii*) The ratio of output frequency of half-wave rectifier and a full wave rectifier when an input frequency of 50 Hz is fed at input is • *Recall* [1]

(a) 1 : 2 (b) 2 : 1 (c) 4 : 1 (d) 1 : 4

(*iii*) **Assertion** Potential difference across each capacitor connected in series is same.

Reason Charge on all the capacitors connected in series is the same. • *Understanding* [1]

(a) Both Assertion and Reason are true and Reason is the correct explanation of the Assertion.

(b) Both Assertion and Reason are true but Reason is not the correct explanation of the Assertion.

(c) Assertion is false and Reason is true.

(d) Both Assertion and Reason are false.

(*iv*) Einstein's photoelectric equation is • *Recall* [1]

(a) $E_{max} = h\lambda - \phi_0$ (b) $E_{max} = \frac{hc}{\lambda} - \phi_0$

(c) $E_{max} = h\nu + \phi_0$ (d) $E_{max} = \frac{hc}{\lambda} + \phi_0$

(*v*) Which of the following graph correctly represents the variation of angle of deviation (δ) with angle of incidence (*i*) for light incident on a prism? • *Analysis* [1]

(a)
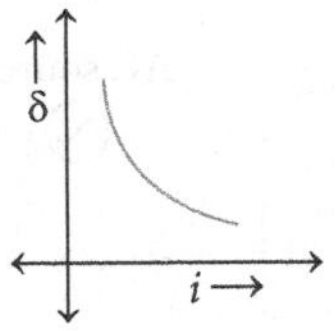

(b)
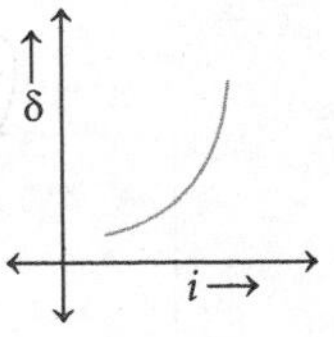

(c)
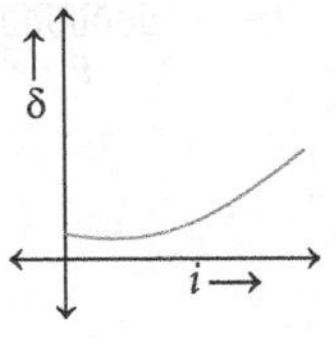

(d)
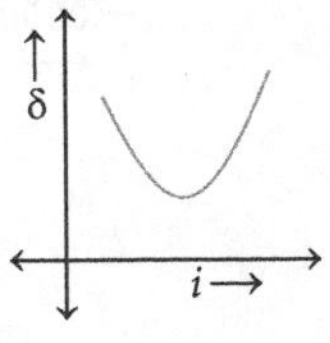

(*vi*) If the length of wire is increased to 4 times, then its resistance will • *Analysis* [1]

(a) increase to 4 times
(b) increase to 16 times
(c) decrease to 1/4 times
(d) decrease to 1/2 times

(*vii*) **Assertion** (A) At resonance, *L-C-R* series circuit have a maximum current.

Reason (R) At resonance, in *L-C-R* series circuit, the current and emf are in phase with each other. • *Analysis* [1]

(a) Both Assertion and Reason are true and Reason is the correct explanation of the Assertion.
(b) Both Assertion and Reason are true but Reason is not the correct explanation of the Assertion.
(c) Assertion is false and Reason is true.
(d) Both Assertion and Reason are false.

B. Answer the following questions briefly.

(*i*) In what way, the behaviour of a diamagnetic material is different from that of a paramagnetic when kept in an external magnetic field? • *Application* [1]

(*ii*) What is the shape of the wavefront generated by a point source? • *Recall* [1]

(*iii*) The following graph shows the variation of charge *Q* with voltage *V*, for two capacitors *K* and *L*. In which capacitor, more electrostatic energy is stored? • *Understanding* [1]

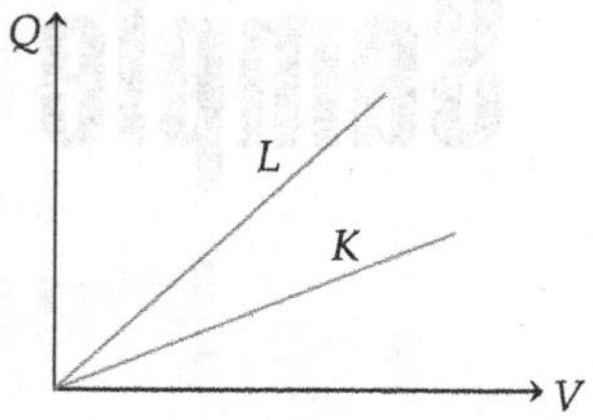

(*iv*) You are provided with six identical cells each of emf 2 V. How will you connect all of them to obtain a battery of emf 2 V? • *Recall* [1]

(*v*) What is the value of magnetic field around a long straight current-carrying conductor? • *Recall* [1]

(*vi*) Two coils of wires *A* and *B* are placed mutually perpendicular. When a current is changed in any one coil, will the current be induced in another coil? • *Recall* [1]

(*vii*) What effects occur on the conductivity of a semiconductor when its temperature is increased? • *Recall* [1]

Section B (14 Marks)

SP-01

2. A coil *Q* is connected to a low voltage bulb *B* and placed near another coil *P* as shown in the figure. Give reasons to explain the following observations • *Application* [2]

(*i*) The bulb *B* lights.

(*ii*) Bulb gets dimmer, if the coil *Q* is moved towards left.

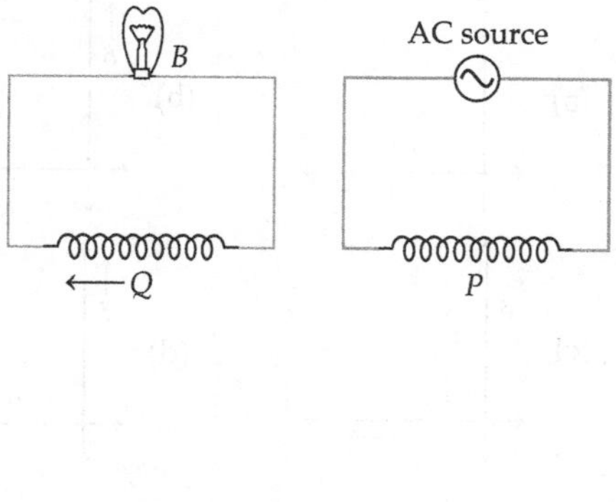

3. Explain, why the reactance offered by an inductor increases with increasing frequency of an alternating voltage? Also, sketch a graph between inductive reactance and frequency. • *Understanding* [2]

Or

A long and an ideal solenoid of length *l*, radius *R* and number of turns *N* carries a steady current *I*. Determine the flux linked with a circular surface C of radius *r* in each of the following cases.

(*i*) $r > R$, plane of coil ⊥ axis of the solenoid • *Recall* [1]

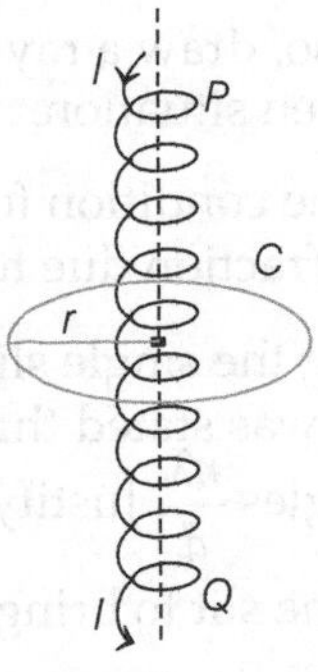

(i)

(*ii*) $r < R$, plane of coil $\perp$ axis of the solenoid • *Recall* [1]

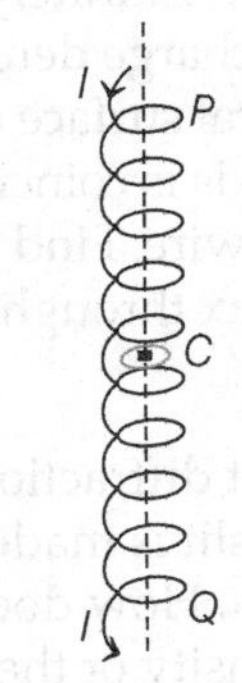

(ii)

4. When an ideal capacitor is charged by a DC battery, no current flows. However, when an AC source is used, the current flows continuously. How does one explain this, based on the concept of displacement current? • *Application* [2]

5. A long horizontal wire P carries a current of 50 A. It is rigidly fixed. Another wire Q is placed directly above and parallel to P as shown in the given figure. The weight/length of wire Q is 0.025 Nm^{-1} and it carries a current of 25 A. Find the distance of wire Q from P, so that the wire Q remains at rest. • *Application* [2]

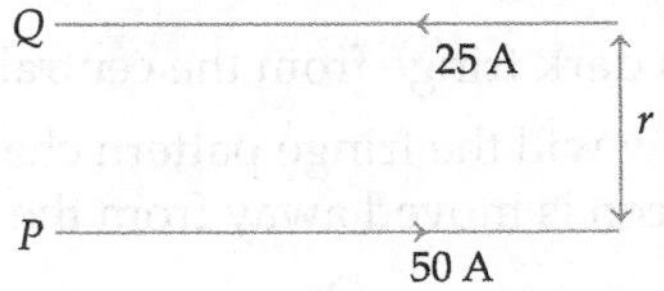

Or

Calculate the force per unit length acting on wire B due to current flowing in wire A and what is the nature of force? • *Recall* [2]

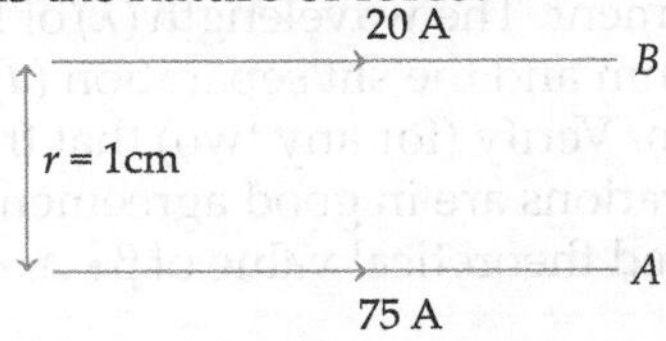

6. Mention any two properties of an L-C-R circuit at resonance. • *Recall* [2]

7. (*i*) Write the expression for equivalent focal length for the following figure. • *Recall* [1]

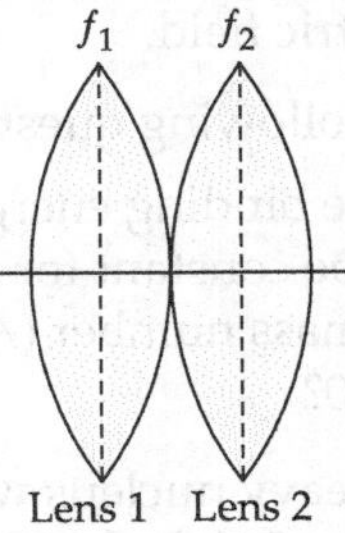

(*ii*) What is the magnification of combination given in part (*i*)? • *Recall* [1]

8. A part of an electric circuit is shown below.

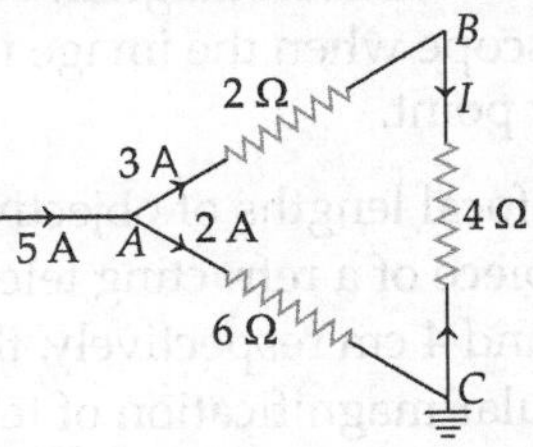

Using Kirchhoff's law, find the current I through 4Ω resistor. • *Application* [2]

Section C (27 Marks)

9. Define the Q-value of a nuclear process. When a nuclear process cannot proceed spontaneously? If both the number of protons and the number of neutrons are conserved in a nuclear reaction, in what way is mass converted into energy (or *vice-versa*) in a nuclear reaction? • *Recall* [3]

10. In Young's double slit experiment, the two slits 0.15 mm apart are illuminated by monochromatic light of wavelength 450 nm. The screen is 1.0 m away from the slits. • *Application* [3]

(*i*) Find the distance of the second

(a) bright fringe

SP-01

(b) dark fringe from the central maxima.

(*ii*) How will the fringe pattern change, if the screen is moved away from the slits?

Or

A student records the following data for the fringe width (β) at different distances (D) from the screen on Young's double-slit experiment. The wavelength (λ) of light used is 600 nm and the slit separation (d) is 0.2 mm. Verify (for any two) that these observations are in good agreement with the expected theoretical value of β. • *Application* [3]

D (m)	1	1.5	2	2.5
β (mm)	3.0	4.5	6.0	7.5

11. Find expressions for force and torque on an electric dipole kept at an angle θ in a uniform electric field. • *Application* [3]

12. Answer the following questions.

(*i*) Why is the binding energy per nucleon found to be constant for nuclei in the range of mass number (A) lying between 30 and 170? • *Recall* [1]

(*ii*) When a heavy nucleus with mass number $A = 240$, breaks into two nuclei of $A = 120$, why energy is released in the process? • *Recall* [2]

13. (*i*) Draw a labelled diagram of astronomical telescope when the image is formed at near point. • *Analysis* [2]

SP-01

(*ii*) The focal lengths of objective lens and eyepiece of a refracting telescope are 100 cm and 4 cm respectively, then find the angular magnification of telescope, when the final image is formed at infinity. [1]

Or

The image obtained with a convex lens is erect and its length is four times the length of the object. If the focal length of the lens is 20 cm, then calculate the object and image distances. Also, draw a ray diagram to depict the given situation. • *Application* [3]

14. (*i*) What is the condition for first minima in case of diffraction due to a single slit? [1]

(*ii*) In deriving the single slit diffraction pattern, it was stated that the intensity is zero at angles $\frac{n\lambda}{d}$. Justify this by suitably dividing the slit to bring out the cancellation. • *Application* [2]

15. (*i*) Define Gauss' law. • *Recall* [1]

(*ii*) A thin straight infinitely long conducting wire having charge density λ is enclosed by a cylindrical surface of radius r and length l, its axis is coinciding with the length of the wire. Find the expression for the electric flux through the surface of the cylinder. • *Recall* [2]

16. (*i*) In a single slit diffraction experiment, the width of the slit is made double the orginal width. How does this affect the size and intensity of the central diffraction band? Explain. • *Application* [2]

(*ii*) When a tiny circular obstacle is placed in the path of light from a distant source, a bright spot is seen at the centre of the obstacle. Explain why? • *Understanding* [1]

17. A horizontal wire AB of length l and mass m carries a steady current I_1, free to move in vertical plane is in equilibrium at a height of h over another parallel long wire CD carrying a steady current I_2, which is fixed in a horizontal plane as shown. Derive the expression for the force acting per unit length on the wire AB and write the condition for which wire AB is in equilibrium. • *Analysis* [3]

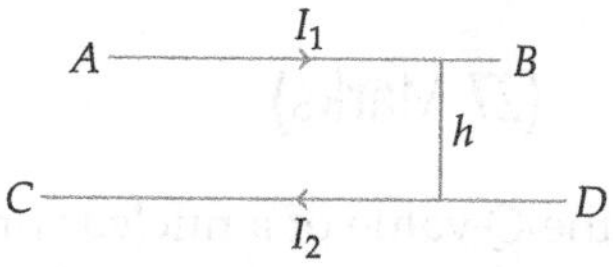

Section D (15 Marks)

18. Shown below is the *V-I* characteristics curve for a forward biased Si diode.

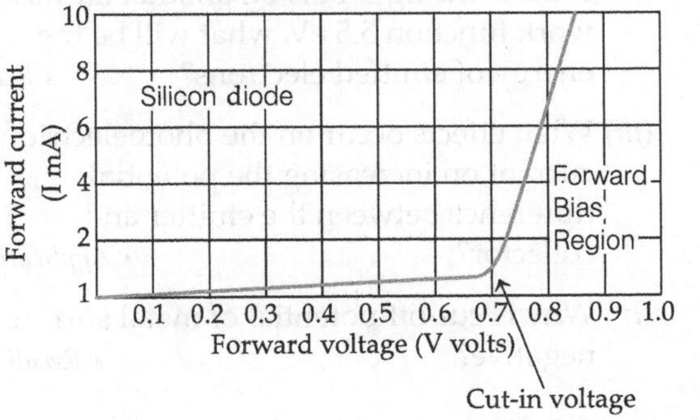

(*i*) A Si diode along with a resistor *R* is connected in series to a battery of 2V. If the value of *R* is 1000 Ω, will the diode now operate above its cut-in voltage? Justify your answer by showing the necesary mathematical calculations. • *Application* [2]

(*ii*) A *p-n* junction diode has a depletion layer of thickness 500 nm and an electric field 16×10^5 V/m.

(a) Find the potential barrier created.

(b) Determine the minimum kinetic energy (in eV) that the conduction electrons must have so that they can diffuse from *n*-side onto *p*-side, in case of the junction is unbiased. • *Application* [3]

Or

Three students *A*, *B* and *C* performed an experiment and study the characteristic curve of an photoelectronic device. They obtained the following graph by changing the intensity (*I*) of light.

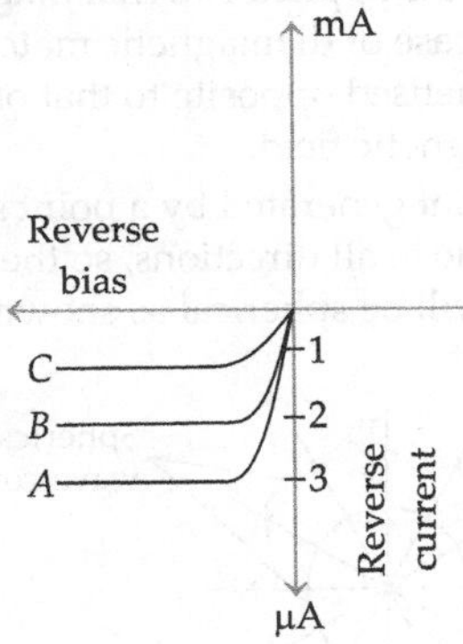

(*i*) What is the name of this device? • *Analysis*

(*ii*) Who uses the minimum intensity of light? • *Analysis*

(*iii*) What did the students concluded about the nature of the reverse current? • *Application*

(*iv*) What is the ratio of intensity of light used by student *A* to the light used by student *C*? • *Analysis* [5]

19. (*i*) Draw a ray diagram to show refraction of a ray of monochromatic light passing through a glass prism. Deduce the expression for the refractive index of glass in terms of angle of prism and angle of minimum deviation. • *Recall* [3]

(*ii*) Explain briefly how the phenomenon of total internal reflection is used in fibre optics. • *Recall* [2]

Or

Light falling on a glass sphere of refractive index *n*, at an angle of incidence α and refracts at angle of refraction β.

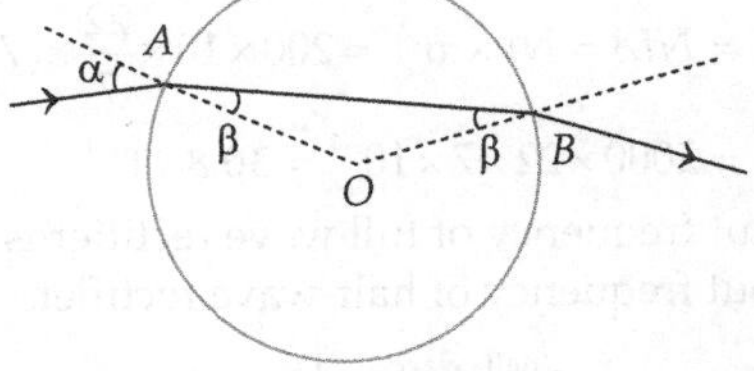

(i) Show that angle of emergence is equal to angle of incidence. • *Recall*

(ii) Complete the given diagram to represent the deviation produced in the incident ray. • *Recall*

(iii) Determine the angle of deviation produced in the incident light as it passes through the glass sphere in terms of α and β. • *Application* [5]

20. The phenomenon of photoelectric emission was discovered in 1887 by Heinrich Hertz during his electromagnetic wave experiments by means of a spark discharge across the detector loop were enhanced.

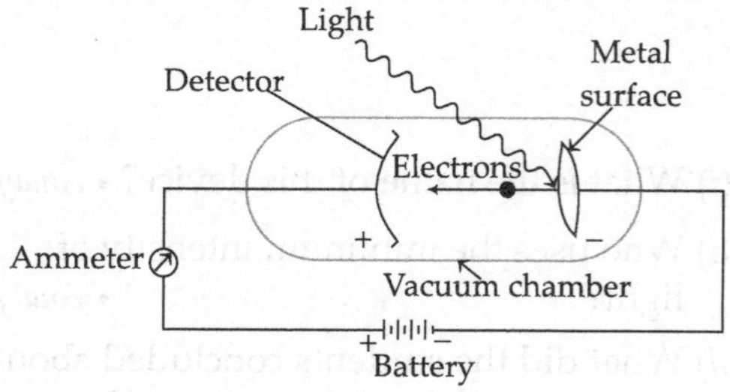

When the emitter plate was illuminated by ultraviolet light from an arc lamp. According to this effect, there is emission of electrons from the surface of metal when a light beam of suitable frequency is incident on it.

(*i*) Light of wavelength 2500 Å falls on a metal surface of work function 3.5 eV. What is the kinetic energy (in eV) of the fastest electrons? • *Application*

(*ii*) If the same light falls on another surface of work function 5.5 eV, what will be the energy of emitted electrons? • *Recall*

(*iii*) What effects occur on the photoelectric current on increasing the potential difference between the emitter and collector? • *Application*

(*iv*) Why is cut-off potential of metal surface negative? • *Recall* [5]

Solutions *in Topper's Style*

My Commitment *I affirm that I am reviewing these solutions only after I have solved the Sample Question Paper 1 on my own. My purpose of looking the solutions is solely to verify whether my answers/solutions were correct or not and to identify my mistakes in case my solutions were wrong or I could not solve that.*

1. A. (*i*) (*c*) Given, number of turns, $N = 200$

Current, $I = 10$ A

Radius, $r = 7\text{ cm} = 7 \times 10^{-2}$ m

$\therefore$ Magnetic moment of the current loop

$$= NIA = NI \times \pi r^2 = 200 \times 10 \times \frac{22}{7} \times (7 \times 10^{-2})^2$$

$$= 2000 \times 22 \times 7 \times 10^{-4} = 30.8 \text{ JT}^{-1}$$

(*ii*) (*a*) Output frequency of full wave rectifier is twice the output frequency of half-wave rectifier.

$$\frac{f_{\text{half-wave}}}{f_{\text{full wave}}} = \frac{1}{2}$$

(*iii*) (*c*) In series combination of capacitors, the charge on each plate of capacitor is same, whereas the potential difference across them are different.

(*iv*) (*b*) According to Einstein's photoelectric equation, maximum kinetic energy of emitted photoelectrons is equal to the difference of energy of incident photons and work function,

i.e. $E_{\max} = h\nu - \phi_0 = \frac{hc}{\lambda} - \phi_0 \quad \left(\because \nu = \frac{c}{\lambda}\right)$

(*v*) (*d*) If the angle of incidence is increased gradually, then the angle of deviation first decreases, attains a minimum value and then starts increasing. So, option (d) is correct.

(*vi*) (*b*) If the length of a wire is increased to n times by stretching it, then its resistance will be increased to n^2 times.

i.e. $R' = n^2 R$

Here, $n = 4$

$\therefore$ $R' = (4^2)R = 16R$

(*vii*) (*b*) Resonance $X_L = X_C$ or $\omega L = \frac{1}{\omega C}$. Because of this, impedance of *L-C-R* series circuit become equal to resistance of circuit ($Z = \sqrt{R^2 + (X_L - X_C)^2}$. Therefore from $I = \frac{E}{Z} = \frac{E}{R}$, at resonance, current in *L-C-R* series circuit is maximum. Correspondingly, phase angle is also equal to zero. Therefore, emf and current are in phase in *L-C-R* series circuit.

B. (*i*) When paramagnetic materials are placed in external magnetic field, these are feebly magnetised in the direction of the applied external magnetic field, whereas in case of diamagnetic materials, these are feebly magnetised opposite to that of applied external magnetic field.

(*ii*) The wavefront generated by a point source should be symmetric in all directions, so the shape of wavefront will be spherical as shown in the figure below.

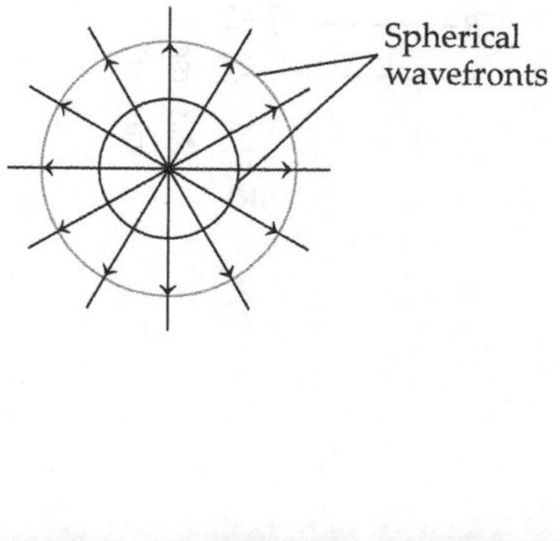

(*iii*) The slope of *Q-V* graph of capacitor gives capacitance ($C = Q/V$). Therefore, capacitor *L* has greater capacitance. The energy stored in a capacitor is given by the formula, $U = \frac{1}{2}CV^2$

At a particular voltage *V* for both capacitors,

$$U \propto C$$

$$\because \quad C_L > C_K \Rightarrow U_L > U_K$$

i.e. capacitor *L* will store more electrostatic energy than capacitor *K*.

(*iv*) On connecting all six identical cells each of emf 2 V in parallel combination by keeping positive terminal at one point and negative terminal at other point, a battery of emf 2 V can be obtained.

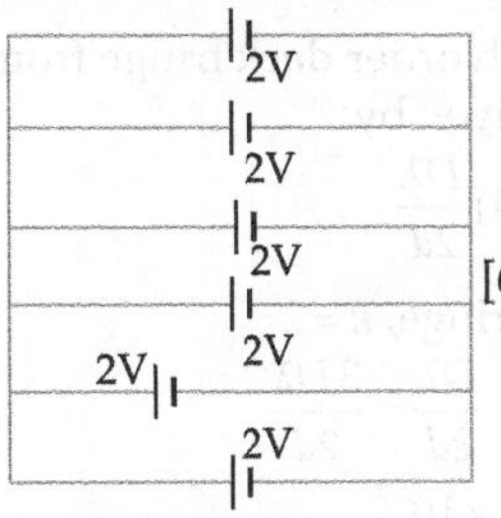

[6 rows, each row contains one cell of emf 2V]

Parallel combination

(*v*) The magnetic field *B* around a long straight current-carrying conductor at any nearby point is given by, $B = \frac{\mu_0}{4\pi}\frac{2I}{r}$, where *I* is the current flowing through the conductor and *r* is the perpendicular distance of the point from the straight conductor. The direction of magnetic field is given by **right hand thumb rule**.

(*vi*) No, this is because the magnetic field due to the current in coil (*A* or *B*) will be parallel to the plane of the other coil (*B* or *A*). Hence, the magnetic flux linked with the other coil will be zero. So, no current will be induced in it.

(*vii*) Conductivity of semiconductor increases on increasing its temperature because resistance of semiconductor decreases with increase of temperature.

2. (*i*) Due to varying current in *P*, the flux linked with *P* changes and hence flux linked with *Q* changes, which in turn induces the emf in *Q* and bulb *B* lights.

(*ii*) When coil *Q* is moved left or it goes away from *P*, the lesser flux change takes place in *Q*. This leads to decrease the value of rate of change of magnetic flux and hence lesser emf and bulb *B* gets dimmer.

3. Inductive reactance of an inductor is given by

$$X_L = \omega L = 2\pi f L$$

It means, it is directly proportional to the inductance *L* and the frequency *f* of the AC current. Thus, if the frequency of AC increases, its inductive reactance also increases.

The graph of inductive reactance *versus* frequency is shown below.

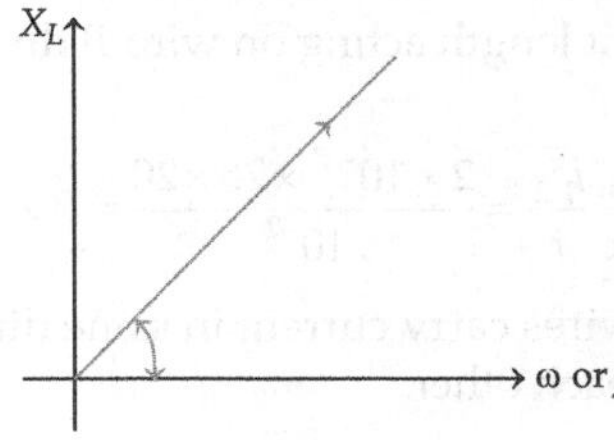

Or

(*i*) Here, $\theta = 0°$,

$$\phi_{in} = B_{in} A \cos\theta$$

$$\phi_{in} = \frac{\mu_0 NI}{l}(\pi R^2)\cos 0° = \frac{\mu_0 NI}{l}(\pi R^2)$$

$$\phi_{out} = 0$$

(Magnetic field outside the solenoid is zero).

$$\phi_C = \phi_{in} + \phi_{out} = \frac{\mu_0 NI}{l}\pi R^2$$

(*ii*) $\phi_{in} = B_{in} A \cos\theta$

$$\phi_{in} = \frac{\mu_0 NI}{l}\pi r^2 \cos 0°$$

$$= \frac{\mu_0 NI}{l}\pi r^2$$

4. If an ideal capacitor is charged by DC battery, then current flows momentarily till capacitor gets fully charged, after that no current flows. However, when an AC source is connected, then conduction current, $I_c = \frac{dq}{dt}$ starts flowing in the connecting wire. As polarity of AC current changes periodically, the capacitor is alternately charged and discharged with time. This causes change in electric field between plates of the capacitor, which changes electric flux. This gives rise to displacement current in the region between plates of capacitor. As displacement current, $I_d = \varepsilon_0 \frac{d\phi_E}{dt}$ and $I_d = I_c$ at all instants. Individually, they are discontinuous but together they possess the property of continuity through any closed circuit.

5. Magnetic force/length on wire *Q* due to current in *P* is

$$\frac{F}{l} = \frac{\mu_0}{2\pi}\frac{i_1 i_2}{r} \text{ N/m}$$

(where, r = distance between *P* and *Q*)

Since, currents in *P* and *Q* are flowing in opposite directions, so *Q* experiences repulsive (upward) force which balances the downward weight of *Q*.

i.e. $$\frac{F}{l} = \frac{\mu_0}{2\pi}\frac{i_1 i_2}{r} = \frac{w}{l} \Rightarrow r = \frac{\mu_0}{2\pi}\frac{i_1 i_2}{w/l}$$

$$\Rightarrow \quad r = \left(\frac{4\pi \times 10^{-7}}{2\pi}\right) \times \frac{50 \times 25}{0.025} = 10^{-2} \text{ m} = 1 \text{ cm}$$

Or

Given, $i_1 = 75\,A$, $i_2 = 20\,A$, $r = 1\,cm = 10^{-2}$ m

Force per unit length acting on wire B due to current in wire A,

$$\frac{F}{l} = \frac{\mu_0}{2\pi}\frac{i_1 i_2}{r} = \frac{2\times10^{-7}\times75\times20}{10^{-2}} = 3\times10^{-2}\ N/m$$

Since, both wires carry current in same direction, so they attract each other.

6. Two special properties of an L-C-R circuit at resonance are as follows

(*i*) At resonance, $X_L = X_C$, so from

$Z = \sqrt{R^2 + (X_L - X_C)^2}$, $Z = R$, that means circuit behaves like a pure resistive circuit.

(*ii*) At resonance, $Z = R$ (min), $\cos\phi = 1$

$\therefore \quad P = I_{rms} V_{rms}$

So, power utilisation in the circuit is maximum.

7. (*i*) The required expression for equivalent focal length of this lens combination is $\frac{1}{f} = \frac{1}{f_1} + \frac{1}{f_2}$ where, f_1 and f_2 are the focal lengths of the lenses in contact.

(*ii*) When two convex lenses are placed in contact, each lens magnifies the image formed by the previous. Thus, the magnification of final image is $m = m_1 \times m_2$.

8. Applying Kirchhoff's second law (or KVL) in the given loop $ABCA$, i.e. net voltage across this loop must be equal to zero.

$\Rightarrow \; -3\times2 - I\times4 + 6\times2 = 0 \Rightarrow 4I = 6$

$\Rightarrow \quad I = \frac{6}{4} = 1.5\ A$

Common Mistakes Generally, we take wrong signs of current, while writing KVL equation. Take negative sign, if actual direction of current is in the assumed direction of loop otherwise take positive sign.

9. The Q-value of a nuclear process refers to the energy released in the nuclear process which can be determined using Einstein's mass-energy relation, $E = mc^2$. The Q-value is equal to the difference of mass of products and reactants multiplied by the square of velocity of light.

The nuclear process cannot proceed spontaneously when Q-value of a process is negative, i.e. the sum of masses of products is greater than the sum of masses of reactants.

Since, the sum of masses of neutrons and protons forming a nucleus is more than the actual mass of nucleus. This difference is called mass defect and appears as equivalent energy Δmc^2, which is liberated during formation of nucleus. This energy is also required to break the nucleus. This is called binding energy.

10. Distance between the two sources,

$d = 0.15\ mm = 1.5\times10^{-4}$ m

Wavelength, $\lambda = 450\ nm = 4.5\times10^{-7}$ m

Distance of screen from source, $D = 1$ m

(*i*) (a) The distance of nth order bright fringe from central fringe is given by

$$y_n = \frac{nD\lambda}{d}$$

For second bright fringe, $n = 2$

$$y_2 = \frac{2D\lambda}{d} = \frac{2\times1\times4.5\times10^{-7}}{1.5\times10^{-4}} = 6\times10^{-3}\ m$$

The distance of the second bright fringe, $y_2 = 6$ mm.

(b) The distance of nth order dark fringe from central fringe is given by

$$y'_n = (2n-1)\frac{D\lambda}{2d}$$

For second dark fringe, $n = 2$

$$y'_2 = (2\times2-1)\frac{D\lambda}{2d} = \frac{3D\lambda}{2d}$$

$$y'_2 = \frac{3}{2}\times\frac{1\times4.5\times10^{-7}}{1.5\times10^{-4}} = 4.5\times10^{-3}\ m$$

The distance of the second dark fringe, $y'_2 = 4.5$ mm.

(*ii*) With increase of D, fringe width also increases as

$$\beta = \frac{D\lambda}{d} \text{ or } \beta \propto D$$

Or

The verify the observations, we use the formula for fringe width (β) in Young's double slit experiment.

$$\beta = \frac{\lambda D}{d}$$

At $D = 1$ m,

$$\beta = \frac{600\times10^{-9}\times1}{0.2\times10^{-3}} = 3.0\times10^{-3}\ m = 3.0\ mm$$

At $D = 1.5$ m,

$$\beta = \frac{600\times10^{-9}\times1.5}{0.2\times10^{-3}} = 4.5\times10^{-3}\ m = 4.5\ mm$$

At $D = 2$ m,

$$\beta = \frac{600\times10^{-9}\times2}{0.2\times10^{-3}} = 6.0\times10^{-3}\ m = 6.0\ mm$$

At $D = 2.5$ m ,

$$\beta = \frac{600\times10^{-9}\times2.5}{0.2\times10^{-3}} = 7.5\times10^{-3} m = 7.5\ mm$$

11. Consider an electric dipole consisting of two charges $-q$ and $+q$ placed in a uniform external electric field of intensity **E**.

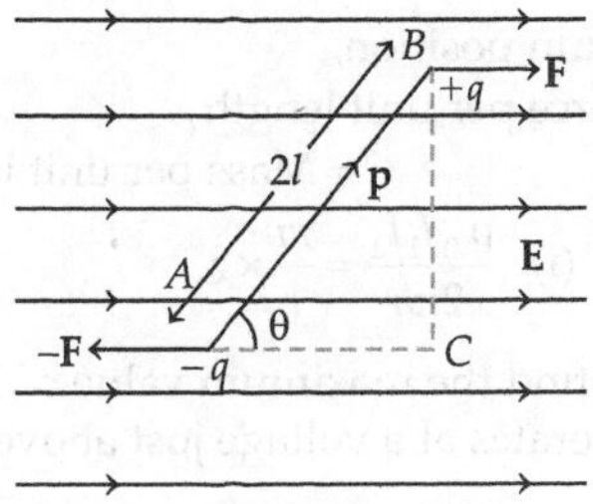

The length of the electric dipole is $2l$. The dipole moment **p** makes an angle θ with the direction of the electric field **E**. Two forces **F** and $-$**F** which are equal in magnitude and opposite in direction act on the dipole.

$$|\mathbf{F}| = |-\mathbf{F}| = qE$$

So, the net force is zero. Since, the two forces are equal in magnitude and opposite in direction and act at different points, therefore they constitute a couple. A net torque τ acts on the dipole about an axis passing through the mid-point of the dipole.

Now, $\tau = F \times BC = qE(2l \sin\theta)$

$$\tau = (q \times 2l) E \sin\theta \text{ or } \tau = pE\sin\theta \qquad (\because p = q \times 2l)$$

12. (*i*) The binding energy per nucleon for nuclei of range, $30 < A < 170$ is close to its maximum value. So, the nuclei belonging to this region have constant binding energy per nucleon and one highly stable. Hence, they do not show radioactivity.

(*ii*) Binding energy per nucleon is smaller for heavier nuclei than the middle ones, i.e. heavier nuclei are less stable. When a heavier nucleus such as nucleus of mass number 240 splits into lighter nuclei (mass number 120), the binding energy per nucleon changes from about 7.6 MeV to 8.4 MeV. Greater binding energy of the product nuclei result in the liberation of energy.

13. (*i*)

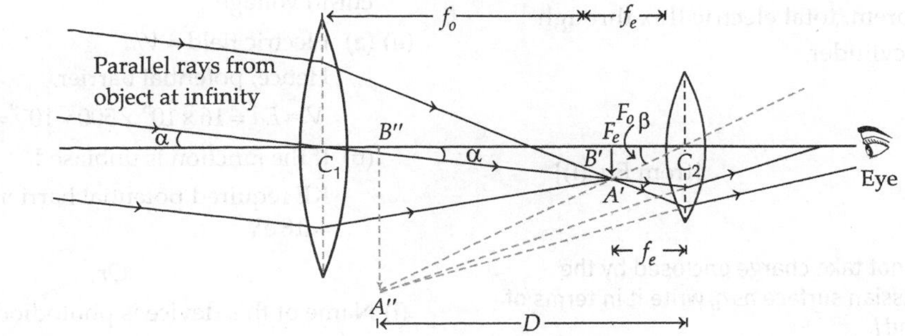

The expression of angular magnification is given by

$$m = \frac{\beta}{\alpha} = \frac{\text{Angle subtended by the final image on the eye}}{\text{Angle subtended by the object on the unaided eye}}$$

(*ii*) Given, $f_o = 100$ cm, $f_e = 4$ cm

When final image is formed at infinity, then

angular magnification, $m = \frac{-f_o}{f_e} = \frac{-100}{4} = -25$

Or

When object is placed between the focus and pole, the image formed by a convex lens is enlarged, virtual and erect and on the same side as that of the object.

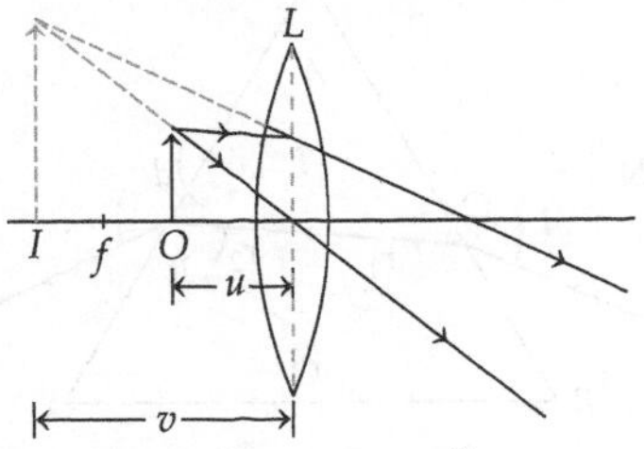

As magnification is given by $m = \frac{v}{u}$

Here, magnification, $m = +4$ and u is the separation of object from lens, whereas v is the separation of image from the lens. The positive sign indicates that object and image formed are on the same side of lens.

By image formula, $\frac{1}{f} = \frac{1}{v} - \frac{1}{u} \Rightarrow \frac{1}{f} = \frac{1}{4u} - \frac{1}{u}$

On substituting the values, we have $\frac{1}{20} = \frac{-3}{4u}$

$\Rightarrow \quad u = -15$ cm

$\Rightarrow \quad v = 4u = -60$ cm

14. (*i*) For first minima,

$$\sin\theta_1 = 1 \times \lambda / a = \lambda / a$$

(*ii*) Angular width, $2\theta = \frac{2\lambda}{a}$

Let the slit be divided into n smaller slits each of

width, $\quad d' = \frac{d}{n}$

Angle, $\quad \theta = \frac{n\lambda}{d} = \frac{n\lambda}{d'n} = \frac{\lambda}{d'}$

Therefore, each of the smaller slit would send zero intensity in the direction of θ. Hence, for the entire single slit, intensity at angle $\frac{n\lambda}{d}$ would be zero.

15. (*i*) According to Gauss' law, total electric flux over a closed surface is equal to $\frac{1}{\varepsilon_0}$ times the total charge enclosed by that surface,

i.e. $\phi_E = \oint \mathbf{E} \cdot d\mathbf{S} = \frac{q}{\varepsilon_0}$

(*ii*) Let q charge be enclosed by the cylindrical surface.

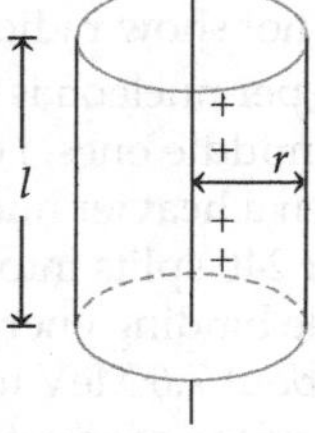

$\therefore$ Linear charge density, $\lambda = \frac{q}{l}$

$\Rightarrow \qquad q = \lambda l \qquad \ldots(i)$

By Gauss' theorem, total electric flux through the surface of cylinder,

$$\phi = \frac{q}{\varepsilon_0}$$

$\therefore \qquad \phi = \frac{\lambda l}{\varepsilon_0} \qquad$ [from Eq. (i)]

Common Mistakes Do not take charge enclosed by the gaussian surface as q, write it in terms of λ and l.

16. (*i*) We know that, width of central maxima $= \frac{2D\lambda}{a}$

where, a = width of slit.

When $a' = 2a$,

width of central maxima $= \frac{2D\lambda}{a'} = \frac{2D\lambda}{2a} = \frac{\lambda D}{a}$.

The intensity of central maxima will become four times, since area of central diffraction band would become one-fourth.

(*ii*) When a tiny circular obstacle is placed in the path of light from a distant source, a bright spot is seen at the centre of the obstacle because the wave diffracted from the edge of circular obstacle interfere constructively at the centre of the shadow resulting in the formation of a bright spot.

17. Magnetic field produced by current I_2 at any point of wire AB is $B_2 = \frac{\mu_0 I_2}{2\pi h}$, normally into force entered on length l of wire AB is $F_m = I_1 l B_2 \sin 90° = \frac{\mu_0 I_1 I_2 \cdot l}{2\pi h}$

$\therefore$ Expression for magnetic force acting per unit length of the wire,

$$\frac{F_m}{l} = \frac{\mu_0 I_1 I_2}{2\pi h} \qquad \text{(upward on } AB)\ldots(i)$$

At equilibrium position,

Magnetic force per unit length

= Mass per unit length $\times g$

From Eq. (i), $\frac{\mu_0 I_1 I_2}{2\pi h} = \frac{m}{l} \times g$

18. (*i*) We shall find the maximum value of R for which the diode operates at a voltage just above its cut-in voltage.

Since, the diode and resistor are connected in series, we get

$$V = V_R + V_D$$

$$V_R = 2 - 0.7 = 1.3 \text{ V}$$

At cut-in voltage, the current through the diode is 1 mA.

$\therefore \qquad R_{max} = V_R / I$

$$R_{max} = 1.3 / 1 \times 10^{-3} = 1.3 \times 1000 = 1300 \Omega$$

Hence, at 1000 Ω, the diode will operate above its cut-in voltage.

(*ii*) (a) Electric field = V/d

Hence, potential barrier,

$$V = Ed = 16 \times 10^5 \times 500 \times 10^{-9} = 0.8 \text{ V}$$

(b) If the junction is unbiased,

KE required potential barrier × charge of electron = 0.8 eV

Or

(*i*) Name of this device is photodiode.

(*ii*) Reverse current produced by photodiode is directly proportional to the intensity of light. Hence, student C uses minimum intensity.

(*iii*) On increasing the reverse bias voltage, current increases and after a certain value, it becomes constant. Hence, reverse saturation current depends on energy of incident photon.

(*iv*) Since, current ∝ intensity

Hence, $\qquad \frac{I_A}{I_C} = \frac{3}{1} = 3:1$

19. (*i*) The figure below shows the passage of light through a triangular prism ABC.

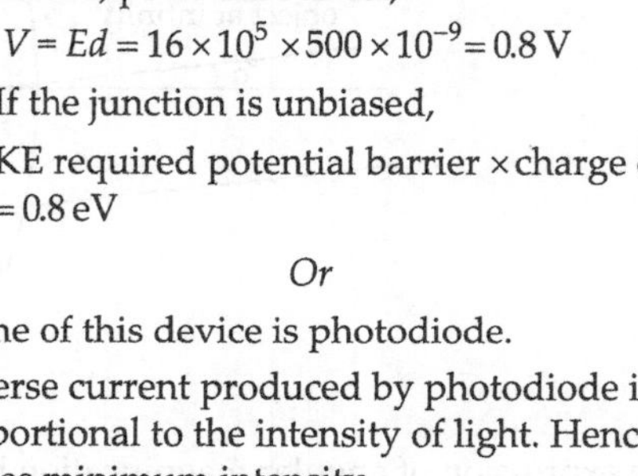

The angles of incidence and refraction at first face AB are i and r_1.

The angle of incidence at the second face AC is r_2 and the angle of emergence is e.

The angle between the emergent ray RS and incident ray PQ is called angle of deviation (δ).

If the angle of incidence is increased gradually, then the angle of deviation first decreases, attains a minimum value (δ_m) and then again starts increasing.

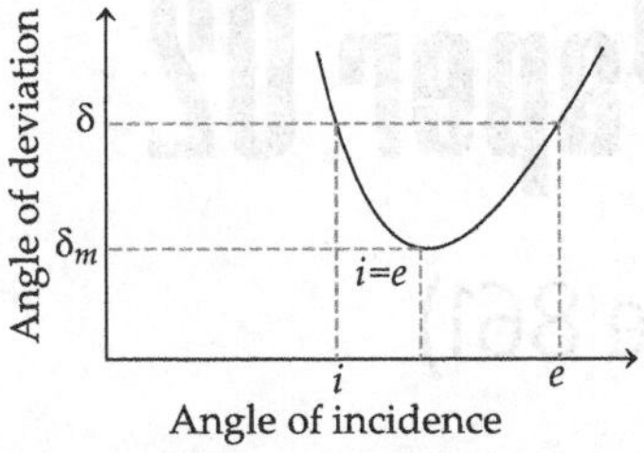

When angle of deviation is minimum, the prism is said to be placed in the minimum deviation position. There is only one angle of incidence for which the angle of deviation is minimum.

When $\delta = \delta_m$
[prism in minimum deviation position]

$$\Rightarrow \quad e = i \text{ and } r_2 = r_1 \quad \text{...(i)}$$

$$\because \quad r_1 + r_2 = A \Rightarrow r + r = A \text{ or } r = \frac{A}{2}$$

Also, we have $A + \delta = i + e$ ...(ii)

Putting $\delta = \delta_m$ and $e = i$ in Eq. (ii), we get

$$A + \delta_m = i + i$$

$$\Rightarrow \quad i = \left(\frac{A + \delta_m}{2}\right)$$

From Snell's law, $\mu = \dfrac{\sin i}{\sin r}$

$$\therefore \quad \mu = \frac{\sin\left(\frac{A + \delta_m}{2}\right)}{\sin \frac{A}{2}}$$

This relation is called a **prism formula.**

For thin prisms (i.e. A is very small), the value of δ_m is also very small.

$$\text{So,} \quad \mu = \frac{\sin\left(\frac{A + \delta_m}{2}\right)}{\sin \frac{A}{2}} \approx \frac{\frac{A + \delta_m}{2}}{A/2}$$

$$\Rightarrow \quad \delta_m = (\mu - 1)A$$

Value Point To get the maximum marks, include following value points.

- Draw the proper ray diagram for the refraction through prism.
- Write all the essential conditions which occurs in the case of minimum deviation.

(*ii*) An optical fibre is a thin tube of transparent material that allows light to pass through, without being refracted into the air or another external medium. Optical fibres make use of total internal reflection.

Optical fibres are fabricated with high quality composite glass/quartz fibres. The refractive index of core is higher than that of the cladding. When a signal in the form of light is directed at one end of the fibre at a suitable angle, it undergoes repeated total internal reflection along the length of the fibre and finally comes out from other end. Due to total internal reflection at each stage, no absorption of light takes place, i.e. there is no appreciable loss in the intensity of light.

Or

(i) For refraction at A,

$$1 \sin \alpha = n \sin \beta \quad \text{...(i)}$$

For refraction at B,

$$n \sin \beta = 1 \sin \gamma \quad \text{...(ii)}$$

Here, γ is the angle of emergence at interface B.

Comparing Eqs. (i) and (ii), we get

$$\gamma = \alpha$$

(ii) Completed ray diagram representing angle of deviation is given below.

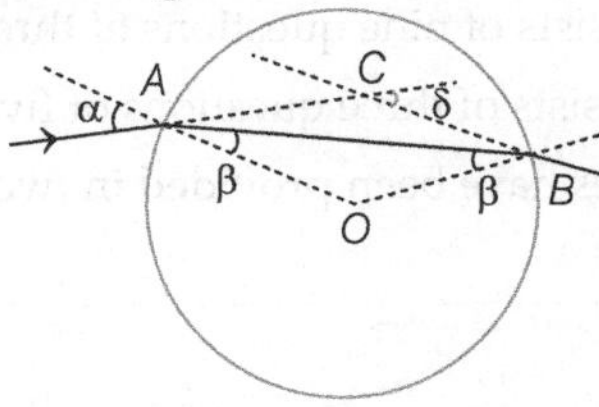

(iii) Angle of deviation,

$$\delta = (\alpha - \beta) + (\alpha - \beta) = 2(\alpha - \beta)$$

[As, exterior angle of a triangle = sum of opposite interior angles]

20. (*i*) Wavelength of incident radiation, $\lambda = 2500$ Å

Work function, $\phi_0 = 3.5\,\text{eV}$

According to Einstein's photoelectric equation,

$$\frac{hc}{\lambda} = \phi_0 + \text{KE}_{\text{max}}$$

$$\Rightarrow \quad \text{KE}_{\text{max}} = \frac{hc}{\lambda} - \phi_0$$

$$= \left[\frac{(6.63 \times 10^{-34})(3 \times 10^8)}{2500 \times 10^{-10}} \times \frac{1}{1.6 \times 10^{-19}} - 3.5\right] \text{eV}$$

$$= (4.97 - 3.5)\,\text{eV} = 1.47\,\text{eV}$$

(*ii*) If the same light (having energy 4.97 eV) falls on a surface of work function 5.5 eV, then no photoelectron will emit.

(*iii*) With the increase in collector potential, it is found that the photoelectric current increases with increase in accelerating (positive) potential and finally saturates or becomes constant.

(*iv*) Free electrons of higher kinetic energy reach anode even at zero plate potential. These electrons can be stopped to reach the anode by negative potential, so the cut-off potential of a metal is negative.

SQP Code : **PB-2/15** Series ***i*-Succeed 2-25/15** Roll No.

Sample Question Paper 02

Physics 12th (Code 861)

General Instructions

1. This paper is divided into four Sections- A, B, C and D. Answer all questions.
2. **Section A** consists of one question having sub-parts of one mark each.
3. **Section B** consists of seven questions of two marks each.
4. **Section C** consists of nine questions of three marks each.
5. **Section D** consists of three questions of five marks each.
6. Internal choices have been provided in two questions each in Section B, Section C and Section D.

Time : 3 Hrs.

Max. Marks : 70

Section A (14 Marks)

1. A. In questions (i) to (vii) below, choose the correct alternative (a), (b), (c) or (d) for each of the questions given below.

(*i*) In charging by induction, • *Recall* [1]

(a) body to be charged must be an insulator

(b) body to be charged must be a semiconductor

(c) body to be charged must be a conductor

(d) any type of body can be charged

(*ii*) In diffraction from a single slit, the angular width of the central maxima does not depend on • *Analysis* [1]

(a) λ of light used

(b) width of slit

(c) distance of slit from the screen

(d) ratio of λ and slit width

(*iii*) **Assertion** The focal length of the mirror is f and distance of the object from the focus is u. The magnification of the mirror is f/u.

Reason Magnification $= \frac{\text{Size of image}}{\text{Size of object}}$

• *Analysis* [1]

(a) Both Assertion and Reason are true and Reason is the correct explanation of the Assertion.

(b) Both Assertion and Reason are true but Reason is not the correct explanation of the Assertion.

(c) Assertion is false and Reason is true.

(d) Both Assertion and Reason is false.

(*iv*) An isolated point charge particle produces an electric field **E** at a point 3 m away from it. The distance of the point at which the field is $\frac{\mathbf{E}}{4}$ will be

• *Understanding* [1]

(a) 2 m (b) 3 m

(c) 4 m (d) 6 m

(*v*) Light waves travel in vacuum along the Y-axis. Which of the following may represent the wavefront? • *Recall* [1]

(a) y = constant

(b) x = constant

(c) z = constant

(d) $x + y + z$ = constant

(*vi*) Light of frequency 6.4×10^{14} Hz is incident on a metal of work function 2.14 eV. The maximum kinetic energy of the emitted electrons is about • *Analysis* [1]

(a) 0.25 eV (b) 0.5 eV
(c) 1.02 eV (d) 0.10 eV

(*vii*) **Assertion** (A) It is essential that all the lines available in the emission spectrum will also be available in the absorption spectrum.

Reason (R) The spectrum of hydrogen atom is only absorption spectrum. • *Understanding* [1]

(a) Both Assertion and Reason are true and Reason is the correct explanation of the Assertion.
(b) Both Assertion and Reason are true but Reason is not the correct explanation of the Assertion.
(c) Assertion is false and Reason is true.
(d) Both Assertion and Reason are false.

B. Answer the following questions briefly.

(*i*) Explain the statement "Light added to light can produce darkness". • *Recall* [1]

(*ii*) A small telescope has an objective lens of focal length 144 cm and an eyepiece of focal length 6.0 cm. What is the magnifying power and length of the tube of this telescope? • *Recall* [1]

(*iii*) The graph shown in the figure represents a plot of current *versus* voltage for a given semiconductor. Identify the region, if any over which the semiconductor has a negative resistance. • *Application* [1]

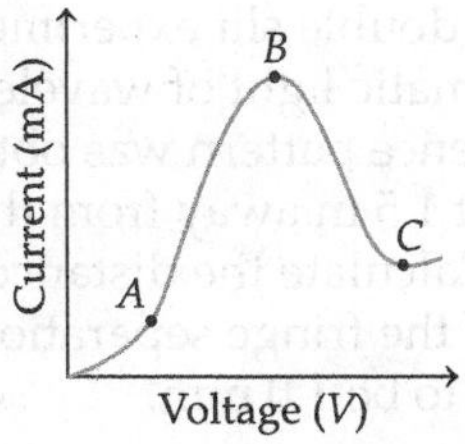

(*iv*) When the voltage drop across a *p-n* junction diode is increased from 0.70 V to 0.71 V, the change in the diode current is 10 mA. What is the dynamic resistance of diode? • *Understanding* [1]

(*v*) Name the series of lines in the hydrogen spectrum which lies in the visible region. • *Recall* [1]

(*vi*) What is the SI unit of magnetic field in terms of *N*, *A* and *m* ? State whether magnetic field is scalar or vector quantity. • *Recall* [1]

(*vii*) The direction of ray of light incident on a concave mirror is shown by *PQ* while directions in which the ray would travel after reflection is shown by four rays marked as 1, 2, 3 and 4 in the figure? Which of the four rays correctly shows the direction of reflected ray? • *Recall* [1]

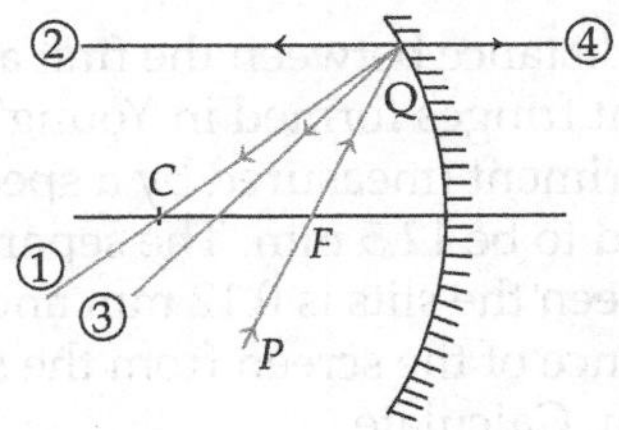

Section B (14 Marks)

2. Give four conclusions of de-Broglie equations. • *Recall* [2]

Or

Show graphically the effect of intensity of light on photoelectric current. • *Application* [2]

3. (*i*) In an electromagnetic wave, how are electric field vector (**E**), magnetic field vector (**B**) and velocity of propagation of the wave (**c**) oriented? • *Recall* [1]

(*ii*) How much time would gamma radiation take to travel from the sun to the earth, a distance of 1.5×10^{11} m? • *Understanding* [1]

4. What is the nuclear radius of ^{125}Fe, if that of ^{27}Al is 6.4 fermi ? • *Recall* [2]

5. A small telescope has an objective lens of focal length 150 cm and eyepiece of focal length 5 cm. What is the magnifying power of the telescope for viewing distant objects in normal adjustments? • *Application* [2]

SP-02

6. In Young's double slit experiment, using monochromatic light of wavelength 700 nm, an interference pattern was obtained on a screen kept 1.5 m away from the plane of two slits. Calculate the distance between the two slits, if the fringe separation or width was found to be 1.0 mm. • *Application* [2]

7. A resistor R and an inductor L are connected in series to a source of voltage $V = V_0 \sin \omega t$. The voltage is found to lead current in phase by $\frac{\pi}{4}$. If the inductor is replaced by a capacitor C, the voltage lags behind current in phase by $\pi/4$. When L, C and R are connected in series with the same source, find the

(i) average power dissipated and • *Recall* [1]

(ii) instantaneous current in the circuit. • *Recall* [1]

8. An element $\Delta l = \Delta x \hat{\mathbf{i}}$ is placed at the origin (as shown in figure) and carries a current $I = 2$ A. Find out the magnetic field at a point P on the Y-axis at a distance of 1.0 m due to the element $\Delta x = w$ cm. Also, give the direction of the field produced. • *Analysis* [2]

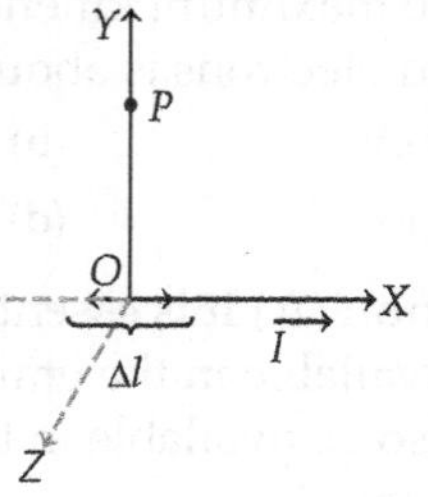

Or

Two long wires carrying currents I_1 and I_2 are arranged as shown in the figure. The one carrying current I_1 is along the X-axis. The other carrying current I_2 is along a line parallel to Y-axis, given by $x = 0$ and $z = d$. Find the force exerted at point O_2 because of the wire along the X-axis. • *Application* [2]

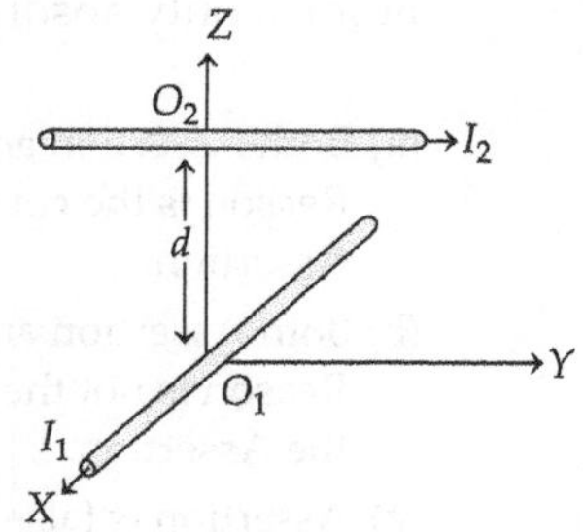

Section C (27 Marks)

9. The distance between the first and the sixth bright fringes formed in Young's double slit experiment (measured by a spectrometer) is found to be 12.5 mm. The separation between the slits is 0.12 mm and the distance of the screen from the slits is 60 cm. Calculate

(*i*) the fringe width and [1]

(*ii*) wavelength of the light used (in nm). • *Understanding* [2]

Or

With the help of suitable ray diagram, derive a relation between the object distance u, image distance v and radius of curvature R for a convex spherical surface, when a ray of light travels from rarer to denser medium. • *Application* [3]

10. (*i*) How does a circular loop carrying current behave as a magnet ? • *Application*

(*ii*) On what factors does the pole strength of a magnet depend ? • *Recall* [3]

11. Sketch the pattern of electric field lines due to

(i) a conducting sphere having negative charge on it. [1½]

(ii) an electric dipole. • *Recall* [1½]

Or

A student records the following data for the electrostatic force (F) between two point charges ($q_1 = 2\,\mu$C and $q_2 = 3\,\mu$C) at different distance (r). Verify (for any two) that these observations are in good agreement with the expected theoretical values of F.

r (cm)	10	20	30	40
F (N)	54	13.5	6	3.375

• *Application* [3]

12. Magnetic field lines are a visual and intuitive realisation of the magnetic field. These are those imaginary lines which continuously represent the direction of the magnetic field. They are in the form of closed loops. Field lines for a bar magnet are as shown in figure below.

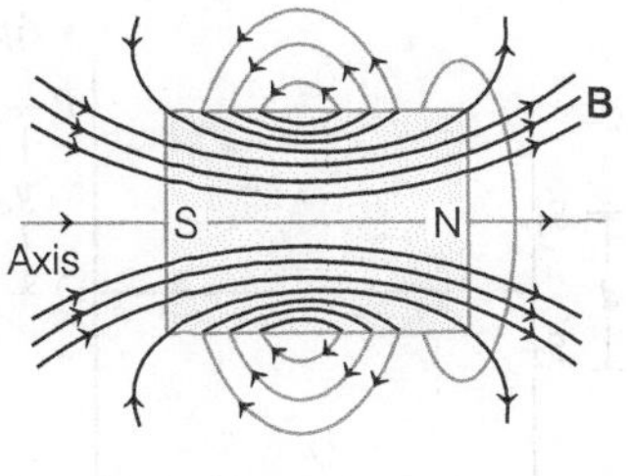

Now, with the help of above information,

(*i*) sketch magnetic field lines around a current carrying finite solenoid.

(*ii*) how is the direction of a magnetic field line represented ?

(*iii*) do these lines resemble to the electric field lines of an electric dipole ? • *Analysis* [3]

13. (*i*) With reference to an electric cell, define

(a) electromotive force (emf) of a cell and [1]

(b) internal resistance (r). • *Recall* [1]

(*ii*) A cell of emf E and internal resistance r is connected across a variable resistor R. Plot a graph showing the variation of terminal potential V with resistance R. • *Application* [1]

14. Study the circuits (a) and (b) shown in the figure and answer the following questions.

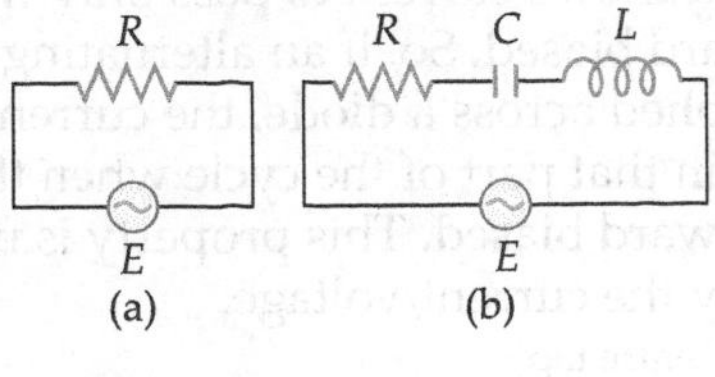

(*i*) Under which conditions would the rms currents in the two circuits be the same?

(*ii*) Can the rms current in circuit (b) be larger than that in (a)? • *Application* [3]

15. In the fusion reaction, ${}_1H^2 + {}_1H^2 \rightarrow {}_2He^3 + {}_0n^1$, the masses of deuteron, helium and neutron expressed in amu are 2.015, 3.017 and 1.009, respectively. If 1kg of deuterium undergoes complete fusion,

then find the amount of total energy released.
(Take, 1 amu $= 931.5\, MeV/c^2$) • *Application* [3]

16. (*i*) In photoelectric effect, what is meant by the terms • *Application*

(a) work function and

(b) stopping potential? [2]

Also specify, how stopping potential is related to kinetic energy of photoelectrons?

(*ii*) Write the Einstein's photoelectric equation? • *Recall* [1]

17. Figure shows two identical capacitors C_1 and C_2 each of $2\ \mu F$ capacitance connected to a battery of 5 V. Initially switch S is left open and dielectric slabs of dielectric constant $K = 5$ are inserted to fill completely the space between the plates of the two capacitors. How will the charge and potential difference between the plates of the capacitors be affected after the slabs are inserted? • *Analysis* [3]

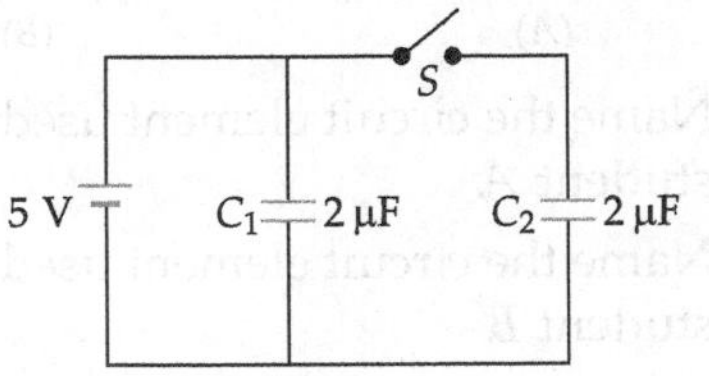

Section D (15 Marks)

18. A uniform magnetic field $B = 0.002T$ acts on a 2 cm long section PQ of an insulated wire. The wire is attached to a spring of spring constant 0.8 N/m as shown in the figure.

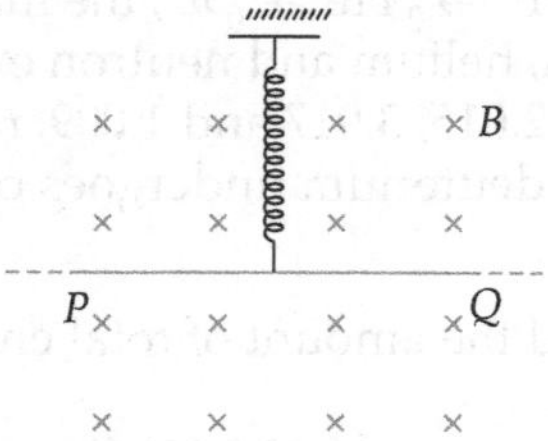

(*i*) What value of current should flow through PQ such that the spring is stretched by 2×10^{-4} m? • *Application* [2]

(*ii*) Identify the possible direction of current through section PQ. • *Application* [1]

(*iii*) The string is released after stretching. Write your observation. • *Application* [1]

(*iv*) Name the phenomenon observed. • *Recall* [1]

Or

Two students *A* and *B* performed an experiment for studying the variation of current with frequency of a series *L-C-R* circuit element.

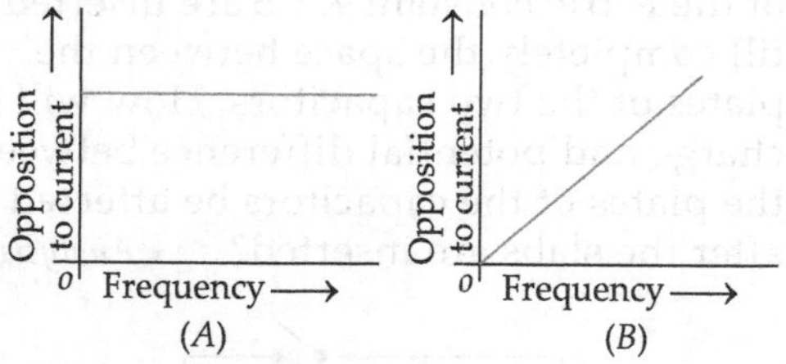

(*i*) Name the circuit element used by student *A*. • *Analysis*

(*ii*) Name the circuit element used by student *B*. • *Analysis*

(*iii*) Write the expression for the impedance offered by the series combination of the above two elements connected across the AC source. • *Application*

(*iv*) Which will be ahead in phase in this circuit voltage of current? • *Analysis* [5]

19. (*i*) When the width of the slit is made double, how would this affect the size and intensity of the central diffraction band? Justify your answer. • *Application* [2]

(*ii*) The intensity at the central maxima (O) in a Young's double slit experiment is I_0. If the distance OP equals two-third of fringe width of the pattern, show that the intensity at point P would be $I_0/4$. • *Application* [3]

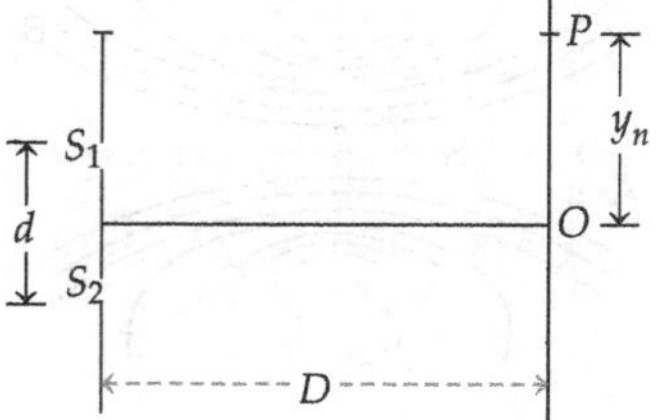

Or

(*i*) A lens whose radii of curvature are different is forming the image of an object on its axis. Will the position of image change, if the lens is placed with its faces reversed? • *Recall* [2]

(*ii*) What happens to a focal length of a cenvex lens, when it is immersed in water? • *Recall* [1]

(*iii*) The radii of curvature of the surfaces of a double convex lens are 20 cm and 40 cm, respectively and its focal length is 20 cm. What is refractive index of the material of the lens? • *Recall* [2]

20. The process of converting alternating voltage/current into direct voltage/current is called rectification. Diode is used as a rectifier for converting alternating current/voltage into direct current/voltage. Diode allows current to pass only when it is forward biased. So, if an alternating voltage is applied across a diode, the current flows only in that part of the cycle when the diode is forward biased. This property is used to rectify the current/voltage.

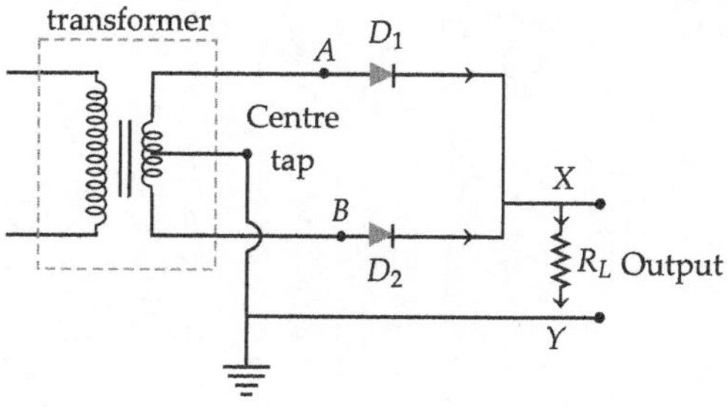

(*i*) In the following diode circuit, input is given between terminals *A* and *C* and output is taken between terminals *B* and *D*. What is the nature of output voltage?
• *Application* [2]

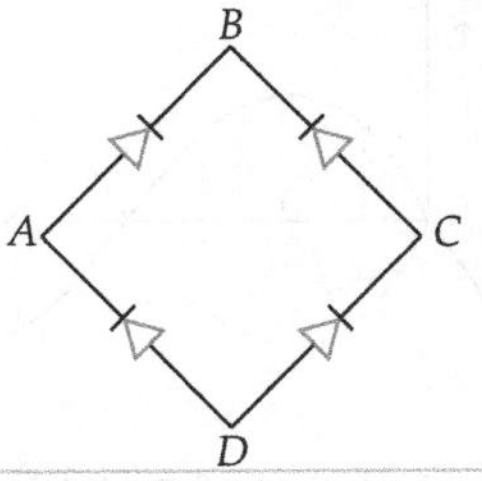

(*ii*) For what purpose, rectifier is used ?
• *Recall* [1]

(*iii*) In the following circuit diagram, what is the use of capacitor *C* ? • *Application* [2]

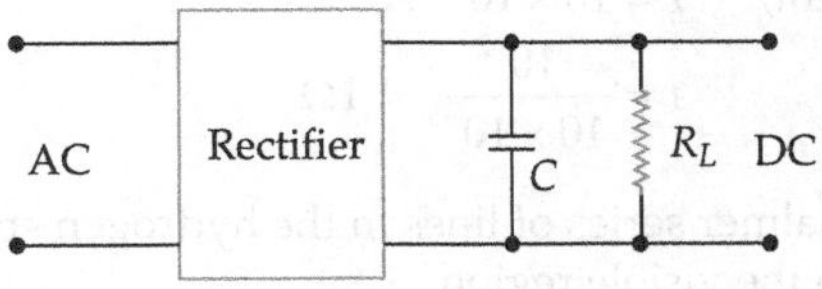

Solutions *in Topper's Style*

My Commitment *I affirm that I am reviewing these solutions only after I have solved the Sample Question Paper 2 on my own. My purpose of looking the solutions is solely to verify whether my answers/solutions were correct or not and to identify my mistakes in case my solutions were wrong or I could not solve that.*

1. A. (*i*) (*c*) Induction requires shifting of free charge carriers which are present only in conductors.

(*ii*) (*c*) Angular width of central maxima, $2\theta = 2\lambda/d$.

where, λ = wavelength and

d = width of slit

Thus, θ does not depend on D, i.e. distance between the slit and the screen.

(*iii*) (*c*) Magnification produced by mirror,

$$m = \frac{\text{Size of image}(I)}{\text{Size of object }(O)} = \frac{f}{f-x}$$

where, x is distance of object from pole.

$$\therefore \quad x = u + f$$

$$\text{and} \quad m = \frac{f}{f-u-f} = \frac{-f}{u}$$

(*iv*) (*d*) Electric field produced by charge particle at a distance of 3 m,

$$E = \frac{1}{4\pi\varepsilon_0} \cdot \frac{q}{r^2}$$

$$E = \frac{1}{4\pi\varepsilon_0} \cdot \frac{q}{3^2} \quad [\text{Here, } r = 3\,\text{m}] \quad \ldots \text{(i)}$$

Let x be the distance from point charge where electric field is $\frac{E}{4}$.

$$\therefore \quad \frac{E}{4} = \frac{1}{4\pi\varepsilon_0} \cdot \frac{q}{x^2} \quad \ldots \text{(ii)}$$

Dividing Eq. (i) by Eq. (ii), we get

$$4 = \frac{x^2}{3^2}$$

$$\Rightarrow \quad x = 2 \times 3 = 6\,\text{m}$$

(*v*) (*a*) As velocity of light is perpendicular to the wavefront and light wave is travelling in vacuum along the *Y*-axis, therefore the wavefront is represented by y = constant.

(*vi*) (*b*) Given, $\nu = 6.4 \times 10^{14}$ Hz, $\phi_0 = 2.14$ eV

The maximum KE of emitted electron

$$= h\nu - \phi_0 = \frac{6.6 \times 10^{-34} \times 6.4 \times 10^{14}}{1.6 \times 10^{-19}} - 2.14$$

$$= 0.5\,\text{eV}$$

(*vii*) (*d*) Emission transitions can take place between any higher energy level and any energy level below it, while absorption transitions start from the lowest energy level only end may end at any higher energy level. Hence, number of absorptions transitions between two given energy is always less than the number of emission transitions between the same two levels.

B. (*i*) If two light waves of equal amplitudes fall at a point in opposite phase, the resultant intensity of light is zero at that point and thus, produces darkness at that point.

(*ii*) According to question,

$$\text{magnification, } m = \frac{f_o}{f_e} = \frac{144}{6} = 24$$

and length of tube, $l = f_o + f_e = 144 + 6 = 150$ cm

(*iii*) Resistance of a material can be calculated by the slope of the curve *V versus I*. In part *BC* of the curve shows the negative resistance as in this region, current decreases by increasing the voltage.

(*iv*) The dynamic resistance is given by, $r = \frac{\Delta V}{\Delta I}$

Given that, change in voltage,

$$\Delta V = 0.71 - 0.70$$
$$\Delta V = 0.01\text{ V} = 10^{-2}\text{ V}$$

Current, $I = 10 \times 10^{-3}$ A

Now, $r = \frac{10^{-2}}{10 \times 10^{-3}} = 1\Omega$

(*v*) The Balmer series of lines in the hydrogen spectrum lies in the visible region.

(*vi*) As $F = qvB\sin\theta$

$\Rightarrow B = \frac{F}{qv\sin\theta}$

$\therefore$ SI unit of $B = \frac{\text{N}}{\text{C-ms}^{-1}}$

$$= \frac{\text{N}}{(\text{Cs}^{-1})\cdot\text{m}} = \frac{\text{N}}{\text{A-m}}$$

SI unit of magnetic field is N/A-m. It is also known as tesla [T]. It is a vector quantity.

(*vii*) The incident ray *PQ* passes through the focus, so the reflected ray is parallel to the principal axis. So, the ray 2 correctly shows the direction of reflected ray.

2. The four conclusions of de-Broglie equations are as follows

(*i*) de-Broglie wavelength, $\lambda \propto \frac{1}{v}$. If the particle moves faster, then the wavelength will be smaller and *vice-versa*.

(*ii*) If the particle is at rest ($v = 0$), then the de-Broglie wavelength is infinity.

(*iii*) de-Broglie waves can't be electromagnetic in nature.

(*iv*) The wavelength of a wave associated with the moving particles defines a region of uncertainity within which the position of the particles is unknown.

Or

Initially, when no light is incident, there will be no electron emission and hence, there will be no photoelectric current. But when the light is incident and its intensity is increased, the number of electrons emitted also increases and hence, photoelectric current increases. So, if we plot a graph in between intensity of light and photoelectric current, we get a straight line with positive slope.

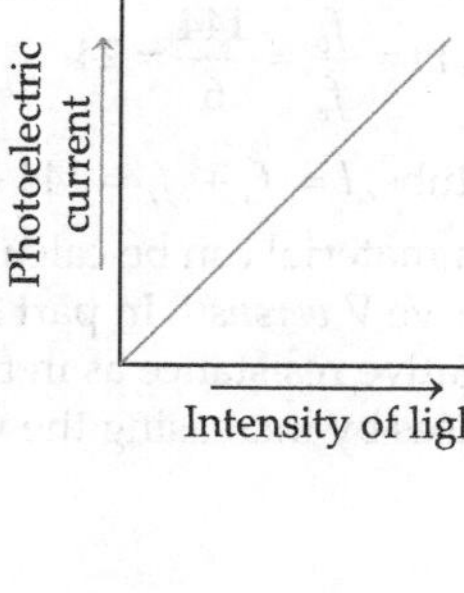

3. (*i*) In an electromagnetic wave, **E** and **B** are perpendicular to each other and **c** (the velocity of propagation of electromagnetic wave) is perpendicular to both **E** and **B**.

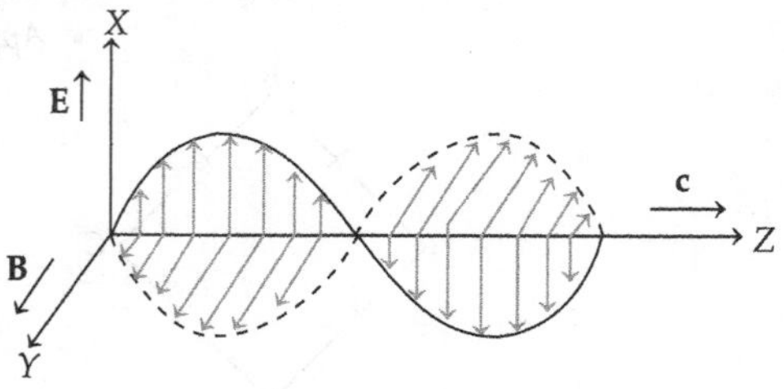

(*ii*) Speed of γ-radiation, $c = 3 \times 10^8$ m/s

Given, distance = 1.5×10^{11} m

Time taken by γ-radiation to travel from the sun to the earth is given by

$$\text{Time} = \frac{\text{Distance}}{\text{Speed}} = \frac{1.5 \times 10^{11}}{3 \times 10^8} = 5 \times 10^2\text{ s}$$

4. Radius of the nucleus is

$$R = R_0 A^{1/3}$$
$$\frac{R_{Fe}}{R_{Al}} = \left(\frac{A_{Fe}}{A_{Al}}\right)^{1/3} = \left(\frac{125}{27}\right)^{1/3}$$

Radius, $R_{Fe} = \frac{5}{3} R_{Al} = \frac{5}{3} \times 6.4 = 10.6\text{ fm}$

5. For telescope

Focal length of objective lens, $f_o = 150$ cm

Focal length of eye piece, $f_e = 5$ cm

If telescope is in normal adjustment, i.e. the final image is at infinity, then its magnification is given by

$$M = \frac{f_o}{f_e}$$

Since, $f_0 = 150$ cm, $f_e = 5$ cm

$$M = \frac{150}{5} = 30$$

6. Given, fringe width, $\beta = 1\text{ mm} = 10^{-3}$ m

Wavelength, $\lambda = 700\text{ nm} = 700 \times 10^{-9}$ m, $D = 1.5$ m, $d = ?$

As we know that, $\beta = \frac{\lambda D}{d}$

So, distance between the two slits, $d = \frac{\lambda D}{\beta}$

$$= \frac{700 \times 10^{-9} \times 1.5}{10^{-3}} = 10.5 \times 10^{-4}\text{ m}$$

7. Given, instantaneous voltage,

$$V = V_0 \sin \omega t$$

As in both cases, the voltage and current differ by a phase of $\frac{\pi}{4}$. So, $\phi = \frac{\pi}{4}$.

(*i*) Average power dissipated,

$$P_{av} = V_{rms} I_{rms} \cos\phi$$
$$= \frac{V_0}{\sqrt{2}} \times \frac{I_0}{\sqrt{2}} \times \cos\phi = \frac{V_0 I_0}{2} \cos\frac{\pi}{4} = \frac{V_0 I_0}{2\sqrt{2}}$$

(*ii*) As R, L and C are in series, therefore at any instant through the three elements, AC has the same amplitude and phase, i.e. instantaneous current, $I = I_0 \sin \omega t$.

8. Biot-Savart's law states that

$$d\mathbf{B} = \frac{\mu_0}{4\pi} \cdot \frac{Id\mathbf{l} \times \hat{\mathbf{r}}}{|\mathbf{r}|^2}$$

Here, $\Delta x = w\text{cm} = w \times 10^{-2}$ m

$\because$ $\Delta\mathbf{l} = \Delta x\hat{\mathbf{i}} = w \times 10^{-2}\hat{\mathbf{i}}$

$\because$ $Id\mathbf{l} = 2w \times 10^{-2}\hat{\mathbf{i}}$ $[\because I = 2\text{A}]$

As, $d\mathbf{B} = \frac{\mu_0}{4\pi} = \frac{Id\mathbf{l} \times \mathbf{r}}{r^3}$

$\Rightarrow$ $d\mathbf{B} = \frac{\mu_0}{4\pi} \cdot \frac{(2 \times w \times 10^{-2}\hat{\mathbf{i}} \times \hat{\mathbf{j}})}{(1)^3}$ $[\because \mathbf{r} = 1\hat{\mathbf{j}}]$

$\Rightarrow$ $d\mathbf{B} = \frac{\mu_0 w}{200\pi}\hat{\mathbf{k}} \Rightarrow |d\mathbf{B}| = \frac{\mu_0 w}{200\pi}$

and direction along + Z-axis.

Or

Here, first we have to find the direction of magnetic field at point O_2 due to the wire carrying current I_1. Use Maxwell's right hand grip (cork screw) rule, the direction of magnetic field at point O_2 due to current I_1 is along Y-axis.

Here, the wire at point O_2 is placed along Y-axis. Now, by the formula, $\mathbf{F} = I_2\,(\mathbf{l} \times \mathbf{B})$

Angle between $\mathbf{l}$ and $\mathbf{B}$ is 0°, since both are at Y-axis, so

$$F = IlB \sin 0° = 0$$

Hence, the force exerted at point O_2 due to the wire along X-axis, is zero.

9. (*i*) We know that, $Y_n = n\frac{D\lambda}{d}$

where, $n = 0, 1, 2, \ldots$

Here, $Y_6 - Y_1 = 12.5$ mm

$\Rightarrow$ $Y_6 - Y_1 = \frac{D\lambda}{d}(6-1) = 5\beta$ $\left(\because \beta = \frac{D\lambda}{d}\right)$

So, fringe width, $\beta = \frac{12.5}{5} = 2.5\text{ mm} = 2.5 \times 10^{-3}$ m

(*ii*) Since, $\beta = \frac{D\lambda}{d}$

Given, $D = 60$ cm $= 0.6$ m, $d = 0.12$ mm $= 0.12 \times 10^{-3}$ m

$\Rightarrow$ $2.5 \times 10^{-3} = \frac{0.6 \times \lambda}{0.12 \times 10^{-3}}$

$\Rightarrow$ $\lambda = 5 \times 10^{-7}\text{ m} = 500\text{ nm}$

Common Mistakes Students get confused in identifying the value of D and d in the fringe width formula, i.e., they put the value of d in place of the value of D and *vice-versa*.

Or

Let us consider that convex spherical surface with centre of curvature C forms the image I of an object O on its principal axis. The rays are incident from a rarer medium of refractive index n_1 to a denser medium of refractive index n_2. The aperture of the surface to be small compared to other distances involved, so that small angle approximation can be made.

Here, i and r are the angles made by incident ray and refracted ray from the normal.

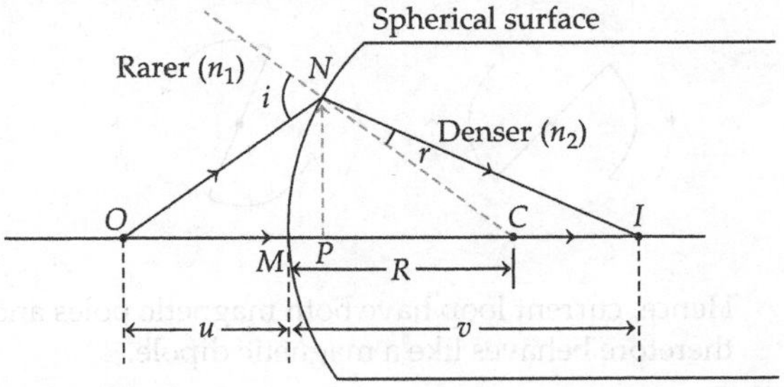

Assumptions

(*i*) The aperture of the surface is small compared to other distance involved.

(*ii*) NM will be taken to be nearly equal to the length of the perpendicular from the point N on the principal axis.

For small angles, $\tan\theta \approx \theta$

$$\tan \angle NOM = \angle NOM = \frac{MN}{OM} \quad \ldots\text{(i)}$$

$$\tan \angle NCM = \angle NCM = \frac{MN}{MC} \quad \ldots\text{(ii)}$$

$$\tan \angle NIM = \angle NIM = \frac{MN}{MI} \quad \ldots\text{(iii)}$$

Now, for ΔNOC, i is the exterior angle,

$\Rightarrow i = \angle NOM + \angle NCM$

$\Rightarrow$ $i = \frac{MN}{OM} + \frac{MN}{MC}$ [from Eqs. (i) and (ii)]

Similarly, $r = \angle NCM - \angle NIM$

$\Rightarrow$ $r = \frac{MN}{MC} - \frac{MN}{MI}$ [from Eqs. (ii) and (iii)]

Snell's law can be written as,

$n_1 \sin i = n_2 \sin r$ or for small angles $n_1 i = n_2 r$

Substituting i and r, we have

$$\frac{n_1}{OM} + \frac{n_2}{MI} = \frac{n_2 - n_1}{MC} \quad \ldots\text{(iv)}$$

Here, OM, MI and MC represent magnitudes of distances. Applying the cartesian sign convention,

$$OM = -u,\ MI = +v,\ MC = +R$$

Substituting these values in Eq. (iv), we get

$$\frac{n_2}{v} - \frac{n_1}{u} = \frac{n_2 - n_1}{R}$$

This equation holds for any curved spherical surface.

To get maximum marks include following value points

Value Point (i) Make the neat and clean ray diagram.

(ii) Use correct sign convention of u, v and R.

10. (*i*) If the current round in the face of the coil is in anti-clockwise direction, then this behaves like a North pole whereas, when it viewed from other side, then current round in it is in clockwise direction necessarily forming South pole of magnet.

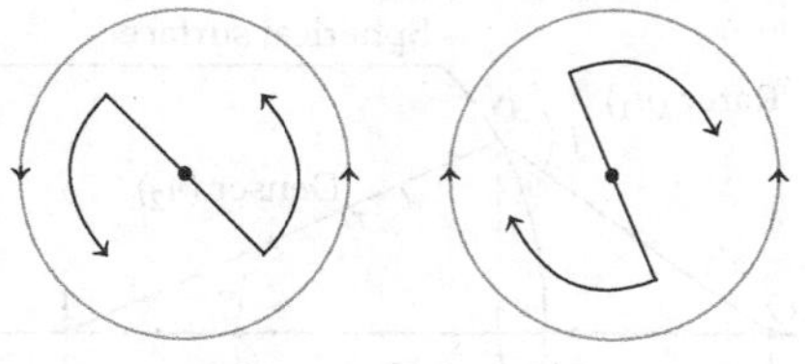

Hence, current loop have both magnetic poles and therefore behaves like a magnetic dipole.

(*ii*) The pole strength of a magnet depends on its cross-section, nature and state of magnetisation.

11. (*i*) Electric field lines due to a conducting sphere are shown in figure.

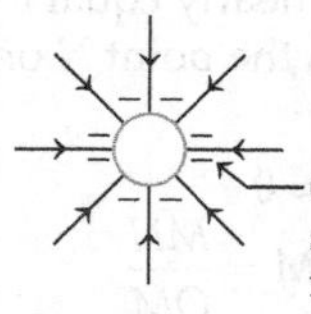

(*ii*) Electric field lines due to an electric dipole are shown in figure.

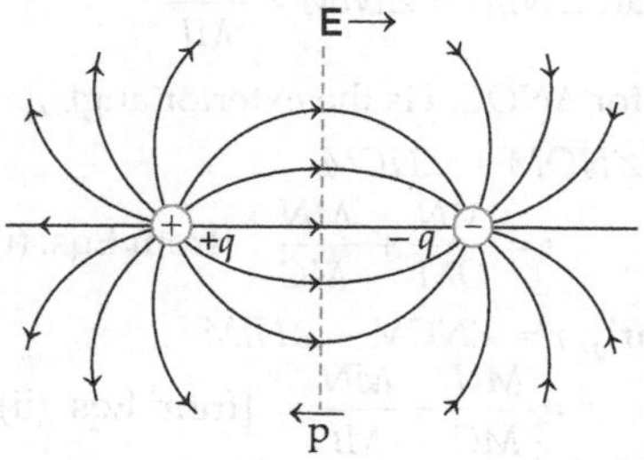

Common Mistakes Do not take charge enclosed by the Gaussian surface as q, write it in terms of λ and l.

Or

To verify the observations, we use Coulomb's law.

$$F = K_e \frac{q_1 q_2}{r^2}$$

where, $K_e = 8.99 \times 10^9 \text{ Nm}^2/\text{C}^2$.

At $r = 10$ cm,

$$F = 8.99 \times 10^9 \times \frac{2 \times 10^{-6} \times 3 \times 10^{-6}}{(0.1)^2}$$

$$= 8.99 \times 10^9 \times \frac{6 \times 10^{-12}}{0.01}$$

$$\approx 54 \text{ N}$$

At $r = 20$ cm,

$$F = 8.99 \times 10^9 \times \frac{2 \times 10^{-6} \times 3 \times 10^{-6}}{(0.2)^2}$$

$$= 8.99 \times 10^9 \times \frac{6 \times 10^{-12}}{0.04}$$

$$\approx 13.5 \text{ N}$$

At $r = 30$ cm,

$$F = 8.99 \times 10^9 \times \frac{2 \times 10^{-6} \times 3 \times 10^{-6}}{(0.3)^2}$$

$$= 8.99 \times 10^9 \times \frac{6 \times 10^{-12}}{0.09}$$

$$\approx 6.0 \text{ N}$$

At $r = 40$ cm,

$$F = 8.99 \times 10^9 \times \frac{2 \times 10^{-6} \times 3 \times 10^{-6}}{(0.4)^2}$$

$$F = 8.99 \times 10^9 \times 3.75 \times 10^{-11} = 3.37125 \text{ N} \approx 3.375 \text{ N}$$

12. (*i*) The magnetic field lines for a solenoid are as shown in figure below.

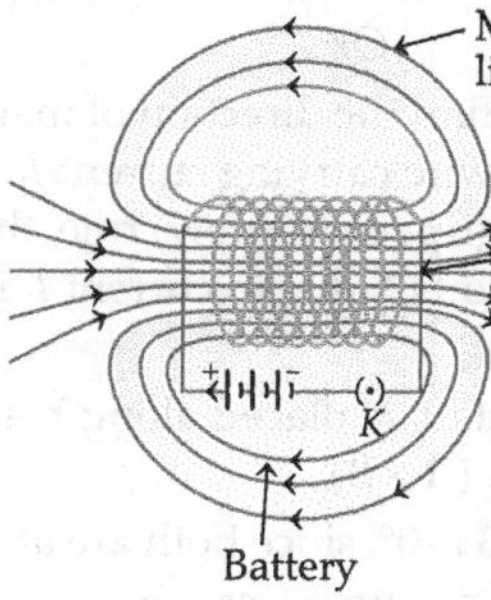

(*ii*) The tangent to the field line at a given point represents the direction of the net magnetic field at that point.

(*iii*) No, these lines are unlike the electric field lines of an electric dipole. Basically, electric field lines begin from a positive charge and end on the negative charge or escape to infinity.

13. (*i*) (a) **Electromotive Force** (emf) **of a Cell** (ε) Electric cell has to do some work in maintaining the current through a circuit. The work done by the cell in moving a unit positive charge through the whole circuit (including the cell) is called the electromotive force (emf) of the cell.

(b) **Internal Resistance** (r) Internal resistance of a cell is defined as the resistance offered by the ions of the electrolyte of the cell to the flow of current through it. It is denoted by r. Its unit is ohm (Ω).

(*ii*) We know that, the terminal potential of a cell is given by

$$V = \frac{E}{1 + \frac{r}{R}} \quad \ldots \text{(i)}$$

where, E is emf of cell, r is internal resistance of cell and R is external resistance used across the cell. Eq. (i) suggests that with increase in R, V approaches/increases close to emf E of cell.

The graph showing the variation of terminal potential V with external resistance R is given below.

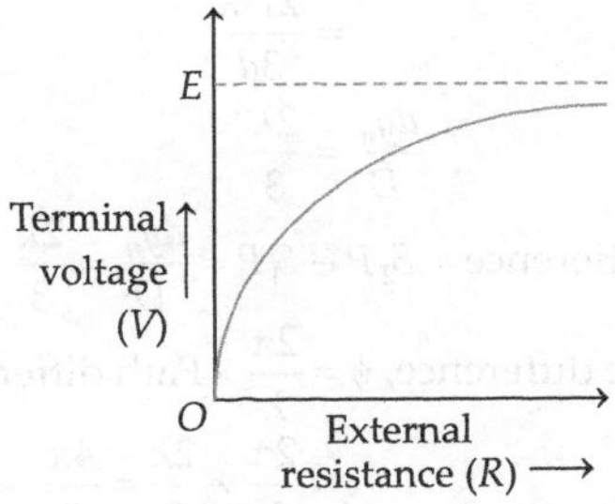

14. Let $(I_{rms})_a$ = rms current in circuit (a)

$(I_{rms})_b$ = rms current in circuit (b)

$$(I_{rms})_a = \frac{V_{rms}}{R} = \frac{V}{R}$$

$$(I_{rms})_b = \frac{V_{rms}}{Z} = \frac{V}{\sqrt{R^2 + (X_L - X_C)^2}}$$

(*i*) When $(I_{rms})_a = (I_{rms})_b$

$$\Rightarrow \quad R = \sqrt{R^2 + (X_L - X_C)^2}$$

$\Rightarrow X_L = X_C$ in resonance condition

(*ii*) As $Z \geq R$

$$\Rightarrow \frac{(I_{rms})_a}{(I_{rms})_b} = \frac{\sqrt{R^2 + (X_L - X_C)^2}}{R} = \frac{Z}{R} \geq 1$$

$$\Rightarrow \quad (I_{rms})_a \geq (I_{rms})_b$$

No, the rms current in circuit (b) cannot be larger than that in (a).

15. Given, fusion reaction, ${}_1H^2 + {}_1H^2 \rightarrow {}_2He^3 + {}_0n^1$

Mass defect, $\Delta m = 2 \times m({}_1H^2) - [m({}_2He^3) + M_n]$

$= [(2 \times 2.015) - (3.017 + 1.009)]$

$= 4 \times 10^{-3}$ amu

Equivalent energy, $E = \Delta mc^2 = \Delta m \times 931.5 \text{ MeV}/c^2 \times c^2$

$= 4 \times 10^{-3} \times 931.5$

$= 3.726$ MeV

Number of atoms in 1 kg of ${}_1H^2$

$$= \frac{\text{Given mass}}{\text{Atomic mass}} \times \text{Avogadro number}$$

$$= \frac{1000}{2} \times 6.023 \times 10^{23}$$

In one reaction, two atoms of ${}_1H^2$ are used.

So, total energy released

$$= \frac{1}{2}\left(\frac{1000}{2} \times 6.023 \times 10^{23}\right) \times 3.726 \times 1.6 \times 10^{-19}$$

$\simeq 9 \times 10^{13}$ J

16. (*i*) (a) The minimum amount of energy of incident radiation required to just eject an electron from the outermost surface of metal is known as work function of the metal. It is given as

$$\phi_0 = h\nu_0 = \frac{hc}{\lambda_0}$$

where, ν_0 and λ_0 are the threshold frequency and threshold wavelength, respectively.

(b) For a particular frequency of the incident radiation, the minimum negative (retarding) potential V_0 given to the metallic plate, so that the maximum kinetic energy of emitted electrons becomes zero or photocurrent becomes zero, is called cut-off or stopping potential. It gives the maximum kinetic energy of an ejected electron.

i.e. $KE_{max} = eV_0$

$$\Rightarrow \quad \frac{1}{2}mv_{max}^2 = eV_0$$

where, v_{max} = velocity of electron

and V_0 = cut-off potential.

(*ii*) Einstein's photoelectric equation is given as

$$KE_{max} = \frac{1}{2}mv_{max}^2 = h\nu - \phi_0$$

where, ν is the frequency of incident photon.

17. Before insertion of dielectric, charge on both capacitors,

$q = 2 \times 5 = 10\ \mu C$

and potential difference between the plates of the capacitors, $V = 5$ V.

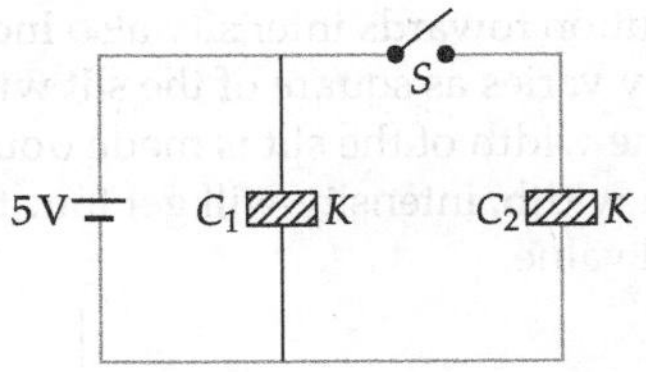

After the insertion of slab, the circuit diagram is shown in the adjacent figure.

Potential difference across C_1, $V_1 = 5$ V(remains same)

Capacitance, $C_1' = KC_1 = 5C_1 = 5 \times 2 = 10\ \mu F$

Charge on C_1, $q_1' = C_1' V_1 = (5C_1)(5) = 25\ C_1$

$= (25)(2) = 50\ \mu C \qquad (\because C_1 = 2\mu F)$

As the switch is opened, C_2 is disconnected from the circuit, so charge on it will remain same.

$\therefore \quad q_2' = q_2 = 10\ \mu C = C_2' V_2'$

Potential difference,

$$V_2' = \frac{q_2'}{C_2'} = \frac{10}{C_2'}$$

$$= \frac{10}{KC_2} = \frac{10}{5 \times 2} = 1 \text{ V}$$

18. (*i*) When the spring is stretched, the restoring force on the spring upwards = the magnetic force acting on the wire PQ downwards

$$F = BIL$$

$$kx = BIL \qquad [\because F = kx]$$

$$I = \frac{kx}{BL} = \frac{0.8 \times 2 \times 10^{-4}}{(0.002 \times 0.02)} = 4 \text{ A}$$

(ii) Direction of current is from Q to P.

(iii) The spring will oscillate up and down. Hence, the direction of current will change from P to Q and Q to P and this will generate alternating current in the wire.

(iv) The phenomenon is electromagnetic induction.

Or

(i) From graph (A), it is clear that resistance is not changing with frequency, i.e. resistance does not depend on frequency of applied voltage, so the circuit element here is pure resistive (R).

(ii) From graph (B), it is clear that resistance increases linearly with frequency, so the circuit element here is inductive in nature.

(iii) Impedance offered by the series combination of resistance (R) and inductor (L).

$$Z = \sqrt{R^2 + X_L^2}$$
$$= \sqrt{R^2 + (2\pi \nu L)^2}$$

(iv) In L-R circuit, the applied voltage leads the current by phase ϕ, where $\tan \phi = \frac{X_L}{R}$.

19. (i) As the number of point sources increases, their contribution towards intensity also increases. Intensity varies as square of the slit width. Thus, when the width of the slit is made double the original width, intensity will get four times of its original value.

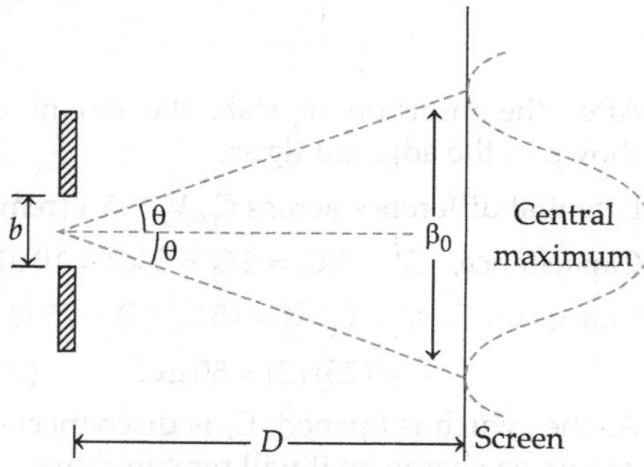

Width of central maximum is given by,

$$\beta = \frac{2D\lambda}{b}$$

where, D = distance between screen and slit,

λ = wavelength of the light

and b = size of slit.

So, with the increase in size of slit, the width of central maxima decreases. Hence, doubling the size of the slit would result as half the width of the central maxima.

(ii) Given, $OP = y_n$

The distance OP equals two-third of fringe width of the pattern,

i.e. $$y_n = \frac{2\beta}{3} = \frac{2}{3}\left(\frac{D\lambda}{d}\right)$$
$$= \frac{2D\lambda}{3d}$$

$$\Rightarrow \quad \frac{dy_n}{D} = \frac{2\lambda}{3}$$

$$\text{Path difference} = S_2P - S_1P = \frac{dy_n}{D} = \frac{2\lambda}{3}$$

$$\therefore \text{Phase difference, } \phi = \frac{2\pi}{\lambda} \times \text{Path difference}$$
$$= \frac{2\pi}{\lambda} \times \frac{2\lambda}{3} = \frac{4\pi}{3}$$

If intensity at central fringe is I_0, then intensity at a point P, where phase difference ϕ, is given by

$$I = I_0 \cos^2 \phi$$
$$I = I_0 \cos^2\left(\frac{4\pi}{3}\right)$$

We know that,

$$\cos\left(\frac{4\pi}{3}\right) = \cos\left(\pi + \frac{\pi}{3}\right) = -\cos\left(\frac{\pi}{3}\right) = -\frac{1}{2}$$

Therefore,

$$I = I_0\left(-\frac{1}{2}\right)^2 = I_0\left(\frac{1}{4}\right) = \frac{I_0}{4}$$

Hence, the intensity at point P would be $\frac{I_0}{4}$.

Or

(i) No, as we know from lens Maker's formula,

$$\frac{1}{f} = (\mu - 1)\left(\frac{1}{R_1} - \frac{1}{R_2}\right)$$

When we interchange R_1 and R_2, the magnitude of f remains same. Hence, the position of the image will not change.

(ii) Focal length f of a convex lens is related to its refractive index as $f \propto \frac{1}{\mu - 1}$.

As ${}^a\mu_g > {}^w\mu_g$, so focal length of convex lens will increase when it is immersed in water.

(iii) Given, $R_1 = 20$ cm, $R_2 = -40$ cm, $f = 20$ cm, $\mu = ?$

We know that, $$\frac{1}{f} = (\mu - 1)\left(\frac{1}{R_1} - \frac{1}{R_2}\right)$$

$$\Rightarrow \quad \frac{1}{20} = (\mu - 1)\left(\frac{1}{20} + \frac{1}{40}\right)$$

$$\Rightarrow \quad \frac{1}{\mu - 1} = 20\left(\frac{2+1}{40}\right) = \frac{3}{2}$$

$$\Rightarrow \quad \mu - 1 = \frac{2}{3} \Rightarrow 3\mu = 5$$

$$\Rightarrow \quad \mu = \frac{5}{3}$$

Hence, the refractive index of the material of the lens is 5/3.

20. (*i*)

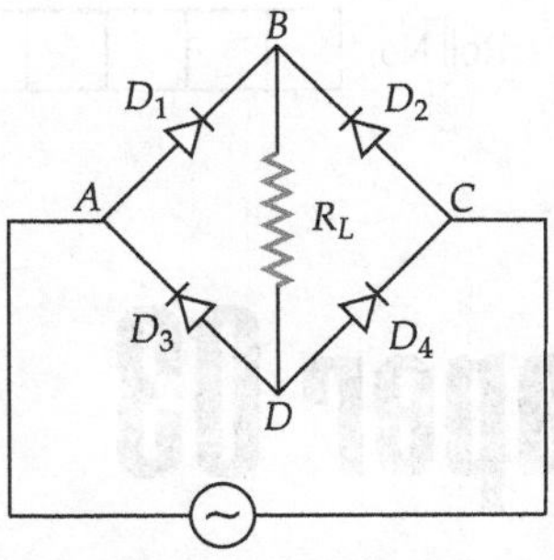

AC input is applied across *A* and *C* and output is taken across *BD*.

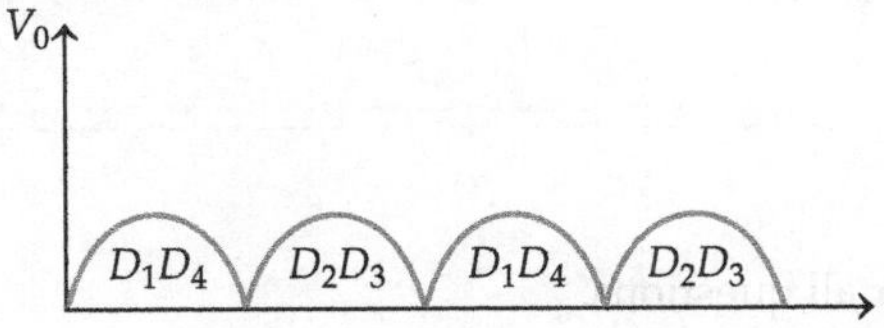

When positive cycle is fed to *AC*, D_1 and D_4 conduct and when negative cycle is fed to *AC*, D_3 and D_2 conduct in the same direction. Output across *BD* is thus full wave rectified.

(*ii*) A rectifier is used to convert AC to DC.

(*iii*) In the given circuit, for the first half-cycle of rectified output when the voltage across *C* will rise, it gets charged. Then, in the presence of R_L, it gets discharged through it and the voltage begins to fall.

In the next half-cycle of rectified output, it again gets charged to peak value and will similarly gets discharged through R_L.

Thus, a steady DC output from pulsating voltage is obtained. In other words, capacitor helps to filter out the AC ripple and give a pure DC voltage or bypass AC component to get DC.

SQP Code : **PB-3/15** Series ***i*-Succeed 3-25/15** Roll No.

Sample Question Paper 03

Physics 12th (Code 861)

General Instructions

1. This paper is divided into four Sections- A, B, C and D. Answer all questions.
2. **Section A** consists of one question having sub-parts of one mark each.
3. **Section B** consists of seven questions of two marks each.
4. **Section C** consists of nine questions of three marks each.
5. **Section D** consists of three questions of five marks each.
6. Internal choices have been provided in two questions each in Section B, Section C and Section D.

Time : 3 Hrs.

Max. Marks : 70

Section A (14 Marks)

1. **A.** In questions (i) to (vii) below, choose the correct alternative (a), (b), (c) or (d) for each of the questions given below.

(*i*) If the current I flowing through a circular coil, its radius R and number of turns N in it, each become four times, then magnetic flux density at its centre becomes • *Recall* [1]

(a) two times (b) four times
(c) eight times (d) sixteen times

(*ii*) The instantaneous magnetic flux linked with a coil is given by $\phi = (5t^3 - 100t + 300)$ Wb. The emf induced in the coil at time $t = 2$ s is • *Analysis* [1]

(a) – 40 V (b) 40 V (c) 140 V (d) 300 V

(*iii*) **Assertion** Mass of a body decreases slightly when it is negatively charged.

Reason Charging is due to transfer of electrons. • *Understanding* [1]

(a) Both Assertion and Reason are true and Reason is the correct explanation of the Assertion.
(b) Both Assertion and Reason are true but Reason is not the correct explanation of the Assertion.
(c) Assertion is false and Reason is true.
(d) Both Assertion and Reason are false.

(*iv*) In a refracting type astronomical telescope, • *Recall* [1]

(a) eyepiece has greater focal length
(b) objective has greater focal length
(c) objective and eyepiece have equal focal length
(d) eyepiece has greater aperture than the objective

(*v*) If photons of frequency ν are incident on the surfaces of metals A and B of threshold frequencies $\frac{\nu}{2}$ and $\frac{\nu}{3}$ respectively, the ratio of the maximum kinetic energy of electrons emitted from A to that from B is • *Understanding* [1]

(a) 2 : 3 (b) 3 : 4 (c) 1 : 3 (d) $\sqrt{3}:\sqrt{2}$

(*vi*) The difference in mass of ^7X nucleus and total mass of its constituent nucleons is 21.00 u. The binding energy per nucleon for this nucleus is equal to the energy equivalent of • *Analysis* [1]

(a) 3 u (b) 3.5 u (c) 7 u (d) 21 u

(*vii*) **Assertion (A)** The magnetic field intensity at the centre of a circular coil carrying current changes, if the current through the coil is doubled.
Reason (R) The magnetic field intensity dependent on current in conductor.
• *Analysis* [1]
(a) Both Assertion and Reason are true and Reason is the correct explanation of the Assertion.
(b) Both Assertion and Reason are true but Reason is not the correct explanation of the Assertion.
(c) Assertion is false and Reason is true.
(d) Both Assertion and Reason are false.

B. Answer the following questions briefly.
(*i*) Two identical balls having same positive charge q coulomb are suspended by two insulating strings of equal length. What would be the effect on the force when a plastic sheet is inserted between the two?
• *Understanding* [1]
(*ii*) At which path, a charge particle moves in a uniform magnetic field when it enters into the uniform magnetic field at an angle • *Recall* [1]
(a) 45°
(b) 90°, from the direction of magnetic field?
(*iii*) What is the formula used for finding refractive index of a prism when its angle of minimum deviation is given? • *Recall* [1]
(*iv*) Graph showing the variation of current *versus* voltage for a material GaAs is shown in the figure. Identify the region
• *Recall* [1]

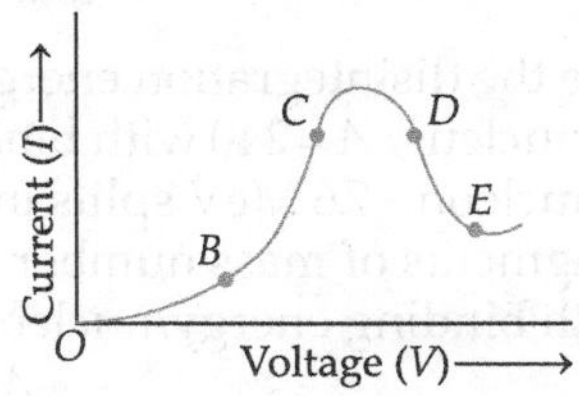

(a) of negative resistance.
(b) where Ohm's law is obeyed.
(*v*) A metallic plug AB is carrying a current I (see figure below). State how the drift velocity of free electrons varies from end A to end B? • *Application* [1]

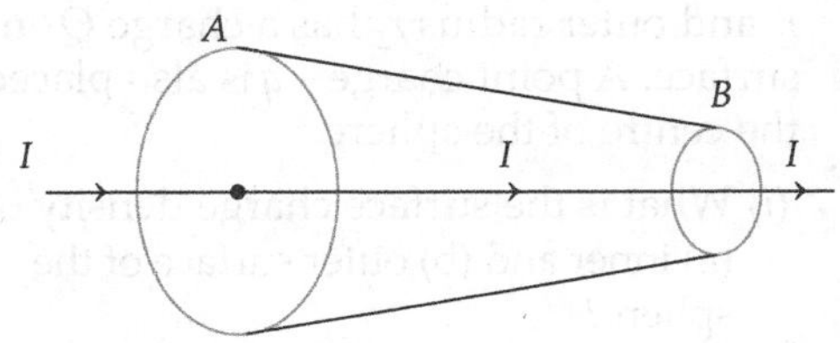

(*vi*) An electric lamp connected in series with a capacitor and an AC source is glowing with a certain brightness. How does the brightness of the lamp change on increasing the capacitance? • *Recall* [1]
(*vii*) In Fraunhofer's single slit diffraction experiment, how does semi-angular width θ of the central bright fringe depend on slit width a? • *Recall* [1]

SP-03

Section B (14 Marks)

2. A solenoid of length 0.5 m has a radius of 1 cm and is made up of 500 turns. It carries a current of 5 A. What is the magnitude of magnetic field inside the solenoid?
• *Application* [2]

Or Equal currents are flowing through two infinitely long parallel wires in the same direction. What will be the magnetic field at a point mid-way between the two wires?
• *Analysis* [2]

3. (*i*) An object of size 3.0 cm is placed at 14 cm from concave lens of focal length 21 cm. Describe the image produced by the lens.
• *Recall* [1]
(*ii*) Find image size. What happens, if the object is moved further away from the lens? • *Recall* [1]

4. A circular coil of closely wound N turns and radius r carries a current I. Write the expressions for the following
(*i*) The magnetic field at its centre. [1]
(*ii*) The magnetic moment of this coil.
• *Recall* [1]

5. (*i*) Identify the electromagnetic waves whose wavelengths vary as
(a) 10^{-12} m $< \lambda < 10^{-8}$ m
(b) 10^{-3} m $< \lambda < 10^{-1}$ m • *Recall* [1]
(*ii*) Write one use for each. • *Recall* [1]

6. A beam of light whose wavelength is 4000Å is diffracted by a single slit of width 0.2 mm. Give the angular position of the second minima. • *Understanding* [2]

7. Calculate the disintegration energy Q when a heavy nucleus, $A = 240$ with binding energy/nucleon ~ 7.6 MeV splits into two equal fragments of mass number $A' = 120$ each, with binding energy/nucleon = 8.5 MeV. • *Application* [2]

Or

Suppose, we think of fission of a $^{56}_{26}$Fe nucleus into two equal fragments of $^{28}_{13}$Al. Is the fission energetically possible? Argue by working out Q of the process.

(Given, $m(^{56}_{26}\text{Fe}) = 55.93494$ u and $m(^{28}_{13}\text{Al}) = 27.98191$ u.) • *Application* [2]

8. Out of the two magnetic materials, A has relative permeability slightly greater than unity while B has less than unity. Identify the nature of the materials A and B. Will their susceptibilities be positive or negative? • *Application* [2]

Section C (27 Marks)

9. A hollow conducting sphere of inner radius r_1 and outer radius r_2 has a charge Q on its surface. A point charge $-q$ is also placed at the centre of the sphere.

   (*i*) What is the surface charge density on the (a) inner and (b) outer surface of the sphere? [1]

   (*ii*) Use Gauss' law of electrostatics to obtain the expression for the electric field at a point lying outside the sphere. • *Application* [2]

10. (*i*) Define Kirchhoff's voltage rule. • *Recall* [1]

   (*ii*) Find the currents I_1, I_2 and I_3 in the circuit shown in figure using Kirchhoff's rule. • *Understanding* [2]

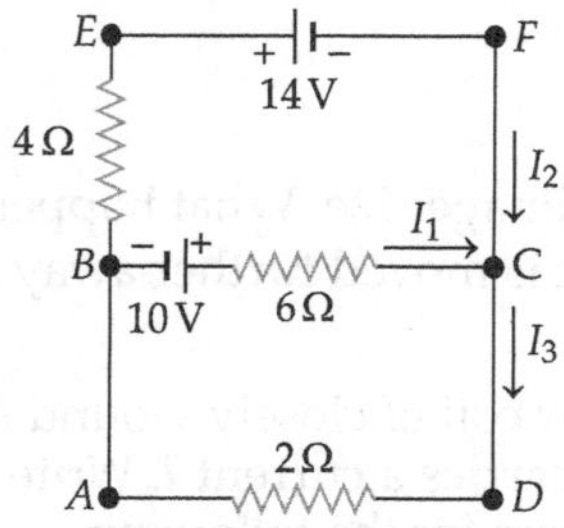

11. (*i*) What are the conditions for constructive and destructive interferences? Give resultant intensity in each case. • *Analysis* [3]

Or (*ii*) A convex lens of focal length 20 cm is placed 15 cm apart coaxially from a convex mirror of focal length 10 cm. A point object O is placed at a distance of 50 cm in front of convex lens. Draw a ray diagram to show the formation of image by the combination and also determine the nature and position of image formed. [3]

12. (*i*) When a forward bias is applied to a *p-n* junction, what happens to its potential barrier across the junction? • *Recall* [1]

   (*ii*) Assuming that the two diodes D_1 and D_2 used in the electric circuit as shown in the figure are ideal, find out the value of the current flowing through 1 Ω resistor. • *Application* [2]

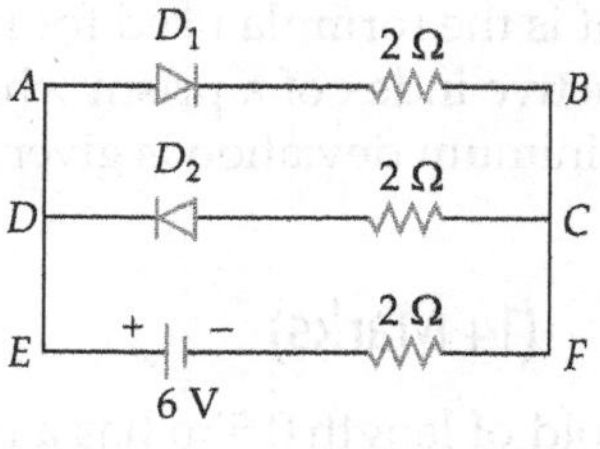

13. (*i*) How is the focal length of a spherical mirror affected when it is immersed in water? • *Recall* [1]

   (*ii*) A convex lens has 10 cm focal length in air. What is its focal length in water? (Refractive index of air-water = 1.33, refractive index of air-glass = 1.5). • *Application* [2]

Or A student records the following data for the image distance (v) produce by a concave mirror of focal length f for different object distance (u). Verify (for any two) that these

observations are in good agreement with the expected theoretical value of v.
• *Application* [3]

u	∞	$2f$	$1.5f$	f
v	f	$2f$	$3f$	No image

14. A student performs an experiment on photoelectric effect, using two materials A and B. A plot of V_{stop} *versus* ν is given in the figure.

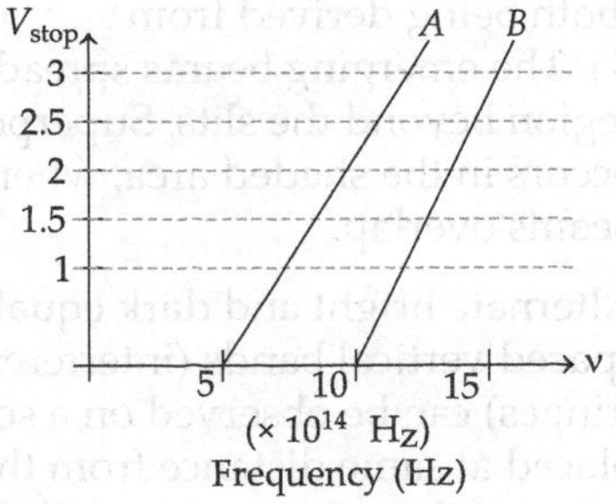

(*i*) Which material (A or B) has a higher work function?

(*ii*) Given the electric charge on an electron $= 1.6 \times 10^{-19}$ C, find the value of h obtained from the experiment for both A and B.

Comment on whether it is consistent with the Einstein's theory . • *Application* [3]

15. What do you mean by the sensitivity of a Wheatstone bridge? On what factor, does it depend? Give an advantage of null point method in this bridge. • *Application* [3]

16. Draw a plot of potential energy between a pair of nucleons as a function of their separation. Mark the regions, where potential energy is

(*i*) positive and

(*ii*) negative • *Understanding* [3]

17. A photon emitted during the de-excitation of electron from a state n to the first excited state in a hydrogen atom, irradiates a metallic cathode of work function 2eV, in a photocell, with a stopping potential of 0.55 V. Obtain the value of the quantum number of the state n. • *Analysis* [3]

Section D (15 Marks)

18. (*i*) Two students A and B performed an experiment for studying the behaviour of inductor and obtained the following graph.

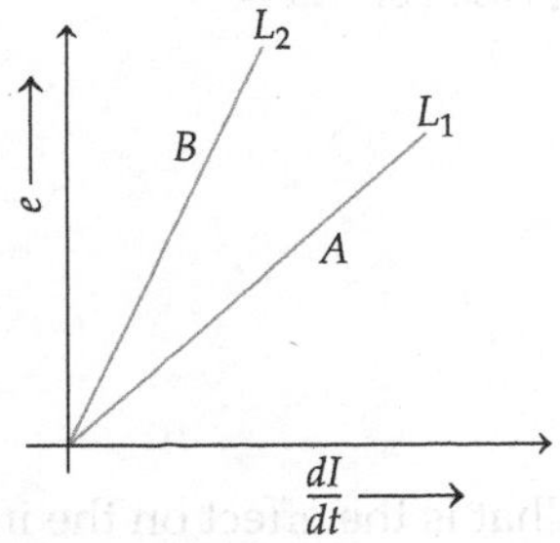

(a) What is induced emf in L_1 in terms of inductance? • *Analysis* [1]

(b) Inductance of which inductor is greater? • *Analysis* [1]

(c) Plot the graph of energy stored *versus* current. • *Analysis* [1]

(d) If L_1 is 12 mH and L_2 is 30 mH, then what is the ratio of energy stored by L_1 w.r.t. L_2. for the same value of current? • *Application* [2]

Or

(*ii*) Two concentric circular loops of are placed co-axially as shown in the figure.

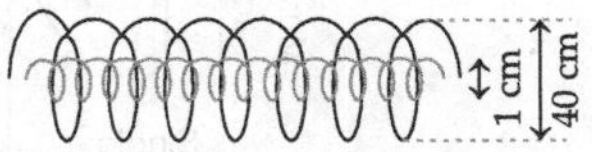

(a) Find mutual inductance of the arrangement. • *Application* [3]

(b) If the current passed through the outer loop is changed at a rate of 5 A/ms, find the emf induced in the inner loop. Assume, the magnetic field on the inner loop to be uniform. • *Application* [2]

19. (*i*) Deduce the expression for the energy density stored in a charged capacitor. • *Application* [2]

(*ii*) Show that the effective capacitance C of a series combination of three capacitors C_1, C_2 and C_3 is given by • *Application* [3]

$$C = \frac{C_1 C_2 C_3}{C_1 C_2 + C_2 C_3 + C_3 C_1}$$

Or

Given is a pair of parallel charged metal plates in the arrangement as shown.

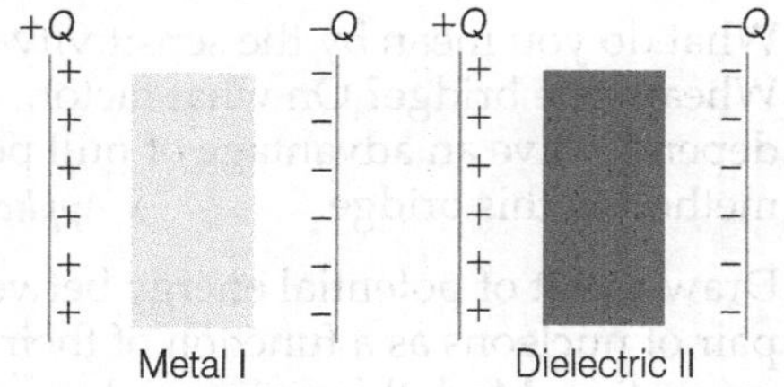

(i) Sketch the electric field lines between the plates in I and II. • *Understanding* [2]

(ii) Mention whether net electric field intensity is zero or non-zero in each case. • *Recall* [1]

(iii) Calculate the electric field, if separation between plates is 1 cm, plate area 100 cm ^{2} and the thickness of metal inserted his 0.9 cm. • *Application* [2]

20. Young's Experiment

In 1801, Thomas Young was the first who demonstrated the interference of light.

In his experimental arrangement (as shown in figure), monochromatic light (single wavelength) from a narrow vertical slit S falls on two other narrow slits S_1 and S_2 which are very close together and equidistant to S. S_1 and S_2 act as two coherent sources (both being derived from S). The emerging beams spread into the region beyond the slits. Superposition occurs in the shaded area, where the beams overlap.

Alternate bright and dark equally spaced vertical bands (interference fringes) can be observed on a screen placed at same distance from the slits. If either of S_1 or S_2 is covered, then the fringes disappear.

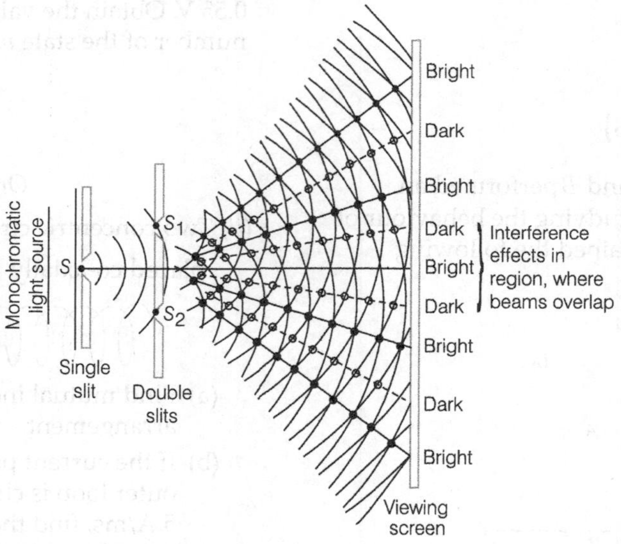

(*i*) Suppose while performing double slit experiment, the space between the slits and the screen is filled with water. How does the interference pattern change? • *Recall* [1]

(*ii*) In Young's double slit experiment, if the distance between the slits is halved, what changes in the fringe width will take place? • *Application* [1]

(*iii*) What is the effect on the interference fringes, if the separation between the two slits is increased ? • *Recall* [1]

(*iv*) The ratio of the widths of two slits in Young's double slit experiment is 4:1. Evaluate the ratio of • *Application* [1]

(a) amplitudes in the interference pattern.

(b) maximum to minimum intensities in interference pattern. [1]

Solutions in Topper's Style

My Commitment *I affirm that I am reviewing these solutions only after I have solved the Sample Question Paper 3 on my own. My purpose of looking the solutions is solely to verify whether my answers/solutions were correct or not and to identify my mistakes in case my solutions were wrong or I could not solve that.*

1. A. (*i*) (*b*) Magnetic flux density at the centre of coil is given by $B=\dfrac{\mu_0 NI}{2R}$

New current, $I'=4I$

New radius, $R'=4R$

New number of turns, $N'=4N$

Thus, magnetic flux density,

$$B'=\frac{\mu_0 N'I'}{2R'}$$

$$\Rightarrow \quad B'=\frac{\mu_0(4N)(4I)}{2(4R)}$$

$$\Rightarrow \quad B'=\frac{4\mu_0 NI}{2R} \Rightarrow B'=4B$$

Thus, the magnetic flux density is increased by 4 times. So, option (b) is correct.

(*ii*) (*b*) Given, $\phi=(5t^3-100t+300)$ Wb, $t=2$ s

Induced electromotive force,

$$e=-\frac{d\phi}{dt}=-\frac{d}{dt}(5t^3-100t+300)$$

$$e=-3\times 5t^2+100=-3\times 5(2^2)+100$$

$$=-3\times 20+100=-60+100=40\text{ V}$$

(*iii*) (*c*) A body acquires charge by the transfer of electrons.

When a body acquires negative charge by gaining more electrons, then its mass increases slightly from its neutral state.

Therefore, Assertion is false but Reason is true.

(*iv*) (*b*) In a refractive type astronomical telescope, the aperture and focal length of an objective lens are kept higher than the aperture and focal length of eyepiece. So, that the most of the light from the distant object enters the objective lens and eyepiece lens magnifies its final image at infinity.

(*v*) (*b*) From Einstein's photoelectric equation, maximum kinetic energy of emitted electrons,

$$K_{max}=h(\nu-\nu_0)$$

where, h is Planck's constant, ν is frequency of incident radiation and ν_0 is threshold frequency of metal surface.

For metal A,

$$K_{(max)A}=h\left(\nu-\frac{\nu}{2}\right) \text{ or } K_{(max)A}=\frac{h\nu}{2} \quad \dots\text{(i)}$$

Similarly, for metal B,

$$K_{(max)B}=h\left(\nu-\frac{\nu}{3}\right)$$

or

$$K_{(max)B}=\frac{2h\nu}{3} \quad \dots\text{(ii)}$$

So, from Eqs. (i) and (ii), the ratio of the maximum kinetic energy of electrons emitted from A to that from B is given as,

$$\frac{K_{(max)A}}{K_{(max)B}}=\frac{\frac{h\nu}{2}}{\frac{2h\nu}{3}}=\frac{1}{2}\times\frac{3}{2}=\frac{3}{4}$$

or

$$K_{(max)A}:K_{(max)B}=3:4$$

(*vi*) (*a*) Given, mass defect, $\Delta m=21.00$ u, $A=7$

Binding energy, $E_b=\Delta mc^2=21\text{u}c^2$

Binding energy per nucleon,

$\dfrac{E_b}{A}=\dfrac{21\text{u}c^2}{7}=3\text{u}c^2$, which is equivalent to 3u.

(*vii*) (*a*) The magnetic field at the centre of circular coil is given by $B=\dfrac{\mu_0 I}{2r}$.

where, I is the current in the coil and r is the radius of the coil.

So if current through coil is doubled, then magnetic field is $B'=2B$.

The magnetic field also get doubled. The magnetic field is directly proportional to the current in conductor.

B. (*i*) According to the question, both the balls have same charge q. Let the balls are separated by a distance r. Hence, according to Coulomb's law, if F and F' are the forces of attraction between balls in air and in medium respectively.

Then, in air, $F=\dfrac{1}{4\pi\varepsilon_0}\cdot\dfrac{q^2}{r^2}$

In medium, $F'=\dfrac{1}{4\pi K\varepsilon_0}\cdot\dfrac{q^2}{r^2}$

$$\therefore \quad F'=F/K$$

where, K is dielectric constant of material. $K>1$ for insulators, hence the force is reduced, when a plastic sheet is inserted.

(*ii*) (a) Helical (b) Circular

(*iii*) The prism formula used for finding its refractive index is

$$\mu=\frac{\sin\left(\frac{A+\delta_m}{2}\right)}{\sin\frac{A}{2}}$$

[where symbols have their usual meanings.]

(*iv*) (a) *DE* is the region of negative resistance, because the slope of curve in this part is negative.

(b) *BC* is the region where Ohm's law is obeyed because in this part, the current varies linearly with the voltage.

(*v*) As we know, current flowing across metallic plug *AB* is $I = neAv_d$

or $$v_d = \frac{I}{neA}$$

For same current, $v_d \propto \frac{1}{A}$

So, drift velocity increases as area of cross-section decreases.

In moving from *A* to *B*, the area of cross-section is decreasing.

Thus, drift velocity of free electrons increases from end *A* to end *B*.

(*vi*) Capacitive reactance is given by

$$X_C = \frac{1}{\omega C} \Rightarrow X_C \propto \frac{1}{C}$$

This means, with the increase in the capacitance, the capacitive reactance decreases. So, if an electric lamp connected in series with a capacitor and an AC source is glowing with certain brightness, then with the increase in the capacitance, the brightness of the lamp increases.

(*vii*) According to Fraunhofer's single slit diffraction experiment, we know

$$\theta = \lambda / a$$

where, λ is wavelength of light and *a* is the slit width.

So, as slit width increases, the semi-angular width of the central bright fringe decreases and *vice-versa*.

2. Given, total number of turns, $N = 500$

Length of solenoid, $l = 0.5\text{ m}$

Current, $I = 5\text{ A}$

Radius, $r = 1\text{ cm} = 10^{-2}\text{ m}$

$\therefore$ Magnetic field, $B = \mu_0 nI = \mu_0 \left(\frac{N}{l}\right) I \quad \left(\because n = \frac{N}{l}\right)$

$$= 4\pi \times 10^{-7} \times \frac{500}{0.5} \times 5$$

or $$B = 6.28 \times 10^{-3}\text{ T}$$

Or

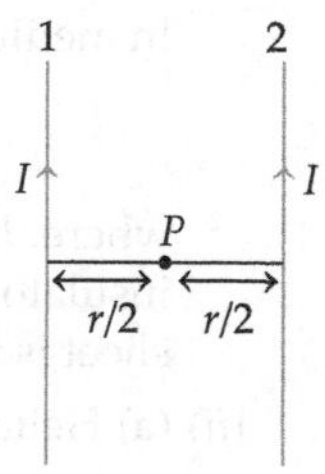

Here, current in wires, $I_1 = I_2 = I$

If *r* be the distance between both wires, then we have to calculate magnetic field at *P* (mid-point).

Magnetic field at point *P* due to current carrying wire 1,

$$B_1 = \frac{\mu_0}{2\pi} \cdot \frac{I}{\frac{r}{2}}$$

$$B_1 = \frac{\mu_0}{2\pi} \cdot \frac{2I}{r} \quad \text{(downward)}$$

Similarly, magnetic field at point *P* due to wire 2,

$$B_2 = \frac{\mu_0}{2\pi} \cdot \frac{2I}{r} \quad \text{(upward)}$$

Since, B_1 and B_2 have equal magnitude, but opposite direction, hence net magnetic field at *P* (mid-point) is zero.

3. (*i*) Using the relation, $\frac{1}{f} = \frac{1}{v} - \frac{1}{u}$, we get

$$\frac{1}{v} = \frac{1}{f} + \frac{1}{u} = \frac{1}{-21} + \frac{1}{(-14)}$$

$$\Rightarrow \quad v = -8.4\text{ cm}$$

$\therefore$ The image is virtual, erect and located at 8.4 cm from the lens on the same side as the object.

(*ii*) We know that, $m = \frac{I}{O} = \frac{v}{u}$

$$\therefore \quad I = \frac{v}{u} \times O = \frac{-8.4}{-14} \times 3 = 1.8\text{ cm}$$

i.e. the image is of diminished size.

If the object is moved away from the lens, the virtual image moves towards the focus of the lens (but never beyond focus).

4. (*i*) Magnetic field at centre due to circular current carrying coil, $B = \mu_0 NI/2r$

(*ii*) Magnetic moment, $M = NIA = NI(\pi r^2)$

$$M = \pi NIr^2$$

where, *r* is the radius of circular coil, *I* is current in coil and *N* is number of turns.

5. (*i*) (a) $10^{-12}\text{ m} - 10^{-8}\text{ m} = 0.01\text{Å}-100\text{Å} \rightarrow$ X-ray.

(b) $10^{-3}\text{ m} - 10^{-1}\text{ m} = 0.1\text{ cm}-10\text{ cm} \rightarrow$ Radiowaves

(*ii*) **X-ray** is used in crystallography.

Radiowaves are used in radio communication.

6. Given, wavelength, $\lambda = 4000\text{ Å}$

Slit width, $a = 0.2\text{ mm} = 0.2 \times 10^{-3}\text{ m}$

Width of second minima, $\theta = ?$

For *n*th minima, $a \sin\theta = n\lambda$

$\therefore 0.2 \times 10^{-3} \sin\theta = 2 \times 4000 \times 10^{-10}$

For θ to be very small; $\sin\theta \approx \theta$

$$\therefore \quad \theta = \frac{2 \times 4000 \times 10^{-10}}{0.2 \times 10^{-3}} = 4 \times 10^{-3}\text{ rad}$$

7. Disintegration energy can be calculated by the difference of the net energies of two fragments and the nucleus.

Binding energy of heavy nucleus $= 240 \times 7.6 = 1824\text{ MeV}$

Binding energy of each fragment

$$= 120 \times 8.5 = 1020\text{ MeV}$$

Binding energy of two fragments

$$= 1020 \times 2 = 2040\text{ MeV}$$

Disintegration energy, $Q = 2040 - 1824 = 216$ MeV

Or

Given, mass of ${}^{28}_{13}Al = 27.98191$ u and mass of ${}^{56}_{26}Fe = 55.93494$ u

Since, the equation is ${}^{56}_{26}Fe \rightarrow {}^{28}_{13}Al + {}^{28}_{13}Al + Q$

But Q = mass converted into energy (in amu) $\times 931.5$ MeV

Therefore, $Q = [m({}^{56}_{26}Fe) - m({}^{28}_{13}Al) - m({}^{28}_{13}Al)] \times 931.5$ MeV

$= [55.93494 - 27.98191 - 27.98191] \times 931.5 \text{ MeV} = -26.90$ MeV

Since, Q-value is negative which implies that fission is not possible.

8. The nature of the material A is paramagnetic and its susceptibility χ_m is positive.

The nature of the material B is diamagnetic and its susceptibility χ_m is negative.

9. (*i*) When a charge $-q$ is placed at the centre of the hollow conducting sphere, then the charge induced on the inner surface is $+q$ and on outer surface is $-q$. But charge Q is already present on its outer surface, so net charge on outer surface is $(Q-q)$ as shown.

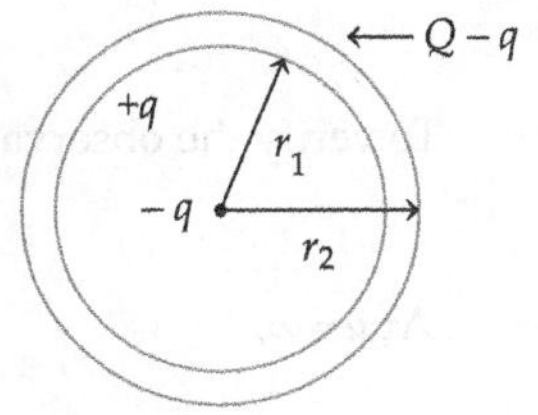

Therefore, surface charge density on

(a) inner surface is $\dfrac{q}{4\pi r_1^2}$

(b) and on outer surface is $\dfrac{Q-q}{4\pi r_2^2}$.

(*ii*) By Gauss' law, at a point lying outside the sphere, the electric flux is given by

$$\phi_E = \oint_s \mathbf{E} \cdot d\mathbf{S} = \frac{q}{\varepsilon_0}$$

where, q is the net charge enclosed.

As **E** and d**S** are in same direction as shown.

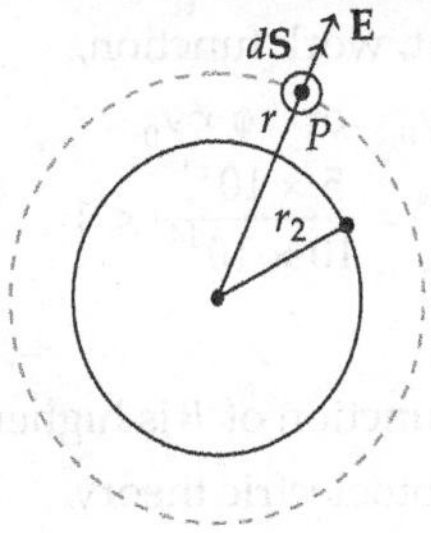

$$\therefore \quad E(4\pi r^2) = \frac{q}{\varepsilon_0} \Rightarrow \text{Electric field, } E = \frac{q}{4\pi\varepsilon_0 r^2}$$

10. (*i*) According to this rule, the algebraic sum of changes in potential around any closed loop involving resistors and cells in the loop is zero. In other words, we can define this rule as the algebraic sum of the emf's is equal to the algebraic sum of the products of the resistances and current flowing through them in any closed part of an electrical circuit (i.e. $\Sigma E = \Sigma IR$).

(*ii*) Applying Kirchhoff's junction rule to junction C, we have

$$I_1 + I_2 = I_3 \quad \text{...(i)}$$

Applying Kirchhoff's loop rule to loops $ABCDA$ and $BEFCB$ and traversing these loops in clockwise, we have

$$10 - (6)I_1 - (2)I_3 = 0 \quad \text{...(ii)}$$

and $$-14 + (6)I_1 - 10 - (4)I_2 = 0 \quad \text{...(iii)}$$

On putting the value of I_3 from Eq. (i) in Eq. (ii), we have

$$10 - (6)I_1 - (2)(I_1 + I_2) = 0$$

or $$10 = (8)I_1 + (2)I_2 \quad \text{...(iv)}$$

Also, $$-12 = (-3)I_1 + (2)I_2 \quad \text{...(v)}$$

[From Eq. (iii)]

On solving Eqs. (iv) and (v), we get

$$I_1 = 2\text{ A}, \; I_2 = -3\text{ A}$$

and $$I_3 = I_1 + I_2 = -1\text{ A}$$

11. (*i*) The condition for **constructive interference** at a point is that the phase difference between the two waves reaching at the point should be zero or an even integral multiple of 2π or path difference should be integral multiple of full wavelength,

i.e. Phase difference $= 2n\pi$, where $n = 0, 1, 2, 3, \ldots$

Path difference $= n\lambda$, where $n = 0, 1, 2, 3, \ldots$

Resultant intensity,

$$I_R = I_1 + I_2 + 2\sqrt{I_1 I_2} = (\sqrt{I_1} + \sqrt{I_2})^2$$

In case of **destructive interference**, the phase difference between the two waves reaching at the point should be an odd integral multiple of π or path difference should be an odd integral multiple of half of the wavelength,

i.e. Phase difference $= (2n-1)\pi$, where $n = 1, 2, 3, \ldots$

Path difference $= (2n-1)\dfrac{\lambda}{2}$, where $n = 1, 2, 3, \ldots$

Resultant intensity,

$$I_R = I_1 + I_2 - 2\sqrt{I_1 I_2} = (\sqrt{I_1} - \sqrt{I_2})^2$$

Or

(*ii*) The ray diagram showing image formation is shown below.

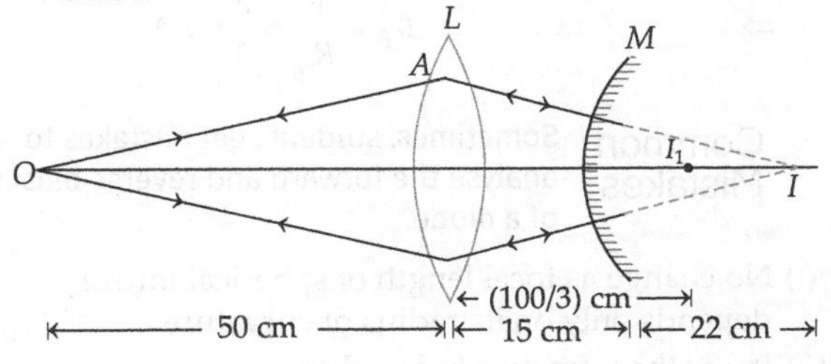

For convex lens, $f=20$ cm, $u=-50$ cm, $v=?$
From lens formula,

$$\frac{1}{v}-\frac{1}{u}=\frac{1}{f} \Rightarrow \frac{1}{v}=\frac{1}{f}+\frac{1}{u}=\frac{u+f}{uf}$$

$$\Rightarrow \quad v=\frac{uf}{u+f}=\frac{-50\times 20}{-50+20}=-\frac{1000}{(-30)}=\frac{100}{3}\text{ cm}$$

In the absence of mirror, the lens would have formed image of O at I_1, which acts as a virtual object for the convex mirror.

For convex mirror, $f=10$ cm,

$$u=\left(\frac{100}{3}-15\right)=\frac{55}{3}\text{ cm, } v=?$$

From mirror formula, $\frac{1}{v}+\frac{1}{u}=\frac{1}{f}$

$$\Rightarrow \quad \frac{1}{v}=\frac{1}{f}-\frac{1}{u}=\frac{u-f}{uf}$$

$$\text{or} \quad v=\frac{uf}{u-f}=\frac{\frac{55\times 10}{3}}{\left(\frac{55}{3}-10\right)}=\frac{550}{55-30}=\frac{550}{25}=22\text{ cm}$$

Hence, the final image I is a virtual image formed at a distance of 22 cm behind the convex mirror.

12. (*i*) When a forward bias is applied to a p-n junction, the width of depletion region decreases and the potential barrier across the junction also decreases, which ultimately vanishes the barrier potential.

(*ii*) According to the question,

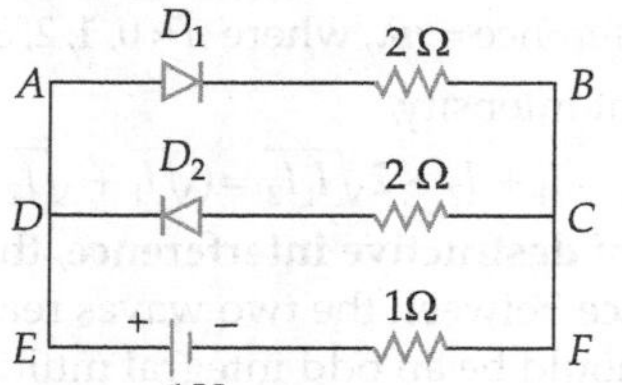

From circuit diagram, diode D_2 is in reverse biased, hence branch DC is useless, therefore new circuit diagram is

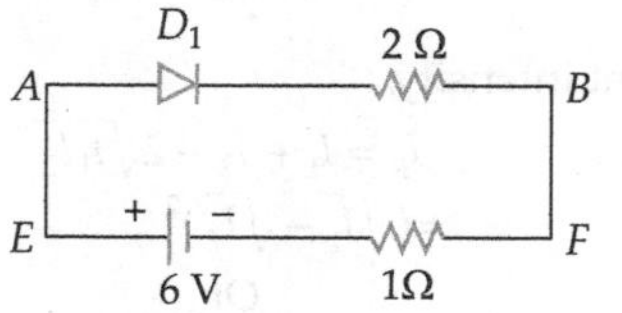

Equivalent resistance, $R_{eq}=2+1=3\Omega$

$$\Rightarrow \quad I_{EF}=\frac{V}{R_{eq}}=\frac{6}{3}=2\text{ A}$$

Common Mistakes Sometimes, students get mistakes to analyse the forward and reverse biasing of a diode.

13. (*i*) No change as focal length of spherical mirror depends only on its radius of curvature.

(*ii*) If μ is the refractive index, then

$$\frac{1}{f_a}=(\mu_{\text{air-glass}}-1)\left(\frac{1}{R}-\frac{1}{R'}\right) \quad \ldots\text{(i)}$$

Given, $\mu_{\text{air-glass}}=1.5=\frac{3}{2}$, $\mu_{\text{air-water}}=1.33=\frac{4}{3}$

$$\therefore \quad \mu_{\text{water-glass}}=\frac{\mu_{\text{air-glass}}}{\mu_{\text{air-water}}}=\frac{(3/2)}{(4/3)}=\frac{9}{8}$$

As, $f_a=10$ cm, then

$$\frac{1}{f_w}=(\mu_{wg}-1)\left(\frac{1}{R}-\frac{1}{R'}\right)$$

$$\Rightarrow \quad \frac{1}{f_w}=\left(\frac{9}{8}-1\right)\left(\frac{1}{R}-\frac{1}{R'}\right) \quad \ldots\text{(ii)}$$

On dividing Eq. (ii) by Eq. (i), we get

$$\frac{f_a}{f_w}=\frac{1}{4}$$

As, $f_a=10$ cm, then

$$\frac{10}{f_w}=\frac{1}{4} \Rightarrow f_w=40\text{ cm}$$

Or

To verify the observations, we use the lens formula

$$\frac{1}{f}=\frac{1}{v}+\frac{1}{u}$$

At $u=\infty$,

$$\frac{1}{f}=\frac{1}{v}+\frac{1}{\infty} \Rightarrow v=f$$

At $u=2f$,

$$\frac{1}{f}=\frac{1}{v}+\frac{1}{2f} \Rightarrow \frac{1}{v}=\frac{1}{f}-\frac{1}{2f}=\frac{1}{2f} \Rightarrow v=2f$$

At $u=1.5f$,

$$\frac{1}{f}=\frac{1}{v}+\frac{1}{1.5f} \Rightarrow \frac{1}{v}=\frac{1}{3f} \Rightarrow v=3f$$

At $u=f$,

$$\frac{1}{f}=\frac{1}{v}+\frac{1}{f} \Rightarrow \frac{1}{v}=0 \Rightarrow v=\infty$$

14. (*i*) Given, threshold frequency of A is,

$$\nu_A=5\times 10^{14}\text{ Hz}$$

and for B, $\nu_B=10\times 10^{14}$ Hz

We know that, work function,

$$\phi=h\nu_0 \quad \text{or} \quad \phi\propto\nu_0$$

$$\text{So,} \quad \frac{\phi_A}{\phi_B}=\frac{\nu_A}{\nu_B}=\frac{5\times 10^{14}}{10\times 10^{14}}<1$$

$$\Rightarrow \quad \phi_A<\phi_B$$

Thus, work function of B is higher than that of A.

(*ii*) Einstein's photoelectric theory,

$$eV_0=h\nu-\phi_0$$

$$V_0=\frac{h}{e}\nu-\frac{\phi_0}{e}$$

Comparing with straight line equation $y=mx+c$, we get

$$\text{Slope,} \quad m=\frac{h}{e}$$

For material A, slope $= \frac{h}{e} = \frac{V_{\text{stop}}}{\nu} = \frac{2}{(10-5) \times 10^{14}}$

or $h = \frac{2 \times e}{5 \times 10^{14}} = \frac{2 \times 1.6 \times 10^{-19}}{5 \times 10^{14}}$
$= 6.4 \times 10^{-34}$ J-s

For material B, slope $= \frac{h}{e} = \frac{2.5}{(15-10) \times 10^{14}}$

or $h = \frac{2.5 \times e}{5 \times 10^{14}}$
$= \frac{2.5 \times 1.6 \times 10^{-19}}{5 \times 10^{14}}$
$= 8 \times 10^{-34}$ J-s

Since, the value of h from experiment for metals A and B is different. Hence, experiment is not consistent with Einstein's theory.

15. A Wheatstone bridge is said to be sensitive, if it shows a large deflection in the galvanometer for a small change of resistance in the resistance arm.

The sensitivity of the Wheatstone bridge depends on the two factors.

(a) The relative magnitudes of the resistance in the four arms of the bridge. The bridge is most sensitive when all the four resistances are of the same order.

(b) The relative position of battery and galvanometer.

The advantage of null point method in a Wheatstone bridge is that the resistance of galvanometer does not affect the balance point.

16. The graph between the potential energy of a pair of nucleons as a function of their separation is given below.

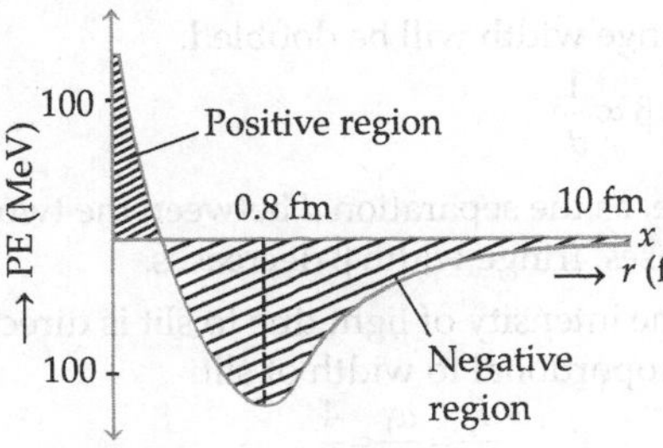

(*i*) For distance less than 0.8 fm, negative PE decreases to zero and then becomes positive.

(*ii*) For distance greater than 0.8 fm, negative PE goes on decreasing.

17. Here, $\phi = 2$ eV

Since, $\frac{1}{\lambda} = R\left(\frac{1}{n_1^2} - \frac{1}{n_2^2}\right)$

$E = \frac{hc}{\lambda} = hcR\left(\frac{1}{n_1^2} - \frac{1}{n_2^2}\right) = \phi + \text{KE}$

Also, $\text{KE} = eV_0$
$n_1 = 2, n_2 = n$

$\Rightarrow hcR\left(\frac{1}{4} - \frac{1}{n^2}\right) = 2 \times 1.6 \times 10^{-19} + 1.6 \times 10^{-19} \times 0.55$

$\Rightarrow 6.62 \times 10^{-34} \times 3 \times 10^8 \times 1.097 \times 10^7 \left(\frac{1}{4} - \frac{1}{n^2}\right)$
$= (3.2 + 0.88) \times 10^{-19}$

$\Rightarrow 21.786 \times 10^{-19} \left(\frac{1}{4} - \frac{1}{n^2}\right) = 4.08 \times 10^{-19}$

$\Rightarrow \frac{1}{4} - \frac{1}{n^2} = 0.187$

$\Rightarrow n \simeq 4$

18. (a) Induced emf in the inductor,
$|e| = L\frac{dI}{dt}$

(b) As, $L = \frac{e}{dI/dt} =$ slope

Hence, $L_2 > L_1$

(c) Energy stored in inductor,
$U = \frac{1}{2}LI^2$

For a given L, $U \propto I^2$

Thus, U *versus* I graph is curved as shown in the following figure.

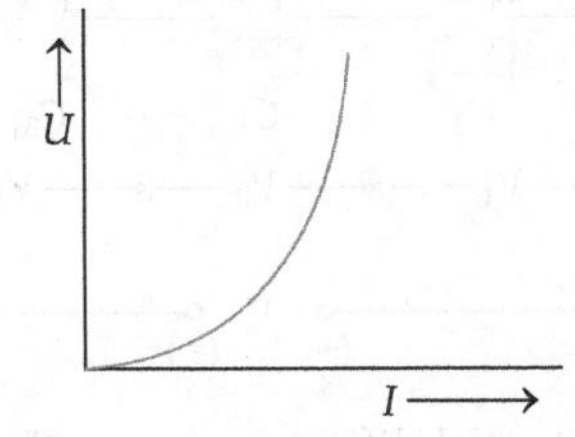

(d) The ratio of energy stored in L_1 and L_2,

$\frac{U_1}{U_2} = \frac{\frac{1}{2}L_1 I^2}{\frac{1}{2}L_2 I^2} = \frac{L_1}{L_2} = \frac{12}{30} = 2:5$

Or

(*ii*) Given, $r_1 = 1\,\text{cm} = 0.01\,\text{m}$
and $r_2 = 20\,\text{cm} = 0.2\,\text{m}$

(a) From the relation, mutual inductance between the two coils, $M = \frac{\mu_0 \pi r_1^2}{2r_2}$

Substituting the given values in above equation, we get

$M = \frac{4\pi \times 10^{-7} \times \pi \times (0.01)^2}{2 \times 0.2} = 9.859 \times 10^{-10}$ H

or $M = 9.86 \times 10^{-10}$ H

(b) Given, time rate of change of current,
$\frac{dI}{dt} = 5\,\text{A/ms} = 5 \times 10^3$ A/s

$\therefore$ emf induced in the inner loop,
$|e| = M\frac{dI}{dt} = 9.86 \times 10^{-10} \times 5 \times 10^3 = 4.93 \times 10^{-6}$ V

19. (*i*) We know that, charge on capacitor, $q = CV$

$\Rightarrow \quad V = q/C$

$\therefore$ The instantaneous work done in moving a charge,

$dW = Vdq = \frac{q}{C}dq$

where, q = instantaneous charge,

C = instantaneous capacitance

and V = instantaneous voltage.

$\therefore$ Total work done in storing charge from 0 to q is given by $W = \int_0^q \frac{q}{C}dq = \frac{q^2}{2C} = \frac{1}{2}CV^2$

This work done is stored as electrostatic potential energy, so energy density is

$$u = \frac{\text{work}}{\text{volume}} = \frac{1}{2}\cdot\frac{CV^2}{A\cdot d}$$

$$= \frac{1}{2}\cdot\frac{\varepsilon_0 A}{d}\cdot\frac{V^2}{A\cdot d} = \frac{1}{2}\varepsilon_0 E^2 \qquad \left[\because E = \frac{V}{d}\right]$$

(*ii*) In series combination of capacitors, same charges lie on each capacitor for any value of capacitance.

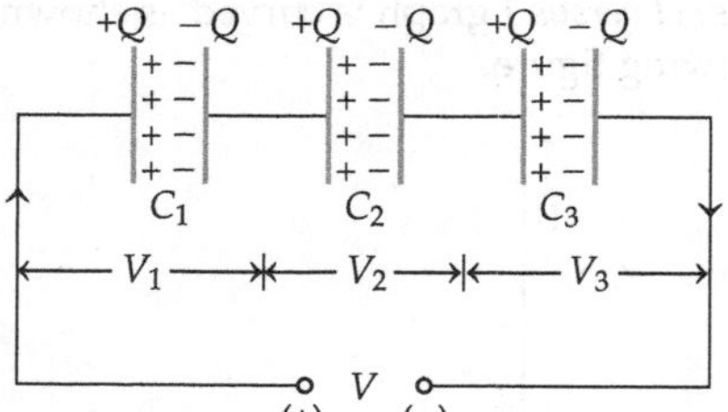

Also, potential difference across the combination is equal to the algebraic sum of potential differences across each capacitor,

i.e. $\quad V = V_1 + V_2 + V_3 \quad \dots(i)$

where, V_1, V_2, V_3 and V are the potential differences across C_1, C_2, C_3 and equivalent capacitor, respectively.

$\therefore \quad q = C_1V_1 \Rightarrow V_1 = \frac{q}{C_1}$

Similarly, $\quad V_2 = \frac{q}{C_2}$ and $V_3 = \frac{q}{C_3}$

$\therefore$ Total potential difference,

$\Rightarrow \quad V = \frac{q}{C_1} + \frac{q}{C_2} + \frac{q}{C_3} \quad$ [from Eq. (i)]

$\Rightarrow \quad \frac{V}{q} = \frac{1}{C_1} + \frac{1}{C_2} + \frac{1}{C_3}$

$\Rightarrow \quad \frac{1}{C} = \frac{1}{C_1} + \frac{1}{C_2} + \frac{1}{C_3}$

$\left[\because \frac{V}{q} = \frac{1}{C}\right.$, where C is the equivalent capacitance of combination]

or $\quad \frac{1}{C} = \frac{C_2C_3 + C_3C_1 + C_1C_2}{C_1C_2C_3}$

$\Rightarrow \quad C = \frac{C_1C_2C_3}{C_1C_2 + C_2C_3 + C_3C_1}$

Or

(*i*)

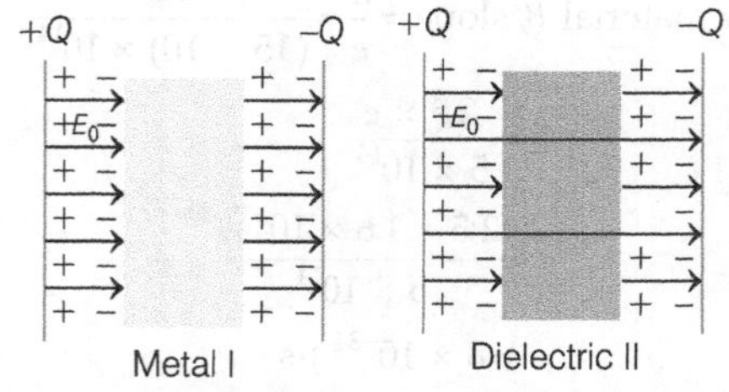

(ii) The net electric field intensity inside a metal is zero. The net electric field intensity inside a dielectric is non-zero.

(iii) Given, $d = 1\text{ cm} = 1\times10^{-2}$ cm

$A = 100\text{ cm}^2 = 100\times10^{-4}\text{ m}^2$

$t = 0.9\text{ cm} = 0.9\times10^{-2}$ m

$$C = \frac{\varepsilon_0 A}{(d-t) + \frac{t}{K}}$$

$\because \quad K = \infty$ for metal,

$$= \frac{8.85\times10^{-12}\times100\times10^{-4}}{(1-0.9)\times10^{-2}}$$

$C = 88.5$ pF

20. (*i*) The pattern will remain the same, but it gets shifted slightly.

(*ii*) Fringe width, $\beta = \frac{D\lambda}{d}$

When $d' = \frac{d}{2}$, then $\beta' = \frac{2D\lambda}{d} = 2\beta$

So, fringe width will be doubled.

(*iii*) Since, $\beta \propto \frac{1}{d}$

Hence, as the separation d between the two slits increases, fringe width β decreases.

(*iv*) (a) The intensity of light due to slit is directly proportional to width of slit.

$\therefore \quad \frac{I_1}{I_2} = \frac{w_1}{w_2} = \frac{4}{1}$

$\Rightarrow \quad \frac{a_1^2}{a_2^2} = \frac{4}{1} \qquad (\because I \propto a^2)$

$\Rightarrow \quad \frac{a_1}{a_2} = \frac{2}{1}$ or 2 : 1

(b) As, $\quad a_1 = 2a_2$

$$\frac{I_{max}}{I_{min}} = \frac{(a_1+a_2)^2}{(a_1-a_2)^2} = \frac{(2a_2+a_2)^2}{(2a_2-a_2)^2} = \frac{9a_2^2}{a_2^2} = 9:1$$

Hence, the ratio of the intensities of maxima and minima is 9 : 1.

SQP Code : **PB-4/15**	Series ***i*-Succeed 4-25/15**	Roll No.							

Sample Question Paper 04

Physics 12th (Code 861)

General Instructions

1. This paper is divided into four Sections- A, B, C and D. Answer all questions.
2. **Section A** consists of one question having sub-parts of one mark each.
3. **Section B** consists of seven questions of two marks each.
4. **Section C** consists of nine questions of three marks each.
5. **Section D** consists of three questions of five marks each.
6. Internal choices have been provided in two questions each in Section B, Section C and Section D.

Time : 3 Hrs.

Max. Marks : 70

Section A (14 Marks)

1. A. In questions (i) to (vii) below, choose the correct alternative (a), (b), (c) or (d) for each of the questions given below.

(*i*) The internal resistance of a 2.1 V cell which gives a current of 0.2 A through a resistance of 10 Ω is • *Analysis* [1]

(a) 0.2 Ω (b) 0.5 Ω (c) 0.8 Ω (d) 1.0 Ω

(*ii*) Masses of nuclei of hydrogen, deuterium and tritium are in ratio • *Recall* [1]

(a) 1 : 2 : 3 (b) 1 : 1 : 1

(c) 1 : 1 : 2 (d) 1 : 2 : 4

(*iii*) **Assertion** When the electric flux through a closed surface is zero, then the net charge inside the surface must be zero.

Reason When the net charge inside a closed surface is zero, then electric field at every point of the Gaussian surface must be zero. • *Analysis* [1]

(a) Both Assertion and Reason are true and Reason is the correct explanation of the Assertion.

(b) Both Assertion and Reason are true but Reason is not the correct explanation of the Assertion.

(c) Assertion is false and Reason is true.

(d) Both Assertion and Reason are false.

(*iv*) A long straight conductor is carrying a current *i*. If the magnetic field at a perpendicular distance *r* is 0.8 T, then magnetic field at a distance 4*r* will be • *Understanding* [1]

(a) 0.4 T (b) 0.1 T (c) 0.5 T (d) 0.2 T

(*v*) An electron accelerated through a potential difference of *V* volt has a wavelength λ associated with it. Mass of proton is nearly 2000 times that of an electron. In order to have the same wavelength for proton, it must be accelerated through a potential difference (in volt) of • *Analysis* [1]

(a) V (b) $\sqrt{2000}\,V$

(c) $2000/\sqrt{V}$ (d) $V/2000$

(*vi*) **Assertion** (A) In a semiconductor diode, the reverse biased current is due to drift of free electron and holes.

Reason (R) The drift of electrons and holes is due to thermal excitations. • *Understanding* [1]

(a) Both Assertion and Reason are true and Reason is the correct explanation of the Assertion.

(b) Both Assertion and Reason are true but Reason is not the correct explanation of the Assertion.

(c) Assertion is false and Reason are true.

(d) Both Assertion and Reason is false.

(*vii*) To a fish under water, viewing obliquely a fisherman standing on the bank of a lake, the man looks • *Recall* [1]

(a) taller than what he actually is
(b) shorter than what he actually is
(c) the same height as he actually is
(d) depends on the obliqueness

B. Answer the following questions briefly.

(*i*) Two thin lenses of power +6 D and −2 D are in contact. What is the focal length of the combination? • *Recall* [1]

(*ii*) Two point charges −4 μC and +4μC are placed at points *A* and *B* respectively, 6 cm apart. Draw the equipotential surface of the system. • *Recall* [1]

(*iii*) For observing Fraunhofer's law of diffraction from a single slit, what type of wavefront should be incident on the slit? • *Recall* [1]

(*iv*) A series combination of an inductor (*L*), a capacitor (*C*) and a resistor (*R*) is connected across an AC source of emf of peak value E_0 and angular frequency (ω). Plot a graph to show variation of impedance of the circuit with angular frequency (ω). • *Application* [1]

(*v*) State two factors on which the sensitivity of a moving coil galvanometer depends. • *Recall* [1]

(*vi*) In a meter bridge, two unknown resistances *R* and *S*, when connected between the two gaps, give a null point at 40 cm from one end. What is the ratio of *R* and *S*? • *Recall* [1]

(*vii*) A bar magnet is cut into two equal parts as shown in the Fig. (a). One part is now kept over the other such that, the P_2 is above P_1 as shown in the Fig. (b).

If *M* is the magnetic moment of the original magnet, what would be the magnetic moment of new combination of magnets so formed? • *Understanding* [1]

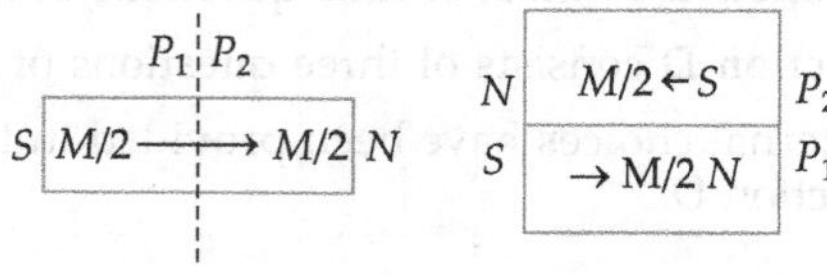

(a) (b)

Section B (14 Marks)

2. The given figure shows tracks of three charged particles in a uniform electrostatic field. Give the signs of the three charges. Which particle has the highest charge to mass ratio? • *Application* [2]

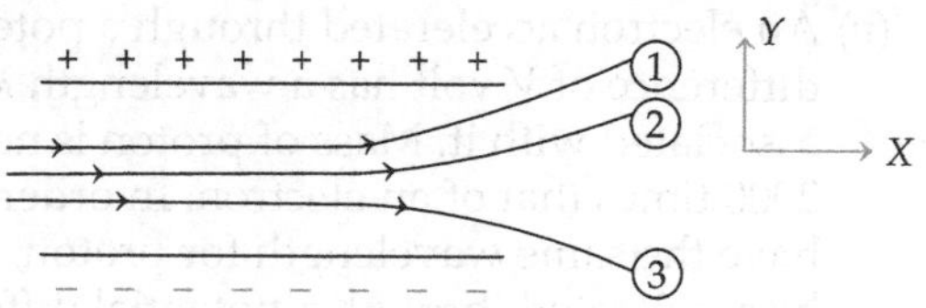

3. An equiconvex lens of focal length *f* is cut into two identical plane convex lenses. How will the power of each part be related to the focal length of the original lens?

A double convex lens of +5 D is made of glass of refractive index 1.55 with both faces of equal radii of curvature. Find the value of its radius of curvature. • *Analysis* [2]

4. How does the mutual inductance of a pair of coil change when

(*i*) distance between the coils is increased by two times and • *Recall* [1]

(*ii*) number of turns in the coils is increased by four times? • *Recall* [1]

5. Show that the radius of a charged particle entering perpendicularly in a magnetic field is directly proportional to its velocity. • *Application* [2]

Or An electron travelling West to East enters a chamber having a uniform electrostatic field in North to South direction. Specify the direction in which a uniform magnetic field should be setup to prevent the electron from deflecting its straight line path. • *Recall* [2]

6. In an electromagnetic wave, the oscillating electric field having a frequency of 3×10^{10} Hz and an amplitude of 30 V/m propagates in the positive *x*-direction. What is the wavelength of the electromagnetic wave? Also, find the amplitude of magnetic field. • *Application* [2]

7. (*i*) Write the necessary conditions for the phenomenon of total internal reflection to occur. • *Recall* [1]

(*ii*) Write the relation between the refractive index and critical angle for a given pair of optical media. • *Recall* [1]

8. Using the relevant Bohr's postulates, show that frequency of electron in a stationary orbit is inversely proportional to the radius of orbit. • *Understanding* [2]

Or The energy of the electron in the ground state of hydrogen is −13.6 eV. Calculate the energy of the photon that would be emitted, if electron was to make a transition corresponding to the emission of the first line of the Lyman series of the H-atom. • *Application* [2]

Section C (27 Marks)

9. A 12 pF capacitor is connected to a 50 V battery. How much electrostatic energy is stored in the capacitor? If another capacitor of 6 pF is connected in series and the same battery is connected across the combination. Find the charge stored and potential difference across each capacitor. • *Analysis* [3]

10. A convex lens of focal length 10 cm is to be used as a simple microscope. Where should an object be kept so that image formed by the lens is formed at least distance D of distinct vision ($D = 25$ cm)? Also, find magnification of lens. • *Application* [3]

11. Draw the energy band diagram of

(*i*) *n*-type and

(*ii*) *p*-type semiconductors at temperature $T > 0$ K.

In the case of *n*-type Si semiconductor, the donor energy level is slightly below the bottom of conduction band, whereas in *p*-type semiconductor, the acceptor energy level is slightly above the top of the valence band. Explain, what role do these energy levels play in conduction and valence bands. • *Application* [3]

12. Suppose while sitting in a parked car, you notice a jogger approaching towards you in the rear view mirror having $R = 2$ m. If the jogger is running at a speed of 5 m/s, how fast is the image of jogger moving, when the jogger is

(*i*) 39 m, (*ii*) 29 m, (*iii*) 19 m and (*iv*) 9 m away? • *Application* [3]

13. A spherical conducting shell of inner radius r_1 and outer radius r_2 has a charge Q.

(*i*) A charge q is placed at the centre of the shell. Find out the surface charge density on the (a) inner and (b) outer surfaces of the shell. • *Recall*

(*ii*) Is the electric field inside a cavity (with no charge) zero, even if the shell is not spherical, but has any irregular shape? Explain. • *Recall* [3]

14. Define the following terms with respect to *p-n* junction diode.

(*i*) Depletion layer • *Recall*

(*ii*) Potential barrier and diffusion current • *Recall* [3]

Or In an experiment, a student measures the conductivity of a doped semiconductor at different doping concentrations. Given the mobility of charge carriers μ is 1400 cm^2/Vs. Verify (for any two) that these observations are in good agreement with the expected theoretical value of doping concentration.

Doping concentration (in cm^3)	Conductivity (in S/cm)
1×10^{16}	0.0224
2×10^{16}	0.0448
3×10^{16}	0.0672
4×10^{16}	0.0896

The theoretical relationship between conductivity σ and doping concentration N_d is given by $\sigma = q\mu N_d$

where, q is the charge of an electron ($q = 1.6 \times 10^{-19}$ C). • *Application* [3]

15. Obtain an expression for v_d, if the current flowing through the conductor of length l has its ends maintained at a potential difference of V volt. • *Application* [3]

Or

In the circuit shown in figure, *E*, *F*, *G* and *H* are cells of emf 2V, 1V, 3V and 1 V respectively, and their internal resistances are 2Ω, 1Ω, 3Ω and 1 Ω, respectively. Calculate

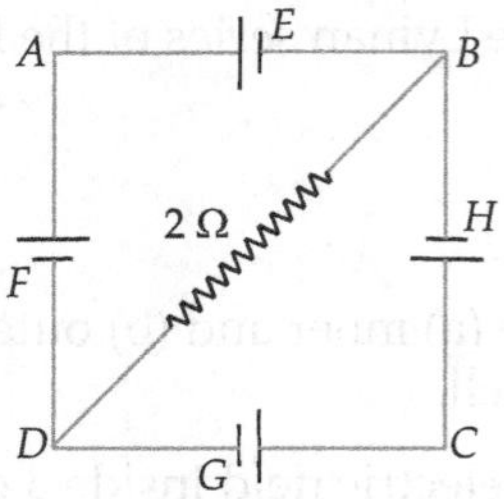

(*i*) the potential difference between *B* and *D* and

(*ii*) the potential difference across the terminals of each of the cells *G* and *H*.

• *Understanding* [3]

16. A beam of monochromatic radiation is incident on a photosensitive surface. Answer the following questions giving reasons.

(*i*) Do the emitted photoelectrons have the same kinetic energy? • *Recall*

(*ii*) Does the kinetic energy of the emitted electrons depend upon the intensity of incident radiation? • *Recall*

(*iii*) On what factors does the number of emitted photoelectrons depend? • *Recall* [3]

17. Two moving coil meters M_1 and M_2 having the following particulars
$R_1 = 10\,\Omega$, $N_1 = 30$, $A_1 = 3.6 \times 10^{-3}\ \text{m}^2$, $B_1 = 0.25\ \text{T}$ and $R_2 = 14\,\Omega$, $N_2 = 42$, $A_2 = 1.8 \times 10^{-3}\ \text{m}^2$, $B_2 = 0.50\ \text{T}$
(The spring constants are identical for the two meters).
Determine the ratio of (*i*) current sensitivity and (*ii*) voltage sensitivity of M_2 and M_1.

• *Analysis* [3]

Section D (15 Marks)

18. The graph below shows the variation in current flowing through two *L-C-R* circuits used in radios *P* and *Q*, with the change in frequency. To prevent adjacent-channel interference while tuning the radio to a particular frequency it is desirable that the frequency of adjacent channels does not lie in the bandwidth region of the selected frequency.

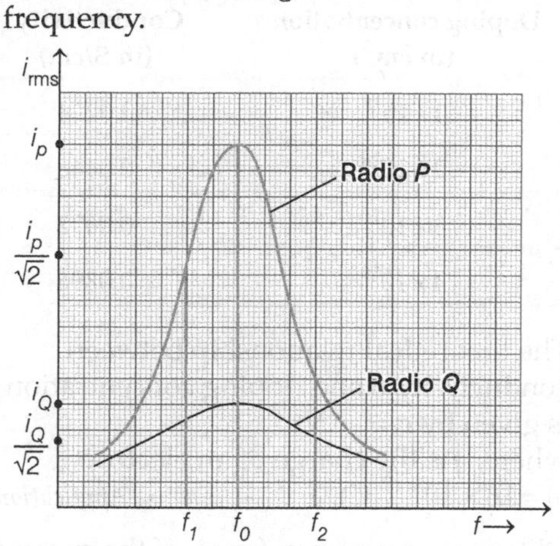

(*i*) Which radio will allow a person to hear a radio channel of frequency f_0, without the interference of other frequencies? Give reason.

(Assume f_1, f_0 and f_2 are the only radio frequencies available and to prevent adjacent-channel interference on the band)

• *Understanding* [2]

(*ii*) Compare the resistance and capacitance of *L-C-R* circuit used in radios *P* and *Q*, if both the circuits have the same inductance. Give reason. • *Application* [2]

(*iii*) Write the condition when *L-C-R* circuit is resistance dominated. • *Recall* [1]

Or

A student performed an experiment to observe the variation of voltage current and power. He connected a device *X* to an AC source $V = V_0 \sin \omega t$ and obtained the following graph.

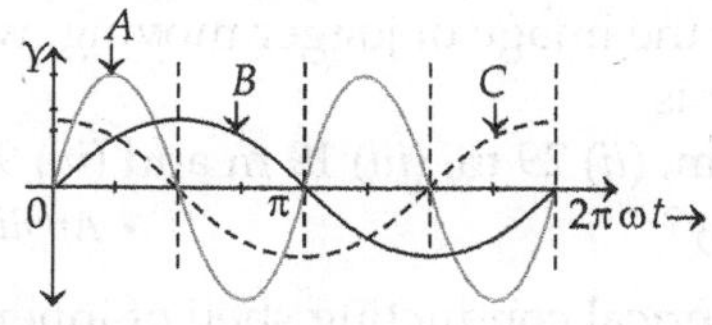

(*i*) Obtain an expression for the current in the circuit and its phase relation with AC voltage. • *Analysis* [1]

(*ii*) Identify the device *X*. • *Analysis* [1]

SP-04

(*iii*) Which of the curves *A*, *B* and *C* represent the voltage, current and the power consumed in the circuit? Justify the answer. • *Application* [1]

(*iv*) How does its impedance vary with frequency of the AC source? Show graphically. • *Application* [2]

19. (*i*) Derive the mathematical relation between refractive indices μ_1 and μ_2 of two radii and radius of curvature *R* for refraction at a convex spherical surface. Consider the object to be a point source lying on the principal axis in rarer medium of refractive index μ_1 and a real image formed in the denser medium of refractive index μ_2. Hence, derive lens Maker's formula. • *Application* [3]

(*ii*) Light from a point source in air falls on a convex spherical glass surface of refractive index 1.5 and radius of curvature 20 cm. The distance of light source from the glass surface is 100 cm. At what position is the image formed? • *Application* [2]

Or A double slit interference experiment is set up using coherent red light ($\lambda = 650 \times 10^{-9}$ m) as illustrated in the figure given below.

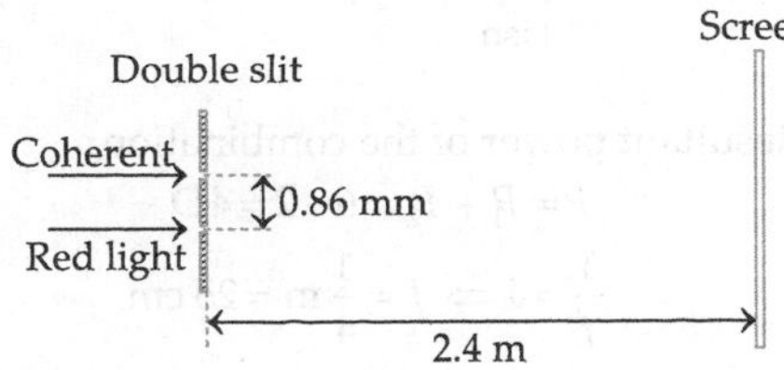

The separation of the slits is 0.86 mm.
The distance of the screen from the double slit is 2.4 m.
A series of light and dark fringes is observed on the screen.

(*i*) State what is meant by coherent light. • *Recall*

(*ii*) Estimate the separation of the dark fringes on the screen. • *Application*

(*iii*) Initially, the light passing through each slit has the same intensity. The intensity of light passing through one slit is now reduced. Suggest and explain the effect, if any, on the dark fringes observed on the screen. • *Understanding* [3]

(*iv*) If intensity of the central bright fringe is *I* and one of the slit is closed, then what will be new intensity at the centre of the screen ? • *Application* [2]

20. Hydrogen spectrum consists of discrete bright lines in a dark background and it is specifically known as hydrogen emission spectrum. There is one more type of hydrogen spectrum that exists where we get dark lines on the bright background, it is known as absorption spectrum.

Balmer found an empirical formula by the observation of a small part of this spectrum and it is represented by

$$\frac{1}{\lambda} = R\left(\frac{1}{2^2} - \frac{1}{n^2}\right),$$

where, $n = 3, 4, 5, \ldots$

For Lyman series, the emission is from first state to *n*th state, for Paschen series, it is from third state to *n*th state, for Brackett series, it is from fourth state to *n*th state and for Pfund series, it is from fifth state to *n*th state.

(*i*) Name the electromagnetic radiation in which Lyman series lies. How many spectral lines are found in hydrogen atom? • *Recall* [1]

(*ii*) Find the ratio of wavelength for $Z \rightarrow 1$ transition in Li^{++}, He^{+} and H. • *Recall* [1]

(*iii*) When an electron jumps from the orbit $n = 2$ to $n = 4$, then find the wavelength of absorbed radiation

(a) in terms of Rydberg's constant *R* and

(b) in metre, if $R = 1.09 \times 10^{7}$ m.

• *Application* [3]

Solutions *in Topper's Style*

My Commitment *I affirm that I am reviewing these solutions only after I have solved the Sample Question Paper 4 on my own. My purpose of looking the solutions is solely to verify whether my answers/solutions were correct or not and to identify my mistakes in case my solutions were wrong or I could not solve that.*

1. A. (*i*) (*b*) As $I = \frac{E}{R+r}$

$\Rightarrow \quad E = I(R+r)$

$\Rightarrow \quad 2.1 = 0.2(10+r)$

$\Rightarrow \quad 10 + r = \frac{2.1}{2} \times 10$

$\Rightarrow \quad r = 10.5 - 10$

$\Rightarrow \quad r = 0.5\Omega$

(*ii*) (*a*) Since, the nuclei of deuterium and tritium are isotopes of hydrogen, so they must contain only one proton each. But the masses of the nuclei of hydrogen, deuterium and tritium are in the ratio of 1 : 2 : 3, because of presence of 1 and 2 neutrons in deuterium and tritium nuclei, respectively.

(*iii*) (*b*) Both Assertion and Reason are true but Reason is not the correct explanation of Assertion.

According to the Gauss' law, $\phi_E = \oint \mathbf{E} \cdot d\mathbf{A} = \frac{q}{\varepsilon_0}$

Since, charge does not reside inside a conductor ($q = 0$), the electric field, $\mathbf{E} = 0$.

Hence, the electric flux through a closed surface will be zero.

(*iv*) (*d*) Magnetic field due to a long straight conductor carrying current i at a perpendicular distance r is given by

$$B = \frac{\mu_0}{4\pi}\left(\frac{2i}{r}\right) \Rightarrow B \propto \frac{1}{r}$$

According to question, $\frac{B'}{B} = \frac{r}{4r}$

[B' is magnetic field at a distance $4r$]

$\Rightarrow \quad B' = B \times \frac{1}{4}$

$\Rightarrow \quad B' = 0.2\text{ T} \qquad [\because B = 0.8\text{ T}]$

(*v*) (*d*) $\frac{1}{2}mv^2 = eV$

$mv = \sqrt{2meV}$

Now, $\lambda_e = \frac{h}{mv}$

$= \frac{h}{\sqrt{2meV}}$

$\lambda_p = \frac{h}{\sqrt{2 \times 2000\, m \times e \times V'}}$

Given, $\lambda_e = \lambda_p$

$\Rightarrow \quad V' = \frac{V}{2000}$

(*vi*) (*d*) A reverse bias on a p-n junction opposes the movement of the majority charge carriers, thus the diffusion current stops. It makes the free electrons and holes to drift cross the junction. Therefore, a small current in μA flows even when the p-n junction is reverse biased. The drift current is due to the thermal excitations of the electrons and holes.

(*vii*) (*a*) When a ray from man O in air (i.e., rarer medium) goes to water (i.e., denser medium), then it bends towards the normal. Extend MN backwards to meet at point O'. Therefore, it appears to the fish as if the man is taller than what he actually is.

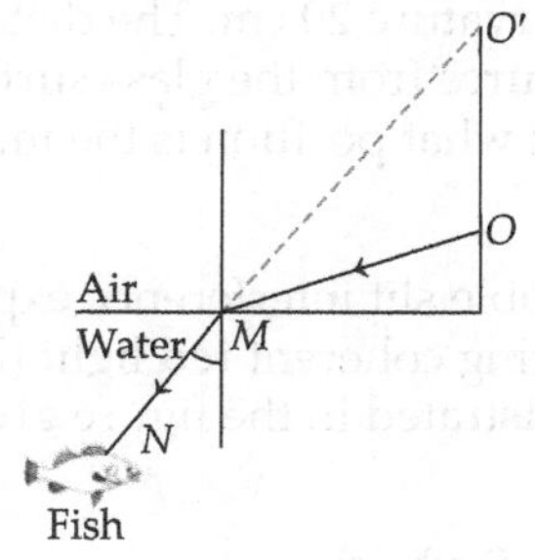

B. (*i*) Resultant power of the combination,

$$P = P_1 + P_2 = 6 - 2 = 4\text{D}$$

$$\therefore \quad \frac{1}{f} = 4 \Rightarrow f = \frac{1}{4}\text{ m} = 25\text{ cm}$$

(*ii*) The equipotential surfaces for the two different point charges of a charge system are shown below.

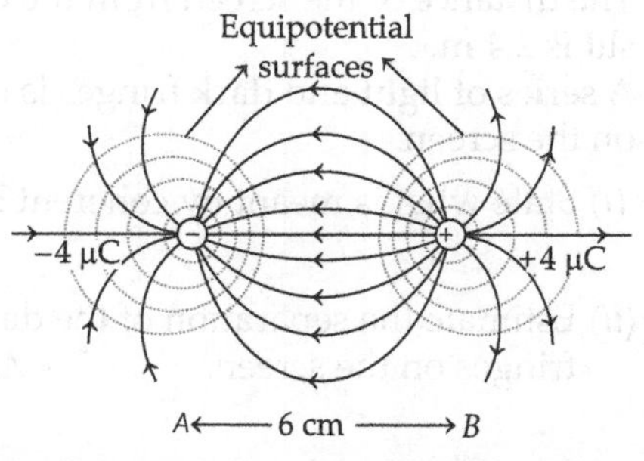

(*iii*) In the Fraunhofer's law of diffraction from a single slit, the incident wavefront should be plane.

(*iv*) Impedance of a series *L-C-R* circuit is given as

$$Z = \sqrt{R^2 + (X_L - X_C)^2} = \sqrt{R^2 + \left(\omega L - \frac{1}{\omega C}\right)^2}$$

So, the graph between impedance (Z) and angular frequency (ω) of the circuit is as shown below.

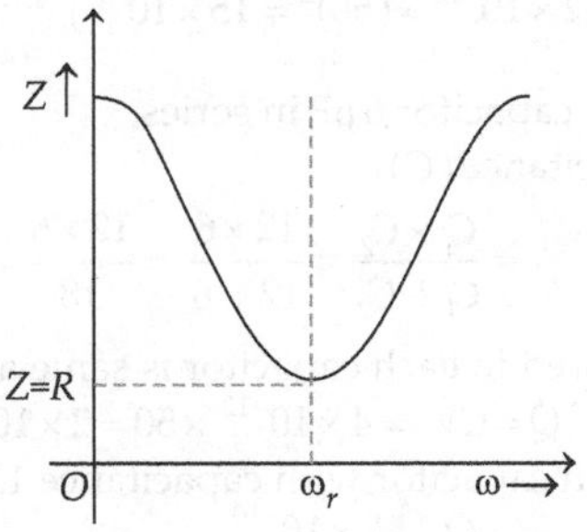

(v) The sensitivity of a moving coil galvanometer depends on

(a) the number of turns of the coil and

(b) the area of the coil.

(vi) As we know, for a meter bridge,

$$\frac{P}{Q}=\frac{R}{S} \Rightarrow \frac{l}{1-l}=\frac{R}{S}$$

$$\Rightarrow \frac{R}{S}=\frac{0.4}{1-0.4}=\frac{0.4}{0.6}=\frac{2}{3} \quad (\because l=40 \text{ cm}=0.4\text{m})$$

$\therefore$ Ratio of R and S is 2 : 3.

(vii) When the bar magnet is cut into two equal parts as shown in the Fig. (a). P_1 behaves as N and P_2 behaves as S and magnetic moment of each part of magnet becomes $M/2$. When pole P_2 is placed over pole P_1 as shown in Fig. (b), the net magnetic moment of the combination is zero, i.e. $\frac{M}{2}-\frac{M}{2}=0$.

2. We know that, a positively charged particle is attracted towards the negatively charged plate and a negatively charged particle is attracted towards the positively charged plate.

Here, particle 1 and particle 2 are attracted towards positive plate that means particle 1 and particle 2 are negatively charged. Particle 3 is attracted towards negatively charged plate, so it is positively charged. As the deflection in the path of a charged particle is directly proportional to the charge/mass ratio.

i.e. $\quad y \propto \frac{q}{m}$

Here, the deflection in particle 3 is maximum. So, the charge to mass ratio of particle 3 is maximum.

3. Given, the focal length of original equiconvex lens is f.

Let the focal length of each part of lens after cutting be F.

Here, $\quad \frac{1}{f}=\frac{1}{F}+\frac{1}{F}$

$$\Rightarrow \frac{1}{f}=\frac{2}{F} \Rightarrow f=\frac{F}{2} \Rightarrow F=2f$$

Power of each part will be given by

$$P=\frac{1}{F} \Rightarrow P=\frac{1}{2f}$$

From lens Maker's formula, we have

$$P=(\mu-1)\left(\frac{1}{R_1}-\frac{1}{R_2}\right)$$

$$\Rightarrow 5=(1.55-1)\left\{\frac{1}{R}-\left(\frac{1}{-R}\right)\right\} \quad \left[\because \begin{matrix} R_1=R \\ R_2=-R \end{matrix}\right]$$

$$\Rightarrow 5=0.55\times\frac{2}{R}$$

$$\Rightarrow R=\frac{0.55\times 2}{5}=0.22 \text{ m}=22 \text{ cm}$$

4. (i) As the flux linked with the coil is $\phi = MI$. With the increase in the distance by two times between the coils, the magnetic flux linked with the secondary coil decreases. Hence, the mutual inductance of the two coils will decrease with the increase of separation between them.

(ii) Mutual inductance of two coils can be found out by $M=\mu_0 N_1 N_2 Al$, i.e. $M \propto N_1 N_2$, so with the increase in number of turns by four times, mutual inductance increases by sixteen times.

5. When a charged particle enters in a uniform magnetic field perpendicularly, central force acts on the particle which provides centripetal force for the circular motion of the particle.

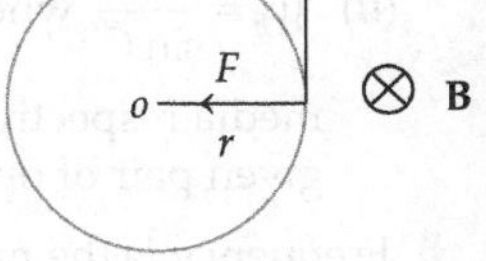

Centripetal force, $F=\frac{mv^2}{r}$

As magnetic force will provide the necessary centripetal force to the charged particle,

i.e. $\quad \frac{mv^2}{r}=qvB$

$$\Rightarrow \frac{mv}{r}=qB$$

$$\Rightarrow r=\frac{mv}{qB} \Rightarrow r \propto v$$

Or

As the electric field is from North to South, that means the plate in North is positive and in South is negative. Thus, the electron (negatively charged) is attracted towards the positive plate that means it moves towards North. If we want that there should be no deflection in the path of electron, then the magnetic force should be in South direction.

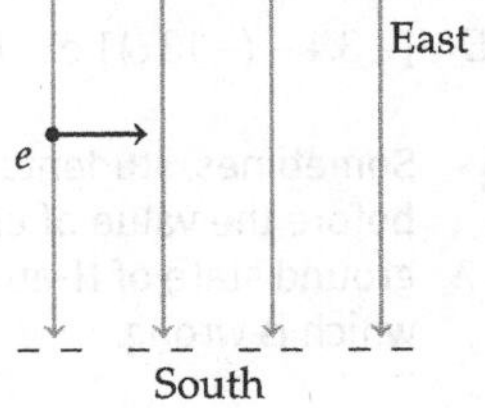

By $F = -e(v \times B)$, the direction of velocity is West to East, the direction of force is towards South, then by using the Fleming's left hand rule, the direction of magnetic field (B) is perpendicularly inwards to the plane of paper.

6. Given, frequency, $\nu = 3 \times 10^{10}$ Hz and velocity of light, $c = 3 \times 10^8$ m/s.

The wavelength of the electromagnetic wave,

$$\lambda = \frac{c}{\nu} = \frac{3 \times 10^8}{3 \times 10^{10}} = 0.01 \text{ m}$$

Since, $E_0 = 30$ V/m

∴ Amplitude of magnetic field,

$$B_0 = \frac{E_0}{c} = \frac{30}{3 \times 10^8} = 10^{-7} \text{ T}$$

7. *(i)* Following are the necessary conditions for total internal reflection.

(a) Light must pass from an optically denser to an optically rarer medium.

(b) Angle of incidence in denser medium must be greater than critical angle for two media.

(ii) ${}^a\mu_b = \frac{1}{\sin C}$, where a and b are the rarer and denser media respectively and C is the critical angle for the given pair of optical media.

8. Frequency is the number of revolutions completed per second by the electron in a stationary orbit around the nucleus.

It is represented by ν.

From $\quad v = r\omega = r(2\pi\nu) \quad [\because \omega = 2\pi\nu]$

$$\therefore \quad \nu = \frac{v}{2\pi r}$$

Putting the values of v and r in above equation, we get

$$\nu = \frac{1}{2\pi r} \cdot \frac{Ze^2}{2h\varepsilon_0} \cdot \frac{1}{n} \Rightarrow \nu = \frac{1}{4\pi\varepsilon_0} \cdot \frac{Ze^2}{nhr}$$

$$\Rightarrow \quad \nu = \frac{kZe^2}{nhr} \quad \left[\because k = \frac{1}{4\pi\varepsilon_0}\right]$$

i.e. $\quad \nu \propto \frac{1}{r}$

Or

Here, energy of electron in ground state of H-atom $= -13.6$ eV i.e. $E_1 = -13.6$ eV

For $\quad n = 2, E_2 = -3.4$ eV $\quad \left[\because E_n = -\frac{13.6}{n^2} \text{ eV}\right]$

The energy of photon corresponding to the first line is given by $\quad E = E_2 - E_1$

$$\therefore \quad E = [-3.4 - (-13.6)] \text{ eV} = 10.2 \text{ eV}$$

Common Mistakes

Sometimes, students apply positive sign before the value of energy of electron in ground state of H-atom, i.e. $E_0 = +13.6$eV, which is wrong.

9. Energy stored in capacitor $= \frac{1}{2} C_1 V^2$

$$= \frac{1}{2} \times 12 \times 10^{-12} \times (50)^2 = 15 \times 10^{-9} \text{ J}$$

With other capacitor 6 pF in series.

Total capacitance (C)

$$= \frac{C_1 \times C_2}{C_1 + C_2} = \frac{12 \times 6}{12 + 6} = \frac{12 \times 6}{18} = 4 \text{ pF}$$

Charge stored in each capacitor is same and is given by

$$Q = CV = 4 \times 10^{-12} \times 50 = 2 \times 10^{-10} \text{C}$$

Potential on capacitor with capacitance 12 pF is

$$= \frac{Q}{C_1} = \frac{2 \times 10^{-10}}{12 \times 10^{-12}} = 16.67 \text{ V}$$

Potential on capacitor with capacitance 6 pF is

$$= \frac{Q}{C_2} = \frac{2 \times 10^{-10}}{6 \times 10^{-12}} = 33.33 \text{ V}$$

10. Given, $f = 10$ cm, $v = D = -25$ cm

[symbols have their usual meanings]

We know that, $\frac{1}{v} - \frac{1}{u} = \frac{1}{f}$ [lens formula]

Substituting f and v with proper sign, we get

$$\frac{1}{D} - \frac{1}{u} = \frac{1}{f}$$

or $\quad \frac{1}{u} = -\left(\frac{1}{25} + \frac{1}{10}\right) = -\frac{7}{50}$

$$\therefore \quad u = -7.14 \text{ cm}$$

The object should be placed at a distance 7.14 cm from the lens.

Magnification, $m = 1 + \frac{D}{f} = 1 + \frac{25}{10} = 3.5$

11. *(i)* For n-type semiconductor,

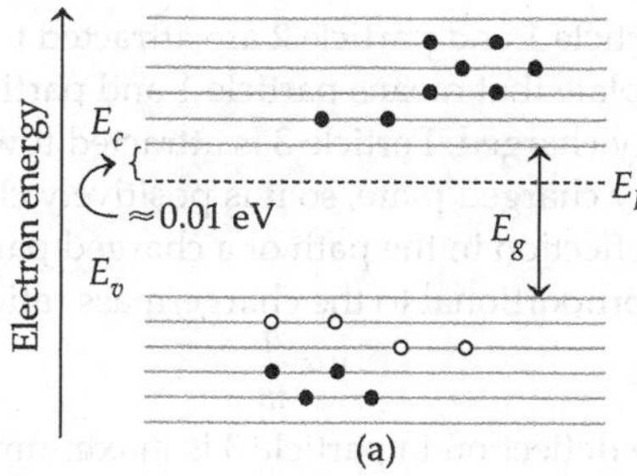

(a)

(ii) For p-type semiconductor,

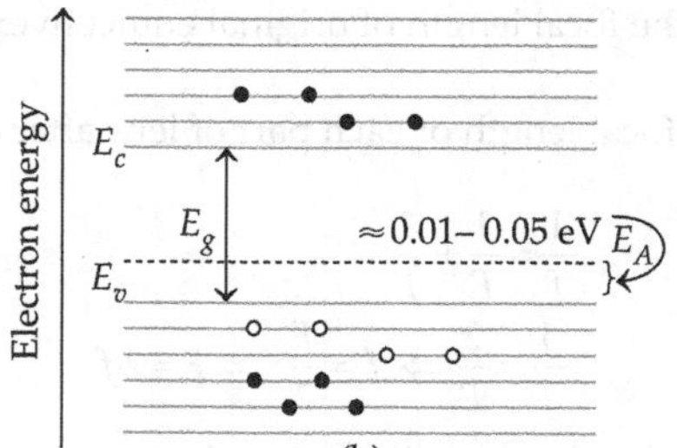

(b)

In n-type extrinsic semiconductors, the number of free electrons in conduction band is much more than the number of holes in valence band. The donor energy level lies just below the conduction band. In p-type extrinsic semiconductor, the number of holes in valence band is much more than the number of free electrons in conduction band. The acceptor energy level lies just above the valence band.

The donor energy level E_D is just below the bottom of the conduction band. At room temperature, this small energy gap is easily converted by the thermally excited electrons. The conduction band has more electrons as they have been contributed both by thermal excitation and donor impurities. Whereas the acceptor energy level E_A lies slightly above the top of the valence band.

At room temperature, many electrons of the valence band get excited to these acceptor energy levels, leaving behind equal number of holes in the valence band. These holes can conduct current. Thus, the valence band has more holes than the electrons in the conduction band.

12. Here, $R = 2\text{m}, f = \frac{R}{2} = \frac{2}{2} = 1\text{ m}$

Using mirror formula, we have

$$\frac{1}{v} + \frac{1}{u} = \frac{1}{f}$$

$$\Rightarrow \quad \frac{1}{v} = \frac{1}{f} - \frac{1}{u}$$

$$\Rightarrow \quad \frac{1}{v} = \frac{u-f}{fu}$$

$$\Rightarrow \quad v = \frac{fu}{u-f} \quad \text{...(i)}$$

When jogger is 39 m away, $u = -39$ m

$$\Rightarrow \quad v = \frac{fu}{u-f} = \frac{1(-39)}{-39-1}$$

$$\Rightarrow \quad v = \frac{39}{40}\text{ m}$$

As the jogger moves at a constant speed of 5 m/s, after 1 s, the position of the image (v) for

$$u = -39 + 5 = -34\text{ m}$$

Using Eq. (i), we have $v = \frac{1(-34)}{-34-1} \Rightarrow v = \frac{34}{35}$ m

Difference in apparent position of jogger in 1 s

$$= \frac{39}{40} - \frac{34}{35} = \frac{1365-1360}{1400} = \frac{1}{280}\text{ m}$$

$\therefore$ Average speed of jogger's image $= \frac{1}{280}$ m/s

Similarly, for $u = -29$ m, -19 m and -9 m, average speed of jogger's image is $\frac{1}{150}$ m/s, $\frac{1}{60}$ m/s, $\frac{1}{10}$ m/s respectively.

The speed of image increases as the jogger approaches the car. This can be experienced by the person in the car.

13. (i) When a charge $+q$ is placed at the centre of spherical shell as shown in the figure, then the charge induced on the inner surface of a shell is $-q$ and the charge induced on the outer surface of shell is $+q$. So,

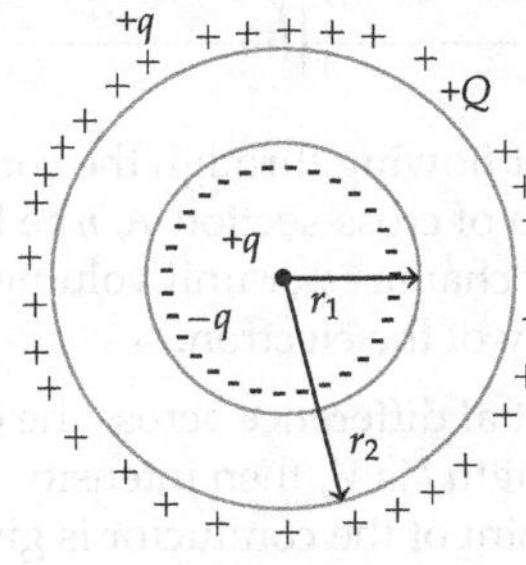

(a) inner surface charge density $= \frac{-q}{4\pi r_1^2}$

(b) outer surface charge density $= \frac{Q+q}{4\pi r_2^2}$

(ii) Yes, the electric field inside a cavity is zero irrespective of shape because the cavity has enclosed zero net charge.

14. (i) The region on either side of the junction which becomes depleted (free) from the mobile charge carriers is called depletion region or depletion layer. The width of depletion region is of the order of 10^{-6} m.

(ii) The potential difference developed across the depletion region is called the potential barrier. It depends on dopant concentration in the semiconductor and temperature of the junction. Due to the diffusion of holes from p-side to n-side and electrons from n-side to p-side at the junction, a current rises from p-side to n-side, which is called as diffusion current.

Or

To verify the conductivity values, we use the formula

$$\sigma = q\mu N_d$$

(i) For $N_d = 1 \times 10^{16}$

$$\sigma = (1.6 \times 10^{-19}) \times (1400 \times 10^{-4}) \times (1 \times 10^{16})$$

$$\sigma = 0.0224\text{ S/cm}$$

(ii) For $N_d = 2 \times 10^{16}$

$$\sigma = (1.6 \times 10^{-19}) \times (1400 \times 10^{-4}) \times (2 \times 10^{16})$$

$$\sigma = 0.0448\text{ S/cm}$$

(iii) For $N_d = 3 \times 10^{16}$

$$\sigma = (1.6 \times 10^{-19}) \times (1400 \times 10^{-4}) \times (3 \times 10^{16})$$

$$\sigma = 0.0672\text{ S/cm}$$

(iv) For $N_d = 4 \times 10^{16}$

$$\sigma = (1.6 \times 10^{-19}) \times (1400 \times 10^{-4}) \times (4 \times 10^{16})$$

$$\sigma = 0.0896\text{ S/cm}$$

15. Consider the diagram as shown below.

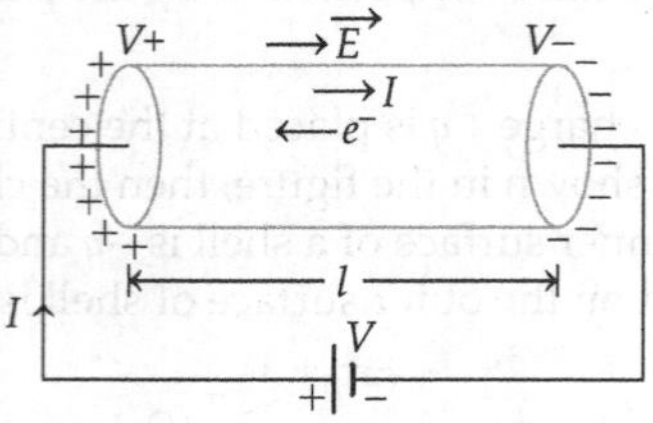

Here, I = current flowing through the conductor of length l and area of cross-section A, n be the number of free electrons of charge e per unit volume and v_d = drift velocity of the electron.

Since, the potential difference across the ends of the conductor of length l is V, then intensity of the electric field at every point of the conductor is given by

$$E = V/l$$

The force experienced by this field on each free electron is given by

$$F = eE = eV/l$$

If the mass of each electron is m, then the acceleration of the electrons due to this force,

$$a = F/m = eV/ml$$

But due to increase in collision rate with atoms, an opposing retarding force $\left(\frac{mv}{\tau}\right)$ also acts on each electron, where τ is known as the relaxation time between two successive collisions. As the accelerating force eE remains constant throughout, very soon the retarding force becomes equal to the accelerating force, and hence the electrons attain steady drift velocity v_d as given below

$$eE = \frac{mv_d}{\tau} \qquad \left(\text{as } F = \frac{dp}{dt}\right)$$

$$\therefore \quad v_d = \frac{e\tau}{m} E = \frac{e\tau}{m} \cdot \frac{V}{l} \text{ or } v_d = \mu \frac{V}{l}$$

where, $\mu = \frac{e\tau}{m}$ is a constant known as mobility of the electron.

Or

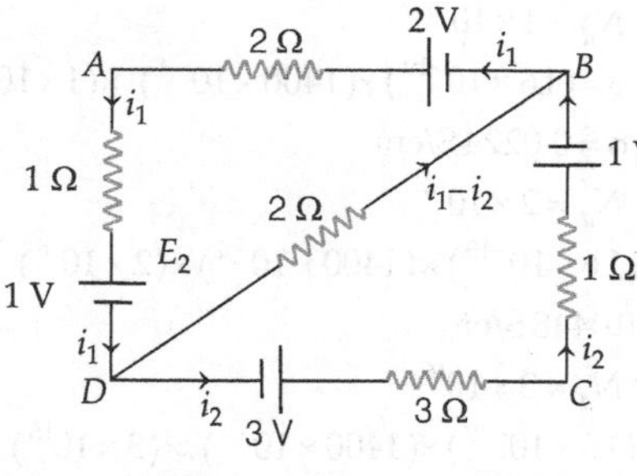

Applying Kirchhoff's second law in loop $BADB$,

$$2 - 2i_1 - i_1 - 1 - 2(i_1 - i_2) = 0 \qquad \text{...(i)}$$

Similarly, applying Kirchhoff's second law in loop $BDCB$,

$$2(i_1 - i_2) + 3 - 3i_2 - i_2 - 1 = 0 \qquad \text{...(ii)}$$

Solving Eqs. (i) and (ii), we get

$$i_1 = \frac{5}{13} \text{ A}, i_2 = \frac{6}{13} \text{ A}$$

and $$i_1 - i_2 = -\frac{1}{13} \text{ A}$$

(*i*) Potential difference between B and D,.

$$V_B + 2(i_1 - i_2) = V_D$$

$$\therefore \quad V_B - V_D = -2(i_1 - i_2) = \frac{2}{13} \text{ V}$$

(*ii*) $V_G = E_G - i_2 r_G = 3 - \frac{6}{13} \times 3 = \frac{21}{13} \text{ V}$

$$V_H = E_H + i_2 r_H = 1 + \frac{6}{13} \times 1 = \frac{19}{13} \text{ V}$$

16. (*i*) Yes, all emitted photoelectrons have same kinetic energy as the kinetic energy of emitted photoelectrons depend upon frequency of the incident radiation for a given photosensitive surface.

(*ii*) No, the kinetic energy of emitted electrons does not depend upon the intensity of incident radiation. If the intensity is increased, number of photons will also increase but energy of each photon remains same as the frequency is also same. The maximum kinetic energy depends upon frequency not on intensity.

(*iii*) The number of emitted photoelectrons depends only on intensity of incident light.

17. Given, $R_1 = 10\Omega$, $N_1 = 30$, $A_1 = 3.6 \times 10^{-3} \text{m}^2$, $B_1 = 0.25 \text{ T}$

and $R_2 = 14\Omega$, $N_2 = 42$, $A_2 = 1.8 \times 10^{-3} \text{m}^2$, $B_2 = 0.50 \text{ T}$

$k_1 = k_2$ (spring constants are same)

(*i*) Using the formula of current sensitivity,

$$I = \frac{NBA}{k}$$

$$\therefore \quad \frac{I_{M_2}}{I_{M_1}} = \frac{N_2 B_2 A_2 k_1}{N_1 B_1 A_1 k_2} = \frac{42 \times 0.50 \times 1.8 \times 10^{-3}}{30 \times 0.25 \times 3.6 \times 10^{-3}} = 1.4$$

(*ii*) Using the formula of voltage sensitivity, $V = \frac{NBA}{kR}$

$$\therefore \quad \frac{V_{M_2}}{V_{M_1}} = \frac{N_2 B_2 A_2 k_1 R_1}{k_2 R_2 N_1 B_1 A_1} = \frac{42 \times 0.50 \times 1.8 \times 10^{-3} \times 10}{14 \times 30 \times 0.25 \times 3.6 \times 10^{-3}} = 1$$

18. (*i*) Radio P will allow the person to hear the radio Channel of frequency f_0, without the interference of other frequencies.

Both frequencies f_1 and f_2 do not lie in the bandwidth of the radio P, while frequency f_1 lies in the bandwidth of radio Q

(*ii*) The maximum current at resonance in an L-C-R circuit is given by

$$i_{\max} = \frac{V}{R}$$

Since, $i_P > i_Q$, the resistance of circuit used in radio P is less than the resistance of the circuit used in radio Q.

The resonance frequency $f_0 = \frac{1}{2\pi\sqrt{LC}}$

As L and f_0 is the same for both circuits the capacitance of both circuits will be the same.

(*iii*) Impedance of an *L-C-R* circuit is,

$$Z = \sqrt{R^2 + (X_C - X_L)^2}$$

when $X_L = X_C$, then $Z = R$ and $\tan \phi = 0$.

Hence, voltage and current are in the same phase. Therefore, *L-C-R* circuit becomes resistance dominated.

Or

(*i*) Current leads voltage by $\frac{\pi}{2}$ rad. Hence, expression of current is $I = I_0 \sin\left(\omega t + \frac{\pi}{2}\right)$.

(*ii*) Device *X* is a capacitor.

(*iii*) As, $E(t) = E_0 \sin \omega t$

Current, $I(t) = I_0 \cos \omega t$

As in the case of capacitor,

$I = I_0 \sin\left(\omega t + \frac{\pi}{2}\right)$ [current is leading voltage]

Average power, $P = E(t)\, I(t) = E_0 I_0 \cos \frac{\phi}{2}$

where, ϕ = phase difference

Hence, curve *A* represents power, curve *B* represents voltage and curve *C* represents current.

(*iv*) $X_C = \frac{1}{C\omega} = \frac{1}{C2\pi\nu}$

The graph of X_C *versus* ν is given below.

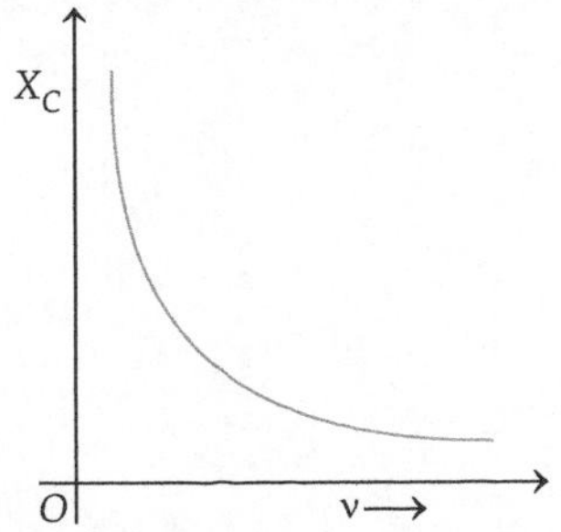

19. (*i*) **Lens Maker's formula**

If a convex lens is made up of two convex spherical refracting surfaces, the final images formed after two refractions. Let μ_2 be the refractive index of the material of the lens and μ_1 be the refractive index of the rarer medium around the lens.

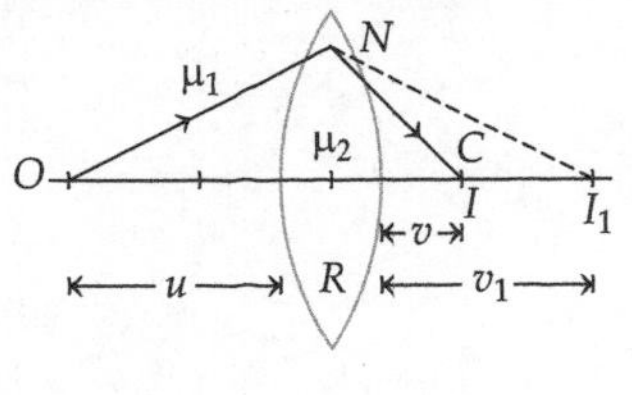

Let R_1 be the radius of curvature of second surface of the lens, I_1 would have been a real image of *O* formed after refraction, then from equation,

$$\frac{\mu_2}{v_1} - \frac{\mu_1}{u} = \frac{\mu_2 - \mu_1}{R_1} \quad \text{... (i)}$$

Let R_2 be the radius of curvature of the second surface of the lens. Refraction is now taking place from denser to rarer medium

$$\frac{\mu_1}{v} - \frac{\mu_2}{v_1} = \frac{\mu_1 - \mu_2}{R_2} \quad \text{... (ii)}$$

Adding Eqs. (i) and (ii), we get

$$\frac{\mu_1}{v} - \frac{\mu_1}{u} = (\mu_2 - \mu_1)\left(\frac{1}{R_1} - \frac{1}{R_2}\right) \quad \text{... (iii)}$$

$$\frac{1}{v} - \frac{1}{u} = \left(\frac{\mu_2}{\mu_1} - 1\right)\left(\frac{1}{R_1} - \frac{1}{R_2}\right) \quad \text{... (iv)}$$

When object on the left of lens is at infinity, then image is formed at the principal focus of the lens.

$\therefore$ When $u = \infty$, $v = f$ = focal length of the lens.

Put $\frac{\mu_2}{\mu_1} = \mu$ = refractive index of material of the lens with respect to surrounding medium, we have

$$\therefore \quad \frac{1}{f} = (\mu - 1)\left(\frac{1}{R_1} - \frac{1}{R_2}\right)$$

This is the lens Maker's formula.

(*ii*) Given, refractive index, $\mu_2 = 1.5$, $\mu_1 = 1$ (air)

Radius of curvature, $R = 20$ cm

Object distance, $u = -100$ cm

So, from surface formula, $\frac{\mu_2}{v} - \frac{\mu_1}{u} = \frac{\mu_2 - \mu_1}{R}$

$$\Rightarrow \quad \frac{1.5}{v} + \frac{1}{100} = \frac{1.5 - 1}{20}$$

$$\Rightarrow \quad \frac{1.5}{v} = \frac{0.5}{20} - \frac{1}{100} \Rightarrow \frac{1.5}{v} = \frac{5}{200} - \frac{1}{100}$$

$$\Rightarrow \quad \frac{1.5}{v} = \frac{5-2}{200} \Rightarrow \frac{1.5}{v} = \frac{3}{200}$$

$$\Rightarrow \quad v = \frac{200 \times 1.5}{3} = \frac{300}{3} = 100 \text{ cm}$$

The image is formed at 100 cm in denser medium.

Or

(*i*) Coherent light refers to light waves that have a constant phase relationship with each other, i.e. the crests and trough of the individual light waves are synchronised.

(*ii*) Wavelength of red light is 650×10^{-9} m, therefore

separation, $x = \frac{\lambda D}{a}$

$$= \frac{(650 \times 10^{-9})\,(2.4)}{0.86 \times 10^{-3}} = 1.81 \times 10^{-3} = 1.81 \text{ mm}$$

(*iii*) Now, amplitude of one wave is larger than the other, so there is no complete destructive interference and the dark fringes are lighter.

(*iv*) For interference of two waves,

$$I = I_1 + I_2 + 2\sqrt{I_1 I_2}\cos\theta$$

For equal intensities from both slits,

$$I = 4I \quad (\because\ \theta = 0° \text{ for central fringe})$$

$$\Rightarrow \quad I_1 = \frac{I}{4}$$

Hence, when one slit is closed, the intensity will be $\frac{I}{4}$.

20. (*i*) Lyman series lies in ultraviolet region.
Number of spectral lines in H-atom is ∞.

(*ii*) Using, $\frac{1}{\lambda} = RZ^2\left(\frac{1}{n_1^2} - \frac{1}{n_2^2}\right)$

$$\Rightarrow \lambda \propto \frac{1}{Z^2}$$

We have, $Z_{Li} = 3$,
$Z_{He} = 2$
and $Z_H = 1$.

So, $\lambda_{Li^{++}} : \lambda_{He^+} : \lambda_H = \frac{1}{9} : \frac{1}{4} : \frac{1}{1} = 4:9:36$

(*iii*) Wavelength is given by

$$\frac{1}{\lambda} = R\left(\frac{1}{n_1^2} - \frac{1}{n_2^2}\right)$$

$$\Rightarrow \frac{1}{\lambda} = R\left(\frac{1}{2^2} - \frac{1}{4^2}\right)$$

$$\Rightarrow \frac{1}{\lambda} = R\left(\frac{1}{4} - \frac{1}{16}\right)$$

$$\Rightarrow \frac{1}{\lambda} = R\left(\frac{4-1}{16}\right)$$

$$\Rightarrow \frac{1}{\lambda} = \frac{3R}{16}$$

(a) $\therefore \quad \lambda = \frac{16}{3R}$

(b) $\lambda = \frac{16}{3 \times 1.09 \times 10^7}$

$= 4.9 \times 10^{-7}$ m

SQP Code : **PB-5/15** Series ***i*-Succeed 5-25/15** Roll No.

Sample Question Paper 05

Physics 12th (Code 861)

General Instructions

1. This paper is divided into four Sections- A, B, C and D. Answer all questions.
2. **Section A** consists of one question having sub-parts of one mark each.
3. **Section B** consists of seven questions of two marks each.
4. **Section C** consists of nine questions of three marks each.
5. **Section D** consists of three questions of five marks each.
6. Internal choices have been provided in two questions each in Section B, Section C and Section D.

Time : 3 Hrs.

Max. Marks : 70

Section A (14 Marks)

1. A. In questions (i) to (vii) below, choose the correct alternative (a), (b), (c) or (d) for each of the questions given below.

(*i*) In the figure, the equivalent capacitance between points *A* and *B* is • *Analysis* [1]

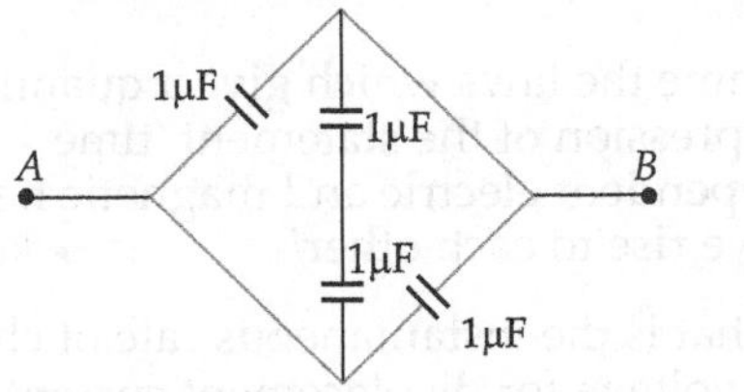

(a) 4 μF (b) 2 .5 μF (c) 2 μF (d) 0.25 μF

(*ii*) An electron of charge (e) is moving parallel to uniform magnetic field B with constant velocity v. The force acting on electron is • *Recall* [1]

(a) Bev (b) Be/v (c) B/ev (d) zero

(*iii*) **Assertion** (A) The electrostatic force increases as the distance between the charges decreases.

Reason (R) The electrostatic force of attraction or repulsion between any two stationary point charges is inversely proportional to the square of the distance between them. • *Analysis* [1]

(a) Both Assertion and Reason are true and Reason is the correct explanation of the Assertion.

(b) Both Assertion and Reason are true but Reason is not the correct explanation for Assertion.

(c) Assertion is false and Reason is true.

(d) Both Assertion and Reason are false.

(*iv*) Carbon, silicon and germanium have four valence electrons. These are characterised by valence and conduction band separated by energy band gap which are equal to $(E_g)_C$, $(E_g)_{Si}$ and $(E_g)_{Ge}$ respectively. Which of the following statement is true? • *Recall* [1]

(a) $(E_g)_{Si} < (E_g)_{Ge} < (E_g)_C$

(b) $(E_g)_C < (E_g)_{Ge} < (E_g)_{Si}$

(c) $(E_g)_C > (E_g)_{Si} > (E_g)_{Ge}$

(d) $(E_g)_C = (E_g)_{Si} = (E_g)_{Ge}$

(*v*) Light from a point source in air falls on spherical glass surface (refractive index of glass, $n = 1.5$ and radius of curvature $= 20$ cm). The distance of the light source from the glass surface is 100 cm. Image distance from the glass surface is • *Understanding* [1]

(a) 20 cm (b) 50 cm (c) 100 cm (d) 75 cm

(*vi*) **Assestion** (A) In the process of photoelectric emission, the photo electrons emitted from the surface of metal have maximum kinetic energy.

Reason (R) The photon transfer its whole energy to the electron of the atom in photoelectric effect. • *Understanding* [1]

(a) Both Assertion and Reason are true and Reason is the correct explanation of Assertion.

(b) Both Assertion and Reason are true but Reason is not the correct explanation the Assertion.

(c) Assertion is false and Reason is true.

(d) Both Assertion and Reason are false.

(*vii*) Which of the following graphs represents the variation of magnetic field B at the axis of a solenoid with current I in it? • *Analysis* [1]

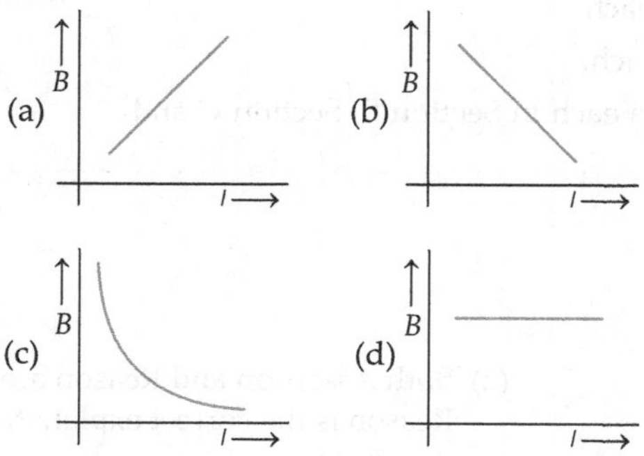

B. Answer the following questions briefly.

(*i*) Name the AC circuit in which wattless current flows. • *Recall* [1]

(*ii*) A converging lens axially in contact with a diverging lens. Both lenses have equal focal length. What is the focal length of the combination? • *Application* [1]

(*iii*) A proton and an electron travelling along parallel paths enter a region of uniform magnetic field, acting perpendicular to their paths. Which of them will move in a circular path with higher frequency? • *Recall* [1]

(*iv*) Write the relation between angle of incidence (i), angle of prism (A) and angle of minimum deviation (δ_m) for a triangular prism. • *Recall* [1]

(*v*) You are provided with six identical cells each of emf 2 V. How will you connect all of them to obtain a battery of emf 2 V? • *Understanding* [1]

(*vi*) Evaluate the total electric flux passing through an encloser of electric dipole. • *Recall* [1]

(*vii*) Why are elemental dopants for silicon or germanium usually chosen from group XIII or group XV? • *Recall* [1]

Section B (14 Marks)

SP-05

2. The susceptibility of a magnetic material is 0.9853. Identify the type of magnetic material. Draw the modification of the field pattern on keeping a piece of this material in a uniform magnetic field. • *Application* [2]

3. The *V-I* characteristic of a silicon diode is as shown in the figure. Calculate the resistance of the diode at

(*i*) $I = 15$ mA and (*ii*) $V = -10$ V.

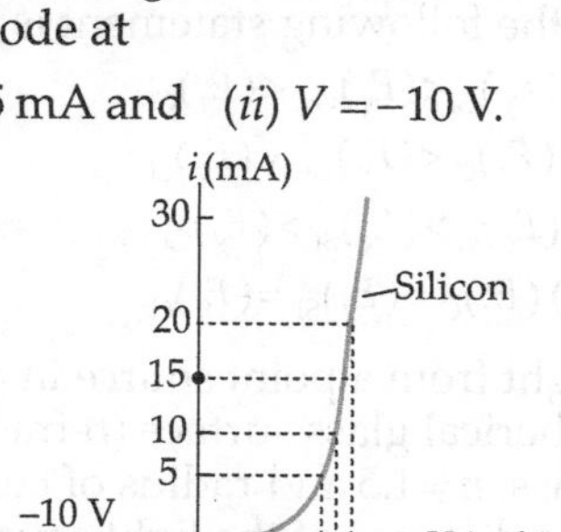

• *Application* [2]

4. (*i*) Name the laws which give a quantitative expression of the statement 'time dependent electric and magnetic fields give rise to each other'. • *Recall* [1]

(*ii*) What is the instantaneous rate of change of voltage for displacement current of 10A in space between the parallel plates of 1μF capacitor? • *Recall* [1]

5. Find the binding energy per nucleon of ${}_{20}\text{Ca}^{40}$ nucleus. Given, $m({}_{20}\text{Ca}^{40}) = 39.962589$ u, $m_n = 1.008665$ u and $m_p = 1.007825$ u. [Take, 1 amu $= 931$ MeV/c^2]. • *Analysis* [2]

6. A beam of light converges at a point P. A concave lens of focal length 16 cm is placed in the path of this beam at 12 cm from point P. Draw a ray diagram and find the location of the point at which the beam would now converge. • *Understanding* [2]

7. (i) Two identical circular loops P and Q, each of radius r and carrying equal currents are kept in the parallel planes having a common axis passing through O. The direction of current in P is clockwise and in Q is anti-clockwise as seen from O, which is equidistant from the loops P and Q. Find the magnitude of the net magnetic field at O. • *Application* [2]

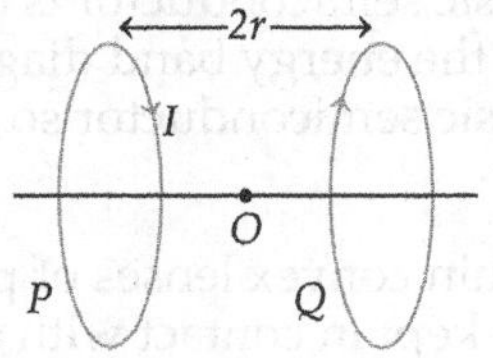

Or

(ii) Find the ratio of the magnitudes of the magnetic field of the centre and at an axial point at a distance $2a$ from the centre of the circular coil of radius a. • *Application* [2]

8. (i) A ray of light suffers minimum deviation, while passing through a prism of refractive index 1.5 and refracting angle 60°. Calculate the angle of incidence. [Given, $\sin^{-1}(0.75) = 48.6°$] • *Analysis* [2]

Or

(ii) What is the shape of the wavefront on the earth for sunlight? Show it by diagram. • *Recall* [2]

Section C (27 Marks)

9. The ground state energy of hydrogen atom is −13.6 eV.

(i) What is the kinetic energy of an electron in the second excited state? • *Recall* [1]

(ii) If the electron jumps to the ground state from the second excited state, calculate the wavelength of the spectral line emitted. • *Recall* [2]

10. Force on a charge due to electric field is given by $\mathbf{F}_E = q\mathbf{E}$ and force due magnetic field is given by $\mathbf{F}_B = q(\mathbf{v} \times \mathbf{B})$. In a certain region of space, both electric and magnetic fields exist mutually perpendicular to each other. If an electron enters this region perpendicular to both **E** and **B** and passes out undeflected, find the velocity of the electron. • *Analysis* [3]

11. (i) A wire of resistivity ρ_1 is plated with a material of resistivity ρ_2, so that its radius changes from r to $2r$. If l is the length of wire, prove that the new wire has a resistance $R = \dfrac{\rho_1 \rho_2 l}{\pi r^2 (3\rho_1 + \rho_2)}$. • *Analysis* [3]

Or (ii) Two conducting wires of the same material having radii in the ratio 2 : 3 and lengths in the ratio 1 : 2 are connected in series with an accumulator. Find the ratio of potential difference across the two conducting wires. • *Analysis* [3]

12. Sketch the graphs showing variation of stopping potential with frequencies of incident radiations for two photosensitive materials A and B having threshold frequencies $\nu_A > \nu_B$. [1]

(i) In which case is the stopping potential more and why? [1]

(ii) Does the slope of the graph depend on the nature of the material used? Explain. • *Application* [1]

Or

A student measures the kinetic energy of emitted electrons in a photoelectric effect experiment using different wavelength of incident light. Given the work function ϕ of the metal is 2.0 eV. Verify (for any two that the experimental data agrees with the theoretical values of KE calculated using the following data. • *Application* [3]

Wavelength (nm)	400	350	300	250
Kinetic energy (eV)	1.1	1.54	2.13	2.96

13. The electric field in a region is given by $\mathbf{E} = (10x + 4)\hat{\mathbf{i}}$ where, x is in metre and **E** is in N/C. Calculate the amount of work done in taking a unit charge from

(i) (5 m, 0) to (10 m, 0)

(ii) (5 m, 0) to (5 m, 10 m) • *Analysis* [3]

SP-05

14. (*i*) For the same angle of incidence, the angles of refraction in three different media *P*, *Q* and *R* are 17°, 27° and 37° respectively. In which medium will the velocity of light be minimum? • *Recall* [2]

(*ii*) Calculate the speed of light in a medium, whose critical angle is 45°. • *Analysis* [1]

15. (*i*) Using Bohr's second postulates of quantisation of orbital angular momentum, show that the circumference of the electron in the *n*th orbital state in hydrogen atom is *n*-times the de-Broglie wavelength associated with it. • *Application* [1]

(*ii*) The electron in hydrogen atom is initially in the third excited state.

What is the maximum number of spectral lines which can be emitted when it finally moves to the ground state? • *Recall* [2]

16. (*i*) Explain the formation of energy bands in crystalline solids. • *Recall* [1]

(*ii*) Draw the energy band diagrams of (a) a metal and (b) a semiconductor. • *Understanding* [1]

(*iii*) In a pure semiconductor crystal of Si, if antimony is added, then what type of extrinsic semiconductor is obtained? Draw the energy band diagram of this extrinsic semiconductor so formed. • *Application* [1]

17. (*i*) Two thin convex lenses of powers P_1 and P_2 are kept in contact with each other. When this combination is used for image formation of an object, find the combined power of combination. • *Application* [2]

(*ii*) If two combined lenses are concave and convex of same power, then find the nature of combination. • *Application* [1]

Section D (15 Marks)

18. A student while performing an experiment with a prism. Plot the following graph.

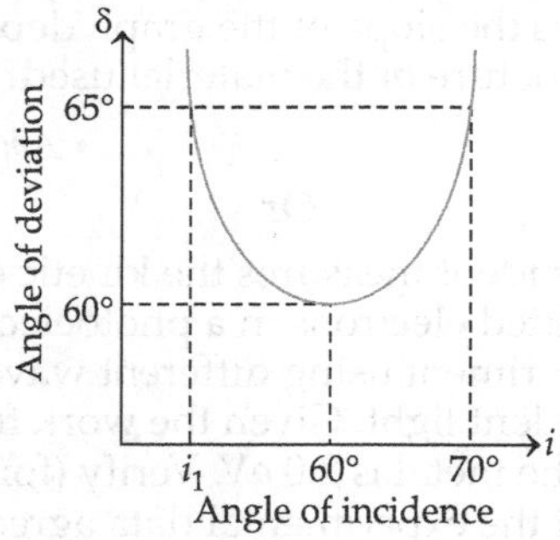

(*i*) What is the angle of prism? • *Analysis*

(*ii*) What is the refractive index of prism? • *Analysis*

(*iii*) Find the angle of emergence for the angle of incidence 70°. • *Analysis*

(*iv*) At which angle the refracted ray parallel to the base of the prism. • *Application* [5]

Or (a) A white light is used to illuminate the two slits in a Young's double slit experiment. It results in the overlapping interference patterns on the screen as each wavelength corresponds to one interference pattern.

[Refer to the figure below for the various parameters of the experimental setup].

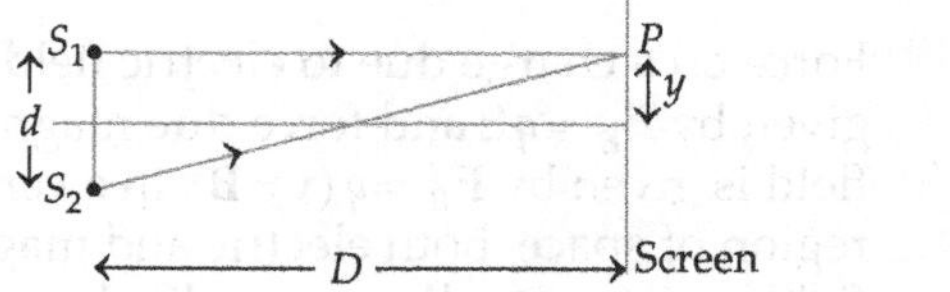

At a point *P*, that is directly opposite to the slit S_1.

(*i*) Find the series of wavelengths that will result in minima. • *Understanding* [2]

(*ii*) If the ratio of slit width is 4 : 1 then what will be the ratio of intensity of maxima to minima close to the central fringe on the screen? • *Application* [3]

19. (*i*) The coil of an AC generator consists of 100 turns of wire each of area 0.5 m^2. The resistance of the wire is 100 Ω. The coil is rotating in a magnetic field of 0.8 T perpendicular to the axis of rotation, at a constant angular speed of 60 rad/s. Calculate the maximum emf generated and power dissipated to the coil. • *Application* [3]

(ii) A long solenoid with 15 turns/cm has a small loop of area 2.0 cm^2 placed inside the solenoid normal to its axis. If the current carried by the solenoid changes steadily from 2.0 A to 4.0 A in 0.1s, then what is the induced emf in the loop while the current is changing? • *Application* [2]

Or (i) Draw a labelled diagram of AC generator and state its working principle. • *Application* [2]

(ii) How is magnetic flux linked with the armature coil changed in a generator? • *Recall* [1]

(iii) Derive the expression for maximum value of the induced emf and state the rule that gives the direction of the induced emf. • *Application* [2]

20. Potential difference (ΔV) between two points A and B separated by a distance x, in a uniform electric field **E** is given by $\Delta V = -Ex$, where x is measured parallel to the field lines. If a charge q_0 moves from A to B, the change in potential energy (ΔU) is given as $\Delta U = q_0 \Delta V$. A proton is released from rest in uniform electric field of magnitude 8.0×10^4 Vm^{-1} directed along the positive X-axis.

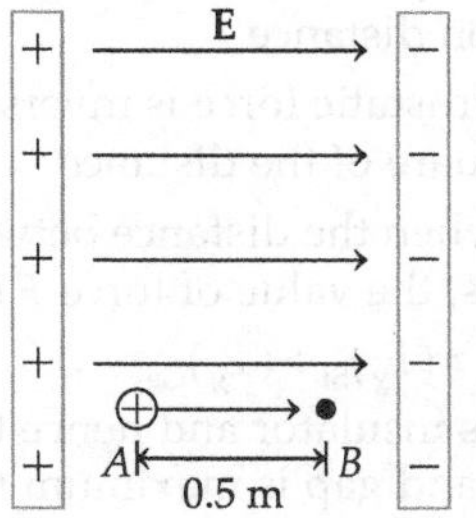

Mass of a proton = 1.66×10^{-27} kg

and charge on a proton = 1.6×10^{-19} C

(i) What effect occurs on the potential energy of proton when it moves from point B to A? • *Recall* [1]

(ii) (a) Find the change in electric potential of the proton in moving between point A and B. • *Recall* [1]

(b) If in place of charged plates, two similar point charges of 1 μC have been kept in air at a distance of 1 m from each other, then find the potential energy of the system. • *Application* [1]

(iii) If proton starts moving from rest, then find its

(a) kinetic energy and

(b) velocity after moving a distance of 0.50 m. • *Application* [2]

Solutions *in Topper's Style*

My Commitment *I affirm that I am reviewing these solutions only after I have solved the Sample Question Paper 5 on my own. My purpose of looking the solutions is solely to verify whether my answers/solutions were correct or not and to identify my mistakes in case my solutions were wrong or I could not solve that.*

1. A. (i) (b) On redrawing, the circuit is

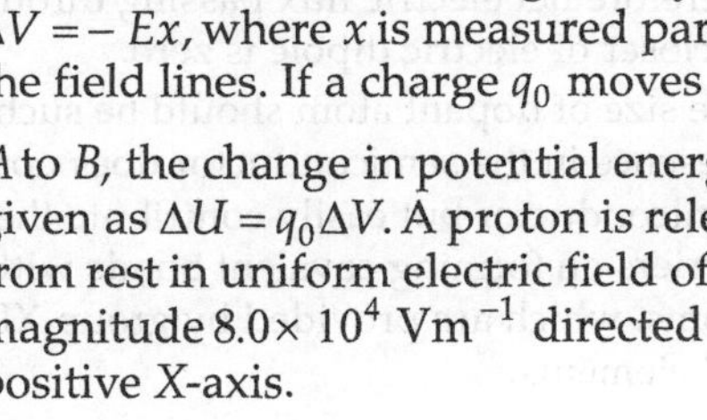

According to the circuit, C_1 and C_2 are in series,

$$\frac{1}{C} = \frac{1}{C_1} + \frac{1}{C_2} = \frac{1}{1} + \frac{1}{1} = 2 \Rightarrow C = \frac{1}{2} \mu F$$

Now, C, C_3 and C_4 are in parallel order.

$$\therefore \quad C_{equivalent} = C + C_3 + C_4 = \frac{1}{2} + 1 + 1 = 2.5 \mu F$$

(ii) (d) The force on electron, $F = qvB\sin\theta$.

The electron is moving parallel to the magnetic field, so $\theta = 0°$

$$\therefore \quad F = qvB\sin 0° = 0$$

(iii) (a) Both A and R are true and R is the correct explanation of A.

The general expression for electrostatic force between two charges is given as

$$F = \frac{q_1 q_2}{4\pi\varepsilon_0 d^2}$$

where, q represents the charge, d represents the separation distance.

The electrostatic force is inversely proportional to the square of the distance.

Hence, when the distance between the charges decreases, the value of force F increases.

(*iv*) (*c*) $(E_g)_C > (E_g)_{Si} > (E_g)_{Ge}$

Carbon is insulator and hence the value of energy band gap is maximum for it. While out of other two semiconductors, the value of energy band gap for germanium is lesser.

(*v*) (*c*) Given, $u = -100$ cm

$v = ?$, $R = +20$ cm

$n_{1\,(\text{for glass})} = 1$ and $n_{2\,(\text{for air})} = 1.5$

According to refraction formula for curved surface,

$$\frac{n_2}{v} - \frac{n_1}{u} = \frac{n_2 - n_1}{R}$$

$$\frac{1.5}{v} - \frac{1}{(-100)} = \frac{1.5 - 1}{20}$$

$$\Rightarrow \frac{1.5}{v} + \frac{1}{100} = \frac{0.5}{20} \Rightarrow v = +100 \text{ cm}$$

(*vi*) (*b*) Only the photoelectrons emitted from the surface of the metal have maximum kinetic energy. The emitted electrons from inside the metal loses some part of their energy in collision with the other atoms.

(*vii*) (*a*) As magnetic field due to a straight solenoid at any point inside the solenoid, $B = \mu_0 nI$ where, n = number of turns per unit length

$$\Rightarrow \quad B \propto I$$

Hence, the graph between B and I is a straight line passing through origin.

$\therefore$ Option (a) is correct.

B. (*i*) In purely inductive, capacitive and inductive-capacitive (*L-C*) circuits, wattless current flows because average power is zero for these circuits. Phase difference between voltage and current is 90°,

i.e. average power, $P_{av} = V_{rms} \times I_{rms} \times \cos 90° = 0$.

(*ii*) Combined focal length of a lens combination,

$\frac{1}{f} = \frac{1}{f_1} + \frac{1}{f_2}$ (for two thin lenses in contact).

As $f_2 = -f_1$ (focal lengths are equal, one is convex and other is concave).

$$\Rightarrow \quad \frac{1}{f} = \frac{1}{f_1} - \frac{1}{f_1} = 0 \Rightarrow f = \infty$$

(*iii*) As we know that in a circular path, frequency of a charged particle is given by

$$\nu = \frac{qB}{2\pi m} \text{ or } \nu \propto \frac{1}{m}$$

Since, $m_p > m_e$, therefore electron will move in circular path with higher frequency.

(*iv*) The relation between the angle of incidence (i), angle of prism (A) and the angle of minimum deviation (δ_m) for a triangular prism is given by

$$i = \frac{A + \delta_m}{2}$$

(*v*) On connecting all six identical cells each of emf 2 V in parallel combination by keeping positive terminal is at a point and negative terminals at other point, a battery of emf 2 V can be obtained.

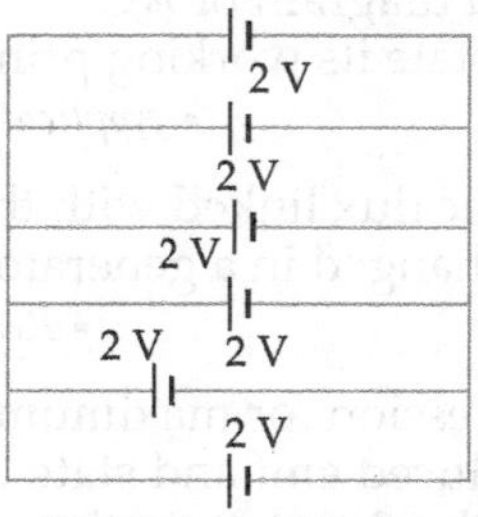

[6 rows, each row contains one cell of emf 2V]

Parallel combination

(*vi*) Since, an electric dipole has two charges of equal magnitude and opposite nature (i.e. positive and negative charges), hence total incoming electric flux is equal to total outgoing electric flux, therefore net electric flux passing through an encloser of electric dipole is zero.

(*vii*) The size of dopant atom should be such that their presence in the semiconductor does not distort the semiconductor but easily contribute the charge carriers on forming covalent bonds with Si or Ge atoms, which are provided by group XIII or group XV elements.

2. Given, susceptibility, $\chi_m = 0.9853$

As the susceptibility of material is positive but small, that's why, the material is paramagnetic in nature.

For paramagnetic material, magnetic field lines of external magnetic field will pass through the material without much deviation, when it is placed in between magnetic poles.

The modification of the field pattern is shown in the following figure.

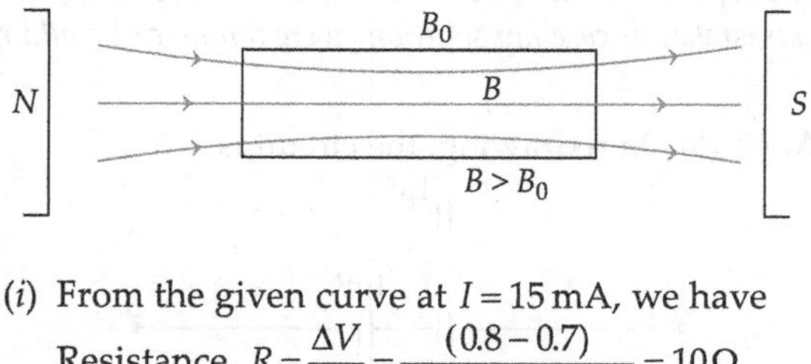

3. (*i*) From the given curve at $I = 15$ mA, we have

$$\text{Resistance, } R = \frac{\Delta V}{\Delta I} = \frac{(0.8 - 0.7)}{(20 - 10) \times 10^{-3}} = 10\,\Omega$$

(*ii*) For $V = -10$ V, we have

$$I = -1\,\mu\text{A} = -1 \times 10^{-6} \text{ A}$$

$$\Rightarrow \quad R = \frac{(-10 - 0)}{(-1 - 0) \times 10^{-6}}$$

$$= 1.0 \times 10^7\,\Omega$$

4. (i) Faraday's law of electromagnetic induction and Ampere-Maxwell's law both gave a quantitative expression of the given statement known as Ampere-Maxwell's circuital law.

$$\oint \mathbf{B}\cdot d\mathbf{l} = \mu_0\left(I_C + \varepsilon_0 \frac{d\phi_E}{dt}\right)$$

(ii) Displacement current, $i_d = \varepsilon_0 \frac{d\phi_E}{dt}$

$$= \varepsilon_0 A \frac{d}{dt}\left(\frac{V}{d}\right)$$

$$= \frac{\varepsilon_0 A}{d} \times \frac{dV}{dt} = C\frac{dV}{dt}$$

$$\Rightarrow \quad \frac{dV}{dt} = \frac{i_d}{C} = \frac{10}{1\times 10^{-6}} = 10^7 \text{ Vs}^{-1}$$

5. In a nucleus of ${}_{20}\text{Ca}^{40}$,

Number of protons = 20

Number of neutrons = 40 − 20 = 20

Total mass of 20 protons and 20 neutrons

$$= 20m_p + 20m_n = 20(m_p + m_n)$$

$$= 20\,(1.007825 + 1.008665) = 40.3298 \text{ u}$$

Mass defect, $\Delta m = 40.3298 - 39.962589 = 0.367211$ u

Total binding energy $= 0.367211 \times 931$

$$= 341.873441 \text{ MeV}$$

Binding energy per nucleon, $E_{bn} = \frac{341.873441}{40}$

$$= 8.547 \text{ MeV/nucleon}$$

6. Given, $u = +12$ cm, $f = -16$ cm, $v = ?$

Using lens formula, $\frac{1}{f} = \frac{1}{v} - \frac{1}{u}$

$$\Rightarrow \quad -\frac{1}{16} = \frac{1}{v} - \frac{1}{12}$$

$$\Rightarrow \quad \frac{1}{v} = \frac{1}{12} - \frac{1}{16} = \frac{4-3}{48} = \frac{1}{48}$$

$$v = 48 \text{ cm}$$

The image of virtual object at P forms at P' at a distance 48 cm from the lens.

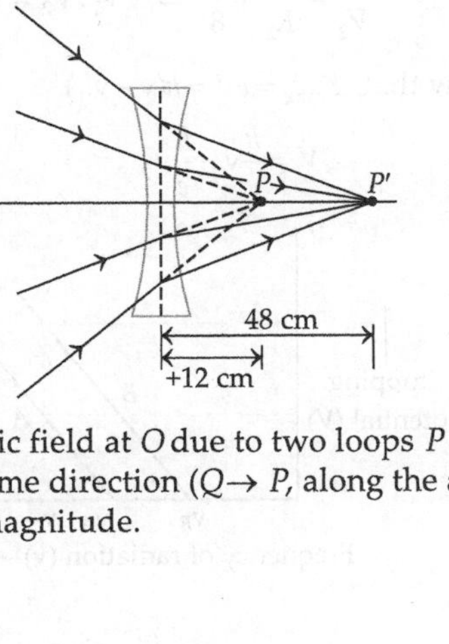

7. (i) Magnetic field at O due to two loops P and Q will be in same direction ($Q \rightarrow P$, along the axis) and of equal magnitude.

$$B = B_1 + B_2, \text{ but } B_2 = B_1$$

$$\Rightarrow \quad B = 2B_1 = 2\left[\frac{\mu_0 I r^2}{2(r^2 + r^2)^{3/2}}\right]$$

$$= \frac{\mu_0 I r^2}{(2r^2)^{3/2}} = \frac{\mu_0 I r^2}{2^{3/2} r^3} = \frac{\mu_0 I}{2^{3/2} r}$$

Or

(ii) Magnetic field at the centre of current carrying circular coil having current I is given by

$$B_1 = \frac{\mu_0 I}{2a}$$

Magnetic field at the axial point at a distance r from the centre is given by

$$B_2 = \frac{\mu_0 I a^2}{2(a^2 + r^2)^{3/2}}$$

Given, $r = 2a$

$$\therefore \quad B_2 = \frac{\mu_0 I a^2}{2(a^2 + 4a^2)^{3/2}}$$

$$= \frac{\mu_0 I a^2}{2 \times 5^{3/2} \times a^3}$$

$$= \frac{\mu_0 I}{2 \times 5^{3/2} \times a}$$

$$\therefore \quad \frac{B_1}{B_2} = \frac{\mu_0 I / 2a}{\mu_0 I / 2 \times 5^{3/2} a} = 5^{3/2}$$

$$\Rightarrow \quad B_1 : B_2 = 5^{3/2} : 1$$

8. (i) Given, refractive index, $\mu = 1.5$

Angle of prism, $A = 60°$,

Angle of deviation, $\delta_m = ?$

Angle of incidence, $i = ?$

We know that,

$$\mu = \frac{\sin\left(\frac{A + \delta_m}{2}\right)}{\sin\left(\frac{A}{2}\right)} = \frac{\sin i}{\sin \frac{A}{2}}$$

$$\left(\because \; i = \frac{A + \delta_m}{2}\right)$$

$$\Rightarrow \quad 1.5 = \frac{\sin i}{\sin\left(\frac{60°}{2}\right)}$$

$$\Rightarrow \quad 1.5 \times \sin 30° = \sin i$$

$$\Rightarrow \quad 1.5 \times 0.5 = \sin i$$

$$\Rightarrow \quad i = \sin^{-1}(0.75)$$

$$\Rightarrow \quad i = 48.6°$$

Or

(ii) We know that, the sun is at a very large distance from the earth. Assuming the sun as spherical, it can be considered as point source situated at infinity. So, the wavefront received on the earth will be plane as shown.

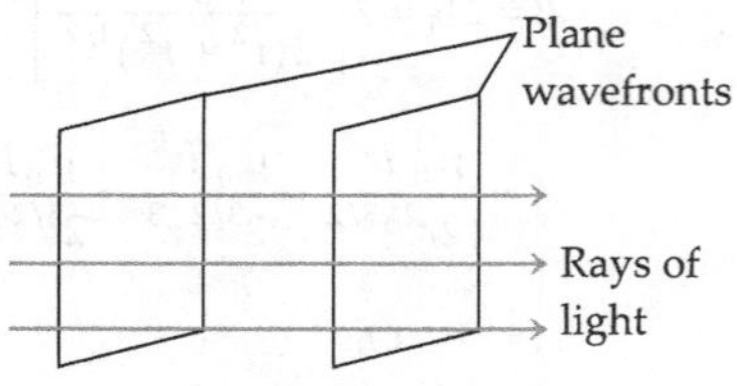

9. (*i*) $E_1 = -13.6\,\text{eV}$, when $n = 1$

Energy of electron in the second excited state i.e. $n = 3$ is

$$E_3 = -\frac{13.6}{n^2} = -\frac{13.6}{9} = -1.51\,\text{eV}$$

$\therefore$ Kinetic energy of electron in the second excited state is given by

$$\text{KE}_3 = -E_3 = 1.51\,\text{eV}$$

(*ii*) Energy of the photon emitted is given by

$$E = E_3 - E_1 = -1.51 - (-13.6) = 12.09\,\text{eV}$$
$$= 12.09 \times 1.6 \times 10^{-19}\,\text{J}$$

Wavelength of the spectral line emitted,

$$\lambda = \frac{hc}{E} = \frac{6.63 \times 10^{-34} \times 3 \times 10^8}{12.09 \times 1.6 \times 10^{-19}}$$
$$= 1.028 \times 10^{-7}\,\text{m}$$

10. As the electron enters perpendicular to electric and magnetic field, then

force due to electric field, $\mathbf{F}_E = e\mathbf{E}$

This will be along the opposite direction of $\mathbf{E}$.

Force due to magnetic field,

$$\mathbf{F}_B = e(\mathbf{v} \times \mathbf{B}) = evB\sin\theta$$
$$= evB\sin 90^\circ = evB \quad (\text{as } \mathbf{v} \perp \mathbf{B})$$

Direction of this force will be given by right hand screw or thumb rule.

As the electron passes undeflected, the force due to the two fields must be equal in magnitude and opposite in direction.

i.e. $F_E = F_B$

$\Rightarrow$ $eE = evB$

$\Rightarrow$ $v = \dfrac{E}{B}$

So, velocity of electron is E/B.

11. (*i*) Let R_1 and R_2 be the resistances of plated parts of wire,

then $$R_1 = \frac{\rho_1 l}{\pi r^2} \quad \text{...(i)}$$

and $$R_2 = \frac{\rho_2 l}{\pi[(2r)^2 - r^2]} \quad \left[\because R = \frac{\rho l}{A}\right] \quad \text{...(ii)}$$

Also, R_1 and R_2 are connected in parallel.

Equivalent resistance, $$R = \frac{R_1 R_2}{R_1 + R_2} \quad \text{...(iii)}$$

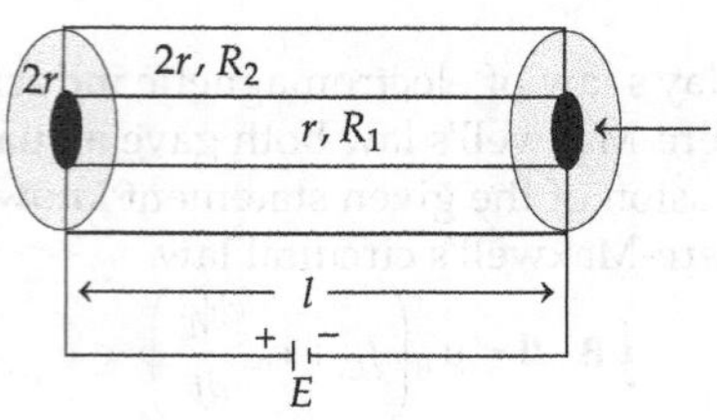

On putting the values of R_1 and R_2 from Eqs. (i) and (ii), we get

$$R = \frac{\left(\frac{\rho_1 l}{\pi r^2}\right)\left(\frac{\rho_2 l}{3\pi r^2}\right)}{\left(\frac{\rho_1 l}{\pi r^2}\right) + \left(\frac{\rho_2 l}{3\pi r^2}\right)} = \frac{\rho_1 \rho_2 l^2}{3\pi^2 r^4} \times \frac{3\pi r^2}{3\rho_1 l + \rho_2 l}$$

$$\Rightarrow \quad R = \frac{\rho_1 \rho_2 l}{\pi r^2 (3\rho_1 + \rho_2)}$$

Or

(*ii*) Resistance of conducting wire 1, can be written as

$$R_1 = \rho \cdot \frac{l_1}{\pi r_1^2}$$

where, l_1 and r_1 are length and radius of wire 1, respectively.

Resistance of conducting wire 2, can be expressed as

$$R_2 = \rho \cdot \frac{l_2}{\pi r_2^2}$$

where, l_2 and r_2 are length and radius of wire 2, respectively.

$$\therefore \quad \frac{R_1}{R_2} = \frac{\rho \cdot \frac{l_1}{\pi r_1^2}}{\rho \cdot \frac{l_2}{\pi r_2^2}} = \frac{l_1}{l_2}\left(\frac{r_2}{r_1}\right)^2 = \frac{1}{2}\left(\frac{3}{2}\right)^2 = \frac{9}{8}$$

$$\left[\text{Given, } \frac{r_1}{r_2} = \frac{2}{3} \text{ and } \frac{l_1}{l_2} = \frac{1}{2}\right]$$

$$\therefore \quad \frac{\text{Potential difference across wire 1}}{\text{Potential difference across wire 2}} = \frac{V_1}{V_2} = \frac{I_1 R_1}{I_2 R_2}$$

[for series, $I_1 = I_2$]

$$\therefore \quad \frac{V_1}{V_2} = \frac{R_1}{R_2} = \frac{9}{8} \Rightarrow V_1 : V_2 = 9 : 8$$

12. We know that, $K_{max} = eV = h(\nu - \nu_0)$

or $$V = \frac{h}{e}\nu - \frac{h}{e}\nu_0$$

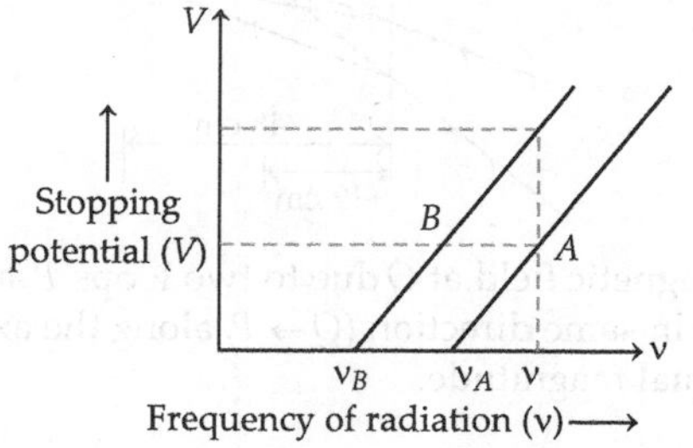

(*i*) From the graph, for the same value of ν, stopping potential is more for material *B*.

As $V = \frac{h}{e}(\nu - \nu_0)$

$\therefore$ *V* is higher for lower value of ν_0. Here, $\nu_B < \nu_A$, so $V_B > V_A$.

(*ii*) Slope of the graph is given by $\frac{h}{e}$, which is constant for all the materials. Hence, slope of the graph does not depend on the nature of the material used.

Or

To verify the kinetic energy values, we use the formula

$$KE = \frac{hc}{\lambda} - \phi$$

(i) For $\lambda = 400$ nm

$$KE = \frac{(4.1357 \times 10^{-15}) \times (3 \times 10^8)}{400 \times 10^{-9}} - 2.0$$

$$KE = \frac{1.2407 \times 10^{-6}}{400 \times 10^{-9}} - 2.0$$

$$KE = 3.10175 - 2.0 = 1.1 \text{ eV}$$

(ii) For $\lambda = 350$ nm

$$KE = \frac{(4.1357 \times 10^{-15}) \times (3 \times 10^8)}{350 \times 10^{-9}} - 2.0$$

$$KE = \frac{1.2407 \times 10^{-6}}{350 \times 10^{-9}} - 2.0$$

$$KE = 3.54486 - 2.0 = 1.54 \text{ eV}$$

(iii) For $\lambda = 300$ nm,

$$KE = \frac{(4.1357 \times 10^{-15}) \times (3 \times 10^8)}{300 \times 10^{-9}} - 2.0$$

$$KE = \frac{1.2407 \times 10^{-6}}{300 \times 10^{-9}} - 2.0$$

$$KE = 4.1357 - 2.0 = 2.13 \text{ eV}$$

(iv) For $\lambda = 250$ nm,

$$KE = \frac{(4.1357 \times 10^{-15}) \times (3 \times 10^8)}{250 \times 10^{-9}} - 2.0$$

$$KE = \frac{1.2407 \times 10^{-6}}{250 \times 10^{-9}} - 2.0$$

$$KE = 4.9628 - 2.0 = 2.96 \text{ eV}$$

13. The amount of work done in taking a unit charge from point *A* to point *B* is given as $W = Q \times V_{AB}$ where, $Q = 1\text{C}$ and V_{AB} is the potential difference between points *A* and *B*, so $W = V_{AB}$.

V_{AB} can be written as

(*i*) From (5 m, 0) to (10 m, 0)

$$V_{AB} = \frac{E_A}{r_A} - \frac{E_B}{r_B}$$

where, $r = \sqrt{x^2 + y^2}$ and $\text{E} = (10x + 4)\hat{\text{i}}$

$$V_{AB} = \frac{10 \times 5 + 4}{\sqrt{5^2}} - \frac{10 \times 10 + 4}{\sqrt{10^2}}$$

$$= \frac{54}{5} - \frac{104}{10} = 10.8 - 10.4 = 0.4 \text{ V}$$

$$W_{AB} = 1 \times 0.4 = 0.4 \text{ J}$$

(*ii*) From, (5m, 0) to (5m, 10m)

$$V_{AB} = \frac{E_A}{r_A} - \frac{E_B}{r_B} = \frac{10 \times 5 + 4}{\sqrt{5^2}} - \frac{10 \times 5 + 4}{\sqrt{5^2 + 10^2}}$$

$$= \frac{54}{5} - \frac{54}{11.18}$$

$$= 10.8 - 4.83 = 5.97 \text{ V}$$

$$\Rightarrow \quad W = 1 \times 5.97 = 5.97 \text{ J}$$

14. (*i*) Refractive index of a medium is given by

$$\mu = \frac{\sin i}{\sin r} = \frac{c}{v}$$

$$\Rightarrow \quad v = \frac{c \sin r}{\sin i}$$

$$\Rightarrow \quad v \propto \sin r$$

i.e. $v_P \propto \sin 17°$, $v_Q \propto \sin 27°$ and $v_R \propto \sin 37°$

But $\sin 17° < \sin 27° < \sin 37°$

$$\therefore \quad v_P < v_Q < v_R$$

Hence, velocity of light is minimum in medium *P*.

(*ii*) Given, $i_c = 45°$

As $\mu = \frac{c}{v} = \frac{1}{\sin i_c}$

$$\Rightarrow \quad v = c \sin i_c$$

$$= 3 \times 10^8 \times \sin 45°$$

$$= 3 \times 10^8 \times \frac{1}{\sqrt{2}} = \frac{3}{\sqrt{2}} \times 10^8 \text{ m/s}$$

Common Mistakes Sometimes, students use $\mu = \frac{v}{c}$ in place of $\mu = \frac{c}{v}$, hence they get wrong results.

15. (*i*) Bohr's second postulate (quantum condition) states that the electron revolves around the nucleus in certain privileged orbit which satisfy certain quantum condition that angular momentum of an electron is an integral multiple of $h/2\pi$, where *h* is Planck's constant,

i.e., $L = mvr = nh/2\pi$

where, *m* = mass of electron, *v* = speed of electron and *r* = radius of orbit of electron

$$2\pi r = n(h/mv) \quad \ldots(i)$$

Since, de-Broglie wavelength associated with an electron is given as

$$\lambda = \frac{h}{p} = \frac{h}{mv} \quad \ldots(ii)$$

From Eqs. (i) and (ii), we get

Circumference of electron in *n*th orbit

$= n \times$ de-Broglie wavelength associated with electron.

(*ii*) Number of spectral lines obtained due to transition of electron from $n=4$ (3rd excited state) to $n=1$ (ground state) is according to formula

$$N=\frac{n(n-1)}{2}$$

$$N=\frac{(4)(4-1)}{2}=6$$

The maximum numbers of spectral lines emitted are 6.

16. (*i*) Since, isolated atoms have discrete energy levels. In a crystalline solid, due to the presence of a large number of atoms, interatomic interactions take place. Due to this, energy levels get modified to energy bands.

(*ii*) (a) **Conductor (Metal)**

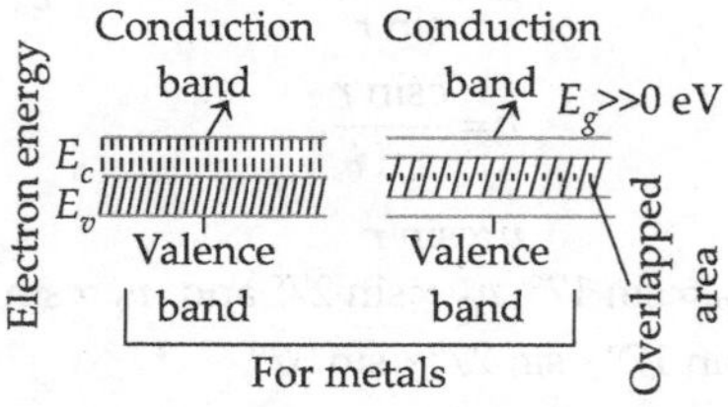

(b) **Semiconductor**

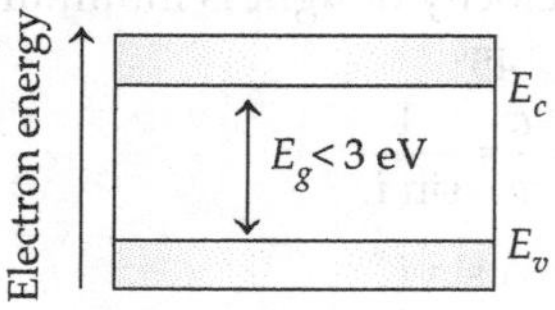

(*iii*) As we know, antimony (Sb) is an element from group 15. When impurities from groups 13 and 15 added to semiconductor to make it better conducting, this type of conductor known as extrinsic semiconductor.

Few points

1. When antimony is added to pure silicon (Si) crystal, then an *n*-type semiconductor would be obtained.
2. It is a pentavalent impurity.

Energy level diagram of *n*-type semiconductor is given below.

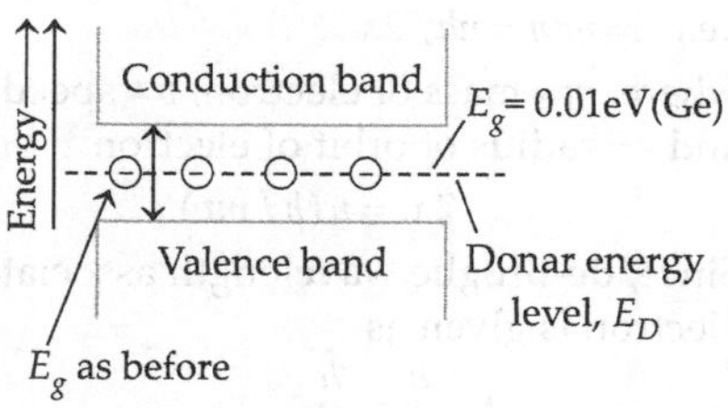

17. (*i*) **Combination of Thin Lenses in Contact**

Consider two lenses *A* and *B* of focal lengths f_1 and f_2 respectively, placed in contact with each other. An object is placed at a point *O* beyond the focus of the first lens *A*.

The first lens produces an image at I_1 (virtual image), which serves as a virtual object for the second lens *B*, producing the final image at *I*.

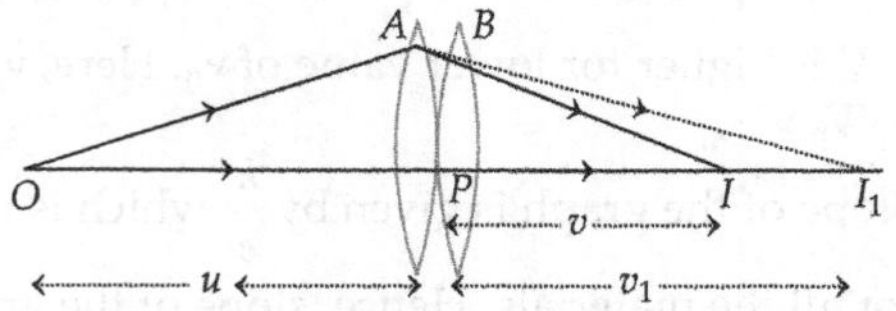

Since, the lenses are thin, we assume the optical centres (*P*) of the lenses to be co-incident.

For the image formed by the first lens *A*, we obtain

$$\frac{1}{v_1}-\frac{1}{u}=\frac{1}{f_1} \quad \text{...(i)}$$

For the image formed by the second lens *B*, we get

$$\frac{1}{v}-\frac{1}{v_1}=\frac{1}{f_2} \quad \text{...(ii)}$$

Adding Eqs. (i) and (ii), we get

$$\frac{1}{v}-\frac{1}{u}=\frac{1}{f_1}+\frac{1}{f_2} \quad \text{...(iii)}$$

If the two lens system is regarded as equivalent to a single lens of focal length *f*, we have

$$\frac{1}{v}-\frac{1}{u}=\frac{1}{f} \quad \text{...(iv)}$$

From Eqs. (iii) and (iv), we get

$$\frac{1}{f}=\frac{1}{f_1}+\frac{1}{f_2} \quad \text{...(v)}$$

i.e. $$P=P_1+P_2 \quad \text{...(vi)}$$

(*ii*) For concave lens, $P_1=-P$

and for convex lens, $P_2=P$

From Eq. (vi), power of combined lens,

$$P=P_1+P_2=-P+P=0$$

$$P=0$$

Hence, combination of lenses behaves like a plane glass.

Value Point

To get maximum marks,

- Draw the proper ray diagram for the combiantion of thin lenses and show the distance *u*, *v* and *f* in the figure.
- Use formula of combined power $P=P_1+P_2$.

18. (*i*) We know that,

Angle of deviation in a prism is given by

$$\delta=i+e-A$$

and for minimum deviation, $i=e$

So minimum deviation, $\delta_m=2i-A$

From the graph, minimum deviation, $\delta_m=60°$ and the corresponding angle of incidence is $i=60°$

So, $60=2\times60-A \Rightarrow A=60°$

So, for the given graph, the angle of the prism is 60°.

(*ii*) Refractive index of the prism is given by

$$n=\frac{\sin\left(\frac{A+\delta_m}{2}\right)}{\sin\frac{A}{2}}$$

$$\Rightarrow \quad n=\frac{\sin\left(\frac{60°+60°}{2}\right)}{\sin\frac{60°}{2}} \Rightarrow n=\frac{\sin 60°}{\sin 30°}$$

$$\Rightarrow \quad n=\frac{\frac{\sqrt{3}}{2}}{\frac{1}{2}} \Rightarrow n=\sqrt{3}$$

So, for the given graph, the refractive index of the prism is $\sqrt{3}$.

(*iii*) For deviation $\delta_1 = 65°$, we get

$\delta_1 = i_1 + e - A$

Substituting the corresponding values from the graph, we get

$$65° = i_1 + 70° - 60° \Rightarrow i_1 = 55°$$

(*iv*) For the angle of minimum deviation, the refracted ray becomes parallel to the base of the prism. Hence, angle of incidence should be 60°.

Or

(*i*) The distance from centre,

$y=\left(\frac{D}{d}\right)\Delta x$, where Δx is the path difference between two light waves reaching at point *P*.

For the missing wavelengths (or minima points) at *P*,

$$\Delta x = \left(n+\frac{1}{2}\right)\lambda, \text{ with } n=0,1,2,3\ldots$$

So, $y=\frac{D}{d}\frac{(2n+1)}{2}\lambda$

As per the given diagram, $\frac{d}{2}=\frac{D}{d}\frac{(2n+1)}{2}\lambda$

$$\lambda=\frac{d^2}{D(2n+1)}$$

for $n=0,1,2,3,\ldots$

So, all $\lambda=\frac{d^2}{D},\frac{d^2}{3D},\frac{d^2}{5D}\ldots$ will form minima at point *P*.

(*ii*) Let I_1 and I_2 are intensities of light coming from two slits.

$I \propto w$ (w= slit width)

$$\frac{I_1}{I_2}=\frac{4}{1} \Rightarrow Ib_1 = 4I_0$$

$$I_2 = I_0$$

$$I_{max} = (\sqrt{I_1}+\sqrt{I_2})^2 = (2\sqrt{I_0}+\sqrt{I_0})^2 = 9I_0$$

$$I_{min} = (\sqrt{I_1}-\sqrt{I_2})^2 = (2\sqrt{I_0}-\sqrt{I_0})^2 = I_0$$

Now, $\frac{I_{max}}{I_{min}}=\frac{9}{1}$

19. (*i*) Given, number of turns, $N = 100$

Area, $A = 0.5\ \text{m}^2$

Resistance, $R = 100\,\Omega$

Magnetic field, $B = 0.8$ T

Angular speed, $\omega = 60$ rad/s

Induced emf $= NBA\omega = 100\times0.8\times0.5\times60$

$$e_0 = 2400\ \text{V} \quad \ldots\text{(i)}$$

Induced current (max), $I_0=\frac{e_0}{R}=\frac{2400}{100}=24$ A

Power dissipated, $P=e_0\times I_0 = 2400\times24=57600$

$$P=576\times10^2\ \text{W}$$

(*ii*) Mutual inductance of solenoid coil system,

$$M=\frac{\mu_0 N_1 N_2 A_2}{l}$$

Here, $N_1=15$, $N_2=1$, $l=1\text{cm}=10^{-2}$ m,

$A_2 = 2.0\ \text{cm}^2 = 2.0\times10^{-4}\text{m}^2$

$$\therefore \quad M=\frac{4\pi\times10^{-7}\times15\times1\times2.0\times10^{-4}}{10^{-2}}$$

$$=120\pi\times10^{-9}\ \text{H}$$

Induced emf in the loop,

$$E_2 = M\frac{\Delta I_1}{\Delta t}\text{(numerically)}$$

$$=120\pi\times10^{-9}\times\frac{(4-2)}{0.1}$$

$$=120\times3.14\times10^{-9}\times\frac{2}{0.1}$$

$$=7.5\times10^{-6}\text{V}=7.5\ \mu\text{V}.$$

Or

(*i*) **Principle** AC generator works on the principle of electromagnetic induction. Whenever amount of magnetic flux linked with a coil changes, an emf is induced in the coil.

It lasts so long as the change in magnetic flux through the coil continues.

Labelled diagram of an AC generator is shown below.

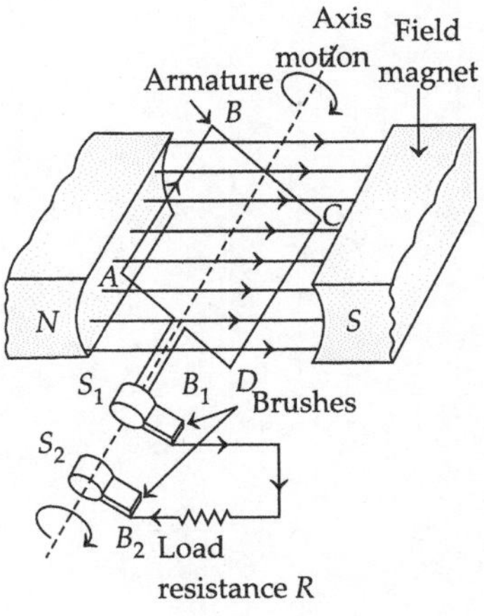

Working When a closed armature coil rotates in a uniform magnetic field with its axis perpendicular to the magnetic field, the magnetic flux linked with the loop changes and emf induces in the coil. Let initially angle between area vector of coil and magnetic field B is 0°. Thereafter, AB comes downward and CD upward, then by Fleming's right hand rule, induced current flows from B to A.

During the next half revolution, when CD comes downward and AB upward, then current flows from C to D. During the first half rotation, current flows through $BAS_2\ B_2\ RB_1S_1\ DC$ and during next half rotation along $CDS_1\ B_1\ RB_2S_2\ AB$. Hence, $e = -Nd\phi/dt = NBA\omega \sin \omega t$, where $e_0 = NBA\omega$

$$i = \frac{e_0}{R}\sin \omega t = i_0 \sin \omega t \quad \left[\text{Here, } \frac{e_0}{R} = i_0\right]$$

(*ii*) The magnetic flux linked with the armature coil is changed by rotating it in the magnetic field between the poles of the magnet.

(*iii*) Let at any instant total magnetic flux linked with the armature coil is given by ϕ.

$$\phi = NBA\cos\theta = NBA\cos\omega t$$

(where, $\theta = \omega t$ is the angle made by area vector of coil with magnetic field.)

$$\therefore \quad \frac{d\phi}{dt} = -NBA\omega \sin \omega t$$

$$\Rightarrow \quad -\frac{d\phi}{dt} = NBA\omega \sin \omega t$$

By Faraday's law of EMI,

$$e = \frac{-d\phi}{dt}$$

Induced emf in coil is given by

$$e = NBA\omega \sin \omega t \Rightarrow e = e_0 \sin \omega t$$

where, $e_0 = NBA\omega$ = peak value of induced emf

Direction of induced emf can be determined using Fleming's right hand rule. If we stretch the thumb and the first two fingers of our right hand in mutually perpendicular directions and if the forefinger points in the direction of the magnetic field, thumb in the direction of motion of the conductor, then the central finger points in the direction of current induced in the conductor.

Common Mistakes In generators, students get confused between the split rings and slip rings. Split rings or commutator are used in DC generator whereas slip rings are used in AC generator.

20. (*i*) Potential energy of the proton increases, as it moves in opposite direction of electric field.

(*ii*) (a) $\Delta V = -E \cdot \Delta x = -8.0 \times 10^4 \times 0.50 = -4 \times 10^4$ V

(b) Electrostatic potential energy of the system,

$$U = 9 \times 10^9 \cdot \frac{q_1 q_2}{r}$$

$$= 9 \times 10^9 \times 1 \times 10^{-6} \times 1 \times 10^{-6} \quad [\because r = 1\,\text{m}]$$

$$= 9 \times 10^{-3}\ \text{J}$$

(*iii*) (a) As, $\Delta K = -\Delta U = 1.6 \times 10^{-19} \times 4 \times 10^4$

$$= 6.4 \times 10^{-15}\ \text{J}$$

(from conservation of energy)

(b) Since, $\Delta K = \frac{1}{2} m v_B^2$

$$\Rightarrow v_B = \sqrt{\frac{2\Delta K}{m}} = \sqrt{\frac{2 \times 6.4 \times 10^{-15}}{1.66 \times 10^{-27}}} = 2.77 \times 10^6\ \text{m/s}$$

SQP Code : **PB-6/15** Series **i-Succeed 6-25/15** Roll No. | | | | | | |

Sample Question Paper 06

Physics 12th (Code 861)

General Instructions

1. This paper is divided into four Sections- A, B, C and D. Answer all questions.
2. **Section A** consists of one question having sub-parts of one mark each.
3. **Section B** consists of seven questions of two marks each.
4. **Section C** consists of nine questions of three marks each.
5. **Section D** consists of three questions of five marks each.
6. Internal choices have been provided in two questions each in Section B, Section C and Section D.

Time : 3 Hrs.

Max. Marks : 70

Section A (14 Marks)

1. A. In questions (i) to (vii) below, choose the correct alternative (a), (b), (c) or (d) for each of the questions given below.

(*i*) Pure silicon at 300 K has equal number of electron (n_e) and hole (n_h), concentration of $1.5\times10^{16}\ m^{-3}$. Doping by indium increases n_h to $4.5\times10^{22}\ m^{-3}$. n_e in doped silicon is (in m^{-3}) • *Recall* [1]

(a) 9×10^5 (b) 5×10^9

(c) 2.25×10^{11} (d) 3×10^{19}

(*ii*) The graph between $(u+v)$ and u or v for real image formed by convex lens will be • *Analysis* [1]

(a) 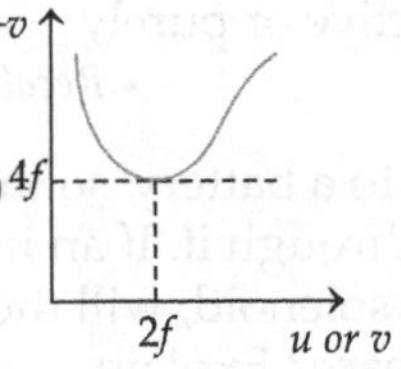

(b) 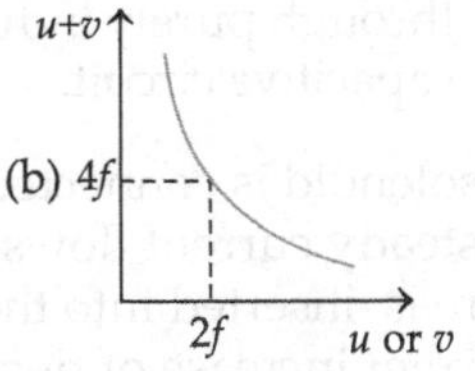

(c) 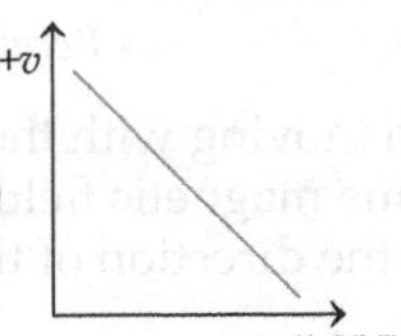

(d) 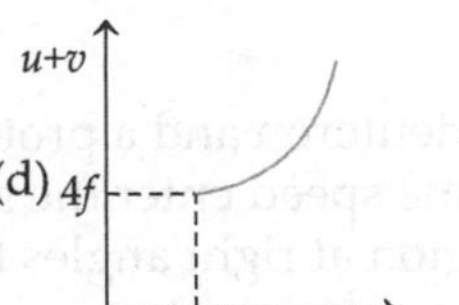

(*iii*) **Assertion** (A) Spherical aberration of a lens can be minimised by blocking the marginal rays.

Reason (R) Spherical aberration arise on account of inability of the lens to focus central and peripheral rays at the same point. • *Understanding* [1]

(a) Both Assertion and Reason are true and Reason is the correct explanation for Assertion.

(b) Both Assertion and Reason are true but Reason is not the correct explanation for Assertion.

(c) Assertion is false and Reason is true.

(d) Both Assertion and Reason are false.

(*iv*) Variation of photoelectric current with intensity of light is • *Analysis* [1]

(a) 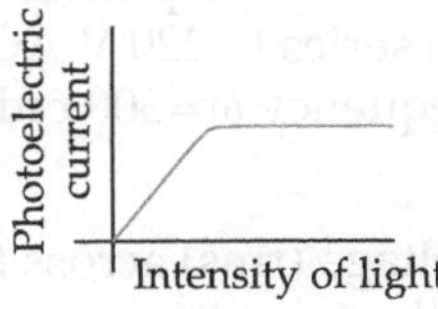

(b) 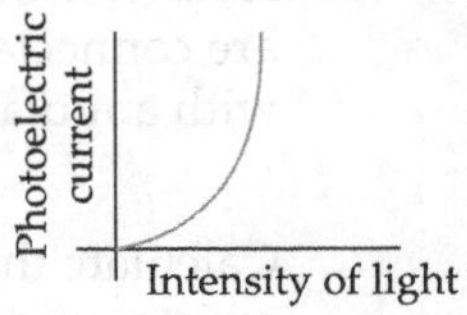

(c) 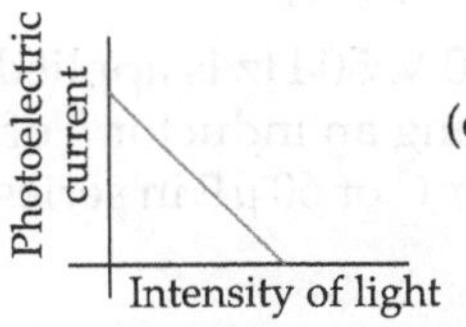

(d) 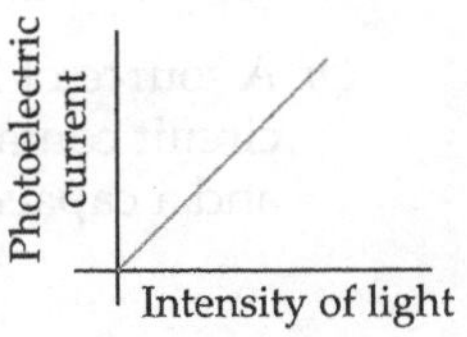

(*v*) The full scale deflection current of a galvanometer of resistance 1 Ω is 5 mA. What is the value of resistance *R*, which is connected in series to convert it into a voltmeter of range 5 V? • *Understanding* [1]

(a) 99Ω (b) 999Ω

(c) 1000Ω (d) 100 Ω

(*vi*) **Assertion** (A) The electrostatic forces weakens the nuclear force.

Reason (R) The nuclear force becomes weak, if the nucleus contains too many protons compared to neutrons.• *Analysis* [1]

(a) Both Assertion and Reason are true and Reason is the correct explanation for Assertion.

(b) Both Assertion and Reason are true but Reason is not the correct explanation for Assertion.

(c) Assertion is false and Reason is true.

(d) Both Assertion and Reason are false.

(*vii*) Consider two point charges $q_1 = 5\ \mu C$ and $q_2 = 2\ \mu C$ located at the distance of $a = 0.1$ m apart. The magnitude of force exerted on q_1 due to q_2 is given by • *Recall* [1]

(a) 90 N (b) 9×10^4 N

(c) 9×10^3 N (d) 9 N

B. Answer the following questions briefly.

(*i*) An electrical lamp connected in series with a capacitor and an AC source is glowing with a certain brightness. How does the brightness of the lamp changes on reducing the capacitance? • *Application* [1]

(*ii*) In a *p-n* junction diode, the forward bias resistance is low as compared to the reverse bias resistance. Give reason. • *Recall* [1]

(*iii*) Which conservation principle is involved with Kirchhoff's second law of electrical circuit? • *Recall* [1]

(*iv*) The objective lens of a telescope has focal length 90 cm and that of eyepiece lens has focal length 0.9 cm. What will be the magnification of the given telescope? • *Recall* [1]

(*v*) What is the function of graphite rods in a nuclear reactor? • *Recall* [1]

(*vi*) In a single slit diffraction experiment, when a tiny circular obstacle is placed in the path of light from a distant source, a bright spot is seen at the centre of the shadow of the obstacle. Explain in brief. • *Recall* [1]

(*vii*) Two particles *A* and *B* of masses *m* and $2m$ have charges *q* and $2q$, respectively. They are moving with velocities v_1 and v_2, respectively in the same direction, enters the same magnetic field *B* acting normally to their direction of motion. If the two forces F_A and F_B acting on them are in the ratio of 1 : 2, find the ratio of their velocities. • *Understanding*[1]

SP-06

Section B (14 Marks)

2. In microwave, UV-rays, X-rays and infrared rays, which of the electromagnetic waves has

(*i*) the highest frequency and [1]

(*ii*) the longest wavelength? • *Application* [1]

3. A resistor of 200 Ω and a capacitor of 40 μF are connected in series to 220 V AC source with angular frequency ω = 300 rad/s. • *Analysis*

Calculate the voltage (rms) across (*i*) the resistor and (*ii*) the capacitor. [2]

Or A source of 230 V, 50 Hz is applied to a circuit containing an inductor *L* of 80 mH and a capacitor *C* of 60 μF in series.

The resistance in the circuit is taken to be zero, then

(*i*) what is the average power transferred to inductor *L* and capacitor *C*? • *Recall* [1]

(*ii*) name the current which is flowing through purely inductive or purely capacitive circuit. • *Recall* [1]

4. A solenoid is connected to a battery, so that a steady current flows through it. If an iron core is inserted into the solenoid, will the current increase or decrease? Explain. • *Recall* [2]

5. A deuteron and a proton moving with the same speed enter the same magnetic field region at right angles to the direction of the field. Show the trajectories followed by the two particles in the magnetic field. Find the ratio of the radii of the circular paths which the two particles may describe.

• *Application* [2]

6. Figure below shows two infinitely long and thin current carrying conductors X and Y kept in vacuum, parallel to each other, at a distance *a*.

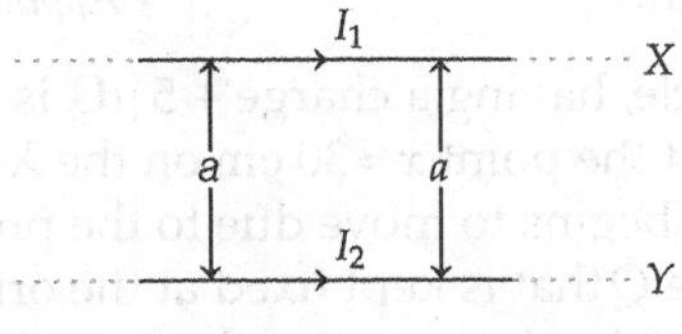

How much force per unit length acts on the conductor Y due to the current flowing through X? Write your answer in terms of $\left(\frac{\mu_0}{4\pi}\right) I_1, I_2$ and *a*.

• *Application* [2]

Section C (27 Marks)

9. Write a short note on

(*i*) LED

(*ii*) Photodiode

(*iii*) Solar cell • *Recall* [3]

10. A screen is placed 90 cm from an object. The image of the object on the screen is formed by a convex lens at two different locations separated by 20 cm. Determine the focal length of the lens. • *Analysis* [3]

Or

What are the need of coherent sources for the production of interference pattern?

• *Application* [3]

11. (*i*) State Gauss' law.

• *Recall* [1]

(*ii*) A thin straight infinitely long conducting wire of linear charge density λ is enclosed by a cylindrical surface of radius *r* and length *l*. Its axis coinciding with the length of the wire. Obtain the expression for the electric field indicating its direction at a point on the surface of the cylinder. • *Application* [2]

7. The work function of Cs is 2.14 eV. Find

• *Understanding* [1]

(*i*) threshold frequency for Cs and

(*ii*) wavelength of incident light if the photocurrent is brought to zero by stopping potential of 0.6V. [1]

8. (*i*) Two metals *A* and *B* have work functions 2eV and 4eV respectively, which metal has lower threshold wavelength for photoelectric effect? • *Recall* [1]

(*ii*) What is the de-Broglie wavelength and momentum of an electron with kinetic energy of 120 eV? • *Application* [1]

Or

A proton and an α-particle have the same de-Broglie wavelength. Determine the ratio of • *Application*

(*i*) their accelerating potentials and [1]

(*ii*) their speeds. [1]

12. A potentiometer wire of length 4 m has a resistance of 20 Ω. When the circuit of potentiometer is connected to 8 V battery in series with resistance of 4 Ω, then find

(*i*) current flowing through the circuit and [1]

(*ii*) emf of the primary cell which gives balance at 40 cm. • *Recall* [2]

Or

A student measures the current flowing through a resistor at different applied voltages. Given the resistance *R* is 5 Ω. Verify (for any two) that the experimental data agrees with Ohm's law using the following data

Voltage (V)	2	4	6	8
Current (A)	0.4	0.8	1.2	1.6

• *Application* [3]

13. (*i*) Is the ratio of number of holes and the number of conduction electrons in an *n*-type extrinsic semiconductor more than, less than or equal to 1?

• *Recall* [1]

(*ii*) What do you mean by reverse current in *p-n* junction diode? • *Recall* [1]

(*iii*) The graph shown in the figure represents a plot of current *versus* voltage for a given semiconductor. Identify the region, if any, over which the semiconductor has a negative resistance. • *Application* [1]

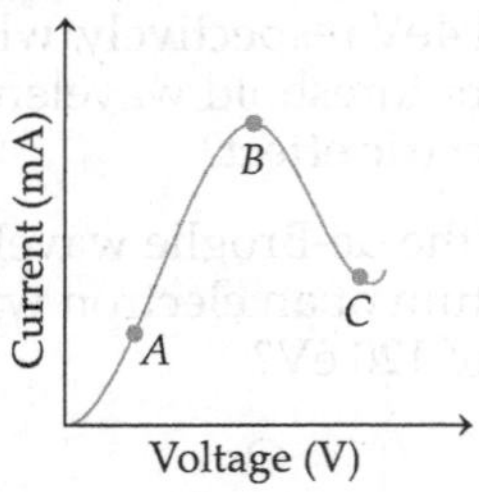

14. A parallel plate capacitor with a plate separation *d* has a capacitance C_0 in the absence of a dielectric material. What is the capacitance, when a slab of dielectric material of dielectric constant *K* and thickness $d/3$ is inserted between the plates as shown in the figure below? • *Application* [3]

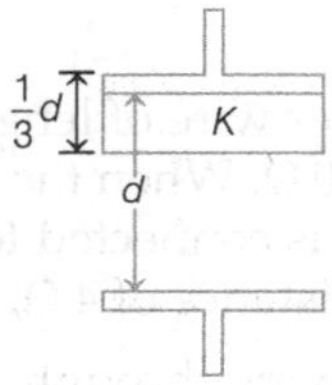

15. (*i*) Monochromatic light of wavelength 589 nm is incident from air on a water surface. If μ for water is 1.33, find the wavelength, frequency and speed of the refracted light. • *Application* [1½]

(*ii*) A double convex lens is made of a glass of refractive index 1.55 with both faces of the same radius of curvature. Find the radius of curvature required, if the focal length is 20 cm. • *Application* [1½]

16. A particle, having a charge + 5 μC, is initially at rest at the point $x = 30$ cm on the *X*-axis. The particle begins to move due to the presence of a charge *Q* that is kept fixed at the origin. Find the kinetic energy of the particle at the instant it has moved 15 cm from its initial position, if • *Understanding* [3]

(i) $Q = +15\ \mu C$ and

(ii) $Q = -15\ \mu C$

17. A beam of light consisting of two wavelengths 560 nm and 420 nm is used to obtain interference fringes in a Young's double slit experiment. Find the least distance from the central maxima, where the bright fringes due to both the wavelengths coincide. The distance between the two slits is 4.0 mm and the screen is at a distance of 1.0 m from the slits. • *Analysis* [3]

Section D (15 Marks)

18. Two students *P* and *Q* while performing an experiment with single slit and double slit obtained the following two graphs.

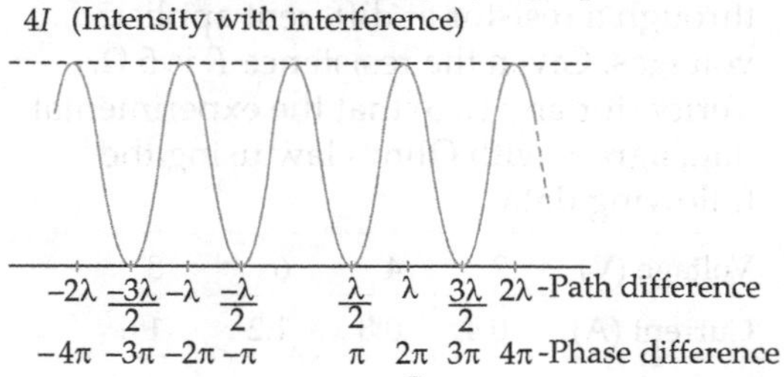

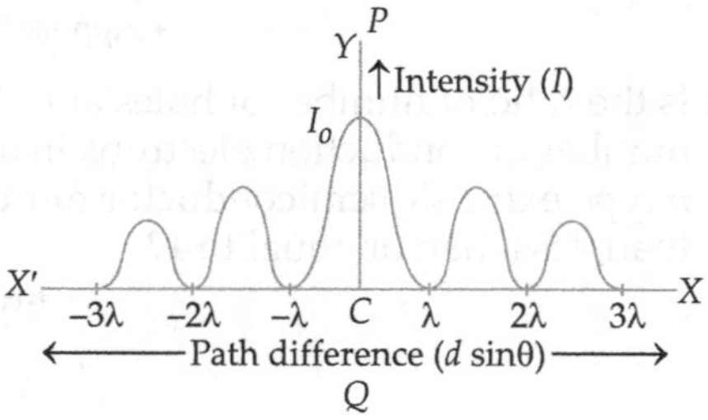

(*i*) Which student is performing experiment with double slit? • *Analysis* [1]

(*ii*) Name the phenomenon which is responsible for the graph obtained by student *Q*. • *Analysis* [1]

(*iii*) In Young's double slit experiment of wave incident at angle 45° and distance between slits is $d = 20\lambda$ (λ = wavelength of light used), then find the angular position, where

(a) central maxima is obtained

(b) third order maxima is obtained. • *Application* [3]

Or

(*i*) What type of lens is an air bubble inside water? • *Recall* [1] (*ii*) A concave lens of refractive index 1.5 is immersed in a medium of refractive index 1.65. What is the nature of the lens? • *Recall* [1]

(*iii*) An equi-convex lens of focal length f is cut into two equal halves as shown in the figure. What is the focal length of each half? • *Application* [3]

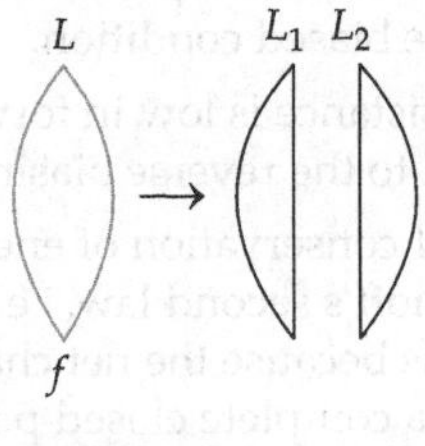

19. (*i*) The ratio of the turns in the primary and the secondary coil, in a given transformer is 1 : 10. If the load resistor draws a current of 1. 2 A from the secondary coil, determine the current in the primary coil assuming that the transformer has an efficiency of only 90% • *Application* [2]

(*ii*) The household power supply is at 200V and 60 Hz. Find the time required for

(a) The value of current to change from 0 to its rms value.

(b) the value of voltage to change from its rms value to 0. • *Application* [3]

Or

In the following diagram, the arm PQ of the rectangular conductor is moved from $x=0$ outwards.

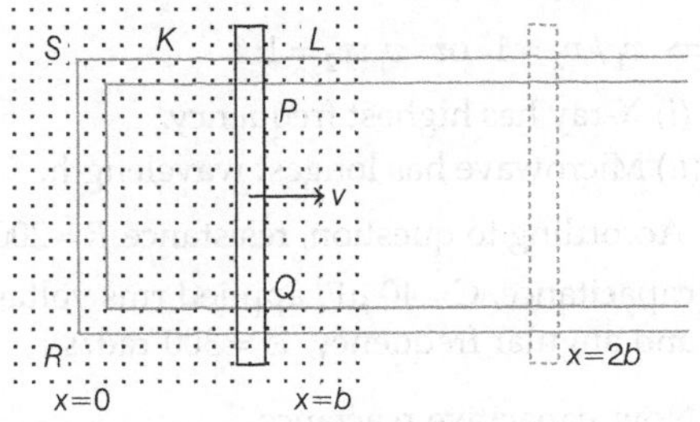

The uniform magnetic field is perpendicular to the plane and extends from $x=0$ to $x=b$ and is zero for $x>b$. Only the arm PQ possesses substantial resistance r. Consider the situation when the arm PQ is pulled outwards from $x=0$ to $x=2b$, and is then moved back to $x=0$ with constant speed v. Obtain expressions for the • *Analysis*

(*i*) electric flux,

(*ii*) the induced emf,

(*iii*) the force necessary to pull the arm and sketch the variation of these quantities with distance. [5]

20. Hydrogen spectrum consists of discrete bright lines in a dark background and it is specifically known as hydrogen emission spectrum.There is one more type of hydrogen spectrum that exists where we get dark lines on the bright background, it is known as absorption spectrum.

Balmer found an empirical formula by the observation of a small part of this spectrum and it is represented by

$$\frac{1}{\lambda}=R\left(\frac{1}{2^2}-\frac{1}{n^2}\right), \text{ where } n=3, 4, 5, \ldots.$$

For Lyman series, the emission is from first state to nth state, for Paschen series, it is from third state to nth state, for Brackett series, it is from fourth state to nth state and for Pfund series, it is from fifth state to nth state.

(*i*) Which series of hydrogen spectrum corresponds to ultraviolet region? • *Recall* [1]

(*ii*) The figure shows energy levels of an atom with six transitions of wavelengths $\lambda_1, \lambda_2, \lambda_3, \lambda_4, \lambda_5$ and λ_6. Which of the following wavelengths occur in absorption spectrum? • *Application* [2]

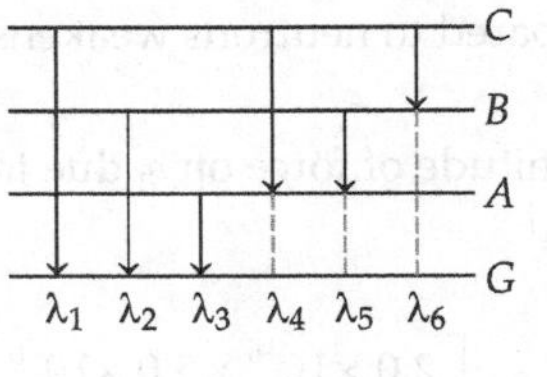

(*iii*) (a) Find the ratio of the wavelength for $2 \rightarrow 1$ transition in Li^{++}, He^{+} and H. • *Recall*

(b) When an electron jumps from the orbit $n=2$ to $n=4$, then find the wavelength of the absorbed radiations? • *Applicaiton* [2]

Solutions in Topper's Style

My Commitment *I affirm that I am reviewing these solutions only after I have solved the Sample Question Paper 6 on my own. My purpose of looking the solutions is solely to verify whether my answers/solutions were correct or not and to identify my mistakes in case my solutions were wrong or I could not solve that.*

1. A. (*i*) (*b*) In an extrinsic semiconductor,

$$n_e n_h = n_i^2$$

$$\Rightarrow \quad n_e \times 4.5 \times 10^{22} = (1.5 \times 10^{16})^2$$

$$\Rightarrow \quad n_e = \frac{2.25 \times 10^{32}}{4.5 \times 10^{22}}$$

$$\Rightarrow \quad n_e = 5 \times 10^9 \text{ m}^{-3}$$

(*ii*) (*a*) For convex lens (for real image) $u + v \geq 4f$
For $u = 2f$, v is also equal to $2f$. Hence, $u + v = 4f$

(*iii*) (*b*) Spherical aberration occurs due to the inability of a lens to converge marginal rays of the same wavelength to the focus because it converges the paraxial rays,but this defect can be removed by blocking the marginal rays.

(*iv*) (*d*) Photocurrent varies linearly with intensity. The photocurrent is directly proportional to the number of photoelectrons emitted per second. This implies that, the graph is a straight line passing through origin.

(*v*) (*b*) Using relation, $V = I_g(G + R)$

$$\Rightarrow R = \frac{V}{I_g} - G = \left(\frac{5}{5 \times 10^{-3}} - 1\right) = 999\,\Omega$$

i.e. A resistance of 999 Ω should be connected in series with the galvanometer to convert it into a voltmeter of desired voltage.

(*vi*) (*c*) Electrostatic force and nuclear force work independently.
Nuclear force are strongest when the nunmber of protons equals the number of neutrons. An excess of proton compared to neutrons weakens the nuclear forces.

(*vii*) (*d*) The magnitude of force on q_1 due to q_2 is given by

$$F_{12} = k\frac{|q_2||q_1|}{a^2}$$

$$= 9 \times 10^9 \times \left[\frac{2.0 \times 10^{-6} \times 5.0 \times 10^{-6}}{(0.1)^2}\right]$$

$$= 9 \text{ N}$$

B. (*i*) Capacitive reactance is given by

$$X_C = \frac{1}{\omega C} \Rightarrow X_C \propto \frac{1}{C}$$

This means, with the decrease in the capacitance, the capacitive reactance increases. So, if an electric lamp connected in series with a capacitor and an AC source, is glowing with certain brightness. Then with the decrease in the capacitance, the brightness of the lamp decreases.

(*ii*) It is because the potential barrier is low in forward biased condition of a *p-n* junction as compared to the reverse biased condition.

So, the resistance is low in forward biasing as compared to the reverse biasing.

(*iii*) The law of conservation of energy is involved with the Kirchhoff's second law, i.e. KVL of electrical circuit. It is because the net change in the energy of a charge in a complete closed path must be zero.

(*iv*) Magnification of telescope

$$= \frac{\text{Focal length of objective lens}}{\text{Focal length of eyepiece lens}}$$

$$\Rightarrow \quad m = \frac{f_o}{f_e} = \frac{90}{0.9} = 100$$

(*v*) The function of graphite rods in a nuclear reactor is as a moderator to control the rate of reaction. It slows down the fast moving secondary neutrons, during fission chain reaction.

(*vi*) When a tiny circular obstacle is placed in the path of light from a distant source, the light waves get diffracted from the edges of circular obstacle. The diffracted waves interfere constructively at the centre of shadow which appears in the form of bright spot at the centre.

(*vii*) Ratio of forces acting on the two particles,

$$\frac{F_A}{F_B} = \frac{qv_1 B\sin 90°}{(2q)v_2 B\sin 90°} = \frac{1}{2} \quad [\text{Given, } B_1 = B_2 = B]$$

$$\Rightarrow v_1 / v_2 = 1 \text{ or } v_1 : v_2 = 1:1$$

2. (*i*) X-ray has highest frequency.
(*ii*) Microwave has longest wavelength.

3. According to question, resistance $R = 200\,\Omega$, capacitance, $C = 40\,\mu\text{F}$, applied rms voltage, $V_{rms} = 220$ V and angular frequency, $\omega = 300$ rad/s

Now, capacitive reactance,

$$X_C = \frac{1}{\omega C} = \frac{1}{300 \times 40 \times 10^{-6}} = 83.33\,\Omega$$

Impedance, $Z^2 = R^2 + X_C^2$

$$= (200)^2 + (83.33)^2$$

$$\Rightarrow \quad Z = \sqrt{46943.88} = 216.6\,\Omega$$

Now, $I_{rms} = \dfrac{V_{rms}}{Z} = \dfrac{220}{216.6} = 1.02$ A

(*i*) Voltage (rms) across resistor R is given by

$$V_{rms} = I_{rms}\, R = 1.02 \times 200 = 204 \text{ V}$$

(*ii*) Similarly, voltage (rms) across capacitor C,

$$V'_{rms} = I_{rms} X_C = 1.02 \times 83.33 = 85\text{ V}$$

To get maximum marks include following value points.

Value Point
- Write the formula used.
- Solve the numerical step by step.

Or

(*i*) Average power transferred per cycle by source to inductor and capacitor is always 0 because the phase difference is $\pi/2$ between alternating voltage and current, for both.

(*ii*) Wattless current because average power in such a circuit, $P_{av} = V_{rms} \times I_{rms} \times \cos\phi$

$$= V_{rms} \times I_{rms} \times \cos 90° = 0$$

4. When the iron core is inserted in the current-carrying solenoid, the magnetic field increases due to the magnetisation of iron core and consequently the flux increases. According to Lenz's law, the emf produced must oppose this increase in flux, which can be done by making decrease in current. So, the current will decrease.

This decreases the relaxation time considerably in metals and consequently resistivity of metal or conductor increases as, $\rho = \frac{1}{\sigma} = \frac{m}{ne^2\tau}$

where *n*, *m*, *e* are number, mass and charge of electron.

5. The trajectory of the two particles in the magnetic field is shown below.

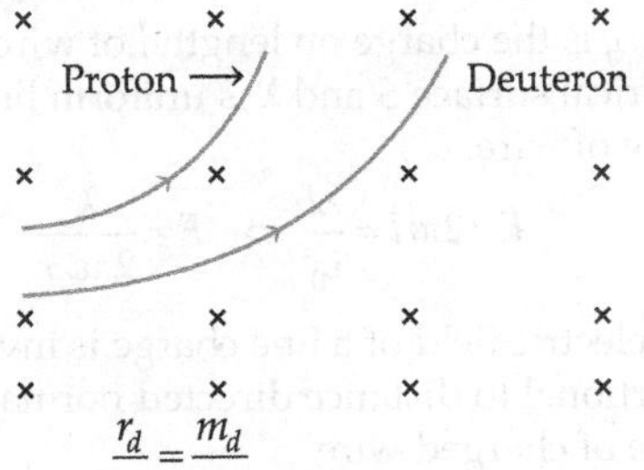

$\because \quad \frac{r_d}{r_p} = \frac{m_d}{m_p}$

$\because \quad m_d = 2m_p$

$\Rightarrow \quad r_d = 2r_p$

or $\quad r_d : r_p = 2:1$

6. Magnetic force between two current carrying parallel conductors per unit length is given by $\frac{F}{l} = \frac{\mu_0}{4\pi}\frac{2I_1I_2}{a}$,

where, I_1 and I_2 are current in **conductors** *X* and *Y* respectively and *a* is distance between the two parallel conductors *X* and *Y*.

7. Given, $\phi_0 = 2.14$ eV

(i) The work function is related with threshold frequency as

$$\phi_0 = h\nu_0$$

$$\therefore \quad \nu_0 = \frac{\phi_0}{h} = \frac{2.14 \times 1.6 \times 10^{-19}}{6.63 \times 10^{-34}}$$

$$= 0.51 \times 10^{15}\text{ Hz}$$

(ii) Stopping potential, $V_0 = 0.6$ V

$\therefore$ By Einstein's photoelectric equation,

$$\frac{hc}{\lambda} = \phi_0 + eV_0 = 2.14 + 0.6 = 2.74\text{ eV}$$

$$\therefore \quad \lambda = \frac{6.63 \times 10^{-34} \times 3 \times 10^8}{2.74 \times 1.6 \times 10^{-19}}$$

$$= 4.53 \times 10^{-17}\text{ m}$$

8. (*i*) We know that, work function, $\phi_0 = \frac{hc}{\lambda_0} \Rightarrow \lambda_0 = \frac{hc}{\phi_0}$

$\therefore \lambda_0 \propto \frac{1}{\phi_0}$, thus metal *B* has lower threshold wavelength because its work function is more than metal *A*.

(*ii*) According to the question,

$$\text{KE} = K = 120\text{ eV}$$

$$= 120 \times 1.6 \times 10^{-19}\text{ J}$$

$$= 1.92 \times 10^{-17}\text{ J}$$

Hence, de-Broglie wavelength, $\lambda = \frac{h}{p} = \frac{6.63 \times 10^{-34}}{p}$

But $p = \text{momentum} = \sqrt{2mK}$

$$= \sqrt{2 \times 9.1 \times 10^{-3} \times 1.92 \times 10^{-17}}$$

$$= 5.91 \times 10^{-24}\text{ kg-ms}^{-1}$$

$$\Rightarrow \quad \lambda = \frac{6.63 \times 10^{-34}}{5.91 \times 10^{-24}} = 0.112\text{ nm}$$

Or

(*i*) de-Broglie wavelength is given by

$$\lambda = \frac{h}{\sqrt{2mqV}} \Rightarrow V = \frac{h}{2mq\lambda^2}$$

$$m_\alpha = 4m_p,\ q_\alpha = 2q_p \text{ and } \lambda_\alpha = \lambda_p$$

$$\Rightarrow \quad \frac{V_p}{V_\alpha} = \frac{m_\alpha q_\alpha}{m_p q_p} = \frac{4m_p \times 2q_p}{m_p q_p}$$

$$\frac{V_p}{V_\alpha} = \frac{8}{1}$$

(*ii*) The de-Broglie wavelength of a particle is given by

$$\lambda = \frac{h}{mv}$$

$$\therefore \quad \lambda_p = \frac{h}{m_p v_p} \quad \text{and} \quad \lambda_\alpha = \frac{h}{m_\alpha v_\alpha}$$

We know that, $m_\alpha = 4m_p$

$\because \quad \lambda_p = \lambda_\alpha$ [given]

$$\therefore \quad \frac{h}{m_p \cdot v_p} = \frac{h}{4m_p \cdot v_\alpha}$$

$$\Rightarrow \quad \frac{v_p}{v_\alpha} = 4$$

9. (*i*) **LED** It is a heavily doped *p-n* junction diode which converts electrical energy into light energy. This diode emits spontaneous radiation under forward biasing.

(*ii*) **Photodiode** It is a special type of junction diode used for detecting optical signals. It is a reverse biased *p-n* junction diode made from a photosensitive material.

(*iii*) **Solar cell** It is a junction diode which converts solar energy into electrical energy and is based on photovoltaic effect. It can be used anywhere as a self-generating source of electricity.

10. Since, the two positions of the lens, for which image is formed at screen are conjugate positions. Assuming object distance from lens in 1st case is z. Therefore, the separation of lens from the screen in the 2nd case be also equal to z. According to question, the image of the object on the screen is formed by a convex lens at two different locations separated by 20 cm.

Now, we have $z + 20 + z = 90$ or $z = 35$ cm

For 1st case,

Object distance from lens, $u = -z = -35$ cm,
$v = 35 + 20 = 55$ cm

Applying lens formula,

$$\frac{1}{f} = \frac{1}{v} - \frac{1}{u}$$

$$\frac{1}{f} = \frac{1}{55} - \frac{1}{-35} = \frac{18}{385}$$

$$\Rightarrow \quad f = \frac{385}{18} = 21.4 \text{ cm}$$

Or

When two monochromatic waves of intensities I_1, I_2 and phase difference ϕ meet at a point, then the resultant intensity is given by

$$I = I_1 + I_2 + 2\sqrt{I_1 I_2} \cos\phi$$

Here, the term $2\sqrt{I_1 I_2}\cos\phi$ is called **interference term.**

There are two possibilities

(*i*) If $\cos\phi$ remains constant with time, then the total intensity at any point will be constant. The intensity will be maximum $(\sqrt{I_1} + \sqrt{I_2})^2$ at points, where $\cos\phi$ is +1 and minimum $(\sqrt{I_1} - \sqrt{I_2})^2$ at points, where $\cos\phi$ is −1. The sources in this case are coherent.

(*ii*) If $\cos\phi$ varies continuously with time assuming both positive and negative values, then the average value of $\cos\phi$ will be zero over time interval of measurement. The interference term averages to zero. There will be same intensity $I = I_1 + I_2$ at every point because there will be general illumination on the screen. The two sources in this case are incoherent.

So, if the sources are not coherent, they cannot emit waves continuously due to zero intensity at some instant of time. Hence, coherent sources are used in interference pattern.

11. (*i*) Gauss' law states that the total flux through a closed surface is $\frac{1}{\varepsilon_0}$ times the net charge enclosed by the closed surface. Mathematically, $\phi_E = \oint_S \mathbf{E} \cdot d\mathbf{S} = \frac{q}{\varepsilon_0}$.

Here, ε_0 is the absolute permittivity of the free space, q is the total charge enclosed by the closed surface and **E** is the electric field at the area element $d\mathbf{S}$.

(*ii*) Electric field intensity due to an infinitely long uniformly charged wire at point P at distance r from it is obtained as follows

Consider a thin cylindrical Gaussian surface S with charged wire on its axis and point P on its surface, then net electric flux through surface S is

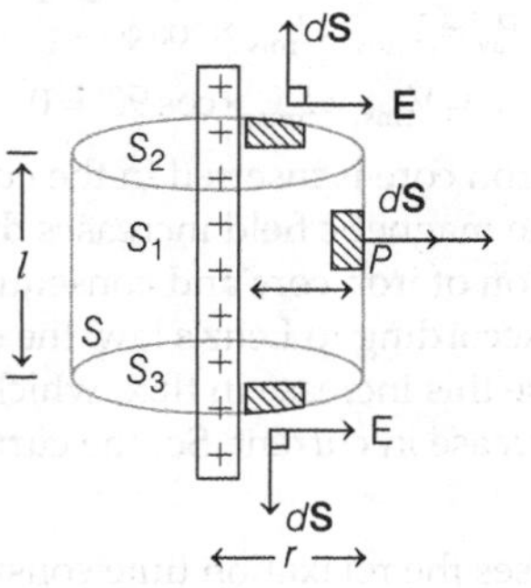

$$\phi = \oint_S \mathbf{E} \cdot d\mathbf{S}$$

$$= \underset{\text{Upper plane face}}{\int EdS\cos 90°} + \underset{\text{Curved surface}}{\int EdS\cos 0°} + \underset{\text{Lower plane face}}{\int EdS\cos 90°}$$

$$\phi = 0 + EA + 0 \text{ or } \phi = E \cdot 2\pi rl$$

But, by Gauss' theorem, $\phi = q/\varepsilon_0 = \lambda l/\varepsilon_0$

where, q is the charge on length l of wire enclosed by cylindrical surface S and λ is uniform linear charge density of wire.

$$\therefore \quad E \times 2\pi rl = \frac{\lambda l}{\varepsilon_0} \Rightarrow E = \frac{\lambda}{2\pi\varepsilon_0 r}$$

Thus, electric field of a line charge is inversely proportional to distance directed normal to the surface of charged wire.

12. Given, length of wire, $l = 4 \text{ m} = 400$ cm

Resistance, $R = 20\Omega$

emf of battery, $\varepsilon = 8$ V

and $R' = 4\Omega$, $x = 40$ cm

(*i*) The current flowing through the circuit,

$$I = \frac{\varepsilon}{R + R'} = \frac{8}{20 + 4} = \frac{1}{3} \text{ A}$$

(*ii*) The terminal potential difference between A and B of the potentiometer will be

$$V_{AB} = IR = \frac{1}{3} \times 20 = \frac{20}{3} \text{ V}$$

$\therefore$ The emf of the primary cell $= \frac{V_{AB}}{l} \times x$

$$= \frac{20}{3 \times 400} \times 40 = \frac{2}{3}\text{ V} \approx 0.66\text{ V}$$

Or

To verify the current values, we use Ohm's law

$$V = IR$$

$$\Rightarrow \quad I = \frac{V}{R}$$

(*i*) For $V = 2\text{ V}$

$$I = \frac{2}{5} = 0.4\text{ A}$$

(*ii*) For $V = 4\text{ V}$

$$I = \frac{4}{5} = 0.8\text{ A}$$

(*iii*) For $V = 6\text{ V}$

$$I = \frac{6}{5} = 1.2\text{ A}$$

(*iv*) For $V = 8\text{ V}$

$$I = \frac{8}{5} = 1.6\text{ A}$$

13. (*i*) The ratio of number of holes and the number of conduction electrons in an *n*-type extrinsic semiconductor is less than 1 because in *n*-type extrinsic semiconductor, number of holes are comparatively less, because electrons are majority charge carriers, i.e. $n_e >> n_h$.

(*ii*) When a *p-n* junction diode is reverse biased, then very small current due to minority charge carriers flows across the junction. This current is called reverse current.

(*iii*) Resistance of a material can be found out by the slope of the curve *V versus I*. Part *BC* of the curve shows the negative resistance as with the increase in voltage, there is a decrease in current.

14. This system can be considered as the series combination of the two capacitors shown in figure given below, in which one having a plate separation $d/3$ and filled with a dielectric constant *K* and the other having a plate separation $2d/3$ and air between its plates.

The capacitances C_1 and C_2 are given by

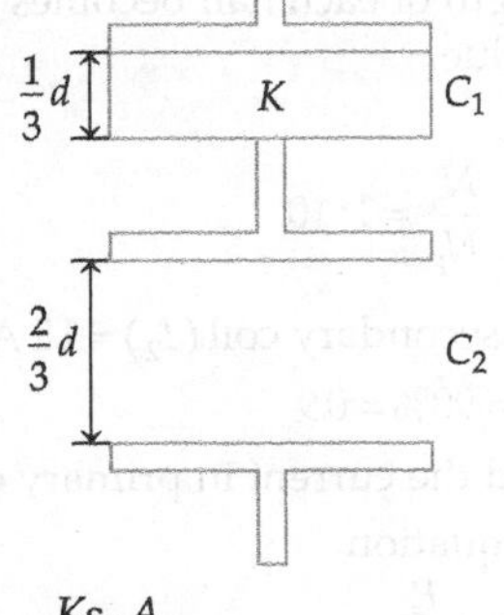

$$C_1 = \frac{K\varepsilon_0 A}{d/3}$$

and $$C_2 = \frac{\varepsilon_0 A}{2d/3}$$

Since, two capacitors are combined in a series combination, so their equivalent capacitance is given by,

$$\frac{1}{C} = \frac{1}{C_1} + \frac{1}{C_2} = \frac{d/3}{K\varepsilon_0 A} + \frac{2d/3}{\varepsilon_0 A}$$

$$\frac{1}{C} = \frac{d}{3\varepsilon_0 A}\left(\frac{1}{K} + 2\right) = \frac{d}{3\varepsilon_0 A}\left(\frac{1+2K}{K}\right)$$

$$C = \left(\frac{3K}{2K+1}\right)\frac{\varepsilon_0 A}{d}$$

Since, the capacitance without the dielectric material is $C_0 = \varepsilon_0 A/d$

We have, $$C = \left(\frac{3K}{2K+1}\right)C_0$$

15. (*i*) In refraction, frequency remains same, so

$$f_{\text{refracted beam}} = f_{\text{incident beam}}$$

Also, $$\mu_{21} = \frac{v_1}{v_2} = \frac{f\lambda_1}{f\lambda_2} = \frac{\lambda_1}{\lambda_2} \qquad [\because v = f\lambda]$$

$$\Rightarrow \quad v_2 = \frac{v_1}{\mu_{21}} = \frac{3 \times 10^8}{1.33} = 2.25 \times 10^8 \text{ ms}^{-1}$$

$$\therefore \quad \lambda_2 = \frac{\lambda_1}{\mu_{21}} = \frac{589}{1.33} = 442.85 \approx 443\text{ nm}$$

So, wavelength of reflected beam ≈ 443 nm and its speed $= 2.25 \times 10^8 \text{ ms}^{-1}$.

(*ii*) For a biconvex lens, using lens Maker's formula,

$$\frac{1}{f} = (\mu - 1)\left(\frac{1}{R_1} - \frac{1}{R_2}\right)$$

Here, $f = 20$ cm, $\mu = 1.55 \Rightarrow R_1 = +R$ and $R_2 = -R$

$\therefore$ We have, $$\frac{1}{f} = (\mu - 1)\frac{2}{R}$$

$$\Rightarrow \quad R = 2(\mu - 1)f = 2 \times (1.55 - 1) \times 20 = 22\text{ cm}$$

$\therefore$ Radius of curvature curvature 22 cm is required.

16. Given that,

Charge $= +5\,\mu\text{C}$

At rest, $x = 30$ cm

From conservation of energy,

$$U_i + K_i = U_f + K_f$$

$$\frac{KQq}{r_i} + 0 = \frac{KQq}{r_f} + K_f$$

$$K_f = KQq\left(\frac{1}{r_i} - \frac{1}{r_f}\right) \quad \ldots \text{(i)}$$

From Eq. (i),

(*i*) When charge is $+15\,\mu\text{C}$,

q will move 15 cm away from it

Hence, $$r_f = 30 + 15 = 45\text{ cm}$$

$$K_f = 9 \times 10^9 \times 15 \times 10^{-6} \times 5 \times 10^{-6}$$

$$\left[\left(\frac{1}{30 \times 10^{-2}}\right) - \left(\frac{1}{45 \times 10^{-2}}\right)\right]$$

$$K_f = 0.75\,\text{J}$$

(*ii*) When charge is $-15\,\mu\text{C}$, q will move 15 cm towards it, hence

$$r_f = 30 - 15 = 15\,\text{cm}$$

$$K_f = 9\times10^9 \times(-15\times10^{-6})\times5\times10^{-6}\left[\left(\frac{1}{30\times10^{-2}} - \frac{1}{15\times10^{-2}}\right)\right]$$

$$K_f = 2.25\,\text{J}$$

17. To find the ponit of coincidence of bright fringes, we can equate the distance of bright fringes from the central maxima, made by both the wavelengths of light.

Given, distance between the screen and slit.

$$D = 1\,\text{m}, \text{ slit width, } d = 4\times10^{-3}\,\text{m}$$
$$\lambda_1 = 560\,\text{nm} = 560\times10^{-9}\,\text{m},$$
$$\lambda_2 = 420\,\text{nm} = 420\times10^{-9}\,\text{m}$$

Let nth order bright fringe of λ_1 coincides with $(n+1)$th order bright fringe of λ_2.

$$\therefore \quad \frac{Dn\lambda_1}{d} = \frac{D(n+1)\lambda_2}{d} \qquad (\lambda_1 > \lambda_2)$$

$$\Rightarrow \quad n\lambda_1 = (n+1)\lambda_2$$

$$\Rightarrow \quad \frac{n+1}{n} = \frac{\lambda_1}{\lambda_2}$$

$$\therefore \quad 1 + \frac{1}{n} = \frac{560\times10^{-9}}{420\times10^{-9}}$$

$$\Rightarrow \quad 1 + \frac{1}{n} = \frac{4}{3}$$

$$n = 3$$

$\therefore$ Least distance from the central fringe where bright fringe of two wavelengths coincides

= Distance of 3rd order bright fringe of λ_1

$$\therefore \quad y_n = \frac{3D\lambda_1}{d} = \frac{3\times1\times560\times10^{-9}}{4\times10^{-3}} = 0.42\times10^{-3}\,\text{m}$$

$$\therefore \quad y_n = 0.42\,\text{mn}$$

3rd bright fringe of λ_1 and 4th bright fringe of λ_2 conicide at 0.42 mm from central fringe.

18. (*i*) Student P because intensity distribution is same for all path difference $0, \pm\lambda, \pm 2\lambda$.

(*ii*) Interference

(*iii*) The given situation is shown in the following diagram.

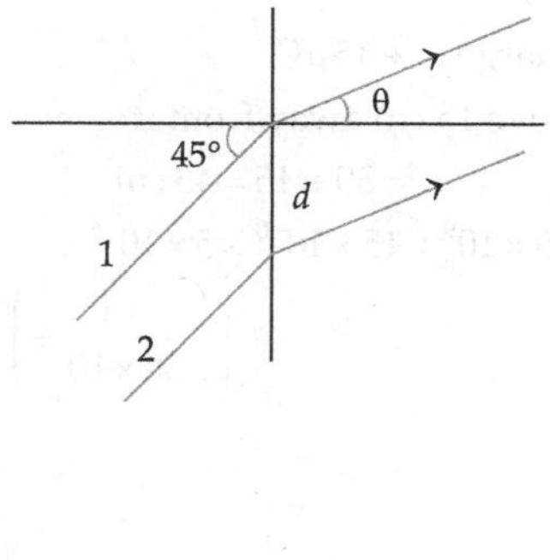

Ray 1 has a longer path than that of ray 2 by a distance $d\sin 45°$, before reaching the slits. Afterwards ray 2 has a path longer than ray 1 by a distance $d\sin\theta$. The net path difference is therefore, $d\sin\theta - d\sin 45°$.

(a) Central maximum is obtained, where net path difference is zero,

$$d\sin\theta - d\sin 45° = 0$$
$$\Rightarrow \quad \theta = 45°$$

(b) Third order maxima is obtained, where net path difference is 3λ, i.e.,

$$d\sin\theta - d\sin 45° = 3\lambda$$
$$\Rightarrow \quad \sin\theta = \sin 45° + \frac{3\lambda}{d}$$

Putting, $d = 20\lambda$, we have

$$\sin\theta = \sin 45° + \frac{3\lambda}{20\lambda}$$
$$\therefore \quad \theta = 59°$$

Or

(*i*) It is clearly visible from the diagram below that air bubble acts as a diverging lens (concave lens) in water.

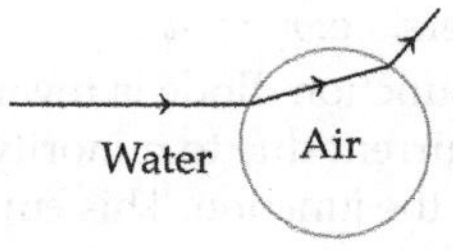

(*ii*) In the given case, concave lens is immersed in a medium having refractive index greater than the refractive index of the material of the lens $(1.65 > 1.5)$. Therefore, it will behave as a converging lens.

(*iii*) Let power of each half of lens is P' and power of whole lens is P.

Hence, $P = P' + P'$

$$P = 2P'$$
$$\frac{1}{f} = \frac{2}{f'}$$
$$f' = 2f$$

$\therefore$ Focal length of each half becomes twice of the original value.

19. (i) Given

turns ratio, $\frac{N_s}{N_p} = 1:10$

Current in secondary coil $(I_2) = 1.2$ A

Efficiency = 90% = 0.9

We can find the current in primary coil (I_P) using the equation,

$$\eta = \frac{P_s}{P_P}$$

$$0.9 = \frac{V_S \cdot I_S}{V_P \cdot I_P}$$

Substitute the given values in I_P, we get

$$I_P = \frac{V_S I_S}{V_P \times 0.9} \qquad \left\{\frac{V_S}{V_P} = \frac{N_S}{N_P}\right\}$$

$$I_P = \frac{1.0 \times 1.2}{0.9} = \frac{120}{9} = 13.33 \text{ A}$$

(ii) (a) Current, $I = I_0 \sin 2\pi v t$

At $t = 0$, $I = 0$

At time $= t$, $\quad I = I_{rms} = \frac{I_0}{\sqrt{2}}$

$$\frac{I_0}{\sqrt{2}} = I_0 \sin 2\pi v t$$

$$\Rightarrow \quad \frac{\pi}{4} = 2\pi v t$$

Solving for t, we get

$$t = \frac{1}{480} = 2 \times 10^{-3} \text{ s}$$

(b) Time taken by current to change from 0 to rms value

= Time taken by the voltage to change from 0 to rms value

= Time taken by voltage to change from rms value to 0.

So, $\quad t = 2 \times 10^{-3}$s as above

Or

According to the given figure,

Variation of the flux

(*i*) When PQ moves forward.

(a) For, $0 \le x < b$

Magnetic field B exists in the region.

Area of loop $PQRS = lx$

Magnetic flux linked with loop $PQRS$,

$$\phi = BA = Blx \qquad \ldots\text{(i)}$$

(b) For, $2b \ge x \ge b$

Magnetic field, $B = 0$

Flux linked with loop $PQRS$ is uniform and given by

$$\phi' = Blb \qquad (\because x = b) \qquad \ldots\text{(ii)}$$

Forward Journey

Thus, for $\quad b > x \ge 0$

Flux, $\quad \phi = Blx$

$\Rightarrow \quad \phi \propto x$

For, $\quad 2b \ge x \ge b$

Flux, $\quad \phi = Bbl \quad$ (constant)

Backward Journey

Flux $\quad b \le x \le 2b$,

$\phi =$ constant $= Bbl$

For, $\quad 0 \le x \le b$,

$\phi = Blx \quad$ (decreasing)

Graphical Representation

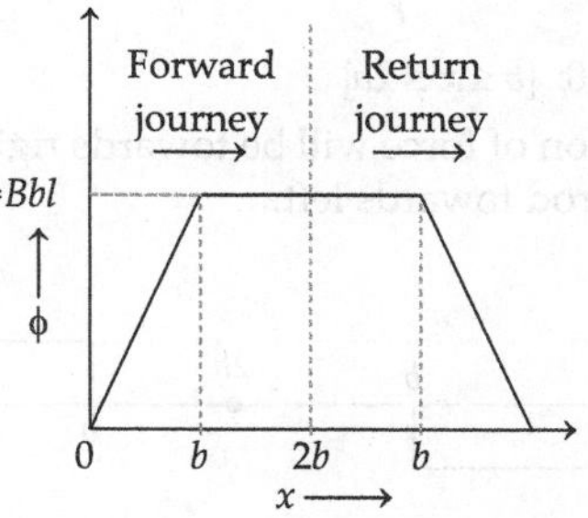

(*ii*) Variation of emf

For, $b > x \ge 0$,

As, $\phi = Blx$

$$\Rightarrow \quad \frac{d\phi}{dt} = Bl\frac{dx}{dt} = Bvl \qquad \left[\because v = \frac{dx}{dt}\right]$$

Induced emf,

$$e = -\frac{d\phi}{dt} = -vBl$$

For, $2b \ge x \ge b$,

As, $\quad \phi' = Bbl$

$$\Rightarrow \quad \frac{d\phi'}{dt} = 0$$

$\Rightarrow \quad e = 0$

Forward Journey

For, $\quad b > x \ge 0$

$\Rightarrow \quad e = -vBl$

For, $\quad 2b \ge x \ge b$

$\Rightarrow \quad e = 0$

Backward Journey

For, $\quad b > x \ge 0$

$\Rightarrow \quad e = vBl$

For, $\quad 2b \ge x \ge b$, $e = 0$

Variation of induced emf

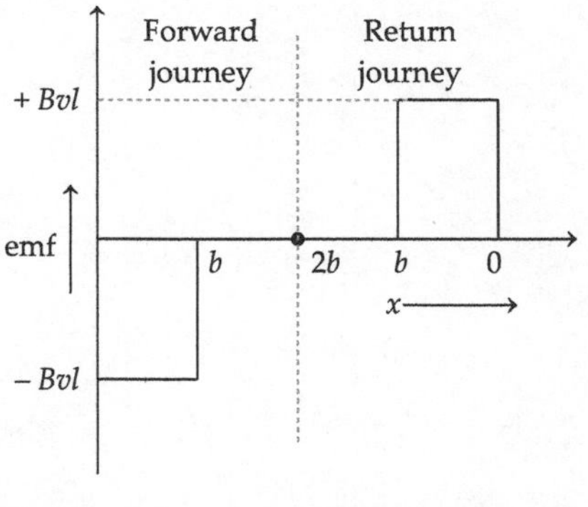

(*iii*) Similarly, the force required to keep arm PQ in constant motion is $F = IlB$. Its direction is to the left. In magnitude,

$$F = IlB = -\frac{B^2l^2v}{r}; \quad [0 \le x < b]$$

$$= 0; \ [b \le x \le 2b]$$

direction of force will be towards right when we move rod towards left.

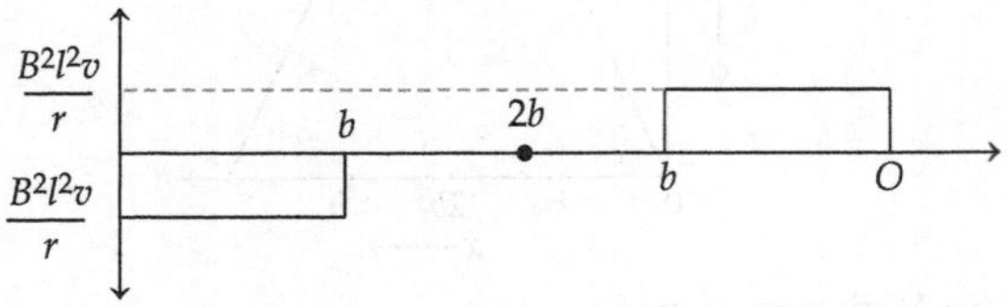

20. (*i*) Lyman series lies in the ultraviolet region.

(*ii*) Absorption lines are obtained when an e^- absorbs a photon in ground state and is excited to a higher state.

Initially e^- is in ground state, so transition states are 1, 2, and 3 and wevelengths are λ_1, λ_2 and λ_3.

(*iii*) (a) $\frac{1}{\lambda} = RZ^2\left(\frac{1}{n_1^2} - \frac{1}{n_2^2}\right) \Rightarrow \lambda \propto \frac{1}{Z^2}$

$\lambda_{Li^{++}} : \lambda_{He^+} : \lambda_H = 4:9:36$

(b) Wavelength is given by $\frac{1}{\lambda} = R\left(\frac{1}{n_1^2} - \frac{1}{n_2^2}\right)$

$$\Rightarrow \quad \frac{1}{\lambda} = R\left[\frac{1}{(2)^2} - \frac{1}{(4)^2}\right]$$

$$\Rightarrow \quad \frac{1}{\lambda} = R\left(\frac{1}{4} - \frac{1}{16}\right) \Rightarrow \quad \frac{1}{\lambda} = R\left(\frac{4-1}{16}\right)$$

$$\Rightarrow \quad \frac{1}{\lambda} = \frac{3R}{16}$$

$$\Rightarrow \quad \lambda = \frac{16}{3R}$$

Common Mistakes Take value of n_1 and n_2 carefully, remembering the initial and final state.

SQP Code : **PB-7/15** Series **i-Succeed 7-25/15** Roll No.

Sample Question Paper 07

Physics 12th (Code 861)

General Instructions

1. This paper is divided into four Sections- A, B, C and D. Answer all questions.
2. **Section A** consists of one question having sub-parts of one mark each.
3. **Section B** consists of seven questions of two marks each.
4. **Section C** consists of nine questions of three marks each.
5. **Section D** consists of three questions of five marks each.
6. Internal choices have been provided in two questions each in Section B, Section C and Section D.

Time : 3 Hrs.

Max. Marks : 70

Section A (14 Marks)

1. A. In questions (i) to (vii) below, choose the correct alternative (a), (b), (c) or (d) for each of the questions given below

(i) SI unit of electrical permittivity is • *Recall* [1]

(a) Nm^2C^{-2} (b) Am^{-2}

(c) NC^{-1} (d) $C^2N^{-1}m^{-2}$

(ii) The angular momentum of an electron in hydrogen atom in ground state is] • *Recall* [1]

(a) $\frac{h}{\pi}$ (b) $\frac{h}{2\pi}$

(c) $\frac{2\pi}{h}$ (d) $\frac{\pi}{h}$

(iii) **Assertion** (A) The magnetic field produced by a current carrying solenoid is independent of its length and cross-sectional area.

Reason (R) The magnetic field inside the solenoid is uniform. • *Analysis* [1]

(a) Both Assertion and Reason are true and Reason is the correct explanation for Assertion.

(b) Both Assertion and Reason are true but Reason is not the correct explanation for Assertion.

(c) Assertion is false and Reason is true.

(d) Both Assertion and Reason are false.

(iv) The resistance of a 10 m long wire is 10Ω. Its length is increased by 25% by stretching the wire uniformly. The resistance of wire will change to • *Analysis* [1]

(a) 12.5 Ω (b) 14.5 Ω

(c) 15.6 Ω (d) 16.6 Ω

(v) A plane wavefront is incident on a concave mirror of radius of curvature R. The radius of the reflected wavefront will be • *Analysis* [1]

(a) $2R$ (b) R (c) $\frac{R}{2}$ (d) $\frac{R}{4}$

(vi) **Assertion** (A) Photoelectric saturation current increases with the increase in frequency of incident light.

Reasion (R) Energy of incident photons increases with increase in frequency and as a result photoelectric current increases. • *Understanding* [1]

(a) Both Assertion and Reason are true and Reason is the correct explanation for Assertion.

(b) Both Assertion and Reason are true but Reason is not the correct explanation for Assertion.

(c) Assertion is false and Reason is true.

(d) Both Assertion and Reason are false.

(*vii*) In an extrinsic semiconductor, the number density of holes is $4 \times 10^{20} \text{ m}^{-1}$. If the number density of intrinsic carriers is $1.2 \times 10^{15} \text{ m}^{-3}$, the number density of electrons in it is • *Understanding*

(a) $1.8 \times 10^{9} \text{ m}^{-3}$

(b) $2.4 \times 10^{10} \text{ m}^{-3}$

(c) $3.6 \times 10^{9} \text{ m}^{-3}$

(d) $3.2 \times 10^{-10} \text{ m}^{-3}$

B. Answer the following questions briefly.

(*i*) Can 8.6×10^{-19} coulomb of charge be given to a conductor? Explain. • *Application* [1]

(*ii*) An emf of 2 V is induced in a coil, when current in it is changed from 0 A to 10 A in 0.4 s. Find the coefficient of self-inductance of the coil. • *Recall* [1]

(*iii*) What is the value of (a) impedance and (b) power factor of *L-C-R* series resonant circuit? • *Recall* [1]

(*iv*) The phase difference between the two light waves reaching at a point is 100π, then what is their path difference? • *Understanding* [1]

(*v*) State the factors on which the refractive index of a material medium for a given wavelength depends. • *Recall* [1]

(*vi*) Can a slab of *p*-type semiconductor be physically joined to another *n*-type semiconductor slab to form *p-n* junction? Justify your answer. • *Recall* [1]

(*vii*) A circular coil having *N* turns carries a current *I*. Write the expression for the magnetic moment of this coil, if its radius is *r*. • *Recall* [1]

Section B (14 Marks)

2. (*i*) Explain the property of a *p-n* junction which makes it suitable for rectifying alternating voltages. • *Recall* [1]

(*ii*) Give two differences between a half-wave and a full wave rectifier. • *Recall* [1]

Or In the following diagram, which bulb out of B_1 and B_2 will glow and why? • *Application* [2]

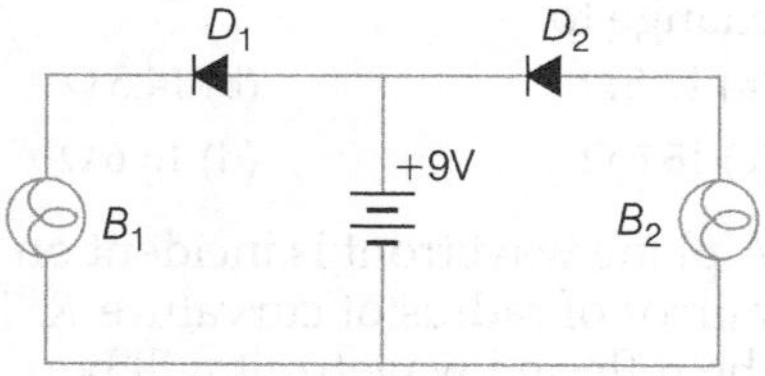

3. In series *L-C-R* circuit, the plot of I_{max} *versus* ω is shown in the figure. Find the bandwidth from the graph shown in figure. • *Application* [2]

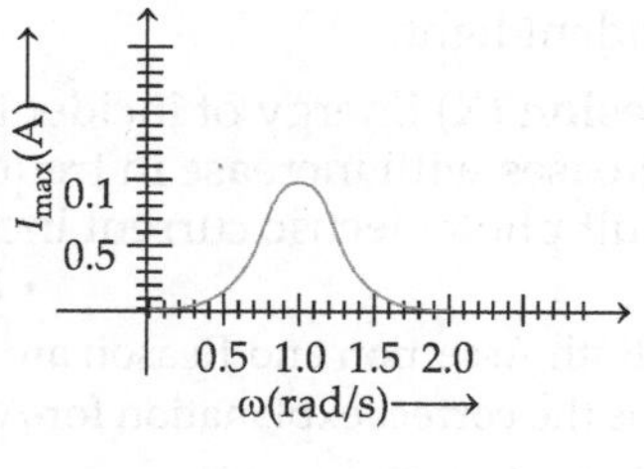

4. (*i*) Why do stable nuclei never have more protons than neutrons? • *Recall* [1]

(*ii*) Which property is responsible for consistency of binding energy per nucleon (E_n)? • *Recall* [1]

5. (*i*) An electromagnetic wave is travelling in a medium with a velocity $\mathbf{v} = v\hat{\mathbf{i}}$. Draw a sketch showing the propagation of the electromagnetic wave indicating the direction of the oscillating electric and magnetic fields. • *Application* [1]

(*ii*) How are the magnitudes of the electric and magnetic fields related to velocity of the electromagnetic wave? • *Recall* [1]

6. Write Einstein's photoelectric equation relating the maximum kinetic energy of the emitted electron to the frequency of the radiation incident on a photosensitive surface. Also, explain the term threshold frequency. • *Application* [2]

7. Calculate the radius of curvature of an equi-concave lens of refractive index 1.5, when it is kept in a medium of refractive index 1.4, to have a power of –5 D ? • *Application* [2]

8. A 100 turns closely wound circular coil of radius 10 cm carries a current of 3.2 A in anti-clockwise direction. What is the *(i)* magnitude and *(ii)* direction of the field at the centre of the coil? • *Application* [2]

Section C (27 Marks)

9. Write the two processes that take place in the formation of a *p-n* junction. Explain with the help of a diagram, the formation of depletion region and barrier potential in a *p-n* junction. • *Application* [3]

10. *(i)* Draw a ray diagram to show image formation when the concave mirror produces a real, inverted and magnified image of the object. • *Recall* [1]

(ii) Obtain the mirror formula. • *Application* [2]

11. A current of 1A is flowing through a copper wire of length 0.1m and cross-section $1 \times 10^{-6}\,\text{m}^2$.

(i) If the specific resistance of copper is $1.7 \times 10^{-8}\ \Omega$-m, then calculate the potential difference across the ends of the wire.

(ii) Determine current density in the wire. (Take, density of copper $= 8.9 \times 10^3$ kg m^{-3}, atomic weight = 63.5 and $N = 6.02 \times 10^{26}$ per kg-atom) • *Understanding* [3]

Or

In an electric circuit shown, a network of resistors is connected across a cell of emf 2V and internal resistance $0.5\,\Omega$.

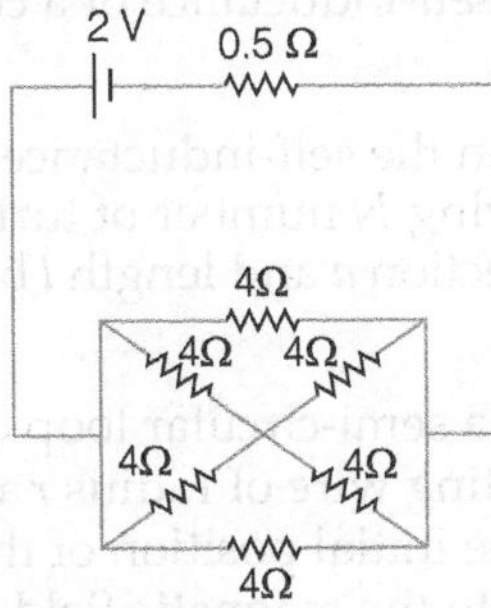

(i) What is the total current drawn from the battery by the circuit?

(ii) What is the power consumed by the circuit from the battery? • *Analysis* [3]

Or A charged particle is moving on a circular path of radius *R* in a uniform magnetic field under the Lorentz force *F*. How much work is done by the force in one round? Is the momentum of particle changing ? • *Understanding* [2]

12. A student records the following data for the angle of minimum deviation δ_m for four different prism with angle $A = 60°$. The refractive index μ of the prism material is calculated for each measurement. Verify (for any two) that these observations are in good agreement with the expected theoretical value of μ. • *Application* [3]

δ_m	30°	35°	40°	45°
μ	1.41	1.46	1.5	1.6

Or

Using Huygens' principle, verify the law of reflection at the plane surface. • *Application* [3]

13. In a parallel plate capacitor with air between the plates, each plate has an area of $6 \times 10^{-3}\,\text{m}^2$ and the distance between the plates is 3 mm.

(i) Calculate the capacitance of the capacitor. [2]

(ii) If this capacitor is connected to a 100 V supply, what is the charge on each plate of the capacitor? • *Recall* [1]

14. Derive an expression for the velocity v_c of a positive ions passing undeflected through a region, where crossed and uniform electric field *E* and magnetic field *B* are simultaneously present.

Draw and justify the trajectory of identical positive ions whose velocity has a magnitude less than $|v_c|$. • *Application* [3]

15. A small telescope has an objective lens of focal length 140 cm and an eyepiece of focal length 5 cm. What is the magnifying power of the telescope for viewing distant objects

(i) when the telescope is in normal adjustment (i.e. when the final image is at infinity). • *Recall*

(*ii*) when the final image is formed at the least distance of distinct vision (25 cm)? • *Recall* [3]

16. (*i*) A dielectric slab of relative permittivity (i.e. dielectric constant) 10 is introduced between the two given charges each of 8 μC charge separated by distance *r* apart. Find the ratio of electrostatic force between them before and after introduction of dielectric medium. • *Understanding* [1]

(*ii*) Write an expression (derivation not required) for intensity of electric field in
(a) axial position
(b) broad-side-on position
of an electric dipole, in terms of its length ($2a$), dipole moment (p) and distance (r) from mid-point of dipole. • *Application* [2]

17. A resistance of *R* draws current from a potentiometer. The potentiometer wire *AB*, has a total resistance of R_0. A voltage *V* is supplied to the potentiometer. Derive an expression for the voltage across *R*, when the sliding contact is in the middle of potentiometer wire. • *Analysis* [3]

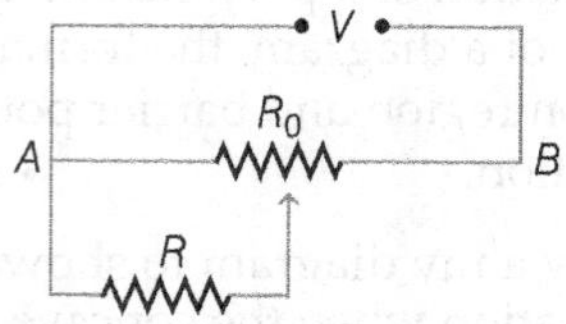

Section D (15 Marks)

18. A plane wavefront of light of wavelength λ, is incident on a narrow slit, an intensity distribution pattern, of the form shown is observed on a screen, suitably kept behind the slit.

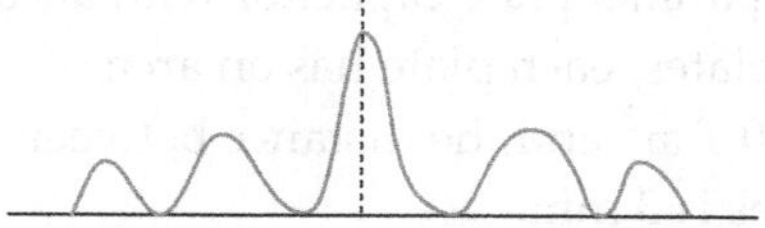

(*i*) Name the phenomenon observed. • *Analysis* [1]

(*ii*) Obtain the conditions for the formation of central maximum and secondary maxima and the minima. • *Analysis* [2]

(*iii*) Why is there significant fall in intensity of the secondary maxima compared to the central maximum, whereas in double slit experiment all the bright fringes are of the same intensity? • *Application* [2]

Or (*i*) With the help of a ray diagram, show the formation of image of a point object by refraction of light at a spherical surface separating two media of refractive indices n_1 and n_2 ($n_2 > n_1$), respectively.
(a) Using a diagram, derive the relation
$$\frac{n_2}{v} - \frac{n_1}{u} = \frac{n_2 - n_1}{R}$$
• *Application* [3]
(b) Write the sign conventions used. • *Application* [1]

(*ii*) An unsymmetrical double convex thin lens forms the image of a point object on its axis. Will the position of the image change, if the lens is reversed? • *Application* [1]

19. (*i*) Derive the expression for the current flowing in an ideal capacitor and its reactance when connected to an AC source of voltage $V = V_0 \sin \omega t$. • *Application* [2]

(*ii*) Draw its phasor diagram. • *Recall* [2]

(*iii*) If resistance is added in series to capacitor, what changes will occur in the current flowing in the circuit and phase angle between voltage and current. • *Application* [1]

Or (*i*) Define self-inductance of a coil. Write its SI unit. • *Recall* [1]

(*ii*) How can the self-inductance of a given coil having *N* number of turns, area of cross-section *a* and length *l* be increased ? • *Analysis* [1]

(*iii*) *ADC* is a semi-circular loop of conducting wire of radius *r* and centred at *O*. The initial position of the loop with respect to the magnetic field is shown in Fig a. The loop is then pulled into the magnetic field (Fig. b) and makes two complete rotations about point *O*.

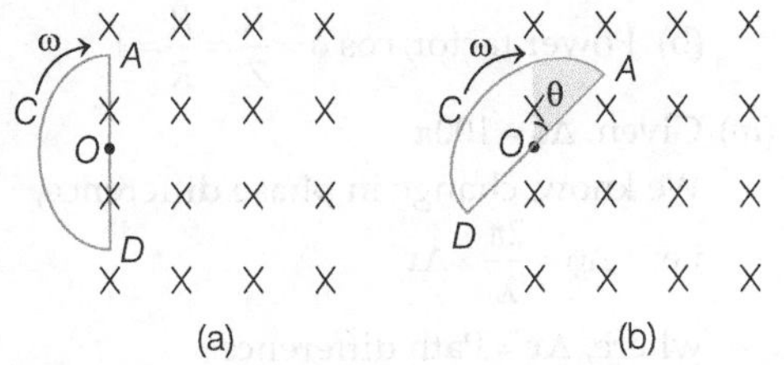

(a) Plot a graph between the induced current I and the angle of rotation θ for two complete periods of rotations. • *Application*

(b) Depict the above graph in case the loop ADC revolves with angular frequency $\omega > \omega'$. Keep all other conditions fixed as earlier. Give a reason for the change depicted in the graph. • *Application* [3]

20. Nuclear fission is the phenomenon of splitting of a heavy nucleus (usually $A > 230$) into two or more lighter nuclei by the bombardment of proton, neutron, α-particle, etc. Energies associated with nuclear processes are about a million times larger than chemical process. In fission, a heavy nucleus like ${}^{235}_{92}U$ breaks into two smaller fragments by the bombardment of thermal neutron (low energy or slow moving).

e.g. $${}^{235}_{92}U + {}^{1}_{0}n \longrightarrow {}^{141}_{56}Ba + {}^{92}_{36}Kr + 3{}_{0}n^{1} + Q$$ (Energy released)

Q-value here refer to the energy released in the nuclear process, which can be determined using Einstein's mass-energy relation, $E = mc^2$. The Q-value is equal to the difference of mass of products and reactants multiplied by square of velocity of light. Energy released per fission of ${}^{235}_{92}U$ is 200.4 MeV. The fragment nuclei produced in fission are highly unstable.

They are highly radioactive and emit β-particle in succession until each reaches to a stable end product.

(*i*) What are moderators? Give few examples. • *Recall* [1]

(*ii*) Define the Q-value of a nuclear process. In which condition, a nuclear process cannot proceed spontaneously? • *Application* [2]

(*iii*) (a) What is multiplicity in nuclear fission? • *Recall*

(b) Write different operation conditions of a reactor depending on the value of multiplicity. • *Application* [2]

Solutions *in Topper's Style*

My Commitment *I affirm that I am reviewing these solutions only after I have solved the Sample Question Paper 7 on my own. My purpose of looking the solutions is solely to verify whether my answers/solutions were correct or not and to identify my mistakes in case my solutions were wrong or I could not solve that.*

1. A. (*i*) (*d*) From Coulomb's law, $F = \frac{1}{4\pi\varepsilon_0} \cdot \frac{q_1 q_2}{r^2}$

$\therefore$ Electrical permittivity,

$$\varepsilon_0 = \frac{q_1 q_2}{4\pi \times F \times r^2} = \frac{C \times C}{N \times m^2}$$

$\therefore$ Unit of electrical permittivity $= C^2N^{-1}m^{-2}$

(*ii*) (*b*) From the formula of angular momentum and Bohr' assumption, $mvr = n\left(\frac{h}{2\pi}\right)$

Here, $n = 1 \Rightarrow mvr = \frac{h}{2\pi}$

(*iii*) (*b*) The magnetic field due to solenoid having n number of turns/m and carrying current I is $B = \mu_0 nI$.

It is obvious that magnetic field is independent of length and cross-sectional area. Also, magnetic field is uniform inside the solenoid.

(*iv*) (*c*) Given, $l_1 = l + \frac{25}{100}l = \frac{5l}{4}$

Since, volume of wire remains unchanged on increasing length, hence

$$\Rightarrow \quad A_1 l_1 = Al$$

$$\Rightarrow \quad A_1 \times \frac{5l}{4} = Al$$

$$\text{or} \quad A_1 = \frac{4}{5}A$$

Given, $R = \frac{\rho l}{A} = 10\Omega$

$$\Rightarrow R_1 = \frac{\rho l_1}{A_1} = \frac{\rho \frac{5l}{4}}{\frac{4A}{5}} = \frac{25\rho l}{16A}$$

$$\therefore \quad R_1 = \frac{25}{16} \times 10 = \frac{250}{16} = 15.6\,\Omega$$

(*v*) (*c*)

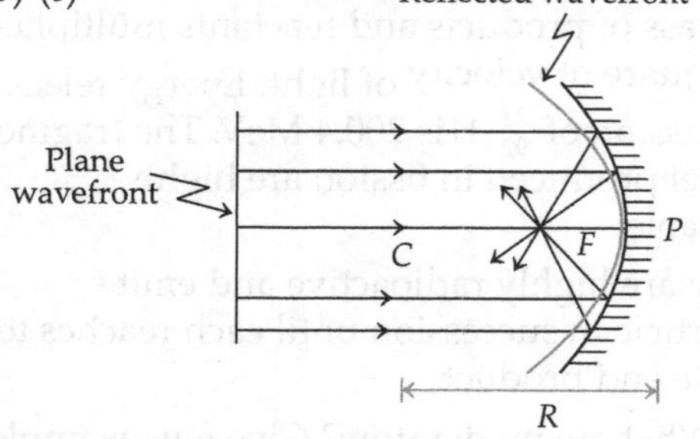

As, the reflected wavefront is a sphere with focal length (f) of concave mirror as its radius.

$\therefore$ The radius of the reflected wavefront is $r = \frac{R}{2}$

(*vi*) (*d*) Photoelectric saturation current increases with increase in intensity of incident light, keeping the frequency of radiation constant and the energy of incident photons increases with increases in frequency, current remaining same.

(*vii*) (*c*) Given

Number density of holes $= 4 \times 10^{20}\ m^{-1}$

Number density of intrinsic carriers $= 1.2 \times 10^{15}\ m^{-3}$

As, $n_i^2 = p \times n$

where, p is the number density of holes and n is the number density of electrons.

$\Rightarrow \quad (1.2 \times 10^{15})^2 = 4 \times 10^{20} \times n$

We get, $n = \frac{(1.2 \times 10^{15})^2}{4 \times 10^{20}} = 3.6 \times 10^9\ m^{-3}$

B. (*i*) Charge on any conductor can be only an integral multiple of charge present on the electron (quantisation of charge), then $q = ne$

where, $n = 1, 2, 3, \ldots$

Now, $n = \frac{8.6 \times 10^{-19}}{1.6 \times 10^{-19}} = 5.4$

[this is a fraction and not an integer]

So, 8.6×10^{-19} coulomb of charge can't be given to a conductor.

(*ii*) Given, $e = 2$ V and change in current, $\frac{di}{dt} = \frac{10}{0.4}$ A/s

$\therefore$ Coefficient of self-inductance of coil is given by

$$L = e \times \frac{dt}{di} \Rightarrow L = 2 \times \frac{0.4}{10} = \frac{0.8}{10} = 0.08\ \text{H}$$

(*iii*) For *L-C-R* series resonant circuit, $X_L = X_C$

(a) Impedance, $Z = \sqrt{R^2 + (X_L - X_C)^2} = \sqrt{R^2 + 0}$

$\Rightarrow \quad Z = R$

(b) Power factor, $\cos\phi = \frac{R}{Z} = \frac{R}{R} = 1$

(*iv*) Given, $\Delta\phi = 100\pi$

We know, change in phase difference,

i.e. $\quad \Delta\phi = \frac{2\pi}{\lambda} \times \Delta x$

where, Δx = Path difference

$$\Rightarrow \quad \Delta x = \Delta\phi \times \frac{\lambda}{2\pi} = 100\pi \times \frac{\lambda}{2\pi} = 50\lambda$$

(*v*) (a) Nature of a medium, i.e. its density (e.g. $\mu_g = 1.5$ and $\mu_w = 1.33$)

(b) With increase in the temperature, the speed of light in medium increases. Therefore, the refractive index of medium decreases.

(*vi*) No, two different slabs of *p*-type and *n*-type semiconductor cannot be physically joined to form *p-n* junction. It is because, two different slabs have different extent of doping of impurity atom in them. So, the characteristics of a *p-n* junction diode are not met by this process.

(*vii*) Magnetic moment of circular coil is given by

$$M = NIA = NI(\pi r^2)$$

$[\because A = \text{area of the coil} = \pi r^2]$

i.e. $\quad M = \pi N I r^2$

2. (*i*) The *p-n* junction is a rectifier diode because it has asymmetric voltage or current characteristics, allowing the current to flow in only one direction.

(*ii*)

Half-wave rectifier	Full wave rectifier
In half-wave rectifier, only one diode is used.	In full wave rectifier two diodes are used.
Electric current is not continuous.	Electric current is continuous.

Or

In the diagram, diode D_1 is in forward bias and diode D_2 in reverse bias. So, current will flow through D_1 and D_2 will not allow flowing the current. So, bulb B_1 will glow and bulb B_2 will not glow.

3. Consider the diagram,

Bandwidth $= \omega_2 - \omega_1$

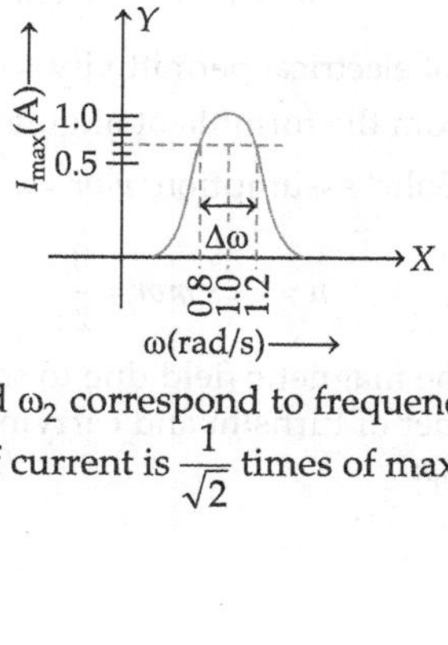

where, ω_1 and ω_2 correspond to frequencies at which magnitude of current is $\frac{1}{\sqrt{2}}$ times of maximum value.

$$I_{rms} = \frac{I_{max}}{\sqrt{2}} = \frac{1}{\sqrt{2}} \approx 0.7 \text{ A}$$

From figure, bandwidth, $\Delta\omega = 1.2 - 0.8 = 0.4$ rad/s

4. (*i*) Because the protons are positively charged, so they repel each other. Since, this repulsion force is more, so that an excess of neutrons are required to reduce this repulsion.

(*ii*) Nuclear forces are saturated in character. This property makes binding energy per nucleon constant for most of the nuclei.

5. (*i*) Given that velocity, $\mathbf{v} = v\hat{\mathbf{i}}$, i.e. the wave is propagating along X-axis, so electric field **E** is along Y-axis and magnetic field **B** is along Z-axis. The propagation of electromagnetic wave is shown in the following figure.

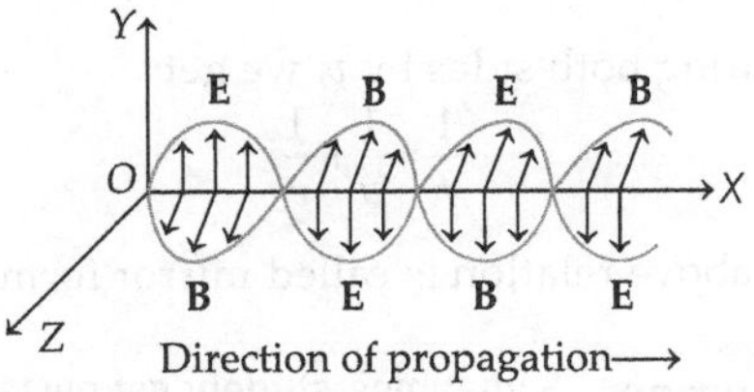

(*ii*) Speed of electromagnetic wave can be given as

$$c = \frac{E_0}{B_0}$$

where, E_0 and B_0 are peak values of E and B, respectively.

6. Einstein's photoelectric equation relating the maximum kinetic energy $\left(KE_{max} = \frac{1}{2}mv_{max}^2\right)$ of the emitted electron to the frequency (ν) of the radiation incident on a photosensitive surface is given by

$$E = \phi + KE_{max} \quad \text{or} \quad h\nu = h\nu_0 + eV_0$$

where, h is the Planck's constant, ν_0 is the threshold frequency, e is the electronic charge and V_0 is the stopping potential.

Threshold Frequency For a given material, there exists a certain minimum frequency of the incident radiation below which no emission of photoelectrons take place. This frequency is called threshold frequency.

7. Given, $\mu_1 = 1.4, \mu_2 = 1.5, P = -5$ D

Using lens Maker's formula,

$$P = \frac{1}{f} = \left(\frac{\mu_2 - \mu_1}{\mu_1}\right)\left(\frac{1}{R_1} - \frac{1}{R_2}\right)$$

$$-5 = \left(\frac{1.5 - 1.4}{1.4}\right)\left(-\frac{1}{R} - \frac{1}{R}\right)$$

(For equi-concave lens, $R_1 = -R$ and $R_2 = R$)

$$-5 = \frac{0.1}{1.4}\left(-\frac{2}{R}\right)$$

$$\Rightarrow \quad R = \frac{1}{14} \times \frac{2}{5} = \frac{1}{35}$$

$$= 0.0286 \text{ m} = 2.86 \text{ cm}$$

8. We know that, the magnetic field at the centre of circular coil of radius R, number of turns N and current I flowing through it, is given by $B = \frac{\mu_0 NI}{2R}$

(*i*) Here, $N = 100$, $I = 3.2$A and $R = 10$ cm $= 0.1$ m

$$\text{Hence, } B = \frac{4\pi \times 10^{-7} \times 100 \times 3.2}{2 \times 0.1}$$

$$= 2\pi \times 3.2 \times 10^{-4} = 2.011 \times 10^{-3} \text{T}$$

$$\simeq 2 \times 10^{-3} \text{T}$$

(*ii*) The direction of the magnetic field is given by the right hand thumb rule, so it is toward upward direction.

Or

When a charged particle is moving on a circular path in a uniform magnetic field, the angle between force **F** due to magnetic field and small displacement $d\mathbf{r}$ is 90°. i.e. The magnetic force is perpendicular to the velocity of the particle. So, work done, $dW = \mathbf{F} \cdot d\mathbf{r} = F \cdot dr \cos 90° = 0$. Since, the velocity of the particle is tangent to the circular path at any point, hence velocity or momentum is changing during circular motion.

9. Two processes that take place during the formation of p-n junction are diffusion and drift of charge carriers.

In a n-type semiconductor, the concentration of electrons is more than that of holes. Similarly, in a p-type semiconductor, the concentration of holes is more than that of electrons. Formation of depletion region during formation of p-n junction and due to the concentration gradient across p and n-sides, holes diffuse from p-side to n-side ($p \to n$) and electrons diffuse from n-side to p-side ($n \to p$). The diffused charge carriers combine with their counterparts in the immediate vicinity of the junction and neutralise each other.

Thus, near the junction, positive charge is built on n-side and negative charge on p-side.

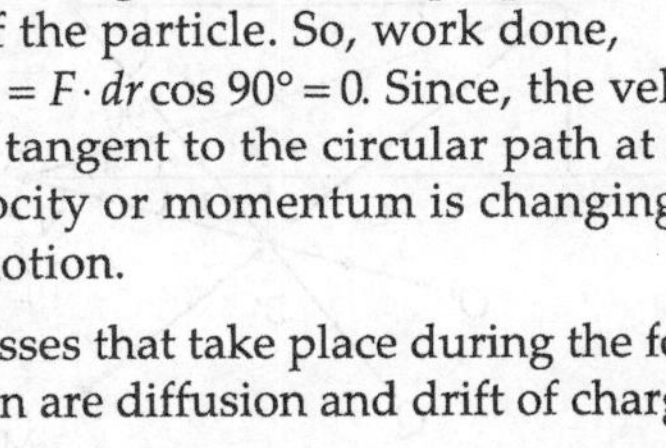

This sets up potential difference across the junction and an internal electric field E_i directed from n-side to p-side. The equilibrium is established when the field E_i becomes strong enough to stop further diffusion of the majority charge carriers (however, it helps the minority charge carriers to drift across the junction).

The region on either side of the junction which becomes depleted (free) from the mobile charge carriers is called **depletion region** or depletion layer. The potential difference developed across the depletion region is called the **potential barrier**.

10. (*i*) Concave mirror form real, inverted and magnified image of an object when it is placed between C and F. The ray diagram is given as

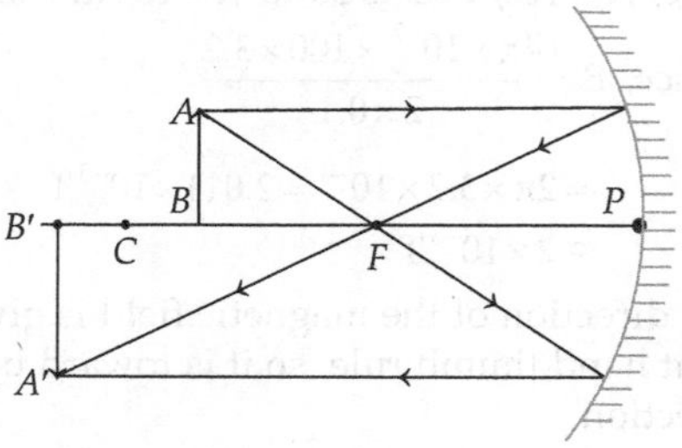

(*ii*) In the given figure, the ray diagram considering three rays for image formation by a concave mirror.

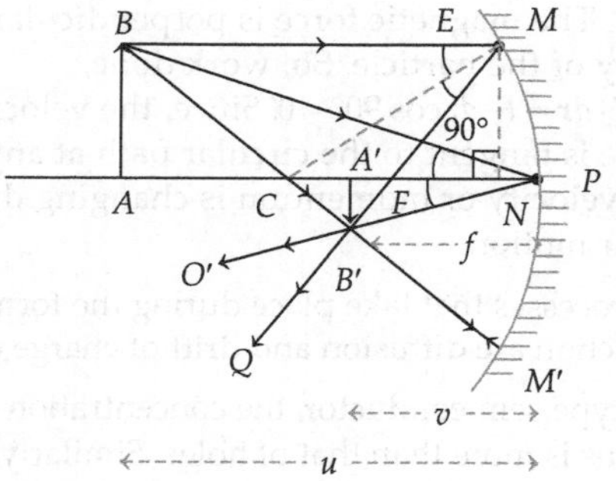

Triangles $A'B'F$ and NEF are similar, then

$$\frac{A'B'}{NE} = \frac{A'F}{NF}$$

As the aperture of the concave mirror is small, the points N and P lie very close to each other.

$$NF \approx PF \text{ and } NE = AB$$

$$\frac{A'B'}{AB} = \frac{A'F}{PF}$$

Since, all the distances are measured from the pole of the concave mirror, we have

$$A'F = PA' - PF$$

$$\therefore \quad \frac{A'B'}{AB} = \frac{PA' - PF}{PF} \quad \ldots\text{(i)}$$

Also, triangles ABP and $A'B'P$ are similar, then

$$\frac{A'B'}{AB} = \frac{PA'}{PA} \quad \ldots\text{(ii)}$$

From Eqs. (i) and (ii), we get

$$\frac{PA' - PF}{PF} = \frac{PA'}{PA} \quad \ldots\text{(iii)}$$

Applying new Cartesian sign convention, we have

$$PA = -u$$

($\because$ distance of object is measured against incident ray)

$$PA' = -v$$

($\because$ distance of image is measured against incident ray)

$$PF = -f$$

($\because$ focal length of concave mirror is measured against incident ray)

Substituting these values in Eq. (iii), we get

$$\frac{-v-(-f)}{-f} = \frac{-v}{-u}$$

$$\Rightarrow \quad \frac{v-f}{f} = \frac{v}{u}$$

$$\Rightarrow \quad \frac{v}{f} - 1 = \frac{v}{u}$$

Dividing both sides by v, we get

$$\therefore \quad \frac{1}{f} = \frac{1}{u} + \frac{1}{v}$$

The above relation is called mirror formula.

Common Mistakes Sometimes, student get mistakes in sign convention during measuring various distances from poles.

11. Given, $I = 1\,\text{A}$, $l = 0.1\,\text{m}$, $A = 1 \times 10^{-6}\ \text{m}^2$,

$$\rho = 1.7 \times 10^{-8}\ \Omega\text{-m},\ d = 8.9 \times 10^{3}\ \text{kg m}^{-3}.$$

(*i*) Resistance of wire, $R = \frac{\rho l}{A} = \frac{1.7 \times 10^{-8} \times 0.1}{1 \times 10^{-6}}$

$$= 1.7 \times 10^{-3}\ \Omega$$

$\therefore$ Potential difference, $V = IR = 1 \times 1.7 \times 10^{-3}$

$$= 1.7 \times 10^{-3}\ \text{V}$$

(*ii*) Current density, $J = \frac{I}{A} = \frac{1}{1 \times 10^{-6}} = 1 \times 10^{6}\ \text{A-m}^{-2}$

Or

(i) Equivalent network,

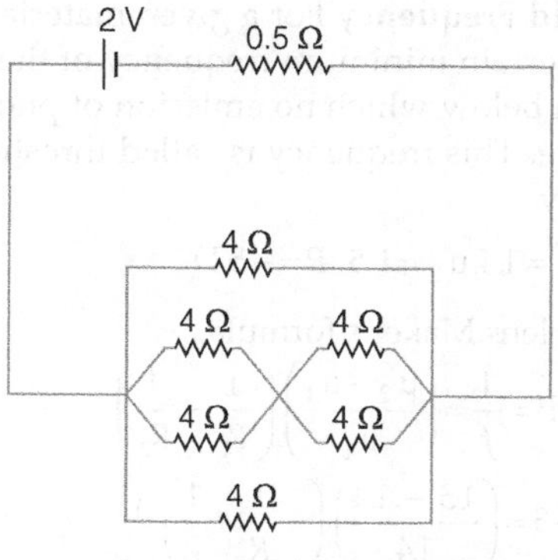

Applying the principle of resistors in parallel and series,

$$R_{eq} = \frac{4}{3}\Omega$$

Current is drawn from the cell due to total resistance

$= \frac{4}{3}\Omega + 0.5\,\Omega$ in series $= \frac{11}{6}\Omega$

$V = RI$

So, current drawn from the cell,

$$I = 2 \times \frac{6}{11} = \frac{12}{11}\text{ A} \approx 1.1\text{ A}$$

(ii) Power consumed by the circuit

$$= I^2 R = \left(\frac{12}{11}\right)^2 \cdot \left(\frac{11}{6}\right) = \frac{24}{11} = 2.2\text{ W}$$

12. The refractive index of the prism material can be determined using the formula

$$\mu = \frac{\sin\left(\frac{A+\delta_m}{2}\right)}{\sin\left(\frac{A}{2}\right)}$$

(i) For $\delta_m = 30°$,

$$\mu = \frac{\sin\left(\frac{60° + 30°}{2}\right)}{\sin\left(\frac{60°}{2}\right)} = \frac{\sin(45°)}{\sin(30°)} = \frac{0.7071}{0.5}$$

$$\mu = 1.414$$

(ii) For $\delta_m = 35°$,

$$\mu = \frac{\sin\left(\frac{60° + 35°}{2}\right)}{\sin\left(\frac{60°}{2}\right)}$$

$$= \frac{\sin(47.5°)}{\sin(30°)} \approx \frac{0.7314}{0.5}$$

$$\mu = 1.463$$

(iii) For $\delta_m = 40°$,

$$\mu = \frac{\sin\left(\frac{60° + 40°}{2}\right)}{\sin\left(\frac{60°}{2}\right)} = \frac{\sin(50°)}{\sin(30°)} = \frac{0.7660}{0.5}$$

$$\mu = 1.532$$

(iv) For $\delta_m = 45°$,

$$\mu = \frac{\sin\left(\frac{60° + 45°}{2}\right)}{\sin\left(\frac{60°}{2}\right)}$$

$$= \frac{\sin(52.5°)}{\sin 30°} = \frac{0.7880}{0.5}$$

$$\mu = 1.576$$

Or

Laws of reflection at a plane surface (On Huygens' principle)

Let, 1, 2 and 3 be the incident rays and 1′, 2′ and 3′ be the corresponding reflected rays.

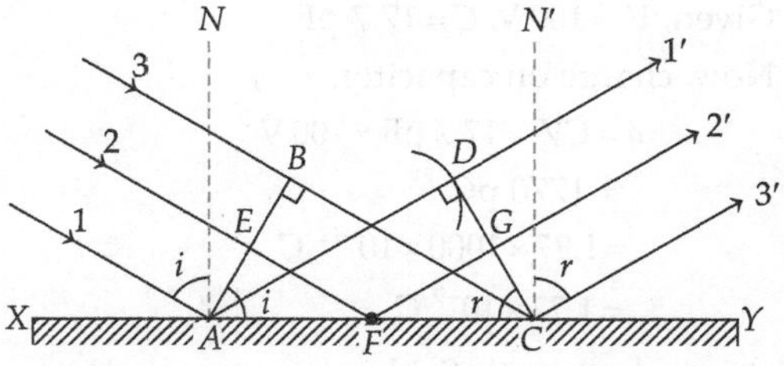

If c is the speed of the light, t is the time taken by light to go from B to C or A to D or E to G through F, then

$$t = \frac{EF}{c} + \frac{FG}{c} \quad \text{...(i)}$$

In ΔAEF, $\sin i = \frac{EF}{AF}$

In ΔFGC, $\sin r = \frac{FG}{FC}$

or $t = \frac{AF \sin i}{c} + \frac{FC \sin r}{c}$

or $t = \frac{AC \sin r + AF(\sin i - \sin r)}{c}$ $\quad (\because FC = AC - AF)$

For rays of light from different parts on the incident wavefront, the values of AF are different. But light from different points of the incident wavefront should take the same time to reach the corresponding points on the reflected wavefront.

So, t should not depend upon AF. This is possible only if

$$\sin i - \sin r = 0$$

i.e. $\sin i = \sin r$

or $\angle i = \angle r$ ...(ii)

which is the **first law of reflection.**

Further, the incident wavefront AB, the reflecting surface XY and the reflected wavefront CD are all perpendicular to the plane of the paper. Therefore, incident ray, normal to the mirror XY and reflected ray all lie in the plane of the paper. This is **second law of reflection.**

13. (i) Given, plate area, $A = 6 \times 10^{-3}\text{ m}^2$, distance between the plates, $d = 3\text{ mm} = 3 \times 10^{-3}\text{ m}$,

$$\varepsilon_0 = 8.85 \times 10^{-12}\text{ C}^2\text{N}^{-1}\text{m}^{-2}$$

The capacitance of a parallel plate capacitor filled with air is given by

$$C = \frac{A\varepsilon_0}{d} \quad \text{...(i)}$$

Substituting the given values in Eq. (i), we get

$$C = \frac{6 \times 10^{-3} \times 8.85 \times 10^{-12}}{3 \times 10^{-3}}$$

$$= 17.7 \times 10^{-12}$$

$$= 17.7\text{ pF}$$

So, capacitance of parallel plate capacitor $= 17.7$ pF

(*ii*) Given, $V = 100\text{ V}, C = 17.7\text{ pF}$

Now, charge on capacitor,

$$q = CV = 17.7\text{ pF} \times 100\text{ V}$$
$$= 1770\text{ pC}$$
$$= 1.77 \times 1000 \times 10^{-12}\text{ C}$$
$$= 1.77 \times 10^{-9}\text{ C}$$

14. Electric and magnetic field,

$$\mathbf{E} = E\hat{\mathbf{j}} \text{ and } \mathbf{B} = B\hat{\mathbf{k}}$$

Force on positive ion due to electric field,

$$\mathbf{F}_E = qE\hat{\mathbf{j}}$$

Force due to magnetic field, $\mathbf{F}_B = q(\mathbf{v}_c \times \mathbf{B})$

For passing undeflected, $\mathbf{F}_E = -\mathbf{F}_B$

$$qE\hat{\mathbf{j}} = -q(v_c \times B\hat{\mathbf{k}})$$

Only possible, when $qv_c \times B\hat{\mathbf{k}} = qv_c\, B\hat{\mathbf{j}}$

or $\quad v_c = \left(\frac{E}{B}\right)\hat{\mathbf{i}}$

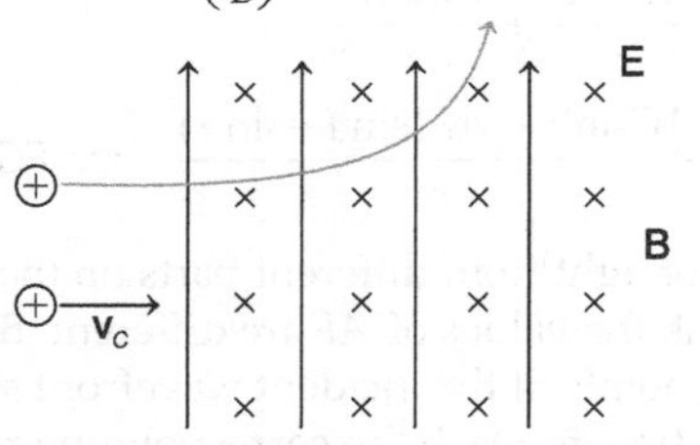

For positive ions with speed $v < v_c$

Force due to electric field, $F'_E = qE$

Due to magnetic field, $F'_B = qvB < F_B$

Since, $v < v_c$

Now, forces are unbalanced, thus ion will experience an acceleration along it. Hence, initial velocity is perpendicular to **E** and the trajectory would be parabolic.

15. (*i*) We know that, in normal adjustment of telescope, magnifying power of telescope is given by

$$m = \frac{f_o}{f_e} \quad \text{...(i)}$$

Given, $f_o = 140$ cm and $f_e = 5$ cm

Substituting these values in Eq. (i), we get

$$m = \frac{140}{5} = 28$$

(*ii*) When the final image is formed at the least distance of distinct vision, then

$$v = D = 25\text{ cm}$$

The magnifying power m of telescope when final image is formed at the least distance of distinct vision (D) is given by

$$m = \frac{f_o}{f_e}\left(1 + \frac{f_e}{D}\right) = 28\left(1 + \frac{5}{25}\right) = 28 \times 1.2 = 33.6$$

16. (*i*) We know that, the electrostatic force between two given charges is inversely proportional to the dielectric constant K of the intervening medium.

i.e. $\quad F \propto \frac{1}{K} \quad$ (Coulomb's law)

If F and F' are electrostatic forces between two charges before and after introduction of dielectric medium, then we have

$$\frac{F}{F'} = K' \quad \text{(Since, } K = 1 \text{ for air or vacuum)}$$

Given, dielectric constant, $K' = 10$

Therefore, $\frac{F}{F'} = K' = 10$

(*ii*) (a) Electric field intensity at a point on the axial position, $E = \frac{1}{4\pi\varepsilon_0} \times \frac{2pr}{(r^2 - a^2)^2}$

If dipole is short, $2a << r$, then $E = \frac{1}{4\pi\varepsilon_0}\frac{2p}{r^3}$

where, p is electric dipole moment.

(b) Electric field intensity at a point on the broad-side-on position,

$$E = -\frac{1}{4\pi\varepsilon_0}\frac{p}{(r^2 + a^2)^{3/2}}$$

If the dipole is short, $2a << r$, then

$$E = \frac{1}{4\pi\varepsilon_0} \times \frac{p}{r^3}$$

17. Total resistance of the circuit $= \frac{R_0}{2} + R_{eq}$

$$\frac{1}{R_{eq}} = \frac{1}{R} + \frac{2}{R_0} = \frac{R_0 + 2R}{RR_0}$$

$$\Rightarrow \quad R_{eq} = \frac{RR_0}{R_0 + 2R}$$

Total resistance

$$= \frac{R_0}{2} + \frac{RR_0}{R_0 + 2R} = \frac{R_0^2 + 2RR_0 + 2RR_0}{2(R_0 + 2R)} = \frac{R_0^2 + 4RR_0}{2(R_0 + 2R)}$$

Current in the circuit

$$= \frac{V}{\frac{R_0^2 + 4RR_0}{2(R_0 + 2R)}} = \frac{2V(R_0 + 2R)}{R_0^2 + 4RR_0}$$

$$\text{Current in } R = \frac{2V(R_0 + 2R)}{(R_0^2 + 4RR_0)} \times \frac{R_0/2}{(R + R_0/2)}$$
$$= \frac{V(R_0 + 2R)}{(R_0^2 + 4RR_0)} \times \frac{2R_0}{(2R + R_0)}$$
$$= \frac{2VR_0}{(R_0^2 + 4RR_0)}$$

$\therefore$ Potential difference across R

$$= \frac{2V\,R_0 R}{(R_0^2 + 4RR_0)} = \frac{2VR}{(R_0 + 4R)}$$

18. (*i*) Observed phenomenon is diffraction. All the secondary wavelets going straight across the slit are focused at the central point of the screen. The wavelets from any two corresponding points of the two halves of the slit reach the point O in the same phase, they add constructively to produce a central bright fringe.

(ii) The condition for first dark fringe is $d \sin\theta_1 = \lambda$. Similarly, the condition for second dark fringe will be $d \sin\theta_2 = 2\lambda$.

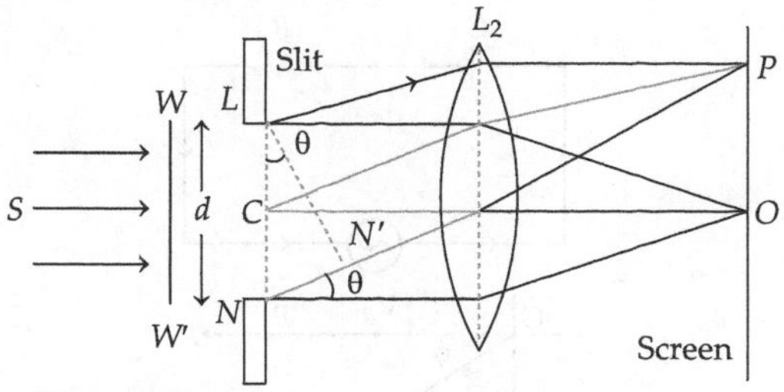

Hence, the condition for nth dark fringe can be written as $d \sin\theta_n = n\lambda$, where $n = 1, 2, 3, ...$

[As $\lambda << d$, so $\sin\theta_n = \theta_n$]

The directions of various minima are given by

$$\theta_n \approx \sin\theta_n = n\frac{\lambda}{d}$$

Suppose the point P is so located that $\theta = \frac{3\lambda}{2}$

When $\theta = \theta_1'$, then $a \sin\theta_1' = \frac{3}{2}\lambda$.

We can divide the slit into three equal parts. The path difference between two corresponding points of the first two parts will be $\frac{\lambda}{2}$. The wavelets from these points will interfere destructively.

However, the wavelets from the third part of the slit will contribute to some intensity forming a secondary maximum. The intensity of this maximum is much less than that of the central maximum. Thus, the condition for the first secondary maximum is $a \sin\theta_1' = \frac{3}{2}\lambda$.

(iii) The reason is that the intensity of the central maximum is due to the constructive interference of wavelets from all parts of the slit, the first secondary maximum is due to the contribution of wavelets from one-third part of the slit, while (wavelets from the remaining two parts interfere destructively). Similarly, the second secondary maximum is due to the contribution of wavelets from the one-fifth part only with (the remaining four parts interfere destructively) and so on. Hence, the intensity of secondary maximum decreases with the increase in the order n of the maximum.

Or

(i) (a) Let a point object O be placed at a distance u from the pole in a medium of refractive index n_1 outside the spherical refracting surface of radius of curvature R. Its real image I is formed at a distance v in denser medium of refractive index n_2. Here, angle of incidence is i and angle of refraction is r.

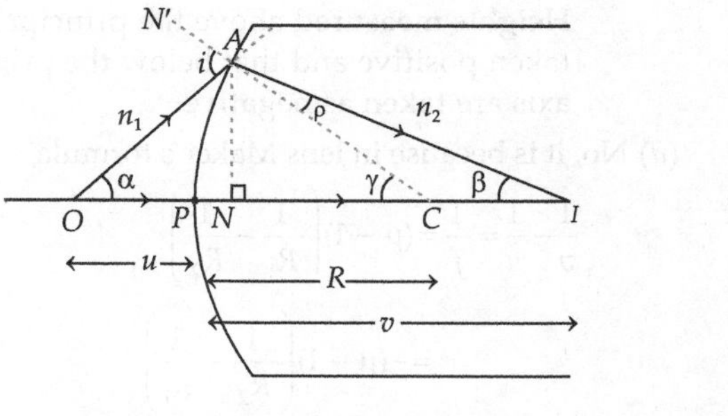

Draw a normal AN on principal axis.

Let $\angle AOC = \alpha$, $\angle AIC = \beta$,

$$\angle ACO = \gamma$$

For ΔAOC, i is the exterior angle

$$i = \alpha + \gamma \quad ...(i)$$

For ΔAIC, γ is the exterior angle

$\therefore$ $$\gamma = r + \beta \text{ or } r = \gamma - \beta \quad ...(ii)$$

According to the Snell's law,

$$\frac{n_2}{n_1} = \frac{\sin i}{\sin r}$$

When angles i and r are very small, then

$$\sin i \approx i \text{ and } \sin r \approx r$$

$\therefore$ $$\frac{n_2}{n_1} = \frac{i}{r}$$

or $$n_1 i = n_2 r$$

Substituting the values of i and r from Eqs. (i) and (ii), we get

$$n_1(\alpha + \gamma) = n_2(\gamma - \beta) \quad ...(iii)$$

If the aperture of the spherical surface is small, then angles α, β and γ will be small and point N will lie near to pole P. Hence,

$$\alpha = \tan\alpha = \frac{AN}{ON} \approx \frac{AN}{OP} = \frac{AN}{(-u)}$$

$$\beta = \tan\beta = \frac{AN}{IN} \approx \frac{AN}{IP} = \frac{AN}{v}$$

$$\gamma = \tan\gamma = \frac{AN}{CN} \approx \frac{AN}{CP} = \frac{AN}{R}$$

Substituting the values of α, β and γ in Eq. (iii), we get

$$n_1 \times AN\left[\frac{1}{(-u)} + \frac{1}{R}\right] = n_2 \times AN\left[\frac{1}{R} - \frac{1}{v}\right]$$

$$-\frac{n_1}{u} + \frac{n_1}{R} = \frac{n_2}{R} - \frac{n_2}{v}$$

$$\Rightarrow \frac{n_2}{v} - \frac{n_1}{u} = \frac{n_2 - n_1}{R}$$

(b) **Sign convention** The distance measured from pole in the direction of propagation of light rays are taken positive and distances measured from pole in opposite direction of propagation of light rays are taken negative.

Heights measured above the principal axis are taken positive and that below the principal axis are taken as negative.

(*ii*) No, it is because in lens Maker's formula,

$$\frac{1}{v}-\frac{1}{u}=\frac{1}{f}=(\mu-1)\left(\frac{1}{R_1}-\frac{1}{R_2}\right)$$

$$=-(\mu-1)\left(\frac{1}{R_2}-\frac{1}{R_1}\right)$$

i.e. On reversing the lens, values and signs of R_1 and R_2 get reversed. Thus, for a given position of object (u), position of image (v) remains unchanged.

19. (*i*) Let alternating voltage, $V=V_0\sin\omega t$ is applied across a capacitor C. At any instant, the potential difference across the capacitor is equal to applied voltage.

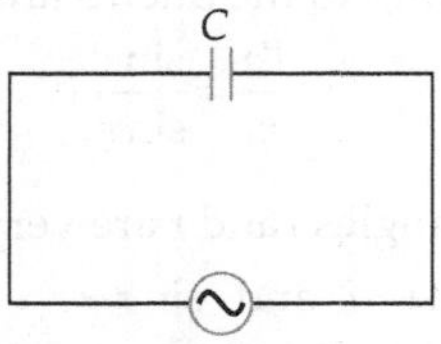

$$V=V_0\sin\omega t \quad \text{...(i)}$$

$\therefore$ V = Potential difference across the capacitor

$$=\frac{q}{C}$$

$\Rightarrow$ $q=CV$ or $q=CV_0\sin\omega t$

$\therefore$ $\frac{dq}{dt}=\omega C V_0\cos\omega t$

or $I=\frac{V_0}{(1/\omega C)}\cos\omega t$

or $I=I_0\sin\left(\omega t+\frac{\pi}{2}\right)$ ...(ii)

where, $I_0=\frac{V_0}{(1/\omega C)}=\frac{V_0}{X_C}$

Capacitive reactance, $X_C=\frac{1}{\omega C}$

(*ii*) As, $V=V_0\sin\omega t$

Then, $I=I_0\sin\left(\omega t+\frac{\pi}{2}\right)$

Phasor diagram

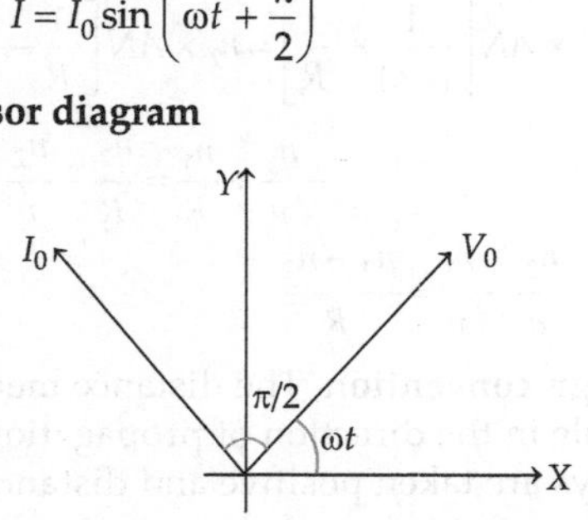

(*iii*) If resistance is added in series to capacitor. The vector sum of two voltage drop is equal to applied voltage.

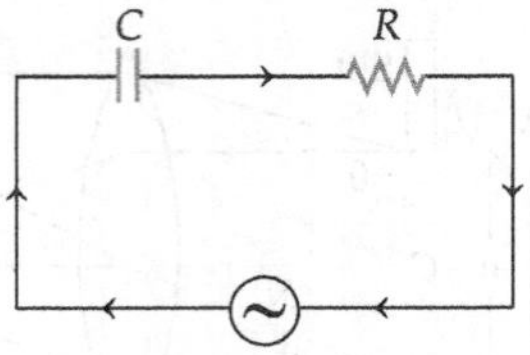

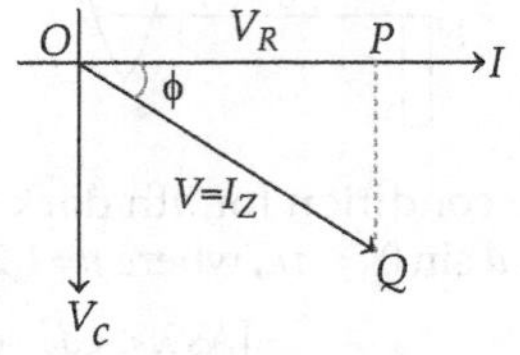

$$V_R=I\times R$$

and $V_C=I\times X_C$

In ΔOPQ, $V=\sqrt{(V_R)^2+(V_C)^2}=\sqrt{(IR)^2+(IX_C)^2}$

$$V=I\sqrt{R^2+X_C^2}$$

Current, $I=\frac{V}{\sqrt{R^2+X_C^2}}$

Phase angle, $\tan\phi=\frac{V_C}{R}=\frac{X_C}{R}$

$$\phi=\tan^{-1}\frac{X_C}{R}$$

Or

(*i*) Self-inductance is the property of a coil by virtue of which, the coil opposes any change in the strength of current flowing through it by inducing an emf in itself. Its SI unit is henry (H).

(*ii*) The self-inductance can be increased with the help of electric fields. It does not depend on the current through circuit but depends upon the permeability of material from which the core is made up off.

(*iii*) (a) The graph between I and angle of rotation θ when the loop revolves with angular frequency ω is shown below.

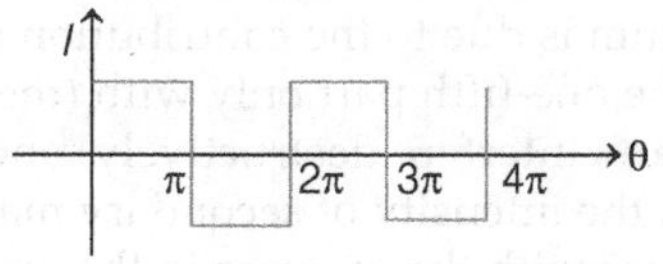

(b) The graph between I and angle of rotation θ when the loop revolves with higher angular frequency ω′

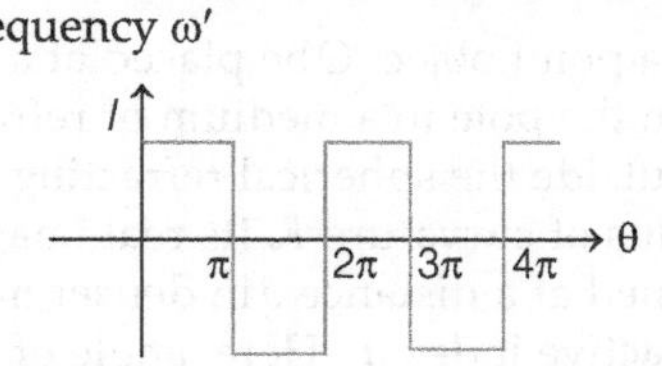

Reason As angular frequency increases, the rate of change in the flux linked with the loop increases. This increases the induced emf and hence the corresponding value of the induced current also increases.

20. (*i*) A moderator is a material used in a nuclear reactor to slow down the neutrons produced from fission.

Some examples of moderators are heavy water (D_2O), boron (B) and cadmium (Cd).

(*ii*) The Q-value of a nuclear process refers to the energy released in the nuclear process which can be determined using Einstein's mass-energy relation, $E = mc^2$. The Q-value is equal to the difference of mass of products and reactant nuclei multiplied by square of velocity of light.

The nuclear process does not proceed spontaneously, when Q-value of a process is negative or sum of masses of product is greater than sum of masses of reactant.

(*iii*) (a) The sustained fissibility of nuclear chain reaction depends on the multiplication factor or simply called multiplicity (K).

$$K = \frac{\text{Rate of production of neutrons}}{\text{Rate of loss of neutrons}}$$

(b) If $K = 1$, the operation of reactor is said to be critical. It is what we wish to be, steady power operation.

If $K > 1$, the reaction rate and reactor power increases exponentially. It is called supercritical and reactor can explode.

If $K < 1$, the reaction gradually stops and the condition is called sub-critical.

SQP Code : **PB-8/15** Series **i-Succeed 8-25/15** Roll No. | | | | | | | |

Sample Question Paper 08

Physics 12th (Code 861)

General Instructions

1. This paper is divided into four Sections- A, B, C and D. Answer all questions.
2. **Section A** consists of one question having sub-parts of one mark each.
3. **Section B** consists of seven questions of two marks each.
4. **Section C** consists of nine questions of three marks each.
5. **Section D** consists of three questions of five marks each.
6. Internal choices have been provided in two questions each in Section B, Section C and Section D.

Time : 3 Hrs.

Max. Marks : 70

Section A (14 Marks)

1. A. In questions (i) to (vii) below, choose the correct alternative (a), (b), (c) or (d) for each of the questions given below.

(*i*) The current in a device varies with time t as $I=4t$, where I is in mA and t is in s. The amount of charge that passes through the device during $t=0$ s, to $t=3$ s is • *Analysis* [1]

(a) 19 mC (b) 18 mC

(c) 24 mC (d) 38 mC

(*ii*) A ray of light strikes an air-glass interface at an angle of incidence ($i=60°$) and gets refracted at an angle of refraction r. On increasing the angle of incidence ($i>60°$), the angle of refraction r • *Recall* [1]

(a) decreases (b) remains same

(c) is equal to 60° (d) increases

(*iii*) **Assertion** (A) For $\nu>\nu_0$ (threshold frequency), photoelectric current is proportional to intensity.

Reason (R) Greater the number of energy quanta available, greater is the number of electrons absorbing the energy quanta and greater is the number of electrons coming out of the metal. • *Analysis* [1]

(a) Both Assertion and Reason are true and Reason is the correct explanation for Assertion.

(b) Both Assertion and Reason are true but Reason is not the correct explanation for Assertion.

(c) Assertion is false and Reason is true.

(d) Both Assertion and Reason are false.

(*iv*) Time taken by sunlight to pass through a window of thickness 4 mm whose refractive index is 3/2, is • *Recall* [1]

(a) 2×10^{-4}s (b) 2×10^{8} s

(c) 2×10^{-11}s (d) 2×10^{11} s

(*v*) Which one of the following graph represent correctly the variation of linear momentum (p) of a charge particle with its de-Broglie wavelength (λ)? • *Analysis* [1]

(a)

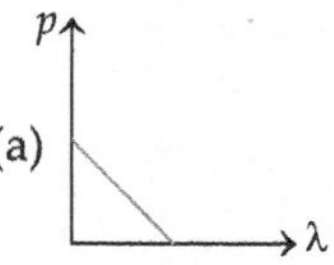

(b)

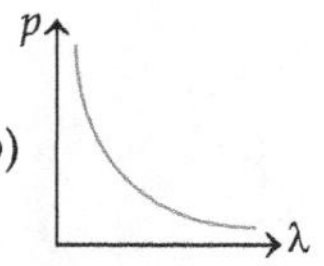

(c)

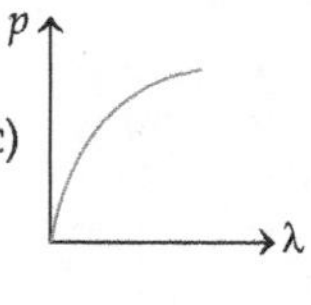

(d)

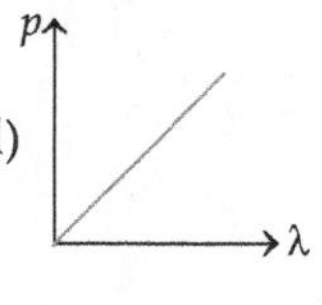

(*vi*) **Assertion** (A) Resistivity of a conductor increases with increase in temperature.
Reason (R) When temperature increases, the random motion of free electrons increases and vibration of ions increases which decreases the relaxation time. • *Understanding* [1]

(a) Both Assertion and Reason are true and Reason is the correct explanation for Assertion.
(b) Both Assertion and Reason are true but Reason is not the correct explanation for Assertion.
(c) Assertion is false and Reason is true.
(d) Both Assertion and Reason are false.

(*vii*) A parallel plate air capacitor has a capacitance 18 μF. If the distance between the plates is tripled and a dielectric medium is introduced, the capacitance becomes 72 μF. The dielectric constant of the medium is • *Understanding* [1]

(a) 4
(b) 9
(c) 12
(d) 6

B. Answer the following questions briefly.

(*i*) Write the two properties of equipotential surface. • *Recall* [1]

(*ii*) The radius of innermost electron orbit of a hydrogen atom is 7.3×10^{-11} m. What is the radius of orbit in the second excited state? • *Recall* [1]

(*iii*) What effects occur on the conductivity of a semiconductor when its temperature is increased? • *Application* [1]

(*iv*) Magnetic flux of 10 μWb is linked with a coil, when a current of 2 mA flows through it. Find self-inductance of the coil. • *Recall* [1]

(*v*) How can the real image of an object be obtained with a convex mirror? • *Recall* [1]

(*vi*) Explain how the intensity of diffraction pattern changes as the order (n) of the diffraction band varies? • *Recall* [1]

(*vii*) An AC generator generates an emf E given by $E = 311 \sin(100\pi t)$ V. Find the rms value of the emf generated by the generator. • *Understanding* [1]

Section B (14 Marks)

2. Two identical circular loops P and Q, each of radius r and carrying equal currents are kept in the parallel planes having a common axis passing through O. The direction of current in P is clockwise and in Q is anti-clockwise as seen from O, which is equidistant from the loops P and Q. Find the magnitude of the net magnetic field at O. • *Application* [2]

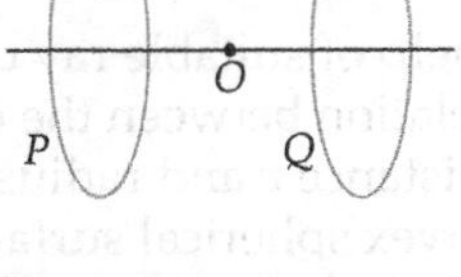

3. The work function of Cs is 2.14 eV. Find

(i) threshold frequency for Cs and
(ii) wavelength of incident light if the photocurrent is brought to zero by stopping potential of 0.2 V. • *Analysis* [2]

4. A concave mirror of small aperture forms a sharper image. Why? • *Recall* [2]

5. Compare the following

(i) Wavelengths of the incident solar radiation absorbed by the earth's surface and the radiation re-radiated by the earth. • *Recall* [1]

(ii) Tanning effect produced on the skin by UV radiation incident directly on the skin and that coming through glass window. • *Application* [1]

6. A parallel beam of light of 500 nm falls on a narrow slit and the resulting diffraction pattern is observed on a screen 1 m away. It is observed that the first minima is at a distance of 2.5 mm from the centre of the screen. Calculate the width of the slit. • *Application* [2]

7. How can elements be identified by the study of the line spectrum? • *Recall* [2]

Or

What is the ratio of radii of the orbits corresponding to second excited state and ground state in a H-atom? • *Understanding* [2]

8. In a Young's double slit experiment, the slits are separated by 0.28 mm and the screen is placed 1.4 m away. The distance between the central bright fringe and fourth bright fringe is measured to be 1.2 cm. Determine the wavelength of light used in the experiment.
• *Application* [2]

Or

The intensity at the central maxima (O) in a Young's double slit experiment is I_0. If the distance OP equals one-third of fringe width of the pattern, then show that the intensity at point P would be $I_0/4$. • *Analysis* [2]

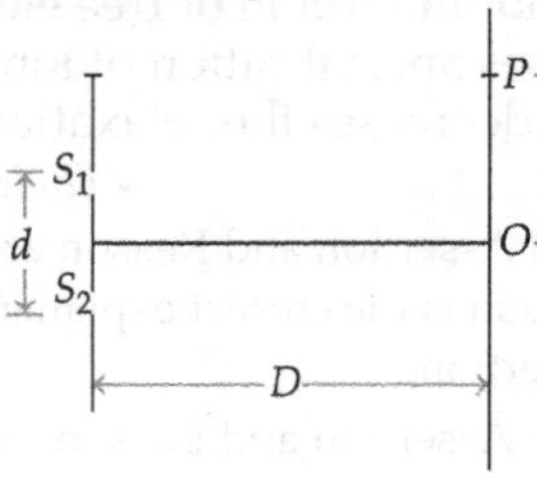

Section C (27 Marks)

9. A rectangular loop of wire of size 2.5 cm × 4 cm carries steady current of 1 A. A straight wire carrying 2 A current is kept near the loop as shown. If the loop and the wire are co-planar, find the (i) torque acting on the loop and (ii) the magnitude and direction of the force on the loop due to the current carrying wire. • *Application* [3]

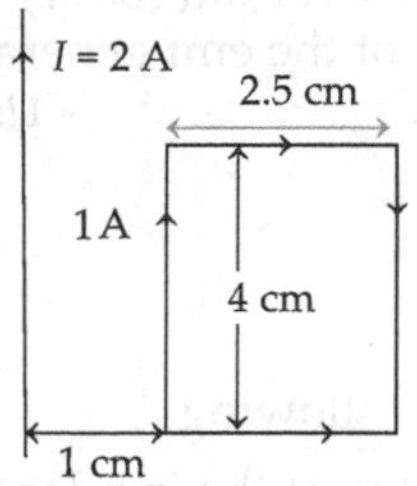

10. Two identical parallel plate capacitors A and B are connected to a battery of V volts with the switch S is closed. The switch is now opened and the free space between the plates of the capacitors is filled with a dielectric of dielectric constant K. Find the ratio of the total electrostatic energy stored in both capacitors before and after the introduction of the dielectric. • *Analysis* [3]

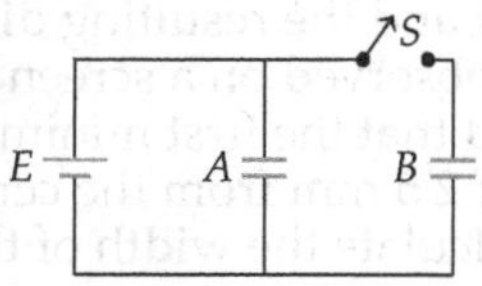

11. In a nuclear reactor, U^{235} undergoes fission releasing energy of 100 MeV. The reactor has 20% efficiency and the power produced is 2000 MW. If the reactor is to function for 5 yr, find the total mass of uranium required.
• *Understanding* [3]

12. (*i*) How does one explain the emission of electrons from a photosensitive surface with the help of Einstein's photoelectric equation? • *Recall* [1]

(*ii*) The work function of the following metals is given as Na = 2.75 eV, K = 2.3 eV, Mo = 4.17 eV and Ni = 5.15 eV. Which of these metals will not cause photoelectric emission for radiation of wavelength 3300 Å from a laser source placed 1 m away from these metals? What happens if the laser source is brought nearer and placed 50 cm away?
• *Application* [2]

13. The distance between the first and the sixth bright fringes formed in Young's double slit experiment (measured by a spectrometer) is found to be 12.5 mm. The separation between the slits is 0.12 mm and the distance of the screen from the slits is 60 cm. Calculate

(*i*) the fringe width and

(*ii*) wavelength of the light used (in nm).
• *Understanding* [3]

Or

With the help of suitable ray diagram, derive a relation between the object distance u, image distance v and radius of curvature R for a convex spherical surface, when a ray of light travels from rarer to denser medium.
• *Application* [3]

14. (*i*) In which condition, force on a moving charged particle is zero in uniform magnetic field. • *Recall* [1]

(*ii*) An α-particle and a proton are moving in the plane of paper in a region of uniform magnetic field B normal to the plane of paper. If the particles have equal linear momentum, what will be the ratio of radii of their trajectories? • *Application* [2]

Or

A student measures the magnetic force F on a current-carrying conductor placed in a uniform magnetic field B for different values I. The conductor is placed perpendicular to the magnetic field. The data collected is recorded as follows. Verify (for any two) that these observations are good agreement with the theoretical values given by $F = BIL$, where, L is the length of the conductor and $B = 0.02$ T, $L = 1$ m. • *Application* [3]

Current (I)	2 A	4 A	6 A	8 A
Magnetic force (F)	4×10^{-2} N	8×10^{-2} N	12×10^{-2} N	16×10^{-2} N

15. A cube with each side a is kept in an electric field, given by $\mathbf{E} = Cx\hat{\mathbf{i}}$ as shown in the figure, where C is a positive dimensionless constant.

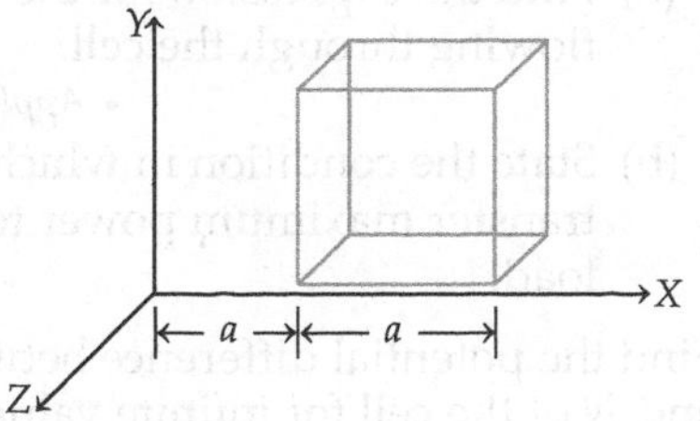

Find out

(*i*) the electric flux through the cube and • *Recall* [2]

(*ii*) the net charge inside the cube. • *Recall* [1]

16. (*i*) Answer the following giving reasons.

(a) A *p-n* junction diode is damaged by a strong current.

(b) Impurities are added in intrinsic semiconductor. • *Recall* [1]

(*ii*) In half-wave rectification, what is the output frequency, if input frequency is 25 Hz? • *Recall* [1]

(*iii*) What is meant by doping of an intrinsic semiconductor? Name the two types of atoms used for doping of Ge/Si. • *Application* [1]

17. A non-ideal diode causes a voltage drop of 0.2 V when in forward bias. The diode burns out, if the current through it exceeds 8 mA through it. In which of the following instances, will this diode run the risk of burning out? Show the working.

(i) A battery of 4.2 V and resistor of 1 kΩ connected in series to the diode.

(ii) A battery of 6.2 V and a resistor of 0.6 kΩ connected in series to the diode.

• *Application* [3]

Section D (15 Marks)

18. (*i*) Draw a ray diagram to show refraction of a ray of monochromatic light passing through a glass prism. Deduce the expression for the refractive index of glass in terms of angle of prism and angle of minimum deviation. • *Application* [3]

(*ii*) Explain briefly how the phenomenon of total internal reflection is used in fibre optics. • *Application* [2]

Or

A student wants to obtain image of a distant object by following set-up. The radius of curvature of curved face in the plano-convex and the plano-concave lens is 15 cm each. The refractve index of the material of the lenses is 1.5.

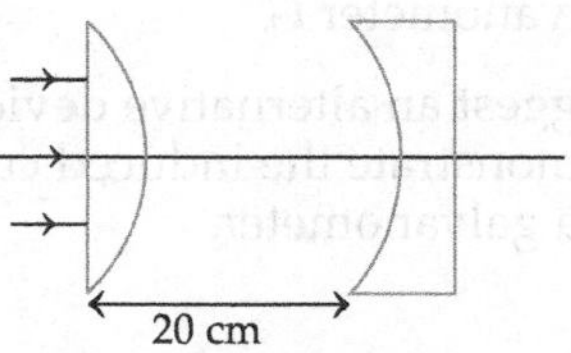

(*i*) What should be the distance of screen from the right lens? • *Analysis* [2]

(*ii*) A real image of size p times the size of an object is formed by a concave mirror of focal length f. What is the object distance from the mirror? • *Analysis* [3]

19. (*i*) AB and CD are two parallel conductors kept 1m apart and connected by a resistance R of 6 Ω, as shown in figure below. They are placed in a magnetic

SP-08

field $B = 3 \times 10^{-2}$T which is perpendicular to the plane of the conductors and directed into the paper. A wire MN is placed over AB and CD and then made to slide with a velocity 2 ms^{-1}. (Neglect the resistance of AB, CD and MN.)

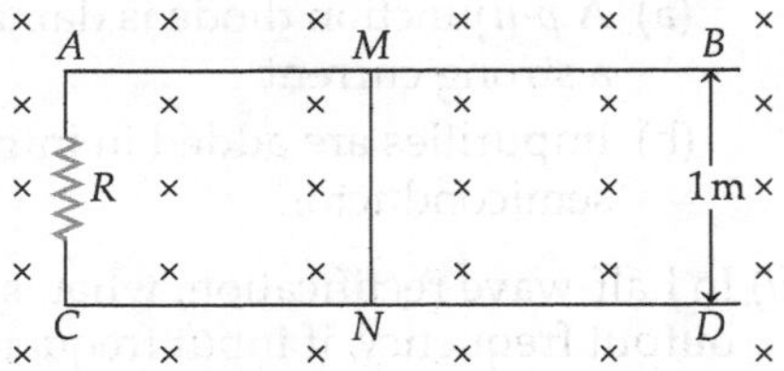

Calculate the induced current flowing through the resistor R. • *Analysis* [3]

(*ii*) State two laws which give the direction of induced current. • *Application* [2]

Or

(*i*) What is a transformer?

(*ii*) State the principle on which it works. • *Application*

(*iii*) A current is induced in coil C_1 due to the motion of current carrying coil C_2. • *Application*

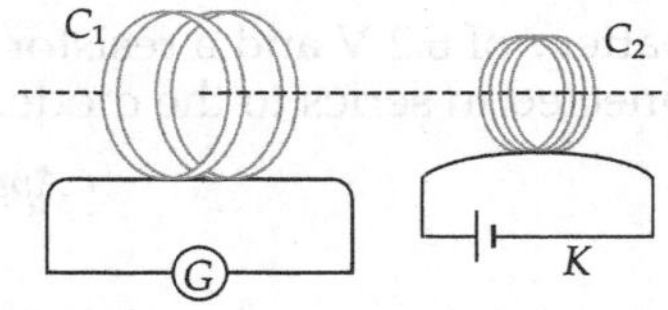

(a) Write any two ways by which a large deflection can be obtained in the galvanometer G. • *Application*

(b) Suggest an alternative device to demonstrate the induced current in place of a galvanometer. • *Recall* [5]

20. An electric cell is a source of energy that maintains a continuous flow of charge in a circuit. It changes chemical energy into electrical energy. It has two electrodes, positive electrode and negative electrode as shown alongside.

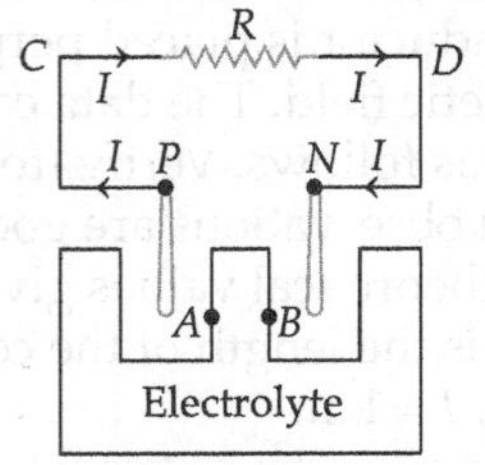

Electric cell has to do some work in maintaining the current through a circuit. The work done by the cell in moving unit positive charge through the whole circuit (including the cell) is called the electromotive force (ε) of the cell. It also has some internal resistance (r).

(*i*) (a) Find the expression for the current flowing through the cell. • *Application* [1]

(b) State the condition in which cell can transfer maximum power to the load. • *Recall* [1]

(*ii*) Find the potential difference between P and N of the cell for infinite value of R. • *Recall* [1]

(*iii*) For the given circuit, suppose the cell has an emf of 2V and the internal resistance of this cell is 0.1Ω. If it is connected to a resistance of 3.9Ω, then find the

(a) current drawn from the cell

(b) potential difference across the resistor. • *Application* [2]

Solutions in Topper's Style

My Commitment *I affirm that I am reviewing these solutions only after I have solved the Sample Question Paper 8 on my own. My purpose of looking the solutions is solely to verify whether my answers/solutions were correct or not and to identify my mistakes in case my solutions were wrong or I could not solve that.*

1. A. *(i)* *(b)* Given, $I = 4t$

$\therefore$ The amount of charge flowing through the device in the time interval t_1 to t_2 is

$$q = \int_{t_1}^{t_2} I dt = \int_0^3 4t\, dt = 4\left[\frac{t^2}{2}\right]_0^3 = 18 \text{ mC}$$

(ii) *(d)* From Snell's law of refraction,

$$^a\mu_g = \frac{\sin i}{\sin r} = \text{constant} \quad \ldots(i)$$

Since, angle of incidence increases, so the angle of refraction has to increase. So, that the ratio of $\left(\frac{\sin i}{\sin r}\right)$ remains constant according to Eq. (i).

(iii) *(a)* Both Assertion and Reason are true and Reason is the correct explanation for Assertion.

According to the Einstein's photoelectric effect, intensity of the radiation is proportional to the number of energy quanta per unit area per unit time. Thus, greater the number of the energy quanta available, greater is the number of electrons absorbing the energy quanta and therefore greater is the number of electrons coming out of the metal.

Hence, for $\nu > \nu_0$, photoelectric current is proportional to intensity.

(iv) *(c)* Given, thickness, $x = 4 \text{ mm} = 4 \times 10^{-3}$ m

Refractive index, $\mu = 3/2$

$\therefore$ Velocity of light in glass,

$$v_g = \frac{c}{\mu} = \frac{3 \times 10^8}{3/2} = 2 \times 10^8 \text{ m/s}$$

$\therefore$ Time taken, $t = \frac{x}{v_g} = \frac{4 \times 10^{-3}}{2 \times 10^8} = 2 \times 10^{-11}$ s

(v) *(b)* de-Broglie wavelength associated with a moving charged particle is given as $\lambda = \frac{h}{p}$.

where, h is planck's constant and p is the linear momentum.

$\Rightarrow \quad p\lambda = h$

This equation is in the form of $yx = c$, which is the equation of a rectangular hyperbola.

(vi) *(a)* When temperature increases, the random motion of electrons and vibration of ions increases which results in more frequent collisions of electrons with the ions. Due to this, the average time between the successive collisions, denoted by τ, decreases which increases ρ.

(vii) *(c)* $C_0 = \frac{\varepsilon_0 A}{d} = 18 \mu\text{F} \quad \ldots(i)$

$$C = \frac{K\varepsilon_0 A}{3d} = 72 \mu\text{F} \quad \ldots(ii)$$

On dividing Eq. (ii) by Eq. (i), we get

$$\frac{K}{3} = \frac{72}{18} = 4$$

$\therefore$ Dielectric constant, $K = 12$

B. *(i)* (a) Work done on moving charge from one point to another point on equipotential surface is zero.

(b) Electric field lines are perpendicular to equipotential surface.

(ii) The radius of atom whose principal quantum number n is given by $r = n^2 r_0$

where, r_0 = radius of innermost electron orbit for hydrogen atom $= 7.3 \times 10^{-11}$ m

For second excited state,

$$n = 3$$

$$\therefore \quad r = 3^2 \times r_0 = 9 \times 7.3 \times 10^{-11}$$

$$r = 6.57 \times 10^{-10} \text{ m}$$

(iii) Conductivity of semiconductor increases on increasing its temperature because resistance of semiconductor decreases with increase of temperature.

(iv) Given, $\phi = 10\ \mu$Wb

$= 10 \times 10^{-6}$ Wb

and $I = 2$ mA

$= 2 \times 10^{-3}$ A

We know that, $\phi = LI$

Self-inductance, $L = \frac{\phi}{I} = \frac{10 \times 10^{-6}}{2 \times 10^{-3}}$

$\Rightarrow \quad L = 5 \times 10^{-3}$ H

$= 5$ mH

(v) A convex mirror produces a real image of a virtual object. Therefore, if a beam of light from a virtual object converges to a point behind the convex mirror, then its real image will be formed in front of the mirror.

(vi) In diffraction pattern, intensity of alternate dark and bright bands decreases as compare to central bright band.

(vii) Given, $E = 311\sin(100\pi t)$ V

Comparing this with standard equation of AC voltage $E = E_0 \sin \omega t$, we get

Peak value of voltage, $E_0 = 311$ V

The rms value of emf generated by the generator,

$$E_{rms} = \frac{E_0}{\sqrt{2}} = \frac{311}{\sqrt{2}} = 219.9 \text{ V}$$

2. Magnetic field at O due to two loops will be in same direction ($Q \to P$, along the axis) and of equal magnitude.

$$B = B_1 + B_2 \text{ but } B_2 = B_1$$

$$\Rightarrow \quad B = 2B_1 = 2\left[\frac{\mu_0 Ir^2}{2(r^2 + 3r^2)^{3/2}}\right]$$

$$= \frac{\mu_0 Ir^2}{(4r^2)^{3/2}} = \frac{\mu_0 Ir^2}{2^3 r^3}$$

$$= \frac{\mu_0 I}{8r}$$

3. Given, $\phi_0 = 2.14$ eV

(i) The work function is related with threshold frequency as

$$\phi_0 = h\nu_0$$

$$\therefore \quad \nu_0 = \frac{\phi_0}{h} = \frac{2.14 \times 1.6 \times 10^{-19}}{6.63 \times 10^{-34}}$$

$$= 0.51 \times 10^{15} \text{ Hz}$$

(ii) Stopping potential, $V_0 = 0.2$ V

$\therefore$ By Einstein's photoelectric equation,

$$\frac{hc}{\lambda} = \phi_0 + eV_0 = 2.14 + 0.2 = 2.34 \text{ eV}$$

$$\therefore \quad \lambda = \frac{6.63 \times 10^{-34} \times 3 \times 10^8}{2.34 \times 1.6 \times 10^{-19}} = 5.31 \times 10^7 \text{ m}$$

4. The rays of light travelling parallel to the principal axis after reflection from a concave mirror meet at a single point only, if the beam of light is narrow or if the mirror is of small aperture. In case, a wide beam of light falls on a concave mirror of large aperture, the rays after reflection from the mirror do not come to focus at a single point. Therefore, it follows that, if the aperture of the concave mirror is small, the image formed will be sharper.

5. (i) Radiation re-radiated by the earth's surface has greater wavelength.

(ii) Tanning effect is significant for direct UV radiation, it is negligible for radiation coming through the glass window.

6. The distance of the nth minima from the centre of the screen is given by $\quad x_n = \dfrac{nD\lambda}{a} \quad$ ...(i)

where, D = distance of slit from screen = 1 m

λ = wavelength of the light = 500 nm

$= 500 \times 10^{-9}$ m,

$n = 1$,

$x_n = 2.5 \text{ mm} = 2.5 \times 10^{-3}$ m,

and $\quad a$ = width of the slit for first minima

Putting these values in Eq. (i), we get

$$2.5 \times 10^{-3} = \frac{(500 \times 10^{-9})}{a}$$

$$\Rightarrow \quad a = 2 \times 10^{-4} \text{ m} = 0.2 \text{ mm}$$

7. Each element has atoms having definite energy levels and they are different from the energy levels of other elements. So, the atoms of an element will emit spectrum of radiation which has lines of certain definite frequencies, different from those of all other elements.

Hence, based on the study of line spectrum, different elements can be easily identified.

Or

For second excited state, $n_2 = 3$

For ground state, $n_1 = 1$

Since, radius of orbit is directly proportional to the square of quantum number n.

i.e., $\quad r \propto n^2$

$$\therefore \quad \frac{r_1}{r_2} = \frac{n_1^2}{n_2^2} = \left(\frac{n_1}{n_2}\right)^2 = \left(\frac{1}{3}\right)^2 = \frac{1}{9}$$

$$\therefore \quad r_1 : r_2 = 1 : 9$$

8. Given, distance between the slits,

$$d = 0.28 \text{ mm} = 0.28 \times 10^{-3} \text{ m}$$

Distance between the slits and the screen, $D = 1.4$ m

Distance between central and fourth fringe, $y = 1.2$ cm $= 1.2 \times 10^{-2}$ m

Order of fringes, $n = 4$

For constructive interference, $y = \dfrac{n\lambda D}{d}$

or wavelength of light,

$$\lambda = \frac{yd}{nD} = \frac{1.2 \times 10^{-2} \times 0.28 \times 10^{-3}}{4 \times 1.4} = 6 \times 10^{-7} = 600 \text{ nm}$$

Value Point

To get maximum marks include following value points.

- write the values of all parameter at starting in SI units.
- write the formula of constructive interference.

Or

In Young's double slit experiment, intensity can be found out if we know the phase difference. Phase difference can be calculated with the help of path difference. So first of all, path difference will be calculated.

Given, $OP = y_n$

The distance OP equals one-third of fringe width of the pattern.

i.e., $y_n = \frac{\beta}{3} = \frac{1}{3}\left(\frac{D\lambda}{d}\right) = \frac{D\lambda}{3d} \Rightarrow \frac{dy_n}{D} = \frac{\lambda}{3}$

Path difference $= S_2P - S_1P = \frac{dy_n}{D} = \frac{\lambda}{3}$

$\therefore$ Phase difference,

$$\phi = \frac{2\pi}{\lambda} \times \text{path difference}$$

$$= \frac{2\pi}{\lambda} \times \frac{\lambda}{3} = \frac{2\pi}{3}$$

If intensity at central fringe is I_0, then intensity at a point P, where phase difference is ϕ, is given by

$$I = I_0 \cos^2 \phi \Rightarrow I = I_0 \left(\cos \frac{2\pi}{3}\right)^2$$

$$= I_0 \left(-\cos \frac{\pi}{3}\right)^2 = I_0 \left(-\frac{1}{2}\right)^2 = \frac{I_0}{4}$$

Hence, the intensity at point P would be $\frac{I_0}{4}$.

9. There will be force of attraction between the straight wire and 4 cm long arm of loop nearer to the straight conductor. Thus,

$$F_1 = \frac{\mu_0}{4\pi} \frac{2 \times 2 \times 1}{(1 \times 10^{-2})} \times (4 \times 10^{-2})$$

$F_1 = 16 \times 10^{-7}$ N [towards straight wire] ...(i)

Similarly, force on other 4 cm arm of loop, away from the straight conductor,

$$F_2 = \frac{\mu_0}{4\pi} \times \frac{2 \times 2 \times 1}{(3.5 \times 10^{-2})} \times (4 \times 10^{-2})$$

$F_2 = 4.57 \times 10^{-7}$ N [away from straight wire] ...(ii)

(i) Since, F_1 and F_2 are of different magnitudes, therefore they do not form couple and torque will be zero.

(ii) The magnitude of net force on loop,

$$F = F_1 - F_2$$

$$F = 16 \times 10^{-7} - 4.57 \times 10^{-7}$$

$$\Rightarrow \quad F = 11.43 \times 10^{-7} \text{ N}$$

The direction of the force would be towards the straight wire.

10. The given figure is shown below.

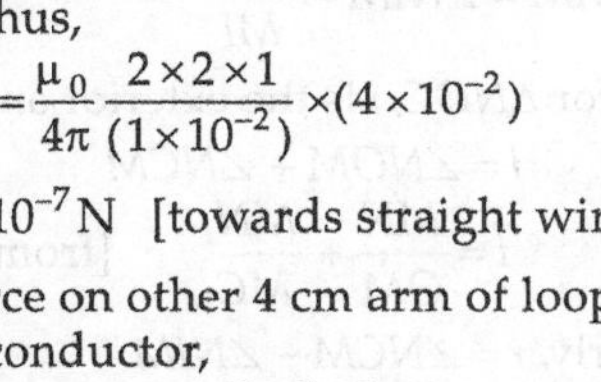

When switch S is closed, the potential difference across capacitors A and B are same

i.e. $V = \frac{Q_A}{C} = \frac{Q_B}{C}$

Initial charges on capacitors $Q_A = Q_B = CV$

When the dielectric is introduced, the new capacitance of each capacitor

$$C' = KC$$

As switch S is opened, the potential difference across capacitor A remains same (V volts).

Let potential difference across capacitor B be V'. When dielectric is introduced with switch S open (i.e. battery disconnected), the charges on capacitor B remains unchanged, so

$$Q_B = CV = C'V'$$

$$\Rightarrow \quad V' = \frac{C}{C'} V = \frac{V}{K} \text{ volt}$$

Initial energy of both capacitors

$$U_i = \frac{1}{2} CV^2 + \frac{1}{2} CV^2 = CV^2$$

Final energy of both capacitors

$$U_f = \frac{1}{2} C'V^2 + \frac{1}{2} C'V'^2$$

$$= \frac{1}{2}(KC)V^2 + \frac{1}{2}(KC)\left(\frac{V}{K}\right)^2$$

$$= \frac{1}{2} CV^2 \left[K + \frac{1}{K}\right] = \frac{1}{2} CV^2 \left(\frac{K^2 + 1}{K}\right)$$

$$\Rightarrow \quad \frac{U_i}{U_f} = \frac{CV^2}{\frac{1}{2} CV^2 \left(\frac{K^2+1}{K}\right)} = \frac{2K}{K^2 + 1}$$

11. Given, output power, $P_o = 2000 \text{ MW} = 2 \times 10^9$ W

$$\text{Efficiency, } \eta = \frac{\text{Output power, } P_o}{\text{Input power, } P_i}$$

$$\Rightarrow \quad \frac{20}{100} = \frac{2 \times 10^9}{P_i} \Rightarrow P_i = 10^{10} \text{ W}$$

Consider the mass of uranium be m.

Number of fissions = Number of atoms

$$= \frac{\text{Given mass}}{\text{Atomic mass}} \times \text{Avogadro number}$$

$$= \frac{m}{A} \times N_A = \frac{m}{235} \times 6.023 \times 10^{23}$$

Energy produced

$$= \text{Number of fissions} \times \text{Energy per fission}$$

$$= \frac{m}{235} \times 6.023 \times 10^{23} \times 100 \text{ MeV}$$

$$= \frac{m}{235} \times 6.023 \times 10^{23} \times 100 \times 1.6 \times 10^{-13} \text{ J}$$

$(\because 1 \text{ MeV} = 1.6 \times 10^{-13} \text{ J})$

$$= m \times 0.041 \times 10^{12} \text{ J}$$

$$= m \times 4.1 \times 10^{10} \text{ J}$$

$$\text{As, Power} = \frac{\text{Energy}}{\text{Time}}$$

$$\Rightarrow \quad 10^{10} = \frac{m \times 4.1 \times 10^{10}}{5 \times 365 \times 24 \times 3600}$$

$$\Rightarrow \quad m = 3.84 \times 10^7 \text{ g} = 38.4 \times 10^3 \text{ kg}$$

12. (*i*) From Einstien's photoelectric equation, we have,

$$K_{max} = h\nu - \phi_0$$

As $K_{max} \geq 0$

So, $h\nu - \phi_0 \geq 0$ or $\nu \geq \frac{\phi_0}{h}$

Thus, photoemission occurs, when frequency is greater than threshold frequency, $\nu \geq \frac{\phi_0}{h}$.

(*ii*) Energy of the incident radiation of wavelength λ

$$E = \frac{hc}{\lambda} = \frac{(6.63 \times 10^{-34}) \times (3 \times 10^8)}{3300 \times 10^{-10} \times 1.6 \times 10^{-19}}$$

$$= 3.76 \text{ eV}$$

This energy of the incident radiation is greater than the work function of Na and K but less than those of Mo and Ni, so photoelectric emission will occur only in Na and K metals and not in Mo and Ni.

If the laser is brought closer, the intensity of incident radiation increases. This does not affect the result regarding Mo and Ni metals, while photoelectric current from Na and K will increase in proportion to intensity.

13. (*i*) We know that, $y_n = n\frac{D\lambda}{d}$

where, $n = 0, 1, 2, \ldots$

Here, $y_6 - y_1 = 12.5$ mm

$\Rightarrow$ $y_6 - y_1 = \frac{D\lambda}{d}(6-1) = 5\beta$ $\left(\because \beta = \frac{D\lambda}{d}\right)$

So, fringe width, $\beta = \frac{12.5}{5} = 2.5$ mm

(*ii*) Since, $\beta = \frac{D\lambda}{d}$

Given, $D = 60$ cm $= 0.6$ m, $d = 0.12$ mm $= 0.12 \times 10^{-3}$ m

$$\Rightarrow \quad 2.5 \times 10^{-3} = \frac{0.6 \times \lambda}{0.12 \times 10^{-3}}$$

$$\Rightarrow \quad \lambda = 5 \times 10^{-7} \text{ m} = 5000 \text{ Å}$$

Common Mistakes Students get confusion in identifying the value of *D* and *d* in the fringe width formula, i.e. they put the value *d* in place of the value *D* and *vice-versa*.

Or

Let us consider that convex spherical surface with centre of curvature *C* forms the image *I* of an object *O* on its principal axis. The rays are incident from a rarer medium of refractive index n_1 to a denser medium of refractive index n_2. The aperture of the surface to be small compared to other distances involved, so that small angle approximation can be made.

Here, *i* and *r* are the angles made by incident ray and refracted ray from the normal.

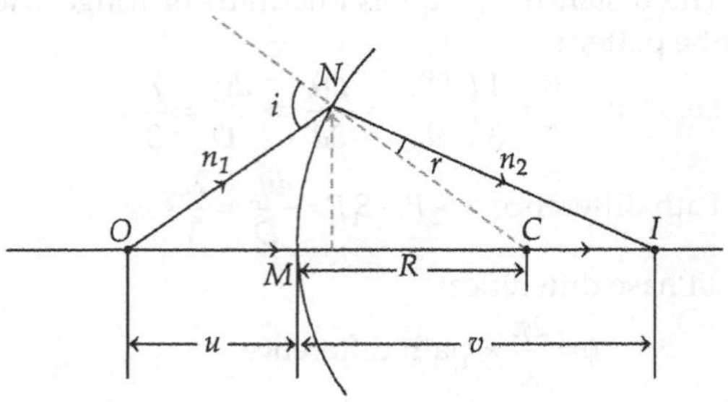

Assumptions

(*i*) The aperture of the surface is small compared to other distance involved.

(*ii*) *NM* will be taken to be nearly equal to the length of the perpendicular from the point *N* on the principal axis.

For small angles, $\tan\theta \approx \theta$

$$\tan\angle NOM = \angle NOM = \frac{MN}{OM} \quad \ldots(i)$$

$$\tan\angle NCM = \angle NCM = \frac{MN}{MC} \quad \ldots(ii)$$

$$\tan\angle NIM = \angle NIM = \frac{MN}{MI} \quad \ldots(iii)$$

Now, for ΔNOC, *i* is the exterior angle,

$\Rightarrow$ $i = \angle NOM + \angle NCM$

$\Rightarrow$ $i = \frac{MN}{OM} + \frac{MN}{MC}$ [from Eqs. (i) and (ii)]

Similarly, $r = \angle NCM - \angle NIM$

$\Rightarrow$ $r = \frac{MN}{MC} - \frac{MN}{MI}$ [from Eqs. (ii) and (iii)]

Snell's law can be written as,

$n_1 \sin i = n_2 \sin r$ or for small angles $n_1 i = n_2 r$

Substituting *i* and *r*, we have

$$\frac{n_1}{OM} + \frac{n_2}{MI} = \frac{n_2 - n_1}{MC} \quad \ldots(iv)$$

Here, *OM*, *MI* and *MC* represent magnitudes of distances. Applying the cartesian sign convention

$OM = -u$, $MI = +v$, $MC = +R$

Substituting these values in Eq. (iv), we get

$$\frac{n_2}{v} - \frac{n_1}{u} = \frac{n_2 - n_1}{R}$$

This equation holds for any curved spherical surface.

Value Point To get maximum marks include following value points

(i) make the neat and clean ray diagram.

(ii) use correct sign convention of *u*, *v* and *R*.

14. (*i*) We know that force on a moving charge particle in uniform magnetic field *B*,

$$F = Bqv\sin\theta$$

F will be zero, if $\theta = 0°$ or $180°$

(ii) Radius of circular path of a charged particle,

$$r = \frac{mv}{qB} = \frac{p}{qB} \qquad (\because p = mv)$$

As linear momentum and magnetic field are same,

so $r \propto \frac{1}{q}$

$$\therefore \quad \frac{r_\alpha}{r_p} = \frac{q_p}{q_\alpha} = \frac{+e}{+2e} = \frac{1}{2}$$

So, the ratio of radii is 1 : 2.

Or

The magnetic force on a current-carrying conductor in a magnetic field is given by $F = BIL$

(i) For $I = 2$ A,

$F = 0.02 \times 2 \times 1 = 0.04$ N

$F = 4 \times 10^{-2}$ N

(ii) For $I = 4$ A,

$F = 0.02 \times 4 \times 1 = 0.08$ N

$F = 8 \times 10^{-2}$ N

(iii) For $I = 6$ A,

$F = 0.02 \times 6 \times 1 = 0.12$

$F = 12 \times 10^{-2}$ N

(iv) For $I = 8$ A,

$F = 0.02 \times 8 \times 1 = 0.16$ N

$F = 16 \times 10^{-2}$ N

15. (i) Given, the electric field, $\mathbf{E} = Cx\,\hat{\mathbf{i}}$ is in x-direction only. So, the face of cube with surface having normal vector perpendicular to this field would give zero electric flux, i.e., $\phi = E\,dS\cos 90° = 0$, through it.

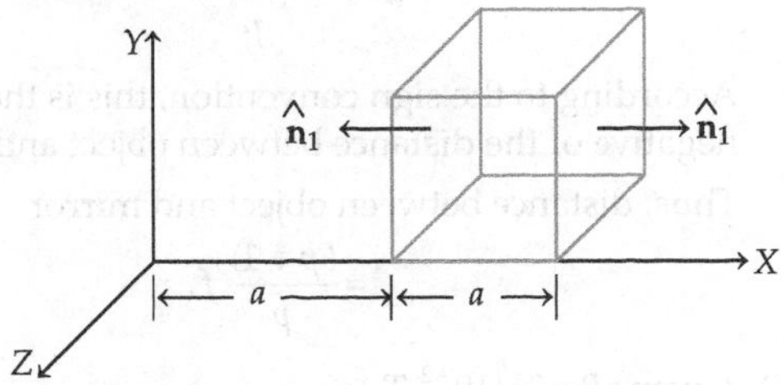

So, flux would be across only two surfaces.

Magnitude of E at left face,

$E_L = Cx = Ca \quad (x = a$ at left face)

Magnitude of E at right face,

$E_R = Cx = C2a = 2aC \qquad (x = 2a$ at right face)

Thus, corresponding fluxes are

$$\phi_L = \mathbf{E}_L \cdot d\mathbf{S} = E_L dS\cos\theta = -aC \times a^2 = -a^3C \qquad (\because \theta = 180°)$$

and $\phi_R = \mathbf{E}_R \cdot d\mathbf{S} = E_R\,dS\cos\theta \qquad (\because \theta = 0°)$

$= 2aCa^2 = 2a^3C$

Now, net flux through cube,

$$\phi = \phi_L + \phi_R = -a^3C + 2a^3C$$
$$= a^3C \text{ N-m}^2\text{C}^{-1} \qquad \ldots\text{(i)}$$

(ii) Again we can use Gauss law to find total charge q inside the cube,

$$\Rightarrow \quad \phi = \frac{q}{\varepsilon_0} \text{ or } q = \phi\varepsilon_0 \Rightarrow q = a^3C\varepsilon_0 \text{ [using Eq. (i)]}$$

16. (i) (a) When a strong current is passed through a semiconductors, it heats up the semiconductor. Due to it, the large number of covalent bonds break up, giving large number of charge carriers. As result of it, the material starts behaving as conductor.

(b) If some impurity is added to intrinsic semiconductor, it will increase the concentration or density of charge carriers and which in turn increase it conductivity.

(ii) Given that, input frequency, $\nu = 25$ Hz
output frequency = 25 Hz
Hence, the output waveform completes one cycle at the same time that of the input. Therefore, the frequency of the output wave is equal to the frequency of the input wave.

(iii) When some desirable impurity is added to intrinsic semiconductor deliberately to increase its conductivity, then this process is called doping and the impurity are called dopants.

Two types of dopants (atoms) are used in doping

(a) Trivalent atoms having 3 valance electrons e.g., Indium, Boron, Aluminium, etc.

(b) Pentavalent atoms having 5 valance electrons e.g., Arsenic, Antimony, Phosphorous, etc.

17. (i) The given non-ideal diode causes a voltage drop of 0.2 V.

So, when a battery of 4.2 V and resistor of 1 kΩ connected in series to the diode, the voltage drop across the resistor will be $4.2 - 0.2 = 4$V

Current through resistor and diode

$$I = 4/1000 = 0.004 = 4 \text{ mA}$$

The diode does not burn out in this case.

(ii) When a battery of 6.2 V and resistor of 0.6 kΩ connected in series to the diode, the voltage drop across the resistor will be $6.2 - 0.2 = 6$ V.

Current through resistor and diode

$= I/600 = 0.01 \text{ A} = 10$ mA

The diode will burn out in this case as the current exceeds the maximum safe limit of 8 mA.

18. (i)

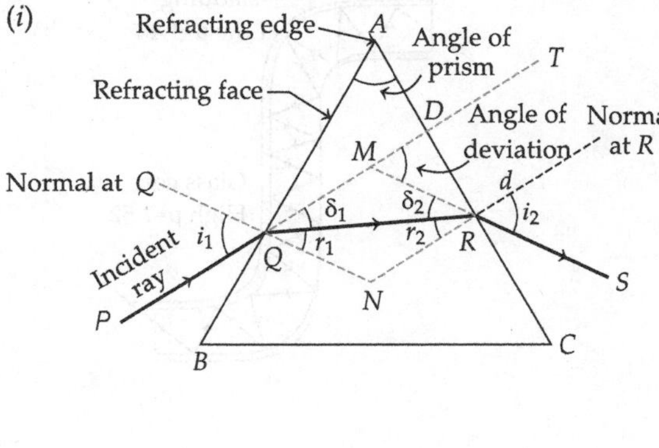

Let incident ray get deviated by δ by prism, i.e.

$$\angle TMS = \delta$$

Suppose δ_1 and δ_2 are deviation produced at refractors taking place at *AB* and *AC*, respectively.

$$\therefore \quad \delta = \delta_1 + \delta_2$$

$$\Rightarrow \quad \delta = (i_1 - r_1) + (i_2 - r_2)$$

$$\delta = (i_1 + i_2) - (r_1 + r_2) \quad \ldots(i)$$

Also, in quadrilateral *AQNR*,

$$A + \angle QNR = 180°$$

[∵ *QN* and *RN* are normal on two surfaces]

Also, In ΔQNR, $\angle QNR + r_1 + r_2 = 180°$

$$\Rightarrow \quad A = r_1 + r_2 \quad \ldots(ii)$$

From Eqs. (i) and (ii), we get

$$\delta = (i_1 + i_2) - A \quad \ldots(iii)$$

Angle of deviation produced by prism varies with angle of incidence. When prism is adjusted at angle of minimum deviation, then

$$i_1 = i_2 = i \quad \text{[say]}$$

At $\quad \delta = \delta_m \Rightarrow r_1 = r_2 = r \quad$ [say]

From Eqs. (i) and (ii), we have

$$\delta_m = 2i - 2r \quad \text{and} \quad 2r = A$$

$$\Rightarrow \quad i = (A + \delta_m)/2 \text{ and } r = A/2$$

∴ Refractive index of material of prism is

$$\mu = \frac{\sin i}{\sin r} = \frac{\sin\left(\frac{A + \delta_m}{2}\right)}{\sin \frac{A}{2}}$$

This is the required expression for the glass prism.

> **Value Point** To get maximum marks, following this point
> - When a ray after passing through a prism suffers minimum deviation, the ray will travel parallel to the base of the prism inside the prism.

(*ii*) When light is incident on one end of the optical fibre at an angle of incidence greater than the critical angle for the glass cladding pair of media. The light suffers repeated total internal reflection and it travels through the optical fibre without any loss of energy from one place to other inside the optical fibre.

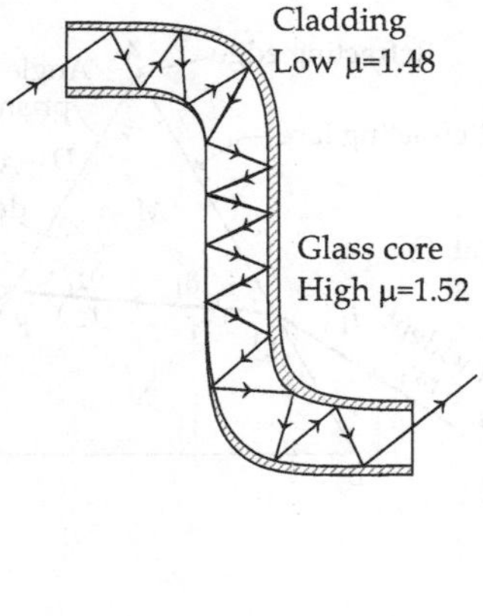

Or

(*i*) For plano-convex lens,

$$\frac{1}{f} = (\mu - 1)\left(\frac{1}{R_1} - \frac{1}{R_2}\right)$$

$$\frac{1}{f} = (1.5 - 1)\left(\frac{1}{15} - \frac{1}{\infty}\right)$$

$$= (0.5)\left(\frac{1}{15} - 0\right) = \frac{5}{10} \times \frac{1}{15} = \frac{1}{30}$$

Plano-concave lens,

$$\frac{1}{f} = (\mu - 1)\left(\frac{1}{R_1} - \frac{1}{R_2}\right)$$

$$\frac{1}{f} = (1.5 - 1)\left(\frac{1}{\infty} - \frac{1}{15}\right)$$

$$= (0.5)\left(0 - \frac{1}{15}\right) = -\frac{1}{30}$$

Given, $\quad u = +20$ cm

$$v = \frac{uf}{u + f} = \frac{20 \times (-30)}{20 - 30} = \frac{-600}{-10}$$

$$\therefore \quad v = +60 \text{ cm}$$

The distance of screen from the right lens is 60 cm.

(*ii*) From the mirror equation, we have

$$\frac{1}{v} + \frac{1}{u} = \frac{1}{f} = \frac{1}{-f} \quad \text{[following sign convention]}$$

Magnification $= \frac{-v}{-u} = p$ [∵ Image is real and inverted]

$$\Rightarrow \quad v = pu$$

Using this in mirror equation, we get

$$u = -\frac{(p+1)f}{p}$$

According to the sign convention, this is the negative of the distance between object and mirror.

Thus, distance between object and mirror

$$= \frac{(p+1)}{p} f.$$

19. (*i*) Given, $B = 3 \times 10^{-2}$ T

$MN = BD = 1$ m (according to the figure)

$$v = 2 \text{ ms}^{-1}$$

The emf induced in the coil, $e = -\frac{d\phi}{dt}$

$$e = -\frac{d(BA)}{dt}$$

where, $\quad A =$ area of the loop $= l \times x$

$$\Rightarrow \quad e = -\frac{d(Bl \times x)}{dt} = -Bl\frac{dx}{dt} = -Blv$$

$$= -3 \times 10^{-2} \times 1 \times 2 = -6 \times 10^{-2} \text{ V}$$

Current, $\quad I = \frac{|e|}{R} = \frac{6 \times 10^{-2}}{6} = 10^{-2} = 0.01$ A

(*ii*) Direction of induced current is given by following laws.

(a) **Lenz's law,** which states that the direction of induced emf (current) is such that it opposes the causes producing it.

(b) **From Fleming right hand rule,** which states that, if we stretch the thumb, the forefinger and the central finger of right hand in such a way that all these three are mutually perpendicular to each other and if thumb represents the direction of motion of the conductor and the forefinger represents the direction of magnetic field, then, central finger will represents the direction of induced current.

Or

(*i*) Transformer is a device which is used for changing the voltage in AC circuits. It is based upon the principle of mutual induction.

(*ii*) It works with AC only. It consists of two coils wound on the same core. The alternating current passing through the primary coil creates a continuously changing flux through the core. This changing flux induces an alternating emf in the secondary coil.

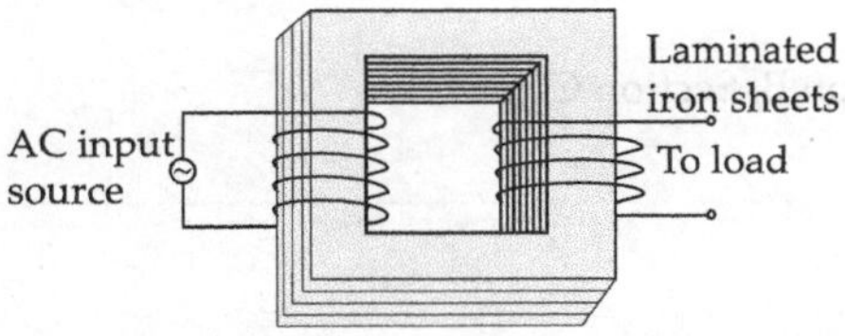

(*iii*) Large deflection means a high current for short time. So, to produce large deflection, induced current should be high and to produce high induced current, rate of change of flux should be also high, i.e. more change in flux in less time.

(a) Large deflection in the galvanometer can be obtained when change in magnetic flux is fast.

Two ways by which a large deflection can be obtained

(I) by moving the coil C_2 quickly towards C_1 or by moving the coil C_2 quickly away from C_1.

(II) by switching OFF and ON the key.

(b) Alternative device in place of galvanometer can be LED or bulb.

20. (*i*) (a) The load resistance and internal resistance are in series, hence same amount of current flows through both of the resistor. The terminal potential ε is given by

$$\varepsilon = IR + Ir$$

$$I(R + r) = \varepsilon$$

$$I = \frac{\varepsilon}{R + r}$$

(b) A cell can transfer maximum power to the load, if its internal resistance (r) is equal to load resistance (R)

i.e. $r = R$

(*ii*) If $R = \infty$, then no current flows in the circuit. Hence, terminal potential is equal to the emf of cell, i.e., $V = \varepsilon$.

(*iii*) Given, emf, $\varepsilon = 2\text{V}$

Internal resistance, $r = 0.1\,\Omega$

Load resistance, $R = 3.9\,\Omega$

(a) Current drawn from cell,

$$I = \frac{\varepsilon}{R + r} = \frac{2}{3.9 + 0.1} = \frac{2}{4} = 0.5\text{ A}$$

(b) Terminal voltage, $V = \varepsilon - Ir$

$$\Rightarrow \quad V = 2 - 0.5 \times 0.1$$

$$= 2 - 0.05 = 1.95\text{ V}$$

SQP Code : **PB-9/15** Series **i-Succeed 9-25/15** Roll No.

Sample Question Paper 09

Physics 12th (Code 861)

General Instructions

1. This paper is divided into four Sections- A, B, C and D. Answer all questions.
2. **Section A** consists of one question having sub-parts of one mark each.
3. **Section B** consists of seven questions of two marks each.
4. **Section C** consists of nine questions of three marks each.
5. **Section D** consists of three questions of five marks each.
6. Internal choices have been provided in two questions each in Section B, Section C and Section D.

Time : 3 Hrs.

Max. Marks : 70

Section A (14 Marks)

1. A. In question (i) to (vii) below, choose the correct alternative (a), (b), (c) or (d) for each of the questions given below.

(*i*) When a voltage measuring device is connected to AC mains, the meter shows the steady input voltage of 220 V. This means • *Recall* [1]

(a) input voltage cannot be AC voltage, but a DC voltage.

(b) maximum input voltage is 220 V.

(c) the meter reads not V but $< V^2>$ and is calibrated to read $\sqrt{< V^2 >}$.

(d) the pointer of the meter is stuck by some mechanical defect.

(*ii*) Lenard observed that no electrons are emitted when frequency of light is less than a certain minimum frequency. This minimum frequency depends on • *Understanding* [1]

(a) potential difference of emitter and collector plates

(b) distance between collector and the emitter plates

(c) size (area) of the emitter plate

(d) material of the emitter plate

(*iii*) **Assertion** (A) According to Bohr's postulate, electrons in stationary orbits around the nucleus do not radiate energy.

Reason (R) According to classical physics all the moving electrons radiate energy. • *Understanding* [1]

(a) Both Assertion and Reason are true and Reason is the correct explanation of Assertion.

(b) Both Assertion and Reason are true but Reason is not the correct explanation of Assertion.

(c) Assertion is false but Reason is true.

(d) Both Assertion and Reason are false.

(*iv*) **Assertion** (A) A diverging lens (in air) cannot be made more diverging whatever be the medium we choose to completely immerse the lens.

Reason (R) The minimum refractive index of any medium is 1. • *Analysis* [1]

(a) Both Assertion and Reason are true and Reason is the correct explanation for Assertion.

(b) Both Assertion and Reason are true but Reason is not the correct explanation for Assertion.

(c) Assertion is false and Reason is true.

(d) Both Assertion and Reason are false.

(*v*) Current sensitivity of a galvanometer is • *Recall* [1]

(a) $\frac{NBA}{k}$ (b) $\frac{k}{NBA}$

(c) $\frac{NBA}{kR}$ (d) $\frac{kR}{NBA}$

(*vi*) The de-Broglie wavelength of an electron in the *n*th Bohr's orbit is related to the radius *R* of the orbit as • *Recall* [1]

(a) $n\lambda = \pi R$ (b) $n\lambda = \frac{3}{2}\pi R$

(c) $n\lambda = 2\pi R$ (d) $n\lambda = 4\pi R$

(*vii*) An electron orbiting in H-atom has energy level -1.51 eV. Its angular momentum will be • *Analysis* [1]

(a) 3.15×10^{-34} J-s (b) 2×10^{-19} J-s

(c) 3.4×10^{-21} J-s (d) 9.94×10^{-34} J-s

B. Answer the following questions briefly.

(*i*) An electron with charge $-e$ and mass m travels at a speed v in a plane perpendicular to a magnetic field of magnitude B. The electron follows a circular path of radius *R*. In a time *t*, the electron travels half-way around the circle. What is the amount of work done by the magnetic field? • *Understanding* [1]

(*ii*) Explain the statement that a capacitor is a conductor at very high frequencies. Compare this behaviour with that of a capacitor in a DC circuit after the steady state. • *Recall* [1]

(*iii*) In the given circuit, *APB* and *AQB* are semi-circles having current as shown. Find magnetic field at the centre *C* of the circular loop. • *Recall* [1]

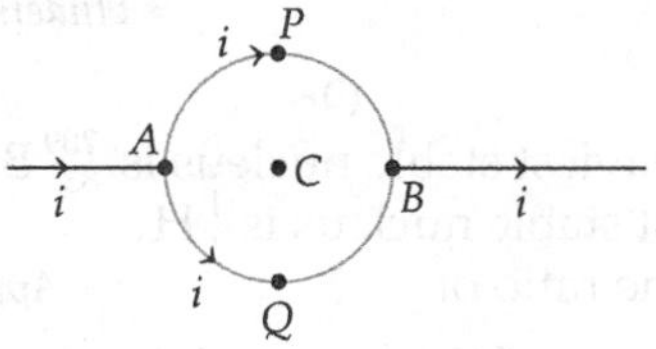

(*iv*) Can a slow neutron produce nuclear fission? Give reason for your answer. • *Recall* [1]

(*v*) Find the radius of curvature of the convex surface of a plano-convex lens, whose focal length is 0.2 m and the refractive index of the material of the lens is 1.2. • *Recall* [1]

(*vi*) If 3×10^{20} electrons pass through an cross-section of a conducting wire in one second, then find the current flowing through the cross-section of wire. • *Recall* [1]

(*vii*) A concave lens made of a material of refractive index μ_1 is immersed in a medium whose refractive index μ_2 is greater than μ_1. How will the emergent rays of incident parallel rays behave? • *Application* [1]

Section B (14 Marks)

2. Sketch the electric field lines for an uniformly charged hollow cylinder as shown in the figure.

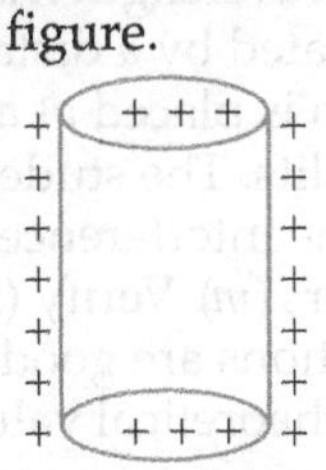

• *Recall* [2]

3. Why does *n*-type semiconductor material is prefered over *p*-type semiconductor material? • *Recall* [2]

Or

The current in the forward bias (mA) is known to be more than the current in the reverse bias (μA). What is the reason to operate the photodiode in reverse bias? • *Application* [2]

4. Suppose the lower half of the concave mirror's reflecting surface is covered with an opaque material. What effect this will have on the image of the object? Explain. • *Application* [2]

Or

The figure shows a ray of light falling normally on the face *AB* of an equilateral glass prism having refractive index 3/2, placed in water of refractive index 4/3. Will this ray suffer total internal reflection on striking the face *AC*? Justify your answer.

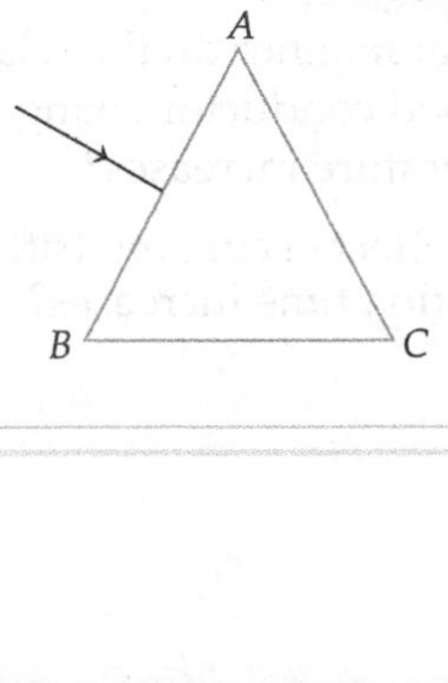

• *Analysis* [2]

5. Calculate the binding energy per nucleon of ${}_{20}Ca^{40}$.

Take, mass of ${}_{20}Ca^{40} = 39.962589$ u
$m_n = 1.008665$ u
$m_p = 1.007825$ u
1 amu = 931 MeV
• *Understanding* [2]

Or

The heavy stable nucleus is ${}^{209}_{83}$Bi and the lightest stable nucleus is ${}^{1}_{1}$H.
Find the ratio of • *Application* [2]

(i) volume of the two nuclei
(ii) density of the two nuclei

6. (*i*) An electromagnetic wave is travelling in a medium, with a velocity $\mathbf{v} = v\hat{\mathbf{i}}$. Draw a sketch showing the propagation of the electromagnetic waves, indicating the direction of the oscillating electric and magnetic fields. • *Recall* [1]

(*ii*) How are the magnitudes of the electric and magnetic fields related to velocity of the electromagnetic wave? • *Recall* [1]

7. Show graphically, the intensity distribution in Fraunhofer's single slit diffraction experiment by labeling the axes. • *Application* [2]

8. Why photoelectric effect cannot be explained on the basis of wave nature of light? Give reason • *Application* [2]

Section C (27 Marks)

9. (*i*) The wire shown in the figure carries a current of 10 A. Determine the magnitude of magnetic field induction at the centre *O*. Given, the radius of bent coil is 3 cm. • *Application* [1]

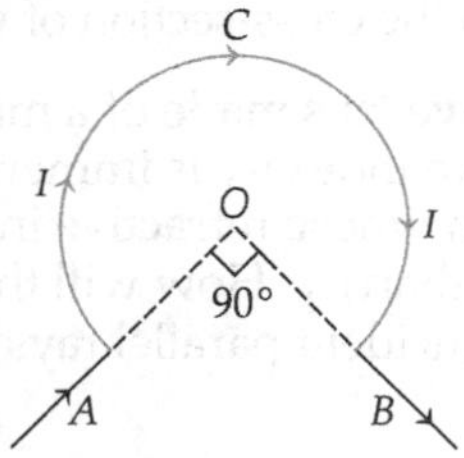

(*ii*) A current 10 A is flowing East to West in a long wire kept horizontally in the East-West direction. Find the magnitude and direction of magnetic field in a horizontal plane at a distance of 10 cm North. • *Application* [1]

(*iii*) A circular coil of wire consisting of 100 turns, each of radius 8.0 cm carries a current of 0.40 A. What is the magnitude of the magnetic field *B* at the centre of the coil? • *Recall* [1]

10. (*i*) A wire of resistivity ρ is stretched to three times its length. What will be its new resistivity? • *Recall* [1]

(*ii*) In what manner do the relaxation time in the good conductor change when its temperature increases? • *Recall* [1]

(*iii*) What effect occurs on drift velocity when relaxation time increases? • *Application* [1]

Or

An electric bulb is marked 200 V, 100 W. Calculate electric resistance of its filament. If five such bulbs are connected in series to a 200 V supply, how much current will flow through them? • *Application* [3]

11. An oil drop of 12 excess electrons is held stationary under a constant electric field of 2.55×10^4 N/C in Millikan's oil drop experiment. The density of the oil is 1.26 g/cm^3. Estimate the radius of the drop. (Take, $g = 9.81 \text{ m/s}^2$, $e = 1.6 \times 10^{-19}$ C).
• *Understanding* [3]

12. A student performs a double-slit experiment with light of wavelength λ is 600 nm. The slits are separated by a distance *d* is 1 mm and the screen is placed at a distance *D* is 2m from the slits. The student records the positions of the interference maxima for different orders (*m*). Verify (for any two) that these observations are good agreement with the expected theoretical values.
• *Application* [3]

m	1	2	3	4
y	12×10^{-4}	24×10^{-4}	36×10^{-4}	48×10^{-4}

Or

(*i*) The phase difference between light waves from two slits of Young's experiment is π radian. Will the centre fringe be dark or bright? • *Application* [1]

SP-09

(*ii*) Show the maximum intensity in interference pattern is four times the intensity due to each slit. • *Application* [2]

13. Write the expression for potential energy stored in a dipole of moment **p**, when placed in an electric field **E** making an angle θ with its direction. How much work will be done in deflecting an electric dipole of moment *p* through (*i*) 90° and (*ii*) 180° in electric field *E*? • *Understanding* [3]

14. An object *AB* is kept in front of a concave mirror as shown in the figure. • *Analysis*

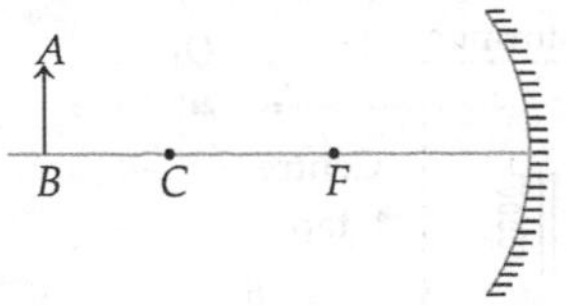

(*i*) Complete the ray diagram showing the image formation of the object. [2]

(*ii*) How will the position and intensity of the image be affected, if the lower half of the mirror's reflecting surface is painted black? [1]

15. (*i*) If the average life time of an excited state of hydrogen is of the order of 10^{-8} s. Estimate how many orbits an electron makes when it is in the state $n=2$ and before it suffers a transition to state $n=1$ (Bohr radius, $a_0 = 5.3\times10^{11}$ m)? • *Application* [2]

(*ii*) Find out the wavelength of the electron orbiting in the ground state of hydrogen atom. • *Recall* [1]

16. Given two coplanar and concentric loops 1 and 2 as shown.

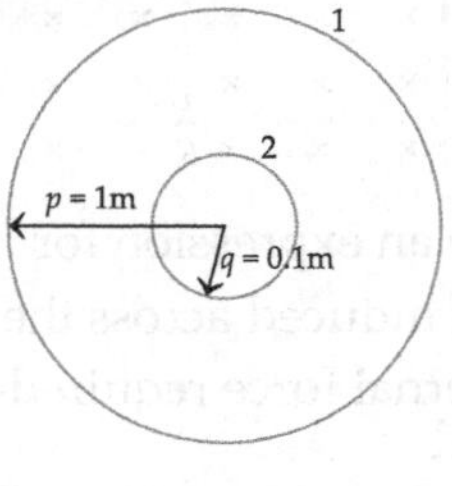

A time-varying voltage $(3+2t)$ is applied to the larger loop 1. If the resistance of the loops is $R_1 = 10\,\Omega$ and $R_2 = 1\,\Omega$, then determine the current induced in the smaller loop. • *Application* [3]

17. In a meter bridge, the balance point is found at a distance l_1 with resistance *R* and *S* as shown in the figure.

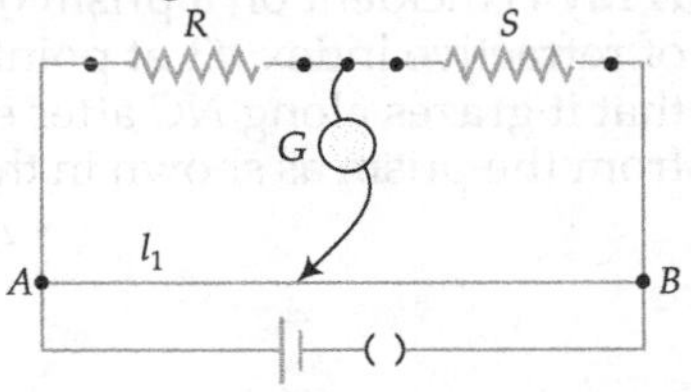

An unknown resistance *X* is now connected in parallel to the resistance *S* and the balance point is found at a distance l_2. Obtain a formula for *X* in terms of l_1, l_2 and *S*. • *Analysis* [3]

Section D (15 Marks)

18. A series *L-C-R* circuit connected to a variable frequency of 250 V source are shown in figure below.

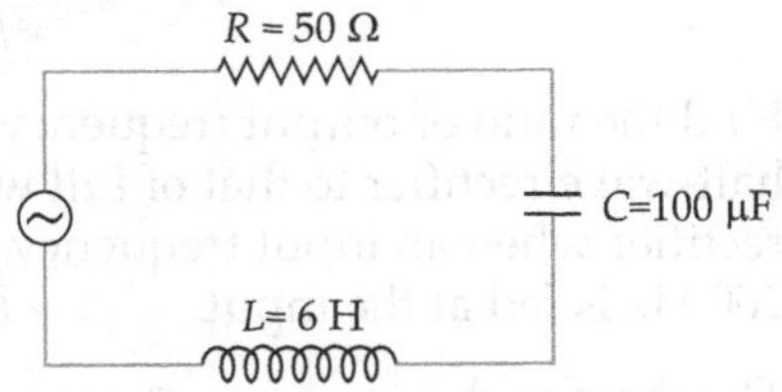

Calculate

(*i*) the source frequency which drives the circuit in resonance. • *Analysis* [1]

(*ii*) the impedance of the circuit and amplitude of current at resonant frequency. • *Analysis* [1]

(*iii*) rms potential drop across the three elements of the circuit. • *Analysis* [1]

(*iv*) In the circuit shown in figure neglecting source resistance, what is the value of voltmeter and ammeter reading? • *Application* [2]

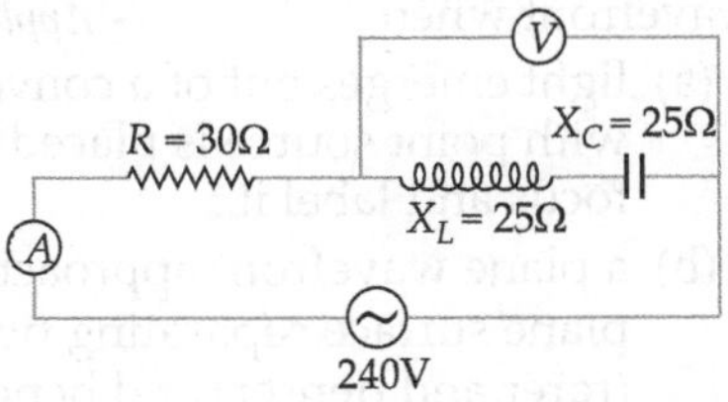

Or

Figure shows a rectangular conducting loop *PQRS* in which arm *RS* of length *l* is movable. The loop is kept in a uniform magnetic field *B* directed downward perpendicular to the plane of the loop.

The arm RS is moved with a uniform speed v. • *Application* [5]

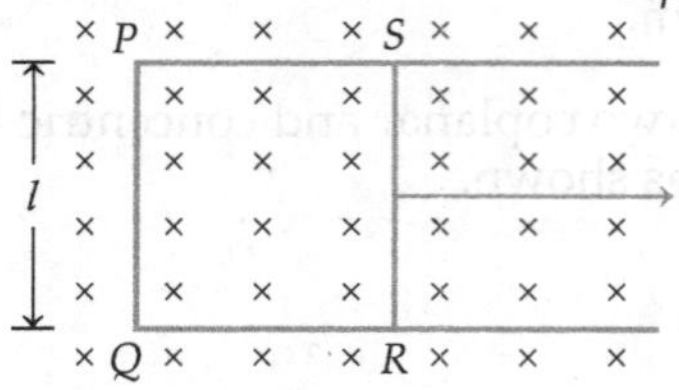

Deduce an expression for

(i) the emf induced across the arm RS

(ii) the external force required to move the arm and

(iii) the power dissipated as heat.

19. (*i*) What do you mean by dispersion of light? • *Recall* [1]

(*ii*) Draw a ray diagram to demonstrate the refraction of a monochromatic ray of light passing through a glass prism. • *Application* [2]

(*iii*) A ray is incident on a prism of material of refractive index $\sqrt{2}$ at point M such that it grazes along NC after emerging from the prism as shown in the figure. • *Application* [2]

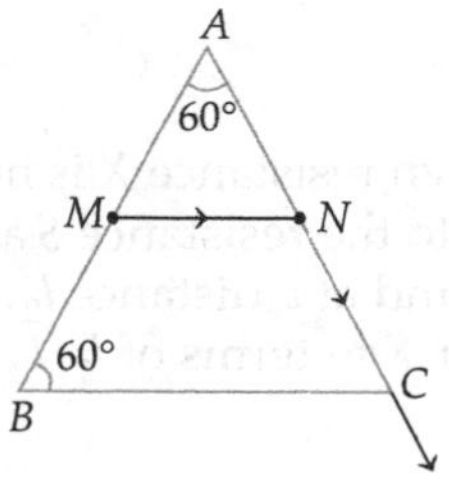

Find (a) the critical angle for the prism and (b) the angle of refraction at face AB.

Or

(*i*) Draw the geometrical shape of a wavefront when • *Application* [2]

(a) light emerges out of a convex lens with point source is placed at its focus and label it.

(b) a plane wavefront approaching a plane surface separating two media (rarer and denser) and hence, construct a refracted wavefront.

(*ii*) Define wavefront. Draw the shape of the wavefront emerging from • *Application* [3]

(a) a point source,

(b) a linear source and

(c) a distant source.

20. Full Wave Rectifier

The process of converting alternating voltage/current into direct voltage/current is called rectification. Diode is used as a rectifier for converting alternating current/voltage into direct current/voltage. Diode allows current to pass only when it is forward biased. So, if an alternating voltage is applied across a diode, the current flows only in that part of the cycle when the diode is forward biased. This property is used to rectify the current/voltage.

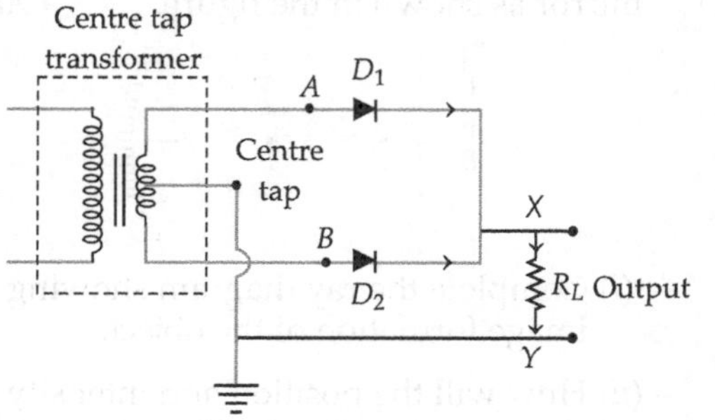

(*i*) In the following diode circuit, input is given between terminals A and C and output is taken between terminals B and D. What is the nature of output voltage? • *Application* [2]

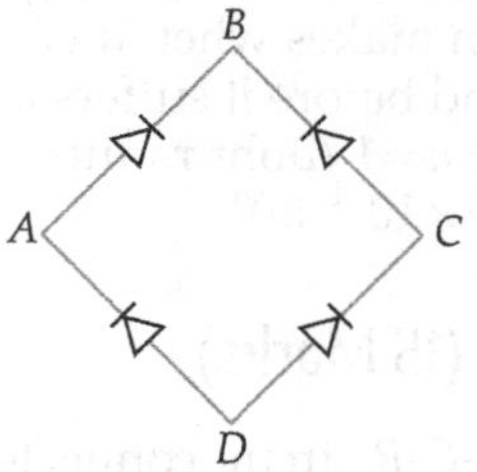

(*ii*) For what puprose, rectifier is used ? Does it convert AC into pure DC? • *Recall* [1]

(*iii*) Find the ratio of output frequency of half-wave rectifier to that of full wave rectifier when an input frequency of 200 Hz is fed at the input. • *Recall* [1]

(*iv*) The threshold voltage for a p-n junction diode used in the circuit is 0.7 V. What is the type of biasing and current in the circuit ? • *Application* [2]

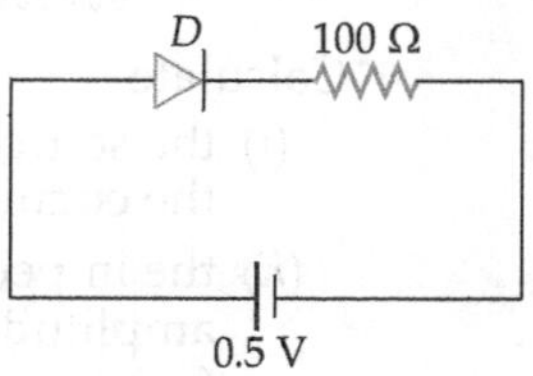

Solutions in Topper's Style

My Commitment *I affirm that I am reviewing these solutions only after I have solved the Sample Question Paper 9 on my own. My purpose of looking the solutions is solely to verify whether my answers/solutions were correct or not and to identify my mistakes in case my solutions were wrong or I could not solve that.*

1. **A.** (*i*) (*c*) The voltmeter connected to AC mains reads mean value ($<V^2>$) and is calibrated in such a way that it gives value of $\sqrt{<V^2>}$, which is multiplied by form factor to give rms value.

(*ii*) (*d*) Hallwachs and Lenard observed that when ultraviolet light fall on the emitter plate, no electrons were emitted at all when the frequency of the incident light was smaller than a certain minimum value, called the threshold frequency. This minimum frequency depends on the nature of the material of the emitter plate.

(*iii*) (*b*) This is one of the Bohr's postulate. According to this, the moving electrons radiate energy only when they go from one orbit to the next lower orbit.

Hence, both Assertion and Reason are true but Reason is not the correct explanation of Assertion.

(*iv*) (*a*) When a diverging lens is immersed in a liquid, then its diverging power will either decrease or it will become converging.

Hence, both Assertion and Reason are true and Reason is the correct explanation of Assertion.

(*v*) (*a*) Current sensitivity of the galvanometer is measured in deflection per unit ampere given as

$$\frac{\phi}{I}=\frac{NBA}{k}$$

(*vi*) (*c*) $n\lambda = 2\pi R$

Only those orbits are possible whose length ($2\pi R$) contains integral number of wavelengths.

(*vii*) (*a*) According to Bohr's second postulate, the angular momentum (L) of the orbiting electron is quantised.

$$L=\frac{nh}{2\pi}$$

where, n = principal quantum number.

Using $E_n=-\frac{13.6}{n^2}=-1.51 \Rightarrow n^2=9 \Rightarrow n=3$

$\therefore$ Angular momentum $=\frac{nh}{2\pi}$

$$=\frac{3\times 6.6\times 10^{-34}}{2\times 3.14}$$

$$=3.15\times 10^{-34}\ \text{J-s}$$

B. (*i*) When an electron with charge e and mass m travel at speed v in plane perpendicular to **B**, then electron follows circular path.

Amount of work done,

$$W = Fs\cos\theta$$

As, $\theta = 90°$

$$W = Fs\cos 90°$$

$\Rightarrow$ $W=0$

(*ii*) By comparison, at very high frequency, the resistance due to capacitor is negligible and hence, it works like a pure conductor of negligible capacitive reactance.

In DC circuits, $\omega=0$ (at steady state)

$$\Rightarrow \quad X_C=\frac{1}{\omega C}=\infty$$

So, it behaves like an open circuit.

(*iii*) Magnetic field due to APB at centre C, $B_1=\frac{\mu_0 I}{4a}\otimes$

where, a = radius of semi-circle.

Magnetic field due to AQB at centre C, $B_2=\frac{\mu_0 I}{4a}\odot$

So, net magnetic field at centre is zero.

(*iv*) Yes, a slow neutron is needed to initiate the process of fission. Unless slowed down, the fast neutrons will escape from fissionable material without causing any fission.

Hence, speed of fast moving neutrons has to be slowed down to occur fission in reactor.

(*v*) Here, $\mu=1.2$, $f=+0.2$ m, $R_1=\infty$, $R_2=-R$

Using lens Maker's formula,

$$\frac{1}{f}=(\mu-1)\left[\frac{1}{R_1}-\frac{1}{R_2}\right]$$

$$\frac{1}{+0.2}=(1.2-1)\left[\frac{1}{\infty}+\frac{1}{R}\right]$$

$$\frac{1}{0.2}=0.20\times\frac{1}{R}$$

or $R=0.04$ m

(*vi*) Given, $n=3\times 10^{20}$ electrons

$$t=1\ \text{s},\ e=1.6\times 10^{-19}\ \text{C}$$

$$\therefore \quad I=\frac{ne}{t}=\frac{3\times 10^{20}\times 1.6\times 10^{-19}}{1}$$

$$=48\text{A}$$

(*vii*) When lens is immersed in medium of greater refractive index, its nature changes, i.e. a concave lens starts behaving as a convex lens. So, the emergent rays will be converging as $\mu_2 > \mu_1$, as per following figure

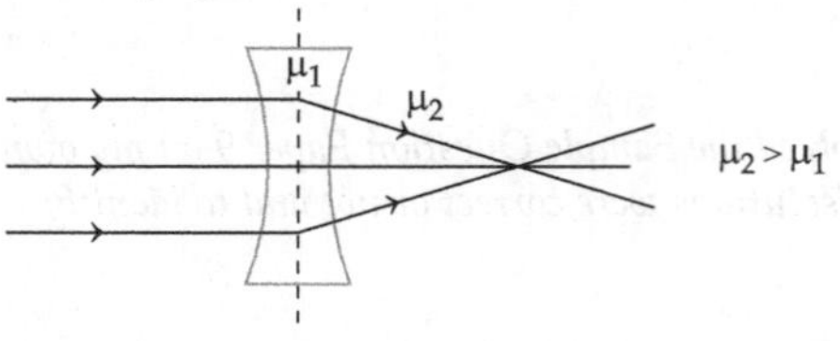

2. Here, the hollow cylinder is positively charged.

We know that, the electric field lines appear to come out from the conductor. Thus, the field lines for an uniformly positive charged hollow cylinder is shown in the figure.

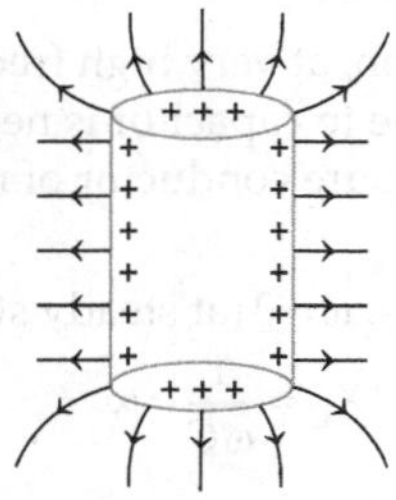

3. In *n*-type semiconductors, electrons are majority charge carriers which have greater mobility than holes (majority charge carriers in *p*-type).

Or

When a photodiode is illuminated with light, then due to breaking of covalent bonds, equal number of additional electrons and holes comes into existence, whereas fractional change in minority charge carrier is much higher than fractional change in majority charge carrier. Since, the fractional change of minority carrier current is measurable significantly in reverse bias than that in forward bias. Therefore, photodiode is connected in reverse bias.

4. We may think that the image will now show only half of the object, but considering the laws of reflection to be true for all points of the remaining part of the mirror, the image will be that of the whole object.

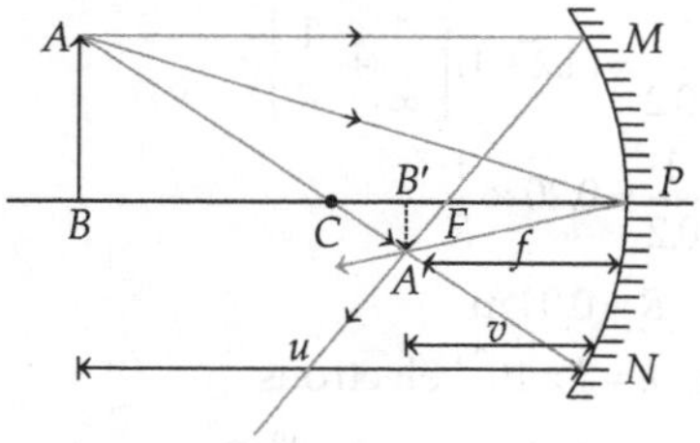

However, as the area of the reflecting surface has been reduced, the intensity of the image will be low, i.e. half.

Or

Given, refractive index of water, $\mu_w = \dfrac{4}{3}$

Refractive index of glass prism, $\mu_g = \dfrac{3}{2}$

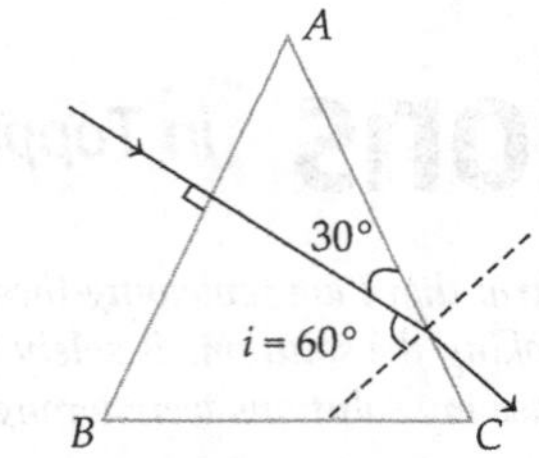

For total internal reflection occurrence the incident angle must be greater than critical angle.

$\therefore$ Let us calculate critical angle *C*.

As we know that, $\sin C = \dfrac{1}{\mu}$

where, $\mu = \dfrac{\text{refractive index of glass } ({}_a\mu_g)}{\text{refractive index of water } ({}_a\mu_w)}$

$\therefore \quad \sin C = \dfrac{1}{\left(\dfrac{{}_a\mu_g}{{}_a\mu_w}\right)} = \dfrac{1}{\left(\dfrac{3/2}{4/3}\right)} = \dfrac{1}{9/8}$ or $\sin C = \dfrac{8}{9} = 0.88$

$\Rightarrow \quad C = 61.6° \quad [\text{As } \sin 60° = \sqrt{3}/2 = 0.86]$

As the critical angle, i.e, 61.6° is greater than the angle of incidence, i.e. 60°, hence TIR will not occurs.

5. Given, mass of ${}^{40}_{20}$Ca nucleus,

$$M = 39.962589 \text{ u}$$

Number of protons in Ca = 20

Number of neutrons in Ca = 40 – 20 = 20

Total mass of 20 protons and 20 neutrons,

$$m = 20(m_p + m_n)$$
$$= 20(1.007825 + 1.008665) \text{ u}$$
$$= 20 \times 2.01649 = 40.3298$$

Mass defect $\Delta m = m - M$

$$= 40.3298 - 39.962589$$
$$= 0.367211 \text{ u}$$

Binding energy = 0.367211 × 931
= 341.873 MeV/nucleon

Or

(i) Radius of nucleus, $R = R_0 A^{\frac{1}{3}}$

where, $R_0 = 1.2 \times 10^{-15}$m

Volume of the nucleus $= \left(\dfrac{4}{3}\right)\pi R^3 = \left(\dfrac{4}{3}\right)\pi R_0^3 \cdot A$

$\therefore \quad \dfrac{\text{Volume of } {}^{209}_{83}\text{Bi}}{\text{Volume of } {}^1_1\text{H}} = \dfrac{209}{1} = 209$

(ii) Density of a nucleus = Mass/Volume

$$= \frac{m_n A}{\frac{4}{3}\pi R_0^3 \cdot A} = \frac{3m_n}{4\pi R_0^3}$$

= constant and independent of *A*.

Ratio of densities of Bi and H is 1.

6. (i)

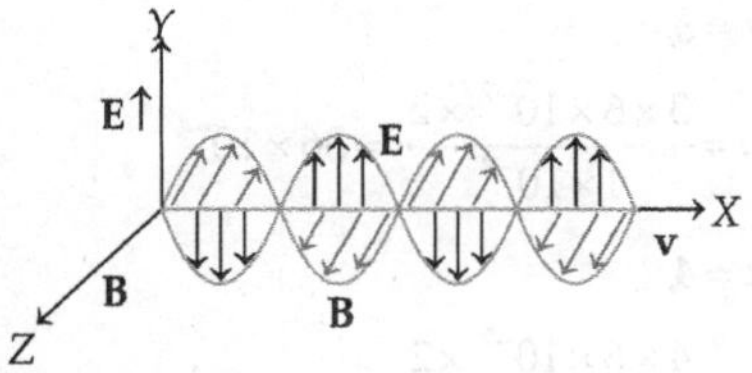

(ii) $B_0 = \frac{E_0}{c}$

where, B_0 = magnitude of magnetic field,

E_0 = magnitude of electric field

and c = speed of light in vacuum.

7. The graph of variation in the intensity of diffracted light in a single slit experiment is shown in the figure. Here, intensity of the central maxima will be maximum and that of other will gradually decreases.

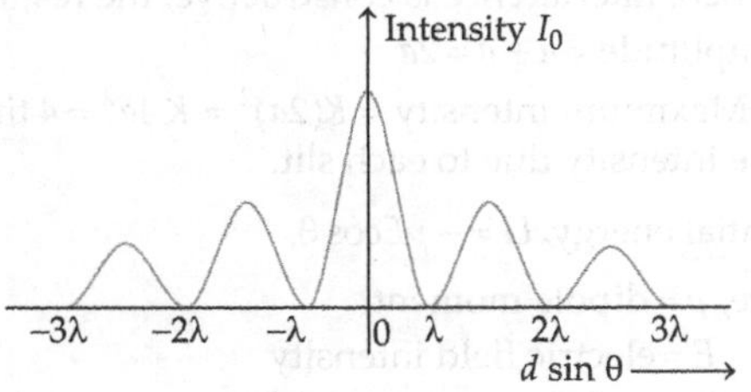

For central bright fringe, $\theta = 0°$

For first dark fringe, $d \sin\theta = \pm\lambda \Rightarrow \sin\theta = \pm\frac{\lambda}{d}$

8. The photoelectric effect cannot be explained on the basis of wave nature of light because wave nature of radiation cannot explain the following concepts.

- The instantaneous ejection of photoelectrons and the existence of threshold frequency for a metal surface.
- In photoelectric effect, emission is not possible till the frequency of light is more than threshold frequency. Whatever be the intensity which is in contrary to wave theory, which explains increase in the intensity of light means more light energy.
- The fact that kinetic energy of the emitted electrons is independent of the intensity of light and depends upon its frequency.

9. (i) Here, $I = 10$ A, $r = 3$ cm,

$r = 3 \times 10^{-2}$ m

Angle subtended by coil at the centre,

$$\theta = 360° - 90° = 270° = \frac{3\pi}{2} \text{ rad}$$

Magnetic field induction at O due to current through circular path ACB is

$$B = \frac{\mu_0}{4\pi} \cdot \frac{I}{r} \theta = 10^{-7} \times \frac{10}{3 \times 10^{-2}} \times \frac{3\pi}{2}$$

$= 1.57 \times 10^{-4}$ T

(ii) Given, current, $I = 10$ A (East to West)

Distance, $r = 10$ cm $= 10 \times 10^{-2}$ m

Magnetic field, $|B| = ?$

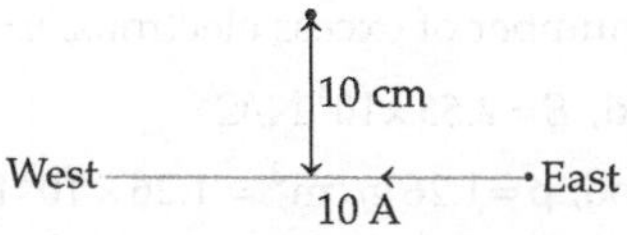

The magnitude of magnetic field $|B|$ for infinite length of wire $= \frac{\mu_0 I}{2\pi r}$

$$\Rightarrow \quad |B| = \frac{4\pi \times 10^{-7} \times 10}{2 \times \pi \times 10 \times 10^{-2}} = 2 \times 10^{-5} \text{T}$$

The direction of magnetic field is given by right hand thumb rule or Maxwell's cork screw rule. So, the direction of magnetic field at point 10 cm North due to flowing current is perpendicularly inwards to the plane of paper.

(iii) Here, $n = 100$, $r = 8$ cm $= 8 \times 10^{-2}$ m and $I = 0.40$ A

$\therefore$ Magnetic field B at the centre,

$$B = \frac{\mu_0}{4\pi} \cdot \frac{2\pi I n}{r} = \frac{10^{-7} \times 2 \times 3.14 \times 0.40 \times 100}{8 \times 10^{-2}}$$

$= 3.1 \times 10^{-4}$ T

10. (i) Resistivity is a property of the material, it does not depend on the dimensions of the wire. Thus, when the wire is stretched to three times, then its resistivity remains same.

(ii) We know that, $R = \frac{ml}{ne^2 \tau A}$

or relaxation time, $\tau = \frac{ml}{ne^2 RA}$

If temperature increases, the resistance (R) of a good conductor increases and hence relaxation time decreases.

(iii) Drift velocity (v_d) of moving electron in the conductor is given by

$$v_d = \frac{eE\tau}{2m}$$

i.e. $\quad v_d \propto \tau$

Hence, on increasing the value of relaxation time, drift velocity increases.

Or

The resistance of the filament of the bulb,

$$R = \frac{V^2}{P} = \frac{200 \times 200}{100} = 400\Omega$$

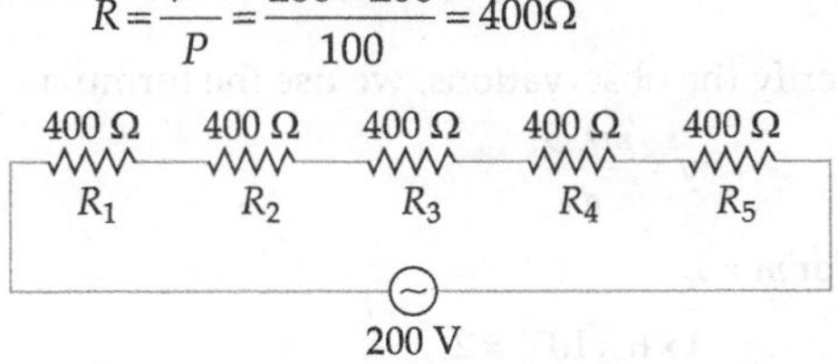

If five bulbs are connected in series, then total resistance of the circuit,

$$R = R_1 + R_2 + R_3 + R_4 + R_5 = 400 \times 5 = 2000\Omega$$

Current, $I = \frac{V}{R} = \frac{200}{2000} = \frac{1}{10} = 0.1$ A

11. Given, the number of excess electrons, $n = 12$

Electric field, $E = 2.55 \times 10^4$ N/C

Density of oil, $\rho = 1.26\ \text{g/cm}^3 = 1.26 \times 10^3\ \text{kg/m}^3$

Electronic charge, $e = 1.6 \times 10^{-19}$ C

$\Rightarrow \quad g = 9.81\ \text{m/s}^2$

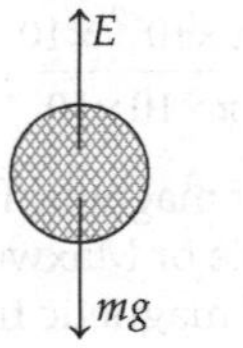

Let the radius of drop be r.

The electrostatic force on drop $= qE = neE \quad [\because q = ne]$

The gravitational force on the drop $= mg$

[where, $m =$ mass of the drop]

$= \text{Volume} \times \text{Density} \times g$

[$\because$ mass = volume × density]

$= \frac{4}{3}\pi r^3 \times \rho \times g$

As the drop is held stationary. So, the net force on the drop is zero.

$\therefore$ Electrostatic force = Gravitational force

$$\Rightarrow \quad neE = \frac{4}{3}\pi r^3 \rho g \Rightarrow r^3 = \frac{3neE}{4\pi\rho g}$$

$$= \frac{3 \times 12 \times 1.6 \times 10^{-19} \times 2.55 \times 10^4}{4 \times 3.14 \times 1.26 \times 10^3 \times 9.81}$$

$$\Rightarrow \quad r^3 = 0.94 \times 10^{-18}$$

$$\Rightarrow \quad r = (0.94 \times 10^{-18})^{1/3} = 9.81 \times 10^{-7}$$

Thus, the radius of the drop is 9.81×10^{-7} m.

Value Point

To get maximum marks, following this point

- Here, oil drop is held stationary under electric field that means the weight of the drop is balanced by the electrostatic force applied on it.

12. To verify the observations, we use the formula

$$y = \frac{m\lambda D}{d}$$

(*i*) **For** $m = 1$,

$$y = \frac{1 \times 6 \times 10^{-7} \times 2}{1 \times 10^{-3}}$$

$$= 12 \times 10^{-4}$$

(*ii*) **For** $m = 2$,

$$y = \frac{2 \times 6 \times 10^{-7} \times 2}{1 \times 10^{-3}} = 24 \times 10^{-4}$$

(*iii*) **For** $m = 3$,

$$y = \frac{3 \times 6 \times 10^{-7} \times 2}{1 \times 10^{-3}} = 36 \times 10^{-4}$$

(*iv*) **For** $m = 4$,

$$y = \frac{4 \times 6 \times 10^{-7} \times 2}{1 \times 10^{-3}} = 48 \times 10^{-4}$$

Or

(*i*) The central fringe will be dark because of initial difference of π radian.

(*ii*) Suppose the amplitude of wave from each slit is a, therefore intensity due to each slit $= Ka^2$.

When, interference is destructive, the resultant amplitude $= a - a = 0$

$\therefore$ Minimum intensity $= 0$

When, interference is constructive, the resultant amplitude $= a + a = 2a$

$\therefore$ Maximum intensity $= K(2a)^2 = K4a^2 = 4$ times of the intensity due to each slit.

13. Potential energy, $U = -pE\cos\theta$

where, $p =$ dipole moment,

$E =$ electric field intensity

and $\theta =$ angle between p and E.

(*i*) Work done in turning through 90°

$= U_f - U_i = -pE\cos 90° - (-pE\cos 0°)$

$= 0 + pE = pE$

(*ii*) Work done in deflecting through 180°

$= U_f - U_i = -pE\cos 180° - (-pE\cos 0°)$

$= pE + pE = 2pE$

Common Mistakes Do not forget the negative sign in the formula of potential energy.

14. (*i*) The ray diagram showing the image formation of the object.

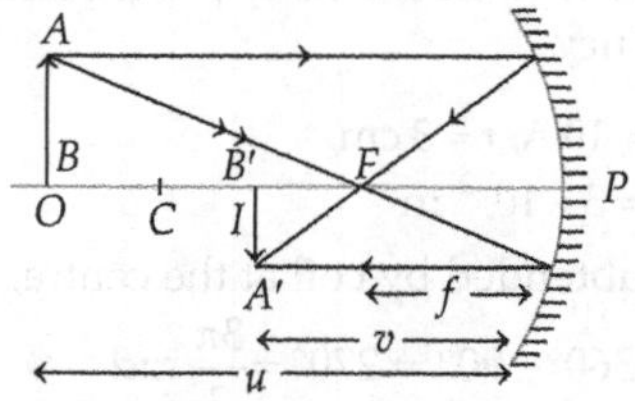

(*ii*) The position of image is unaffected but the intensity of image is reduced as number of rays reduced.

15. (*i*) Angular momentum of an electron in nth orbit $= \frac{nh}{2\pi}$

By Bohr's hypothesis, we have

$$mvr = \frac{nh}{2\pi} \Rightarrow v = \frac{nh}{2\pi mr}$$

Time period to complete a revolution in an orbit,

$$T = \frac{2\pi r}{v} = \frac{2\pi r(2\pi mr)}{nh} = \frac{4\pi^2 mr^2}{nh}$$

Since, radius of the orbit is proportional to n^2, hence

$$r \propto n^2 \Rightarrow r = a_0 n^2$$

$$\therefore \quad T = \frac{4\pi^2 m a_0^2 n^4}{nh} = \frac{4\pi^2 m a_0^2 n^3}{h}$$

$\therefore$ Number of orbits completed in 10^{-8} s

$$= \frac{10^{-8}}{T} = \frac{10^{-8} \times h}{4\pi^2 m a_0^2 n^3}$$

$$= \frac{10^{-8} \times 6.6 \times 10^{-34}}{4 \times (3.14)^2 \times 9.1 \times 10^{-31} \times (5.3 \times 10^{-11})^2 \times (2)^3}$$

$$= 8 \times 10^6$$

(*ii*) For an electron revolving in nth orbit of radius r_0, then we have, $n\lambda = 2\pi r_0$

For electron orbiting in ground state, $n = 1$.

$$1\lambda = 2\pi r_0 = 2\pi \times 0.5\,\text{Å} \qquad [\because r_0 = 0.5\,\text{Å}]$$

$$\lambda = \pi\,\text{Å}$$

$$\lambda = 3.14\,\text{Å}$$

16. Current in loop 1,

$$I_1 = \frac{V}{R_1} = \frac{(3+2t)}{10}$$

Magnetic field at the centre of the loop 1 due to current I_1,

$$B_1 = \frac{\mu_0 I_1}{2R_1} = \frac{\mu_0(3+2t)}{20}$$

Flux linked with loop 2,

$$\phi_2 = B_1 A_2 = \frac{\mu_0}{20}(3+2t)\,\pi\,(0.1)^2$$

Emf induced in loop 2,

$$e_2 = \frac{d\phi_2}{dt}$$

$$= \frac{\mu_0 \pi}{2000}\frac{d(3+2t)}{dt} = \frac{\mu_0 \pi}{1000}$$

Induced current in loop 2,

$$I_2 = \frac{e_2}{R_2}$$

$$= \frac{\mu_0 \pi}{1000}\,\text{A}$$

17.

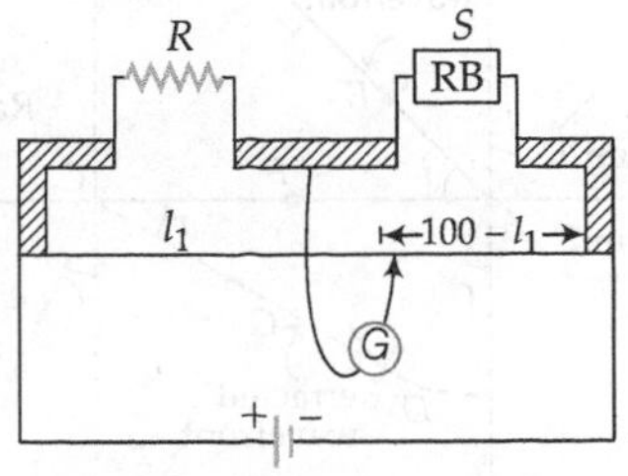

In given meter bridge, initially

$$\frac{R}{l_1} = \frac{S}{100 - l_1} \text{ at balance condition} \quad \ldots\text{(i)}$$

When a resistance X is placed in parallel with S, then net resistance in gap $= \dfrac{SX}{S+X}$.

Hence, for balance condition, $\dfrac{R}{l_2} = \dfrac{\left(\dfrac{SX}{S+X}\right)}{100 - l_2}$ $\quad \ldots$(ii)

Substitute the value of R from Eq. (i) to Eq. (ii), we get

$$\frac{l_1}{l_2(100 - l_1)} = \frac{X}{(S+X)(100 - l_2)}$$

$$\Rightarrow \quad S + X = X\left\{\frac{l_2(100 - l_1)}{l_1(100 - l_2)}\right\}$$

$$\Rightarrow \quad \frac{S}{X} + 1 = \frac{l_2(100 - l_1)}{l_1(100 - l_2)}$$

$$\Rightarrow \quad \frac{S}{X} = \frac{l_2(100 - l_1) - l_1(100 - l_2)}{l_1(100 - l_2)}$$

$$\therefore \quad X = \frac{S l_1 (100 - l_2)}{100(l_2 - l_1)}\,\Omega$$

18. Given that, $L = 6\,\text{H}$, $C = 100\,\mu\text{F} = 100 \times 10^{-6}\,\text{F}$, $R = 50\,\Omega$

and $\quad V_{rms} = 250\,\text{V}$

(*i*) Resonance angular frequency,

$$\omega_r = \frac{1}{\sqrt{LC}} = \frac{1}{\sqrt{6 \times 100 \times 10^{-6}}} = \frac{100}{\sqrt{6}}\,\text{rad/s}$$

(*ii*) Impedance, $Z = \sqrt{R^2 + \left(\omega L - \dfrac{1}{\omega C}\right)^2}$

At resonance, $X_L = X_C \Rightarrow \omega L = \dfrac{1}{\omega C}$

$$\therefore \quad Z_r = R = 50\,\Omega$$

Amplitude of current at resonant frequency,

$$I_0 = \frac{V_0}{Z_r} = \frac{\sqrt{2} \times 250}{50} = 5\sqrt{2}\,\text{A}$$

$$\Rightarrow \quad I_{rms} = \frac{I_0}{\sqrt{2}} = \frac{5\sqrt{2}}{\sqrt{2}} = 5\,\text{A}$$

(*iii*) Potential difference across L,

$$V_L = I_{rms} \times X_L = I_{rms} \times (\omega_r \times L)$$

$$= 5 \times \left(\frac{100}{\sqrt{6}} \times 6\right)$$

$$\approx 500\sqrt{6}\,\text{V} = 1224.7\,\text{V}$$

Potential difference across C,

$$V_C = I_{rms} \times X_c = I_{rms} \times \frac{1}{\omega_r C}$$

$$= \frac{5}{40 \times 100 \times 10^{-6}} = 1250\,\text{V}$$

Potential difference across R,

$$V_R = I_{rms} \times R = 5 \times 50 = 250\,\text{V}$$

(*iv*) Since, $X_L = X_C = 25\,\Omega$

So, V_L and V_C are equal and opposite in phase, i.e. voltmeter reading $= 0$ V. Ammeter reading,

$$I=\frac{V}{\sqrt{R^2+(X_L-X_C)^2}}=\frac{240}{30}=8\text{ A}$$

Or

According to the question,

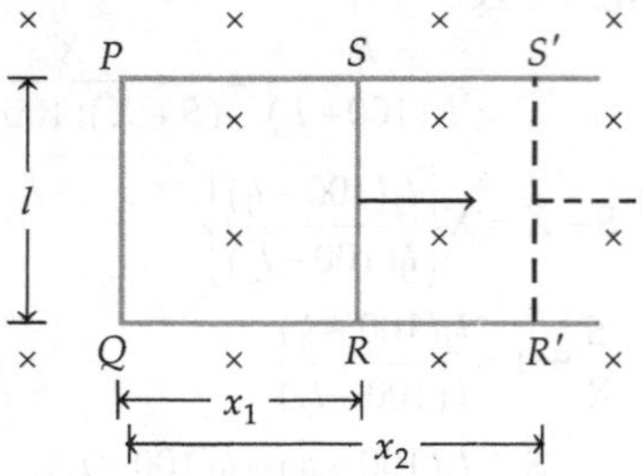

(*i*) Let RS moves with speed v rightward and also RS is at distances x_1 and x_2 from PQ at instants t_1 at t_2, respectively.

$\therefore$ At t_1, flux linked with loop 1, i.e. $PQRS$, $\phi_1=B(lx_1)$

Similarly, at instant t_2, flux linked with loop 2, i.e. $PQR'S'$, $\phi_2=B(lx_2)$

$\therefore$ Change in flux, $\Delta\phi=\phi_2-\phi_1=Bl(x_2-x_1)=Bl\Delta x$

$$\Rightarrow \frac{\Delta\phi}{\Delta t}=Bl\frac{\Delta x}{\Delta t}=Blv\quad\left[\because v=\frac{\Delta x}{\Delta t}\right]$$

By Faraday's law, magnitude of induced emf, $e=vBl$.

(*ii*) If resistance of loop is R, then $I=\dfrac{vBl}{R}$

$$\therefore \text{Magnetic force}=IBl\sin 90^\circ=\left(\frac{vBl}{R}\right)Bl$$

$$=\frac{vB^2l^2}{R}\qquad[\because \sin 90^\circ=1]$$

$\therefore$ External force must be equal to magnetic force and in opposite directions.

$$\therefore \text{External force}=\frac{vB^2l^2}{R}$$

(*iii*) As, $P=I^2R=\left(\dfrac{vBl}{R}\right)^2\times R=\dfrac{v^2B^2l^2}{R^2}\times R$

$$\therefore\quad P=\frac{v^2B^2l^2}{R}$$

19. (*i*) The phenomenon of splitting of light into its constituent colours after passing through a prism is called dispersion of light.

(*ii*) **Refraction of light through a prism**

The figure below shows the passage of light through a triangular prism ABC.

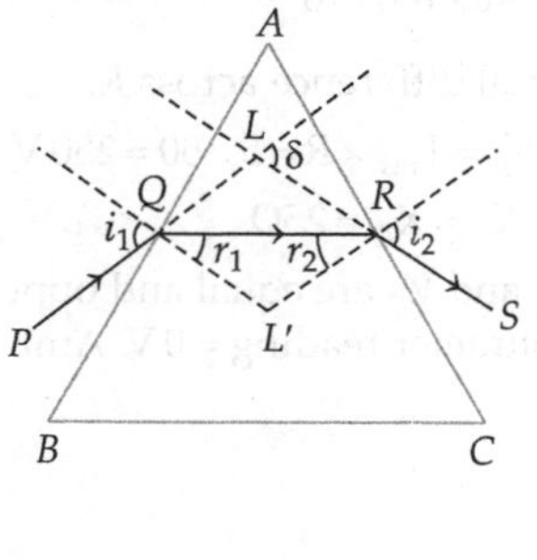

(*iii*) (a) Given, $\mu=\sqrt{2}$

As ray grazes along NC, so the critical angle for prism is

$$\sin c=\frac{1}{\mu}\Rightarrow c=\sin^{-1}\left(\frac{1}{\mu}\right)=\sin^{-1}\left(\frac{1}{\sqrt{2}}\right)=45^\circ$$

(b) In a prism, the angle, $A=r_1+r_2$

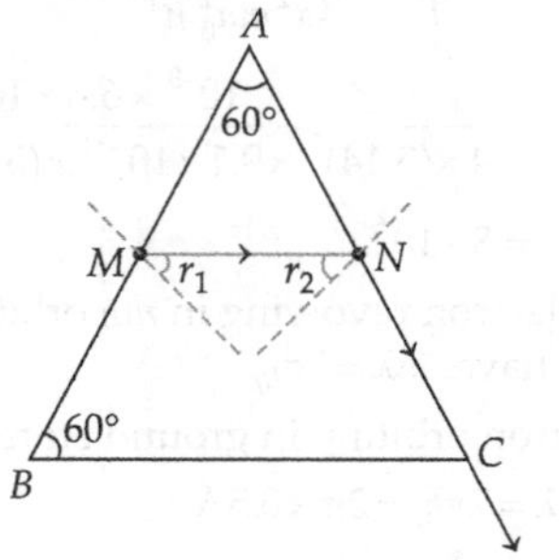

Since, the ray MN is parallel to the base,

so, $\quad r_1=r_2\Rightarrow A=2r_1$ or $r_1=\dfrac{A}{2}=\dfrac{60}{2}=30^\circ$

Hence, $r_1=r_2=30^\circ$

Or

(*i*) (a) The wavefront when light emerges out is shown below in figure.

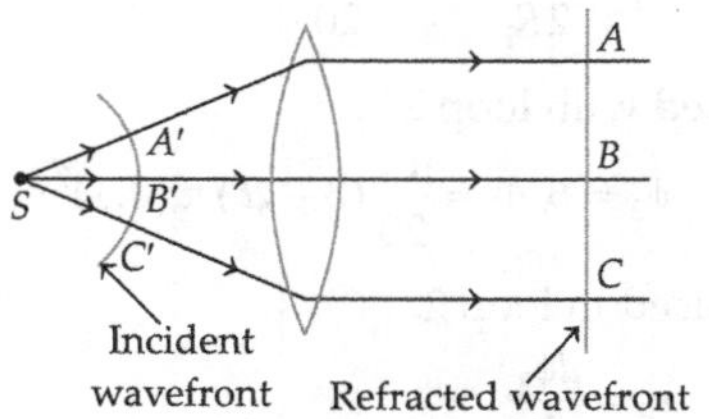

or a convex lens with point source (S) which is placed at its focus (F).

(b) Huygens' principle is used to explain refraction showing refracted wavefront below.

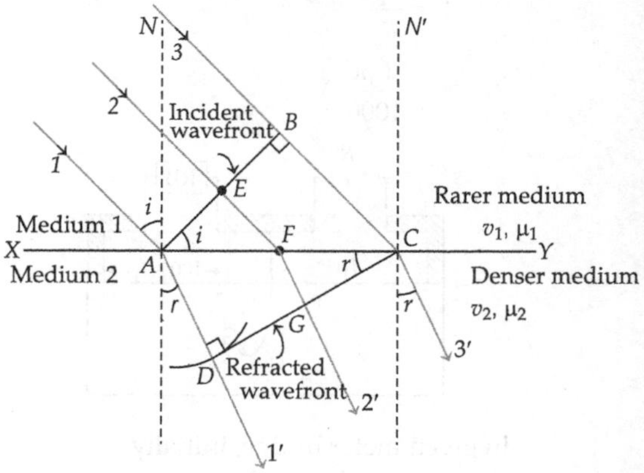

(*ii*) The locus of all those points where the wave is in the same phase at any instant is called wavefront.

(a) When the source of light is a point source, the wavefront is a sphere with source at the centre of the sphere. It is called a spherical wavefront.

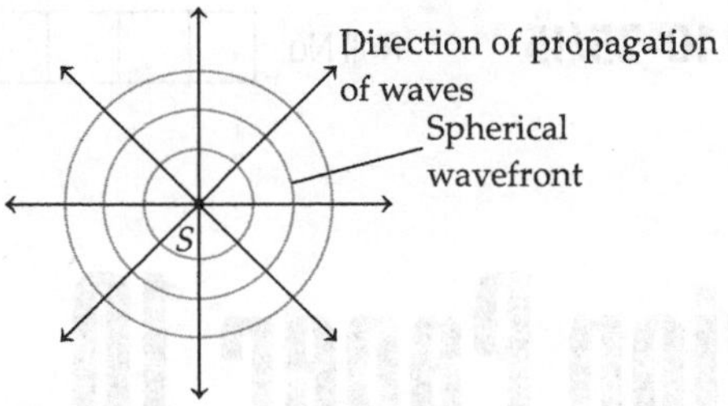

(b) When, the source of light is linear as given in the figure below, all the points equidistant from the source lie on a cylindrical surface. Therefore, the wavefront is cylindrical.

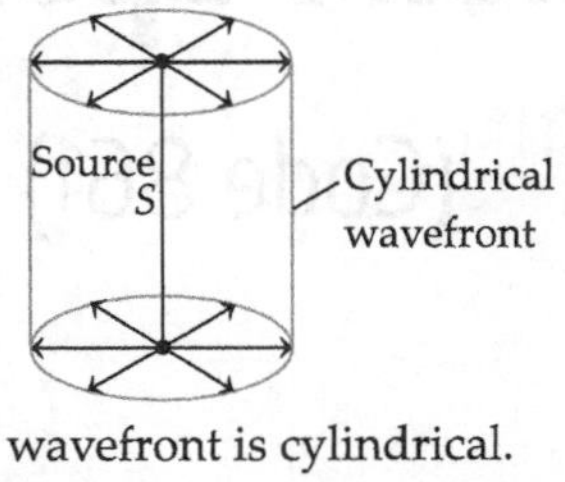

(c) When, the point source or linear source of light is at a very large distance, a small portion of spherical or cylindrical wavefront appears to be plane. Such a wavefront is called a plane wavefront.

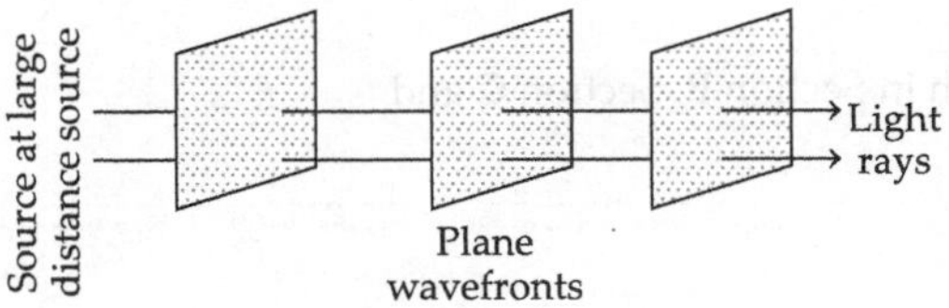

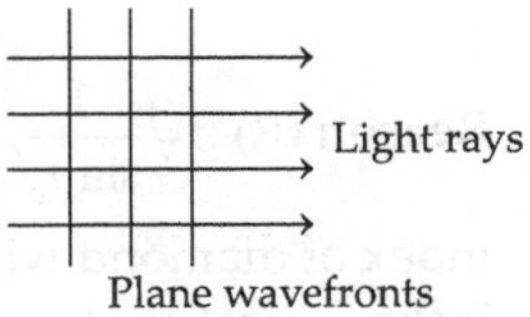

Value Point To get maximum marks, show the direction of propagation of wave and wavefront in the diagram.

20. (*i*)

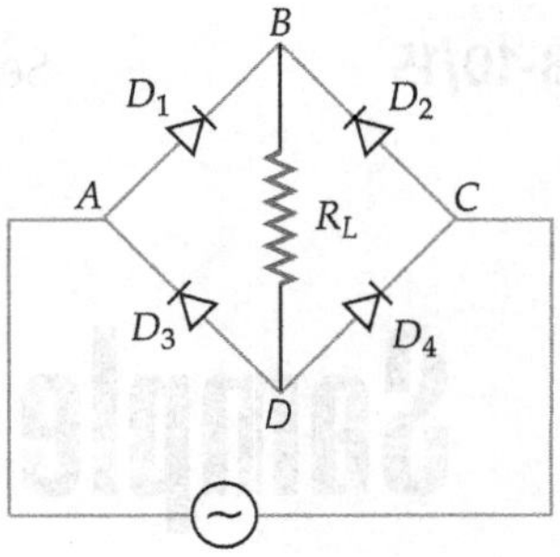

AC input is applied across A and C and output is taken across BD.

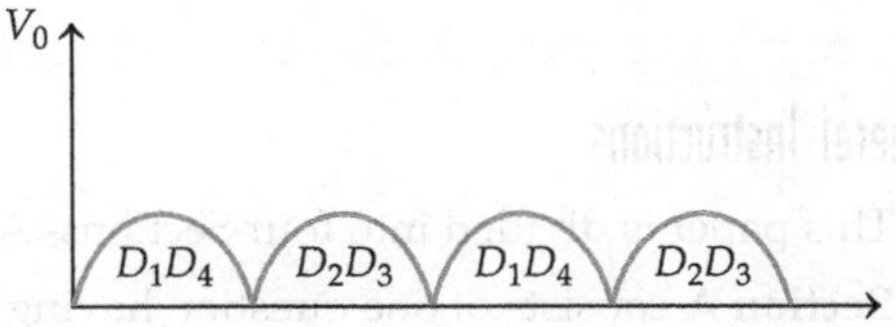

When positive cycle is fed to AC, D_1 and D_4 conduct and when negative cycle is fed to AC, D_3 and D_2 conduct in the same direction. Output across BD is thus full wave rectified.

(*ii*) A rectifier is used to convert AC to DC. No, output has some AC component.

(*iii*) Output frequency of full wave rectifier is twice the output frequency of half-wave rectifier.

$$\therefore \quad \frac{f_{\text{half-wave}}}{f_{\text{full wave}}} = \frac{1}{2}$$

(iv) Here, diode is forward bias.

Threshold voltage = 0.7 V

Input voltage = 0.5 V

Since, $0.7 > 0.5$

No current flow, so forward biasing, 0A.

SQP Code : **PB-10/15** | Series **i-Succeed 10-25/15** | Roll No. | | | | | | | |

Sample Question Paper 10

Physics 12th (Code 861)

General Instructions

1. This paper is divided into four Sections- A, B, C and D. Answer all questions.
2. **Section A** consists of one question having sub-parts of one mark each.
3. **Section B** consists of seven questions of two marks each.
4. **Section C** consists of nine questions of three marks each.
5. **Section D** consists of three questions of five marks each.
6. Internal choices have been provided in two questions each in Section B, Section C and Section D.

Time : 3 Hrs.

Max. Marks : 70

Section A (14 Marks)

1. **A.** In questions (i) to (vii) below, choose the correct alternative (a), (b), (c) or (d) for each of the questions given below.

(*i*) A beam of protons with a velocity of $4\times 10^5 \text{ms}^{-1}$ moves in the direction of uniform magnetic field. It makes an angle of 37° with the magnetic field and follows a helical path. If the time period of helix is 2×10^{-7} s, then its pitch will be • *Understanding* [1]

(a) 2 cm (b) 4 cm

(c) 8 cm (d) 6 cm

(*ii*) Long thin strips of white paper, which are lightly ironed, when brought near TV screen or computer monitor (in switched ON situation), these paper strips • *Recall* [1]

(a) get attracted to screen

(b) are repelled by screen

(c) become black

(d) melt down

(*iii*) **Assertion** (A) The refractive index of diamond is $\sqrt{6}$ and that of liquid is $\sqrt{3}$. If the light travels from diamond to the liquid, it will totally reflected when the angle of incidence is 45°.

Reason (R) $n=\dfrac{1}{\sin i_c}$, where n is the refractive index of diamond with respect to liquid and i_c is the critical angle. • *Analysis* [1]

(a) Both Assertion and Reason are true and Reason is the correct explanation for Assertion.

(b) Both Assertion and Reason are true but Reason is not the correct explanation for Assertion.

(c) Assertion is false and Reason is true.

(d) Both Assertion and Reason are false.

(*iv*) Which of the following is true for rays coming from infinity? • *Recall* [1]

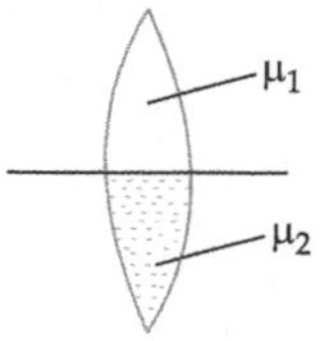

(a) Two images are formed at two different points

(b) Continuous image is formed between focal points of upper and lower lens

(c) One image is formed by the lens

(d) None of the above

(*v*) Two particles of masses m_a and m_b having same charges are projected in a perpendicular magnetic field. They travel along circular paths of radii r_a and r_b such that $r_a > r_b$, then which is true? • *Analysis* [1]

(a) $m_a v_a > m_b v_b$

(b) $m_a > m_b$ and $v_a > v_b$

(c) $m_a = m_b$ and $v_a > v_b$

(d) $m_b v_b > m_a v_a$

(*vi*) In which of the following transitions the wavelength will be minimum? • *Analysis* [1]

(a) $n = 5$ to $n = 4$ (b) $n = 4$ to $n = 3$

(c) $n = 3$ to $n = 2$ (d) $n = 2$ to $n = 1$

(*vii*) **Assertion** (A) The temperature coefficient of resistance is positive for metals and negative for *p*-type semiconductors.

Reason (R) The charge carriers in metals are negatively charged whereas the majority charge carriers in *p*-type semiconductors are positively charged. • *Understanding* [1]

(a) Both Assertion and Reason are true and Reason is the correct explanation for Assertion.

(b) Both Assertion and Reason are true but Reason is not the correct explanation for Assertion.

(c) Assertion is false and Reason is true.

(d) Both Assertion and Reason are false.

Section B (14 Marks)

2. Define magnetic dipole moment. Also, write its SI unit. • *Recall* [2]

Or

Obtain an expression of magnetic flux density **B** at the centre of a circular coil of radius *R* having *N* turns and carrying a current *I*. • *Application* [2]

3. You are given three lenses L_1, L_2 and L_3 each of focal length 10 cm. An object is kept at 15 cm in front of lens L_1, as shown in figure. The final real image is formed at the focus of L_3. Find the separation between L_1, L_2 and L_3. • *Analysis* [2]

B. Answer the following questions briefly.

(*i*) Figure shows three point charges $+2q, -q$ and $+3q$. Two charges $+2q$ and $-q$ are enclosed within a surface *S*. What is the electric flux due to this configuration through the surface *S*? • *Application* [1]

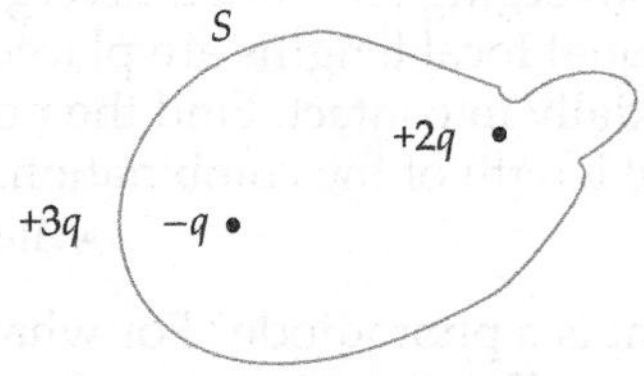

(*ii*) Find the ratio of nuclear densities of nuclei of $^{40}Ca_{20}$ and $^{16}O_8$. • *Recall* [1]

(*iii*) A polythene piece rubbed with wool is found to have a negative charge of 3×10^{-7} C. Estimate the number of electrons transferred from which to which? • *Recall* [1]

(*iv*) To convert a pure semiconductor into *n*-type semiconductor, what type of impurity is added to it? • *Recall* [1]

(*v*) What consideration led de-Broglie to suggest that material particles can also shown wave property? • *Recall* [1]

(*vi*) Name the material which is used as a moderator in nuclear reactor. • *Recall* [1]

(*vii*) A particle of mass 1 mg has the same wavelength as an electron moving with a velocity of 3×10^6 ms^{-1}. What is the velocity of the particle? • *Understanding* [1]

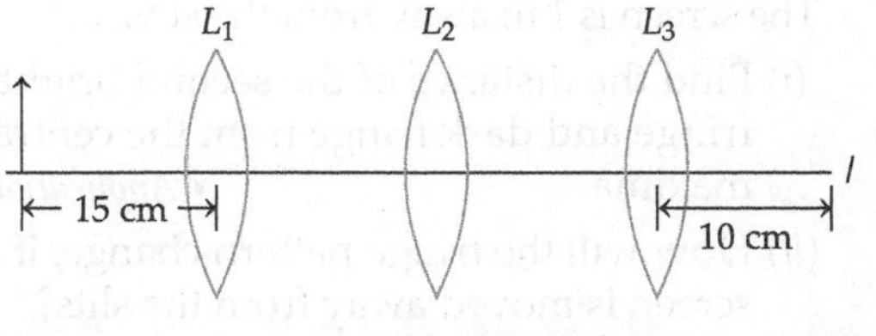

4. When an ideal capacitor is charged by a DC battery, no current flows. However, when an AC source is used, the current flows continuously. How does one explain this, based on the concept of displacement current? • *Application* [2]

5. (*i*) (a) Write the necessary conditions for the phenomenon of total internal reflection to occur. • *Recall*
(b) Write the relation between refractive index and critical angle for a given pair of optical media. • *Recall*
(*ii*) A converging lens and a diverging lens of equal focal lengths are placed coaxially in contact. Find the power and focal length of the combination. • *Application* [2]

6. (*i*) What is a photodiode? For what purpose is it used? • *Recall*
(*ii*) Why is photodiode operated in reverse bias? Draw its *V-I* characteristic for different intensities of illumination. • *Application* [2]

7. Draw a rough sketch showing the variation of binding energy per nucleon with mass number of various nuclei. Label the graph and state the region where the nuclei are most stable. • *Application* [2]

Or (*i*) Why is the density of nucleus more than that of atoms? • *Application* [1]
(*ii*) The mass of nucleus is less than the sum of masses of nucleons forming it, why? • *Recall* [1]

8. In a meter bridge, the null point is found at a distance of 40 cm from end *A*. If a resistance of 12Ω is connected in parallel with *S*, the null point occurs at 50 cm from *A*. Determine the values of resistances *R* and *S*. • *Understanding* [2]

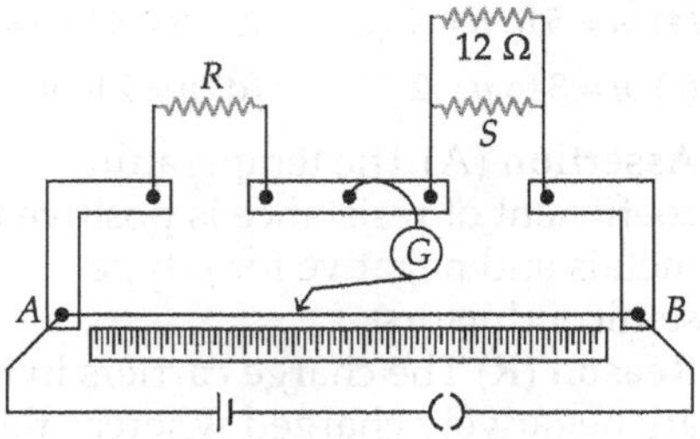

Section C (27 Marks)

9. An electric dipole of dipole moment **p** is placed in a uniform electric field **E** with its axis inclined to the field. Write an expression for the toque τ experienced by the dipole in vector form. Show diagrammatically, now the dipole should be kept in the electric field so that the torque acting on it is • *Application* [3]
(*i*) maximum
(*ii*) minimum

SP-10

10. In Young's double slit experiment, the two slits 0.15 mm apart are illuminated by monochromatic light of wavelength 450 nm. The screen is 1 m away from the slits.
(*i*) Find the distance of the second bright fringe and dark fringe from the central maxima. • *Application* [2]
(*ii*) How will the fringe pattern change, if the screen is moved away from the slits? • *Recall* [1]

11. Briefly describe the formation of image by compound microscope with the help of suitable ray diagram. • *Application* [3]

12. Draw *V-I* characteristics of a *p-n* junction diode. Answer the following questions giving reasons. • *Application*
(*i*) Why is the current under reverse bias almost independent of the applied potential upto a critical voltage?
(*ii*) Why does the reverse current show a sudden increase at the critical voltage? [3]

Or

A student records the following data for the resistivity (ρ) of a semiconductor at different doping concentration (N_d). Verify (for any two) that these observations are in good agreement with the expected theoretical values of ρ. • *Application* [3]

N_d(cm^{-3})	1×10^{16}	2×10^{16}	4×10^{16}	8×10^{16}
ρ (Ω cm)	ρ_0	$\frac{\rho_0}{2}$	$\frac{\rho_0}{4}$	$\frac{\rho_0}{8}$

13. A circular coil of 200 turns and radius 10 cm is placed in a uniform magnetic field of 0.5 T, parallel to the plane of the coil. If the current in the coil is 3 A. Assume the area of cross-section of the wire to be 10^{-5} m^2 and the free electron density is 10^{29} m^{-3}.
Calculate the • *Analysis* [3]
(*i*) total torque on the coil,

(*ii*) total force on the coil and

(*iii*) average force on each electron in the coil, due to the magnetic field.

14. (*i*) For wiring in the home, one should use Cu wires or Al wires. What? considerations are involved in this? • *Recall* [1]

(*ii*) Write two characteristics of manganin which make it suitable for making standard resistances. • *Recall* [1]

(*iii*) The relaxation time τ is nearly independent of applied electric field, whereas it changes significantly with temperature T. First fact is responsible for Ohm's law, whereas the second fact leads to variation of ρ with temperature. Elaborate why? • *Recall* [1]

15. State Bohr's quantisation condition of angular momentum. Calculate the longest wavelength of the Brackett series and state to which part of the electromagnetic spectrum does it belong.

• *Application* [3]

Or

A photon emitted during the de-excitation of electron from a state n to the first excited state in a hydrogen atom, irradiates a metallic cathode of work function 2eV, in a photocell, with a stopping potential of 0.55 V. Obtain the value of the quantum number of the state n.

• *Application* [3]

16. Why is wave theory of electromagnetic radiation not able to explain photoelectric effect ? How does photon picture resolve this problem? • *Understanding* [3]

17. State the significance of negative value of electrostatic potential energy of a system of charges.

Three charges are placed at the corners of an equilateral triangle ABC of side 2.0 m as shown in figure. Calculate the electric potential energy of the system of three charges. • *Analysis* [3]

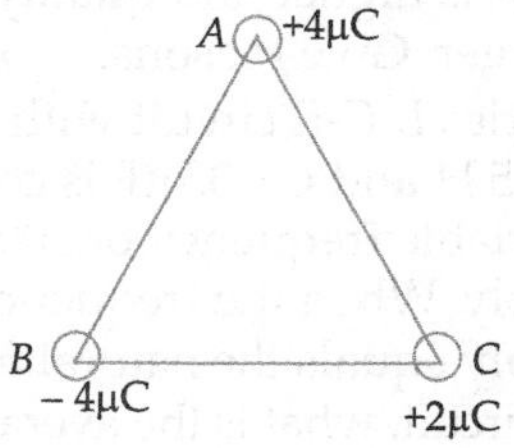

Section D (15 Marks)

18. (*i*) How does the angle of minimum deviation of a glass prism vary, if the incident violet light is replaced by red light? Give reason. • *Recall* [1]

(*ii*) A light ray enters in a prism through the side PR. PQR is a cross-section of the prism. The emergent ray lies along the boundary OQ, $\angle P = 90°$ and $PQ = PR$. The ray diagram has been given, then calculate the critical angle of the prism. • *Application* [2]

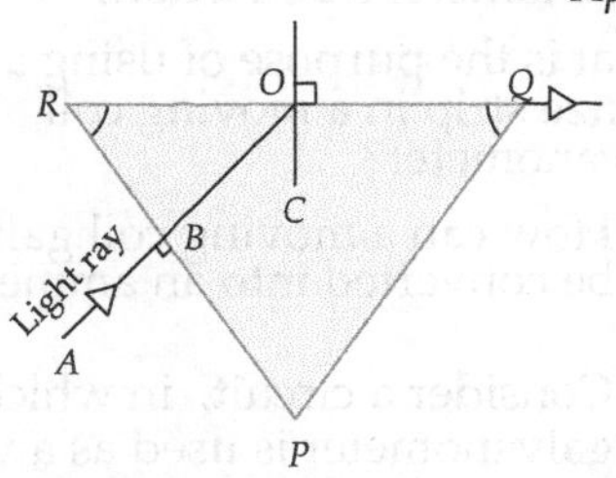

(*iii*) (a) A ray of light incident on face AB of an equilateral glass prism, shows minimum deviation of 30°. Calculate the speed of light through the prism. • *Application*

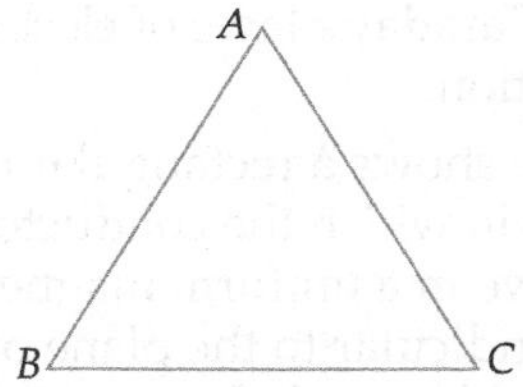

(b) Find the angle of incidence at face AB, so that the emergent ray grazes along the face AC. • *Application* [2]

Or (*i*) Give three points of difference between interference and diffraction. • *Recall* [2]

(*ii*) Graphically show the variation in intensity of light with angular position for both the phenomena. • *Application* [2]

(*iii*) How will the diffraction pattern change, if monochromatic light of smaller wavelength is used? • *Recall* [1]

19. (*i*) Two students A and B performed an experiment and depict the variation of current i_{rms} with angular frequency ω for two different series L-C-R circuits.

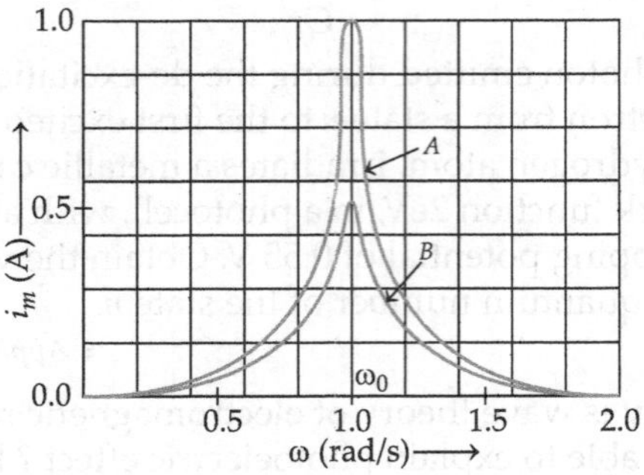

Observe the graph carefully and answer the given questions.

(a) What is the condition for resonance in the *L-C-R* circuit? • *Analysis* [1]

(b) State the relation between *L* and *C* values of the two circuits when the current in two circuits is maximum. • *Analysis* [1]

(c) Indicate the circuit for which power factor is higher and quality factor (Q) is larger. Give reasons. • *Analysis* [1]

(d) A series *L-C-R* circuit with $R = 20\,\Omega$, $L = 1.5$ H and $C = 35\,\mu$F is connected to a variable frequency of 200 V AC supply. When the frequency of the supply equals the natural frequency of the circuit, what is the average power transferred to the circuit in one complete cycle? • *Application* [2]

Or (*i*) State Faraday's laws of electromagnetic induction. • *Recall* [1]

(*ii*) Figure shows a rectangular conductor *PQRS* in which the conductor *PQ* is free to move in a uniform magnetic field *B* perpendicular to the plane of the paper. The field extends from $x = 0$ to $x = b$ and is zero for $x > b$. Assume that only the arm *PQ* possesses resistance *r*. When the arm *PQ* is pulled outward from $x = 0$ to $x = 2b$ and is then moved backward to $x = 0$ with constant speed *v*, obtain the expressions for the flux and the induced emf. • *Application* [4]

Sketch the variation of these quantities with distance $0 \le x \le 2b$.

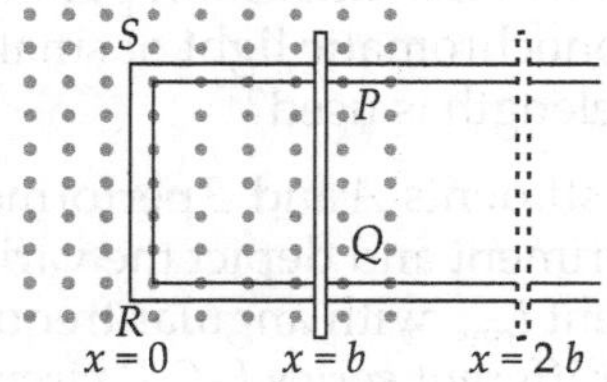

SP-10

20. The galvanometer consists of a coil, with many turns, free to rotate about a fixed axis, in a uniform radial magnetic field. There is a cylindrical soft iron core which not only makes the field radial but also increases the strength of the magnetic field. The galvanometer can be used in a number of ways. It can be used as a detector to check if a current is flowing in the circuit. In this usage the neutral position of the pointer (when no current is flowing through the galvanometer) is in the middle of the scale and not at the left end. Depending on the direction of the current, the pointer's deflection is either to the right or the left. The galvanometer cannot as such be used as an ammeter to measure the value of the current in a given circuit. This is for two reasons : (i) Galvanometer is a very sensitive device, it gives a full scale deflection for a current of the order of μA. (ii) For measuring currents, the galvanometer has to be connected in series, and as it has a large resistance, this will change the value of the current in the circuit.

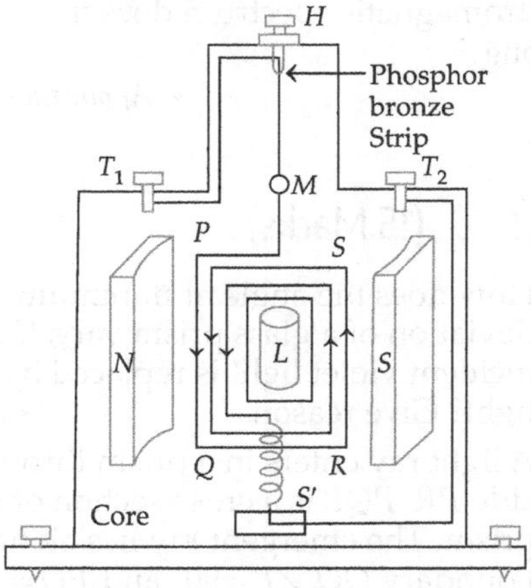

(*i*) What is the effect of increasing the magnetic field strength on the galvanometer's deflection? • *Recall* [1]

(*ii*) What is the purpose of using a phosphor bronze strip in a moving coil galvanometer? • *Recall* [2]

(*iii*) (a) How can a moving coil galvanometer be converted into an ammeter? • *Recall* [2]

(b) Consider a circuit, in which the galvanometer is used as a voltmeter by connecting a high resistance R_V in series with it. If the galvanometer has a resistance of $50\,\Omega$ and gives full scale deflection at $20\,\mu$A, and we want to measure up to 50 V, what should be the value of R_V? • *Application*

Solutions *in Topper's Style*

My Commitment *I affirm that I am reviewing these solutions only after I have solved the Sample Question Paper 10 on my own. My purpose of looking the solutions is solely to verify whether my answers/solutions were correct or not and to identify my mistakes in case my solutions were wrong or I could not solve that.*

1. A. (*i*) (*c*) Velocity of protons in the direction of B,

$$\mathbf{v}_{||} = 4\times10^5 \text{ ms}^{-1}$$

Time period of helix $= 2\times10^{-7}$ s

Pitch $= \mathbf{v}_{||}\times T = 4\times10^5\times2\times10^{-7} = 0.08 \text{ m} = 8 \text{ cm}$

(*ii*) (*a*) Charge on TV screen or computer monitor attracts charge in paper strips. They remain stuck to screen for a while.

(*iii*) (*a*) Refractive index of diamond with respect to liquid,

$$^{d}n_l = \frac{1}{\sin i_c} = \frac{n_d}{n_l}$$

$$\Rightarrow \quad \frac{\sqrt{6}}{\sqrt{3}} = \frac{1}{\sin i_c}$$

$$\Rightarrow \quad \sin i_c = \frac{1}{\sqrt{2}} = \sin 45°$$

$$\therefore \quad i_c = 45°$$

This means that, when the ray of light while travelling from diamond to liquid is incident at an angle of 45°, then it will be totally reflected due to TIR.

Therefore, both A and R are correct and R is the correct explanation of A.

(*iv*) (*a*) As we know, lens is made up of two layers of different refractive indices, hence for a given wavelength of light, it will have two different focal lengths or will have two images at two different points as $\frac{1}{f} \propto (\mu - 1)$ (from lens Maker's formula).

(*v*) (*a*) Radius of circular path,

$$r_a = \frac{m_a v_a}{qB} \text{ and } r_b = \frac{m_b v_b}{qB}$$

According to the question, $r_a > r_b$

$$\therefore \quad \frac{m_a v_a}{qB} > \frac{m_b v_b}{qB}$$

or $\quad m_a v_a > m_b v_b$

(*vi*) (*d*) Wavelength of emitted photon is given by

$$\frac{1}{\lambda} = R\left[\frac{1}{n_f^2} - \frac{1}{n_i^2}\right]$$

The wavelength will be minimum for which $\left(\frac{1}{n_f^2} - \frac{1}{n_i^2}\right)$ is maximum or n_f and n_i are minimum.

(*vii*) (*b*) For metals, the temperature coefficient of resistance is positive because charge carriers in metals are negatively charged but in semiconductor (*p*-type), it is negative because majority charge carriers in *p*-type semiconductor are positively charged.

B. (*i*) According to Gauss' theorem, total electric flux linked with closed gaussian surface S is equal to $1/\varepsilon_0$ times the total charge enclosed by the gaussian surface. The total charge enclosed is $(+2q - q = +q)$. Therefore, electric flux due to this configuration through the surface S is q/ε_0. Charge $+3q$ is outside the closed surface S, hence Gauss' theorem will not be applicable here.

(*ii*) Mass density of nuclear matter is a constant quantity for all elements. It does not depend on element's mass number or atomic radius.

$\therefore$ The ratio of mass densities of $^{40}Ca_{20}$ and $^{16}O_8$ is 1 : 1.

(*iii*) Given, negative charge on polythene piece,

$$q = 3\times10^{-7} \text{C}$$

Since, charge is negative, therefore electrons are transferred from wool to polythene.

So, number of electrons,

$$n = \frac{q}{e} = \frac{3\times10^{-7}}{1.6\times10^{-19}}$$

$$= 1.875\times10^{12}$$

Hence, 1.875×10^{12} electrons have been transferred from wool to polythene.

(*iv*) A pentavalent impurity is to be added to form *n*-type semiconductor whose majority carriers are electrons. e.g. Sb, P or As is added to Ge (or Si).

(*v*) The following considerations led de-Broglie to suggest that material particles can also show wave property.

(a) The Einstein's mass-energy relationship $E = mc^2$, i.e. matter can be converted into energy and *vice-versa*.

(b) From symmetry, consideration particles like electrons, protons should exhibit wave nature when in motion.

(*vi*) Heavy water graphite is used as a moderator in nuclear reactors.

(*vii*) de-Broglie wavelength, $\lambda = \frac{h}{mv}$

As, both particle and electron are having same wavelength therefore their momentum will be equal.

$$m_p v_p = m_e v_e$$

$$\Rightarrow \quad v_p = \frac{m_e v_e}{m_p}$$

$$= \frac{9.1 \times 10^{-31} \times 3 \times 10^6}{10^{-6}}$$

$$\Rightarrow \quad v_p = 2.7 \times 10^{-18} \text{ ms}^{-1}$$

2. The magnetic dipole moment of a magnet is a quantity that determines the torque, it will experience in an external magnetic field. If a coil has N number of turns, then magnetic dipole moment, $M = NIA$. Its SI unit is A-m^2.

Or

According to Biot-Savart's law, the magnetic field $d\mathbf{B}$ at the centre O of the coil having radius R due to the current element Idl is given by, $d\mathbf{B} = \frac{\mu_0}{4\pi} \frac{I\,(d\mathbf{l} \times \mathbf{R})}{R^3}$

The magnitude of $d\mathbf{B}$ at the centre O,

$$dB = \frac{\mu_0}{4\pi} \cdot \frac{IdlR \sin\theta}{R^3}$$

$$\Rightarrow \quad dB = \frac{\mu_0}{4\pi} \frac{Idl \sin\theta}{R^2}$$

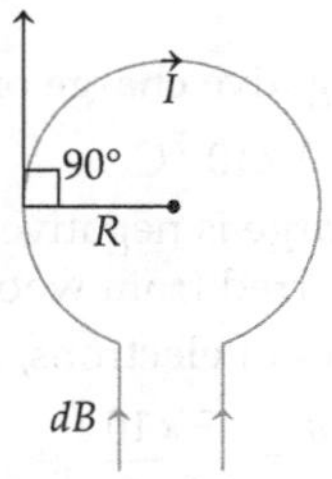

$$\Rightarrow \quad B = \int dB = \int \frac{\mu_0}{4\pi} \frac{Idl \sin\theta}{R^2}$$

$\because \quad \theta = 90°$ and $\sin 90° = 1$

$$\therefore \quad B = \frac{\mu_0}{4\pi} \frac{I}{R^2} \int dl$$

$\int dl$ = total length of the coil = $2\pi R$

$$\Rightarrow \quad B = \frac{\mu_0}{4\pi} \frac{I}{R^2} (2\pi R) = \frac{\mu_0 I}{2R}$$

If the coil has N turns, $B = \frac{\mu_0 NI}{2R}$

> **Value Point** To get maximum marks, write the general formula of Biot-Savart's law and draw the diagram.

3. For lens L_1, $\frac{1}{f} = \frac{1}{v} - \frac{1}{u}$

Given, $u = -15$ cm, $f = +10$ cm, $v = ?$

$$\therefore \quad \frac{1}{10} = \frac{1}{v} + \frac{1}{15}$$

$$\Rightarrow \quad \frac{1}{v} = \frac{1}{10} - \frac{1}{15} \Rightarrow \frac{1}{v} = \frac{1}{30}$$

Distance of image from lens L_1, $v = 30$ cm

For lens L_3, $\frac{1}{f''} = \frac{1}{v''} - \frac{1}{u''}$

Distance of image from lens L_3, $v'' = 10$ cm

$$\therefore \quad \frac{1}{10} = \frac{1}{10} - \frac{1}{u''}$$

$$\Rightarrow \quad \frac{1}{u''} = 0 \Rightarrow u'' = \infty$$

The refracted rays from lens L_2 becomes parallel to principal axis. It is possible only when image formed by L_1 lies at first focus of L_2, i.e. at a distance of 10 cm from L_2.

$\therefore$ Separation between L_1 and $L_2 = 30 + 10 = 40$ cm

The distance between L_2 and L_3 may take any value.

4. If an ideal capacitor is charged by a DC battery, current flows momentarily till capacitor gets fully charged after that no current flow. However, when an AC source is connected, then conduction current, $I_c = \frac{dq}{dt}$ starts flowing in the connecting wire. As charging polarity of AC current changes, the capacitor is alternatively charged and discharged with time. This causes change in electric field between plates of the capacitor which causes electric flux to change and gives rise to displacement current in the region between plates of capacitor, as displacement current, $I_d = \varepsilon_0 \frac{d\phi_E}{dt}$ and $I_d = I_c$ at all instants.

5. (*i*) (a) Necessary conditions for total internal reflection to take place are as

I. The ray incident on the interface of two media should travel in the denser medium.

II. The angle of incidence should be greater than critical angle for the two media.

(b) The relation between angle of incident and critical angle is given by $\mu = \frac{1}{\sin i_c}$.

(*ii*) Let f and $-f$ be the focal lengths of the converging and diverging lenses, respectively.

As, power, $P = \frac{1}{\text{focal length, } (f)}$

So, $\quad P_{net} = P_1 + P_2 = \frac{1}{f} + \frac{1}{-f} = 0$

Thus, focal length of the combination,

$$f = \frac{1}{P} = \frac{1}{0} = \infty$$

6. (*i*) Photodiode is a special type of diode which converts light energy into electrical energy. It is used to detect optical signals.

(*ii*) It is operated in reverse bias as small reverse bias current is more sensitive to the variation in intensity of light than the large forward bias current.

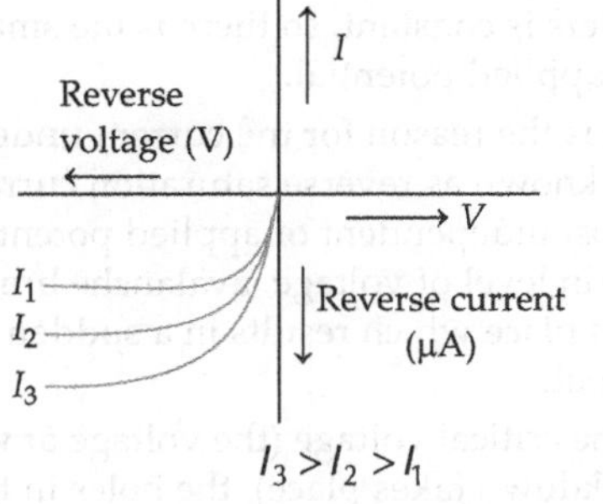

7.

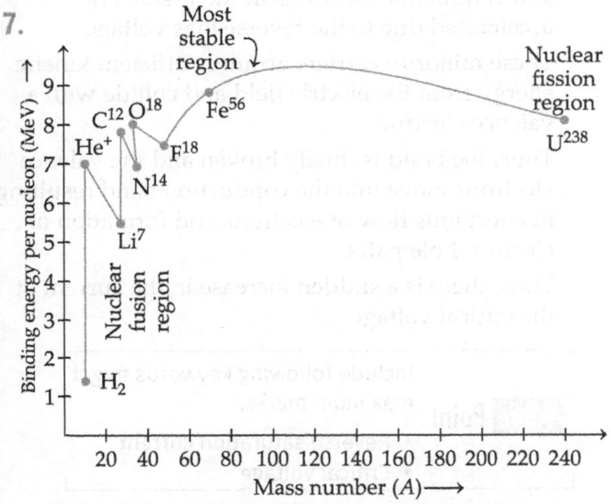

The nuclei having mass number between 50 to 80, are most stable whose binding energy/nucleon is about 8.8 MeV.

Or

(*i*) A nucleus contains neutrons and protons. It is of size of the order of 10^{-14}m. On the other hand, an atom consists of neutrons, protons and electrons. The size of the atom is of the order 10^{-10}m. It means the size of the atom is 10^4 times the size of nucleus. Since, mass of atom is slightly greater than the mass of nucleus, hence the density of the atom is very small as compared to that of nucleus as density is mass/volume.

(*ii*) In the formation of nucleus, the neutrons and the protons have to collect in a very small space whose size is of the order of 10^{-14}m. The energy required for this purpose is spent by the nucleons at the cost of their masses. As a result of this, the mass of the nucleus formed becomes less than the sum of the masses of the individual nucleons.

8. Applying the condition of balanced meter bridge, we have

$$\frac{R}{S} = \frac{l}{100 - l} = \frac{40}{100 - 40} = \frac{40}{60} = \frac{2}{3}$$

$$\frac{R}{S} = \frac{2}{3} \qquad \ldots\text{(i)}$$

The equivalent resistance of 12 Ω and S Ω in parallel is $\dfrac{12\,S}{12 + S}$ Ω.

Again, applying the condition here, we get

$$\frac{R}{\left(\dfrac{12\,S}{12+S}\right)} = \frac{50}{50} = 1$$

$$\Rightarrow \quad R = \frac{12\,S}{12 + S} \qquad \ldots\text{(ii)}$$

From Eqs. (i) and (ii), we get

$$\Rightarrow \quad \frac{2}{3}S = \frac{12\,S}{12 + S}$$

$$\Rightarrow \quad 12 + S = 18 \quad \text{or} \quad S = 6$$

$$\Rightarrow \quad R = \frac{2}{3}S = \frac{2}{3} \times 6 \Rightarrow R = 4\,\Omega$$

9. Torque on an electric dipole placed in a uniform electric field (**E**)

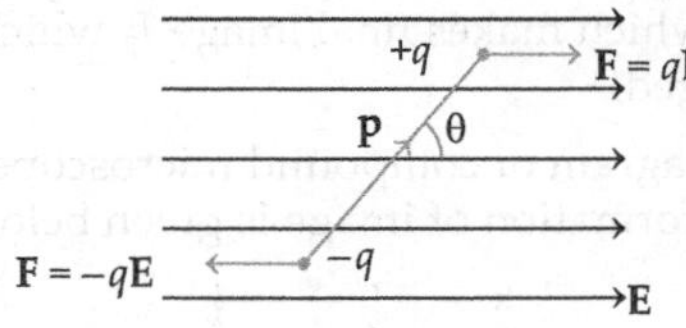

Torque, $\tau = \mathbf{p} \times \mathbf{E} \Rightarrow |\tau| = pE\sin\theta$

$\tau = pE\sin\theta$

(*i*) For maximum torque, $\sin\theta = 1$ or $\theta = 90°$

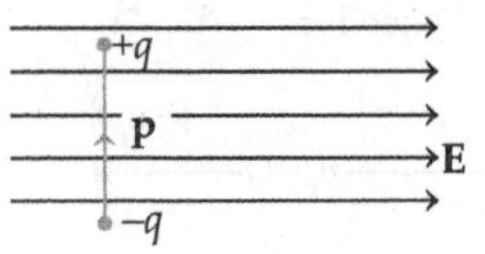

So, dipole should be kept perpendicular to the electric field.

(*ii*) For minimum torque $\theta = 0°$ or π (180°)

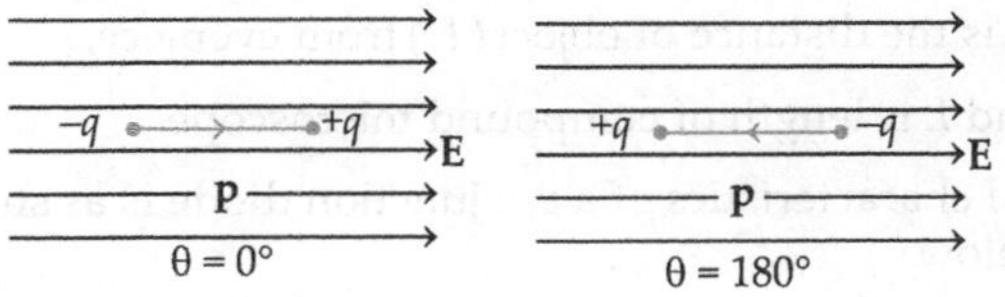

10. Distance of screen from source, $D = 1$m

(*i*) The distance of nth order bright fringe from central fringe is given by

$$y_n = \frac{Dn\lambda}{d}$$

For second bright fringe, $y_2 = \dfrac{2D\lambda}{d}$

$$\Rightarrow \quad y_2 = \frac{2 \times 1 \times 4.5 \times 10^{-7}}{15 \times 10^{-5}}$$

$$\Rightarrow \quad y_2 = 6 \times 10^{-3}\ \text{m}$$

The distance of the second bright fringe from the central fringe, $y_2 = 6$ mm

The distance of nth order dark fringe from central fringe is given by

$$y'_n = (2n-1)\frac{D\lambda}{2d}$$

For second dark fringe, i.e., $n = 2$

$$y'_n = (2 \times 2 - 1)\frac{D\lambda}{2d} = \frac{3D\lambda}{2d}$$

$$\Rightarrow \quad y'_n = \frac{3}{2} \times \frac{1 \times 4.5 \times 10^{-7}}{15 \times 10^{-5}} = 4.5 \times 10^{-3} \text{ m}$$

(*ii*) The distance between fringe, i.e., β increases or decreases in accordance to distance D between slits and screen.

As $\beta \propto D$

fringe width,

$$\beta = \frac{\lambda D}{d}$$

11. From the figure, objective lens makes the real image of tiny object between focus and optical centre of eyepiece and this image works as an object for eyepiece which makes final image I_2 which is virtual and enlarged.

The ray diagram of compound microscope with complete formation of image is given below

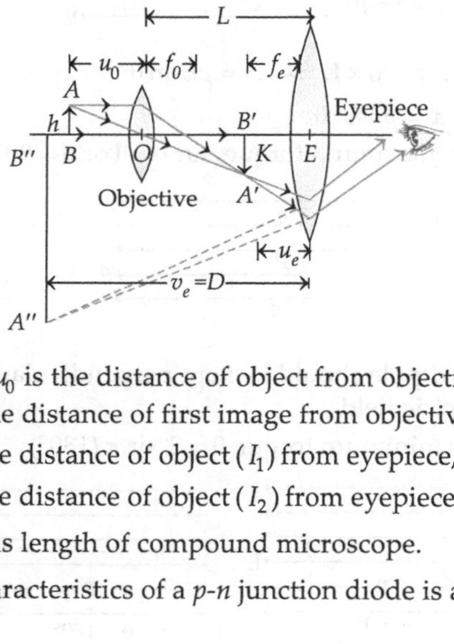

Here, u_0 is the distance of object from objective,
v_0 is the distance of first image from objective,
u_e is the distance of object (I_1) from eyepiece,
v_e is the distance of object (I_2) from eyepiece,
and L is length of compound microscope.

12. *V-I* characteristics of a *p-n* junction diode is as shown below

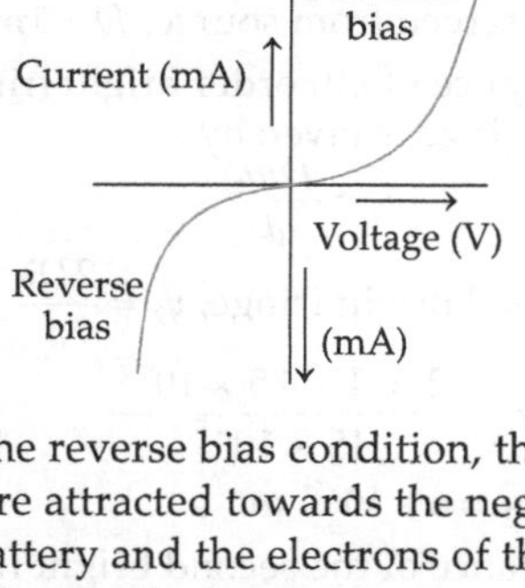

(*i*) Under the reverse bias condition, the holes of *p*-side are attracted towards the negative terminal of the battery and the electrons of the *n*-side are attracted towards the positive terminal of the battery. This increases the depletion layer and the induced potential barrier is also increased.

However, the minority charge carriers are drifted across a junction producing a small current. At any temperature, a number of minority charge carriers is constant, so there is the small current at any applied potential.

This is the reason for the current under reverse bias known as reverse saturation current, which is almost independent of applied potential. At the certain level of voltage, avalanche breakdown takes place which results in a sudden flow of large current.

(*ii*) At the critical voltage (the voltage at which breakdown takes place), the holes in the *n*-side and conduction electrons in the *p*-side are accelerated due to the reverse bias voltage.

These minority carriers acquire sufficient kinetic energy from the electric field and collide with a valence electron.

Thus, the bond is finally broken and the valence electrons move into the conduction band resulting in enormous flow of electrons and formation of electron-hole pairs.

Thus, there is a sudden increase in the current at the critical voltage.

> **Value Point** Include following keywords to get maximum marks.
> - Reverse saturation current
> - Critical voltage

Or

To verify the observations, we use the formula $\rho = \frac{1}{q\mu N_d}$, where q is charge of electron and μ is mobility of charge carriers.

(i) For $N_d = 1 \times 10^{16}$ cm^{-3},

$$\rho = \frac{1}{q\mu\,(1 \times 10^{16})} = \rho_0$$

(ii) For $N_d = 2 \times 10^{16}$ cm^{-3},

$$\rho = \frac{1}{q\mu\,(2 \times 10^{16})} = \frac{\rho_0}{2}$$

(iii) For $N_d = 4 \times 10^{16}$ cm^{-3},

$$\rho = \frac{1}{q\mu\,(4 \times 10^{16})} = \frac{\rho_0}{4}$$

(iv) For $N_d = 8 \times 10^{16}$ cm^{-3},

$$\rho = \frac{1}{q\mu\,(8 \times 10^{16})} = \frac{\rho_0}{8}$$

13. Given, $N = 200$, $r = 10$ cm $= 0.1$ m, $B = 0.5$ T, $\theta = 90°$ and $I = 3$A

(*i*) As, $\tau = NIAB$

$= 200 \times 3 \times [\pi(0.1)^2] \times 0.5$ $\quad [\because A = \pi r^2]$

$\Rightarrow \tau = 9.42$ N-m

(*ii*) The net magnetic force on the circular loop is zero.

(*iii*) Average force on each electron,

$F = ev_d B \sin 90°$

But $I = neAv_d$

[where, A = cross-section of the wire]

$v_d = \frac{I}{neA}$

$\therefore \quad F = e\left(\frac{I}{neA}\right)B$

$F = \frac{IB}{nA} = \frac{3 \times 0.5}{10^{29} \times 10^{-5}}$

$\Rightarrow \quad F = \frac{1.5}{10^{24}}$

$\Rightarrow \quad F = 1.5 \times 10^{-24}$ N

14. (*i*) The Cu wires or Al wires are used for wiring in the home. The main considerations involved in this process are cost of metal and good conductivity of metal.

(*ii*) Two properties of manganin are as follows

(a) Low temperature coefficient of resistance.

(b) High value of resistivity of material of manganin make it suitable for making a standard resistor.

(*iii*) Relaxation time is inversely proportional to the velocities of electrons and ions. The applied electric field produces the insignificant change in velocities of electrons at the order of 1 mm/s, whereas the change in temperature T affects velocities at the order of 10^2 m/s.

This decreases the relaxation time considerably in metals and consequently resistivity of metal or conductor increases as, $\rho = \frac{1}{\sigma} = \frac{m}{ne^2\tau}$

15. According to Bohr's quantisation condition, electrons are permitted to revolve in only those orbits in which the angular momentum of electron is an integral multiple of $\frac{h}{2\pi}$. i.e. $mvr = \frac{nh}{2\pi}$, where $n = 1, 2, 3, \ldots$,

m, v, r are mass, speed and radius of electron and h being Planck's constant.

For Brackett series, $\frac{1}{\lambda} = R\left(\frac{1}{4^2} - \frac{1}{n^2}\right)$, where $n = 5, 6, 7, \ldots$

For longest wavelength, $n = 5$

$\Rightarrow \quad \frac{1}{\lambda} = 1.097 \times 10^7 \left(\frac{1}{16} - \frac{1}{25}\right)$

$= 1.097 \times 10^7 \times \frac{9}{16 \times 25}$

$= 0.0246 \times 10^7$

$\Rightarrow \quad \lambda = 40.650 \times 10^{-7} \simeq 4065$ nm

It lies in infrared region of electromagnetic spectrum.

Common Mistakes In such type of problems, students put $n = \infty$, for the determination the longest wavelength, which is wrong.

Or

Given, work function, $\phi = 2$ eV

$\frac{1}{\lambda} = R\left(\frac{1}{n_1^2} - \frac{1}{n_2^2}\right)$

$E = \frac{hc}{\lambda} = hcR\left(\frac{1}{n_1^2} - \frac{1}{n_2^2}\right) = \phi + \text{KE}$

Also, $\text{KE} = eV_0$

$n_1 = 2, n_2 = n$

$hcR\left(\frac{1}{4} - \frac{1}{n^2}\right) = 2 \times 1.6 \times 10^{-19} + 1.6 \times 10^{-19} \times 0.55$

$\Rightarrow 6.62 \times 10^{-34} \times 3 \times 10^8 \times 1.097 \times 10^7 \left(\frac{1}{4} - \frac{1}{n^2}\right) = (3.2 + 0.88) \times 10^{-19}$

$\Rightarrow 21.786 \times 10^{-19}\left(\frac{1}{4} - \frac{1}{n^2}\right) = 4.08 \times 10^{-19}$

$\frac{1}{4} - \frac{1}{n^2} = 0.187$

$\Rightarrow \quad n \simeq 4$

16. The wave theory of light is not able to explain the observed features of photoelectric current because of following reasons

(*i*) According to wave nature of light, the free electrons at the surface of the metal absorb the radiant energy continuously.
The greater the intensity of radiation, the greater should be the energy obtained by each electrons. The maximum kinetic energy of the photoelectrons on the surface is then expected to increase with increase in intensity. But according to experimental facts, the maximum kinetic energy of ejected photoelectrons is independent of intensity of incident radiation.

(*ii*) Wave theory states that, energy carried by wave is independent of frequency of light wave and hence wave of high intensity and low frequency (less than threshold frequency) should stimulate photoelectric emission but practically, it does not happen.

Considering the following few properties of photon, the given problem was resolved.

(*i*) In interaction of radiation with matter, radiation behaves as if it is made up of particle called **photon**.

(*ii*) Energy of a photon is directly proportional to the frequency of the incident light.

17. Potential energy of two unlike charges is negative. As the electrostatic force is attractive, so a positive amount of work has to be done against this force to take the charge from the given location to infinity. For this, negative amount of work is needed to bring back the charges from infinity to a specific location. Hence, potential energy is negative.

Given that,

Side of triangle, $a = 2.0$ m

Potential energy, $PE = \frac{1}{4\pi\varepsilon_0} \frac{q_1 q_2}{r}$ ...(i)

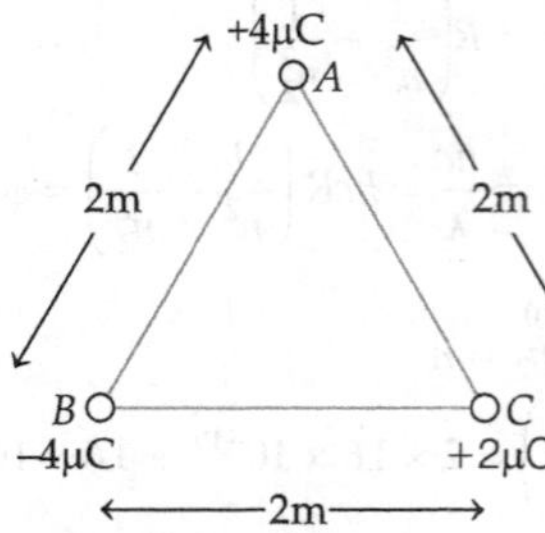

From Eq. (i), for all three charges (say AB, BC and AC),

$$PE = \frac{1}{4\pi\varepsilon_0}\left[\frac{AB}{2} + \frac{BC}{2} + \frac{AC}{2}\right]$$

$$= \frac{1}{4\pi\varepsilon_0}\left[\frac{4\times(-4)}{2} + \frac{(-4)\times(2)}{2} + \frac{4\times 2}{2}\right]$$

$$= 9\times10^9\left[-\frac{16}{2} + \frac{(-8)}{2} + \frac{8}{2}\right]$$

$$= 9\times10^9[-8-4+4]$$

$$= -72\times10^9 \text{ J}$$

18. (*i*) Wavelength of violet light is smaller than that of red light. Also, angle of minimum deviation,

$$\delta_m = (\mu - 1)A$$

$\Rightarrow$ $\delta_m \propto \mu$

As, $\mu_R < \mu_V$

$\Rightarrow$ $(\delta_m)_R < (\delta_m)_V$

As deviation is less for red light, hence angle of deviation decreases.

(*ii*) Given, $\angle P = 90°$ and $PQ = PR$.

Therefore, $\angle R = \angle Q$

$$\angle R + \angle Q = 90°$$

$$\angle R = \angle Q = 45°$$

$$\angle OBR = 90°$$

Therefore, $\angle BOR = 45°$, $\angle BOC = 45°$

Hence, the critical angle is 45°.

(*iii*) (a) Given, angle of minimum deviation, $\delta_m = 30°$

$\therefore$ Angle of prism, $A = 60°$

By prism formula, refractive index,

$$\mu = \frac{\sin\frac{\delta_m + A}{2}}{\sin A/2} = \frac{\sin\frac{30° + 60°}{2}}{\sin 30°}$$

$$= \frac{\sin 45°}{\sin 30°}$$

$$= \frac{1}{\sqrt{2}} \times 2 = \sqrt{2}$$

Also, $\mu = \frac{\text{speed of light in vacuum } (c)}{\text{speed of light in prism } (v)}$

$\Rightarrow$ $v = c/\mu = (3\times10^8/\sqrt{2})$ m/s

Hence, speed of light through prism is $(3\times10^8/\sqrt{2})$ m/s.

(b) Critical angle i_c is given as

$$\sin i_c = \frac{1}{\sqrt{2}} \qquad \left[\because \sin i_c = \frac{1}{\mu}\right]$$

$\Rightarrow$ $i_c = 45°$

$$A = r + i_c = 60°$$

$\Rightarrow$ $r = 60° - 45° = 15°$

Using Snell's law, $\frac{\sin i}{\sin r} = \sqrt{2}$

$\Rightarrow$ $\sin i = \sqrt{2}\sin r = \sqrt{2} \times \sin 15°$

$\therefore$ $i = \sin^{-1}(\sqrt{2}\sin 15°)$

Or

(*i*)

Interference	Diffraction
It takes place due to superposition of light waves from two monochromatic sources.	It takes place due to superposition of several waves from a single slit.
For path difference $n\lambda$, bright fringes obtained.	For path difference $n\lambda$, dark fringes obtained.
Width of all fringes is same.	Width of central maxima is twice of successive maxima.

(ii) **Interference**

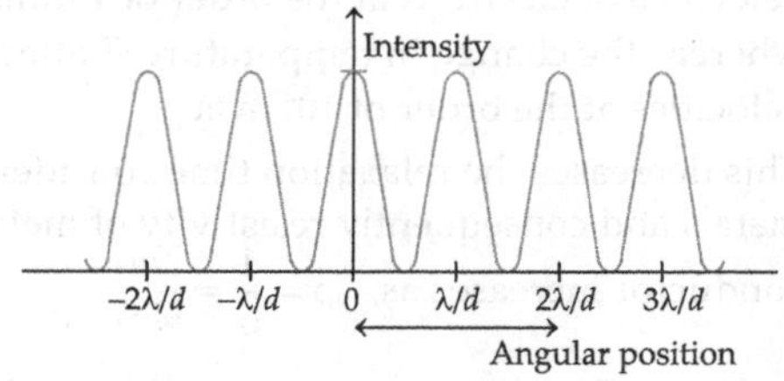

Diffraction

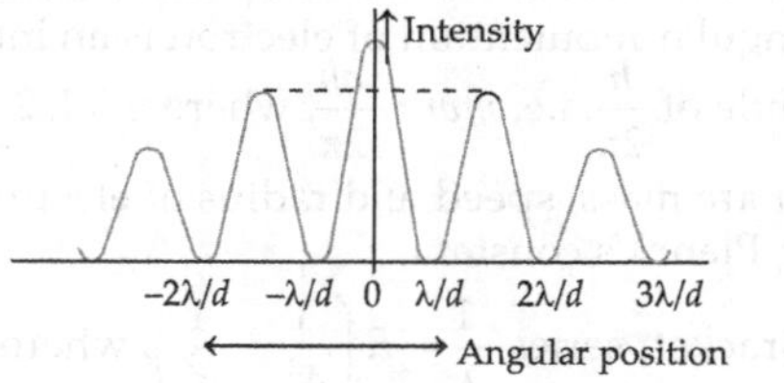

(*iii*) Fringe width is directly proportional to wavelength λ of the light i.e., $\beta = \frac{\lambda D}{a}$

So, as λ decreases, fringe width decreases.

19. (*i*) (a) The condition for resonance in the series L-C-R circuit is when phase (ϕ) between current and voltage is zero, is

$$X_L = X_C$$

$\Rightarrow$ $\omega_0 L = \frac{1}{\omega_0 C}$

$\Rightarrow$ $\omega_0^2 = \frac{1}{LC}$

$\Rightarrow \quad \omega_0 = \dfrac{1}{\sqrt{LC}}$

or $\quad \nu_r = \dfrac{1}{2\pi\sqrt{LC}} \quad (\because \omega = 2\pi\nu)$

where, ν_r = resonating frequency.

(b) When the current in the two circuits is maximum, the L-C-R circuit is in condition of resonance. Therefore, for the same resonant frequencies, $\omega_1 = \omega_2$

$\Rightarrow \quad \dfrac{1}{\sqrt{L_1C_1}} = \dfrac{1}{\sqrt{L_2C_2}}$

or $\quad \dfrac{L_1}{L_2} = \dfrac{C_2}{C_1}$

(c) Power factor, $\cos\phi \propto R$.

The peak value of current is higher for graph (I) than graph (II), $I_{m1} > I_{m2}$.

This implies that $R_1 < R_2$ i.e, the circuit (ii) has higher power factor being of higher resistance.

Quality factor,

$$Q = \frac{V_L}{V_R} = \frac{1}{R}\sqrt{\frac{L}{C}}$$

Since, $\quad L/C$ = constant

$Q \propto 1/R$

Since, $\quad R_1 < R_2$

Therefore, the circuit (I) has higher quality factor being of smaller resistance.

(d) When the frequency of the supply equals to the natural frequency of the circuit, then resonance occurs.

$\therefore \quad Z_r = R = 20\,\Omega$

$$I_{rms} = \frac{V_{rms}}{Z_r} = \frac{200}{20} = 10\text{ A}$$

$\therefore$ Average power transferred/cycle,

$$P_{av} = V_{rms}\, I_{rms} \cos\phi$$

$= 200 \times 10 \times \cos 0° \quad [\because \phi = 0°]$

$= 2000$ W

$= 2$ kW

Or

(*i*) **Faraday's laws of EMI**

Whenever the amount of magnetic flux linked with a circuit changes, an emf is induced in the circuit. The induced emf last so long as the change in magnetic flux continues.

(*ii*) According to the given figure,

Case I When PQ moves forward.

(a) For $0 \le x < b$,

Magnetic field B exists in the region.

Area of loop $PQRS = lx$

$\therefore$ Magnetic flux linked with loop $PQRS$,

$\phi = BA = Blx$

$\Rightarrow \quad \phi = Blx \quad$ ...(i)

(b) For $2b \ge x \ge b \ (b > x \ge 0)$,

$B = 0$

$\therefore$ Flux linked with loop $PQRS$ is uniform and given by

$\phi' = Blb \quad$ ...(ii)

$\because \quad x = b$

Forward journey

Thus, for $b > x \ge 0$

Flux, $\quad \phi = Blx \Rightarrow \phi \propto x$

For $\quad 2b \ge x \ge b$

Flux, $\quad \phi = Bbl \quad$ [constant]

Backward journey

For $\quad b \le x \le 2b$,

ϕ = constant $= Bbl$

For $\quad 0 \le x \le b$,

$\phi = Blx \quad$ [decreasing]

Graphical representation

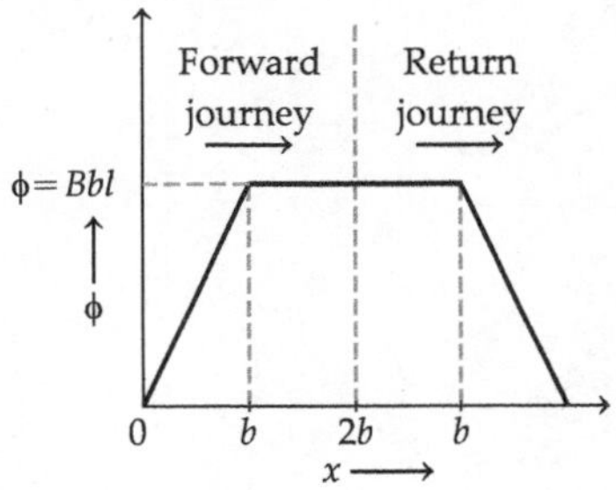

Case II For $\quad b > x \ge 0,\ B = 0$

As, $\quad \phi = Blx$

$\Rightarrow \quad \dfrac{d\phi}{dt} = Bl\dfrac{dx}{dt} = Bvl \quad \left[\because v = \dfrac{dx}{dt}\right]$

Induced emf, $e = -\dfrac{d\phi}{dt} = -vBl$

For $\quad 2b \ge x \ge b$,

As, $\quad \phi' = Bbl$

$\Rightarrow \quad \dfrac{d\phi'}{dt} = 0$

$\Rightarrow \quad e = 0$

Forward journey

For $\quad b > x \ge 0$

$\Rightarrow \quad e = -vBl$

For $\quad 2b \ge x \ge b$

$\Rightarrow \quad e = 0$

Backward journey

For $\quad b > x \ge 0$

$\Rightarrow \quad e = vBl$

For $2b \geq x \geq b,\ e = 0$

Variation of induced emf,

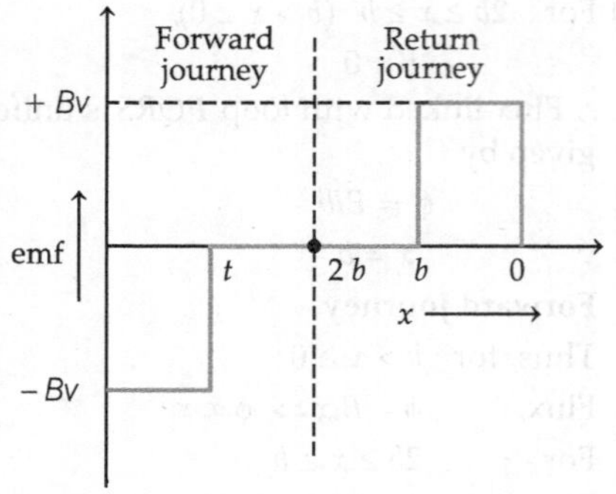

20. (*i*) Increasing the magnetic field strength, increases the torque for a given current, thus increasing the deflection.

(*ii*) The phosphor bronze strip provides a restoring torque and also serves as a lead to conduct current to the coil.

(*iii*) (a) By connecting a low resistance (shunt) in parallel with the galvanometer, it can be converted into an ammeter to measure large currents.

(b) Full scale deflection current, $I_g = 20\ \mu A$

Maximum voltage to be measured, $V = 50\ V$

The total resistance needed in series with the galvanometer,

$$R_{total} = \frac{V}{I_g}$$

$$R_{total} = \frac{50}{20 \times 10^{-6}}$$

$$R_{total} = 2.5 \times 10^6$$

Since, galvanometer itself has a resistance $R_g = 50\ \Omega$, the series resistance required is

$$R_V = R_{total} - R_g$$

$$R_V = 2.5 \times 10^6 - 50$$

$$R_V = 2.49995 \times 10^6\ \Omega$$

$$\approx 2.5 \times 10^6\ \Omega$$

SQP Code : **PB-11/15** Series **i-Succeed 11-25/15** Roll No. | | | | | | | | |

Sample Question Paper 11

Physics 12th (Code 861)

General Instructions

1. This paper is divided into four Sections- A, B, C and D. Answer all questions.
2. **Section A** consists of one question having sub-parts of one mark each.
3. **Section B** consists of seven questions of two marks each.
4. **Section C** consists of nine questions of three marks each.
5. **Section D** consists of three questions of five marks each.
6. Internal choices have been provided in two questions each in Section B, Section C and Section D.

Time : 3 Hrs.

Max. Marks : 70

Section A (14 Marks)

1. **A.** In questions (i) to (vii) below, choose the correct alternative (a), (b), (c) or (d) for each of the questions given below

(i) When a current carrying conductor of length l is placed parallel to the magnetic field, the magnitude of force due to current carrying conductor is equal to • *Analysis* [1]

(a) zero (b) IlB (c) $\frac{IlB}{2}$ (d) $-IlB$

(ii) In Rutherford's nuclear model of the atom, if F_e indicates electrostatic force between electron and nucleus and F_c indicates the centripetal force on revolving electron, then • *Recall* [1]

(a) $F_e = F_c$ (b) $F_e > F_c$

(c) $F_e < F_c$ (d) $F_e = \infty$ and $F_c = 0$

(iii) **Assertion** (A) The mass of an alpha particle is less than the sum of the masses of its constituent nucleons.

Reason (R) The binding energy per nucleon of an alpha particle is very high.

• *Understanding* [1]

(a) Both Assertion and Reason are true and Reason is the correct explanation for Assertion.

(b) Both Assertion and Reason are true but Reason is not the correct explanation for Assertion.

(c) Assertion is false and Reason is true.

(d) Both Assertion and Reason are false.

(iv) **Assertion** (A) In electrostatic, electric lines of force can never be closed loops.

Reason (R) The number of electric line of force originating or terminatings on a charge is proportional to the magnitude of charge. • *Analysis* [1]

(a) Both Assertion and Reason are true and Reason is the correct explanation for Assertion.

(b) Both Assertion and Reason are true but Reason is not the correct explanation for Assertion.

(c) Assertion is false and Reason is true.

(d) Both Assertion and Reason are false.

(*v*) Total electric flux coming out of a unit positive charge kept in air is • *Recall* [1]

(a) ε_0 (b) ε_0^{-1}

(c) $(4p\varepsilon_0)^{-1}$ (d) $4\pi\varepsilon_0$

(*vi*) A charge particle after being accelerated through a potential difference V enters in a uniform magnetic field and moves in a circle of radius r. If V is doubled, then the radius of the circle will become • *Understanding* [1]

(a) $2r$ (b) $\sqrt{2}\,r$

(c) $4r$ (d) $\frac{r}{\sqrt{2}}$

(*vii*) If the velocity of charged particle has both perpendicular and parallel components while moving through a magnetic field, what is the path followed by a charged particle? • *Analysis* [1]

(a) Circular

(b) Elliptical

(c) Linear

(d) Helical

B. Answer the following questions briefly.

(*i*) The drift velocity of the electrons in a copper wire of length 2m under the application of a potential difference of 220 V is 0.5 ms^{-1}. Find the mobility of electron. • *Understanding* [1]

(*ii*) Two thin lenses of power +4 D and −2 D are in contact. What is the focal length of the combination? • *Application* [1]

(*iii*) A magician during a show makes a glass lens $n = 1.47$ disappear in a liquid. What is the refractive index of the liquid? Could the liquid be water? • *Recall* [1]

(*iv*) What is the principle of operation of a nuclear reactor? • *Recall* [1]

(*v*) Define the term reactive power. • *Recall* [1]

(*vi*) A proton is placed in a uniform electric field directed along the positive *Y*-axis. In which direction, will it tend to move? • *Recall* [1]

(*vii*) What is commercial unit of electrical power? Give its value. • *Recall* [1]

Section B (14 Marks)

2. (*i*) Give the dependence of magnetic field produced by a current conductor. • *Recall* [1]

(*ii*) A circular coil of wire consisting of 100 turns, each of radius 8.0 cm carries a current of 0.40 A. What is the magnitude of the magnetic field B at the centre of the coil? • *Application* [1]

3. What is the minimum energy that must be given to an H-atom in ground state, so that it can emits an H_γ line in Balmer series? • *Recall* [2]

Or States Bohr's second and third postulates. • *Understanding* [2]

4. Define one tesla using the expression for the magnetic force acting on a particle of charge q moving with velocity v in a magnetic field **B**. • *Understanding* [2]

5. The coefficient of self-inductance of a coil is 2 H. What do you understand by this statement? • *Recall* [2]

6. A convex lens is put 10 cm from a light source and it makes a sharp image on a screen, kept 10 cm from the lens. Now a glass block (refractive index 1.5) of 1.5 cm thickness is placed in contact with light source. To get the sharp image again, the screen is shifted by a distance *d*. Calculate the distance between screen and slit. • *Application* [2]

Or

Show that a light ray will pass through an equilateral glass prism ($\mu = 1.5$), if the angle of incidence is greater than 30°. • *Analysis* [2]

7. Name the electromagnetic waves used in LASIK eye surgery and why? • *Recall* [2]

8. Assuming that the two diodes D_1 and D_2 used in the electric circuit shown in the figure are ideal, find out the value of the current flowing through 1Ω resistor.

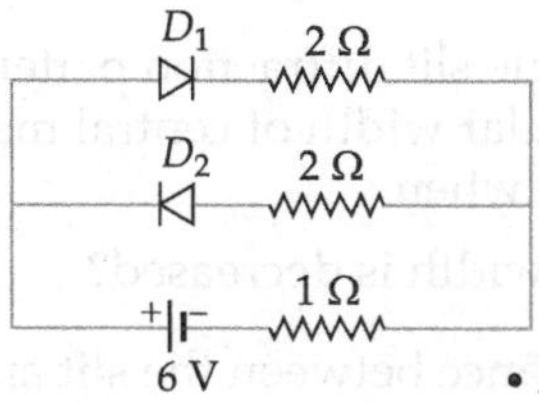

• *Application* [2]

Section C (27 Marks)

9. In the circuit shown below, initially K_1 is closed and K_2 is opened, what are the charges on each of the capacitors? Then, K_1 was opened and K_2 was closed (order is important), what will be the charge on each capacitor now? [Given, $C = 1\,\mu F$] • *Analysis* [3]

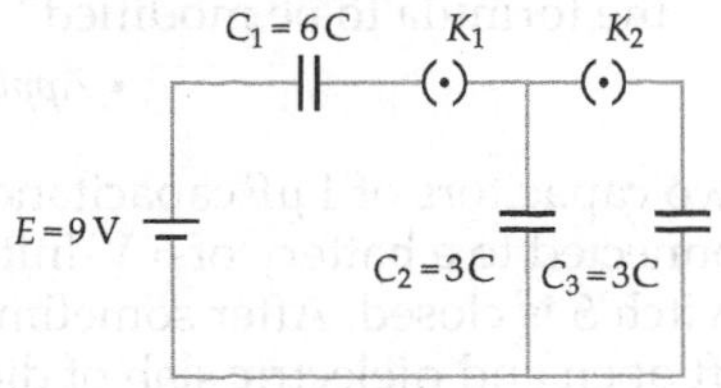

10. (*i*) White light is incident on one of the refracting surface of a prism of angle 5°. If the refractive indices for red and blue colours are 1.641 and 1.659 respectively, then what will be the angular separation between these two colours when they emerge out? • *Application* [1]

(*ii*) How does the magnification of a magnifying glass differ from its magnifying power? • *Recall* [1]

(*iii*) The focal length of a thin biconvex lens is 20 cm. When an object is moved from a distance of 25 cm in front of it to 50 cm, the magnification of its image changes from m_{25} to m_{50}. Find the ratio of $\frac{m_{25}}{m_{50}}$. • *Application* [1]

11. (*i*) In H-atom, an electron undergoes transition from second excited state to the first excited state and then to the ground state. Identify the spectral series to which these transitions belong. • *Understanding* [1]

(*ii*) Find out the ratio of the wavelengths of the emitted radiations in the two cases. [2]

12. In a Young's double slit experiment, red light of wavelength 6000 Å is used and the *n*th bright fringe is obtained at point *P* on the screen. Keeping the same setting, the source is replaced by a green light of 5000 Å and now $(n+1)$th bright fringe is obtained at *P*. Calculate the value of *n*. • *Understanding* [3]

13. It is found that when $R = 4\,\Omega$, the current is 1 A and when *R* is increased to 9 Ω, the current reduces to 0.5 A. Find the values of the emf *E* and internal resistance *r*. • *Understanding* [3]

Or

A student measures the power dissipated in a resistor at different currents. Given, the resistance *R* is 10 Ω. Verify (for any two) that the experimental data agrees with the theoritical values using the following data. • *Application* [3]

Current (A)	1	2	3	4
Power (W)	10	40	90	160

14. Two concentric circular coils *x* and *y* of radii 16 cm and 10 cm respectively, lie in the same vertical plane containing the North to South direction. Coil *x* has 20 turns and carries a current of 16 A, coil *y* has 25 turns and carries a current of 18 A. The sense of the current in *x* is anti-clockwise and clockwise in *y*, for an observer looking at the coils facing West. Find the magnitude and direction of the net magnetic field due to the coils at their centre. • *Application* [3]

15. In a single slit diffraction pattern, how does the angular width of central maximum changes when • *Application*

(*i*) slit width is decreased? [1]

(*ii*) distance between the slit and screen is increased? [1]

(*iii*) light of smaller visible wavelength is used? Justify your answer in each case. [1]

Or

(*i*) (a) Two independent monochromatic sources of light cannot produce a sustained interference pattern. Give reason. • *Recall*

(b) Light waves each of amplitude a and frequency ω, emanating from two coherent light sources superpose at a point. If the displacements due to these waves is given by $y_1 = a\cos\omega t$ and $y_2 = a\cos(\omega t + \phi)$, where ϕ is the phase difference between the two, obtain the expression for the resultant intensity at the point. • *Application*

(*ii*) In Young's double slit experiment, using monochromatic light of wavelength λ, the intensity of light at a point on the screen, where path difference is λ, is K units. Find out the intensity of light at a point where path difference is $\lambda/3$. • *Application* [3]

16. (*i*) Estimate the speed with which electrons emitted from a heated emitter of an evacuated tube impinge on the collector maintained at a potential difference of 500 V with respect to the emitter. Ignore the small initial speeds of the electrons. The specific charge of the electron, i.e. its e/m is given to be 1.76×10^{11} C/kg. • *Analysis* [2]

(*ii*) Use the same formula you employ in (i) to obtain electron speed for a collector potential of 10 MV. Do you see what is wrong? In what way is the formula to be modified? • *Application* [1]

17. Two capacitors of 1 μF capacitance are connected to a battery of 6 V. Initially, switch S is closed. After sometime, S is left open and dielectric slab of dielectric constant K=3 are inserted to fill completely the space between the plates of the two capacitors. How will the (*i*) charge and (*ii*) potential difference between the plates of the capacitors be affected after the slabs are inserted? Analysis [3]

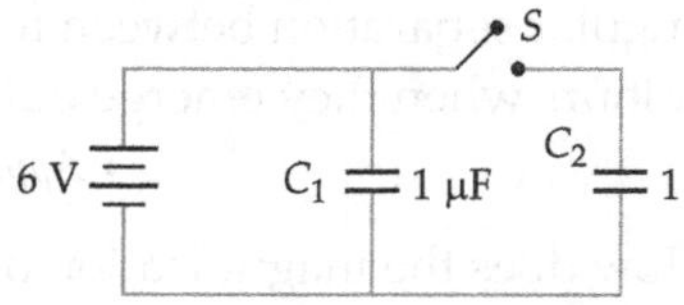

SP-11

Section D (15 Marks)

18. A curious student purchased a small bulb and connected to an inductor L=10 mH is an AC circuit with an input rms voltage of 100 V as shown in the figure.

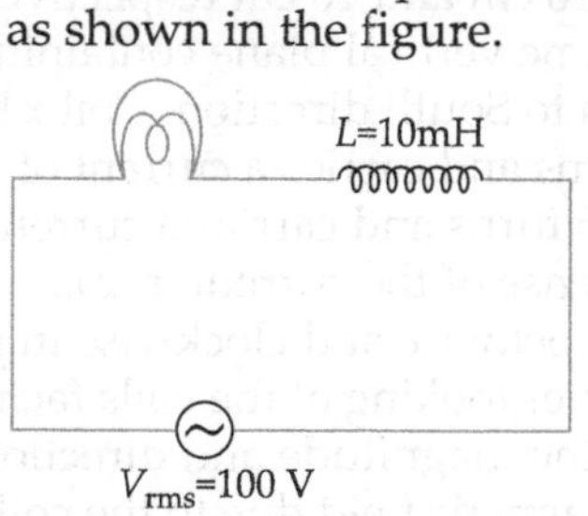

If resistance of the bulb is negligible and the frequency of input AC voltage is increased from 50Hz to 50kHz.

(*i*) What is the percentage change in the rms current in the AC circuit? • *Analysis* [1]

(*ii*) Will the bulb glow brighter or dimmer? Explain your answer. • *Analysis* [1]

(*iii*) In *L-C-R* circuit, the capacitance is changed from C to 4C. To keep the same resonant frequency, what should be the value of inductance (L)? • *Application* [3]

Or (*i*) Draw a graph showing variation of amplitude of circuit current with changing frequency of applied voltage in a series *L-C-R* circuit for two different values of resistances R_1 and $R_2 (R_1 > R_2)$. • *Application* [1]

(*ii*) A capacitor of 100μF and a coil of resistance 50Ω and inductance 0.5 H are connected in series with a 110 V -50 Hz source. Calculate the rms value of current in the circuit. • *Understanding* [2]

(*iii*) A small town with a demand of 800 kW and 200 V of electric power is situated 15 km away from the electric plant generating power of 440 V_0. A wire (electric power line of 0.5 Ω per km) connects the town with the plant. The town receives the power from the line through a 4000-200V step-down transformer of a sub-station located in the town. Estimate the power loss in the form of heat. • *Application* [2]

19. (*i*) Write the difference between electron current and hole current. • *Recall* [2]

(*ii*) What is the voltage across a capacitor, if a diode is connected to 220 V (rms) AC in series with it? • *Recall* [1]

(*iii*) As we know that, an *n*-type semiconductor has large number of electrons but it is still electrically neutral. Why? • *Recall* [2]

Or (*i*) What is a photodiode? • *Recall* [1]

(ii) Explain its working principle. Why is a photodiode operated in reverse bias? • *Application* [2]

(*iii*) There are two semiconductor materials *A* and *B* which are made by doping germanium crystal with indium and arsenic, respectively. As shown in the figure, the junction of two is biased with a battery. Will the junction be forward bias and reverse bias? • *Application* [2]

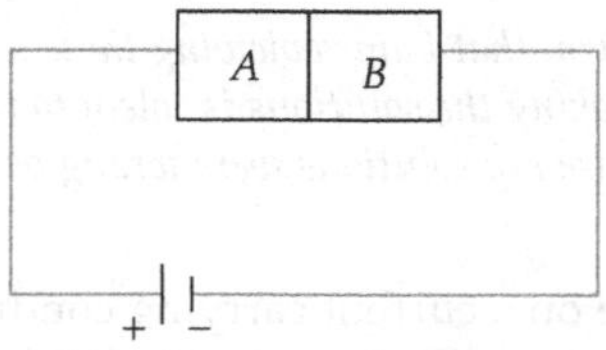

20. Refraction involves change in the path of light due to change in the medium. When a beam of light encounters another transparent medium, a part of light gets reflected back into the first medium, while the rest enters the other. The direction of propagation of an obliquely incident ray of light, that enters the other medium, changes at the interface of two media. This phenomenon is called refraction of light.

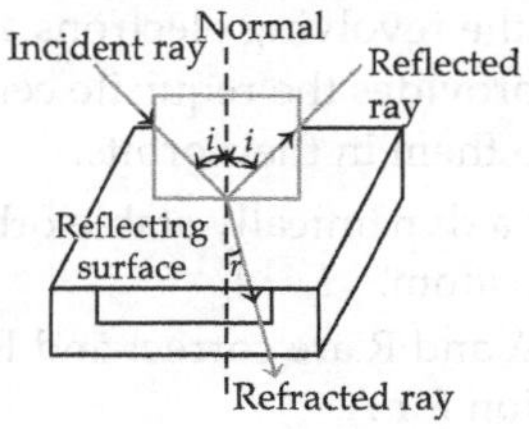

(*i*) For the same value of angle of incidence, the angles of refraction in three media *A*, *B* and *C* are 15°, 25° and 35°, respectively. In which medium, would the velocity of light be minimum? • *Application* [1]

(*ii*) Why does a crack in a glass window pane appear silvery? • *Recall* [1]

(*iii*) The refractive index of diamond is much higher than that of glass. How does a diamond cutter make use of this fact? • *Recall* [2]

(*iv*) What is the apparent position of an object below a rectangular block of glass 6 cm thick, if a layer of water 4 cm thick is on the top of the glass? (Take, $n_{ga} = 1.5$ and $n_{wa} = 1.3$) • *Application* [1]

Solutions *in Topper's Style*

My Commitment *I affirm that I am reviewing these solutions only after I have solved the Sample Question Paper 11 on my own. My purpose of looking the solutions is solely to verify whether my answers/solutions were correct or not and to identify my mistakes in case my solutions were wrong or I could not solve that.*

1. A. (*i*) (*a*) Force on a current carrying conductor when placed on a uniform magnetic field,

$$F = I(\mathbf{l} \times \mathbf{B}) \Rightarrow F = IlB\sin\theta$$

where, I = current flowing in the conductor,
l = length of the conductor
and B = uniform magnetic field.

If conductor is parallel to the magnetic field, then $\theta = 0°$.

$$\Rightarrow \quad F = IlB\sin 0° = 0$$

Hence, force will be zero.

(*ii*) (*a*) The electrostatic force of attraction (F_e) between the revolving electrons and the nucleus provides the requisite centripetal force F_c to keep them in their orbits.

Thus, for a dynamically stable orbit in a hydrogen atom, $F_e = F_c$

(*iii*) (*a*) Both A and R are correct and R is the correct explanation for A.

The masses of an α-particle (which consists of 2 protons and 2 neutrons) is less than the sum of the individual masses of 2 protons and 2 neutrons.

The binding energy per nucleon in an α-particle is very high, which means a large amount of energy is released when the nucleons come together to form the α-particle, resulting in a mass deficit.

(*iv*) (*b*) Electrostatic field lines of force can never form any closed loop because electric field originate from positive charge and terminates on negative charge.

(*v*) (*b*) By Gauss' law, ϕ = electric flux through closed surface area $= \frac{q_{\text{enclosed}}}{\varepsilon_0}$, if $q_{\text{enclosed}} = 1$ unit

$$\Rightarrow \quad \phi = \frac{1}{\varepsilon_0} = \varepsilon_0^{-1}$$

(*vi*) (*b*) For the given charged particle, the radius of the circular path, $r = \frac{mv}{Bq} = \frac{\sqrt{2qVm}}{Bq}$ ... (i)

[Since, momentum, $p = \sqrt{2mK} = \sqrt{2mqV}$]

Keeping q, B and m fixed, if V is doubled, then

$$r' = \frac{\sqrt{2q(2V)m}}{Bq} = \frac{\sqrt{2}\sqrt{2qVm}}{Bq} = \sqrt{2}r$$

[From Eq. (i)]

(*vii*) (*d*) Suppose, the velocity **v** of the particle entering the magnetic field **B** makes some angle with **B**.

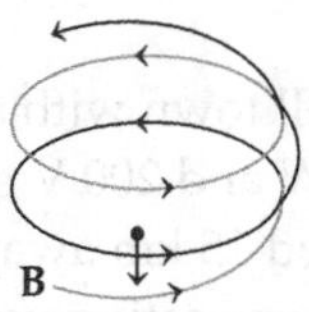

Then, **v** may be resolved into two components, $\mathbf{v}_{\|} = v\cos\theta$ parallel to **B** and $\mathbf{v}_{\perp} = v\sin\theta$ perpendicular to **B**.

The component $\mathbf{v}_{\|}$ gives a linear path and the component $\mathbf{v}_{\perp}$ gives a circular path to the particle. The resultant of these two paths is a helical path whose axis is parallel to the magnetic field.

B. (*i*) We know that, drift velocity,

$$v_d = \mu E$$

$$v_d = \mu\frac{V}{l} \qquad \left[\because E = \frac{V}{l}\right]$$

$$\mu = \frac{v_d \times l}{V} = \frac{0.5 \times 2}{220} = 4.5 \times 10^{-3}\ \text{m}^2\text{V}^{-1}\text{s}^{-1}$$

(*ii*) Given, power of lenes, $P_1 = +4\text{D}$ and $P_2 = -2\text{D}$

As, $\frac{1}{f} = \frac{1}{f_1} + \frac{1}{f_2}$

$\because$ Power of lens, $P = \frac{1}{f}$

So, $\frac{1}{f} = P_1 + P_2$

$$\Rightarrow \quad f = \frac{1}{P_1 + P_2} = \frac{1}{4-2} = \frac{1}{2} = 0.5\ \text{m}$$

Hence, the focal length of combination is 0.5 m.

(*iii*) If $\mu_1 = \mu_2$, then $f = \infty$

Hence, the lens in the liquid acts like a plane sheet, when refractive index of the lens and the surrounding medium is the same. Therefore, $\mu_1 = \mu_2 = 1.47$.

So, the liquid medium is not water, refractive index for water = 1.33.

(*iv*) Nuclear reactor is a device that can initiate a self-sustaining controlled chain reaction of fissionable material. ^{235}U and ^{239}Pu are the nuclear fuels, which cause the chain reaction with the emission of neutrons.

(*v*) If the load is purely reactive, then the voltage and current are 90° out of phase. For half of each cycle, power is positive but on other half-cycle, power is negative. Hence, the average energy flow is zero. This power is known as reactive power.

(*vi*) As, proton has positive charge on it, so it moves in the direction of electric field, i.e. in positive direction of *Y*-axis.

(*vii*) Commercial unit of electrical power is horse power (HP).

Its value is 1 HP = 746W.

2. (*i*) Magnetic field produced by a current conductor is

(a) Directly proportional to the current flowing through the conductor, length of the element and sine of the angle between the length of the element and line joining the element to the point

(b) Inversely proportional to the square of the distance between the element and the point.

(*ii*) Here, $n = 100$, $r = 8\text{ cm} = 8\times10^{-2}$ m and $I = 0.40$ A

$\therefore$ Magnetic field B at the centre.

$$B = \frac{\mu_0}{4\pi}\cdot\frac{2\pi In}{r}$$

$$= \frac{10^{-7}\times2\times3.14\times0.40\times100}{8\times10^{-2}} = 3.1\times10^{-4}\text{T}$$

3. As, wavelength emitted in Balmer series,

$$\frac{1}{\lambda} = R\left[\frac{1}{4}-\frac{1}{n^2}\right]$$

where, $n = 3, 4, 5, \ldots$

So, for H_γ line in Balmer series taking, $n = 5$

$$\frac{1}{\lambda} = R\left[\frac{1}{4}-\frac{1}{5^2}\right] = \frac{21R}{100}$$

$$\Rightarrow \quad \lambda = \frac{100}{21R}$$

$$\Rightarrow \quad \lambda = \frac{100}{1.097\times10^7\times21}$$

$$= 4.34\times10^{-7}\text{ m} = 4340\text{ Å}$$

Hence, energy, $E_{\min} = \dfrac{12400}{\lambda(\text{in Å})}\text{eV} = \dfrac{12400}{4340} = 2.85\text{ eV}$

Common Mistakes There is a confusion in the value of n for minimum energy of $H\gamma$ line in Balmer series. The correct value is $n = 5$ not $n = 3$.

Or

Bohr's second postulate states that the electron revolves around the nucleus only in those orbits for which the angular momentum is some integral multiple of $h/2\pi$, where h is the Planck's constant ($= 6.63\times10^{-34}$ J-s).

Thus, the angular momentum (L) of the orbiting electron is quantised, i.e. $L = \dfrac{nh}{2\pi}$

As, angular momentum of electron = mvr

$\therefore$ For any permitted (stationary) orbit,

$$mvr = \frac{nh}{2\pi}$$

where, n = any positive integer 1, 2, 3, ...

It is also called principal quantum number.

Bohr's third postulate states that an electron might make a transition from one of its specified non-radiating orbits to another of lower energy. When it does, so a photon is emitted having energy equal to the energy difference between the initial and final states.

The frequency of the emitted photon is given by

$$h\nu = E_i - E_f$$

where, E_i and E_f are the energies of the initial and final states and $E_i > E_f$.

4. The magnetic force acting on a particle of charge q, moving with velocity v in a magnetic field B is given by expression, $\quad F = q(\mathbf{v}\times\mathbf{B})$

$$\Rightarrow \quad B = \frac{F}{qv} \Rightarrow 1\text{T} = \frac{1\text{N}}{(1\text{C})(1\text{ ms}^{-1})}$$

If a force of 1 N acts on a particle of charge 1C, moving with velocity 1 ms^{-1}, then it shows the presence of 1 T magnetic field perpendicular to its velocity.

5. We know that, self-inductance, $e = L\cdot\dfrac{\Delta I}{\Delta t}$

If $L = 2$H, then $e = 2\cdot\dfrac{\Delta I}{\Delta t}$

If $\dfrac{\Delta I}{\Delta t} = 1\text{ As}^{-1}$, then $e = 2$ V

Hence, self-induction of 2H states, that an induced emf of 2 V is set-up in it when the current in it, changes at the rate of one ampere per second.

6. ***Case* I** $u = -10$ cm, $v = 10$ cm, $f = ?$

Using lens formula, $\quad \dfrac{1}{f} = \dfrac{1}{v} - \dfrac{1}{u}$

$$\Rightarrow \quad \frac{1}{f} = \frac{1}{10} + \frac{1}{10} = f = 5\text{ cm}$$

***Case* II** Due to introduction of slab shift in source

$$= t\left[1-\frac{1}{\mu}\right] = 1.5\left[1-\left(\frac{2}{3}\right)\right] = 0.5$$

Now, $u = -9.5$ cm, $v = 10.55$ cm,

$d = 10.55 - 10$

$d = 0.55$ cm away from the lens.

Common Mistakes Sometimes, students would not assign proper sign in taking the value of u, v and f. So, they get wrong result.

Or

From Snell's law, $\mu = \dfrac{\sin i}{\sin r}$

If the light is incident at 30°, then

$$\sin r = \frac{\sin i}{\mu} = \frac{\sin 30°}{1.5} = \frac{0.5}{1.5} = 0.33$$

$\Rightarrow$ $r = \sin^{-1}(0.33) \simeq 19°$

Angle of incidence at second face,

$$i' = A - r = 60° - 19° = 41°$$

which is just less than the critical angle 42° for glass-air interface. If $i < 30°$, then $r' > i_C$ and the ray will suffer total internal reflection at the second face and will not emerge through the prism.

7. In LASIK eye surgery, ultraviolet rays are used because of their short wavelength, they can be focused into very narrow beam, with high precision.

8. According to given circuit diagram, diode D_2 is in reverse biased, hence is ineffective. Therefore, redrawing the circuit diagram as

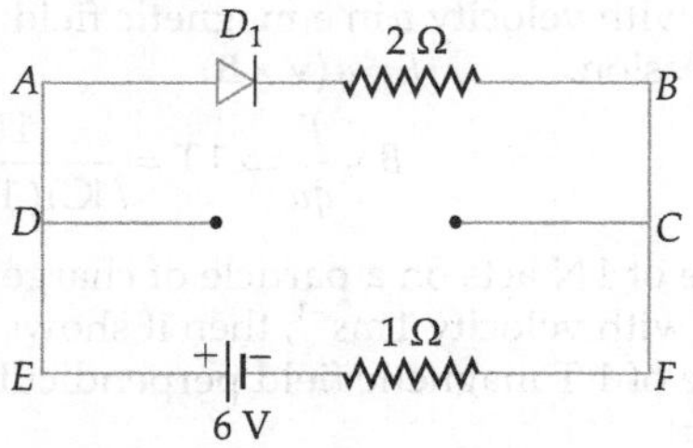

Resistances 2 Ω and 1 Ω are in series,

$$R = 2 + 1 = 3\Omega$$

$\therefore$ Current through 1 Ω resistance,

$$I = \frac{V}{R} = \frac{6}{3} = 2 \text{ A}$$

9. In the circuit, when initially K_1 is closed and K_2 is opened, the capacitor C_1 and C_2 acquire potential difference V_1 and V_2, respectively. So, we have

$$V_1 + V_2 = E$$

and $\quad V_1 + V_2 = 9\text{V}$

Also, in series combination, $V \propto 1/C$

$$V_1 : V_2 = \frac{1}{6} : \frac{1}{3} = 1 : 2$$

On solving,

$\Rightarrow$ $V_1 = 3\text{V}$ and $V_2 = 6\text{V}$

$\therefore$ $Q_1 = C_1V_1 = 6 \times 3 = 18\mu\text{C}$

$\Rightarrow$ $Q_2 = C_2V_2 = 3 \times 6 = 18\mu\text{C}$

and $\quad Q_3 = 0$

When K_1 was opened and K_2 was closed, the parallel combination of C_2 and C_3 in series with C_1.

[Charge on C_1 remains unchanged]

i.e. $\quad Q_1' = Q_1 = 18\mu\text{C}$

Charge on C_2 is shared between C_2 and C_3 in parallel.

As, $\quad Q_2' = Q_3'$

$\therefore$ $Q_2' = Q_3' = \frac{Q_2}{2} = \frac{18}{2} = 9\mu\text{C} \quad [\because Q_2 = 18\mu\text{C}]$

10. (*i*) Angle of prism, $A = 5°, \mu_R = 1.641, \mu_B = 1.659$

As we know that, $\delta = (\mu - 1)A$

So, $\quad \delta_B = (\mu_B - 1)A$ and $\delta_R = (\mu_R - 1)A$

$\therefore$ $\quad \delta_B - \delta_R = (\mu_B - \mu_R)A = (1.659 - 1.641) \times 5 = 0.09°$

(*ii*) The **magnification** of a magnifying glass depends upon, where it is placed between the user's eye and the object being viewed and the total distance between them, while the **magnifying power** is equivalent to angular magnification.

(*iii*) Since, magnification, $m = \frac{f}{f + u}$

$\Rightarrow$ $m_{25} = \frac{20}{20 - 25} = -4$

Similarly, $m_{50} = \frac{20}{20 - 50} = \frac{-2}{3}$

Therefore, $\frac{m_{25}}{m_{50}} = (-4)\left(\frac{-3}{2}\right) = 6$

11. (*i*) An electron undergoes transition from second excited state the first excited state, is Balmer series and then to the ground state, is Lyman series.

(*ii*) The wavelength of the emitted radiations in the two cases.

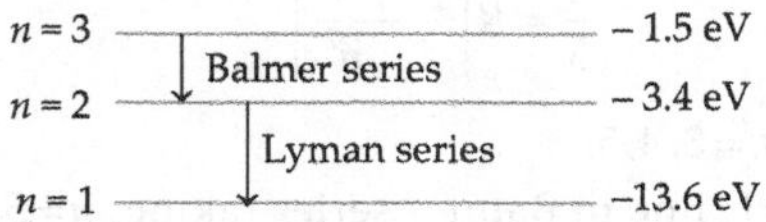

We know that, $\lambda = \frac{hc}{\Delta E}$

From $n_3 \rightarrow n_2$,

$$\lambda_1 = \frac{hc}{E_3 - E_2} = \frac{hc}{(-1.5) - (-3.4)} = \frac{hc}{1.9}$$

From $n_2 \rightarrow n_1$,

$$\lambda_2 = \frac{hc}{E_2 - E_1} = \frac{hc}{(-3.4) - (-13.6)} = \frac{hc}{10.20}$$

$\therefore$ $\frac{\lambda_1}{\lambda_2} = \frac{10.20}{1.9} = 5.368$

12. Let x be the distance of point P from the centre of screen.

When red light ($\lambda = 6000$ Å) is used, nth bright fringe is obtained at point P.

$\therefore$ $x = \frac{nD\lambda}{d} = \frac{nD \times 6000 \times 10^{-10}}{d}$

When green light ($\lambda' = 5000$ Å) is used, $(n + 1)$th the bright fringe is obtained at the same point P.

$\therefore$ $x = \frac{(n+1)D\lambda'}{d} = \frac{(n+1)D \times 5000 \times 10^{-10}}{d}$

Equating the two values of x, we get

$$\frac{nD \times 6000 \times 10^{-10}}{d} = \frac{(n+1)D \times 5000 \times 10^{-10}}{d}$$

$$6n = 5(n+1)$$
$$\therefore \quad n = 5$$

Value Point To get maximum marks, start the solution by writting the formula, $x = \frac{nD\lambda}{d}$

13. Given, $R = 4\Omega$, $I_1 = 1\text{A}$

$$\therefore \quad I_1 = \frac{E}{R+r}$$

$$I_1(R+r) = E \quad \Rightarrow \quad 1(4+r) = E$$

$$\Rightarrow \quad r = E - 4 \quad \ldots\text{(i)}$$

According to second condition,

$$R' = 9\Omega \text{ and } I_2 = 0.5\text{A}$$

$$\therefore \quad I_2 = \frac{E}{R'+r}$$

$$I_2(R'+r) = E \quad \Rightarrow \quad 0.5(9+r) = E$$

$$r = 2E - 9 \quad \ldots\text{(ii)}$$

From Eqs. (i) and (ii), we get

$$\Rightarrow \quad 2E - 9 = E - 4$$

$$\Rightarrow \quad E = 5\text{V}$$

From Eq. (i),

$$r = 5 - 4 = 1\Omega$$

Or

To varify the power values, we use the formula

$$P = I^2 R$$

(i) For $I = 1\text{A}$
$$P = I^2 \times 10 = 10\text{W}$$

(ii) For $I = 2\text{A}$
$$P = 2^2 \times 10 = 40\text{W}$$

(iii) For $I = 3\text{A}$
$$P^2 = 3^2 \times 10 = 90\text{W}$$

(iv) For $I = 4\text{A}$
$$P = 4^2 \times 10 = 160\text{W}$$

14. For coil *x*

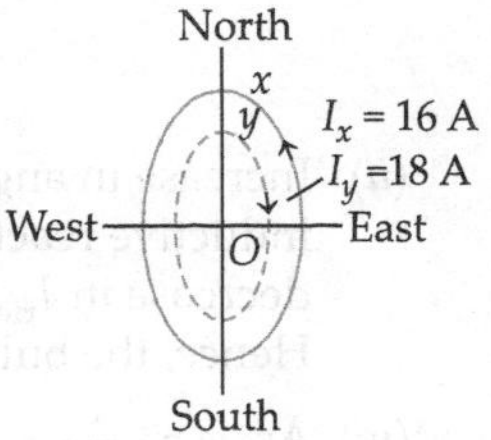

Radius of coil, $r_x = 16 \text{ cm} = 0.16\text{m}$

Number of turns, $n_x = 20$

Current in the coil, $I_x = 16\text{ A}$ (anti-clockwise)

For coil *y*

Radius of coil, $r_y = 10 \text{ cm} = 0.1\text{ m}$

Number of turns, $n_y = 25$

Current in the coil, $I_y = 18\text{ A}$ (clockwise)

The magnitude of the magnetic field at the centre of coil *x*,

$$B_x = \frac{\mu_0}{4\pi} \cdot \frac{2I_x \pi n_x}{r_x} = \frac{10^{-7} \times 2 \times 16 \times \pi \times 20}{0.16}$$
$$= 4\pi \times 10^{-4}\text{T}$$

The direction of magnetic field due to the coil *x* at centre *O* is towards right, i.e. East, according to right hand thumb rule. The magnitude of the magnetic field at the centre of coil *y*,

$$B_y = \frac{\mu_0}{4\pi} \cdot \frac{2\pi I_y n_y}{r_y} = \frac{10^{-7} \times 2 \times \pi \times 18 \times 25}{0.1}$$
$$= 9\pi \times 10^{-4}\text{T}$$

The direction of magnetic field due to coil *y* at centre *O* is towards left, i.e. West, according to right hand thumb rule. Here, the magnitude of B_y is greater than B_x, so the resultant magnetic field will be in the direction of B_y, i.e. left (West).

Net magnetic field at the centre,

$$B = B_y - B_x$$
$$= (9\pi - 4\pi)\, 10^{-4}\text{T} = 5\pi \times 10^{-4}\text{T}$$
$$[\because B_y \text{ and } B_x \text{ are opposite to each other}]$$
$$= 1.6 \times 10^{-3}\text{ T} \quad \text{[towards West]}$$

15. We know that, angular width of central maximum of diffraction pattern of a single slit is given by

$$2\theta = \frac{2\lambda}{a}$$

(i) If slit width *a* is decreased, the angular width will increase, because $2\theta \propto \frac{1}{a}$.

(ii) If the distance between the slit and the screen increases, then it does not affect the angular width of diffraction maxima.

(iii) If the light of smaller visible wavelength is used, the angular width is decreased because $2\theta \propto \lambda$.

Or

(i) (a) Two independent monochromatic sources of light cannot produce a sustained interference pattern because their relative phases change randomly. When *d* is negligibly small, fringe width β is proportional to $1/d$ may become too large. Even a single fringe may occupy the screen.

Hence, the pattern cannot be detected.

(b) Given, $y_1 = a\cos(\omega t)$

and $y = a\cos(\omega t + \phi)$

$\therefore$ Resultant, $R = \sqrt{a^2 + b^2 + 2ab\cos\phi}$

[Using parallelogram law]

$$= \sqrt{a^2 + a^2 + 2a^2\cos\phi} \quad [\because a = b]$$
$$= \sqrt{2a^2(1+\cos\phi)} = \sqrt{2a^2 \times 2\cos^2\frac{\phi}{2}}$$
$$= 2a\cos\frac{\phi}{2}$$

$$I_1 \propto a^2 \quad \text{and} \quad I_2 \propto a^2$$
$$I_{net} \propto R^2$$

$$\therefore \quad \frac{I_{net}}{I} = \left(\frac{R}{a}\right)^2 = \left(2\cos\frac{\phi}{2}\right)^2 \Rightarrow I_{net} = 4I\cos^2\frac{\phi}{2}$$

(ii) Intensity of light at a point on the screen is given by, $I_R = I_1 + I_2 + 2\sqrt{I_1 I_2}\cos\phi$

For the path difference λ, phase difference is 2π.

As, source are coherent and taken out L of the same source in Young's double slit experiment,

$$I_1 = I_2 = I \Rightarrow I_R = 2I + 2I\cos 2\pi$$

$$I_R = 4I \Rightarrow 4I = K \text{ unit} \quad \text{....(i)}$$

For the path difference, $\frac{\lambda}{3}$ corresponds to phase difference of $\frac{2\pi}{3}$,

$$I_R = 2I + 2I\cos\frac{2\pi}{3} = 2I - I = I \quad \text{...(ii)}$$

From Eqs. (i) and (ii), we conclude

$$I_R = \frac{K}{4} \text{ unit}$$

16. (i) Given, potential difference, $V = 500$ V

Specific charge of the electron,

$$e/m = 1.76 \times 10^{11} \text{ C/kg}$$

Kinetic energy of an electron,

$$\text{KE} = \frac{1}{2}mv^2 = eV$$

$$\Rightarrow \quad v = \sqrt{\frac{e}{m} \times 2V} \quad \text{...(i)}$$

$$= \sqrt{1.76 \times 10^{11} \times 2 \times 500}$$

$$= 1.326 \times 10^7 \text{ m/s}$$

(ii) Potential, $V = 10$ MV $= 10^7$ V

Again from Eq. (i), $v = \sqrt{\frac{2e}{m}V}$

$$= \sqrt{2 \times 1.76 \times 10^{11} \times 10^7}$$

$$= 1.8762 \times 10^9 \text{ m/s}$$

This speed is greater than the speed of light, which is not possible. As v approaches to c, then mass

$$m = \frac{m_0}{\sqrt{1 - \frac{v^2}{c^2}}}$$

17. (i) According to the diagram, when the switch S is closed, the two capacitors C_1 and C_2 in parallel will be charged by the same potential difference V.

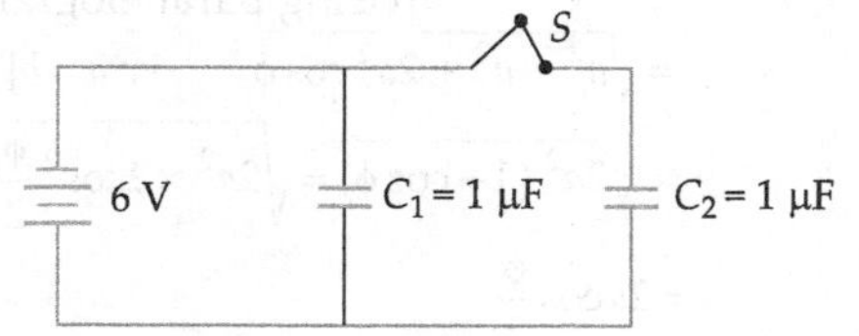

So, charge on capacitor C_1,

$$q_1 = C_1 V = 1 \times 6 = 6\,\mu\text{C} \quad \text{...(i)}$$

and charge on capacitor C_2,

$$q_2 = C_2 V = 1 \times 6 = 6\,\mu\text{C} \quad \text{...(ii)}$$

Hence, total charge on capacitor,

$$q = q_1 + q_2 = 6 + 6 = 12\,\mu\text{C}$$

(ii) When switch S is opened and dielectric is introduced, then

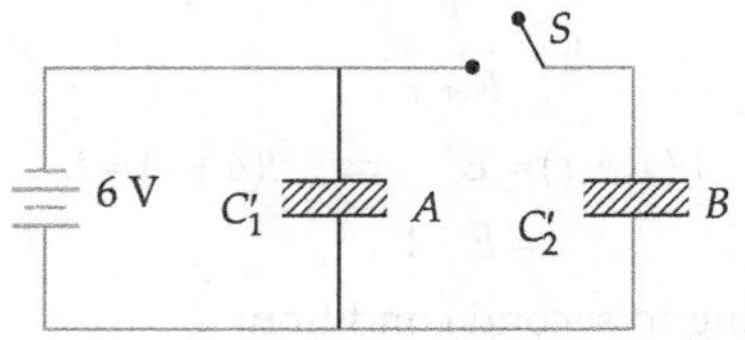

Capacity of both the capacitors becomes K times i.e. $C_1' = C_2' = KC = 3 \times 1 = 3\,\mu\text{F}$ (as $C_1' = C_2'$)

Capacitor A remains connected to battery

$$\therefore \quad V'_1 = V = 6\text{V}$$

$$q_1' = Kq_1 = 3 \times 6\mu\text{C} = 18\mu\text{C}$$

Capacitor B becomes isolated

$$\therefore \quad q_2' = q_2$$

or $\quad C_2'V_2' = C_2 V_2$

or $\quad (KC)V_2' = CV$

or $\quad V_2 = \left(\frac{V}{K}\right) = \frac{6}{3} = 2\,\text{V}$

18. (i) For angular frequency, $\nu = 50$ Hz

Inductive reactance,

$$X_L = \omega L = 2\pi \times 50 \times 10 \times 10^{-3} = \pi\Omega$$

$$I_{\text{rms}} = (V_{\text{rms}} / X_L) = (100/\pi)\text{A}$$

For angular frequency, $\nu = 50$ kHz

Inductive reactance,

$$X_L' = \omega L = 2\pi \times 50 \times 10^3 \times 10 \times 10^{-3}$$

$$= 1000\pi\Omega$$

$$I_{\text{rms}}' = (V_{\text{rms}} / X_L) = (1/10\pi)\text{A}$$

$$\% \text{ decrease in } I_{\text{rms}} = \{|\Delta I_{\text{rms}}|/I_{\text{rms}}\} \times 100$$

$$= \{999\pi/(10\pi \times 100)\} \times 100$$

$$= 99.9\%$$

(ii) Increase in angular frequency, increases the inductive reactance that further results in the decrease in I_{rms} current flowing through the bulb. Hence, the bulb glows dimmer.

(iii) As $\omega = \frac{1}{\sqrt{LC}}$

For $\omega = \text{constant} = \sqrt{LC} = \text{constant}$

$$\frac{L_2}{L_1} = \frac{C}{4C} \Rightarrow L_2 = \frac{L}{4}$$

Therefore, if C is made $4C$, then L should be reduced to $L/4$.

Or

(*i*) Graph showing the variation of amplitude of circuit current with changing frequency is given below.

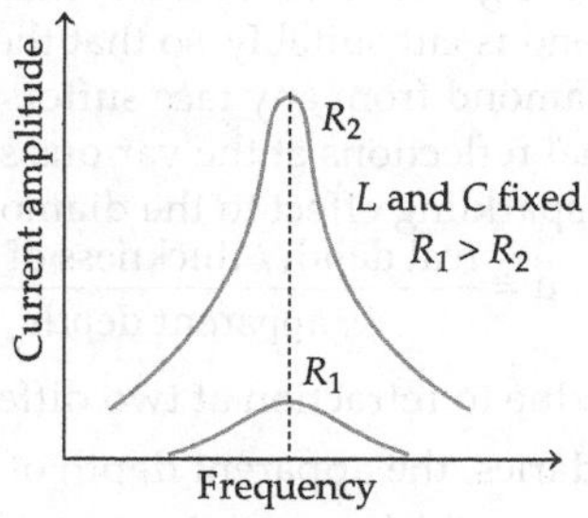

(*ii*) Given, capacitance, $C = 100\,\mu\text{F} = 100 \times 10^{-6}\,\text{F} = 10^{-4}\,\text{F}$

Resistance, $R = 50\,\Omega$

Inductance, $L = 0.5\,\text{H}$

RMS value of voltage, $E_V = 110\,\text{V}$

Frequency, $\nu = 50$ Hz

Since, capacitive reactance,

$$X_C = \frac{1}{\omega C} = \frac{1}{2\pi\nu C}$$

$$= \frac{1}{2 \times 3.14 \times 50 \times 10^{-4}}$$

$$X_C = 31.85\,\Omega$$

and inductive reactance,

$$X_L = \omega L = 2\pi\nu L = 2 \times 3.14 \times 50 \times 0.5 = 157\,\Omega$$

$\because$ Impedance, $Z = \sqrt{R^2 + (X_L - X_C)^2}$

$$= \sqrt{(50)^2 + (157 - 31.85)^2} = 134.77\,\Omega$$

$$\Rightarrow \quad I_V = \frac{E_V}{Z} = \frac{110}{134.77} = 0.816\text{ A}$$

(*iii*) Transformer voltage $= (4000 - 200)$ V

Length of two conductors $= 15 \times 2 = 30$ km

Resistance of the conductor $= 0.5 \times 30 = 15\,\Omega$

and power $= 800$ kW $= 800 \times 10^3$ W

As, $\quad VI = \text{Power}$

$\Rightarrow \; 4000 \times I = 800 \times 10^3$

$\Rightarrow \quad I = 200$ A

Now, power loss in the form of heat

$$P = I^2 R = 200 \times 200 \times 15$$

$$= 600000 = 600\text{ kW}$$

19. (*i*) Drift of the free electrons in conduction band in a direction opposite of the electric field when an electric field is applied across a semiconductor is known as electron current. At the same time, drift of bound electrons from one vacant place to next in opposite direction of field takes place. This motion of bound electrons is equivalent to the motion of holes in direction of applied field and constitutes hole current.

(*ii*)

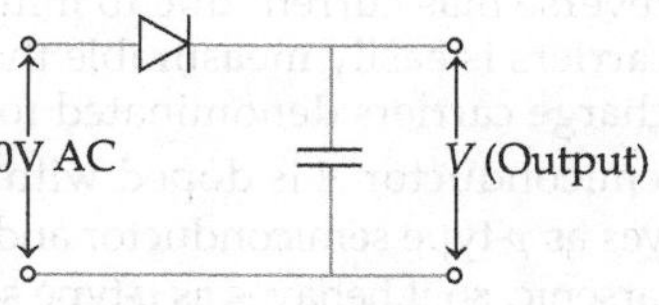

When diode is forward biased, i.e. during positive half-cycle of input AC, the capacitor voltage, $V = V_0 = \sqrt{2}\,V_{\text{rms}} = \sqrt{2} \times 220 = 311.1$ V.

Here, capacitor charges itself the peak value of supply voltage 220 V.

(*iii*) n-type semiconductor is formed by doping it with pentavalent impurities. These impurities or dopant takes the atoms in the crystal and its four electrons take part in chemical bonding with four electrons of intrinsic semiconductor or pure semiconductor. Whereas, the last electrons are left free. Since, whole atom is electrically neutral, so n-type semiconductor is also neutral.

Or

(*i*) A p-n junction diode is made up of photosensitive semiconductors designed to operate in reverse bias and its reverse current increases, when light of suitable frequency and intensity is incident on it, and is known as photodiode.

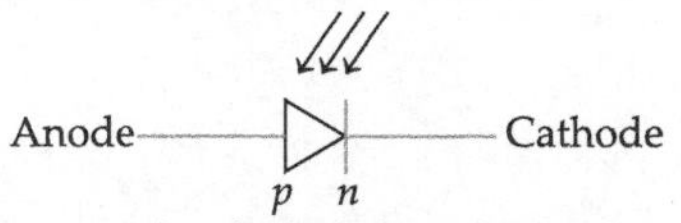

(a) Symbol of photodiode

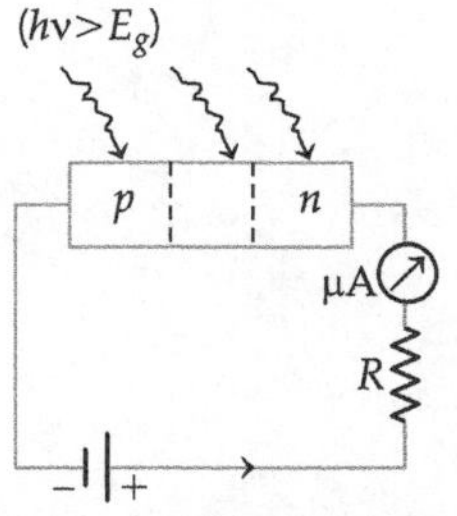

(b) Reverse biased photodiode

(*ii*) When light of suitable frequency (ν) is incident on the junction such that energy of photon is greater than the band gap of the semiconductor, then more electron-hole pairs are generated and hence, reverse current increases. The saturation value of reverse current increases with the increase in the intensity of incident light.

The photodiode is operated in reverse bias because

(a) fractional charge of minority charge carriers becomes much higher than the fractional charge carriers when the light of suitable frequency and intensity is incident on it.

(b) reverse bias current due to minority charge carriers is easily measurable than majority charge carriers denominated forward current.

(*iii*) As, semiconductor A is doped with indium, so it behaves as p-type semiconductor and B is doped with arsenic, so it behaves as n-type semiconductor. Thus, the figure given shows that it is forward bias condition.

20. (*i*) From Snell's law, $\mu = \dfrac{\sin i}{\sin r} = \dfrac{c}{v}$

$\Rightarrow v \propto \sin r$, for given value of i.

Smaller the angle of refraction, smaller the velocity of light in medium.

Velocity of light is minimum in medium A, as the angle of refraction is minimum, i.e. 15°.

(*ii*) Whenever rays of light travels through glass, they strike the glass-air interface at an angle greater than critical angle of glass. They are totally reflected, hence crack appears silvery.

(*iii*) The refractive index of diamond is much higher than that of glass. Due to high refractive index, the critical angle for diamond-air interface is low. The diamond is cut suitably, so that the light entering the diamond from any face suffers multiple total internal reflections at the various surfaces. This gives sparkling effect to the diamonds.

(*iv*) Here, $\mu = \dfrac{\text{real depth / thickness of object}}{\text{apparent depth}}$

Now, due to refraction at two different boundaries, the apparent depth of object

$$= \frac{\text{thickness of glass}}{\mu_{\text{glass}}} + \frac{\text{thickness of water}}{\mu_{\text{water}}}$$

$$= \frac{6}{1.5} + \frac{4}{1.3} = 4 + 3 = 7\text{ cm}$$

SQP Code : **PB-12/15** Series **i-Succeed 12-25/15** Roll No. | | | | | | | |

Sample Question Paper 12

Physics 12th (Code 861)

General Instructions

1. This paper is divided into four Sections- A, B, C and D. Answer all questions.
2. **Section A** consists of one question having sub-parts of one mark each.
3. **Section B** consists of seven questions of two marks each.
4. **Section C** consists of nine questions of three marks each.
5. **Section D** consists of three questions of five marks each.
6. Internal choices have been provided in two questions each in Section B, Section C and Section D.

Time : 3 Hrs.

Max. Marks : 70

Section A (14 Marks)

1. **A.** In questions (i) to (vii) below, choose the correct alternative (a), (b), (c) or (d) for each of the questions given below.

(*i*) In modern microscopes, the quality of image is improved by • *Recall* [1]

(a) minimising optical aberrations in lens
(b) increasing focal length of objective lens
(c) decreasing focal length of objective lens
(d) increasing the radius of curvature of objective lens

(*ii*) A ray passing through or directed towards centre of curvature of a spherical mirror is reflected such that it trace back of its path, because • *Recall* [1]

(a) it does not follow law of reflection
(b) angle of incidence is 0°
(c) centre of curvature is midway between object and pole
(d) distance of centre of curvature from focus is equal to its distance from pole

(*iii*) **Assertion** (A) The poles of magnet cannot be separated by breaking into two pieces.
Reason (R) The magnetic moment will be reduced to half, when a magnet is broken into two equal pieces. • *Understanding* [1]

(a) Both Assertion and Reason are true and Reason is the correct explanation for Assertion.
(b) Both Assertion and Reason are true but Reason is not the correct explanation for Assertion.
(c) Assertion is false and Reason is true.
(d) Both Assertion and Reason are false.

(*iv*) **Assertion** (A) A given transformer can be used to step-up or step-down the voltage.
Reason (R) The output voltage depends upon the ratio of the number of turns of the two coils of the transformer. • *Analysis* [1]

(a) Both Assertion and Reason are true and Reason is the correct explanation for Assertion.
(b) Both Assertion and Reason are true but Reason is not the correct explanation for Assertion.
(c) Assertion is false and Reason is true.
(d) Both Assertion and Reason are false.

(*v*) Total energy of an electron in the ground state of hydrogen atom is –13.6 eV. Its total energy when hydrogen atom is in the first excited state, is • *Understanding* [1]

(a) + 13.6eV (b) + 3.4 eV

(c) – 3.4 eV (d) – 54.4 eV

(*vi*) One requires 11 eV of energy to dissociate a carbon monoxide molecule into carbon and oxygen atoms. The minimum frequency of the appropriate electromagnetic radiation to achieve the dissociation lies in • *Analysis* [1]

(a) visible region (b) infrared region

(c) ultraviolet region (d) microwave region

(*vii*) A 900 pF capacitor is charged by 100 V battery in the figure. How much electrostatic energy is stored by the capacitor? • *Analysis* [1]

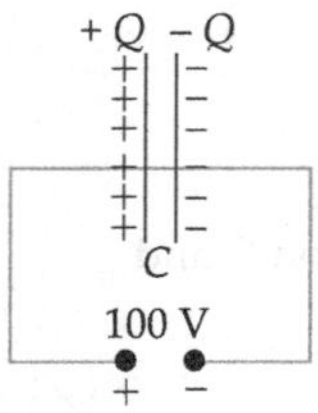

(a) 45×10^{-6} J (b) 4.5×10^{6} J

(c) 4.5×10^{-6} J (d) 0.45×10^{5} J

B. Answer the following questions briefly.

(*i*) Will an induced current develop in a conductor moving in a direction parallel to magnetic field? • *Recall* [1]

(*ii*) Sketch the graph to show, how the reactance of a capacitor varies as a function of frequency ? • *Understanding* [1]

(*iii*) A coil has a self-inductance of 0.05 H. Find magnitude of the emf induced in it, when the current flowing through it is changing at the rate of 100 As^{-1}. • *Recall* [1]

(*iv*) A charged particle oscillates about its mean position with frequency 10^9 Hz. What is the frequency of electromagnetic wave produced by the oscillator? • *Recall* [1]

(*v*) When does a moving charged particle not experience any force while moving through a uniform magnetic field? • *Recall* [1]

(*vi*) Is electrostatic potential necessarily zero at a point, where electric field strength is zero? Illustrate your answer. • *Recall* [1]

(*vii*) Show on the graph, the variation of resistivity with temperature for a typical semiconductor. • *Application* [1]

Section B (14 Marks)

2. (*i*) How can an *n*-type semiconductor be obtained from a pure crystal of germanium? • *Recall* [1]

(*ii*) What is meant by energy gap in solids? • *Recall* [1]

Or Explain with the help of a circuit diagram the working of a photodiode. Write briefly, how it is used to detect the optical signals? • *Application* [2]

3. (*i*) How does a diamagnetic material behave when it is cooled at very low temperature? • *Recall* [1]

(*ii*) Why does a paramagnetic sample display greater magnetisation when cooled? Explain. • *Recall* [1]

4. Calculate the energy released when an electron annihilates a positron. • *Understanding* [2]

Or

Consider two different hydrogen atoms. The electron in each atom is in an excited state. Is it possible for the electrons to have different energies but same orbital angular momentum according to the Bohr model? Justify your answer. • *Application* [2]

5. (*i*) What are matter waves? • *Recall* [1]

(*ii*) Show with the help of a labelled graph how their wavelength (λ) varies with their linear momentum (*p*)? • *Application* [1]

6. A ray of light passing through an equilateral triangular glass prism from air undergoes minimum deviation, when the angle of incidence is (3/4)th of the angle of prism. Calculate the speed of light in the prism. • *Analysis* [2]

7. Calculate de-Broglie wavelength of the following cases. • *Application*

(*i*) A stone of mass 0.020 kg travelling at a speed of 500 m/s. [1]

(*ii*) A ball of mass 0.050 kg moving at a speed of 600 m/s. [1]

8. Experimentally it is found that energy required to separate a H-atom into a proton and an electron be 13.6 eV. • *Application*

Calculate

(*i*) orbital radius and [1]

(*ii*) velocity of the electron in H-atom. [1]

Section C (27 Marks)

9. Obtain the relation, $I = I_0 \sin(\omega t + \pi/2)$ and $X_C = 1/\omega C$ for a pure capacitor across which an AC emf of $E = E_0 \sin \omega t$ is applied as shown in the figure. Draw a phasor diagram showing emf ε, current I and their phase difference ϕ. • *Application* [3]

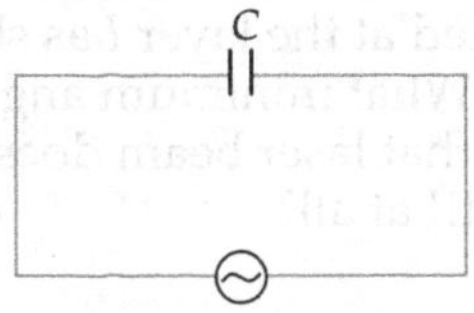

10. (*i*) An electric lamp is connected in series with a capacitor and an AC source is glowing with a certain brightness. How does the brightness of the lamp change on increasing the capacitance? • *Recall* [1]

(*ii*) Which of the following 120 V AC devices cost more to operate (a) one that draws an rms current of 10 A or (b) one that draws a peak current of 12 A? Explain the reason for your answer. • *Application* [1]

(*iii*) In an AC circuit, the rms voltage is $100\sqrt{2}$ V. Determine the peak value of voltage and its mean value during a positive half-cycle. • *Recall* [1]

11. Three charges $1\,\mu C, 1\,\mu C$ and $2\,\mu C$ are kept at vertices *A*, *B* and *C* of an equilateral triangle *ABC* of 10 cm side respectively. What will be the resultant force on the charge at *C*? • *Understanding* [3]

12. In the circuit shown, $R_1 = 4\ \Omega$, $R_2 = R_3 = 5\ \Omega$, $R_4 = 10\ \Omega$ and $E = 6$ V. Find out the equivalent resistance of the circuit and the current in each resistor. • *Application* [3]

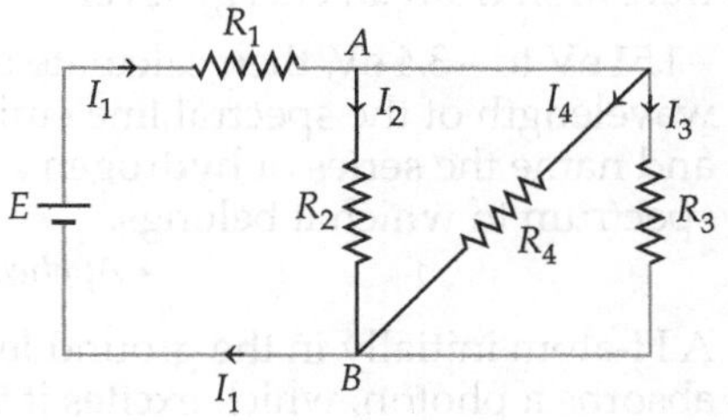

Or

Find the change in power dissipated in the $4\,\Omega$ resistor after the switch *S* is closed. • *Application* [3]

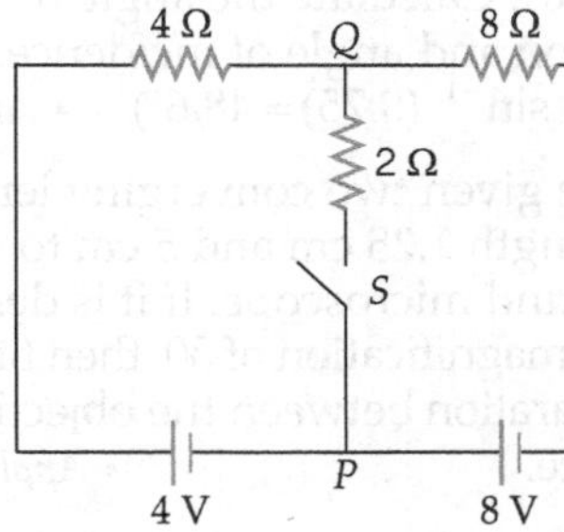

13. A ray of light falls normally on the surface of glass prism as shown in figure. Draw ray diagram of light passing through prism. If refractive index of the material of prism is $\sqrt{3}$, then find the value of the angle of emergence. • *Analysis* [3]

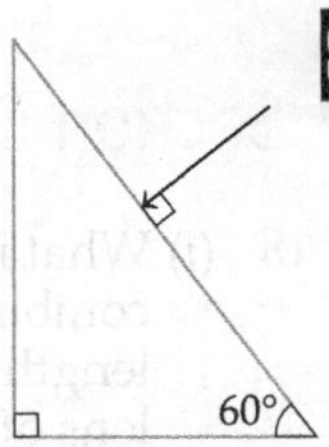

Or

A student records the following data for the image distance (v) of a convex mirror with focal length f at different object distance u. Verify (for any two) that these observations are in good agreement with the expected theoretical value of v. • *Application* [3]

SP-12

u	$2f$	$3f$	$4f$	$5f$
v	$2f$	$\frac{3f}{2}$	$\frac{4f}{3}$	$\frac{5f}{4}$

14. Find the electrostatic potential energy of the configuration of four charges $+q, -q, +q$ and $-q$ placed at four corners A, B, C and D of a square of side a. • *Understanding* [3]

15. (*i*) The ground state energy of hydrogen atom is -13.6 eV. If an electron makes a transition from an energy level -1.51 eV to -3.4 eV, then calculate the wavelength of the spectral line emitted and name the series of hydrogen spectrum to which it belongs. • *Application* [2]

(*ii*) A H-atom initially in the ground level absorbs a photon, which excites it to the $n = 4$ level. Determine the wavelength and frequency of photon. • *Understanding* [1]

16. (*i*) A ray of light suffers minimum deviation, while passing through a prism of refractive index 1.5 and refracting angle 60°. Calculate the angle of deviation and angle of incidence. (Given, $\sin^{-1}(0.75) = 48.6°$) • *Analysis* [2]

(*ii*) You are given two converging lenses of focal length 1.25 cm and 5 cm to design a compound microscope. If it is desired to have a magnification of 30, then find out the separation between the objective and eyepiece. • *Application* [1]

17. (*i*) A ray of light is incident at the glass-water interface at an angle i, it emerges finally parallel to the surface of water, then what would be the value of μ_g ? • *Recall* [1]

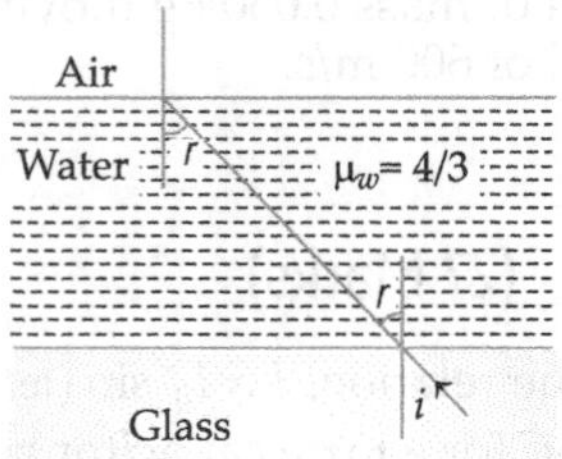

(*ii*) A transparent container contains layers of 3 immiscible transparent liquids of different refractive indices. A laser beam is pointed at the layer I as shown in the figure. What minimum angle of θ_1 will ensure that laser beam does not enter region III at all? • *Application* [2]

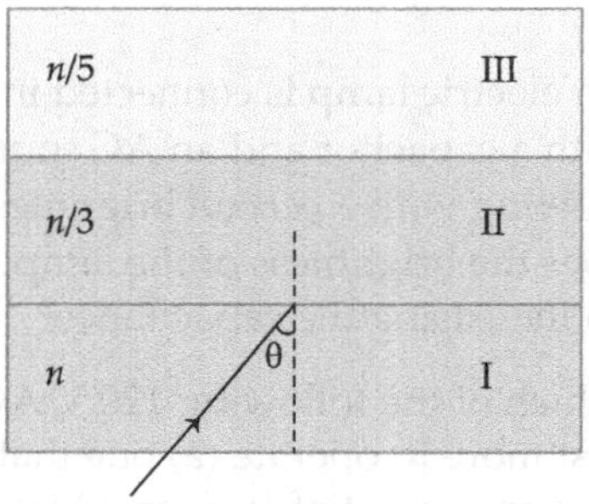

SP-12

Section D (15 Marks)

18. (*i*) What is the focal length of the combination of a convex lens of focal length 30 cm in contact with a concave lens of focal length 20 cm? Is the system a converging or a diverging lens? Ignore thickness of the lenses. • *Application* [2]

(*ii*) At what angle should a ray of light be incident on the face of a prism of refracting angle 60°, so that it just suffers total internal reflection at the other face? The refractive index of the material of the prism is 1.524. • *Application* [3]

Or (*i*) In Young's double slit experiment using monochromatic light L_1 of wavelength 700 nm, 10th bright fringe was obtained at a certain point P on a screen.

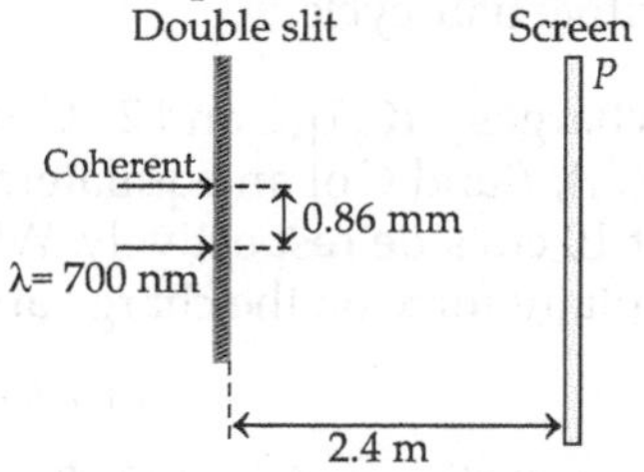

(a) Which bright fringe will be obtained at the same point P, if monochromatic light of wavelength 500 nm is used in place of L_1? (No other alterations were made in the experimental set-up). • *Analysis* [2]

(b) Monochromatic light of wavelength 650 nm falls normally on a slit of width 1.3×10^{-4} cm and the resulting Fraunhofer diffraction is obtained on a screen. Find th angular width of the central maxima. • *Application* [3]

19. (*i*) The forward characteristic curve of a junction diode is shown in figure below.

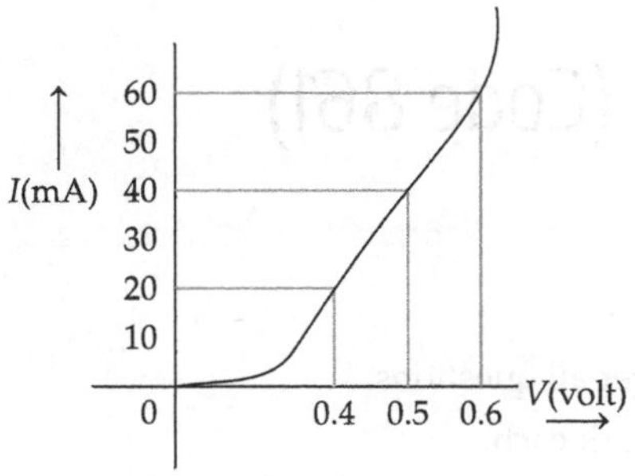

Calculate the resistance of the diode at

(a) $V = 0.5$ V (b) $I = 60$ mA • *Analysis* [2]

(*ii*) Draw separate energy band diagrams for conductors, semiconductors and insulators and label each of them. • *Application* [3]

Or (*i*) Draw a labelled circuit diagram of a half-wave rectifier and give its output waveform. • *Application* [3]

(*ii*) Find the ratio of output frequencies of the ripple voltage obtained in full wave and half-wave rectifiers. • *Application* [2]

20. A charged particle moving in an external magnetic field experiences a force, which is called Lorentz force, i.e. $\mathbf{F} = q(\mathbf{v} \times \mathbf{B})$, where q is the charge on the particle and v is the velocity of the particle.

The direction of the force is given by the cross product of velocity vector and magnetic field vector at any time.

The charge particle travels in a special trajectory called helical path. Because, the force is always perpendicular to the velocity vector and the magnetic field can do no work on an isolate charge. Hence, the linear velocity always remains the same.

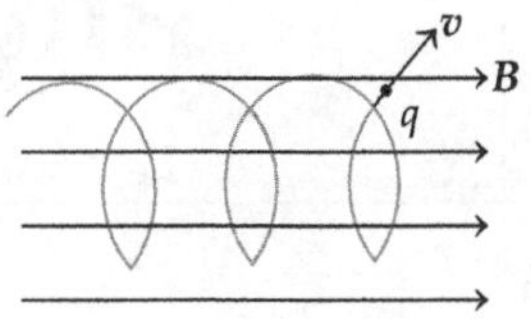

(*i*) State the condition in which force on a moving charge particle is zero. • *Recall* [1]

(*ii*) (a) Find the trajectory of charged particle in uniform magnetic field when it enters at any angle except 90°, 0° or 180°. • *Application* [1]

(b) A radioactive nuclei emits β-rays. In a uniform magnetic field shown in the figure, describe the path of β-rays. • *Recall* [1]

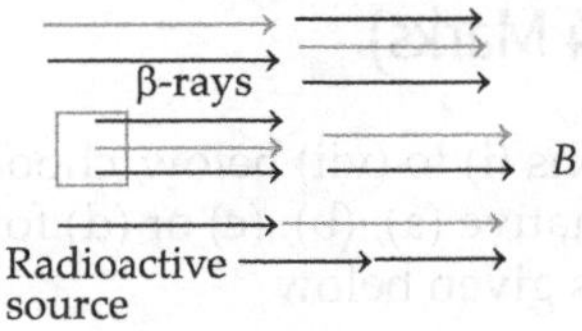

(*iii*) (a) What do you mean by pitch? • *Recall* [1]

(b) What is the radius of helical path ? • *Recall* [1]

SP-12

Answers

1. A (i) (a) (ii) (b) (iii) (b) (iv) (a) (v) (c) (vi) (c) (vii) (c)

B. (iii) 5V (iv) 10^9Hz **4.** 1. 0125 MeV

6. 2.1×10^8 m / s

7. (i) 6.63×10^{-35}m (ii) 2.21×10^{-35}m

8. (i) 5.3×10^{-11}m (ii) 2.2×10^6m / s

10. (iii) 127.4 V **11.** 3.12N

12. 6Ω, 1A, $\frac{2}{5}$A, $\frac{2}{5}$A, $\frac{1}{5}$A Or 0 W.

13. 60° **15.** (i) 656 nm (ii) 3.1×10^{15}Hz

16. (i) 48.6° (ii) 7.5 cm

18. (i) $f = -60$ cm (ii) 29° 75′

Or (i) (a) $n_2 = 14$ (b) 1 rad

19. (i) (a) 12.5Ω (b) 10Ω *Or* (ii) 2 : 1

For Detailed Solutions, scan the given QR code.

SQP Code : **PB-13/15** Series **i-Succeed 13-25/15** Roll No. | | | | | | | | |

Sample Question Paper 13

Physics 12th (Code 861)

General Instructions

1. This paper is divided into four Sections- A, B, C and D. Answer all questions.
2. **Section A** consists of one question having sub-parts of one mark each.
3. **Section B** consists of seven questions of two marks each.
4. **Section C** consists of nine questions of three marks each.
5. **Section D** consists of three questions of five marks each.
6. Internal choices have been provided in two questions each in Section B, Section C and Section D.

Time : 3 Hrs.

Max. Marks : 70

Section A (14 Marks)

1. A. In questions (i) to (vii) below, choose the correct alternative (a), (b), (c) or (d) for each of the questions given below.

(i) The figure shows some of the electric field lines corresponding to an electric field. The figure suggests • *Analysis* [1]

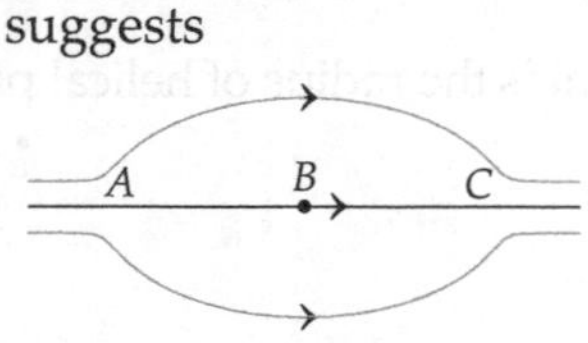

(a) $E_A > E_B > E_C$ (b) $E_A = E_B = E_C$

(c) $E_A = E_C > E_B$ (d) $E_A = E_C < E_B$

(ii) The energy bands of three substances are given in the diagram, where V is valence band and C is conduction band. These substances are, respectively • *Analysis* [1]

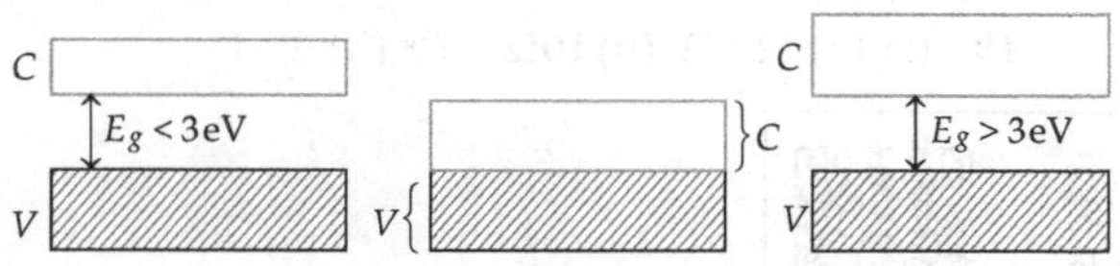

(a) conductor, semiconductor and insulator

(b) semiconductor, insulator and conductor

(c) insulator, conductor and semiconductor

(d) semiconductor, conductor and insulator

(iii) **Assertion** (A) The energy of electron in first excited state of hydrogen atom is – 3.4 eV.

Reason (R) When electrons jumps from any higher state to first excited state in hydrogen atom, then balmer series are obtained. • *Analysis* [1]

(a) Both Assertion and Reason are true and Reason is the correct explanation for Assertion.

(b) Both Assertion and Reason are true but Reason is not the correct explanation for Assertion.

(c) Assertion is false and Reason is true.

(d) Both Assertion and Reason are false.

(iv) Net emf across A and B shown in the figure below is • *Understanding* [1]

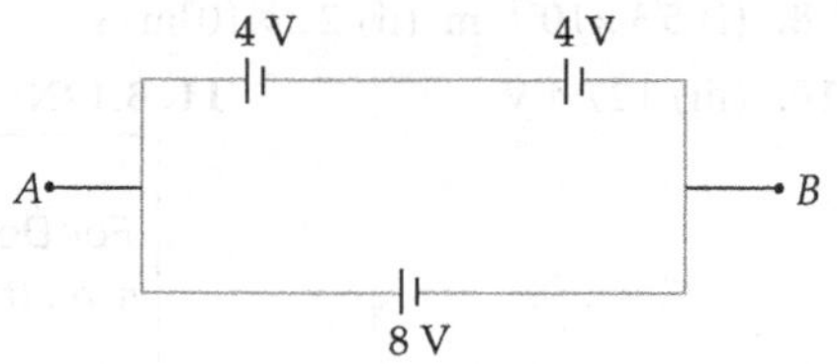

(a) 4 V (b) 2 V (c) 8 V (d) 0 V

(*v*) If the electric field is given by $(5\hat{\mathbf{i}} + 4\hat{\mathbf{j}} + 9\hat{\mathbf{k}})$, the electric flux through a surface area of 20 units lying in the YZ-plane will be • *Recall* [1]

(a) 100 units (b) 80 units
(c) 180 units (d) 20 unit

(*vi*) **Assertion** (A) The focal length of an equi-convex lens placed in air is equal to radius of curvature of either face. Lens is made up of material of refractive index 1.5.
Reason (R) For an equi-convex lens, radius of curvature of both face is same. • *Understanding* [1]

(a) Both Assertion and Reason are true and Reason is the correct explanation for Assertion.
(b) Both Assertion and Reason are true but Reason is not the correct explanation for Assertion.
(c) Assertion is false and Reason is true.
(d) Both Assertion and Reason are false.

(*vii*) The de-Broglie wavelength of a particle of kinetic energy K is λ. What will be the wavelength of the particle, if its kinetic energy is $\frac{K}{9}$? • *Recall* [1]

(a) λ (b) 2λ (c) 3λ (d) 4λ

B. Answer the following questions briefly.

(*i*) Why is it necessary to introduce a cylindrical soft iron core inside the coil of a galvanometer? • *Applicaiton* [1]

(*ii*) The ratio of intensities of two interfering waves is 25 : 9. Find the ratio of their amplitudes. • *Recall* [1]

(*iii*) Find the value of resistance X in the circuit shown below, so that the junctions M and N are at the same potential. • *Analysis* [1]

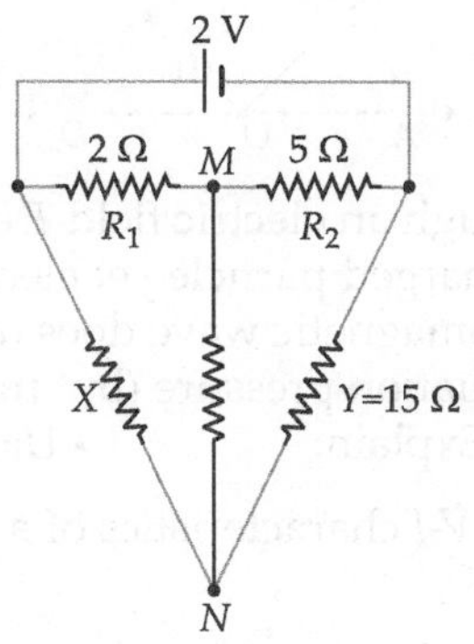

(*iv*) The magnifying powers of two telescopes are same but the aperture of their objectives are different. What will be the difference in the final image formed by them? • *Recall* [1]

(*v*) A wire of length L metre carrying a current of I ampere is bent in the form of a circle. Find its magnetic moment. • *Recall* [1]

(*vi*) Fraunhofer diffraction from single slit of width 1.24×10^{-6} m is observed with the light of wavelength 6200Å. Calculate the angular width of the central maximum. • *Recall* [1]

(*vii*) Is the ratio of number of holes and the number of conduction electrons in an n-type extrinsic semiconductor more than, less than or equal to 1? • *Understanding* [1]

Section B (14 Marks)

2. At room temperature (27°C), the resistance of a heating element is 100 Ω. What is the temperature of the element, if the resistance is found to be 117 Ω, given that the temperature coefficient of the material of the resistor is $1.70 \times 10^{-4}\,°C^{-1}$. • *Application* [2]

3. When an object is placed at a distance of 15 cm from a concave mirror, then its image is formed at 10 cm in front of the mirror. Find the focal length of the mirror. • *Application* [2]

Or

Name the principle on which the working of an optical fibre is based. What are the necessary conditions for this phenomenon to occur? What is the relation between critical angle and refractive index of a material? Does critical angle depends on the colour of light? • *Recall & Application* [2]

4. The wire loop $ABCD$ formed by joining two semicircular wires of radii, R_1 and R_2 carrying a current i as shown in figure. Find the magnitude of the magnetic field at the centre *O*. • *Analysis* [2]

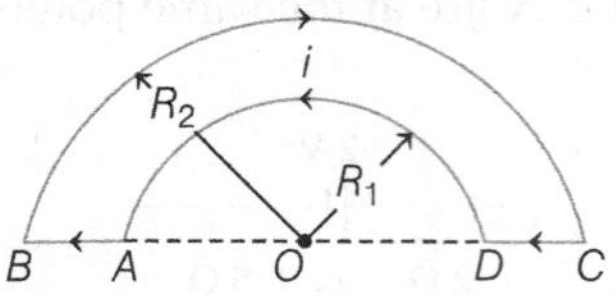

5. Even though an electric field *E* exerts a force *qE* on a charged particle yet electric field of an electromagnetic wave does not contribute to the radiation pressure (but transfers energy). Explain. • *Understanding* [2]

6. (i) Draw *V-I* characteristics of a *p-n* junction diode. • *Recall* [1]

   (ii) Why is the current under reverse bias almost independent of the applied potential upto a critical voltage? • *Application* [1]

Section C (27 Marks)

9. Given figure shows a charge array known as an electric quadrupole. For a point on the axis of the quadrupole, obtain the dependence of potential on *r* for $r/a >> 1$ and contrast your results with that due to an electric dipole and an electric monopole (i.e. a single charge).

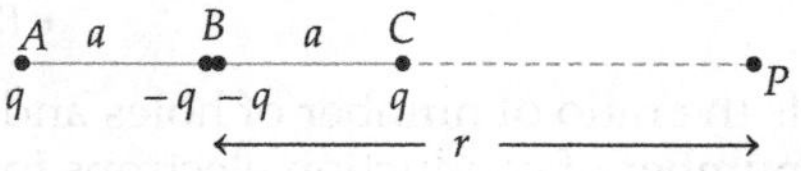

• *Application* [3]

SP-13

10. (i) A particle of mass 1 mg has the same wavelength as an electron moving with a velocity of $3 \times 10^6 \text{ms}^{-1}$. What is the velocity of the particle? • *Application* [1]

   (ii) What is the
   (a) momentum,
   (b) speed and
   (c) de-Broglie wavelength of an electron with kinetic energy of 120 eV? • *Recall* [2]

11. Find the magnitude of the resultant force on a charge of 1 μC held at *P* due to two charges of $+ 2 \times 10^{-8}$C and -10^{-8}C at *A* and *B*, respectively. Given, *AP* = 10 cm, *BP* = 5 cm and $\angle APB = 90°$,

7. A choke coil and a bulb are connected in series to a DC source. If an iron core is inserted in the choke coil, is there any change in the brightness of the bulb? • *Recall* [2]

Or

If the lamp is connected in series with a capacitor. Predict your observations for DC and AC connections. What happens in each case, if capacitance of capacitor is reduced? • *Recall* [2]

8. If an electron has total energy in first excited state of the H-atom of about −3.4 eV, then calculate the (*i*) kinetic energy and (*ii*) potential energy of the electron in this state. • *Analysis* [2]

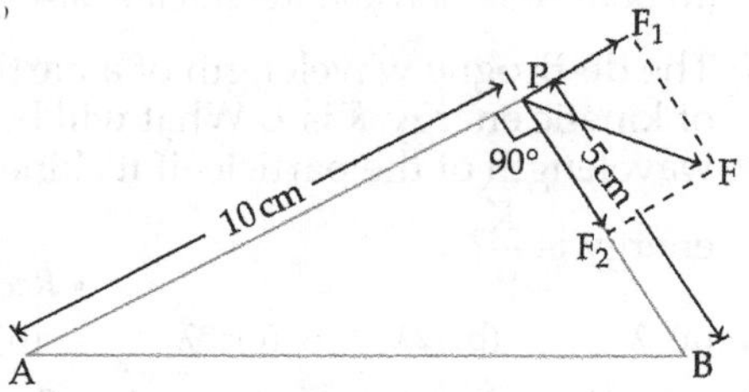

• *Application* [3]

Or

Two equal positive charges, each of 2 μC interact with a third positive charge of 3 μC situated as shown in figure.

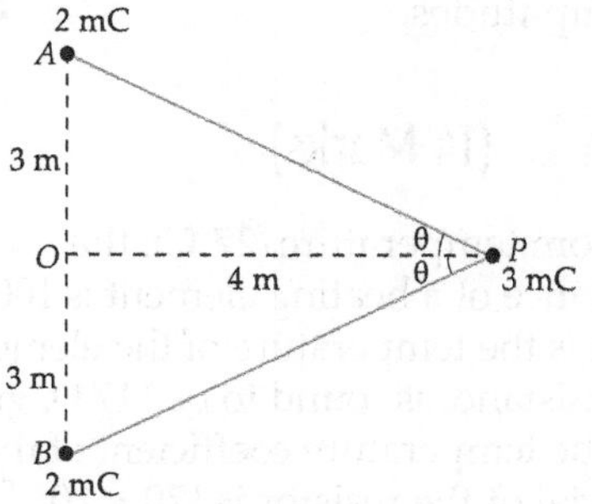

Calculate the magnitude and direction of the force on the 3 μC charge. • *Application* [3]

12. Show that spherical mirror formula is applicable to a plane mirror. • *Recall* [3]

13. A charged parallel plate capacitor having plate charge Q.

(*i*) If the separation between the plates of the capacitor is halved keeping the same area. What will be the effect on the capacitance of the capacitor? • *Application* [1]

(*ii*) If the separation between the plates remains unchanged and its area is halved. What will be the effect on the capacitance? • *Recall* [1]

(*iii*) If the separation between the plates of the capacitor is increased to doubled and area is reduced to half. What will the effect on the capacitance of the capacitor? • *Recall* [1]

14. (i) What is the critical angle for a material of refractive index $\sqrt{2}$? • *Recall*

(ii) Light of wavelength 5000 Å falls on a plane reflecting surface. What are the wavelength and frequency of reflected light? For what angle of incidence is the reflected ray normal to the incident ray? • *Application* [2]

Or

A student records the following data for the magnitudes of the image distance v for different object distance u the centre of a convex lens with focal length f. Verify (for any two) that these observations are in good agreement with expected theoretical value of B. • *Application* [3]

u	f	$2f$	$3f$	$4f$
v	$\frac{f}{2}$	$\frac{2f}{3}$	$\frac{3f}{4}$	$\frac{4f}{5}$

15. Answer the following.

(*i*) Why is the binding energy per nucleon found to be constant for nuclei in the range of mass number (A) lying between 30 and 170? • *Understanding* [1]

(*ii*) Explain in brief, why Rutherford's model cannot account for the stability of an atom? • *Understanding* [2]

16. Obtain the first Bohr's radius and the ground state energy of a muonic H-atom [i.e., an atom in which a negatively charged muon (μ) of mass about 207 m_e orbits around a proton]. • *Application* [3]

17. The image below shows a circuit with three diodes and three resistors connected to an AC source with an rms voltage V.

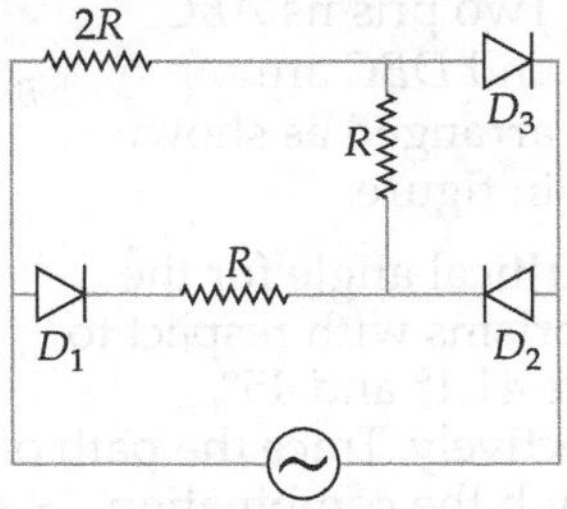

What is the average power delivered over one full cycle of AC in the above circuit? Show your calculations and arrive at the final answer in terms of V and R. (Assume the diode is ideal) • *Application* [3]

Section D (15 Marks)

18. A student is performing an experiment with a conducting loop of resistance 10 Ω and area 10 cm^2 the loop is removed from an external magnetic field acting normally and the variation of induced current in the loop with time is plotted as shown in the figure.

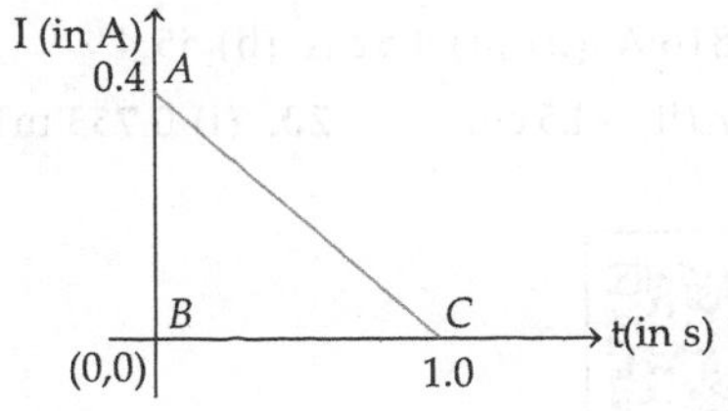

Find the

(*i*) total charge passed through the loop, • *Analysis* [2]

(*ii*) change in magnetic flux through the loop and • *Analysis* [1]

(*iii*) magnitude of the magnetic field applied. • *Application* [2]

Or (*i*) A capacitor of 100 μF and a coil of resistance 50 Ω and inductance 0.5H are connected in series with a 110V-50Hz source. Calculate the rms value of current in the circuit. • *Application* [2] (*ii*) A resistor of 12 Ω, a capacitor of reactance 14Ω and a pure inductor of inductance 0.1H are joined in series and placed across 200V-50Hz AC supply. Calculate (a) current in the circuit and (b) phase angle between current and voltage. • *Application* [3]

19. (*i*) A point object is placed at *O* in front of a glass sphere as shown in figure.

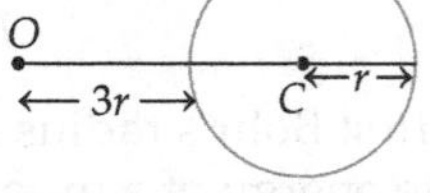

Show the formation of image by the sphere.
• *Application* [2]

(*ii*) (a) Write two necessary conditions for total internal reflection.

(b) Two prisms *ABC* and *DBC* are arranged as shown in figure.

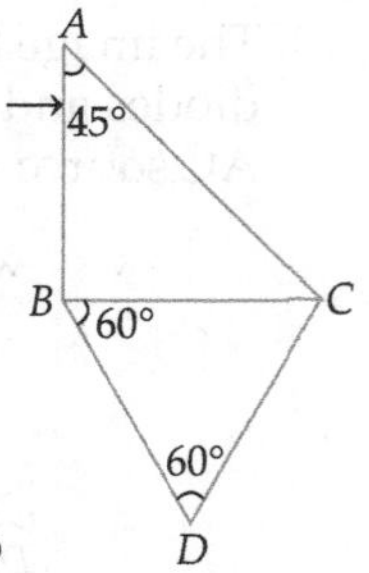

The critical angle for the two prisms with respect to air are 41.1° and 45°, respectively. Trace the path of the ray through the combination. • *Application* [2]

Or

(*i*) How is the working of a telescope different from that of a microscope? • *Recall* [3]

(*ii*) The focal lengths of the objective and eyepiece of a microscope are 1.25 cm and 5 cm, respectively. Find the position of the object relative to the objective in order to obtain an angular magnification of 30 in normal adjustment. • *Application* [3]

20. Mohan tightly wound a very long copper wire on a PVC pipe and carefully took the pipe out. The two ends of the copper wire then attached to a battery.

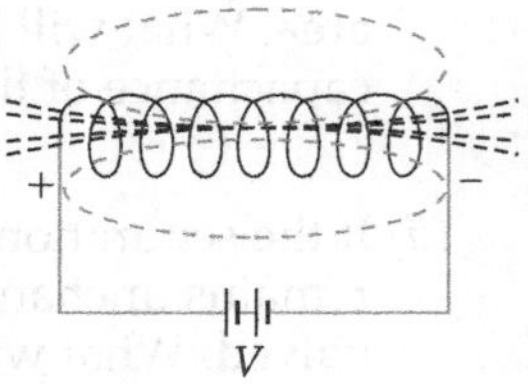

This cylindrical shape of copper wire showed few properties of a bar magnet. Later he found that it is called a solenoid and this solenoid is used in several devices such as door bell, relay switch, etc. The magnetic field of a solenoid is given below.

The magnetic field strength of a solenoid having *n* turns is $B = \mu_0 nI$, where *I* is the current flowing in the solenoid.

(*i*) A long solenoid having 400 turns is used as electromagnet. If 1.5 A current is flowing through the solenoid, then find the strength of solenoid. • *Application* [1]

(*ii*) State the four factors which increases the strength of magnetic field of solenoid. • *Recall* [2]

(*iii*) (a) At which position, magnetic field due to current carrying solenoid is zero? • *Recall* [1]

(b) State the nature of magnetic field lines inside the solenoid. • *Application* [1]

Answers

1. A. (i) (c), (ii) (d), (iii) (b), (iv) (c), (v) (a), (vi) (b), (vii) (c)

B. (ii) 5 : 3 (iii) $X = 6\Omega$ (vi) 60°

2. 1027°C **3.** 6 cm

8. (i) 3.4 eV (ii) − 6.8 eV

10. (i) 2.7×10^{-18} ms^{-1}

(ii) (a) 5.91×10^{-24} kg-ms^{-1} (b) 6.5×10^{6} ms^{-1}

(c) 1.12×10^{-10} m

11. 4.0×10^{-2} *Or* 3.5×10^{-3}

14. (i) 45° (ii) 45° **16.** − 2.8152 keV

18. (i) 0.2 C (ii) 2 Wb (iii) 0.2×10^{4} Wbm^{-2}

Or (i) 0.816 A (ii) (a) 9.52 A (b) 55.4°

19. *Or* (ii) −1.5 cm **20.** (i) 0.753 mT

For Detailed Solutions, scan the given QR code.

SQP Code : **PB-14/15**	Series **i-Succeed 14-25/15**	Roll No.

Sample Question Paper 14

Physics 12th (Code 861)

General Instructions

1. This paper is divided into four Sections- A, B, C and D. Answer all questions.
2. **Section A** consists of one question having sub-parts of one mark each.
3. **Section B** consists of seven questions of two marks each.
4. **Section C** consists of nine questions of three marks each.
5. **Section D** consists of three questions of five marks each.
6. Internal choices have been provided in two questions each in Section B, Section C and Section D.

Time : 3 Hrs.

Max. Marks : 70

Section A (14 Marks)

1. A. In questions (*i*) to (*vii*) below, choose the correct alternative (a), (b), (c) or (d) for each of the questions given below.

(*i*) A metal wire is subjected to a constant potential difference. When the temperature of the metal wire increases, then the drift velocity and thermal velocity of the electron in it, respectively • *Recall* [1]

(a) increases and decreases

(b) decreases and decreases

(c) increases and increases

(d) decreases and increases

(*ii*) A circular coil carrying a current *I* has radius *R* and the number of turns *N*, if all of three, (i.e. the current *I*, radius *R* and number of turns *N*) are doubled, then magnetic field at its centre becomes • *Analysis* [1]

(a) double (b) half

(c) four times (d) one-fourth

(*iii*) **Assertion** (A) Though light of a single frequency (monochromatic) is incident on a metal, the energies of emitted photoelectrons are different.

Reason (R) The energy of electron emitted from inside the metal surface, is lost in collision with the other atom in the metal. • *Understanding* [1]

(a) Both Assertion and Reason are true and Reason is the correct explanation for Assertion.

(b) Both Assertion and Reason are true and Reason is not the correct explanation for Assertion.

(c) Assertion is false and Reason is true.

(d) Both Assertion and Reason are false.

(*iv*) In Bohr's model of hydrogen atom, radius of the first orbit of an electron is r_0. Then, radius of the third orbit is • *Recall* [1]

(a) $\frac{r_0}{9}$ (b) r_0 (c) $3r_0$ (d) $9r_0$

(*v*) Einstein's photoelectric equation is • *Understanding* [1]

(a) $E_{max} = h\lambda - \phi_0$

(b) $E_{max} = \frac{hc}{\lambda} - \phi_0$

(c) $E_{max} = h\nu + \phi_0$

(d) $E_{max} = \frac{hc}{\lambda} + \phi_0$

(*vi*) **Assertion** (A) The permeability of a ferromagnetic material is independent of the magnetic field.
Reason (R) Permeability of a material is a constant quantity. • *Analysis* [1]

(a) Both Assertion and Reason are true and Reason is the correct explanation for Assertion.
(b) Both Assertion and Reason are true and Reason is not the correct explanation for Assertion.
(c) Assertion is false and Reason is true.
(d) Both Assertion and Reason are false.

(*vii*) The stopping potential needed to stop the most energetic electron depends on • *Analysis* [1]

(a) intensity of incident light
(b) photocurrent
(c) frequency of incident light
(d) plate potential

B. Answer the following questions briefly.

(*i*) What do you mean by controlled chain reaction? • *Recall* [1]

(*ii*) Complete the following reaction
$${}^{9}_{4}\text{Be} + {}^{4}_{2}\text{He} \rightarrow {}^{1}_{0}n + ...$$ • *Recall* [1]

(*iii*) Define knee voltage. • *Recall* [1]

(*iv*) Red light is incident on a converging lens of focal length f. State with reason, how f will change, if red light is replaced by blue light? • *Understanding* [1]

(*v*) When a wave undergoes reflection into a rarer medium from the surface of a denser medium, what will be the phase change? • *Recall* [1]

(*vi*) Explain, why the electric conductivity of pure semiconductor increases on heating? • *Recall* [1]

(*vii*) Imagine removing one electron from He^4 and He^3. Their energy levels, as worked out on the basis of Bohr's model will be very close. Explain, why? • *Application* [1]

Section B (14 Marks)

2. An electron is moving vertically upwards in the uniform magnetic field. The velocity of the electron is 2.0×10^6 m/s. Magnetic field of 0.32×10^{-4} T is directed horizontally. Obtain the magnitude and direction of the force on the electron. • *Application* [2]

3. The focal length of objective and eye lens of a microscope are 4 cm and 8 cm respectively. If the least distance of distinct vision is 24 cm and object distance is 4.5 cm from objective lens, then what is the magnifying power of the microscope? • *Application* [2]

Or

Write the two conditions of sustained interference. • *Recall* [2]

4. State Lenz's law. A metallic rod held horizontally along East-West direction, is allowed to fall under gravity. Will there be an emf induced at its ends? Justify your answer. • *Application* [2]

5. The given graph represents the variation of intensity of magnetisation (M) with magnetic field strength (H) for substances P and Q.

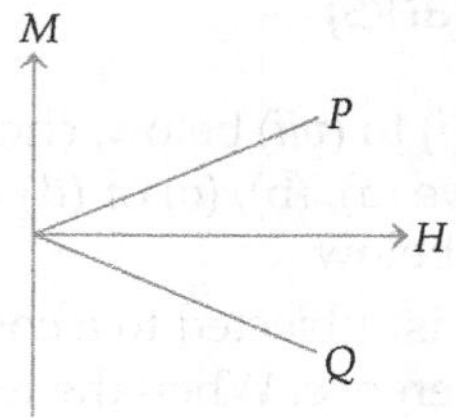

Which of the two substances is most likely to be attracted when taken near a magnet? • *Analysis* [2]

6. (*i*) In which direction do the electric and magnetic field vectors oscillate in an electromagnetic wave propagating along the X-axis? • *Recall* [1]

(*ii*) How is the speed of electromagnetic waves in vacuum determined by the electric and magnetic fields? • *Recall* [1]

Or

In which way, you can establish an instantaneous displacement current of 1.0 A in the space between the parallel plates of 1 μF capacitor ? • *Application* [2]

SP-14

7. What will be the effect on the width of the central bright fringe in the diffraction pattern of a single slit, if

(*i*) the monochromatic light of smaller wavelength is used. • *Recall* [1]

(*ii*) slit is made narrower. • *Recall* [1]

8. Two long and parallel straight wires A and B carrying currents of 8 A and 5 A respectively in the same direction, are separated by a distance of 4 cm. Estimate the force on a 10 cm section of wire A. • *Understanding* [2]

Section C (27 Marks)

9. An angular magnification (magnifying power) of 24 is desired using an objective of focal length 1.25 cm and an eyepiece of focal length 5 cm. How will you set up the compound microscope? • *Application* [3]

10. Two small identical dipoles AB and CD, each of dipole moment **p** are kept at an angle of 120° as shown in the figure. What is the resultant dipole moment of this combination?

If this system is subjected to electric field **E** directed along positive x-direction, what will be the magnitude and direction of the torque acting on this? • *Understanding* [3]

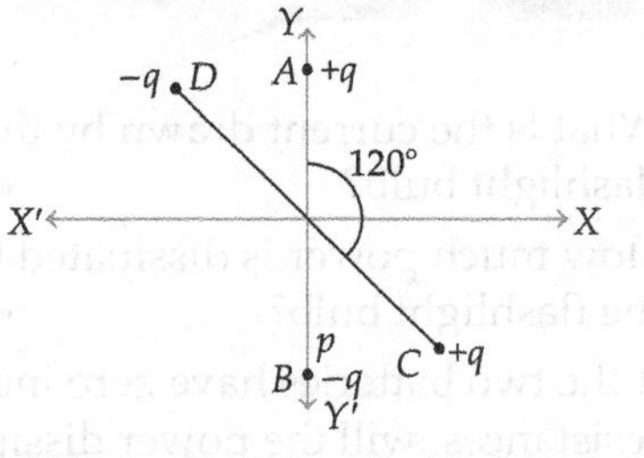

11. Obtain the binding energy per nucleon of the nuclei $^{56}_{26}Fe$ and $^{209}_{83}Bi$ in units of MeV from the following data • *Application* [3]

(*i*) $m\,(^{56}_{26}Fe) = 55.934939$ u

(*ii*) $m\,(^{209}_{83}Bi) = 208.980388$ u

(Take $m_p = 1.00783$ u, $m_n = 1.00867$u)

12. A network of four capacitors each of 12 μF capacitance is connected to a 500 V supply as shown in the figure. • *Analysis* [3]

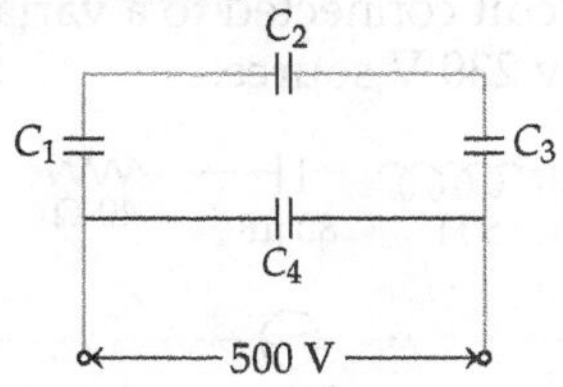

Determine,

(*i*) the equivalent capacitance of the network and

(*ii*) the charge on each capacitor.

Or An electric dipole of dipole moment **p** is parallel to a uniform electric field **E** as shown in figure.

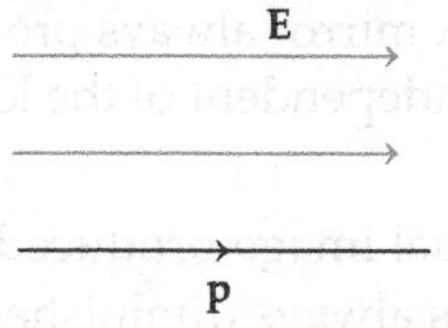

Derive an expression for work done on the dipole when it is rotated through 180°. • *Application* [3]

13. What is the de-Broglie wavelength of

(*i*) a bullet of mass 0.040 kg travelling at the speed of 1.0 km/s ? [1]

(*ii*) a ball of mass 0.060 kg moving at a speed of 1.0 m/s ? [1]

(*iii*) a dust particle of mass 1.0×10^{-9} kg drifting with a speed of 2.2 m/s ? [1]

14. Two identical parallel plate capacitors A and B are connected to a battery of V volts with the switch S is closed. The switch is now opened and the free space between the plates of the capacitors is filled with a dielectric of dielectric constant K. Find the ratio of the total electrostatic energy stored in both capacitors before and after the introduction of the dielectric. • *Analysis* [3]

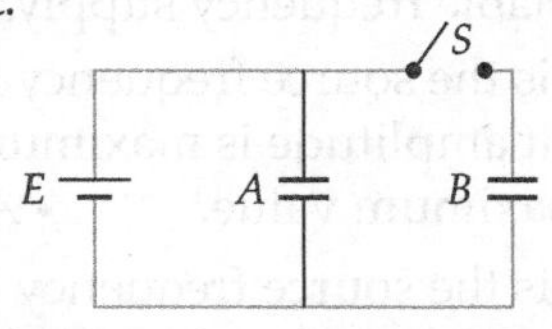

15. A student records the following data for the position y of the bright fringes in a Young's double slit experiment. The wavelength of light is λ, the slit separaton is d and the distance between the screen and the slits is D. Verify (for any two) that these

SP-14

observations are good agreement with the expected theoritical values for fringe positions y_n for different fringe orders n.

Fringe order (n)	Measured (y_n)
$n=0$ (Central)	0
$n=1$	$\lambda D/d$
$n=2$	$2\lambda D/d$
$n=3$	$3\lambda D/d$

• *Application* [3]

Or

Use the mirror equation to deduce that

(*i*) a convex mirror always produces a virtual image independent of the location of the object. • *Recall* [1]

(*ii*) the virtual image produced by a convex mirror is always diminished in size and is located between the focus and the pole. • *Recall* [1]

(*iii*) an object placed between the pole and focus of a concave mirror produces a virtual and enlarged image. • *Recall* [1]

16. (*i*) AB and CD are two parallel conductors kept 1 m apart and connected by a resistance R of 6 Ω, as shown in figure below. They are placed in a magnetic field $B = 3 \times 10^{-2}$ T which is perpendicular to the plane of the conductors and directed into the paper. A wire MN is placed over AB and CD and then made to slide with a velocity 2 ms^{-1}. (Neglect the resistance of AB, CD and MN.) • *Analysis* [2]

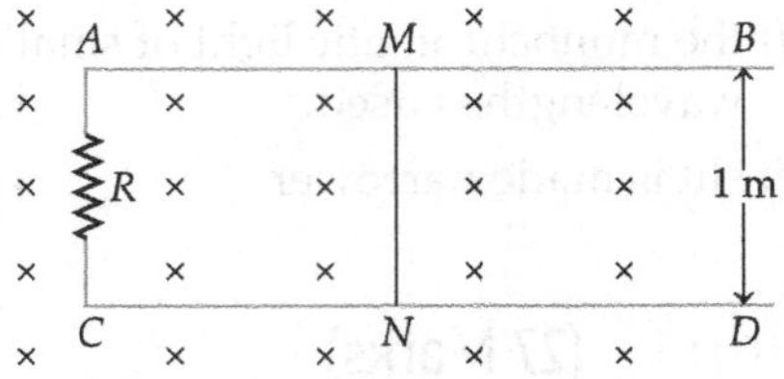

Calculate the induced current flowing through the resistor R.

(*ii*) In an ideal transformer, an output of 66 kV is required when an input voltage of 220 V is available. If the primary coil has 300 turns, how many turns should the secondary coil have? • *Recall* [1]

17. A flashlight uses two batteries, each of emf 2 V and internal resistance 0.1 Ω, in series. The flashlight bulb has a resistance of 10 Ω.

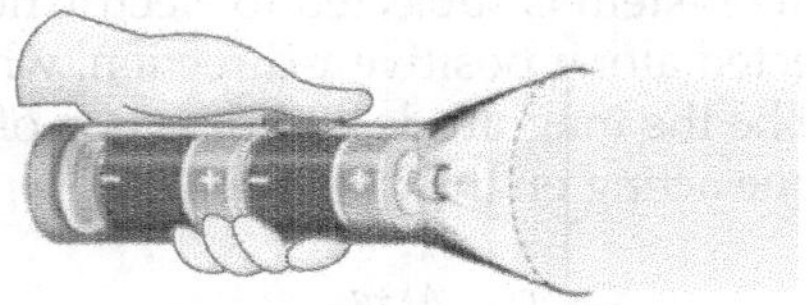

(*i*) What is the current drawn by the flashlight bulb? • *Recall* [1]

(*ii*) How much power is dissipated through the flashlight bulb? • *Recall* [1]

(*iii*) If the two batteries have zero internal resistances, will the power dissipated through the flashlight bulb be more or less? Calculate the difference. • *Application* [1]

Section D (15 Marks)

18. A series L-C-R circuit with $L = 0.12$ H, $C = 480$ nF, $R = 23\,\Omega$ is connected to a 230 V variable frequency supply.

(*i*) What is the source frequency for which current amplitude is maximum? Obtain this maximum value. • *Application* [2]

(*ii*) What is the source frequency for which average power absorbed by the circuit is maximum? Obtain the value of maximum power. • *Application* [1]

(*iii*) For which frequency of the source is the power transferred to the circuit half the power at resonant? What is the current amplitude at these frequencies? • *Application* [2]

Or The given circuit diagram shows a series L-C-R circuit connected to a variable frequency 230 V source.

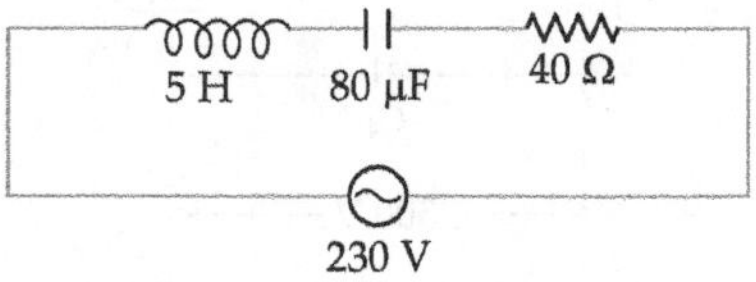

(*i*) Determine the source frequency which derives the circuit in resonance. • *Analysis* (*ii*) Obtain the impedance of the circuit and the amplitude of current at the resonating frequency. • *Analysis*

(*iii*) Determine the rms potential drop across the three elements of the circuit. • *Analysis*

(*iv*) How do you explain the observation that the algebraic sum of the voltage across the three elements in circuit is greater than the supplied voltage? • *Application* [5]

19. (*i*) Draw a labelled diagram of half-wave rectifier circuit. Describe its working in short. • *Application* [2]

(*ii*) Sketch its input and output waveforms. [2]

(*iii*) A 5 V battery is connected across the points *X* and *Y*. Assume D_1 and D_2 to be normal silicon diodes. Find the current supplied by the battery, if the +ve terminal of the battery is connected to point X.

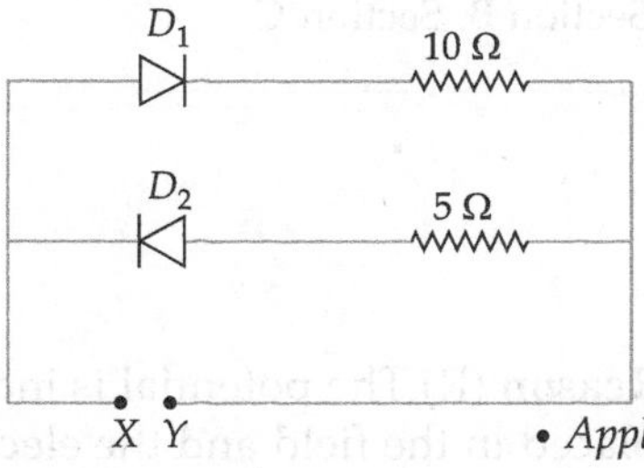

• *Application* [1]

Or

(*i*) The number of silicon atoms per m^3 is 5×10^{28}. This is doped simultaneously with 5×10^{22} atoms per m^3 of arsenic and 5×10^{20} atoms per m^3 of indium. Calculate the number of electrons and holes. Given that, $n_i = 1.5\times10^{16}\ m^{-3}$.

Is the material *n*-type or *p*-type? • *Application* [2]

(*ii*) A *p-n* junction photodiode is fabricated from a semiconductor with a band gap of 2.8 eV. How much wavelength can it detect? • *Application* [1]

(*iii*) Draw the symbol, *I-V* characteristics of a solar cell and explain its construction and *I-V* characteristics in short. • *Application* [2]

20. An optical fibre is a thin tube of transparent material that allows light to pass through, without being refracted into the air or another external medium. It makes use of total internal reflection.

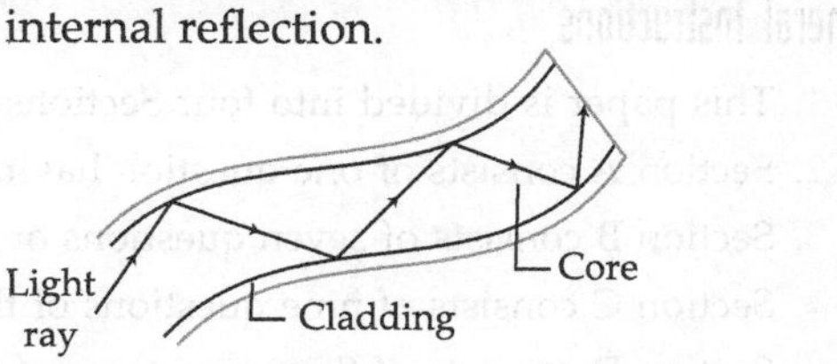

These fibres are fabricated in such a way that, light reflected at one side of the inner surface strikes the other at an angle larger than critical angle. Even, if fibre is bent, light can easily travel along the length.

(*i*) State the conditions for total internal reflection. • *Application* [2]

(*ii*) (a) If angle of incidence is equal to critical angle in core, then find the angle of refraction. • *Recall* [1]

(b) Give two examples based on the phenomenon of total internal reflection. • *Recall* [1]

(*iii*) Find the speed of light in medium for which critical angle is 30°. • *Application* [1]

SP-14

Answers

1. A. (i) (d), (ii) (a), (iii) (a), (iv) (d), (v) (b), (vi) (d), (vii) (c)

6. *Or* $10^6\ Vs^{-1}$ **8.** 2×10^{-5} N

11. (i) 8.790 MeV (ii) 7.848 MeV

12. (i) 16 μF

16. (i) 0.01 A (ii) 90000 turns

18. *Or* (i) 7.96 Hz (ii) 8.13 A (iii) 1437.2 V

19. (iii) 0.43A *Or* (ii) 440 nm

20. (ii) (a) 90° (iii) 1.5×10^8 m/s

For Detailed Solutions, scan the given QR code.

SQP Code : **PB-15/15** Series **i-Succeed 15-25/15** Roll No.

Sample Question Paper 15

Physics 12th (Code 861)

General Instructions

1. This paper is divided into four Sections- A, B, C and D. Answer all questions.
2. Section A consists of one question having sub-parts of one mark each.
3. Section B consists of seven questions of two marks each.
4. Section C consists of nine questions of three marks each.
5. Section D consists of three questions of five marks each.
6. Internal choices have been provided in two questions each in Section B, Section C and Section D.

Time : 3 Hrs.

Max. Marks : 70

Section A (14 Marks)

1. A. In questions (*i*) to (*vii*) below, choose the correct alternative (a), (b), (c) or (d) for each of the questions given below.

(*i*) According to Huygens' principle, light is a form of • *Recall* [1]

(a) rays (b) waves

(c) particles (d) None of these

(*ii*) Which of the following statements about nuclear forces is not true? • *Recall* [1]

(a) The nuclear force between two nucleons falls rapidly to zero as their distance is more than a few femtometres.

(b) The nuclear force is much weaker than the coulomb force.

(c) The force is attractive for distances larger than 0.8 fm and repulsive, if they are separated by distances less than 0.8 fm.

(d) The nuclear force between neutron-neutron, proton-neutron and proton-proton is approximately the same.

(*iii*) **Assertion** (A) The potential at a point is characteristic of the electric field at a point only, whereas electric potential energy at a point is characteristic of the charge-field system.

Reason (R) The potential is independent of a placed in the field and the electric potential energy is due to an interaction between the electric field at the point and the charged particle placed in the field at that point. • *Understanding* [1]

(a) Both Assertion and Reason are true and Reason is the correct explanation for Assertion.

(b) Both Assertion and Reason are true but Reason is not the correct explanation for Assertion.

(c) Assertion is false and Reason is true.

(d) Both Assertion and Reason are false.

(*iv*) A short linear object of length b lies along the axis of a concave mirror of focal length f at a distance u from the pole of the mirror. The size of the image is approximately equal to • *Understanding* [1]

(a) $b\left(\frac{u-f}{f}\right)^{1/2}$ (b) $b\left(\frac{f}{u-f}\right)^{1/2}$

(c) $b\left(\frac{u-f}{f}\right)$ (d) $b\left(\frac{f}{u-f}\right)^{2}$

(*v*) A sinusoidal voltage of peak value 283 V and frequency 50 Hz is applied to a series L- C- R circuit in which $R = 3\,\Omega$,

$L = 25.48$ mH and $C = 796$ μF, then the power dissipated at the resonant condition will be • *Analysis* [1]

(a) 39.70 kW (b) 26.70 kW
(c) 13.35 kW (d) zero

(*vi*) **Assertion** (A) A proton and an electron with same momentum, enter in a magnetic field in a direction at right angles to the lines of the force. The radius of the paths followed by them will be same.

Reason (R) Electron has less mass than the proton. • *Analysis* [1]

(a) Both Assertion and Reason are true and Reason is the correct explanation for Assertion.
(b) Both Assertion and Reason are true but Reason is not the correct explanation for Assertion.
(c) Assertion is false and Reason is true.
(d) Both Assertion and Reason are false.

(*vii*) An observer looks a distant tree 15 m high through a telescope of magnifying power of 12, the tree appears to him • *Analysis* [1]

(a) 12 times taller (b) 15 times taller
(c) 12 times nearer (d) 15 times shorter

B. Answer the following questions briefly.

(*i*) In a single diffraction pattern observed on a screen placed at D m distance from the slit of width d m, then what is the ratio of the width of the central maxima to the width of other secondary maxima? • *Recall* [1]

(*ii*) Why are the field lines repelled (expelled) when a diamagnetic material is placed in an external uniform magnetic field? • *Recall* [1]

(*iii*) If the number of turns in coil increases to double, then what changes occur in its self-inductance? • *Recall* [1]

(*iv*) A ray of light strikes on air-glass interface at an angle of incidence ($i < 60°$) and gets refracted at an angle of refraction ($r < 30°$). What will happen to the angle of refraction on increasing the angle of incidence? • *Recall* [1]

(*v*) What is meant by doping of an intrinsic semiconductor ? Name the two types of atoms used for doping of Ge/Si. • *Application* [1]

(*vi*) Energy of electron in first excited state in hydrogen atom is –3.4 eV. Find KE and PE of electron in the ground state. • *Recall* [1]

(*vii*) Threshold frequency of a certain metal for photoelectric emission is 5×10^{14} Hz. Calculate its work function. • *Understanding* [1]

Section B (14 Marks)

2. A rectangular loop of area $5\,m^2$, has 50 turns and carries a current of 1 A. It is held in a uniform magnetic field of 0.1T, at an angle of 30°. Calculate the torque experienced by the coil. • *Recall* [2]

3. The impurity levels of dopped semiconductor are 30 eV below the conduction band. Determine whether the semiconductor is n-type or p-type. At the room temperature, thermal collisions occur as a result of which, the extra electron loosely bound to the impurity ion gets an amount of energy kT and hence this electron can jump into conduction band. What is the value of T ? Take, k is Boltzmann constant $= 8.62 \times 10^{-5}$ eV/K. • *Application* [2]

4. Lyman series of hydrogen is available both in emission and absorption, but Balmer series is available only in emission, not in absorption. Give reason. • *Application* [2]

Or

Mention the conclusion of Rutherford's α-scattering experiment. • *Application* [2]

5. The sun is believed to be getting its energy from the fusion of four protons to form a helium nucleus and a pair of positrons. Calculate the release of energy per fusion in MeV.

Mass of proton = 1.007825 amu, mass of positron = 0.000549 amu, mass of helium nucleus = 4.002604 amu. (Take, 1 amu = 931.5 MeV) • *Analysis* [2]

6. Write any one use for each of the following mirrors. • *Recall* [2]

(*i*) Convex (*ii*) Concave

Or The deviation produced for violet, yellow and red lights for crown glass are 3.75°, 3.25° and 2.86°, respectively. Calculate the dispersive power of the crown glass. • *Application* [2]

7. In accordance with the Bohr's model, find the quantum number that characterises in the earth's revolution around the sun in an orbit of radius 1.5×10^{11} m with orbital speed 3×10^4 m/s. (Mass of the earth = 6×10^{24} kg) • *Understanding* [2]

8. (*i*) What is the ratio of the speed of gamma rays to that of radio waves in vacuum? • *Recall* [1]

(*ii*) Name an electromagnetic wave which is used in the radar system for aircraft navigation. • *Recall* [1]

Section C (27 Marks)

9. For a glass prism ($\mu = \sqrt{3}$), the angle of minimum deviation is equal to the angle of the prism. Find the angle of the prism. • *Recall* [3]

Or

A student records the following data for the length of an astronomical telescope *L* (which is the distance between the objective and eyepiece) for different focal lengths of the objective lens f_0, while keeping the focal length of the eyepiece f_e = 20 cm constant. Verify (for any two) that these observations are in good agreement with the expected theoretical values of *L*. • *Application* [3]

f_0 (cm)	50	100	150	200
L (cm)	70	120	170	220

10. A battery of emf 10 V and internal resistance 3Ω is connected to a resistor. If the current in the circuit is 0.5 A, what is the resistance of resistor? What is the terminal voltage and power of the battery when the circuit is closed? • *Application* [3]

Or

In the figure shown, an ammeter *A* and a resistor of 4 Ω are connected to the terminals of the source. The emf of the source is 12 V having an internal resistance of 2 Ω. Calculate the voltmeter and ammeter readings. • *Analysis* [3]

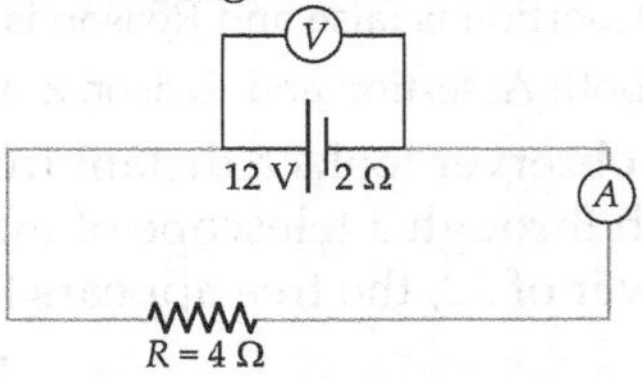

11. Photoelectrons are emitted from a metal surface when UV-light of wavelength λ = 300 nm is incident on it. The minimum negative potential required to stop the emission of electrons is 0.54 V. Calculate • *Application*

(*i*) the energy of the incident photons. [1]

(*ii*) the maximum kinetic energy of the photoelectrons emitted. [1]

(*iii*) the work function of the metal. [1]

12. (*i*) From molecular view point, discuss the temperature dependence of susceptibility for diamagnetism, paramagnetism and ferromagnetism. • *Application*

(*ii*) The magnetic field *B* due to a current carrying circular loop of radius 12 cm at its centre is 0.5×10^{-4} T. Find the magnetic field due to this loop at a point on the axis at a distance of 5.0 cm from the centre. • *Understanding* [3]

13. A potential barrier of 0.4 V exists across *p-n* junction.

(*i*) If the depletion region is 4.0×10^{-7} m wide, what is the intensity of the electric field in this region? • *Recall* [1]

(*ii*) In half-wave rectification, what is the output frequency, if the input frequency is 50 Hz? What is the output frequency of a full wave rectifier for the same input frequency? [1]

(*iii*) Why are Si and GaAs preferred materials for solar cells? • *Recall* [1]

14. An infinitely long rod lies along the axis of a concave mirror of focal length *f*. The near end of the rod is at a distance $u > f$ from the mirror, then what will be the length of the image of the rod? • *Application* [3]

15. Figure shows two identical capacitors C_1 and C_2, each of 2 μF capacitance, connected to a battery of 5 V. Initially switch *S* is closed. After sometime, *S* is left open and dielectric slabs of dielectric constant $K = 5$ are inserted to fill completely the space between the plates of the two capacitors. How will the charge and potential difference between the plates of the capacitors be affected after the slabs are inserted? • *Analysis* [3]

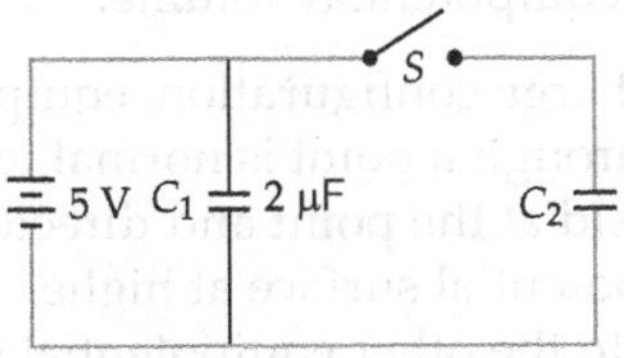

16. (*i*) A long straight wire is bent as shown in the given figure. Find the resultant magnetic field *B* at the centre C of the circular path of radius 2 cm, if a current *I* of 5 A is passed through the wire as shown. • *Application* [2]

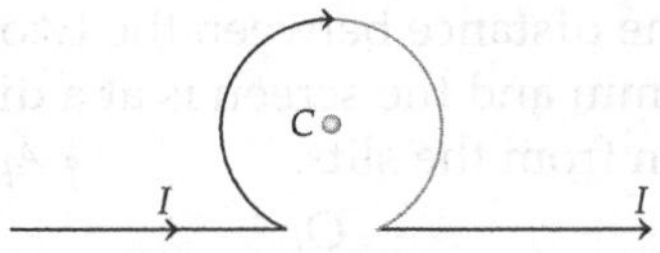

(*ii*) When would a moving charged particle travel undeviated in a uniform magnetic field? • *Recall* [1]

17. Given two resistors R_1 and R_2 connected in series in circuit 1 and in parallel in circuit 2 across identical batteries of terminal voltage *V* with some internal resistance.

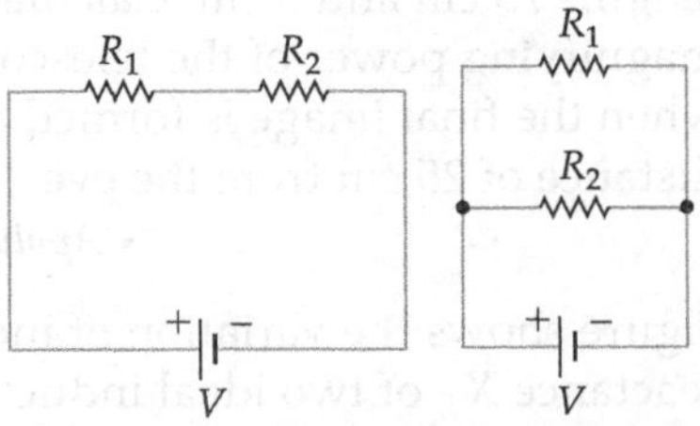

Circuit 1 Circuit 2

A third unknown resistor R_3 is added in series in circuit 1 and in parallel in circuit 2. [3]

(i) Does the current in the battery increase, decrease or remain the same in each of the two circuits? Give a reason for your answer. • *Application*

(ii) Does the terminal voltage of the battery increase, decrease or remain the same in each of the two circuits? Give a reason for your answer. • *Application*

SP-15

Section D (15 Marks)

18. An experimental set up is arranged according to the following diagram.

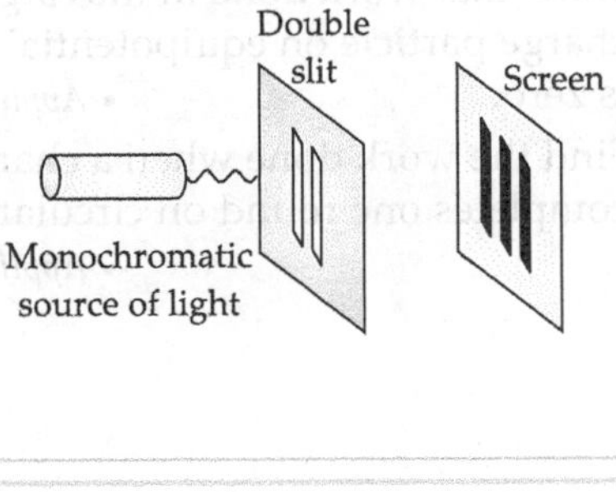

(*i*) How will the fringe pattern change, if the screen is moved away from the slits? • *Analysis* [1]

(*ii*) How does the fringe width will change when the distance of separation between the slits and screen is doubled? • *Analysis* [1]

(*iii*) A beam of light consisting of two wavelengths 560 nm and 420 nm, is used to obtain interference fringes in a Young's double slit experiment. Find the least distance from the central maxima, where the bright fringes due to both the wavelengths coincide. The distance between the two slits is 4 mm and the screen is at a distance of 1m from the slits. • *Application* [3]

Or

(*i*) Mention two differences between telescope and microscope. • *Recall*

(*ii*) Is it possible to increase the range of a telescope by increasing the diameter of the objective lens? • *Recall* [2]

(*iii*) Define magnifying power of an optical instrument. An astronomical refracting telescope consists of two lenses of focal lengths 75 cm and 5 cm. Calculate the magnifying power of the telescope when the final image is formed at a distance of 25 cm from the eye.

• *Application* [3]

19. (*i*) Figure shows the variation of inductive reactance X_L of two ideal inductors of inductances L_1 and L_2, with angular frequency ω. Calculate the value of $\frac{L_1}{L_2}$.

• *Application* [1]

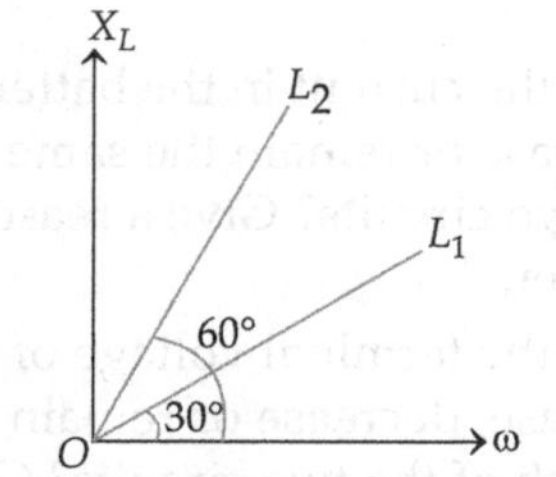

SP-15

(*ii*) The figure shows variation of R, X_L and X_C with frequency f in a series L-C-R circuit, then for what frequency point, the circuit is inductive? • *Analysis* [2]

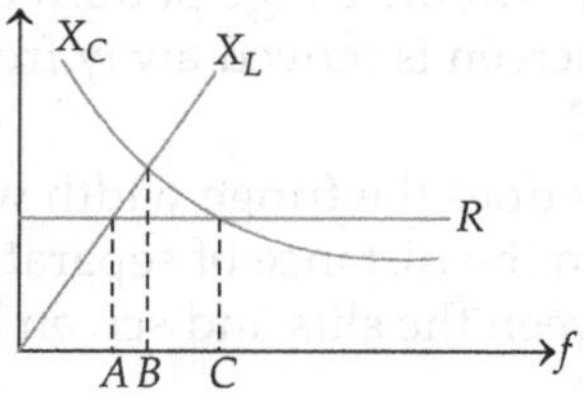

(*iii*) What are the different types of energy losses in a transformer? State how to minimise any one of them?

• *Application* [2]

Or

(*i*) In the given figure, a bar magnet is quickly moved towards a conducting loop having a capacitor. Predict the polarity of the plates *A* and *B* of the capacitor. • *Application* [2]

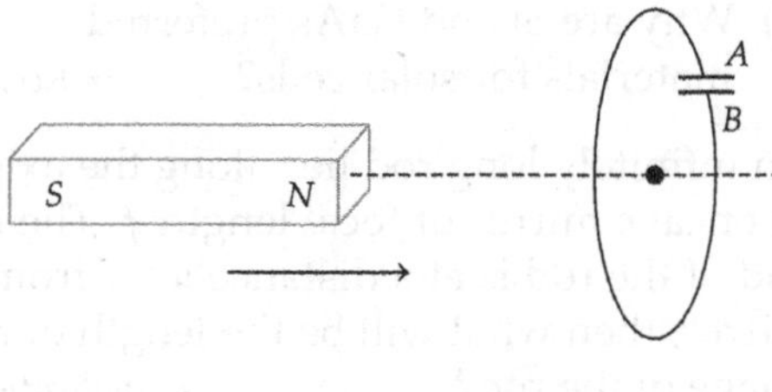

(*ii*) Derive the formula for motional emf using Faraday's law of electromagnetic induction. • *Application* [3]

20. Equipotential in terms of Physics is defined as a region in space in which every specified point has same potential. If these points are connected by a line or curve, it is known as an equipotential line. When such points lie on a surface,then it is called an equipotential surface and when they lie in space or a volume, then it is called an equipotential volume.

For any charge configuration, equipotential surface through a point is normal to the electric field at the point and directed from one equipotential surface at higher potential to the other equipotential surface at lower potential.

(*i*) (a) Find the shape of equipotential surface for a point charge. • *Recall*

(b) What is the angle between electric field and plane of equipotential surface? • *Recall* [2]

(*ii*) Show that work done in moving a charge particle on equipotential surface is zero. • *Application* [2]

(*iii*) Find the work done when a charge completes one round on circular path.

• *Application* [1]

Answers

1. **A.** (i) (b) (ii) (b) (iii) (a) (iv) (d) (v) (c) (vi) (b) (vii) (c)

   B. (i) 2:1 (vi) KE = 13.6 eV, PE = 27.2 eV

   (vii) 2.07 eV

2. $12.5\sqrt{3}$ N-m

3. 348.02 K

5. 25.7 MeV

6. *Or* 0.274°

7. 2.6×10^{74}

9. 60°

10. 17 Ω, 8.5 V, 4.25 W *Or* 2 A, 8 V

11. (i) 4.12 eV (ii) 0.54 eV (iii) 3.58 eV

12. (ii) 3.9×10^{-5} T

13. (i) 1×10^6 V/m (ii) 50 Hz, 100 Hz

16. (i) 10.7×10^{-5} T, inward direction

18. (iii) 0.42 mm *Or* (iii) 18

19. (i) $\frac{1}{3}$

20. (i) (b) 90° (iii) zero

For Detailed Solutions, scan the given QR code.

Knowledge Booster Zone

Welcome to the Knowledge Booster Zone !

This section is dedicated to enhancing your understanding of key concepts. Here, you will find chapter-wise revision notes designed to solidify your **foundational knowledge**. Use these notes to review and reinforce what you've learned, ensuring you're well-prepared for each topic.

Progress Tracker Tick the papers as you complete them.

- ☐ Electric Charges and Fields
- ☐ Electrostatic Potential and Capacitance
- ☐ Current Electricity
- ☐ Moving Charges and Magnetism
- ☐ Magnetism and Matter
- ☐ Electromagnetic Induction
- ☐ Alternating Current
- ☐ Electromagnetic Waves
- ☐ Ray optics and Optical Instrument
- ☐ Wave Optics
- ☐ Dual Nature of Radiation and matter
- ☐ Atoms
- ☐ Nuclei
- ☐ Semiconductor and Electronic Devices

Chapter 1 Electric Charges and Fields

1. Electric Charge

The property of electrons and protons which gives rise to electric force between them is called **electric charge**.

Charge is a scalar quantity and its dimensional formula is $[M^0L^0TA]$.

When two unlike objects like amber and wool are rubbed against each other, two types of charges namely, positive charge and negative charge are produced. This is called **frictional electricity**. These names were given by Benjamin Franklin.

Transfer of electrons is the cause of frictional electricity. It is also known as **electron theory of electrification.**

2. Units of Electric Charge

(i) SI unit is coulomb (C)

(ii) In CGS system

(a) Electrostatic unit, i.e., esu of charge or stat-coulomb (stat-C)

$1\ C = 3 \times 10^9$ stat-C

(b) Electromagnetic unit, i.e., emu of charge or ab-coulomb (ab-C)

1 ab-C $= 10\ C$

3. Quantisation of Electric Charge

Charge exists in discrete amount rather than continuous value and hence it is quantised. Mathematically, charge on an object is given by, $q = \pm ne$ where, n is the number of electrons and e is the electronic charge $(1.6 \times 10^{-19}\ C)$.

4. Additivity of Charges

Charges are scalar quantities and they add up like real numbers. It means, if a system consists of n charges $q_1, q_2, q_3, \ldots, q_n$, then total charge on the system will be

$$Q = q_1 + q_2 + q_3 + \ldots + q_n.$$

5. Conservation of Charge

The total charge of an isolated system always remains conserved, i.e., initial and final charges of the system will be same.

6. Conductor and Insulator

Conductors are those substances which can be used to carry or conduct electric charges from one point to other inside it. e.g. silver, copper, iron, etc.

Insulators are those substances which cannot conduct electricity. They are also called as **dielectrics**. e.g. glass, rubber, plastic, mica, etc.

7. Electrostatic Induction

It is the process of redistribution of electric charges on an object caused by the influence of nearby charged object.

8. Coulomb's Law

It states that the electrostatic force of attraction or repulsion acting between two stationary point charges is directly proportional to the product of their magnitudes and inversely proportional to the square of the distance between them. It is given by

$$F_{vacuum} = \frac{1}{4\pi\varepsilon_0} \cdot \frac{|q_1||q_2|}{r^2}$$

where, $|q_1|$ and $|q_2|$ are the magnitudes of charge on stationary point charges and r is the distance of separation between them in air or vacuum and F is the magnitude of force of attraction (when $q_1q_2 < 0$) or repulsion (when $q_1q_2 > 0$).

Also, ε_0 = permittivity of free space

$= 8.85419 \times 10^{-12}\ C^2 / N\text{-}m^2$

and $K = \frac{1}{4\pi\varepsilon_0} = 9 \times 10^9\ N\text{-}m^2/C^2$

In a medium of permittivity (ε) and relative permittivity (ε_r)

$$F_{medium} = \frac{1}{4\pi\varepsilon} \frac{|q_1||q_2|}{r^2} = \frac{|q_1||q_2|}{4\pi\varepsilon_0\varepsilon_r r^2}$$

$$\left[\because \frac{\varepsilon}{\varepsilon_0} = \varepsilon_r\right]$$

9. Comparison of Coulomb's Law with Newton's Law of Gravitation

- *Both the laws are inverse square law.*

The equations of these laws are as below.

Newton's law of gravitation	Coulomb's law
$F_G = \frac{Gm_1m_2}{r^2}$	$F_E = \frac{kq_1q_2}{r^2}$

- *The coulombic force is much stronger than the gravitational force between two electrons, i.e.,*

$$F_E = 10^{39} F_G$$

- *The coulombic force can be attractive or repulsive, while gravitational force is only attractive.*

10. Direction of Electrostatic Force or Coulombic Force

The direction of electrostatic force between the two point charges is along the line joining them. It may be either attractive (for unlike charges) or repulsive (for like charges).

11. Electrostatic Forces are Conservative (Non-Dissipative Forces)

The work done during a round trip by an electrostatic force is always zero. The workdone does not depend on the path followed by the charge, however it depends on the initial and final positions of the charge. So, electrostatic force is called as a conservative force.

12. Principle of Superposition of Electrostatic Forces

This principle states that the net electric force experienced by a given charge particle q_0 due to a system of n charged particles is equal to the vector sum of all the forces exerted on it individually due to all the other charged particles of the system.

i.e., $$\mathbf{F}_{net} = \mathbf{F}_{01} + \mathbf{F}_{02} + \cdots + \mathbf{F}_{0n}$$

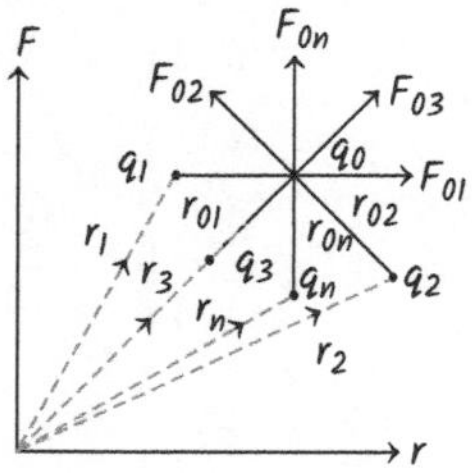

where, $\mathbf{F}_{net}$ is the net force on charge q_0 and $\mathbf{F}_{01}, \mathbf{F}_{02}, \mathbf{F}_{03}, \ldots, \mathbf{F}_n$ are individual forces on charge q_0 due to charges $q_1, q_2, q_3, \ldots, q_n$, respectively.

Now, we can write net force,

$$\mathbf{F}_{net} = \frac{1}{4\pi\varepsilon_0}\left[\frac{q_1q_0}{|\mathbf{r}_{01}|^3}\mathbf{r}_{01} + \frac{q_2q_0}{|\mathbf{r}_{02}|^3}\mathbf{r}_{02} + \ldots + \frac{q_nq_0}{|\mathbf{r}_{0n}|^3}\mathbf{r}_{0n}\right]$$

where, $\mathbf{F}_{01}$ = force on q_0 due to q_1 and $\mathbf{r}_{01} = \mathbf{r}_0 - \mathbf{r}_1$

Similarly, $\mathbf{r}_{0n} = \mathbf{r}_0 - \mathbf{r}_n$ and $\mathbf{F}_{0n}$ = force on q_0 due to q_n.

Hence, net force ($\mathbf{F}_{net}$) in terms of position vectors can be written as

$$\mathbf{F}_{net} = \frac{q_0}{4\pi\varepsilon_0}\left[\sum_{i=1}^{n}\frac{q_i}{|\mathbf{r}_0 - \mathbf{r}_i|^3}(\mathbf{r}_0 - \mathbf{r}_i)\right]$$

where, q_i and $\mathbf{r}_i$ are the magnitude and position vector, respectively of the ith charge and also $(\mathbf{r}_0 - \mathbf{r}_i)$ is a vector pointing in the direction from q_i to q_0.

13. Electrostatic Force due to Continuous Charge Distribution

Charge Distribution	Formula
Linear charge distribution (λ)	$dq = \lambda dl$ $\Rightarrow \mathbf{F} = \frac{q_0}{4\pi\varepsilon_0}\int_l \frac{\lambda dl}{\lvert \mathbf{r}\rvert^2}\hat{\mathbf{r}}$ 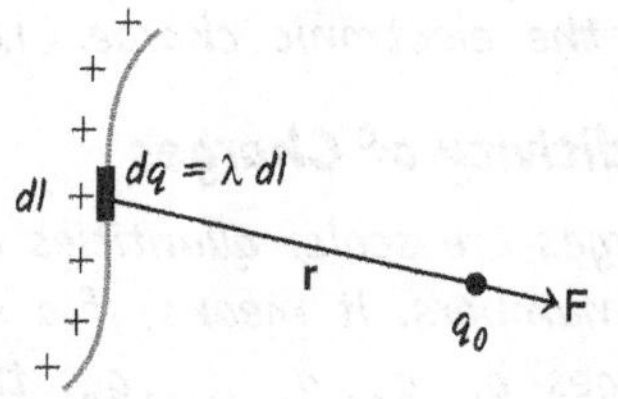
Surface charge distribution (σ)	$dq = \sigma dS$ $\Rightarrow \mathbf{F} = \frac{q_0}{4\pi\varepsilon_0}\int_S \frac{\sigma dS}{\lvert \mathbf{r}\rvert^2}\hat{\mathbf{r}}$ 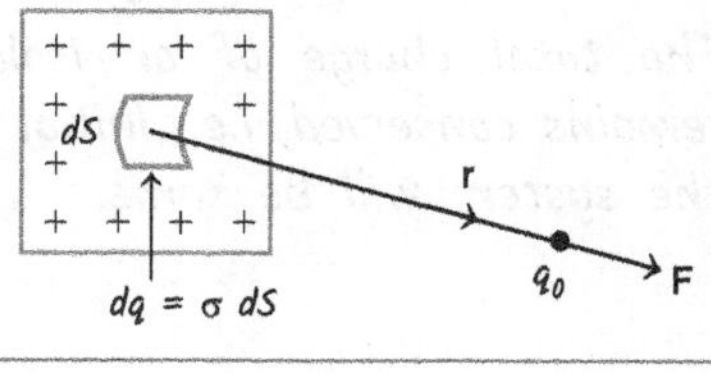

Charge Distribution	Formula
Volume charge distribution (ρ)	$dq = \rho\, dV$ $\Rightarrow \mathbf{F} = \dfrac{q_0}{4\pi\varepsilon_0} \displaystyle\int_V \dfrac{\rho\, dV}{\lvert \mathbf{r} \rvert^2}\, \hat{\mathbf{r}}$

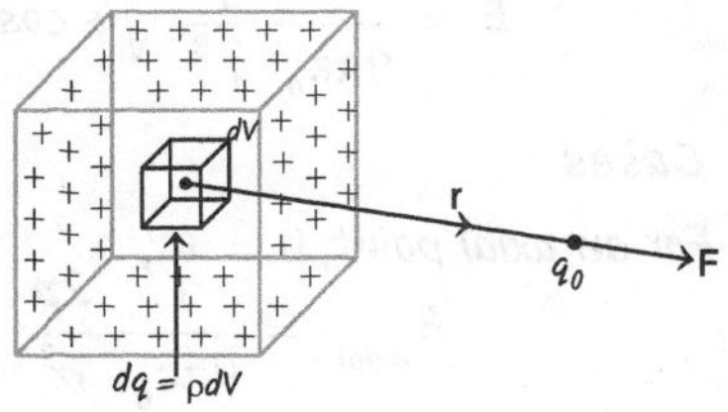

14. Electric Field

The space around a charge in which its effect can be felt significantly, i.e., the area which produces attractive or repulsive force on another charge placed in that area is called electric field.

15. Electric Field Intensity

The electric field intensity at any point due to a source charge is defined as the force experienced per unit positive test charge placed at that point without disturbing the source charge. It is expressed as

$$E = \lim_{q_0 \to 0} \frac{F}{q_0}$$

Here, $q_0 \to 0$, i.e., the test charge q_0 must be small, so that it does not produce its own electric field.

SI unit of electric field intensity $\mathbf{E}$ is N/C and it is a vector quantity having dimensions $[MLA^{-1}T^{-3}]$.

16. Electric Field Intensity due to a Point Charge

Electric field intensity at point P due to a point charge q at O,

$$\mathbf{E}_P = \frac{1}{4\pi\varepsilon_0} \frac{q}{\lvert r^2 \rvert} \hat{\mathbf{r}}$$

If $q > 0$, i.e., for positive charge, $\mathbf{E}$ is directed away from the source charge.

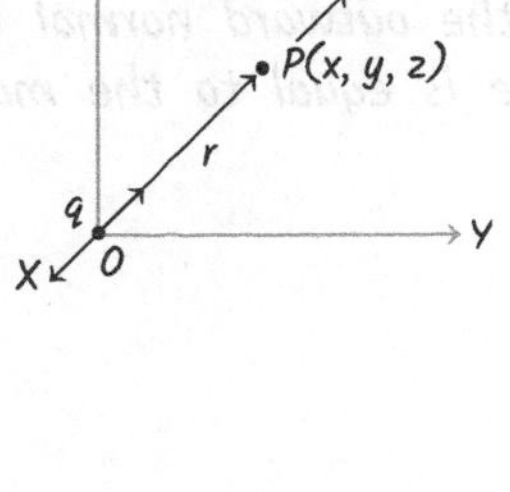

While on the other hand, if $q < 0$, i.e., for negative charge, $\mathbf{E}$ is directed towards the source charge.

17. Electric Field due to System of Charges

This is same as in the case of electrostatic force. Here also we will apply principle of superposition, i.e.,

$$E = E_1 + E_2 + E_3 + \cdots + E_n$$

$$\Rightarrow \quad E = \frac{1}{4\pi\varepsilon_0} \sum_{i=1}^{n} \frac{q_i}{\lvert r_i \rvert^2} \hat{r}_i$$

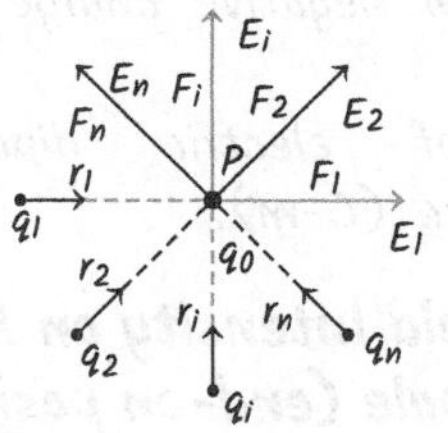

18. Electric Field Lines

"An electric field line is an imaginary line on curve drawn through a region of space so that its tangent at any point is in the direction of the electric field vector at that point.

The relative closeness of the lines at some place gives an idea about the intensity of electric field at that point."

Electric field lines always start from positive charge and end on negative charge.

Two electric field lines can never intersect each other.

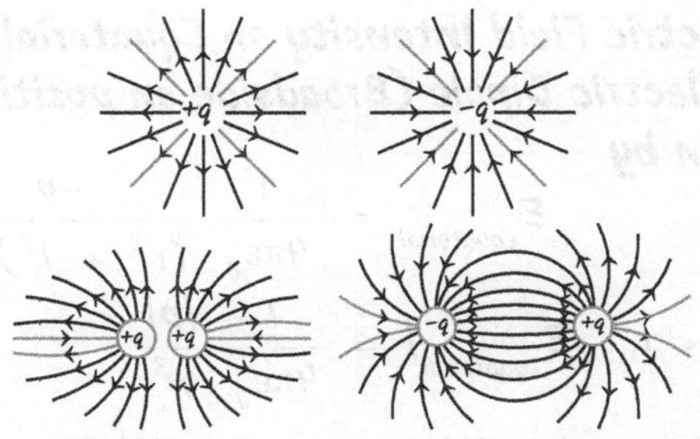

Field lines due to two equal positive charges

Field lines due to an electric dipole

Different electric field lines

19. Electric Dipole

Two point charges of same magnitude and opposite nature separated by a small distance form an electric dipole.

20. Electric Dipole Moment

The strength of an electric dipole is measured by a vector quantity known as electric dipole moment **p** which is the product of magnitude of either charge *q* and separation between the two charges, i.e., 2*l*.

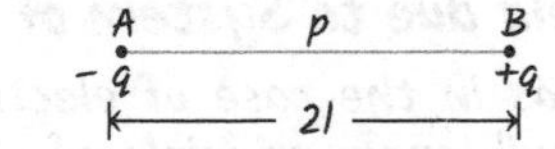

It is expressed as $\mathbf{p} = q \times 2l$

$$\Rightarrow \quad |\mathbf{p}| = q\,(2l)$$

Direction The direction of electric dipole moment is taken from negative charge $(-q)$ to positive charge $(+q)$.

SI unit of electric dipole moment is coulomb-metre (C-m).

21. Electric Field Intensity on Axial Line of Electric Dipole (end-on position) is Given by

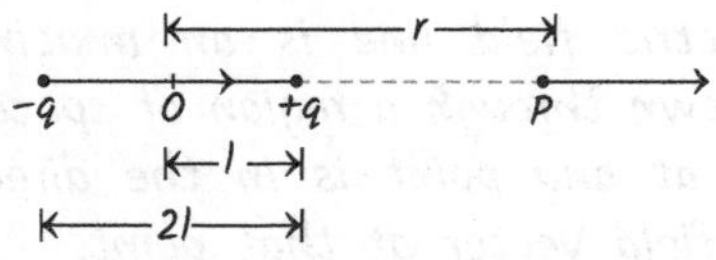

$$E_{axial} = \frac{1}{4\pi\varepsilon_0} \frac{2\,p\,r}{(r^2 - l^2)^2}$$

When $l << r$,

$$E_{axial} = \frac{1}{4\pi\varepsilon_0} \frac{2p}{r^3}$$

$$[\because r^2 - l^2 \simeq r^2]$$

22. Electric Field Intensity on Equatorial Line of Electric Dipole (Broadside on position) is Given by

$$E_{equatorial} = \frac{1}{4\pi\varepsilon_0} \frac{-p}{(r^2 + l^2)^{3/2}}$$

If $l << r$, $$|E_{equatorial}| = \frac{1}{4\pi\varepsilon_0} \frac{|p|}{r^3}$$

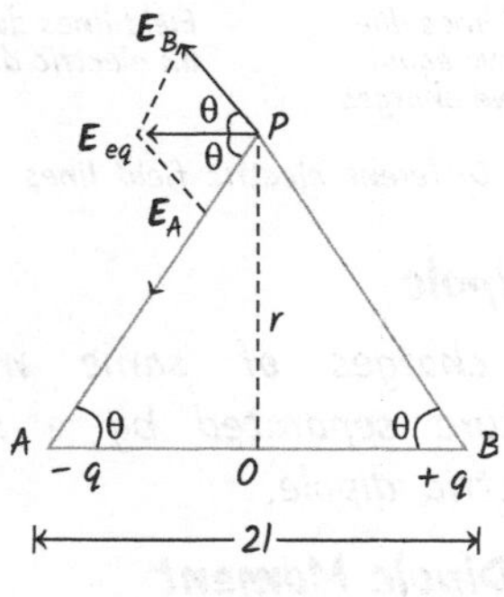

23. Electric Field Intensity at a General Point (r, θ) due to a Short Electric Dipole is Given by

$$E = \frac{1}{4\pi\varepsilon_0} \frac{p}{r^3} \sqrt{3\cos^2\theta + 1}$$

Cases

- For an axial point, $\theta = 0°$,
$$E_{axial} = \frac{1}{4\pi\varepsilon_0} \frac{2p}{r^3}$$
- For an equatorial point, $\theta = 90°$,
$$E_{equatorial} = \frac{1}{4\pi\varepsilon_0} \frac{p}{r^3}$$
- $E_{axial} = 2 \times E_{equatorial}$

24. Torque on a Dipole Placed in a Uniform Electric Field

Torque on an electric dipole placed in a uniform electric field E is given by

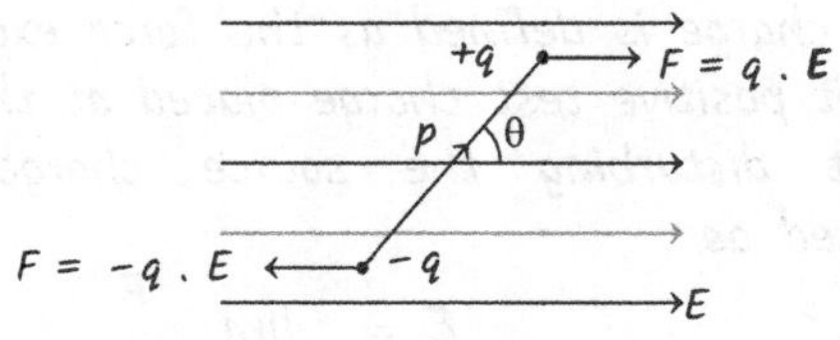

Torque, $\tau = \mathbf{p} \times \mathbf{E} \Rightarrow \tau = pE\sin\theta$

The SI unit of torque is newton-metre (N-m) and its dimensional formula is $[ML^2T^{-2}]$.

Cases

- Minimum torque experienced by electric dipole in electric field, when $\theta = 0°$ or π, then $\tau = \tau_{min} = 0$
- Maximum torque, $\tau = \tau_{max}$ when $\sin\theta = 1$, i.e. $\theta = \frac{\pi}{2} \Rightarrow \tau_{max} = pE$

Dipole is in stable equilibrium in uniform electric field when angle between **p** and **E** is 0° and in unstable equilibrium when angle θ is 180°.

Note The net force on electric dipole placed in a uniform electric field is zero.

25. Area Vector

The vector associated with every area element of a closed surface is taken to be in the direction of the outward normal to that surface. Its magnitude is equal to the magnitude of area.

26. Electric Flux

Electric flux linked with any surface is proportional to the total number of electric field lines that normally pass through that surface. It is a scalar quantity.

SI unit of electric flux is
$N - m^2C^{-1}$ *or* $J - mC^{-1}$ *or* $V - m$.

CGS unit of electric flux is $dyne\text{-}cm^2 / stat - C$.

27. Gaussian Surface

Any hypothetical closed surface enclosing a charge is called the Gaussian surface of that charge. It is chosen to evaluate the surface integral of the electric field produced by the charge enclosed by it, which in turn gives the total flux through the surface.

28. Gauss's Law

The total electric flux linked with a closed surface S is

$$\phi_E = \oint \mathbf{E} \cdot d\mathbf{S} = \frac{q}{\varepsilon_0}$$

where, q is the total charge enclosed by the closed Gaussian (an imaginary) surface.

29. Applications of Gauss's Theorem

(i) Electric field intensity due to infinitely long uniformly charged wire with linear charge density λ

We have considered cylindrical Gaussian surface.

From Gauss's law,

$$\oint \mathbf{E} \cdot d\mathbf{S} = \frac{q}{\varepsilon_0} = \frac{\lambda l}{\varepsilon_0}$$

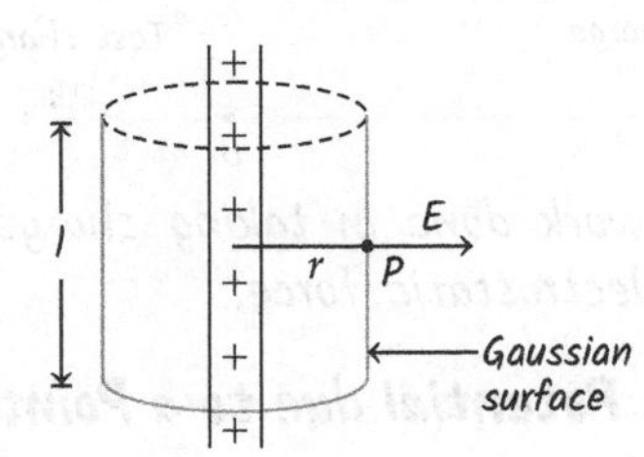

$$\Rightarrow \quad E = \frac{\lambda}{2\pi\varepsilon_0 r} \quad (\because \oint dS = 2\pi rl)$$

where, r is the perpendicular distance from the charged wire and $E \propto \frac{1}{r}$.

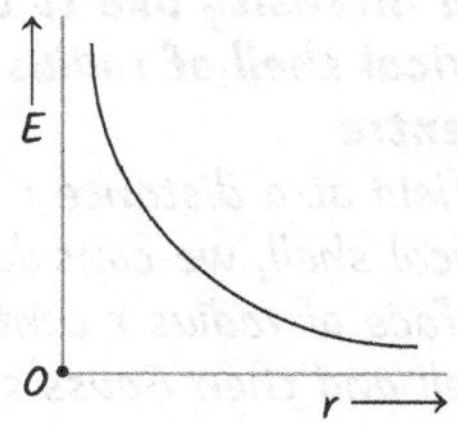

(ii) (a) Electric field intensity due to a thin infinite plane sheet of charge with uniform surface charge density σ at any nearby point

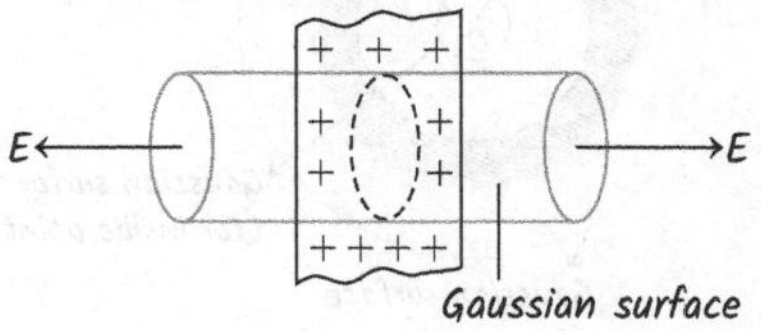

$E = \frac{\sigma}{2\varepsilon_0}$ *[for a plane sheet of charge]*

and $E = \frac{\sigma}{\varepsilon_0}$ *[for a charged conducting surface]*

Note *E does not depend on r.*

(b) Electric field intensity due to two equally and oppositely charged parallel plane sheet of charge density (σ)

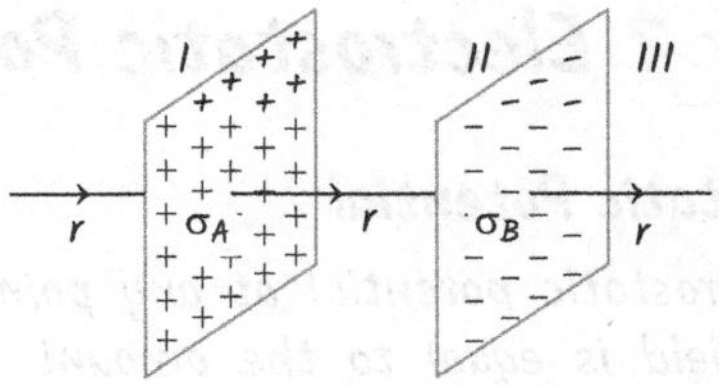

In region I $E = -\frac{\sigma_A}{2\varepsilon_0} + \frac{\sigma_B}{2\varepsilon_0}$

$$= +\frac{1}{2\varepsilon_0}(\sigma_B - \sigma_A)$$

In region II $E = \frac{1}{2\varepsilon_0}(\sigma_A + \sigma_B)$

In region III $E = \frac{1}{2\varepsilon_0}(\sigma_A - \sigma_B)$

Special Case *If* $\sigma_A = \sigma_B = \sigma$, *then electric field is zero in regions I and III, while in the region I,* $E = \frac{\sigma}{\varepsilon_0}$.

(iii) Electric field intensity due to a thin charged hollow spherical shell of radius R at a distance r from its centre

To find the field at a distance r from the centre of the spherical shell, we consider a spherical Gaussian surface of radius r centered at the centre of shell and then Gauss's law is applied.

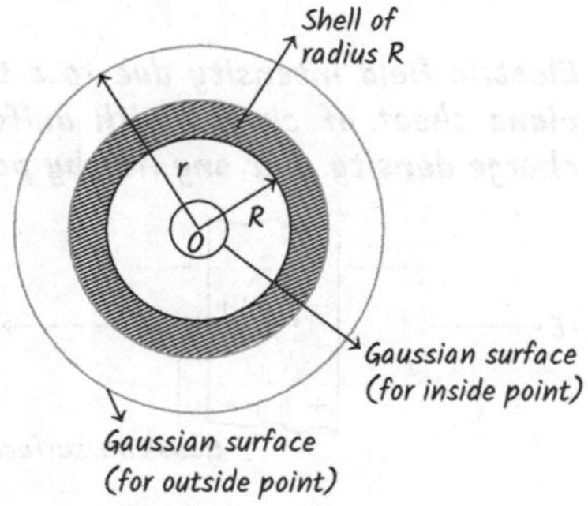

(a) Electric field intensity at a point inside the shell ($r < R$)

As, $q = 0 \Rightarrow \mathbf{E} = 0$

[$\because$ from Gauss's law, $\oint \mathbf{E} \cdot d\mathbf{S} = \dfrac{q}{\varepsilon_0}$]

(b) For points lying outside the shell ($r > R$)

By Gauss's law,

$$\oint \mathbf{E} \cdot d\mathbf{S} = \frac{q}{\varepsilon_0}$$

$$\Rightarrow E \times 4\pi r^2 = \frac{\sigma \times (4\pi R^2)}{\varepsilon_0}$$

$[q = \sigma \times 4\pi R^2]$

$$\Rightarrow E = \frac{\sigma R^2}{\varepsilon_0 r^2} \quad ...(i)$$

$$\therefore E \propto \frac{1}{r^2}$$

(c) Electric field intensity at a point on the surface ($r = R$)

On putting $r = R$ in Eq. (i),

$$E = \frac{\sigma}{\varepsilon_0}$$

where, surface charge density, $\sigma = \dfrac{q}{4\pi R^2}$.

The variation of E with r is shown in diagram given below.

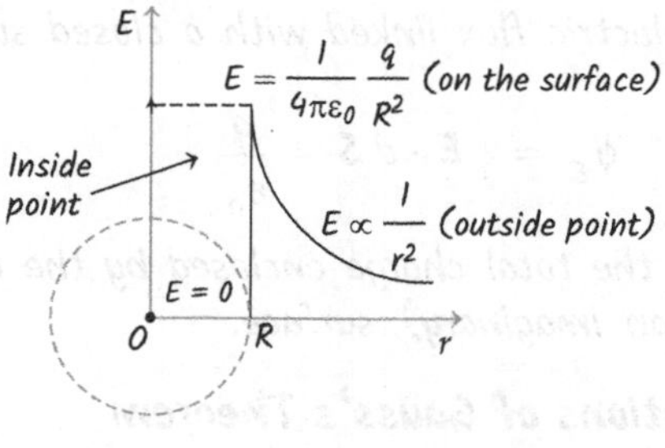

Chapter 2 Electrostatic Potential and Capacitance

1. Electrostatic Potential

The electrostatic potential at any point in an electric field is equal to the amount of work done in bringing the unit positive test charge without acceleration from infinity to that point.

$$\text{Electrostatic potential, } V = \frac{\text{Work done } (W)}{\text{Charge } (q)}$$

It is a scalar quantity having unit JC^{-1} and its dimensional formula is $[ML^2T^{-3}A^{-1}]$.

2. Electrostatic Potential Difference

The potential difference between two points in an electric field is defined as the amount of work done in moving a unit positive test charge from one point to the other, against the electrostatic force without any acceleration, i.e.,

$$V_B - V_A = \frac{W_{AB}}{q_0}$$

where, W_{AB} is work done in taking charge q_0 from A to B against electrostatic force.

3. Electrostatic Potential due to a Point Charge

Potential due to a point charge q at any point P lying at a distance r from it, is given by,

$$V = \frac{1}{4\pi\varepsilon_0} \cdot \frac{q}{r}$$

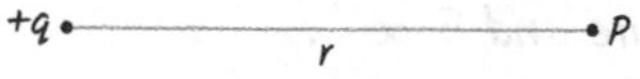

4. Electrostatic Potential at any Point (whose Position Vector is r) due to a System of Point Charges

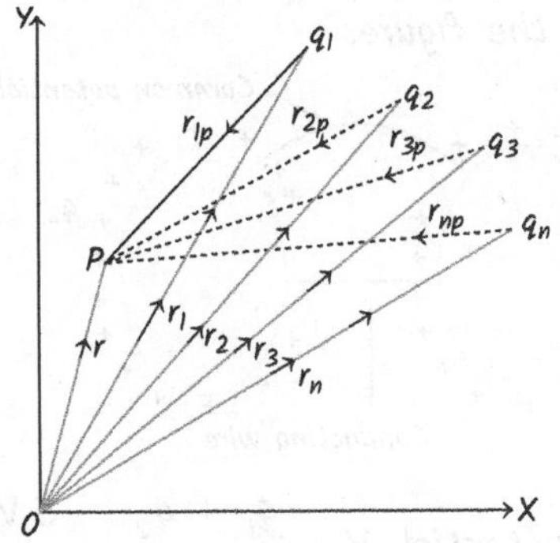

The electrostatic potential at point P due to a system of point charges $q_1, q_2, \ldots, q_n$ whose position vectors are $\mathbf{r}_1, \mathbf{r}_2, \ldots, \mathbf{r}_n$ respectively, is given by

$$V = \frac{1}{4\pi\varepsilon_0} \sum_{i=1}^{n} \frac{q_i}{|\mathbf{r} - \mathbf{r}_i|}$$

where, $|\mathbf{r} - \mathbf{r}_i|$ is the distance between location of charge and point of potential calculations.

5. Electrostatic Potential due to an Electric Dipole

At any point P whose position vector is $\mathbf{r}$ w.r.t. mid-point of the dipole, the electrostatic potential is given by

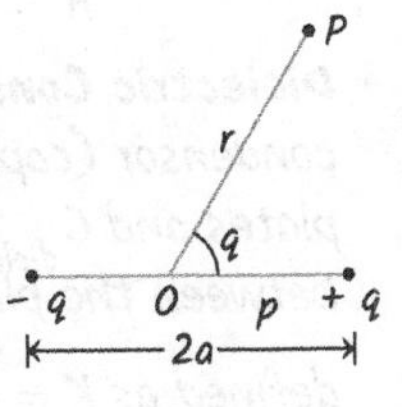

$$V = \frac{1}{4\pi\varepsilon_0} \cdot \frac{p \cos\theta}{r^2}$$

$$= \frac{1}{4\pi\varepsilon_0} \frac{\mathbf{p} \cdot \mathbf{r}}{r^3}$$

where, θ is the angle between $\mathbf{r}$ and $\mathbf{p}$.

Cases

- The electrostatic potential on the perpendicular bisector due to an electric dipole is zero. Since, $\theta = 90°$ or $\cos 90° = 0$, so $V = 0$.
- The electrostatic potential at the axial point due to an electric dipole is maximum, since $\theta = 0°$.

$$\therefore \quad V_{max} = \frac{1}{4\pi\varepsilon_0} \frac{p \cos 0°}{r^2} = \frac{1}{4\pi\varepsilon_0} \cdot \frac{p}{r^2}$$

6. Equipotential Surface

A surface which has same electrostatic potential at every point on it, is known as equipotential surface. It is spherical for a point charge, cylindrical for a line charge and planar for distant charges.

7. Relationship between Electric Field and Potential

$$V = -\int \mathbf{E} \cdot d\mathbf{r} \quad \text{or} \quad E = -\frac{dV}{dr}$$

i.e. potential decreases in the direction of electric field.

8. Electrostatic Potential Energy

The work done against electrostatic force gets stored as potential energy. This is called electrostatic potential energy U.

$$\Delta U = U_B - U_A = W_{AB}$$

9. Potential Energy in an External Field

(i) Potential energy of a single charge in external field

Potential energy of a single charge q at a point with position vector $\mathbf{r}$ in an external field

$$= q \cdot V(\mathbf{r})$$

where, $V(\mathbf{r})$ is potential at that point due to the external electric field E.

(ii) Potential energy of a system of two charges in an external field

$$U = q_1 \cdot V(\mathbf{r}_1) + q_2 \cdot V(\mathbf{r}_2) + \frac{q_1 q_2}{4\pi\varepsilon_0 r_{12}}$$

where, q_1, q_2 are two point charges at position vectors $\mathbf{r}_1$ and $\mathbf{r}_2$, respectively to origin.

(iii) Potential energy of a system of three charges is given by

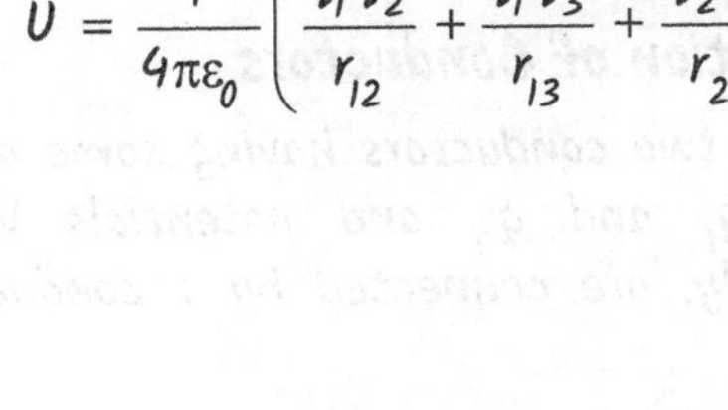

$$U = \frac{1}{4\pi\varepsilon_0}\left(\frac{q_1 q_2}{r_{12}} + \frac{q_1 q_3}{r_{13}} + \frac{q_2 q_3}{r_{23}}\right)$$

The values of q_1, q_2 and q_3 must be put with proper sign.

10. Potential Energy of Electric Dipole in a Uniform Electric Field

Potential energy of electric dipole when it rotates from $\theta_1 = 90^\circ$ to $\theta_2 = \theta$

$$U = pE(\cos 90^\circ - \cos\theta)$$
$$= -pE\cos\theta = -\mathbf{p}\cdot\mathbf{E}$$

If $\theta_2 = 180^\circ$, then $U = pE$

where, $\mathbf{p}$ = dipole moment and $\mathbf{E}$ = external electric field.

11. Conductors and Insulators

Conductor contains a large number of free charge carriers, i.e., electrons to conduct electricity, while insulator does not have any free charge carriers to conduct electricity. Examples of conductors are metals, the earth, etc. Plastic, rubber, mica, wood, etc., are the examples of insulator.

12. Capacitor

A capacitor is a device which is used to store electrostatic potential energy or charge. It comprises of two conductors separated by an insulating medium.

13. Capacitance of a Conductor

If charge q is given to an insulated conductor, which leads to increase in its potential by V, such that

$$q \propto V \Rightarrow q = CV$$

where, C is known as capacitance of conductor. The capacitance depends on shape, size and geometry of conductor, nature of surrounding medium and presence of other conductors in the neighbourhood of it.

- Its SI unit is farad (F).

  Here, $1 \text{ farad} = \dfrac{1 \text{ coulomb}}{1 \text{ volt}} \Rightarrow 1\text{ F} = 1\text{ CV}^{-1}$

- F(farad) is a very large unit of capacitance. So, μF is usually taken.
- The dimensional formula of capacitance is are $[M^{-1}L^{-2}T^4A^2]$.

14. Connection of Conductors

Whenever two conductors having some amounts of charges q_1 and q_2 and potentials V_1 and V_2 respectively, are connected by a conducting wire, then potential of each conductor becomes same after the connection. So, the redistribution of charges takes place and charges are redistributed such that, they acquire common potential V as shown in the figure.

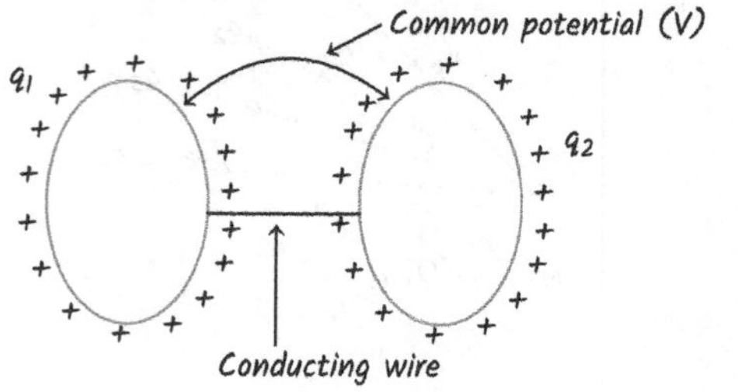

$$\text{Common potential, } V = \frac{q_1 + q_2}{C_1 + C_2} = \frac{C_1V_1 + C_2V_2}{C_1 + C_2}$$

15. Parallel Plate Capacitor

The most common among all capacitors is parallel plate capacitor. It consists of two metal plates of same area A and separated by distance d filled with air or some other medium.

- Capacitance of a parallel plate capacitor is given by

  $$C = \frac{\varepsilon_0 A}{d}$$

  where, d = separation between the plates,
  A = area of each plate

- **Dielectric Constant** If C_{vacuum} be the capacity of a condensor (capacitor) with vacuum or air between its plates and $C_{dielectric}$ be the capacity with dielectric between the plates, then dielectric constant K is defined as $K = \dfrac{C_{dielectric}}{C_{vacuum}}$.

  Dielectric constant is also known as ***specific inductive capacity of the dielectric*** or ***relative permittivity***.

- When a dielectric medium of dielectric constant K is inserted between the plates of capacitor and fully occupies the intervening region, then capacitance

  $$C = \frac{KA\varepsilon_0}{d}$$

  - If a dielectric material of dielectric constant K and thickness t is placed in between the plates of capacitor, then

    $$C = \frac{\varepsilon_0 A}{d - t + \dfrac{t}{K}}$$

    where, K = dielectric constant,

t = thickness of dielectric

- When a metallic conducting slab is partially filled in capacitor, then capacitance of capacitor becomes

$$C = \frac{\varepsilon_0 A}{d - t}$$

where, t = thickness of metallic slab,
d = separation between two plates

16. Series Combination of Capacitors

The charge on each capacitor is same for any value of capacitance and equal to the charge across the combination.

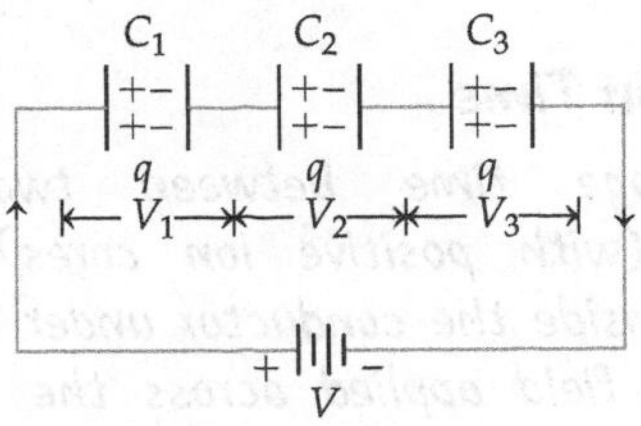

(i) The potential difference across the combination is equal to the algebraic sum of potential differences across each capacitor ,i.e.,

$$V = V_1 + V_2 + V_3$$

(ii) The potential difference is divided across capacitors in inverse ratio of their capacitances, i.e.,

$$V_1 : V_2 : V_3 = \frac{1}{C_1} : \frac{1}{C_2} : \frac{1}{C_3}$$

(iii) The equivalent capacitance is given by

$$\frac{1}{C_s} = \frac{1}{C_1} + \frac{1}{C_2} + \frac{1}{C_3}$$

(iv) The equivalent capacitance of n identical capacitors each of capacitance C is $C_s = \frac{C}{n}$.

17. Parallel Combination of Capacitors

The potential difference across each capacitor is same for any value of capacitance and equal to the potential difference across the combination.

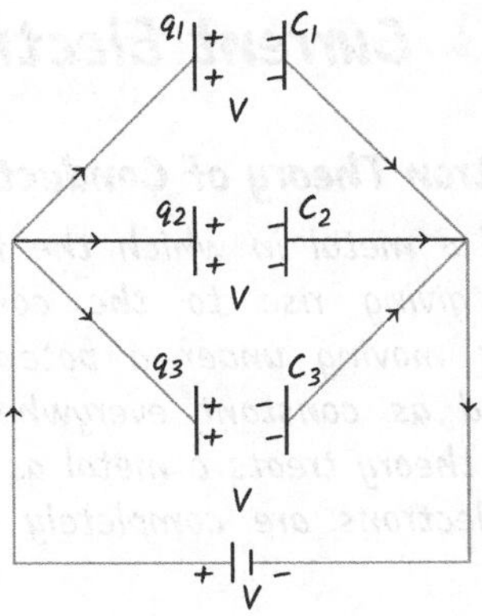

(i) The total charge on combination is equal to the algebraic sum of charges on each capacitor, i.e.,
$q = q_1 + q_2 + q_3$

(ii) The equivalent capacitance (C_p) is given by,
$C_p = C_1 + C_2 + C_3$

(iii) The total charge on the capacitors is divided in the ratio of their capacitances
i.e. $q \propto C$

$$\Rightarrow q_1 : q_2 : q_3 = C_1 : C_2 : C_3$$

(iv) The equivalent capacitance of n identical capacitors each of capacitance C connected in parallel combination is $C_p = nC$.

18. Energy Stored in Capacitor

The energy of a charged capacitor is the measure of total work done in charging the capacitor to a given potential. The electrostatic energy stored in a capacitor is given by,

$$U = \frac{1}{2} CV^2 = \frac{1}{2} qV = \frac{q^2}{2C}$$

where, q = charge on capacitor, C = capacitance,
V = potential difference across capacitor

19. Energy Density

The energy stored per unit volume in an electric field E is known as energy density and it is given by

$$U_E = \frac{1}{2}\varepsilon_0 E^2$$

Chapter 3 Current Electricity

1. Free Electron Theory of Conduction

A model of a metal in which the free electrons, i.e., those giving rise to the conductivity are regarded as moving under a potential which is approximated as constant everywhere inside the metal. This theory treats a metal as gas container in which electrons are completely free to move within it.

2. Acceleration of Free Electron in an External Electric Field

Electron placed in an external electric field experiences a force, hence the acceleration,

$$a_e = \frac{eE}{m_e}$$

where, m_e = mass of electron, E = electric field and e = charge on an electron.

3. Electric Current

It is defined as the rate of flow of electric charge through any cross-section of a conductor. If ΔQ charge flows in Δt time, then current at any time t is

$$I = \lim_{\Delta t \to 0} \frac{\Delta Q}{\Delta t} = \frac{dQ}{dt}$$

Charge can be written as

$\Delta Q = ne$ [quantisation of charge]

where, n = number of free electrons and

e = charge on an electron (1.6×10^{-19} C)

The current is a scalar quantity. The SI unit of current is ampere (A).

4. Current Density

Current density at a point in a conductor is the ratio of the current at that point to the area of cross-section of the conductor at that point, provided area is held normal to the direction of flow of current.

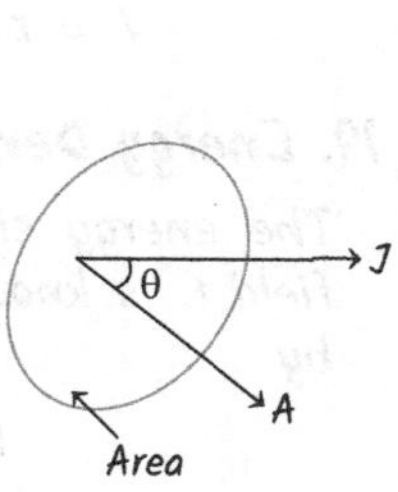

Current density, $J = \frac{\Delta I}{\Delta A}$

Also, $I = \int \mathbf{J} \cdot d\mathbf{A} = \int J dA \cos\theta$

Its SI unit is A/m^2.

5. Drift Velocity

It is defined as the minimum average velocity with which the free electrons in a conductor get drifted towards the positive end of the conductor under the influence of an electric field applied across the conductor. It is denoted by v_d.

Thus, $v_d = \frac{-eE}{m}\tau$

where, τ = relaxation time.

The drift velocity of an electron is of the order of 10^{-4} ms^{-1}.

6. Relaxation Time

The average time between two successive collisions (with positive ion cores) of drifting electrons inside the conductor under the influence of electric field applied across the conductor, is known as relaxation time (τ).

7. Relation between Electric Current and Drift Velocity

Electric current in terms of drift velocity

$I = neAv_d$

where, n = number density of free electrons,

e = electronic charge,

A = cross-sectional area and

v_d = drift velocity of an electron.

8. Current Density in Terms of Drift Velocity

Current density at any point of conductor,

$J = \frac{I}{A} = nev_d$

9. Mobility

It is defined as the magnitude of drift velocity per unit electric field. It is expressed as

$$\mu = \frac{\text{Drift velocity } (v_d)}{\text{Electric field } (E)} = \frac{eE\,\tau/m}{E} = \frac{e\tau}{m}$$

where, τ is the average relaxation time of the electron while drifting towards the opposite electrode and m is the mass of the electron.

Its SI unit is $m^2/(V\text{-}s)$.

10. Ohm's Law

At constant temperature, the potential difference V across the ends of a given metallic wire (conductor) in a circuit (electric) is directly proportional to the current flowing through it.

$$V \propto I \Rightarrow V = RI$$

where, R is a constant known as resistance of the conductor.

Such a conductor is known as ohmic conductor. Its graph between V and I is a straight line as shown in the figure.

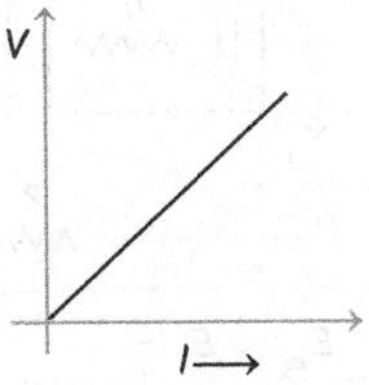

Whereas, a non-ohmic conductor does not obey Ohm's law, i.e., the graph between V and I is not a straight line.

11. Resistance of a Conductor

It is defined as the ratio of the potential difference applied across the conductor to the current flowing through it. The resistance of a conductor is directly proportional to the length of conductor (l) and inversely proportional to the cross-sectional area of conductor (A).

i.e. $$R \propto \frac{l}{A}$$

So, resistance, $$R = \rho \frac{l}{A}$$

where, ρ is resistivity of conductor and it does not depend on the dimensions of conductor, i.e., it depends on the nature of conductor.

SI unit of resistance (R) is ohm (Ω).

SI unit of resistivity (ρ) is Ω- m.

12. Conductance

It is defined as the reciprocal of resistance of a conductor. It is expressed as $G = \frac{1}{R}$.

Its SI unit is mho (Ω^{-1}) or Siemen (S).

The dimensional formula of conductance is $[M^{-1}L^{-2}T^3A^2]$.

13. Conductivity

It is defined as the reciprocal of resistivity of a conductor. It is expressed as $\sigma = \frac{1}{\rho}$.

SI unit is mho per metre $(\Omega\text{-}m)^{-1}$.

14. Relation between J, σ and E

$$J = \sigma E$$

This is also called Ohm's law in vector form.

15. Temperature Coefficient of Resistance

It is defined as the increase in resistance per unit original resistance per degree celsius (or kelvin) rise in temperature.

- **Temperature coefficient** of resistance is given by,

$$\alpha = \frac{R_2 - R_1}{R_1(t_2 - t_1)}$$

where, R_1 and R_2 are the resistances at t_1°C and t_2°C respectively.

SI unit of α is per degree celsius (°C^{-1}).

- **For metals**, the value of α is **positive**, therefore resistance of the metal increases with rise in temperature.
- **For semiconductors**, the value of α is **negative**, therefore resistance of semiconductor decreases with rise in temperature.

16. Resistivity

- It is the resistance of a unit length with unit area of cross-section of the material of the conductor.
- **Relationship between resistivity and relaxation time**

$$\rho = \frac{m}{ne^2\tau}$$

where, τ = relaxation time.

Specific resistance or resistivity (ρ) depends on the material of conductor, not on the length and cross-sectional area (A), i.e. geometry of conductor.

- **Effect of Temperature on Resistivity**

For metals, resistivity increases with increase in temperature.

For semiconductors, resistivity decreases with increase in temperature.

17. Electrical Energy

It is defined as the total work done (W) by the source of emf (E) in maintaining the electric current (I) in the given circuit for a specified time t.

i.e. $$E = VIt = I^2Rt = \frac{V^2t}{R}$$

Its SI unit is joule (J).

18. Electric Power

The rate of consumption of electrical energy or production of heat energy is known as electric power.

SI unit of electric power is watt (W).

Electric power,

$$P = I^2R = \frac{V^2}{R} = VI$$

Note Commercial unit of electric energy is 1 Unit $= 1 \text{ kWh} = 3.6 \times 10^6 \text{ J}$

19. Cells

The electric cell is a source of energy that maintains a continuous flow of charge in a circuit. Electric cell changes chemical energy into electrical energy.

20. Electromotive Force (EMF) of a Cell (E)

The work done by cell in moving unit positive charge through the whole circuit (including the cell) is called **electromotive force** (emf) of the cell.

EMF of the cell, $E = W/q$

Its SI unit is joule/coulomb or volt.

21. Terminal Voltage (V) of a Cell

Work done in moving the unit charge in the external circuit (excluding the cell) is called terminal voltage (V) of the cell.

22. Internal Resistance (r)

Internal resistance of a cell is defined as the resistance offered by the electrolyte of the cell to the flow of current through it. It is denoted by r. Its SI unit is ohm (Ω).

23. The Relationship among r, R, E and V

Internal resistance, $r = R\left(\frac{E}{V} - 1\right)$

where, R = external resistance, E = emf of cell and V = terminal voltage of cell

Note When cell is discharging, then $V = E - ir$.
When cell is charging, then $V = E + ir$.

24. Combination of Cells

There are following types of combination of cells

Combination of cells	
Series combination	$E_{eq} = E_1 + E_2 + \ldots + E_n$
	$r_{eq} = r_1 + r_2 + \ldots r_n$ $i = ne(R + nr)$ 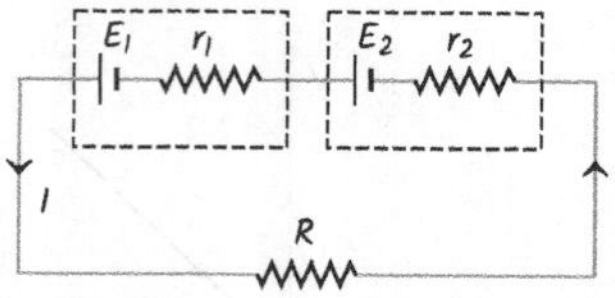
Parallel combination	$E_{eq} = E$
	$\frac{1}{r_{eq}} = \frac{1}{r_1} + \frac{1}{r_2} + \ldots + \frac{1}{r_m}$ (upto m terms)
	$I = \frac{mE}{(r + mR)}$ 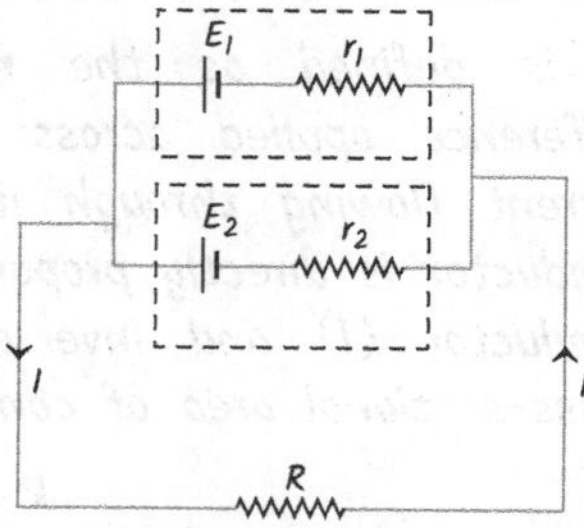
Mixed Grouping	$E_{eq} = nE$
If n cells, each of emf E and internal resistance r are connected in series and such m rows are connected in parallel, then	$r_{eq} = \frac{nr}{m}$ $I = \frac{mnE}{mR + nr}$ 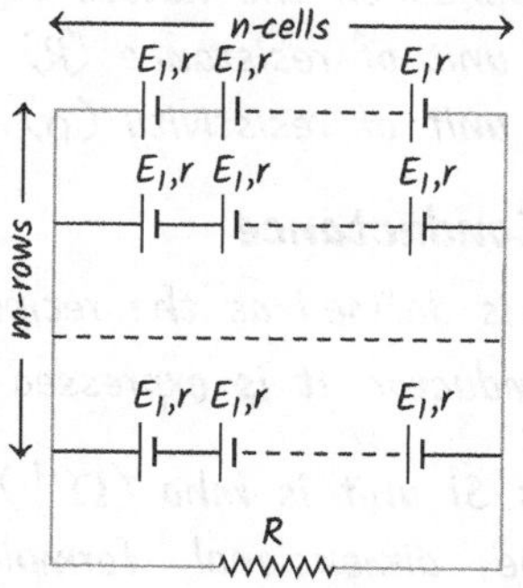

25. Kirchhoff's First Law/Junction Law/Current Law

The sum of currents entering into a junction is equal to the sum of currents leaving the junction. It supports the law of conservation of charge.

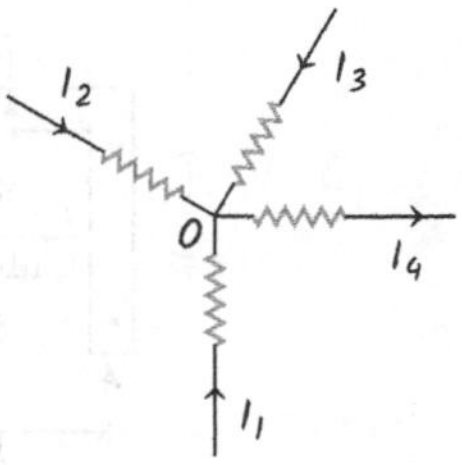

e.g. $\Sigma I = 0$

$\therefore \quad I_1 + I_2 + I_3 - I_4 = 0$

26. Kirchhoff's Second Law or Voltage Rule

In any closed loop of electrical circuit, the algebraic sum of emfs of the cell and the product of currents and resistance is always equal to zero, i.e., $\Sigma E + \Sigma IR = 0$. Kirchhoff's second law supports the law of conservation of energy. Because the net change in the energy of a charge, after the charge completes a closed path must be zero.

Sign convention for Kirchhoff's second law:

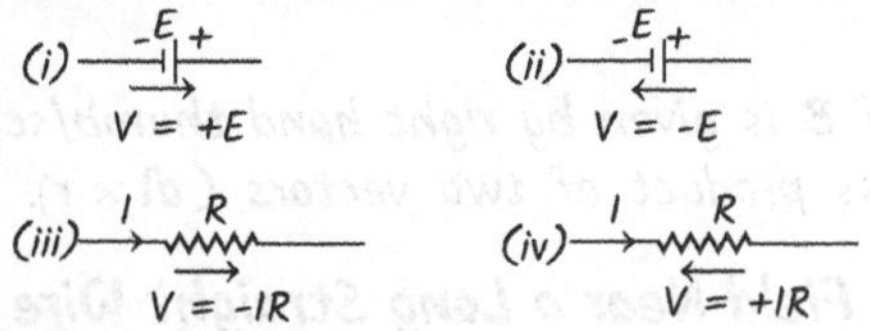

27. Potentiometer

It is an electrical device which can be used to measure potential difference with greater accuracy as well as for the following purposes:

- The emfs of two primary cells can be compared using potentiometer as

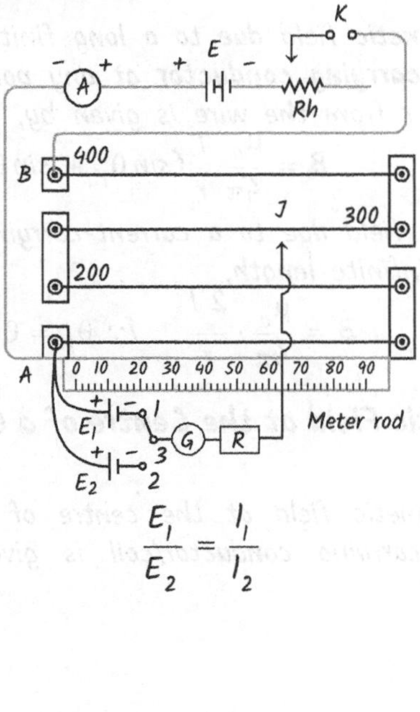

$$\frac{E_1}{E_2} = \frac{l_1}{l_2}$$

where, l_1 and l_2 are the balancing lengths corresponding to the cells of emf's E_1 and E_2 respectively.

- The internal resistance of a cell can be determined using potentiometer. If l_1 and l_2 are the balancing lengths when key K_1 is opened and closed respectively, and resistance R is applied in safety resistance box (SRB), then internal resistance of primary cell is given by

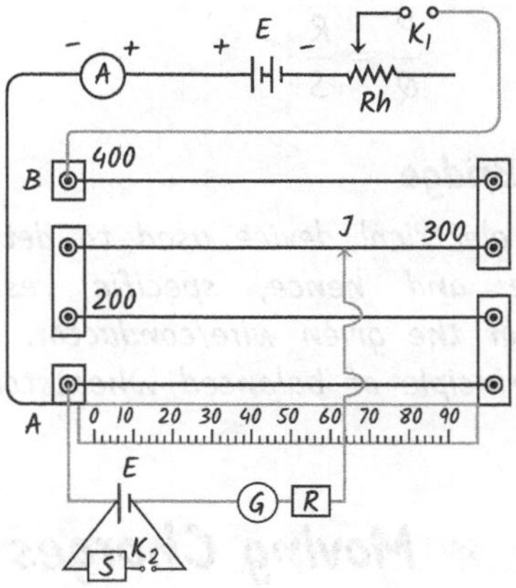

$$r = R\left(\frac{l_1}{l_2} - 1\right)$$

The sensitivity of a potentiometer refers to the capability of measuring very small potential difference and exhibit change in balancing length even on very small change in potential difference. The sensitivity of potentiometer can be increased by increasing the length of potentiometer wire and decreasing the value of potential gradient.

28. Wheatstone Bridge

It is an arrangement of four resistances connected to form the arms of quadrilateral ABCD as shown in figure.

A battery with key and galvanometer are connected along its two diagonals respectively, where, P, Q = ratio arms, R = known resistance and S = unknown resistance.
The bridge is said to be balanced, when

(i) $V_B = V_D$

(ii) there is no flow of current through the galvanometer. In the balanced condition, ratio of resistances of adjacent arms are equal.

i.e. $\frac{P}{Q} = \frac{R}{S}$

29. Meter Bridge

It is an electrical device used to determine the resistance and hence, specific resistance of material of the given wire/conductor. It is based on the principle of balanced Wheatstone bridge.

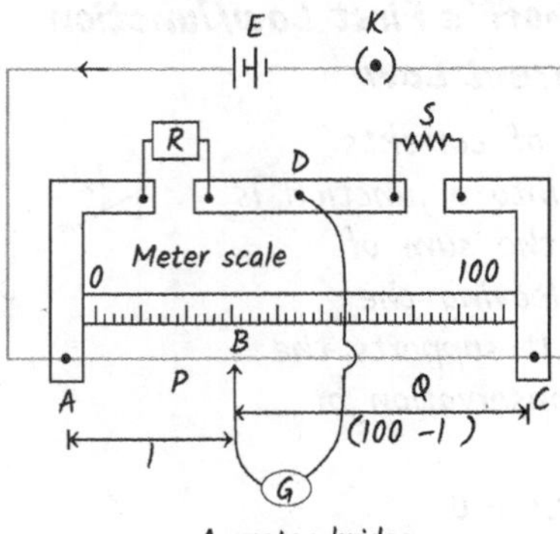

A meter bridge

At balanced situation of bridge

$$\frac{P}{Q} = \frac{R}{S} \text{ or } \frac{l}{100-l} = \frac{R}{S}$$

where, l is the balancing length, and P, Q, R and S are the arm resistances of a balanced Wheatstone bridge.

Chapter 4 Moving Charges and Magnetism

1. Magnetic Field

The space around a magnet on a current-carrying conductor in which its magnetic influence can be experienced is called magnetic field. Its SI unit is tesla (T).

2. Oersted's experiment

HC Oersted observed by his experiment that a current-carrying conductor deflects magnetic compass needle placed near it.

2. Biot-Savart's Law

According to this law, the magnetic field due to the small current carrying element dl at any nearby point P is given by,

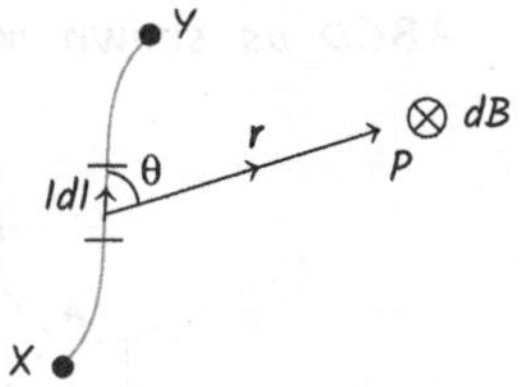

$$d\mathbf{B} = \frac{\mu_0}{4\pi} \cdot \frac{I d\mathbf{l} \times \mathbf{r}}{|r|^3}$$

or $$|d\mathbf{B}| = \frac{\mu_0}{4\pi} \cdot \frac{I\,dl\,\sin\theta}{r^2}$$

where, $Id\mathbf{l}$ = current element (vector quantity)
and r = displacement vector from current element to the point P.

*Direction of **B** is given by right hand thumb/screw rule or cross product of two vectors ($d\mathbf{l} \times \mathbf{r}$).*

3. Magnetic Field Near a Long Straight Wire

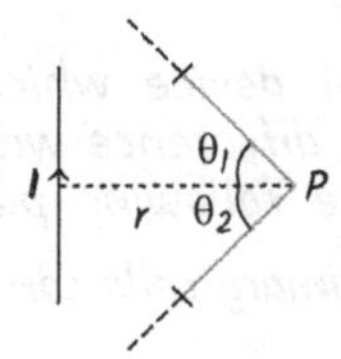

*The magnetic field due to a long finite **straight current-carrying conductor** at any point P at a distance r from the wire is given by,*

$$B = \frac{\mu_0}{4\pi}\frac{I}{r}(\sin\theta_1 + \sin\theta_2)$$

Magnetic field due to a current-carrying straight wire of infinite length,

$$B = \frac{\mu_0}{4\pi} \cdot \frac{2I}{r} \quad [\because \theta_1 = \theta_2 \approx 90°]$$

4. Magnetic Field at the Centre of a Circular Loop

The magnetic field at the centre of a circular current carrying conductor/coil is given by,

$$B = \frac{\mu_0 I}{2r}$$

For N number of turns, $B = \frac{\mu_0 NI}{2r}$

5. Magnetic Field on the Axis of Circular Loop

The magnetic field at any point P(r) lying on the axis of a circular current (I) carrying conductor (loop) of radius a is given by $B = \frac{\mu_0 NIa^2}{2(r^2 + a^2)^{3/2}}$

where, N = number of turns in the loop.

6. Ampere's Law

According to this law, the line integral of magnetic field along the closed path is μ_0 times the net current enclosed by the path, i.e.,

$$\oint B \cdot dl = \mu_0 \Sigma I$$

7. Magnetic Field Due to a Straight Solenoid

The magnetic field at any point inside a solenoid is given by,

$$B = \mu_0 nI$$

where, n = number of turns per unit length
and I = current flowing through the solenoid.

8. Magnetic Force

If a charged particle carrying a positive charge q and moving with velocity v through a particular point in a magnetic field B, it experiences a deflecting force F, given by the equation

$$F = q(\mathbf{v} \times \mathbf{B})$$

9. Motion of Charged Particle in Magnetic Field

As force on particle $F = qvB \sin\theta$

(i) If $\theta = 90°$, motion of particle will be circular.

(ii) If $\theta \neq 90°$, motion of particle will be helical.

Frequency of revolution,

$$f = \frac{qB}{2\pi m}$$

where, m = mass of charged particle.

10. Lorentz Force

Force on a moving charge in a uniform magnetic and electric field is given by,

$$v_{Lorentz} = F_{electric} + F_{magnetic}$$
$$= q\,[E + \mathbf{v} \times \mathbf{B}]$$

11. Force on a Current-Carrying Conductor in a Uniform Magnetic Field

Each electron of the wire experiences an average magnetic force $|e\,\mathbf{v}_d \times \mathbf{B}|$, where e is electronic charge, $\mathbf{v}_d$ is drift velocity and **B** is magnetic field. Total force on the wire can be calculated by summing all the forces on all electrons of a wire of length l or due to current by that number of electrons is given by

$$d\mathbf{F} = I d\mathbf{l} \times \mathbf{B}$$
$$\Rightarrow \quad F = I\mathbf{l} \times \mathbf{B} = IlB \sin\theta \hat{n}$$
$$\therefore \quad |F| = IlB \sin\theta$$

If $\theta = 0°$ or $180°$,
then $F = 0$, hence no force.
If $\theta = 90°$, then $F = IlB$,
hence maximum force.

12. Force between Two Parallel Current Carrying Conductors

Magnetic force per unit length between two straight parallel current carrying conductors is given by,

$$f = \frac{F}{l} = \frac{\mu_0}{4\pi} \cdot \frac{2I_1I_2}{r} = \frac{\mu_0 I_1 I_2}{2\pi r}$$

where, I_1 and I_2 are currents in the wires, r is the distance between wires and l is length of each conductor. The force will be of attractive in nature, if currents in the wires are in same direction and it will be repulsive, if these currents are in opposite directions.

13. Torque on a Current Loop Placed in External Field

A loop of cross-sectional area **A**, placed in an external magnetic field **B**, experiences a torque τ, given by

$$\tau = NI\mathbf{A} \times \mathbf{B}$$

where, **A** = area vector
and N = number of turns of loop.

14. Moving Coil Galvanometer

It is a device used to detect the current in an electrical circuit. Its working is based on the principle that a current-carrying loop placed in a uniform magnetic field experiences a torque.

Also, deflecting couple = restoring couple

$$I = \frac{C\theta}{NAB} = K\theta$$

where, $K = \frac{C}{NAB}$ = galvanometer constant.

- **Current sensitivity** It is the deflection per unit current flowing through a galvanometer, $I_s = \frac{NAB}{C}$

where, C = restoring torque per unit twist,
A = area of loop
and N = number of turns.

- **Voltage sensitivity** It is the deflection per unit voltage of a galvanometer, $V_s = \frac{NAB}{CR}$

where, R = resistance.

- **Ammeter** It is an instrument used to measure the current in electrical circuits directly in ampere (A).

Conversion of Galvanometer into an Ammeter

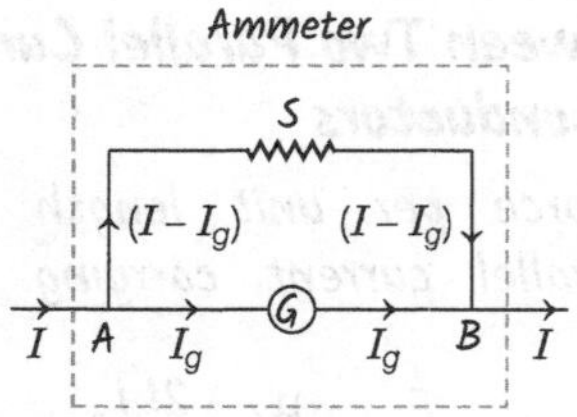

A galvanometer can be converted into an ammeter by connecting a very low resistance (shunt S) in parallel with galvanometer whose value is given by

$$S = \frac{I_g G}{I - I_g}$$

where, G = resistance of galvanometer,
I_g = current in galvanometer,
I = current in ammeter

- **Voltmeter** It is an instrument used to measure potential difference between two points in electrical circuits directly in volt (V).

Conversion of Galvanometer into a Voltmeter

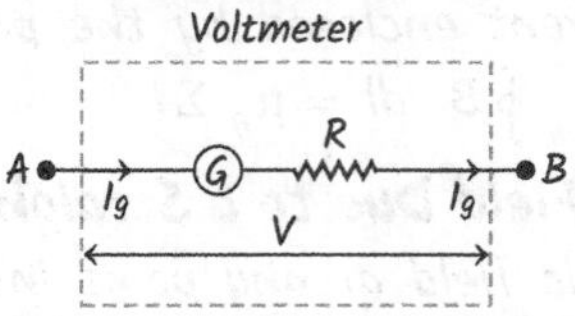

A galvanometer can be converted into voltmeter by connecting a very high resistance R in series with galvanometer which is given by $R = \frac{V}{I_g} - G$

where, I_g = current in galvanometer,
G = resistance of galvanometer and
V = range of voltmeter.

Chapter 5 Magnetism and Matter

1. Bar Magnet

It has two poles similar to the positive and negative charges of an electric dipole.

•N	S•

where, N and S are North and South poles respectively.

2. Magnetic Dipole Moment

The magnetic dipole moment of a magnetic dipole is given by,

$$M = m \times 2l$$

where, m is pole strength and $2l$ is dipole length directed from S to N. SI unit of magnetic dipole moment is $A - m^2$ or J/T.

3. Magnetic Dipole Moment of Revolving Electron

A current loop behaves as a magnetic dipole. The magnetic dipole moment of the loop is given by,

$$\mathbf{M} = NI\mathbf{A}$$

where, I = current through the loop,
$\mathbf{A}$ = area of the loop. (vector)
and N = number of turns in the loop

Magnetic dipole moment of a revolving electron,

$$M = \frac{evr}{2}$$

where, v = speed of electron on a circular path of radius r

or $$M = \frac{e}{2m}L$$

where, L is angular momentum and given as $L = mvr$.

4. Magnetic Field Lines

The magnetic field lines in a magnetic field are those imaginary lines which continuously represent the direction of magnetic field at a point, which is directed along the tangent drawn at the point. These field lines never intersect and *form continuous closed loops. The diagram shows magnetic field lines associated with a bar magnet.*

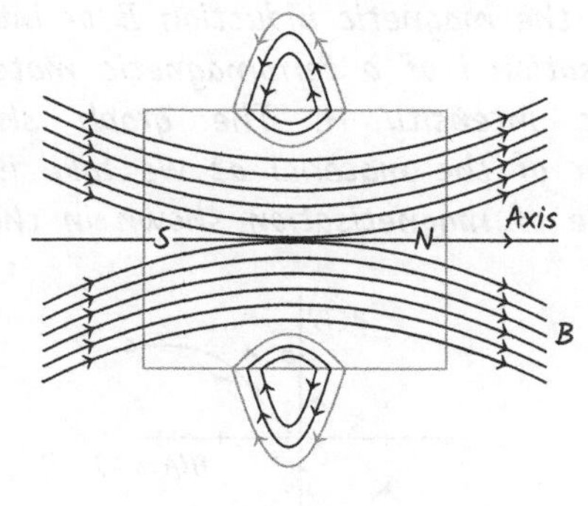

5. Magnetic Field due to a Bar Magnet

(i) On axial point (end-on-position)

$$B = \frac{\mu_0}{4\pi} \frac{2\,Mr}{(r^2 - l^2)^2} \approx \frac{\mu_0}{4\pi} \cdot \frac{2M}{r^3}$$

[$\because r >> l$]

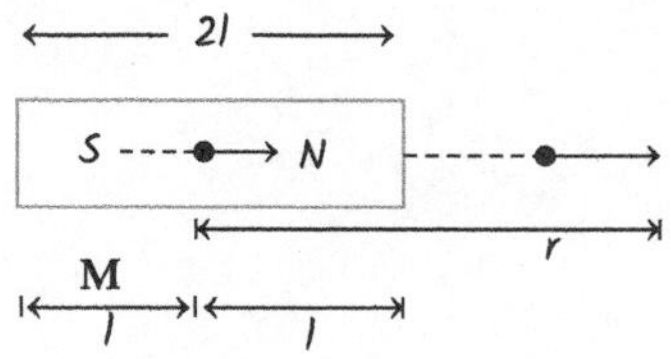

(ii) On equatorial point (broad side-on-position)

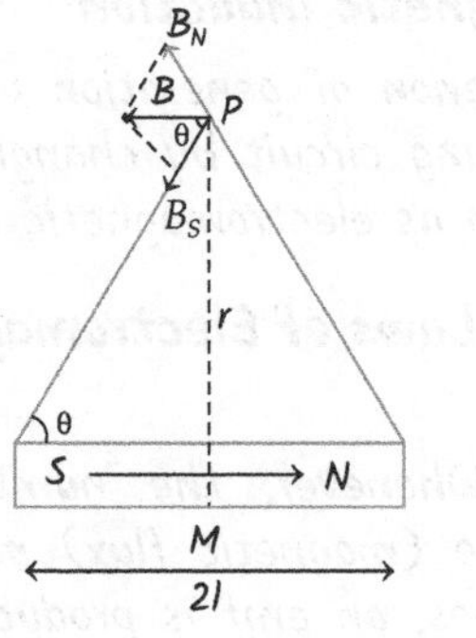

$$\mathbf{B} = \frac{\mu_0}{4\pi} \frac{-\mathbf{M}}{(r^2 + l^2)^{3/2}}$$

$$= \frac{\mu_0}{4\pi} \cdot \frac{(-\mathbf{M})}{r^3}$$

[$\because r >> l$]

6. Important Formulae Regarding Magnetic Dipole

- **Torque** on a magnetic dipole (bar magnet) in uniform magnetic field is

$$\tau = \mathbf{M} \times \mathbf{B}$$
$$= MB \sin\theta$$

where, θ is the angle between **M** and **B**.

7. Diamagnetism

Diamagnetic substances are those substances which have a tendency to move from stronger to the weaker part of the external magnetic field.

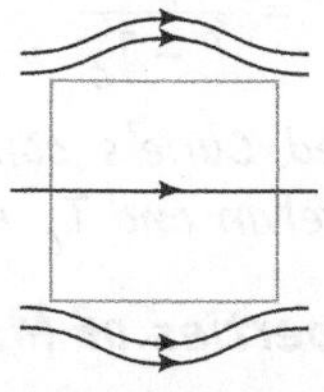

When a bar of diamagnetic material is placed in an external magnetic field, the field lines are repelled or expelled and the field inside the material is reduced.

8. Paramagnetism

The substances which get weakly magnetised in the direction of external field, when placed in an external magnetic field are called paramagnetic substances. These substances have the tendency to move from a region of weak magnetic field to strong magnetic field, i.e., they get weakly attracted to a magnet.

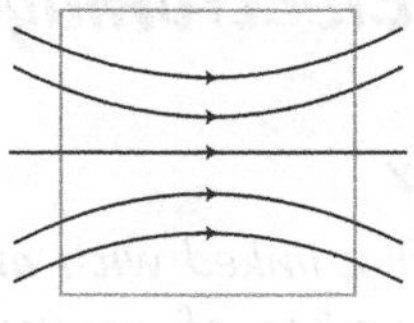

9. Curie's Law

Magnetisation of a paramagnetic material is inversely proportional to the absolute temperature (T),

$$I = C\frac{B_0}{T} \quad \text{or equivalently} \quad \chi_m = \frac{C\mu_0}{T}$$

where, C is called Curie's constant.

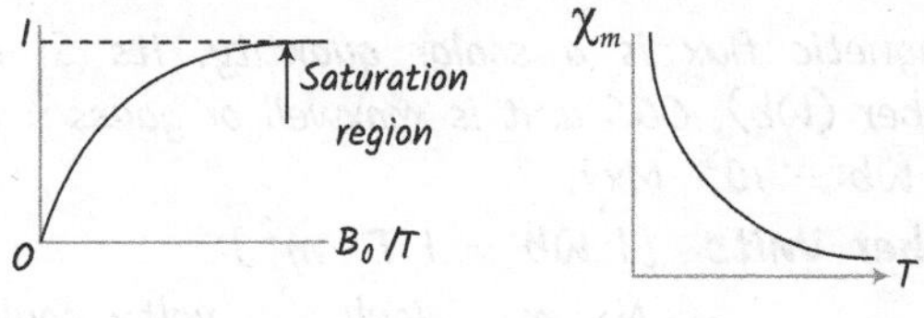

10. Ferromagnetism

The substances which get strongly magnetised when placed in an external magnetic field are called ferromagnetic substances. They have strong tendency to move from a region of weak magnetic field to strong magnetic field, i.e., they get strongly attracted to a magnet.

11. Curie-Weiss Law

This describes the magnetic susceptibility χ_m of a ferromagnet in the paramagnetic region above the Curie point. It is expressed as

$$\chi_m = \frac{C}{T - T_C} \quad [\because T > T_C]$$

where, C is called Curie's constant, T is absolute temperature in kelvin and T_C is Curie temperature.

12. Magnetic Properties of Materials

Materials can be classified as diamagnetic, paramagnetic and ferromagnetic on the basis of susceptibility (χ_m).

Diamagnetic	Paramagnetic	Ferromagnetic
$-1 \le \chi_m < 0$	$0 < \chi_m < \varepsilon$	$\chi_m >> 1$
$0 \le \mu_r < 1$	$1 < \mu_r < 1 + \varepsilon$	$\mu_r >> 1$
$\mu < \mu_0$	$\mu > \mu_0$	$\mu >> \mu_0$

Here, ε is a small positive number introduced to quantify paramagnetic materials.

13. Hysteresis Curve

The hysteresis curve represents the relation between the magnetic induction B or intensity of magnetisation I of a ferromagnetic material with magnetic intensity H. The graph shows the behaviour of the material as we take it through one cycle of magnetisation shown in the figure.

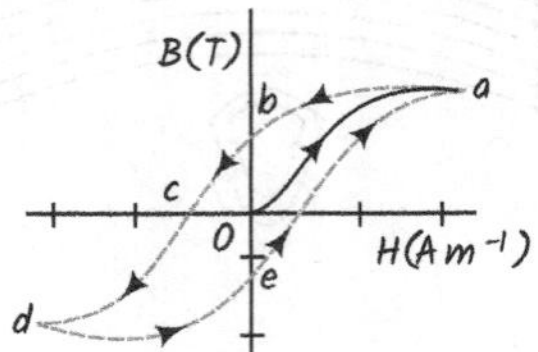

Then, at $H = 0$, $B \neq 0$ (curve ab), the value of B at $H = 0$ is called **retentivity**.

- at $B = 0, H \neq 0$ (Curve bc), the value of H at $B = 0$ is called **coercivity**.

Chapter 6 Electromagnetic Induction

1. Magnetic Flux

The magnetic flux linked with any surface is equal to the total number of magnetic lines of force passing normally through it.

Net flux through surface, $\phi = \oint \mathbf{B} \cdot d\mathbf{A} = BA \cos\theta$, where θ is the angle between area vector and magnetic field vector.

If $\theta = 0°$, then $\phi = BA$ and if $\theta = 90°$, then $\phi = 0$

2. Unit and Dimensions

Magnetic flux is a scalar quantity. Its SI unit is weber (Wb), CGS unit is maxwell or gauss × cm^2, (1 Wb = 10^8 Mx).

Other Units [1 Wb = 1 T-m^2]

$$\text{Tesla} \times m^2 = \frac{N \times m}{A} = \frac{\text{joule}}{\text{ampere}} = \frac{\text{volt} \times \text{coulomb}}{\text{ampere}}$$

$$= \text{volt} \times \text{second} = \text{ohm} \times \text{coulomb}$$

$$= \text{henry} \times \text{ampere}$$

Its dimensional formula is $[\phi] = [ML^2T^{-2}A^{-1}]$.

3. Electromagnetic Induction

The phenomenon of generation of current or emf in a conducting circuit by changing the magnetic flux is known as electromagnetic induction (EMI).

4. Faraday's Laws of Electromagnetic Induction

First law Whenever, the number of magnetic lines of force (magnetic flux) passing through a circuit changes, an emf is produced in the circuit called induced emf. The induced emf persists only as long as there is a change of magnetic flux.

Second law The magnitude of induced emf in a closed loop or circuit, is directly proportional to the rate of change of magnetic flux linked with the closed loop or circuit,

i.e. $$e \propto \frac{\Delta\phi}{\Delta t}$$

$$\Rightarrow \quad e = -N\frac{\Delta\phi}{\Delta t}$$

where, N = total number of turns in the loop.

5. Lenz's Law

The direction of induced emf or induced current is such that it always opposes the cause that produces it.

Note *Lenz's law is a consequence of the law of conservation of energy.*

6. Motional Emf

The potential difference induced in a conductor of length l moving with velocity v, in a direction perpendicular to magnetic field B is given by,

$$\varepsilon = \int (v \times B)\, dl = vBl \sin\theta$$

For maximum value of ε, $\theta = 90°$

$$\therefore \quad \varepsilon_{max} = Bvl$$

7. Fleming's Right Hand Rule

If the thumb, forefinger and middle finger of right hand are held mutually perpendicular, then the forefinger represents the direction of magnetic field, thumb represents the direction of velocity of the conductor then middle finger will represent the direction of induced current.

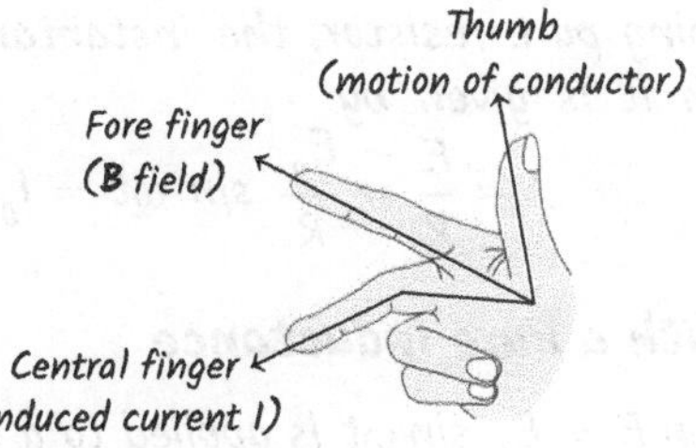

8. Eddy Current

Eddy currents are the currents induced in a bulk pieces of the conductors when the magnetic flux linked with the conductor changes and their flow patterns resemble eddies in water.

9. Self-Induction

Self-inductance of a long solenoid is given by,

$$L = \frac{\mu_0 N^2 A}{l}$$

where, N = *total number of turns,*
A = *area of solenoid,*
l = *length of the solenoid and*
μ_0 = *permeability in free space.*

10. Mutual Induction

The phenomenon of generation of induced emf in secondary coil when current linked with primary coil changes.

Mutual inductance (M) of two closely wound solenoids,

$$M = \frac{\mu_0 N_1 N_2 A}{l}$$

where, N_1 *and* N_2 = *number of turns in primary and secondary solenoids,*
A = *area of smaller solenoid*
and l = *length of solenoid*

SI unit of inductance is henry (H).

$$1 \text{ henry (H)} = 1 \text{ V-s/A or } 1 \text{ Tm}^2/\text{A}.$$

Chapter 7 Alternating Current

1. Direct and Alternating Currents

- *An alternating current or voltage is one, whose magnitude changes continuously with time between zero and a maximum value and whose sense of flow reverses periodically.*
- *When a battery is connected to a circuit, the current moves steadily in only one sense, from positive terminal to negative terminal. This is called a* ***direct current*** *or DC.*

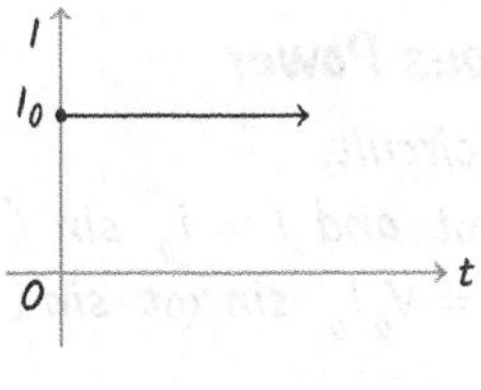

Current/voltage remains constant with time as shown below graphically.

Electric generator and power plants produce alternating current or AC. An alternating current varies sinusoidally with time as shown graphically.

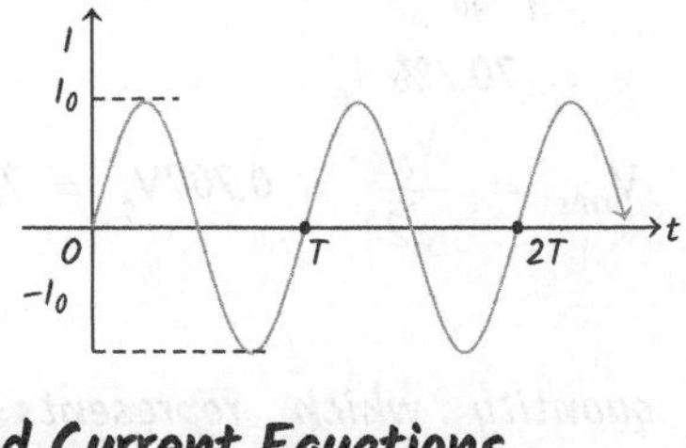

2. EMF and Current Equations

Alternating emf is given by,

$$V = V_0 \sin \omega t = V_0 \sin 2\pi ft$$

$$= V_0 \sin \frac{2\pi}{T} t$$

Similarly, alternating current is given by,

$$I = I_0 \sin \omega t = I_0 \sin \frac{2\pi}{T} t$$

where, I and V = instantaneous values of current and voltage respectively,

I_0 and V_0 = peak (maximum) values of current and voltage, respectively,

f = frequency in hertz,

T = time period,

ω = angular frequency (in rad/s) and

t = time

3. Peak Value

Peak Value (i_0 or V_0) The maximum value of alternating quantity (i or V) is called its peak value or amplitude.

4. Mean Square Value

Mean Square Value ($\bar{V}^2$ or $\bar{i}^2$) The average of squares of instantaneous values in one cycle is called mean square value. It is always positive for one complete cycle.

e.g. $\bar{V}^2 = \frac{i}{T}\int_0^T V^2 dt = \frac{V_0^2}{2}$ or $\bar{i}^2 = \frac{i_0^2}{2}$

5. Root Mean Square

Root Mean Square (rms) value The root of mean square of voltage or current in an AC circuit for one complete cycle is called root mean square (rms) value. It is denoted by V_{rms} or I_{rms}.

$$I_{\text{rms}} = \sqrt{\frac{i_1^2 + i_2^2 + \cdots + i_n^2}{n}} = \sqrt{\bar{i}^2}$$

$$= \sqrt{\frac{\int_0^T i^2 dt}{\int_0^T dt}} = \frac{i_0}{\sqrt{2}} = 0.707\, i_0$$

$$= 70.7\%\; i_0$$

Similarly, $V_{rms} = \frac{V_0}{\sqrt{2}} = 0.707V_0 = 70.7\%$ of V_0

6. Phase

Physical quantity which represents both the instantaneous value and direction of alternating quantity at any instant is called its phase. It is a dimensionless quantity and its unit is radian.

7. Phasor

A quantity which varies sinusoidally with time can be represented as projection of a rotating vector is called a phasor.

This is rotating vector, relating with angular velocity (ω) about the origin.

8. Phase Difference or Phase Constant

The difference between the phase of current and voltage is called phase difference. If alternating voltage and current are given by, $V = V_0 \sin(\omega t + \phi_1)$ and $I = I_0 \sin(\omega t + \phi_2)$, then phase difference, $\phi = (\phi_1 - \phi_2)$ related to current or $\phi = (\phi_2 - \phi_1)$ related to voltage.

9. Time Difference

If the phase difference between alternating current and voltage is ϕ, then time difference between them is given as, $TD = \frac{T}{2\pi} \times \phi$

10. AC with a Pure Resistance

When $E = E_0 \sin \omega t$ is applied to a circuit containing pure resistor, the instantaneous current through it is given by

$$I = \frac{E}{R} = \frac{E_0}{R} \sin \omega t = I_0 \sin \omega t$$

11. AC with a Pure Inductance

(i) When $E = E_0 \sin \omega t$ is applied to a circuit containing pure inductor, the instantaneous current in pure inductive load is given by

$$I = I_0 \sin\left(\omega t - \frac{\pi}{2}\right)$$

(ii) Inductive reactance, $X_L = \omega L = 2\pi f L$.

12. AC with a Pure Capacitance

(i) Instantaneous current in a circuit containing pure capacitance is given by $I = I_0 \sin\left(\omega t + \frac{\pi}{2}\right)$, when applied AC voltage is $E = \sin \omega t$

(ii) Capacitive reactance, $X_C = \frac{I}{C\omega} = \frac{I}{2\pi f C}$.

13. Instantaneous Power

Suppose in a circuit,

$V = V_0 \sin \omega t$ and $I = I_0 \sin(\omega t + \phi)$, then

$P_{inst} = VI = V_0 I_0 \sin \omega t \sin(\omega t + \phi)$.

14. Average Power or True Power

The average of instantaneous power in an AC circuit over a full cycle is called average power. Its unit is watt.

$$P_{av} = V_{rms} \cdot I_{rms} \cos\phi = I_{rms}^2 Z \cos\phi$$

15. Power Factor

(i) It may be defined as cosine of the angle of lag or lead (i.e. $\cos\phi$).

(ii) It is also defined as the ratio of resistance and impedance $\left(\text{i.e. } \frac{R}{Z}\right)$.

(iii) For a purely resistive circuit,

$$\phi = 0° \Rightarrow \cos\phi = \cos 0° = 1$$

$$\therefore P_{resistor} = V_{rms} I_{rms}$$

(iv) For a pure inductor and pure capacitor, $\phi = \frac{\pi}{2}$ and $-\frac{\pi}{2}$, respectively.

$$\Rightarrow \cos\phi = \cos\frac{\pi}{2} = 0$$

$$\therefore P_{inductor} \text{ or } P_{capacitor} = V_{rms} I_{rms} \cos\frac{\pi}{2} = 0$$

In an inductor or capacitor, power dissipated is zero and the current flowing through inductor or capacitor is called **wattless current.**

16. Series R-L Circuit

(i) Applied voltage (V)	$V = \sqrt{V_R^2 + V_L^2}$
(ii) Impedance (Z)	$Z = \sqrt{R^2 + X_L^2} = \sqrt{R^2 + \omega^2 L^2}$ $[\because X_L = \omega L]$
(iii) Current (i)	$I = I_0 \sin(\omega t - \phi)$
(iv) Peak current (i_0)	$I_0 = \frac{V_0}{Z} = \frac{V_0}{\sqrt{R^2 + X_L^2}} = \frac{V_0}{\sqrt{R^2 + 4\pi^2 f^2 L^2}}$
(v) Phase difference (ϕ)	$\phi = \tan^{-1}\left(\frac{X_L}{R}\right) = \tan^{-1}\left(\frac{\omega L}{R}\right)$
(vi) Power factor	$\cos\phi = \frac{R}{\sqrt{R^2 + X_L^2}}$

17. Series R-C Circuit

(i) Applied voltage (V)	$V = \sqrt{V_R^2 + V_C^2}$
(ii) Impedance (Z)	$Z = \sqrt{R^2 + X_C^2} = \sqrt{R^2 + \left(\frac{1}{\omega C}\right)^2}$ $\left[\because X_C = \frac{1}{\omega C}\right]$
(iii) Current (I)	$I = I_0 \sin(\omega t + \phi)$
(iv) Peak Current (i_0)	$I_0 = \frac{V_0}{Z} = \frac{V_0}{\sqrt{R^2 + X_C^2}} = \frac{V_0}{\sqrt{R^2 + \frac{1}{4\pi^2 f^2 C^2}}}$
(v) Phase difference (ϕ)	$\phi = \tan^{-1}\left(\frac{X_C}{R}\right) = \tan^{-1}\left(\frac{1}{\omega CR}\right)$
(vi) Power factor	$\cos\phi = \frac{R}{\sqrt{R^2 + X_C^2}}$

18. Series L-C-R Circuit

(i) For an L-C-R circuit,

$$\tan\phi = \frac{(X_L - X_C)}{R} \text{ and}$$

$$\phi = \tan^{-1}\frac{(X_L - X_C)}{R}$$

$$\Rightarrow \cos\phi = \text{power factor} = \frac{R}{Z}$$

$$= \frac{R}{\sqrt{R^2 + \left(\omega L - \frac{1}{\omega C}\right)^2}}$$

$$\text{So, } P_{L\text{-}C\text{-}R} = V_{rms} \cdot I_{rms} \cos\phi$$

(ii) For an L-C-R circuit at resonance,

$$X_L = X_C \Rightarrow \phi = 0°$$

Power factor, $\cos\phi = 1$

$$\therefore P_{L\text{-}C\text{-}R\,(resonance)} = V_{rms} I_{rms}$$

19. Resonance in L-C-R Circuit

(i) At resonance	$X_L = X_C$ $Z = R$
(ii) Power factor	$\cos\phi = \frac{R}{Z} = \frac{R}{R} = 1$

(iii) Angular frequency at resonance	$\omega = \frac{1}{\sqrt{LC}}$
(vi) Quality factor (Q- factor) or sharpness of Resonance	Q – Factor $= \frac{\omega_0}{2\Delta\omega} = \frac{1}{\omega_0 CR} = \frac{\omega_0 L}{R}$ $= \frac{1}{R}\sqrt{\frac{L}{C}}$ Q – factor $= 2\pi \times \frac{\text{Maximum energy stored}}{\text{Energy dissipated}}$

20. AC Generator

A generator produces electrical energy from mechanical work, just the opposite of what a motor does.

Principle An AC generator is based on the phenomenon of electromagnetic induction which states that whenever magnetic flux linked with a conductor (or coil) changes, an emf is induced in the coil.

If e is the emf induced in the coil, then

$\varepsilon = NBA\,\omega \sin \omega t$

where, N = number of turns in the coil,
B = strength of magnetic field,
A = area of each turn of the coil,
ω = angular velocity of rotation and
$\varepsilon = \varepsilon_0 \sin \omega t$

Here, $\varepsilon_0 = NBA\omega$ = peak value of emf.

21. Transformer

It is a device which is used for changing the voltage level in AC circuits without changing the frequency of AC voltage. It is based on the principle of mutual induction.

Type of transformer

(i) **Step-up transformer** It converts low alternating voltage into high alternating voltage.

(ii) **Step-down transformer** It converts high alternating voltage into low alternating voltage.

For ideal transformer,

$$P_{out} = P_{in}$$

or $$V_s i_s = V_p i_p$$

$$\Rightarrow \quad \frac{V_s}{V_p} = \frac{i_p}{i_s}$$

where, V_s = voltage across secondary coil,
V_p = applied (input) voltage to primary coil,
i_p = current in primary coil and
i_s = current in secondary coil .

22. Efficiency of Transformer

It is defined as the ratio of output to the input power. It is expressed as

$$\eta\,(\%) = \frac{P_{out}}{P_{in}} \times 100 = \frac{V_s i_s}{V_p i_p} \times 100$$

In practice, η can be achieved from 90% to 99%.

23. Loss of Energy in Transformer

(i) **Flux leakage** There is always some leakage of flux that is not all of the flux due to primary passes through the secondary. This is due to poor design of the core or the air gaps in the core. It can be reduced by winding the primary and secondary coils one over the other.

(ii) **Resistance of the windings** The wire used for the windings has some resistance and so, energy is also lost due to heat (I^2R) produced in the wire. In high current, low voltage windings, energy losses are minimised by using thick wire.

(iii) **Hysteresis** The magnetisation of the core is repeatedly reversed by an alternating magnetic field. The resulting expenditure of energy in the core appears as heat and is kept to a minimum by using a magnetic material which has a low hysteresis loss.

Chapter 8 Electromagnetic Waves

1. Electromagnetic Waves

Electromagnetic waves are the transverse waves which are produced due to the **electric field (E)** and **magnetic field (B)** changing sinusoidally and propagating through space such that the two fields are perpendicular to each other and also perpendicular to the direction of wave propagation.

2. Displacement Current

It is that current which comes into play in a region where the electric field and electric flux (ϕ_E) are changing with time,

i.e., $$I_d = \varepsilon_0 \frac{d\phi_E}{dt}$$

where, ε_0 = permittivity of free space.

3. Transverse nature of EM waves

Since, the electric and magnetic fields in an electromagnetic wave are perpendicular to each other and also to the direction of wave propagation, hence an electromagnetic wave is transverse in nature.

4. Electromagnetic Spectrum

The orderly arrangement of EM wave in increasing or decreasing order of wavelength of frequency is called electromagnetic spectrum. The range varies from 10^{-12} m to 10^{-1} m, i.e., from X-rays to radio waves.

5. Different Types of Electromagnetic Waves

Type	Wavelength range	Production	Detection
Radio wave	>0.1 m	Rapid acceleration and deceleration of electrons in aerials	Receiver's aerials
Microwave	0.1m to 1 mm	Klystron valve or magnetron valve	Point contact diodes
Infrared wave	1 mm to 700 nm	Vibration of atoms and molecules	Thermopiles bolometer, infrared photographic film
Light	700 nm to 400 nm	Electrons in atom emit light when they move from higher energy level to a lower energy level	The eye, photocells, photographic film
Ultraviolet rays	400 nm to 1 nm	Inner shell electrons in atoms moving from one energy level to a lower level	Photocells, photographic film
X-rays	1 nm to 10^{-3} nm	X-ray tubes or inner shell electrons	Photographic film, geiger tubes, ionisation chamber
Gamma rays	<10^{-3} nm	Radioactive decay of the nucleus	Compton scattering, gamma-ray spectrum

Chapter 9 Ray Optics and Optical Instruments

1. Laws of Reflection

According to these laws,

(i) the incident ray, reflected ray and the normal, all lie in the same plane, and

(ii) the angle of incidence, $\angle i$ = angle of reflection, $\angle r$.

2. Important Points

(i) Light propagates in straight line in homogeneous media.

(ii) Rays do not disturb each other upon intersection.

(iii) Rays retrace their path when their direction is reversed (i.e., when they are incident normally).

3. Mirror Formula

$$\frac{1}{v} + \frac{1}{u} = \frac{1}{f}$$

where u, v and f represent object distance, image distance and focal length, respectively.

4. Focal Length of Mirror

$$f = \frac{\text{Radius of Curvature}}{2} = \frac{R}{2}$$

5. Linear Magnification

Magnification, $m = \frac{h_i}{h_o} = -\frac{v}{u} = \frac{f}{u-f}$

where, h_i = height of image and

h_o = height of object.

6. Magnification (m)

It is negative for real image and positive for virtual image.

7. Refraction

The phenomenon of changing the path of light as it goes from one transparent medium to another is called refraction.

8. Laws of Refraction

Two laws of refraction are given below :

(i) The incident ray, refracted ray and the normal to the refracting surface at the point of incidence, all lie in the same plane.

(ii) The ratio of the sine of the angle of incidence to the sine of the angle of refraction is constant for the two given media. This constant is denoted by μ and is called the relative refractive index.

$${}_1\mu_2 = \frac{\sin i}{\sin r}$$

where, ${}_1\mu_2$ is refractive index of the second medium with respect to first medium.

9. Refractive index

$$\mu = \frac{\text{Speed of light in the vacuum}}{\text{Speed of light in the material}} = \frac{c}{v}$$

10. Refraction Through Parallel Multiple Media

$${}_1\mu_3 = {}_1\mu_2 \times {}_2\mu_3$$

where, ${}_q\mu_p$ = refractive index of medium p with respect to medium q.

11. Laws of Refraction at a Plane Surface

$$\frac{\sin i}{\sin r} = \frac{v_1}{v_2} = \mu$$

This is also kown as Snell's law.

12. Critical Angle (i_c)

$$\mu = \frac{1}{\sin i_c}$$

where, μ = refractive index of denser medium, when rarer medium is air.

13. Refraction of Light Through a Prism

$$\mu = \frac{\sin\left(\frac{\delta_m + A}{2}\right)}{\sin\frac{A}{2}}$$

where, δ_m = angle of minimum deviation through the prism,

μ = refractive index of material of prism

and A = angle of prism.

14. Dispersion

The phenomenon of splitting of light into its component colour is known as dispersion.

- Angular dispersion, $\theta = (\mu_v - \mu_r) A$
- Dispersive power, $\omega = \frac{(\mu_v - \mu_r)}{\mu_y - 1}$

15. Total Internal Reflection

When a ray of light travelling from denser medium to rarer medium is incident at the interface of two medium at an angle greater than the critical angle for the two media, the ray is totally reflected back to the denser medium. This phenomenon is called total internal reflection.

It occurs only when angle of incidence in denser medium is greater (not equal) than critical angle, i.e., $i > i_c$.

Optical fibre, mirage, sparkling of diamond, totally reflecting prism, etc. work on the principle of total internal reflection.

16. Refraction Formula

(i) For refraction by convex or concave spherical refracting surface,

$$\frac{n_2}{v} - \frac{n_1}{u} = \frac{n_2 - n_1}{R}$$

where n_1 & n_2 are refractive indices of rarer & denser medium respectively and u, v and R are to be taken with their proper signs.

(ii) When refraction takes place from denser to rarer medium, then

$$\frac{n_1}{v} - \frac{n_2}{u} = \frac{n_1 - n_2}{R}$$

17. Lens Maker's Formula

It is given by, $\frac{1}{f} = (\mu - 1)\left(\frac{1}{R_1} - \frac{1}{R_2}\right)$

where, μ is refractive index of material of lens w.r.t. surrounding media and R_1, R_2 is the radii of curvature of two surfaces.

18. Thin Lens Formula

It is given as, $\frac{1}{v} - \frac{1}{u} = \frac{1}{f}$

where, v = image distance,
u = object distance
and f = focal length of the lens.

19. Power of a Lens

$$P = \frac{1}{f(\text{in metre})}$$

where, f is focal length.
The SI unit of power of lens is dioptre (D).
Note Power of convex lens is positive and negative of concave lens.

20. Linear Magnification Produced by a Lens

$$m = \frac{\text{Height of image } (I)}{\text{Height of object } (O)} = \frac{v}{u}$$

21. Combination of Thin Lenses in Contact

Equivalent power of the system,

$$P = P_1 + P_2$$

Combined focal length is given by

$$\frac{1}{f} = \frac{1}{f_1} + \frac{1}{f_2}$$

22. Magnification by Combination of Lenses

$$m = m_1 \times m_2$$

where, m_1 and m_2 are linear magnification of lenses.

23. (i) Optical Instruments

(a) Simple microscope (Magnifying glass)

It is a single convex lens of small focal length.

If the image is formed at near point of eye, then

$$m = \left(1 + \frac{D}{f}\right)$$

But, if the image is formed at infinity, then

$$m = \frac{D}{f}.$$

(b) Compound microscope

It consists of an objective lens of small focal length f_0 and small aperture and eyepiece of small focal length f_e and large aperture.

I. If m_o and m_e be the magnifications produced by objective and eye piece respectively, then total magnification of microscope,

$$m = m_o \times m_e$$

II. If final image is formed at near point (D) of eye, then

$$m = -\frac{v_o}{u_o}\left(1 + \frac{D}{f_e}\right)$$

or

$$m = -\frac{L}{f_o}\left(1 + \frac{D}{f_e}\right) \text{ (approx.)}$$

III. If final image is formed at infinity, then

$$m = -\frac{v_o}{u_o} \cdot \frac{D}{f_e} = -\frac{L}{f_o} \cdot \frac{D}{f_e} \text{ (approx.)}$$

(ii) Astronomical telescope

(a) Refracting telescope

I. It consists of an objective lens of large focal length f_o and large aperture. The eye piece consists of a convex lens of small aperture and small focal length f_e.

II. Distance between the two lenses is maintained as

$$L = f_o + f_e$$

III. In normal adjustment, the final image is formed at infinity and magnifying power of telescope is given by

$$m = -\frac{f_o}{f_e}$$

IV. In practical adjustment, the final image is formed at near point of the observer's eye.

In this arrangement, $m = -\frac{f_o}{f_e}\left(1 + \frac{f_e}{D}\right)$

(b) ***Reflecting telescope***

I. It consists of an objective which is a large paraboloid concave mirror of maximum possible focal length f_o and the eye piece is a convex lens of small focal length and small aperture.

Magnifying power, $m = -\frac{f_o}{f_e}$

II. **Reflecting type telescope** is considered superior as it is free from spherical and chromatic aberrations, it is easy to install and maintain and can produce image of greater intensity.

Chapter 10 Wave Optics

1. Wavefront

The locus of all those particles which are vibrating in the same phase at any instant is called wavefront. Thus, wavefront is a surface having same phase of vibrating particles at any instant at every point on it.

2. The Shape of Wavefront due to a

(i) point source is spherical,

(ii) line source is cylindrical and

(iii) source at infinity is plane.

3. The direction of rays are always perpendicular to the wavefront along the direction of propagation of wave.

4. Huygens' Principle

Huygens' principle is essentially a geometrical construction which gives the shape of the wavefront in a later time.

According to Huygens' principle

(i) Each point on the given wavefront (called primary wavefront) is the source of a secondary disturbance (called secondary wavelets) and the wavelets emanating from these points spread out in all directions with the same speed as that of the wave.

(ii) A surface touching these secondary wavelets, tangentially in the forward direction at any instant gives the new wavefront at that instant. This is called secondary wavefront.

5. Interference

The phenomenon of redistribution of energy in the region of superposition of waves is called **interference.** The points of maximum intensity in the regions of superposition of waves are said to be in **constructive interference** whereas the points of minimum intensity are said to be in **destructive interference.**

(i) **Conditions for constructive interference**

If initial phase difference is zero, then the necessary conditions for constructive interference of waves are

(a) phase difference $= (2n)\pi$, where $n = 0, 1, 2, 3, \ldots$

(b) path difference $= n\lambda$, where $n = 0, 1, 2, 3\ldots$

(ii) **Conditions for destructive interference**

Assuming, initial phase difference = 0

Necessary conditions for destructive interference of waves are

(a) phase difference $= (2n-1)\pi$, where $n = 1, 2, 3, \ldots$

(b) path difference $= (2n-1)\frac{\lambda}{2}$, where $n = 1, 2, 3, \ldots$

6. Young's Double Slit Experiment

(i) Separation of nth order bright fringe from central fringe is given by

$$y_n = \frac{Dn\lambda}{d}, \text{ where } n = 1, 2, 3, 4, \ldots$$

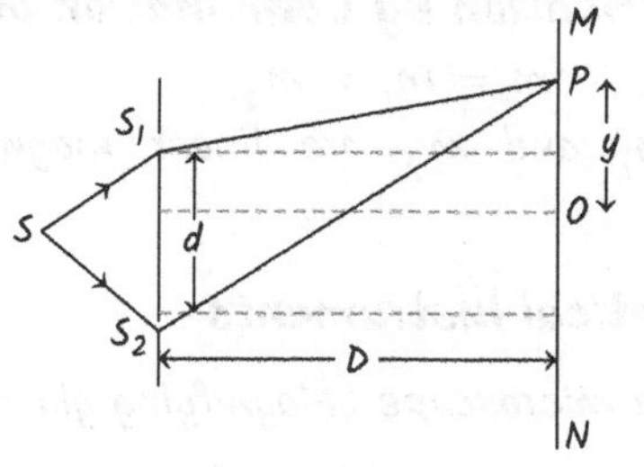

(ii) Separation of nth order dark fringe from central fringe is given by

$$y_n = (2n - 1)\frac{D\lambda}{2d}$$

where, $n = 1, 2, 3, 4$ ......

(iii) **Fringe width** It is the separation between two consecutive bright or dark fringes. It is given by

$$\beta = \frac{D\lambda}{d}$$

and angular fringe width is given by,

$$\theta = \frac{\beta}{D} = \frac{\lambda}{d}.$$

7. Diffraction of Light at a Single Slit

The width of central maxima is the distance between the first secondary minima on either side of the central bright fringe.

- Angular width of central maxima = $2\lambda / d$
- Linear width of central maxima, $\beta_0 = \frac{2D\lambda}{d}$
- Angular width of secondary maxima or minima = λ / d
- Linear width of secondary maxima or minima = $D\lambda / d$

Chapter 11 Dual Nature of Radiation and Matter

1. Quantisation of Radiation

According to the Planck's photon hypothesis, the electromagnetic radiation comes in the form of discrete particles called photons. This is called quantisation of radiation.

Energy of photon, $E = h\nu$

where, h = Planck's constant = 6.33×10^{-34} J - s

and ν = frequency of electromagnetic radiation.

2. Photoelectric Effect

It is the phenomenon of emission of electron from the surface of metals when light radiation of suitable frequency is incident on them.

3. Work function

Work function, $\phi = h\nu_0 = \frac{hc}{\lambda_0}$

where, ν_0 and λ_0 are the threshold frequency and threshold wavelength, respectively.

Work Function of Some Metals

Metal	Work function, ϕ_0 (eV)	Metal	Work function, ϕ_0 (eV)
Cs	2.14	Al	4.28
K	2.30	Hg	4.49
Na	2.75	Cu	4.65
Ca	3.20	Ag	4.70
Mo	4.17	Ni	5.15
Pt	4.25	Pt	5.65

From the above table, it can be concluded that, the work function of platinum is the highest (ϕ_0 = 5.65 eV), while it is the lowest for caesium (ϕ_0 = 2.14 eV).

4. Cut-off Potential/Stopping Potential

$$KE_{max} = eV_0 \Rightarrow \frac{1}{2} mv_{max}^2 = eV_0$$

where, v_{max} = maximum velocity of emitted electron and V_0 = cut-off potential.

5. Cut-off Frequency/Threshold Frequency

The minimum frequency of the light which can emit photoelectrons from a photosensitive material is called threshold frequency or cut-off frequency of that material. It is denoted by ν_0.

6. Cut-off Wavelength/Threshold Wavelength

The maximum wavelength of light which can emit photoelectrons from a material is called threshold wavelength or cut-off wavelength of that material. It is denoted by λ_0.

7. Einstein's Photoelectric Equation

Einstein explained photoelectric effect on the basis of Planck's photon hypothesis (i.e. energy falls on a metallic surface in the form of discrete packets each having energy $h\nu$). According to Einstein's photoelectric equation,

$$K_{max} = h\nu - \phi$$

where, $h\nu$ = energy of photon, ϕ = work function and K_{max} = maximum kinetic energy of emitted electrons.

8. de-Broglie Wavelength

$$\lambda = \frac{h}{p}$$

where, p is the momentum of the particle and h is Planck's constant.

(i) According to Planck's quantum theory, the energy of the photon is $E = h\nu = \frac{hc}{\lambda}$.

(ii) If a material particle of mass (m) is moving with velocity (v), then momentum of the particle, $p = mv$ and the equation becomes

$$\lambda = \frac{h}{p} = \frac{h}{mv} = \frac{h}{\sqrt{2mE_K}}$$

where, E_K = kinetic energy of the particle.

(iii) If an electron is accelerated through a potential difference V, then wave associated with the electron is given by $\lambda = \frac{h}{\sqrt{2meV}}$

where, e = electron charge

and m = mass of electron.

9. Relation between de-Broglie Wavelength (λ) and Temperature (T)

From Kinetic theory of matter, the average kinetic energy of a particle at a given temperature T (kelvin) is given by $K = \frac{3}{2} k_B T$

where, k_B = Boltzmann constant.

If a particle of mass m is moving with velocity v, then its kinetic energy, $K = \frac{1}{2} mv^2$

Momentum of particle is

$$p = mv = \sqrt{2mK}$$
$$= \sqrt{2m \times \frac{3}{2} k_B T} = \sqrt{3mk_B T}$$

de-Broglie wavelength,

$$\lambda = \frac{h}{p} = \frac{h}{\sqrt{3mk_B T}}$$

10. de-Broglie Wavelength of an Electron

de-Broglie wavelength of an electron accelerated by a potential difference V is given by

$$\lambda = \frac{h}{\sqrt{2eVm_e}}$$

where, m_e = mass of electron.

Chapter 12 Atoms

1. Atoms

The smallest invisible particle of an element that can exist is known as atom. Atoms consist of a small dense nucleus of protons and neutrons surrounded by revolving electrons in different orbits. Every atom is a sphere of radius of the order 10^{-10} m. Atom is electrically neutral and contains equal amount of positive and negative charges.

2. α-particles Scattering Experiment by Rutherford

This experiment was suggested by Rutherford in 1911 as given in the figure.

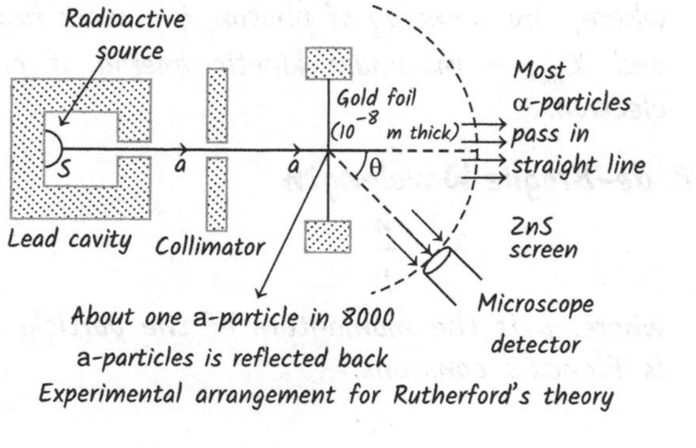

Experimental arrangement for Rutherford's theory

In this experiment, H. Geiger and E. Marsden had taken $^{214}_{83}Bi$ as a source for α-particles. A collimated beam of α-particles of energy 5.5 MeV was allowed to fall on 2.1×10^{-7} m thick gold foil. The scattered α-particles were observed through a rotatable detector consisting of a zinc sulphide screen and a microscope.

These scattered α-particles produced scintillations on the zinc sulphide screen. Now, these scintillations were counted at different angles from the direction of incident beam.

3. Observations from the Experiment

Rutherford made following observations from his experiment

(i) Most of the α-particles pass through the gold foil without any appreciable deflection.

(ii) Only about 0.14% of the incident α-particles scatter by more than 1°.

(iii) About one α-particle in every 8000 α-particles deflects by more than 90°.

(iv) The number of α-particles scattered per unit area $N(\theta)$ at scattering angle θ varies inversely as $\sin^4(\theta/2)$, i.e., $N(\theta) \propto \frac{1}{\sin^4(\theta/2)}$

4. Conclusions from the Experiment

On the basis of his experiment, Rutherford concluded that

(i) Atom has a lot of empty space and practically, the entire mass of the atom is confined to an extremely small central core called nucleus whose size is about 10^{-15} m to 10^{-14} m.

(ii) Scattering of α-particles (positively charged) is due to the Coulomb's law for electrostatic force of repulsion between the positive charge of nucleus and α-particles.

(iii) Distance between electrons and nucleus is 10^4 to 10^5 times the size of the nucleus itself.

(iv) More is the distance of the velocity vector of an α-particle from the central line of the nucleus, lesser is the angle of scattering.

5. Rutherford's Model of Atom

The essential features of Rutherford's nuclear model of the atom or planetary model of the atoms are as follows

(i) Every atom consists of a central core, called the atomic nucleus in which the entire positive charge and almost entire mass of the atom is concentrated.

(ii) The size of nucleus is of the order of 10^{-15} m which is very small as compared to the size of the atom which is of the order of 10^{-10} m.

(iii) The atomic nucleus is surrounded by certain number of electrons. Atom is electrically neutral, so the total negative charge of electrons surroundings the nucleus is equal to total positive charge on the nucleus.

(iv) These electrons revolve around the nucleus in various circular orbits as the planets do around the sun. The centripetal force required by electrons for revolution is provided by the electrostatic force of attraction between the electrons and nucleus.

6. Bohr's Model of Atom

Bohr's combined classical and quantum concepts and gave his models on the basis of three postulates

(i) As long as electron revolves in an atom, it does not radiate any energy. So, these orbits are called stationary states and they have fixed energy.

(ii) Electron can revolve only in those orbits in which its angular momentum is integral multiple of $h/2\pi$, where h is the Planck's constant ($h = 6.63 \times 10^{-34}$ J – s)

(iii) When an electron makes a transition from one energy level to another, a photon equal to energy of the difference of two levels is emitted.

7. The Equation of Energy Difference from Bohr's Model

The energy of the emitted photon ΔE, when it jumps from higher energy level n_2 to lower energy level n_1 is given by

$$\Delta E = E_2 - E_1 = R_H hc \left(\frac{1}{n_1^2} - \frac{1}{n_2^2} \right)$$

where, R_H = Rydberg constant, n_1 = lower energy orbit and n_2 = higher energy orbit.

8. Radius of Different Orbits

$$r_n = \frac{\varepsilon_0 n^2 h^2}{2\pi m e^2}$$

where, r_n = radius of nth orbit,
h = Planck's constant,
m = mass of an electron,
e = charge on an electron and
Z = 1 (for hydrogen atom)

9. Velocity of Electron

The orbital velocity of electron is given by

$$v_n = \frac{Ze^2}{2\varepsilon_0 nh}$$

10. Wavelength

If an electron jumps from higher energy state n_2 to lower energy state n_1, then corresponding wavelength of emitted radiation is given by

$$\frac{1}{\lambda} = R_H \left(\frac{1}{n_1^2} - \frac{1}{n_2^2} \right)$$

11. Frequency of Electron

Orbital frequency is given by,

$$f_n = \left(\frac{me^4}{4\varepsilon_0^2 h^3} \right) \frac{1}{n^3}$$

$$= \frac{f_0}{n^3}$$

12. Energy Level

The total energy of the orbital electron is

$$E_n = \frac{-me^4}{8\varepsilon_0^2 n^2 h^2}$$

For hydrogen atom, if $n = 1$,

$$E_1 = -13.6 \text{ eV}$$

So, $$E_n = \frac{-13.6}{n^2} \text{ eV}$$

13. Line Spectra of Hydrogen Atom

Series	Found in	Wavelength Formula	Value of n_1 and n_2
Lyman Series	Ultraviolet region	$\frac{1}{\lambda} = R\left(\frac{1}{1^2} - \frac{1}{n_2^2}\right)$	$n_1 = 1$, $n_2 = 2, 3, 4, 5...$
Balmer Series	Visible spectrum	$\frac{1}{\lambda} = R\left(\frac{1}{2^2} - \frac{1}{n_2^2}\right)$	$n_1 = 2$, $n_2 = 3, 4, 5, 6...$
Paschen Series	Infrared region	$\frac{1}{\lambda} = R\left(\frac{1}{3^2} - \frac{1}{n_2^2}\right)$	$n_1 = 3$, $n_2 = 4, 5, 6, 7...$
Brackett Series	Infrared region	$\frac{1}{\lambda} = R\left(\frac{1}{4^2} - \frac{1}{n_2^2}\right)$	$n_1 = 4$, $n_2 = 5, 6, 7, 8...$
Pfund Series	Infrared region	$\frac{1}{\lambda} = R\left(\frac{1}{5^2} - \frac{1}{n_2^2}\right)$	$n_1 = 5$, $n_2 = 6, 7, 8, 9...$

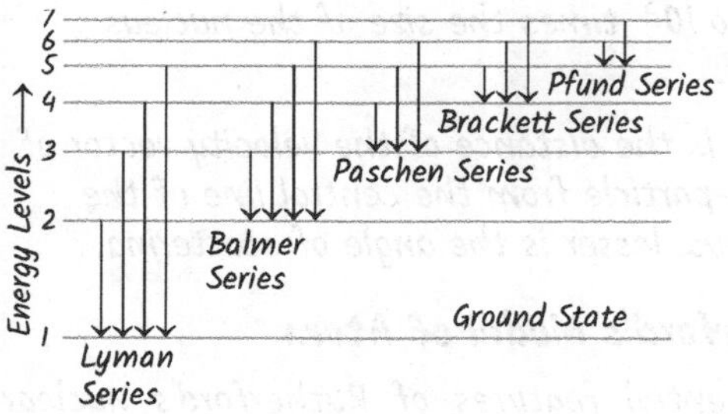

Chapter 13 Nuclei

1. Nucleus

In every atom, the positive charge and mass are densely concentrated at the central core of the atom which forms its nucleus.

The radius of the nucleus is smaller than the radius of an atom by a factor of 10^4. This means that the volume of a nucleus is about 10^{-12} times the volume of the atom.

2. Atomic Mass Unit (amu)

The unit of mass used to express mass of an atom is called atomic mass unit.

i.e., 1 amu or 1 u $= 1.67377 \times 10^{-27}$ Kg

Atomic masses are measured by an instrument called mass spectrometer.

3. Relation between amu and MeV

1 amu = 931 MeV

4. Atomic Number (Z)

Atomic number, Z = Number of protons

= Number of electrons (in a neutral atom)

5. Mass Number (A)

Mass number = Number of protons + Number of neutrons

$$\Rightarrow \quad A = Z + N$$

6. Nuclear Density (ρ)

Density of nuclear matter,

$$\rho = \frac{\text{Mass of nucleus}}{\text{Volume of nucleus}} = \frac{3m}{4\pi R_0^3}$$

Note Nuclear density is independent with mass number.

7. Mass Defect and Binding Energy

$$\Delta m = Zm_p + (A - Z)\, m_n - M$$

where, Z = atomic number, A = mass number,

m_p = mass of proton,
m_n = mass of neutron and M = mass of nucleus.

8. Mass-energy Relation

It is given by $E = mc^2$
where, m = mass of the body, c = speed of the light and E is the energy.

9. Isotopes or Isoprotons

The atoms of same element whose nuclei have the same number of protons but different number of neutrons.
Oxygen : ${}_8O^{16}, {}_8O^{17}$

10. Isobars

Atoms of different elements whose nuclei have the same number of nucleons (i.e. mass number), but different number of protons and neutrons are called isobars.
${}_1H^3$ and ${}_2H^3$ and ${}_{11}Na^{23}$ and ${}_{12}Mg^{23}$

11. Isotones

Atoms of different elements whose nuclei have equal number of neutrons are called isotones.
${}_3Li^7$ and ${}_4Be^8$

12. Binding Energy

$$\Delta E_b = [Zm_p + (A - Z)m_n - M]\,c^2$$

where, $c = 3 \times 10^8$ m/s

13. Binding Energy per Nucleon

$$BE/Nucleon = \frac{\text{Total binding energy}}{\text{Number of nucleons (A)}}$$

14. Binding Energy Curve

It is a plot of the binding energy per nucleon E_{bn} versus the mass number A for a large number of nuclei as shown below.

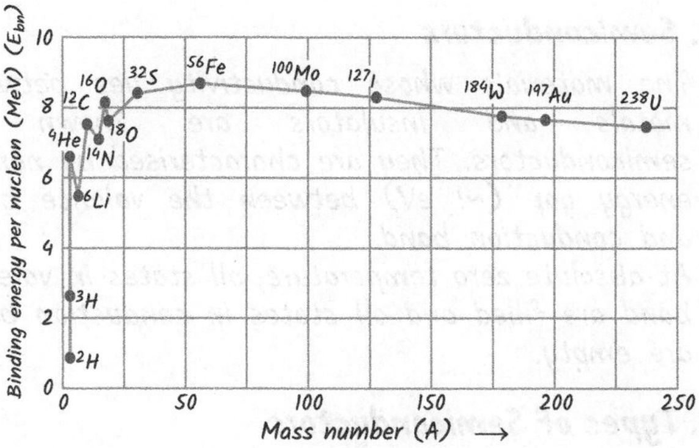

15. Nuclear Fission

The phenomenon of splitting of heavy nuclei (mass number > 120) into smaller nuclei of nearly equal masses is known as nuclear fission.
e.g. ${}^{235}_{92}U + {}^{1}_{0}n \rightarrow {}^{141}_{56}Ba + {}^{92}_{36}Kr + 3\,{}^{1}_{0}n + Q$ (energy)

16. Nuclear Fusion

The phenomenon of conversion of two lighter nuclei into a single heavy nucleus is called nuclear fusion.
e.g.
${}_1H^3 + {}_1H^2 \longrightarrow {}_2He^4 + {}_1^1n + 17.6$ MeV (Energy)

17. Nuclear Chain Reaction

In the nuclear fission reaction, there is a release of extra neutron. The extra neutron in turn initiates fission process, producing still more neutrons and so on. Thus, a chain of nuclear fission is set up called nuclear chain reaction.
The chain reaction may be of two types
(i) Uncontrolled chain reaction .
(ii) Controlled chain reaction.

Chapter 14 Semiconductor and Electronic Devices

1. Types of Material

Types of Material	Resistivity (ρ)	Conductivity (σ)	Conclusion
(i) Conductors (metals)	10^{-2} to $10^{-8}\Omega$-m	10^2 to 10^8 Sm^{-1}	low resistivity, high conductivity
(ii) Insulators	10^{11} to $10^{19}\Omega$-m	10^{-11} to 10^{-19}Sm^{-1}	high resistivity, zero conductivity
(iii) Semiconductors	10^{-5} to $10^{6}\Omega$-m	10^{+5} to 10^{-6}Sm^{-1}	resistivity and conductivity intermediate to metals and insulator

2. Semiconductors

The materials whose conductivity lies between metals and insulators are known as semiconductors. They are characterised by narrow energy gap (~1 eV) between the valence band and conduction band.
At absolute zero temperature, all states in valence band are filled and all states in conduction band are empty.

3. Types of Semiconductors

(i) **Elemental semiconductors**

These semiconductors are available in natural form. e.g. Silicon(Si) and germanium(Ge).

(ii) **Compound semiconductors**

These semiconductors are made by compounding the metals. e.g. CdS, GaAs, CdSe, InP, anthracene, polyaniline, etc.

4. Intrinsic Semiconductors

Pure semiconductors in which $n_e = n_h = n_i$
where, n_e and n_h are number densities of electrons and holes respectively and n_i is called intrinsic carrier concentration.

5. Extrinsic Semiconductors

The process of adding impurities to an intrinsic semiconductor in a controlled manner is called **doping**. A doped semiconductor is called extrinsic semiconductor.

6. n-type Semiconductor

In n-type semiconductor, majority charge carriers are electrons and minority charge carriers are holes, i.e. $n_e > n_h$.

7. p-type Semiconductor

In p-type semiconductor, majority charge carriers are holes and minority charge carriers are electrons, i.e. $n_h > n_e$.

8. Equation for Extrinsic Semiconductors

- Current, $I = eA\,(n_e v_e + n_h v_h)$
where, A is area of cross-section, while v_e and v_h are speeds of electrons and holes, respectively.
- Mobility of charge carriers, $\mu = \frac{v}{E}$, where E is applied electric field and v is velocity of electron or holes.
- Electrical conductivity, $\sigma = \frac{1}{\rho} = e\,(\mu_e n_e + n_h \mu_h)$

where, n_e and n_h are concentrations of electrons and holes respectively, μ_e and μ_h are mobilities of electrons and holes, respectively.

9. **Semiconductor diode or p-n junction diode** It is basically a p-n junction with metallic contact provided at the ends for the application of an external voltage. It is a two terminal device.

A p-n junction diode is represented (as),

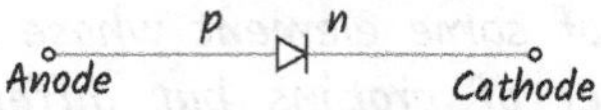

In forward bias (n-side is connected to negative terminal of the battery and p-side is connected to positive), the barrier is decreased while the barrier increases in reverse bias. Hence, forward bias current is more (mA) while it is very small (μA) in a p-n junction diode.

10. V-I Characteristics of a Diode

Graph between applied voltage V and current I through the diode when a voltage is applied across it is called V-I characteristics.
The DC resistance on of a junction diode,

$$r_{DC} = \frac{V}{I}$$

The dynamic resistance or AC resistance of a junction diode, $r_{AC} = \frac{DV}{DI}$

11. Diode as Rectifier

The process of converting alternating voltage or current into direct voltage or current is called rectification.
There are two ways of using a diode as a rectifier
(i) half-wave rectifier (ii) full wave rectifier

12. Photodiode

It is used for detecting optical signals by converting light into electrical energy. It is enclosed in a transparent window. It is also operated under reverse bias.

13. Light Emitting Diode (LED)

It is a heavily doped p-n junction diode which converts electrical energy into light energy. It emits spontaneous radiation under forward biasing.

14. Solar Cell

It is a diode that converts solar energy into electrical energy. It is not given any biasing. It has a large surface area to allow maximum sunlight to fall on it.